Family Violence Across the Lifespan

An Introduction

Ola W. Barnett
Cindy L. Miller-Perrin
Robin D. Perrin

SAGE Publications
International Educational and Professional Publisher
Thousand Oaks   London   New Delhi

For information address:

 SAGE Publications, Inc.
2455 Teller Road
Thousand Oaks, California 91320
Phone: 805-499-0721
E-mail: order@sagepub.com

SAGE Publications Ltd.
6 Bonhill Street
London EC2A 4PU
United Kingdom

SAGE Publications India Pvt. Ltd.
M-32 Market
Greater Kailash I
New Delhi 110 048 India

Printed in the United States of America

Library of Congress Cataloging-in-Publication Data

Barnett, Ola W.
  Family violence across the lifespan: An introduction / authors,
Ola W. Barnett, Cindy L. Miller-Perrin, and Robin D. Perrin.
      p.   cm.
  Includes bibliographical references and index.
  ISBN 0-8039-5615-0 (cloth: acid-free paper)—ISBN 0-7619-0707-6 (pbk.: acid-free paper)
  1. Family violence.   I. Miller-Perrin, Cindy L. (Cindy Lou),
1962- II. Perrin, Robin D.   III. Title.
HV6626.B315   1997
362.82′92—dc20   96-35666

This book is printed on acid-free paper.

  99 00 01 02 10 9 8 7 6

Acquiring Editor: C. Terry Hendrix
Editorial Assistant: Dale Grenfell
Developmental Editor: Ann West
Production Editor: Diana E. Axelsen
Production Assistant: Sherrise Purdum
Typesetter & Designer: Andrea D. Swanson
Indexer: Trish Wittenstein
Cover Designer: Ravi Balasuriya
Print Buyer: Anna Chin

Family
Violence
Across
the Lifespan

Editorial Review Board

BRIEF CONTENTS

DETAILED CONTENTS

To the victims of family abuse
and to the dedicated individuals in every walk of life
who are working to end the violence.

Introduction

Family violence is not a new phenomenon—it has probably existed in families since the beginning of time. Only recently, however, has violence in the family against children, spouses, and elderly persons become recognized as a social problem by professionals and society at large.

One major event occurring in this century propelled the problem into public view. This was the well-publicized findings of Dr. C. Henry Kempe of Colorado of the multiple bone fractures appearing in the X rays of abused children. Another was the advent of the women's movement in the 1970s, which helped spawn the shelter movement. The vast number of reports of family violence made to the police and other officials also heightened public and professional concern about the problem of family violence.

Progress within the field has been rapid as many grassroots organizations, mental health workers, university researchers, lawmakers, legal and medical personnel, criminal justice personnel, book writers, and the media have mobilized their efforts to understand family violence. The combined efforts of all these groups have led to a growing national concern about family violence. In the past two decades, the general public has become more familiar with family violence through news coverage of highly publicized cases, cover stories in magazines, television programs, and movies. Although media exposure has helped make people more aware of family violence and researchers have made great strides in understanding the problem, much is still unknown about this complex and multifaceted problem.

This textbook, *Family Violence Across the Lifespan,* was written to continue the "discovery" of this social problem that occurs behind closed doors. We, as authors, want to continue to bring the topic into the mainstream of public knowledge. To achieve these goals, we have drawn together a voluminous research literature that describes the magnitude of family violence, how family violence is assessed, the consequences of family violence, and what is known about the many factors that contribute to family violence. Other topics cover the professional and social responses to family violence, including clinical treatments, educational efforts within the schools, the ways social agencies respond to disclosures of family violence, and the approaches taken to prevent family violence.

Because of the breadth of the topic and the enormous amount of available literature, the information in this volume is organized to present a broad overview and summary of research findings. Throughout the book, we have attempted to keep our commitment to responsible scholarship by presenting the data relevant to both sides of a debatable issue. Along the way, we have enlivened statistical accounts with graphic case histories, and we have highlighted a number of current controversies within boxed inserts. For readers who are interested in obtaining further details on specific topics, additional references and resources can be found in appendixes at the end of the book.

Each chapter features an interview of a nationally or internationally known expert that provides an example of the variety of philosophies and training typical of the many professionals working in the field of family violence. Our desire, as authors, is to acknowledge this diversity and to point out that individuals with different personal backgrounds can still work together to eradicate family violence. We hope that this book provides these professionals with a comprehensive overview and access to the growing body of research in the field.

We also hope that we have presented the content in such a way that readers can find their own personal roles in the struggle to end family violence. We invite you, our readers, to contact us to express your impressions about the book, to send us your personal case histories, or to provide us with additional references and resources. Furthermore, we hope the book offers information to victims and perpetrators that will change their lives for the better. Finally, we hope this text in some measure decreases the pain and suffering of family violence victims and ultimately leads to solutions that end family violence.

Ola W. Barnett
Cindy Miller-Perrin
Robin D. Perrin

Acknowledgments

We have many people to thank for their contributions to this text.

First, we wish to acknowledge C. Terry Hendrix, Senior Editor at Sage Publications. Without his support and guidance we could not have brought this book to the public. We wish to formally recognize the vital contributions he has made toward ending family violence through his editorial accomplishments in publications. His leadership in this area has promoted a growing recognition of the scope of family violence and its devastating aftermath.

We also wish to thank Ann West for her work in developing the text into a final cohesive whole. Ann is the kind of "Wonder Woman" whose unique ideas, expertise, organizational skills, and devotion to the project helped make the text more illuminating and interesting. Kate Peterson, our copy editor, is another "super hero" in our estimation. Her expertise and diligence added consistency and clarity to every facet of the manuscript. She also managed the Herculean chore of checking the formatting of the hundreds of references in the text.

Along similar lines, Carol V. Harnish offered continual assistance in reading, rereading, and rereading once again every word in every chapter. She provided the authors with a "common man's" (woman's, in this case) reaction to the text's content and clarity. She provided a plethora of up-to-date references, assembled the foundation for the appendix on related readings, and served as an invaluable creative consultant in advancing ideas about the selection of information presented in the text.

The reviewers deserve everlasting praise for their careful reading of the text, first in part, and then again in its entirety. Their extensive knowledge of the field and constructive comments provided the authors with new insights and directions. Although readers should not hold the reviewers responsible for the final content of the text, the reviewers provided considerable feedback about the selection and highlighting of information and the appropriate framework for its presentation. They also helped motivate us as we forged ahead toward completing those final pages.

We are especially indebted to the scholars who granted us permission to interview them. Their professionalism in conveying their personal, and sometimes controversial, viewpoints within a field where final truths about family violence have yet to emerge is commendable. Although sometimes disagreeing with each others' methodologies or research interpretations, these professionals are totally united in their commitment to ending family violence. They serve as models to the generations of scholars to follow.

We also wish to thank the staff at Sage Publications and Pepperdine University for their work in executing the many detailed tasks that accompany a publication of this size. Finally, we wish to thank our families for their encouragement and support while undertaking this project.

History and Definitions of Family Violence

CHAPTER OUTLINE

Introduction

CASE HISTORY: O.J. SIMPSON

At 29 years of age, O.J. Simpson was already a football legend. He was a two-time all-American and Heisman Trophy winner at the University of Southern California. As a professional, he won four rushing titles and in 1973 had become the first running back to run for over 2,000 yards. Nicole Brown was 18 and a recent high school graduate when she met O.J. in 1977. In 1979, O.J. and his first wife were divorced, and in 1985 O.J. married Nicole in a lavish ceremony at Simpson's Brentwood, California, home. "They were a stunning couple," remembered former Los Angeles Rams General Manager Don Klosterman. "She was beautiful. He was O.J. When they entered the room, heads turned" (Farrell & Hall, 1994, p. A18).

In 1992, after 7 years of marriage, they divorced. Yet in the years following the divorce, people often saw them together. From time to time, friends even speculated that they might be getting back together. Sometime in 1994, however, Nicole reportedly told O.J. that it was over between them (Farrell & Hall, 1994).

On the evening of June 12, 1994, O.J. and Nicole separately attended the dance recital of their daughter, Sydney. After the recital, Nicole met family and friends at an upscale West Los Angeles restaurant, the Mezzaluna. On returning home, Nicole called the restaurant to see if anyone had found her mother's lost glasses. The manager located them at 9:45 p.m., and her friend and Mezzaluna waiter Ronald Goldman left the restaurant to return the glasses ("O.J. Simpson," 1994).

At 12:10 a.m., neighbors found the bodies of Nicole Brown Simpson and Ron Goldman near the steps of her Brentwood condominium. Both had been stabbed numerous times, and reports indicated that their throats had been slashed. The evidence quickly led police to O.J. Simpson, and on Friday evening, June 17, following a dramatic nationally televised car chase, they arrested Simpson and charged him with "double murder, under special circumstances" ("O.J. Simpson," 1994).

Americans responded with shock: "Not O.J. Simpson, not *our* O.J. The O.J. we knew was amiable, courteous, friendly, even gentle. The O.J. we knew 'never spiked a ball. He was among the first running backs to bestow gifts and recognition upon his blockers. He once jokingly called himself the Angel of Death for his frequent visits to terminally ill children in Buffalo hospitals. Nobody signed more autographs with as much good

humor' " (Lieber & Steptoe, 1994, p. 20). The O.J. we knew impressed us as a genuinely nice guy. The O.J. we knew could not have killed his wife, the mother of his children. Friends who knew him more intimately responded similarly. "It's unbelievable, so shocking," said former teammate Steve Grady. "He never showed a tendency toward what's described. He didn't even have a temper" (Gustkey, 1994, p. A8). "This was my roommate. I know this guy," said another former teammate. "For him to get in that kind of a rage and to do this to someone—they'll have to prove it beyond a shadow of a doubt to me" (Gustkey, 1994, p. A8).

As more about O.J. Simpson came to light, it became clear just how limited and fanciful our view of him had been. Friends reported that the Simpsons had often argued and that Nicole was sometimes bruised. Nicole had even called the police on many occasions. When the police responded to a call during a January 1, 1989, argument, Nicole ran out from some bushes in her front yard screaming, "He's going to kill me, he's going to kill me! You never do anything about him. You talk to him and then leave." Angered that the police were intervening, an indignant Simpson screamed, "The police have been out here eight times before and now you're going to arrest me for this? This is a family matter. Why do you want to make a big deal out of it when we can handle it?" He then got in his white Bentley and drove off (Meyer, 1994, p. A24). The police did arrest O.J. for spousal assault this time, and he eventually pleaded no contest to spousal assault.

Simpson dismissed the charge as a "bum rap." "We had a fight," he said, "that's all" (Meyer, 1994, p. A24). Friends also came to Simpson's defense, alleging that Nicole Brown was no saint and definitely knew how to "push his buttons." People should be careful not to judge O.J. too harshly for the abuse, cautioned high school friend Calvin Tennyson: "You put a man and a woman in the same house, day in and day out, and from time to time someone gets slapped. I don't think that made O.J. outstanding in America. It's not exactly an uncommon thing" (Gustkey, 1994, p. A9).

The television station NBC apparently did not worry that the abuse conviction tarnished O.J. Simpson's image, and in July 1989 they hired Simpson as a football analyst. Rental car company Hertz, for whom Simpson had been a spokesperson for many years, was also unperturbed and dismissed the assault as a private issue between the couple. Certainly, there was no real outcry of public condemnation of O.J. and his behavior. *Sports Illustrated* quoted a former employee at NBC sports as saying, "People at NBC Sports used to always remark about the beating, shaking their heads and saying, 'Here's a man who used to beat his wife, and none of America cares or remembers.' People refused to believe it because they thought he was such a nice guy" (Lieber & Steptoe, 1994, p. 20).

* * *

For family violence experts who followed the O.J. Simpson saga, it was a chilling sign of society's continuing reluctance to define marital violence as a serious problem. Simpson was a football star, surely not a wife beater. The "spats" he had with his wife were a "normal" part of a "rocky" marriage. There was no reason to believe that he was a violent man. Of course, Simpson eventually was acquitted of murder charges. However, as advocates for women reminded us, his acquittal does not change the fact that he was a wife beater and that society seemed not to care that he was a wife beater.

In the weeks following Simpson's arrest, the world heard the 9-1-1 calls for help. The world heard about O.J. Simpson's violence. Experts spoke out and reminded the world that although "everyone is acting as if this is so shocking, [it] happens all the time" (Debbie Tucker, director of the National Domestic Violence Coalition on Public Policy, as quoted in Smolowe, 1994, p. 20). Many abused women, some of whom saw something of themselves in the life of Nicole Simpson, called domestic violence hotlines in record numbers (Smolowe, 1994). Domestic violence was on the cover of every major news magazine and at the forefront of America's consciousness.

Violence:
As American as Apple Pie?

By almost any measure, the United States is a violent country. The U.S. murder rate, which during the 1980s and 1990s ranged from a 1980 high of 10.2 for every 100,000 people to a 1994 rate of 9 for every 100,000 people, is by far the highest in the industrialized world (U.S. Bureau of the Census, 1994, p. 198; also see Lacayo, 1996). If the U.S. rate were as low as England's, there would have been approximately 2,500 murders and non-negligent homicides in 1992, rather than the actual figure of 22,540 (Maguire & Pastore, 1994; Siegel, 1995). Recent surveys suggest that Americans are well aware of the violence

problem in American society and now consider violence to be the most urgent problem confronting the nation (Hart, 1994).

It is easy to think of the family as being relatively immune from violence, a place of safe harbor, a place where a loving family provides sustenance and care. The family is supposed to protect us from the violent world. All too often, however, this is not the case. In 1994, it is estimated that 1,271 children died as a result of abuse and/or neglect (Weise & Daro, 1995). Many others were physically, sexually, and emotionally abused and neglected. In 1992, of the 13,805 U.S. homicides where the relationship between the offender and the victim was known; (15%) were committed by an intimate (spouse or ex-spouse, boyfriend or girlfriend), and 1,480 (11%) were committed by another relative. There were 9,371 homicides where the victim-offender relationship was unknown. Even more dramatic, of the 3,454 female homicides in which the offender could be identified, 1,415 (41%) were committed by an intimate, and 510 (15%) were committed by another relative (Bachman & Saltzman, 1996).[1] Many other women, of course, were physically assaulted or emotionally abused by their partners. In fact, according to the National Crime Victimization Survey, 29% of all violence against women by a lone offender is committed by an intimate (Bachman & Saltzman, 1996). Research consistently demonstrates that many women and children are actually more likely to be assaulted *in their own homes* than on the streets in the most violent American cities (Bachman & Saltzman, 1996; Hotaling, Straus, & Lincoln, 1990; Straus, Gelles, & Steinmetz, 1980).

Rather than seeing family violence and street violence as separate entities, it is probably helpful to view them as interconnected. Some evidence for such an overlap has arisen from studies showing that men who are violent in the home, for example, are especially likely to be violent outside the home (e.g., Hotaling et al., 1990; Shields, McCall, & Hanneke, 1988). Family violence and street violence are probably also interconnected causally. Although many factors such as the influence of peers, unemployment, poverty, ethnic diversity, gun ownership, media violence, intrapersonal characteristics, and biological factors may contribute to violence in society, one could reasonably argue that family influence is the single most likely determinant of an individual's level of violence.

The family is, after all, the most important agent of socialization. Early philosophers certainly recognized the important role family plays. To capture the importance of childhood experiences, Freud (1895/1961) coined the phrase "The child is father of the man." Sarte agreed: "One is never finished with the family. It's like smallpox—it catches you in childhood and marks you for life." So important is the family that it can often be considered the "cradle of violence" (Newman, 1979). A recent 4-year longitudinal study of 1,000 adolescents offers compelling evidence for these precepts. In the study, which was conducted by the Office of Juvenile Justice and Delinquency Prevention (OJJDP; 1995), 38% of youths from nonviolent families self-reported involvement in some type of violence, and 78% of youths exposed to maltreatment, violence by parents, and a general family climate of hostility self-reported participation in violent acts.

Other evidence further confirms the intergenerational patterns of violence. Indeed, the adage "violence begets violence," although no doubt overly simplistic, seems generally true. Children who are victims of assault within the family are, when compared to children who are not victimized, more likely to be adult murderers, rapists, and assaulters outside the family (Hotaling et al., 1990). The greater the severity and frequency of the victimization, the greater the likelihood of severe and frequent violent offending outside the family (Straus, 1994). Although the relationship between childhood victimization and adult perpetration is far from perfect, research evidence continues to point to the profound influence childhood victimization plays in producing the next generation of abusers (e.g., Burke, Stets, & Pirog-Good, 1989). All of these haunting and perplexing patterns of violence within and outside the home illustrate the compelling need for a textbook on family violence. As OJJDP administrator Shay Bilchik (cited in "Violence in Families," 1995) recognizes, the research seems clear: "If we can reduce family violence—not just abuse and neglect—we can prevent future violence by its young victims" (p. 6). Clearly, family violence is worthy of our attention.

Discovering the Family Violence Problem: Understanding the Social Construction of Social Problems

Few would dispute the fact that family violence is a social problem. Academia has begun to include coverage of the topic in most social problems textbooks, and a few

---

So important is the family that it can often be considered the "cradle of violence."

---

separate family violence courses emerged in the 1980s. Beginning in the mid-1980s, several new journals devoted specifically to family and intimate violence appeared. Perhaps most telling of all, the most accepted social commentators of our time, from U.S. Senator Joseph Biden to talk show host Oprah Winfrey, clearly have defined family violence as a social problem.

Yet it is important to recognize that family violence was a *social condition* long before it was recognized as a *social problem*. Family violence is not the only contemporary problem that has not always been defined as such. Racial and gender inequality or environmental problems, for example, probably would not have been identified as social problems 100 years ago.

Many sociologists point out that social problems are socially constructed (Spector & Kitsuse, 1977). From a social constructionist perspective, there is no way to identify "social problems" objectively. This perspective holds that *societal reactions* are central to the process of redefining a social condition as a social problem. Societal reaction includes all of the ways individuals within a society respond to social conditions. Societal reactions can come from any of a number of different sources: churches, social movement organizations, political interest groups, and the media, to name but a few.

These various interest groups, or *claims-makers,* are actively engaged in the process of raising awareness about a particular social condition. Claims-making refers to the "activities of individuals or groups making assertions of grievances or claims with respect to some putative condition" (Spector & Kitsuse, 1977, p. 75). Generally speaking, the process begins when a claims-maker or interest group attempts to increase awareness and arouse controversy about a particular condition that it sees as unacceptable (Best, 1989). Claims-makers may have a vested interest, or they may be "moral entrepreneurs" engaged in a purely moral crusade (Becker, 1963). As the cause of the particular complainant group

comes to be recognized by society more generally, the social condition becomes a social
problem. Social problems, then, are essentially "discovered" through this process of
societal reactions and social definition. From
this perspective, social problems come and
go as societal reactions change (Studer, 1984).

The social constructionist perspective provides helpful insights into why violence is
sometimes condemned as abuse in some cultures but not others. In Japan, for example,
although male-to-female intimate violence is
common, it is essentially unrecognized. It is
a widespread social condition, but it is not
recognized as a social problem. There is, in
fact, no word in the Japanese language for
the English concept "domestic violence" or
"husband/boyfriend violence" (Yoshihama
& Sorenson, 1994). Because there is no societal condemnation of male-to-female intimate violence, it is not viewed as a social
problem.

Social constructionism also explains how
certain empirical generalizations come to be
accepted as fact. Although one might hope
that research findings could stand on their
own, the reality is that the "facts" are often
interpreted differently by competing claims-
makers. Experts continue to debate, for example, the effectiveness of spanking (Chapter 3), the existence of repressed memories
and satanic ritual abuse (Chapter 4), the
mutual nature of marital violence (Chapter
8), and the prevalence of date rape (Chapter
7). Each side is armed with its own set of
empirical findings it espouses as the truth.
From a social constructionist perspective, whoever wins the empirical battle earns the right
to define "the truth" to the general public.

The significance of the social construction process also becomes obvious in historical accounts of family violence. Family violence has been a social condition for as long
as there have been families, but only recently
has the social condition of family violence
developed into a social problem.

Discovering Child Victimization

Physical Child Abuse and Neglect. Since ancient times, reports have documented maltreatment of children (Bakan, 1971). Many
societies, for example, practiced infanticide
for population control or to eliminate children with birth defects. Abandoning or drown-
ing unwanted babies was not uncommon.

Some contemporary scholars maintain that
infanticide was the most frequent crime in
all of Europe until about 1800 (Piers, 1978).
The era of industrialization in modern Western cultures evidenced the abusive use of
children in the labor force. Children were
employed in textile mills, mines, and other
industries involving dangerous, exhausting,
and unhealthy work. Children as young as 5
years of age worked 10 to 14 hours a day, 6
days a week. Even today, in some societies,
child maltreatment remains common. In some
rural areas of China, for example, female
infanticide remains a common practice (Walsh,
1995).

Importantly, however, these acts are not
always viewed as abusive. Rather, they are
accepted as legitimate adult-child interactions. Many factors have likely contributed to
society's lack of recognition of physical child
abuse. First, the political powerlessness of
children as a group provided a basis for adults
to establish rules and laws governing their
treatment and care. (Wolfe, 1991). In addition, societies historically have regarded children as the property of their parents and
subsequently allowed adults to treat their
property as they saw fit, without independent
status or rights (Walker, Bonner, & Kaufman,
1988). Parents sometimes viewed their children as liabilities in terms of their economic
drain on the family, one more mouth to feed
and body to clothe. High rates of death and
disease further diminished the bond of affection and concern for one's children (Walker
et al., 1988).

The first court case of child abuse was not
tried until 1874 (Bremner, 1971). A woman
who discovered that 8-year-old Mary Ellen
Wilson was being beaten and starved on a
daily basis by her stepmother brought the
case to Henry Bergh, the founder of the
Society for the Prevention of Cruelty to Animals. The woman sought Bergh's assistance
after attempting to seek help from several
other sources without success. A courtroom
full of concerned New Yorkers, most of them
upper-class women, heard the shocking details of Mary Ellen's life. She had been beaten
almost daily and had not been allowed to
play with friends or to leave the house. She
had an unhealed gash on the left side of her
face, a result of a blow to the head with a pair
of scissors. The jury took only 20 minutes to
find the stepmother guilty of assault and
battery (Pleck, 1987).

The case of Mary Ellen attracted considerable attention, and the resulting public

outcry eventually led to the 1874 founding of the Society for the Prevention of Cruelty to Children (SPCC) (Pagelow, 1984). Through the advocacy of the SPCC, state legislatures passed child protective statutes, criminalizing abusive and neglectful behavior and specifying procedures for meeting the needs of abused and neglected children (Pleck, 1987). Because reporting of child abuse was not required, however, most child abuse remained unacknowledged until the early 1960s. In 1962, Kempe and his colleagues described the "battered child syndrome" and suggested that physicians should report abuse (Kempe, Silverman, Steele, Droegemueller, & Silver, 1962).

Kempe, Silverman, Steele, et al. (1962) defined child abuse as a clinical condition with diagnosable medical and physical symptoms resulting from deliberate physical assault. The seminal battered-child-syndrome article had a significant effect on the recognition of physical child abuse as a widespread problem, but the definition was restricted to acts of physical violence that produced a diagnosable pattern of injury. Finally, in 1974, Congress enacted the Child Abuse Prevention and Treatment Act to encourage reform. This law provided federal funds to fight child abuse for states that passed laws requiring certain professionals, such as teachers and health care personnel, to report suspected abuse.

As concern about maltreatment grew during the 1900s, several child protection organizations emerged. National organizations include the National Committee to Prevent Child Abuse (formerly the National Committee for Prevention of Child Abuse), the Family Resource Coalition, the Children's Defense Fund, the National Center for Missing and Exploited Children, and the Child Welfare League of America.

Child Sexual Abuse. Sexual abuse shares much of its history with the child saving movement of the 1800s. Throughout history and in some cultures, sexual interactions involving children have been commonplace. In fact, during some periods, a few societies did not typically view these types of interactions as wrong or harmful, but as "appropriate" and, in some cases, even "healthy" for children. For example, Aristotle claimed that masturbation of boys by adult males hastened their manhood (DeMause, 1974). Even today, sexual contact between adults and children is common in some societies. The Sambia of Papua New Guinea, for example, believe young boys must ingest semen from older boys and men if they are to grow into manhood. In other words, a boy only becomes a "man"—masculine, strong, sexually attractive to women—if he performs fellatio (Herdt, 1987).

Even in North America, there are those who believe that adult-child sexual interactions are appropriate and healthy. One extreme minority perspective is expressed by the North American Man-Boy Love Association (NAMBLA), an organization founded in December 1978 (Hechler, 1988), which supports adult-child sexual interactions or "transgenerational sex." Robert Rhodes, a NAMBLA spokesperson, made the following comments when asked whether the organization views itself as an advocacy group for children:

Yes. Considering the legitimacy of sexual relationships with children, there's two main theories that you can work from. One was the classical Greek theory—that is to say that the older partner in a sexual relationship served as initiator and tutor of the younger partner. You can also take a children's liberationist's viewpoint—that is to say that children insofar as is possible—and it's far more possible than the current structure allows—should be given liberty to run their own lives as they choose, including the ability to determine how and with whom they should have sex. (cited in Hechler, 1988, pp. 193-194)

This sexual liberation perspective represents a minority view, of course. It also represents a criminal view. Sexual exploitation statutes now offer children considerable protection (see Wurtele & Miller-Perrin, 1992). The 1978 Protection of Children Against Sexual Exploitation Act and the 1986 Child Sexual Abuse and Pornography Act make it a federal crime to sexually exploit a child, or to permit a child to engage in child pornography.

Discovering Adult Victimization

Wife Beating. Historically, men have dominated and controlled women. With respect to the family, early marriage laws actually gave men the legal right to hit their wives (Dobash & Dobash, 1979). According to Sigler (1989), English common law held that women were inferior to men. A woman had no legal existence apart from her husband.

Her husband owned and controlled her. Early British rape laws also reflected the propertied status of women. The law held that when a woman was raped, restitution should be paid to the husband (or if the woman was unmarried, to her father) for damage done to his property (Sigler, 1989). Men were also held responsible for their wives' behavior. Because the man was expected to control his wife, the law allowed him a degree of latitude in the use of force. The "rule-of-thumb" law gave the husband the right to hit his wife with a rod no thicker than his thumb (Sigler, 1989).

In this country, concern about domestic violence began to grow in the late 1800s. The most significant wave of legal reforms occurred in the 1870s, when Alabama and Massachusetts introduced the first spouse abuse laws. With these new laws, it became illegal to "beat a wife with a stick, pull her hair, choke her, spit in her face, or kick her to the floor" (Pagelow, 1984, p. 284).

During the late 1960s and 1970s, violence directed at women received renewed attention, largely as a part of the women's movement (Pleck, 1987). Recognition of equal status for women in areas such as jobs and pay spread to a growing pressure for equality in marital relationships. The first shelter for battered women and their children, Haven House in Pasadena, California, was established in 1964. In 1971 in England, Chiswick Women's Aid became the first widely publicized shelter for battered women (Johnson, 1980). One of the founders of Chiswick, Erin Pizzey, published the influential book *Scream Quietly or the Neighbors Will Hear* in 1974. Through this book, and the subsequent radio and television exposure that it generated, the battered women's movement gained considerable momentum. In 1976, over 200 women from 33 countries attended the International Tribunal on Crimes Against Women. A 1986 study indicated that there were over 700 shelters across the United States (Berk, 1986).

Women's organizations were also increasingly active in the United States during the 1970s. In 1974, the National Organization for Women (NOW) decided to make battered wives a priority issue. Organizations such as the National Coalition Against Domestic Violence, which focused specifically on battered women, began political efforts to establish better social services for battered wives and to force alterations in legal statutes that failed to protect women from spouse abuse (Studer, 1984). With increasing ur-

gency, shelters began to open in this country just as they had in England (Pagelow, 1984).

Several organizations, including the Displaced Homemakers Network, the National Association of Women and Law (in Canada), the National Organization for Victim's Assistance, the National Clearing House for the Defense of Battered Women, and the National Council on Child Abuse and Family Violence, actively fought for the rights of women. Although it would be incorrect to assume that each of these organizations has the same social and political agenda, their combined effort raised awareness of the significance of domestic violence as a social problem, and today concern for battered women seemingly is at an all-time high. For example, on March 21, 1995, President Bill Clinton announced plans to begin implementation of the Violence Against Women Act, a bill first introduced by Delaware Senator Joseph Biden and later included as part of the Clinton crime bill. The Violence Against Women Act provides the 50 states with funds to help reduce the level of violence against women ("$26 Million in Grants Announced," 1995). One month later, on April 9, 1995, over 50,000 people marched in Washington in an effort to raise awareness about violence against women and to celebrate the successful designation of April as Domestic Violence Awareness Month.

Marital Rape. The women's movement has also played an influential role in the recent discovery of another form of domestic violence: marital rape. Historically, rape laws pertained only to unmarried individuals. In the 1700s, Sir Matthew Hale (1736/1874) originated the marital exemption law, holding that by mutual matrimonial consent and contract, the wife had given her consent and could not retract it. Other beliefs such as the need for marital privacy, the need to promote marital reconciliation, and the fear of excessive litigation that would clog the court system have all contributed to the acceptability of forced sex within marriage (see Barshis, 1983).

The first successful conviction of a husband for marital rape occurred in 1979 in Massachusetts in *State v. Chretien* (see Barshis, 1983). Of the 50 states, marital exemption laws still exist in 3, have been completely abolished in 24, and are qualified in the remaining 23 states by such circumstances as living apart or by having initiated divorce proceedings (Small & Tetreault, 1990).

Courtship Violence and Date Rape. In 1981, Makepeace published a seminal study on courtship violence and, in 1986, an article on date rape. The apparent similarity in victimization of women in both dating violence and marital violence led advocates for battered women to view the association as just one more example of male domination of women (Dobash & Dobash, 1979). For family violence researchers, dating violence seemed to present a microcosm of the larger problem of marital violence. Advocates and researchers have been quite successful in their claims-making, and today there are education and prevention programs on many high school and college campuses (Levy, 1991).

Elder Abuse. Elder abuse was among the last forms of family violence to receive attention from the research community. The academic world discovered child abuse in the 1960s and marital violence in the 1970s, but elder abuse did not begin to receive attention until the 1980s. The first family elder abuse research did not appear in the *Social Science Index* until 1981-1982 (Baumann, 1989). By 1989, however, a scholarly journal dedicated solely to elder abuse became available (*Journal of Elder Abuse & Neglect*). Elder abuse lagged behind other forms of family violence in legislative interest as well. In 1980, several years after the implementation of mandatory reporting laws for children, only 16 states had similar laws for elders. By the late 1980s, 36 states had mandatory reporting laws for elder abuse (Wolf & Pillemer, 1989).

Other Emerging Cultural Issues

DISCOVERING CROSS-CULTURAL VIOLENCE

Any examination of the historical record clearly indicates that the rights of women and children throughout the world have been subordinated to those of adult males. Research has uncovered a vast array of cultural practices that victimize women and children (e.g., genital mutilation, foot binding, dowry death, selective malnourishment, female infanticide, forced prostitution, and violent pornography) (Heise, 1989; Holloway, 1994). In the 1980s, Broude and Greene (1983) documented wife beating in 57 of 71 societies, thus revealing how common and unexceptional wife beating is throughout the world.

Whereas some cultural attitudes (e.g., equal treatment of women, education of women) appear to decrease spouse abuse (Holloway, 1994; Levinson, 1988), others (e.g., economic dependency, prohibition against female-initiated divorce) increase wife assault (Brown, 1992). The cultural support for violence against family members also varies widely from one country to the next. Acceptance of male-to-female sexual aggression may be less in China than in the United States (Tang, Critelli, & Porter, 1993). In India, certain customs (e.g., giving

> *One study documented wife beating in 57 of 71 societies, thus revealing how common and unexceptional wife beating is throughout the world.*

away one's property as preparation for the next world) make financial exploitation of elders much easier (Shah, Veedon, & Vasi, 1995).

As new as family violence research is in America, it is even newer and more preliminary in other countries. Some nations do not as yet recognize family violence as a social problem. Only recently have Singaporean women's groups, for instance, attempted to rally government support for spouse abuse intervention. Fortunately, these organizations have made some headway in influencing the police to take a more active role (Choi & Edleson, 1995; Edleson, 1992). Cross-cultural research tends to pose a few methodological problems that are distinct from those in the United States. Illustrative of these difficulties is that government officials in some countries might not even categorize infanticide as homicide (Gartner, 1993).

Very few estimates of the frequency of abuse are available worldwide. Current reports suggest that the annual incidence of spouse abuse in Canada (15%–36%) (e.g., Kennedy & Dutton, 1989; Smith, 1987) is somewhat higher than in the United States (16%) (Straus & Gelles, 1986). On the other hand, elder abuse in Canada appears to be comparable to that of the United States (Podkieks, 1992). In South Africa, the general level of violence is so high that violence against certain subgroups (e.g., elders) is characterized as a "blip on a radar screen" (Eckely & Vilakazi, 1995).

DISCOVERING INTERPARTNER VIOLENCE IN GAY AND LESBIAN PARTNERS

Possibly the newest form of interpartner violence to attract research attention is gay and lesbian violence. The rate of violence for gay or lesbian relationships is about the same as that for heterosexual couples. For gay male couples, estimates of annual rates extend from 11% to 20% (Bourg & Stock, 1994; Island & Letellier, 1991). Estimates for lesbian interpartner violence ranged from 17% to 26% (Lie, Schlitt, Bush, Montagne, & Reyes, 1991; Loulan, 1987).

EXAMINING MULTICULTURAL VIOLENCE IN THE UNITED STATES

Information about family violence in different ethnic groups is sparse and extremely variable. Some researchers report more severe violence among minorities and others do not (see Neff, Holamon, & Schluter, 1995; Stets, 1990). Some experts attribute any discernible racial differences to either police behaviors or to socioeconomic status; others cite findings that minorities call police and shelters for help more frequently (Cronin, 1995; Hutchison, Hirschel, & Pesackis, 1994; Kantor, Jasinski, & Aldarondo, 1994). Discussions that are relevant to various subfields (e.g., child abuse, wife abuse) appear in the forthcoming chapters.

UNRECOGNIZED COSTS OF FAMILY VIOLENCE

The discovery of all these forms of family violence underscores the sweeping nature of this heretofore hidden violence. Also hidden from view are the many costs associated with family violence. Table 1.1 represents a fresh look at the many costs and consequences of criminal behavior. Although not limited in scope to family violence, the table provides a composite of the vast number of monetary and nonmonetary costs of crime to victims, perpetrators, and society (Miller, Cohen, & Wiersema, 1996).

Defining Family Violence: Understanding the Social Construction of Deviance Definitions

The claims-making process is not only important in the discovery of a social problem,

but it also helps clarify conceptualizations of the problem. Indeed, "claims-makers do more than simply draw attention to particular social conditions. *Claims-makers shape our sense of just what the problem is*" (Best, 1989, p. xix, emphasis added). Clearly, because competing claims-makers are rarely in agreement, there is not one universal definition of family violence or family abuse. Ultimately, researchers employ a diversity of definitions, depending on their particular research requirements and findings, as well as on their own theoretical and personal viewpoints.

One illustration will help clarify the point. Some people believe that spanking is a serious form of family violence and should be stopped (e.g., Straus, 1994). They are claims-makers attempting to influence societal definitions of abuse. If they are completely successful in their claims-making, then spanking would be defined as abusive and could be criminalized, as it is in Scandinavia (Straus, 1994). At the other end of the spectrum are people who believe that children are their property and that society has no right to tell them what they can and cannot do (Hechler, 1988). They too are claims-makers attempting to influence societal definitions of abuse. Importantly, from a social constructionist perspective, the answer to the question, "What is child abuse?" is that it depends on whom one asks. From this perspective, definitions are negotiated by competing claims-makers in society. This ambiguity presents several problems for those charged with the task of studying violence and controlling abuse in society. Police, judges, prosecutors, child protective services workers, and adult protective services workers must have definitions with which to work.

Researchers, likewise, must operationally define family violence. An operational definition is a definition of a concept in terms of the methods used to measure that concept. Operational definitions of abuse might focus on any of a number of criteria, including the nature of the act itself (severity, form, frequency), the physical or psychological consequences of an act, or the intent of the perpetrator (Emery, 1989).

Probably the most common strategy among researchers is to focus on the *severity and frequency* of violence in the home. Violence can be defined as "an act carried out with the intention of, or an act perceived as having the intention of, physically hurting another person" (Steinmetz, 1987, p. 729). Although it is certainly possible to define violence more

Table 1.1 Comprehensive List of Costs and Consequences of Crime

Costs of Crime		Cost of Society's Response to Crime	
Cost Category	Party Who Directly Bears Cost	Cost Category	Party Who Directly Bears Cost
Direct property losses		**Precautionary expenditures/effort**	
1. Losses not reimbursed by insurance	Victim		
2. Losses reimbursed by insurance	Society	Fear of crime	Potential victim
3. Administrative cost: Insurance reimbursement	Society	**Criminal justice system**	
4. Recovery by police	Society	1. Police and investigative costs	Society
		2. Prosecutors	Society
Medical and mental health care		3. Courts	Society
1. Costs not reimbursed by insurance	Victim, victim's family, and society	4. Legal fees	
		a. Public defenders	Society
		b. Private	Offenders
2. Costs reimbursed by insurance	Society	5. Incarceration costs	Society
3. Administrative overhead of insurance coverage (2) above	Society	6. Nonincarceration sanctions	Society
		7. Victim time	Victim
		8. Jury and witness time	Jury and witnesses
Victim services			
1. Expenses charged to victim	Victim		
2. Expenses paid by agency	Society	**Victim services**	
3. Temporary labor and training of replacements	Society	1. Victim services organizations	Society
		2. Victim service volunteer time	Volunteers
		3. Victim compensation programs	Society and offender
Lost workdays		4. Victim time	Victim
1. Lost wages for unpaid workday	Victim		
2. Lost productivity	Society and employer	**Other noncriminal programs**	
		1. Hotlines and public service announcements	Society
Lost School Days		2. Community treatment programs	Society
1. Forgone wages due to lack of education	Victim	3. Private therapy and counseling	Society and offender
2. Forgone nonpecuniary benefits of education	Victim		
3. Forgone social benefits due to lack of education	Society	**Incarcerated offender costs**	
		1. Lost wages	Offender and family
Lost housework	Victim	2. Lost tax revenue and productivity	Society
1. Pain and suffering and lost quality of life[a]	Victim	3. Value of lost freedom	Offender
2. Loss of affection/enjoyment[a]	Victim's family	4. Psychological cost to family; loss of consortium	Family of offender
Death		**"Overabundance" costs**	
1. Lost quality of life	Victim	1. Innocent individuals accused of offense	Innocent individuals
2. Loss of affection/enjoyment	Victim's family	2. Restriction of legitimate activity	Innocent individuals
3. Funeral and burial expenses	Victim's family	3. Actions taken by offenders to avoid detection (e.g., kill robbery victims to reduce chance of being caught)	Society, offender, and victim
4. Psychological injury/treatment	Victim's family		
Legal costs associated with tort claims	Victim or victim's family	**"Justice costs"**	
"Second-generation costs"		1. Constitutional protections to avoid false accusations	Society
1. Future victims of crime committed by earlier victims	Future victims	2. Cost of increasing detection rate to avoid differential punishment	Society
2. Future social costs associated with (1) above	Society, victims, and so on		

SOURCE: From *Victim Costs and Consequences: A New Look* by T. R. Miller, M. A. Cohen, and B. Wiersema, 1996, p. 11. U.S. Department of Justice (NCJ No. 155282).
a. The monetary estimates in this report combine the categories of pain, suffering, and lost quality of life to the victim and the loss of affection/enjoyment to families categories.

Table 1.2 Four Types of Family Violence

Legitimate-expressive	**Illegitimate-expressive**
Violence is a catharsis. This is reflected in the belief that it is sometimes "better to spank a child than to 'hold in' one's anger" (Gelles & Straus, 1979, p. 558).	This is the most recognized and publicized kind of family violence, including child abuse, wife beating, and murder.
Legitimate-instrumental	**Illegitimate-instrumental**
This is the most widely occurring type of family violence. It includes, but is not limited to, physical punishment of children.	This is punishment that the parent might claim is "for the child's own good" but that society defines as abuse.

SOURCE: Adapted from Gelles and Straus (1979), in *Contemporary Theories About the Family,* Volume 1, edited by W. R. Burr, R. Hill, F. I. Nye, & I. L. Keiss. Used with permission of the Free Press, a division of Simon & Schuster. Copyright © 1979 by The Free Press.

broadly to include, for example, emotional abuse, or more narrowly to exclude, for example, spanking, this definition offers a clear and concise starting point.

To further illuminate the matter, Gelles and Straus (1979) proposed that family violence can be conceptualized along two sepa-

---

Limiting family abuse only to physical aggression fails to capture the true gamut of harmful family interactions.

---

rate continuums. The legitimate-illegitimate continuum represents the degree to which social norms legitimize violence. The instrumental-expressive continuum represents the degree to which violence is used as a means to an end—"to induce another person to carry out or refrain from an act" (Gelles & Straus, 1979, p. 557)—or as an end in itself (e.g., hitting someone out of anger). These two continuums result in a four-cell taxonomy of family violence (Table 1.2).

These four types of violence are reflected in the words of a young mother, who shares her views of discipline with family violence researcher Steinmetz (1987):

I've heard that you shouldn't spank when you're angry, but I can't agree with that because I think that's the time you should spank; before you have a chance to completely cool off, too. I think that the spanking helps the mother or dad as well as impresses the child that they did something wrong, and when they do something bad, they are going to be physically punished for it. You don't hit them with a stick or a belt, or a hairbrush, but a good back of the hand . . . they remember it. (p. 729)

This mother spanks her child, at least in part, because it is a catharsis—it helps her get the frustration out of her system (legitimate-expressive). She also spanks because she wants to impress on the child that he has done something wrong (legitimate-instrumental). This mother also indicated where she draws the line between legitimacy and illegitimacy, stating that some behaviors (spanking with a stick, belt, or hairbrush) are not acceptable (Steinmetz, 1979, pp. 729-730). Although each of these cells represents family violence, this book will focus on violence that crosses the legitimacy line—violence society regards as abusive.

It quickly becomes obvious, however, that limiting family abuse only to physical aggression fails to capture the true gamut of harmful family interactions. Sexual abuse, for example, may only occasionally involve physical violence but can have damaging effects that last a lifetime (Malinosky-Rummell & Hansen, 1993). Child neglect and emotional abuse are forms of maltreatment that can be even more devastating than physical violence, according to some reports (see Gleason, 1993). A woman can be psychologically tormented and controlled by a man who never touches her. Elders, likewise, can be neglected without being physically assaulted. If severity of physical injury is the sole criterion on which a definition is based, then these cases would be excluded from definitions of abuse (Graham, Dinwall, & Wolkind, 1985).

In each of the following chapters, definitions of specific forms of abuse will be discussed in more detail. It will quickly become obvious that defining and assessing family violence constitutes one of the most extensive, ongoing, and controversial areas of inquiry in the study of family violence (see Hamberger, 1994).

Common Myths About Family Violence

We conclude this first chapter by considering some of the myths commonly associated with family violence. Family violence is a topic that has unleashed a flood of opinion. These opinions, however, are not always well informed. Without sufficient knowledge about family violence, people are likely to develop nonscientific explanations or myths (Gelles & Cornell, 1990). A major function of myths is to reduce people's fears of personal vulnerability by implying that these kinds of events happen only to "other" kinds of people (Brownmiller, 1975). Myths also provide convenient and overly simplistic explanations of social issues that are very complex. When repeated often enough, myths become "conventional wisdom" and take on the semblance of well-established fact. Myths about family violence have been particularly hard to dispel because many of them contain a kernel of truth. Providing information about what is and is not accurate about myths is one important role of the social scientist. The first six of the following myths were first identified in Gelles and Cornell (1985, 1990).

Myth 1: Family Violence Is Rare

Because family violence is hidden and difficult to measure, it is impossible to estimate precisely how frequently it occurs. However, the fact that it is rarely seen should not be taken to mean that it rarely occurs. In fact, if there is one point about which family violence experts seemingly all agree, it is that family violence is far more common than we realize. Concerning child maltreatment, for example, data from the annual survey conducted by the National Committee to Prevent Child Abuse indicated that 3,140,000 children experienced some form of abuse (i.e., physical, sexual, neglect, emotional maltreatment) in 1994. In a national survey of parents, Gelles and Straus (1986) estimate that 11% had been severely violent (kicked, bit, hit with fist, hit or tried to hit with something, beat up) toward their children in the previous year. Of course, if one conceptualizes violence more broadly to include all forms of parental violence (including spanking), then almost all North American parents are violent. Straus (1991c) estimates, in fact, that over 95% of parents in the United States have, at some point in their children's lives, used physical punishment.

In regard to spouse abuse, approximately 28% of American couples experience at least one act of violence during their marriage, 16% experience at least one act of violence a year, and 6% experience severe violence in any given year (Straus & Gelles, 1986). These estimates suggest that maltreatment is not rare.

Myth 2: Only Poor People Are Violent

A substantial body of evidence does show higher rates of family violence in lower socioeconomic groups. Using the data from the National Family Violence Survey, Straus et al. (1980) estimated that families living at or below the poverty line had a marital violence rate that was 5 times that of families above the poverty line. Wauchope and Straus (1990b) estimate that the rate of child abuse among "blue collar" parents is approximately twice that among "white-collar" parents. Kantor and Straus (1990) similarly estimate that more of blue-collar husbands (13.4%) were violent the previous year than were white-collar husbands (10.4%). Because this research suggests that poor families are *more likely* to be violent, it contributes to the erroneous conclusion that *only* poor families are violent. It also contributes to unfair stereotypes that poor families are always violent. This simply is not true.

Another reason the myth that poor families are the only violent families is so commonly accepted is because family violence that comes to the attention of agents of social control is overwhelmingly from the underclass. People who are poor and lack other resources must turn to police and social service agencies more frequently than people who have money. This visibility is reflected in official estimates of family violence and seems to further reinforce the myth that only poor people are violent (also see Hampton & Newberger, 1988).

Myth 3: Abused Children Always Become Abusive Parents

As is discussed in the next chapter, perhaps the most commonly understood cause of child abuse is being a victim of child abuse. There is considerable truth in this generalization, because research consistently demonstrates that abusive parents have been exposed to significantly more childhood violence than nonabusive parents (Egeland, 1993). There are many reasons, however, to be cautious about accepting intergenerational patterns of abuse, in and of themselves, as completely explanatory.

Widom (1989) points to the many methodological problems with the research. First, there has been an overreliance on self-report and retrospective research. Retrospective reports are problematic because they rely on the memories and perceptions of violent adults concerning their childhood abuse experiences. Second, there has been a general lack of comparison groups of nonviolent adults also asked to provide retrospective, self-reports. When researchers sample general populations instead of only violent samples, the strength of the evidence declines. Perhaps most important of all is the simple fact that childhood abuse is neither a necessary nor sufficient cause of adult violence. Adoption of an abusive parenting style undoubtedly has a number of causes, not just exposure to abuse in one's childhood. At best, the data suggest that children who were abused, or who witnessed abuse, are more likely to be abusive adults. They are not predetermined to be abusive adults. In fact, the majority of abused children do not grow up to be abusive adults (Kaufman & Zigler, 1993; Widom, 1989).

Myth 4: Battered Women "Ask for It"

Some members of society have viewed wife assault as a problem affecting only certain types of women (Andrews & Brewin, 1990). Presumably, women who get battered "are nags," "drink too much," "come from dysfunctional families" (Tilden, 1989), "are masochistic martyrs" who actually enjoy being beaten (Shainess, 1979), or "are psychiatrically disturbed" (Snell, Rosenwald, & Robey, 1964). These criticisms of battered women recur in terms of blaming them for not "just leaving" violent men. Implicit in many of these assertions are assumptions that something must be wrong with battered women or that they somehow deserve the violence directed at them. Research has not generally supported these claims (see Hotaling & Sugarman, 1990).

Overall, battered women do not come from substantially more abusive homes than those of nonbattered women (Hotaling & Sugarman, 1990). Battered women are no more "alcoholic" than nonbattered women, but they may drink in response to abusive episodes (Barnett & Fagan, 1993). Research on self-esteem is difficult to interpret, because the studies finding low self-esteem in battered women cannot rule out the probability that its occurrence is a consequence of the beatings, rather than a precipitating factor. In light of these findings, the question of whether battered women's childhood experiences impel them to select abusive men to marry becomes moot.

Myth 5: Alcohol and Drugs Are the Real Cause of Family Violence

Men and women who drink are more likely to hit each other and to hit their children (Steinmetz, 1987). The rate of husband-to-wife violence is approximately 3 times higher for "binge" drinkers (19.2%) than for abstainers (6.8%), and alcohol is involved in roughly one out of four instances of wife beating (Kantor & Straus, 1990). Although alcohol or drug usage typifies abusive individuals, it is probably not the root cause of family violence (Yegidis, 1992; Zubretsky & Digirolamo, 1994). Abusive individuals are abusive whether sober or drunk (Browne, 1987; Walker, 1984) and may use alcohol or drugs as a response to the violence rather than as a precursor (e.g., Barnett & Fagan, 1993). Drunkenness can also serve as a justification or explanation for the abuse, thus allowing the couple to maintain the belief that their marriage is healthy (LaBell, 1979). Finally, the vast majority of men who drink do not hit their wives (Kantor & Straus, 1990).

Myth 6: Violence and Love Cannot Coexist

People tend to believe that love and violence are so opposite that one cannot exist in the presence of the other. In reality, love does not seem to preclude violence. As early as infancy, some children learn that the people who love them also hit them (Straus, 1977b). Violent couples also often express love for one another (Muldary, 1983). The statement, "If he ever lays a hand on me, I'll leave" does not mirror reality. Physical aggression does not herald the demise of a marriage (Lloyd, 1988; Margolin & Fernandez, 1987). Indeed, the average battering relationship lasts about 6 years, the same length of time as the average marriage (Browne, 1983).

Myth 7: Women Who Claim Date Rape Are "Lying," "Deserve What They Got," or Were "Asking for It"

Probably the most common myth about women who report date rape is that they are lying (Burt, 1991). Implicit in this myth is the assumption that the raped woman actually consented to intercourse. In truth, rape is such an underreported crime that exaggeration and false reports are especially unlikely (National Victims Center, 1992). Given the prevalence of date rape, the myth that only "loose" girls become victims seems unfounded also (Warshaw, 1988). Rape myths may serve to cloud interpretations about consent, shift the blame from the rapist to the victim, or absolve men of self-blame and accountability (Burt, 1991).

Summary

The point of this first chapter, in part, is to impress on the reader the significance and prevalence of violence in society. Arguably, the United States is the most violent industrialized country in the world (Siegel, 1995). A remarkably high proportion of this violence, furthermore, *occurs within the family* (Hotaling et al., 1990). There is also considerable evidence suggesting that family violence and street violence are causally connected (OJJDP, 1995). If so, then reducing family violence could help prevent "the future violence by its young victims" ("Violence in Families," 1995, p. 6).

It is also important to understand the history of the family violence problem. Examining this history serves as an illustration of how social conditions come to be defined as social problems. History is filled with accounts of the mistreatment of children and women (DeMause, 1974; Dobash & Dobash, 1979; Pleck, 1987). Quite remarkably, the mistreatment of children only began to receive serious attention during the child saving move-

ment of the mid- to late 1800s (Pleck, 1987), and the research community essentially ignored child abuse until the 1960s (Kempe, Silverman, Steele, et al., 1962). The victimization of women was similarly ignored until the late 1800s, and battered women were not discovered until the early 1970s (Pleck, 1987). Other forms of family violence—sibling violence, courtship violence, marital rape, date rape, and elder abuse—were largely ignored until the 1980s.

Today, as a result of the successful claims-making by many advocacy groups and organizations, family violence is generally recognized as a serious social problem. This recognition is reflected in the words of President Bill Clinton (quoted in "$26 Million in Grants Announced," 1995b):

If children aren't safe in their homes, if college women aren't safe in their dorms, if mothers can't raise their children in safety, then the American Dream will never be real for them. Domestic violence is now the number one health risk for women between the ages of 15 and 44 in our country. It's a bigger threat than cancer or car accidents. And we know, too, that often when a spouse is beaten, the children are beaten as well. (p. 6)

Defining family violence is inherently problematic. Definitions are subjective and constantly changing. Although words like *abuse* and *battering* and *assault* are often used as if everyone agrees on their meaning, it is important to recognize that no such consensus exists. Despite disagreement, however, definitions are a crucial part of any research endeavor. Social scientific progress depends, to some extent, on a shared definitional understanding of family violence.

A number of myths about family violence have prospered. The existence of these myths underscores the dearth of public knowledge about family violence and their relevance in helping people cope with violence. Myths are likely to remain in the background, influencing a number of important judgments that people make about family violence unless theoretical formulations and clear research data are available to counteract them.

Goals of the Book

There are many reasons for writing a book like this. Certainly, we hope to summarize and present available information on the topic of family violence so that readers will gain a substantive knowledge. Second, we hope to foster understanding of the magnitude of the problem and the devastation it causes (see Boxed Insert: "Personalizing Family Violence Research"). We realize that along the way, we must confront a number of controversial issues that have sparked debate among experts and that we will encounter numerous areas where future research is crucial. We trust that in providing numerous sources of information, student researchers who have an interest in family violence will have a foundation for their work. We also hope to help researchers and advocates currently working in the field to achieve greater interface to promote dialogue about solutions. Last, of course, we hope to continue the process of outlining some possible solutions. Just as we have felt compelled to write this textbook, we anticipate generating interest and concern in readers. We want the readers' exploration of the field to be stimulating and worthwhile.

Note

1. Because in almost 40% of all homicides the offender is not identified, these statistics should be interpreted with caution. Assuming that the offenders in intimate homicides are more likely to be identified, the actual proportion of women, for example, who are killed by intimates or other relatives is probably somewhere between 39% (where the denominator includes all homicides) and 56% (where the denominator includes only homicides where the victim-offender relationship could be identified).

PERSONALIZING FAMILY VIOLENCE RESEARCH

Scientific study has a way of depersonalizing the tragedy of family violence. Indeed, when reading research it is easy to distance oneself from the words on the page, to think of the victims and perpetrators of family violence as merely subjects in a research study. It is important to remember, however, that behind every research finding there are real people. Given the high rate of domestic violence, child maltreatment, elder abuse, and date rape in the general population, it is highly likely that someone you know has been associated in some way with one or more types of family violence. In reading the following chapters of this text, don't forget that family violence affects real victims, real people.

Robert Sandifer was a real 11-year-old boy, nicknamed "Yummy" because of his love for cookies. Robert's story, which ended when he was shot in the head by his own gang, attracted national attention in the fall of 1994. Illinois children's services first came into contact with Robert when he was less than a year old. At age 3, he was removed from his home, with bruises (apparently from an electrical cord) and burns (from cigarettes) covering his body. From that point on, he lived with his grandmother in a home that sometimes contained as many as 19 children. What was the reason for his murder? Robert had killed a 14-year-old neighbor, and his gang, fearing he would become a liability, gunned him down (Braun & Pasternak, 1994).

Elisa Izquierdo was another real-life person. Her life and death, at age 6, also attracted national attention when her picture appeared on the cover of *Time* magazine (Van Biema, 1995). To all who knew her, Elisa was a bright, happy, beautiful girl with limitless potential. For most of her life, she had lived with her father, Gustavo, who loved and doted on his daughter. However, on weekend visits with her mother, Awilda Lopez, she was being abused. Elisa began to urinate and defecate uncontrollably, and she developed sores on her vagina. Gustavo petitioned the court to deny Awilda visitation rights, but before he could follow through on the petition, he died of cancer in 1994. Despite the evidence of abuse and the pleas from Gustavo's family, Awilda was granted permanent custody. While living with her mother, Elisa's condition quickly deteriorated. School officials noticed that she was often bruised and had trouble walking. Neighbors reported hearing her pleas: "Mommy, Mommy, please stop! No more! No more! I'm sorry!" The Child Welfare Administration investigated but reported that everything looked fine. Elisa eventually stopped attending school altogether, and on November 23, police were called to Elisa's home: "When the police arrived, she [Awilda] confessed to killing Elisa by throwing her against a concrete wall. She confessed that she had made Elisa eat her own feces and that she had mopped the floor with her head. The police told reporters that there was no part of the 6-year-old's body that was not cut or bruised. Thirty circular marks that at first appeared to be cigarette burns, turned out to be impressions left by the stone in someone's ring" (Van Biema, 1995, p. 36).

These stories about Robert and Elisa are tragedies, so horrific that they made headlines in the national press. There are, of course, thousands of other tragedies that never attract media attention. Consider Markus, a cute and precocious 7-year-old boy who went to live with his father and stepmother after his biological mother abandoned him at age 5. Markus's father asked that Markus be admitted to the inpatient psychiatric unit because he and his wife were unable to keep him from running away from their home in the middle of the night. Markus's father admitted that they had sometimes resorted to shackling Markus to his bed so that he would not run away. Markus's stepmother also revealed that she and her husband had never really wanted Markus to move into their home because they already had two children of their own. Young Markus, at age 7, had now been rejected by both his mother and father. Imagine being 7 years old and being faced with the realization that your mother and father neither love you nor want you. No wonder he wanted to run away! (Author's case history)

2

Theories and Methodology

Investigating the Problem of Family Violence

CHAPTER OUTLINE

An Interview
With Kersti Yllö

"I feel that I have become a translator between mainstream sociologists and those concerned with feminist analysis."

KERSTI YLLÖ is a widely recognized feminist scholar, teaching and conducting sociological research at Wheaton College in Norton, Massachusetts, just outside of Boston. She is the Dorothy Reed Williams Professor of Sociology, an endowed chair that supports faculty in the social sciences whose works and research connect to the community. She has published primarily in the areas of cohabitation, the status of women, and wife abuse. She completed her undergraduate work at Dennison University. In 1980, she earned her Ph.D. in sociology from the University of New Hampshire, where she also held a postdoctoral fellowship at the Family Violence Research Program.

Q: What sparked your interest in the area of family violence?

A: While I was an undergraduate, I took the first course ever offered in women's studies at Dennison University and a family course that looked at power issues. When I later entered graduate school, it was when Murray Straus was just beginning his national survey work on family violence. I was given the opportunity to obtain a predoctoral grant with the stipulation that my work be connected to family violence. I found the topic to be the most compelling focus of family power issues, and I've been fascinated with the subject ever since.

Q: Looking back, what is your most influential contribution to the area of family violence?

A: One area is my work with David Finkelhor and our book, *License to Rape: Sexual Abuse of Wives.* At the time we began our work, there were no published articles on marital rape, although legislatures were beginning to debate whether marital rape should be criminalized. Many people thought of marital rape as a contradiction in terms. Our in-depth interviews with women provided such a rich source of data that we ended up testifying before lawmakers in support of criminalization. Through the work of many women's advocates, marital rape has finally been crimi-

nalized in all 50 states. In 1993, North Carolina was the last state to enact marital rape laws. Unfortunately, the laws stop short of full criminalization by incorporating many restrictions and time limits and allowing too many loopholes. The laws still do not treat marital rape like "real" rape.

Q: How do you see marital rape as intersecting with power issues?

A: I think that marital rape at its core is about the use of sexuality in the power relationship whether it occurs in the midst of a very violent, injurious attack accompanied by the use of weapons, whether it is a means of humiliation and degradation, or whether it is a nonviolent coercive action, the one way for the husband to win a power battle. Marital rape actually receives very little attention. Probably because it is at the heart of power, sex, and intimacy in marriage, it is too hard to address.

Q: Have you run across students who have said, "She doesn't have a right to say 'No.' Maybe she shouldn't have gotten married in the first place"? People are not seeing the difference between consensual marital sex and rape.

A: Yes. I've also heard, "She has had sex with him a thousand times before. What is one more time?" I think these questions reflect a misunderstanding of rape. Rape is not a sexual violation as much as it is a coercive act that destroys trust.

Q: What do you see as your role in the field of family violence, where you have been and where you are going?

A: Working at the University of New Hampshire [UNH] and with people like Murray

Straus, I became well acquainted with the mainstream approach of sociologists and I understand their thinking. Although I disagree with some of the tenets of this school, Murray has always been supportive of my work and my approach. I also disagree with those who feel that the mainstream approach has done more harm than good. I think that these kinds of criticisms by some feminists and other family violence researchers have been very hurtful to the people at UNH.

On the other hand, I understand the viewpoint of those involved in feminist analysis. I am very close to this group of feminist researchers. In fact, my interest in developing feminist perspectives on family violence research grew out of my interactions with others at the Third National Family Violence Research Conference here at UNH. I feel that I have become a translator between these two groups—the mainstream sociologists and those concerned with feminist analysis. I hope to continue in this role.

Introduction

As interest in family violence has heightened, the field has expanded beyond its initial academic borders of sociology, psychology, and criminology to encompass a large number of academic fields such as women's studies and victimology, as well as professional fields such as medicine and law enforcement. In addition, advocates working with victims of family violence have emerged as a forceful group of activists with a specific moral and political agenda. Each of these claims-maker groups brings its own perspectives to bear on the problem.

While academic researchers in these fields spent years in graduate school learning procedures for studying phenomena like family violence, activists spent years on the firing line, trying to awaken the public, legislators, and law enforcement personnel to the plight of victims. Inclusion of so many groups (researchers, professionals, activists), with such a diversity of backgrounds and goals, has posed a serious challenge for the field in terms of accommodating opposing points of view (Geffner, 1987; Jacobson, 1994; Schechter, 1988).

Characteristic contentions have also arisen between experts schooled within divergent academic disciplines and between academicians and clinicians. These experts have applied differing research methodologies, have collected data from separate sources, and have formulated alternative definitions and theoretical frameworks (Fagan, 1988). Although thoughtful diversity of opinion is one cornerstone of science, fractious debate generated by opposing academic and political groups in the field of family violence has exceeded customary levels and has occasionally created an atmosphere of distrust and acrimony (see Gelles & Loseke, 1993). Murray Straus of the Family Violence Laboratory at the University of New Hampshire, for instance, received a bomb threat from someone trying to stop a presentation of his research findings (Straus, 1991d).

Much of the dispute has erupted over divergent views about the causes of family violence (e.g., patriarchy, childhood learning, psychopathology) and hence the most effective solutions. Probably the most impassioned argument between diverse groups (e.g., researchers, practitioners, criminal justice personnel, advocates) has stemmed from competition over limited funds (Dobash & Dobash, 1988; Schechter, 1988).

Child molestation provides an exemplar of funding dilemmas. Should whatever money that is available go to a treatment program for child molesters who, without treatment, will go on to molest hundreds of other children? Alternatively, should funds be expended on a treatment program for molested children whose lives have been shattered by their victimization and whose futures are in jeopardy? Should funding support research to identify prevention strategies? Should funding go to longer prison sentences for child molesters? Because of varying experiences and needs, people hold antagonistic opinions about such matters, leading them to actions to ensure that their side will prevail. Altogether, there is a great need for social scientists to shed light on all aspects of family violence through research. They need to conduct their research in a manner that informs policy and helps resolve the problems of all affected groups.

Studying Family Violence: A Multidisciplinary Approach

No one social institution has been able to come to grips with the enormity of the family violence problem. Many, however, have tried: the criminal justice system, the medical community, the mental health community, social welfare, the schools, and academicians. Not surprisingly, practitioners from these diverse areas have offered different kinds of solutions to the problems. Some suggest prison, some medication, some counseling, some castration.

The diversity of approaches has resulted in a knowledge base that looks very much like a colossal jigsaw puzzle. Some parts of the picture seem clear, some are obscured, some do not fit together, some seem as if they will never fit together, and some are totally missing. To be sure, there is a considerable wealth of research findings, but insufficient synthesis of the field as a whole (Gelles & Loseke, 1993; Ohlin & Tonry, 1989; Steinman, 1991).

One of the goals of this book is to bring together this wealth of knowledge. A brief summary of the various academic and professional paradigms that dominate the study of family violence is a prerequisite to comprehension of the field. In fact, the various interviews with leading experts in the field that appear in all but the first chapter reflect the diversity of their training and theoretical backgrounds. It may be helpful to view these various perspectives as claims-making, where advocates and academicians often compete with one another for the ear of the nation.

Sociological Research

Sociologists were the first academicians to grapple with the problems of family violence. Sociologists in this field usually survey large numbers of people about interpersonal violence (e.g., Straus, 1977b) and postulate various structural theories to account for the rates and patterns of violence (age, gender, class) (Gelles, 1993d). A typical topic of study by a sociologist is the examination of the relationships between marital power and violence among couples (Coleman & Straus, 1986).

Criminological Research

Criminologists who study family violence are most frequently sociologists with a special focus on family crime. They gather and study very large banks of crime statistics and

other official reports funded by government agencies such as the Federal Bureau of Investigations (FBI) or the Bureau of Justice Statistics (BJS). Historically, criminologists viewed their role as studying stranger violence. They perceived family violence as a distinct prob-

---

There is a considerable wealth of research findings but insufficient synthesis of the field as a whole.

---

lem; they did not categorize violent acts between family members as a crime until the 1970s (Morash, 1986). A typical criminal justice study would be an inquiry about the role of police in domestic violence cases (Ferraro, 1989).

Psychological Research

Psychologists and social workers usually collect data from small, clinical samples. They center their inquiries primarily on individual factors such as psychopathology or the dynamics of interpersonal functioning. They also specialize in treatment and prevention. Typical of studies undertaken by psychologists in the field of child sexual abuse, for example, is the study of sex differences in experiences of child sexual victimization (Levesque, 1994).

Legal Research

Because of a great escalation in the reporting of family violence incidents, and the mounting pressure to prevent family violence, legal scholars have increasingly reviewed the legal issues surrounding family violence. Attorneys have offered advice about needed changes in the law, for example, how to ease the burden on children testifying in court (Walker, 1993).

Research in Medical Settings

Physicians took the lead in recognition of child abuse (Kempe, Silverman, & Steele, 1962) and continue to have a role in describing abuse, in mandatory reporting, in treatment, and in offering medical testimony in court on behalf of victims (Lawson & Chaffin, 1992; Murdock, 1992). A typical study in a medical setting is the analysis of treatments received by battered women in emergency rooms (Stark & Flitcraft, 1985).

Advocacy Positions

Advocates for women and children have also played an important role in understanding family violence. Their calls for greater awareness and prevention efforts have contributed to the increased societal attention to the problem. Feminists represent one such advocate influence. *Feminist,* however, is not an academic title but a label applied to a sub-group of individuals who can be found in any discipline. They act from their perception that "empirical" information includes a patriarchal bias damaging to women (Dutton, 1994).

Feminist theories of marital violence attribute violence to patriarchy because of the perceived inequality of power between the sexes. In particular, questions arise among feminists about the reasons men physically assault women and what function these acts serve for a given society (Bograd, 1988). The main theme expressed by this group is that men beat women because they can get away with it (Gelles & Straus, 1988) and because control is a powerful resource (Allen & Straus, 1980).

Intermediate Chapter Summary

Family violence as a topic has attracted the attention and study of numerous segments of society. A number of academicians representing various disciplines (e.g., sociology, criminology, psychology), experts within various professions (e.g., law, medicine), and other groups (e.g., activists) have become highly involved in finding solutions to the problem of family violence.

Compartmentalization has led to insufficient integration of research and summarization of ideas, making it difficult to obtain a comprehensive overview of family violence (see Gelles & Straus, 1979). According to Ohlin and Tonry (1989), for example, the separation of criminological research from social science research may have contributed to a belated recognition of violent acts within families as crimes. On the other hand, distinctions between **academic disciplines, professionals,** and **advocates** are actually more blurred than current categorization might imply. The desire to find solutions has, in many instances, united various groups and their agendas.

Macrotheory: Explaining Patterns of Family Violence

In many respects, family violence is incomprehensible. How could a husband who supposedly loves his wife be physically violent? How could a mother purposely hurt her child? Research suggests, nevertheless, that family violence is far from uncommon. Given these empirical realities, it may be fruitful to consider the many social and cultural conditions that not only make violence comprehensible but also, in some respects, make it a "normal" (i.e., culturally approved) part of family life. The task of macrotheories is to identify the structural factors that make families prone to violence.

Cultural Explanations

Broad macroexplanations of violence include cultural factors, structural characteristics of the family (e.g., family stress), deterrence factors (e.g., low costs of family violence), and social structural factors (e.g., poverty).

Cultural Acceptance of Violence. On many levels, violence is an accepted, encouraged, and even glorified form of cultural expression (Heath, Kruttschnitt, & Ward, 1986). It is probable that violence in the home mirrors society's tolerance for victimizing vulnerable people (Wyatt, 1994). There may be a spill-over effect in which the acceptance of violence in the culture contributes to violence in the family (Straus, 1977a). Social approval of corporal punishment, for example, is consonant with the moral obligation that parents have to use enough force to train, protect, and control their children. From this perspective, violence against children is "normative" (Witt, 1987). Some argue that it is this cultural support of violence that lays the groundwork for child abuse (Straus, Gelles, & Steinmetz, 1980).

Hitting a spouse is less tolerable than hitting a child, and hitting a woman is less acceptable than hitting a man (Arias & Johnson, 1989; Greenblat, 1983). Still, a sizable minority of Americans think that hitting a spouse is permissible, whereas hitting a stranger is an unacceptable form of violence, if not a criminal act. In a national survey of family violence, Dibble and Straus (1980a) documented that 27.6% of respondents thought that slapping a spouse could be necessary, normal, or good (also see Briere, 1987; Gentemann, 1984).

Patriarchy. Complaints about patriarchy have been at the foundation of the domestic violence movement since its inception. Patriarchy is a cultural belief system that allows men to hold greater power and privilege than women on a social hierarchy. In its extreme form, it literally gives men the right to dominate and control women and children (Dobash & Dobash, 1979).

Although some might argue that patriarchy is dead and no longer dictates male-female interactions, many disagree. Straus (1976), in fact, identifies a number of contemporary, cherished cultural standards that not only permit but also encourage husband-to-wife violence: (a) the greater authority of men in our culture; (b) male aggressiveness and the notion that aggression positively correlates to maleness and that aggression is not only an acceptable tool for a man but also a way to demonstrate male identity; (c) the wife/mother role as the preferred status for women; and (d) male domination and orientation of the criminal justice system that provides little legal relief for battered women.

Subculture of Violence. Cultural norms vary within a society so that certain groups may accept violence more than other groups. Proponents of the "subculture of violence" theory maintain that there is a greater acceptance of violence among families in the lower class. From this perspective, violence is a cultural norm—a way of life (Wolfgang & Ferracuti, 1972).

Structural Characteristics of the Family—Family Stress

Many researchers have focused their etiological quest on the structural factors that make families particularly prone to violence (Brinkerhoff & Lupri, 1988; Gelles & Straus, 1979). Family life can be so stressful that many families are unable to cope with their

---

A factor that naturally arouses conflict is the power differential that exists between family members.

---

problems (Denzin, 1984). The "time risk" of spending a disproportionate amount of time with family members, along with the intensity of these interactions, makes families susceptible to violence. Emotional investment is sometimes one-sided, and the emotionally invested person may be especially vulnerable to violence (Brinkerhoff & Lupri, 1988).

Another factor that naturally arouses conflict in the family is the power differential that exists between family members. Children are always subordinate to parents and women are often subordinate to men. Conflict emerges naturally out of this power imbalance (Gelles, 1993d). One way to relieve conflict in interpersonal interactions is to dissolve the relationship. Family relationships, however, are relatively involuntary and difficult to dissolve. Divorce is complicated and children cannot divorce their parents (Gelles, 1993d).

Finally, the privacy of families makes violence relatively easy to hide and dictates a "hands off" policy when it comes to family matters (Brinkerhoff & Lupri, 1988). Lack of public surveillance of families decreases accountability of family members. Somewhat germane to issues of privacy are issues of social isolation and lack of social support. Abusive parents have reported high levels of social isolation (Garbarino & Gilliam, 1980), and battered women have reported lack of social support (Barnett, Martinez, & Keyson, 1996). The boxed insert titled "Does Stress Cause Elder Abuse?" illustrates a controversy in attributing family violence to structural characteristics of the family.

DOES STRESS CAUSE ELDER ABUSE?

At the basis of the stress model of elder abuse is the belief that elders who become abused are those who create inordinate levels of stress for family caregivers. When an elder's impairments necessitate reliance on family members to fulfill financial, physical, or emotional support needs, it creates an intolerable burden of stress for these caregivers (Hickey & Douglass, 1981a).

In a study substantiating the dependency-induced stress thesis, Alzheimer's-impaired elders were at greater risk for abuse than were elders without the disease (Paveza et al., 1992). Additional congruent evidence arose from a study of 107 abused elders contrasted with 147 nonabused elders (Fulmer & O'Malley, 1987). Dependency was a strong predisposing factor for abuse (also see Biegel, Sales, & Schulz, 1991; Coyne, Reichman, & Berbig, 1993).

Other studies, however, have produced contradictory results by showing that impaired, dependent elders, those who presumably create high levels of caregiver stress, are not significantly more abused than nonimpaired elders (e.g., Phillips, 1986; Wolf, Godkin, & Pillemer, 1986). Elder abuse victims in one study (Pillemer, 1986), in fact, were distinctly less likely to rely for assistance on the abuser (26%) than on someone else (63%). Using six measures (e.g., financial, housing), elder abuse victims were significantly less dependent on the abuser than elder nonvictims in five of the areas assessed (also see Bristowe & Collins, 1989; Phillips, 1983).

In reality, the dependency of the victim may simply be a catalyst for abuse in a caretaker who cannot cope effectively (e.g., Movsas & Movsas, 1990; Pillemer, 1986). In other words, abusive behavior may stem from a "problem" caregiver rather than from an elder with "problems." Furthermore, citing victim impairment and dependency may be yet one more disguised attempt to blame victims for the abusive behavior of others (Pillemer, 1993).

The use of vastly different samples and other methodological differences has most likely produced the divergence in findings and thus fueled the debate (Fulmer, 1990). Professional report data arising from samples drawn from agencies support a caregiver-stress model (e.g., Paveza et al., 1992). In contrast, interview data arising from victims drawn from general population surveys do not support a caregiver-stress model (Pillemer, 1986). More research is needed to resolve the debate about stress-induced violence.

Deterrence Theory: Low Costs of Family Violence

From a social control standpoint, deviant behavior is common when there are few social or legal costs. According to Travis Hirschi (1969), humans, being basically antisocial at birth, are held in check by their "stakes in conformity." *Stakes in conformity* refers to commitments to conventional goals, involvement in conventional activities, attachments to significant others, and beliefs that violence is wrong. People who have few stakes in conformity are free to commit deviant acts.

The criminal justice system is based on much the same principle. Deterrence theory assumes that humans will rationally weigh the costs and benefits of a behavior (Gibbs, 1975). Therefore, increasing the legal costs of antisocial behavior will inevitably lead to a decrease in the amount of antisocial behavior. Many scholars argue that the reason family violence is so common is that the potential cost of committing a violent act against a family member is too low.

Even when the violence is reported, arrest is uncommon (Gelles & Straus, 1988). Historically, police have taken as little action as possible in family violence (LaFave, 1965). Cases in which children are beaten, for example, are more likely to be turned over to child protection services than to the criminal justice system (Gelles & Straus, 1988). In fact, the number of police interventions that result in arrest is probably less than 10%. In short, the cost of family violence is so minimal that it does not deter potential offenders (Gelles & Straus, 1988).

Social Structural Factors— Environmental Stress

Social structural theories begin with the recognition that rates of family violence are higher in lower-income families. The unequal distribution of opportunities, along with the inevitable stressors associated with poverty (e.g., financial worries, ill health, crowded living conditions), produces high levels of frustration in lower-class families (Farrington, 1980; Straus, 1980a). This stress and frustration sometimes result in aggression directed at innocent, yet convenient victims (i.e., children, spouses).

Psychologists have formulated a frustration-aggression hypothesis to refer to aggression following frustration caused by blocked goals (Dollard, Doob, Miller, & Sears, 1939). When the person or situation responsible for the frustration is not available as a target of the aroused aggression, people sometimes displace their aggression onto an innocent person, or scapegoat. The assumption, then, is that "frustration and/or strain experienced as a result of structural contingencies can result in aggressive actions towards others,

---

Deterrence theory assumes that humans will rationally weigh the costs and benefits of a behavior.

---

such as a spouse" (Howell & Pugliesi, 1988, p. 17). Research demonstrating a significant relationship between stress and family violence supports this theoretical expectation (Barnett, Fagan, & Booker, 1991; Straus, 1980a; Webster, Goldstein, & Alexander, 1985). When used to explain racial or ethnic differences, however, one study found stress accounts were overly simplistic (Neff, Holamon, & Schluter, 1995).

Intermediate Chapter Summary

Macrotheories account for family violence by explaining how broad, cultural forces may allow or promote it. **Cultural acceptance theory** assumes that violence is the product of widespread social approval. Parents regularly spank their children and some people approve of slapping a spouse. Violence is so generally acceptable that low levels are considered "normative." **Patriarchal formulations** attribute family violence to male privilege and power. Patriarchy gives men the "right," if not the moral obligation, to dominate and control women and children. **Feminist analysis** focuses on gender inequality of power. This viewpoint assumes that men beat women because they can get away it. Some groups may accept violence more than others in a so-called **subculture of violence.**

Structural characteristics of the family may also account for family violence. The continual interaction and power imbalances inherent in family living create stress and seemingly provoke violent assaults by family members on each other. Furthermore, family privacy conceals violence from other members of society, thus making its occurrence more probable. **Deterrence theory** assumes that the low costs of family violence make it easy to abuse a family member and get away with it. For example, police intervention exerts so little pressure on people to conform that the costs of violence are too low to be effective. **Social structural factors,** such as poverty, may account for family violence by creating frustration, and hence aggression.

Microtheory: Explaining the Behavior of Violent Family Members

Cultural and structural factors may successfully explain why family violence exists in a society, or why some segments of society experience more violence than others, but they fail to explain why individual family members are violent. Some of the single-dimensional theories that address these issues are learning principles, individual (intrapersonal) differences, and interpersonal interaction.

Socialization or Learning Explanations

A large body of research within the fields of sociology, criminology, and psychology has revealed the importance of childhood socialization in the developmental problems of family-violent offenders (see Ohlin & Tonry, 1989). Children learn specific forms or techniques for using violence as well as attitudes and cognitions that justify violence. Furthermore, adult persistence in abusive relationships can be linked theoretically to reinforcement- and punishment-based learning during childhood.

Classical and Operant Conditioning. An obvious application of operant conditioning (shaping behavior in a step-by-step fashion) is that a victim's compliance with a perpetrator's demands reinforces (rewards) the perpetrator's use of violence. In other words, a perpetrator gets what he wants (e.g., dinner cooked on time) by using violence. Because the victim's compliance is reinforcing, the perpetrator will increase his violence (see Felson, 1992; Ganley, 1989). Along the same lines, the failure to punish aggressive behavior of a perpetrator allows the perpetrator (e.g., child who hits a sibling) to gain practice using violent interpersonal skills (Patterson, 1982).

Operant principles also apply to the question of why battered women stay in abusive relationships (Barnett & LaViolette, 1993). The most famous application has been L. E. Walker's (1977) analogy between *learned helplessness* in laboratory dogs (a type of failure to avoid shock) and battered women's passive acceptance of the violence directed at them. Learned helplessness is a condition frequently used as an explanatory variable in battered women's decisions to stay with an abuser. Applications based on laboratory findings about the effects of intermittent reinforcement and punishment also help explain how an abusive male partner's inconsistent behavior keeps the female partner engaged in the relationship (see Barnett & LaViolette, 1993, for a review).

Social Learning—Modeling. A widely accepted explanation of how socialization plays a role in family violence rests on social learning theory. A process called *modeling,* in which a person learns social and cognitive behaviors by simply observing and imitating others, resides at the core of this theory (Bandura, 1971). In addition, learning in the *observer* is strengthened through observation of rewards and punishment dispensed to the *model.* As applied specifically to family violence, observation of violence (e.g., father hits mother

for "mouthing off") and reinforcement of violence within a social context (i.e., mother "shuts up") teaches children exactly how to be abusive.

The popularity of social learning theory rests on several observations. First, violence tends to perpetuate itself from one generation to the next, "like father, like son" (Straus et al., 1980). Second, a wealth of laboratory experiments with humans (e.g., schoolchildren) lends strong validation to the claim that aggression can be learned through modeling (e.g., Bandura, Ross, & Ross, 1961). Finally, a large number of family violence studies have successfully linked exposure to violence in one's childhood, either directly or through observation, to violence in adulthood (e.g., Hotaling & Sugarman, 1986; Rosenbaum & O'Leary, 1981a). Straus et al. (1980), for example, found that sons who had witnessed their fathers' violence had a 1,000% greater battering rate than those who had not (also see Kalmuss, 1984).

Researchers have increasingly postulated more specific learning vehicles. Children in violent families, for example, have inadequate opportunities to learn appropriate conflict resolution skills and nonviolent assertion behaviors (M. S. Rosenberg, 1987) that might be related to anger control deficits as seen in adult batterers (Kenning, Merchant, & Tomkins, 1991). Violence in the home further legitimizes the right to use force (Straus, 1991c; Tontodonato & Crew, 1992). The use of aggression as a problem-solving technique might be the nexus between observation of interparental abuse and dating violence (Riggs & O'Leary, 1989). In one study, Barnett, Martinez, and Bleustein (1996) conjectured that childhood exposure to aggression fostered the learning of dependent and jealous interactional styles that, in turn, precipitated wife assault (see Langhinrichsen-Rohling, Neidig, & Thorn, 1995).

The exact link between parental violence and the child's violence is a matter of considerable speculation. Several variables and their interactions influence these associations: (a) *type of childhood experience* (direct abuse or exposure to interparental abuse), (b) *type of involvement in adult violence* (victimization or perpetration), and (c) *gender of adult parent/partner* (male or female). Specifically, research findings are unclear about whether direct childhood abuse by parents and childhood exposure to interparental violence are equally predictive of adult violence. It is also inconclusive whether direct childhood abuse or childhood exposure to interparental violence is associated more clearly with perpetration of or victimization in adult violence. Finally, whether these variables affect males differently than females is uncertain. The gender of the parent perpetrator is probably important also, but its effects have not been documented carefully (see Langhinrichsen-Rohling et al., 1995; Silvern, Karyl, Waelde, et al., 1995).

One study of dating couples did examine these factors more closely. The family-of-origin features that predicted high levels of courtship aggression were as follows: frequency and severity of family-of-origin violence, the effect of aggression, identification with parents, model and observer gender, and whether the aggression was witnessed or experienced. The more features present, the greater the level of courtship violence (MacEwen, 1994).

Individual (Intrapersonal) Differences Theories

In an attempt to define the etiology of family violence, other researchers have searched for explanations in the individual/intrapersonal differences among offenders (and sometimes victims), including psychopathology, psychological traits, and biological characteristics. Social exchange theory also offers a more individually based explanation of family violence than do other theories.

Psychopathology. One recurrent explanation for family violence is psychopathology (also referred to as abnormal behavior or mental disorder; see Bolton & Bolton, 1987). Psychopathology theories propose that various forms of family violence, such as child abuse or spouse abuse, are committed by individuals who are seriously disturbed by some form of mental illness, personality disorder, or some other individual defect. The individual's psychopathology might distort his or her view of the world or serve as a disinhibitor to prohibited behavior. Some research has supported the psychopathology model of family violence by demonstrating higher rates of various psychological disorders in family violence offenders relative to comparison groups (e.g., Hamberger & Hastings, 1986a). Others hold that psychopathology, as an explanation, may explain only a small part of the violence (see Pagelow, 1992).

Examinations of sexual abuse perpetrators, for example, show that they experience stronger deviant sexual arousal (e.g., penile responses to child-adult sexual interactions) than nonperpetrators (Marshall, Barbaree, & Christophe, 1986). In addition, about 80% to 90% of men court ordered to treatment for marital violence are diagnosable with some form of psychological disorder (primarily personality disorders) (Dutton & Starzomski, 1993; Hamberger & Hastings, 1986a; Saunders, 1992).

Psychological Traits. Other research has focused on psychological (personality) traits of the perpetrators of family violence that are less severe and would not be officially defined as psychopathology. These theories propose that the psychological traits that characterize offenders contribute to their perpetration of family violence. Because traits are measurable on personality tests (e.g., hostility) and differentiate individuals, they help to explain (not justify) abusive behaviors. Those who possess negative traits, for example, impulsivity, are more prone to commit violent acts. Although traits are constructs (labels) that do not actually exist, they describe the typical ways in which people behave in different situations. They help predict behavior and also provide a clear point of therapeutic intervention.

Child sexual abuse perpetrators, for example, may exhibit feelings of vulnerability, dependency, inadequacy, loneliness, or cognitive distortions (e.g., Hanson, Gizzarelli, & Scott, 1994; Seidman, Marshall, Hudson, & Robertson, 1994). These characteristics appear to lead offenders to turn to children to avoid the demands of adult relationships to have their relationship needs satisfied. Studies have also identified several psychological traits in assaultive partners such as low self-esteem, anger and hostility, poor problem-solving skills, and emotional dependency (see Barnett et al., 1991; Barnett & Hamberger, 1992; Dutton & Strachan, 1987; Goldstein & Rosenbaum, 1985).

Biological Theories. Possible biological bases for family violence have received almost no study until recently (DiLalla & Gottesman, 1991). In the area of child abuse, for example, recent research has suggested that perpetrators of physical child abuse show hyperresponsive physiological activity to both positive and negative child stimuli (Milner & Chilamkurti, 1991). Such unusual hyperresponsiveness might contribute to decreased tolerance for proximity to children in such individuals and, in turn, lead to physical aggression. Neglectful parenting has also been associated with intellectual deficits in parents (Crittenden, 1992). Intellectually deficient parents may lack the knowledge and skills necessary to parent adequately.

Researchers have further identified unique biological characteristics potentially related to the etiology of spouse abuse, including organic problems, head injuries, and birth complications (see Faulk, 1974; Kandel & Mednick, 1991; Rosenbaum & Hoge, 1989). Finally, genetic studies have uncovered some controversial evidence for a gene-crime association (Walters, 1992).

Interpersonal Interaction Theories

Violence may be a product of the interactions between individuals in a specific relationship rather than the result of the behavior of only one individual (i.e., the perpetrator) (Giles-Sims, 1983). Lane and Russell (1989), for example, contend that one cannot separate a victim from the victimizer, dominance from submission, or aggression from passivity. In other words, specific aspects about relationships, in and of themselves, may contribute to family violence.

Dyadic Stress. A number of experts, for example, have pinpointed marital dysfunction as a dyadic stressor and have assumed that certain intimate relationships are more likely to promote violence than others. From this point of view, a violent spouse's behavior is a response to the behaviors of the other spouse and is maintained by the interactions of both partners to preserve the homeostatic balance of the relationship (Giles-Sims, 1983).

Support for this view often rests on studies showing that violent couples experience high rates of marital discord or have problems in communication skills (e.g., Babcock, Waltz, Jacobson, & Gottman, 1993; Margolin, John, & Gleberman, 1988). Some research has also demonstrated high stress levels in violent dating partners (e.g., Makepeace, 1987; Marshall & Rose, 1987). The correlational nature of the data in these studies, however, precludes assumptions about causality. Consequently, whether these negative characteristics serve as antecedents or consequences of interpart-

ner abuse is uncertain. In addition, contradictory evidence has shown that men scoring above the median on marital satisfaction tests may still beat their wives, and those scoring below may not (e.g., Barnett & Hamberger, 1992; Rosenbaum & O'Leary, 1981b). Furthermore, longitudinal data of early marriages demonstrate that relationship discord does not precede the occurrence of aggression. Instead, repeated aggressive incidents are linked with relationship dissatisfaction (Murphy & O'Leary, 1987; O'Leary et al., 1989).

Parent-Child Interactional Stress. Researchers have also applied interpersonal interaction theories as an explanation for child abuse and neglect. Theorists, for example, have increasingly focused on the reciprocal nature of the parent-child relationship as it may initiate and maintain abusive and neglectful interactions (Wolfe, 1987). Difficult child behaviors (e.g., continual whining and complaining) might interact with behavior problems of parents (e.g., anger control problems) to result in physical abuse of a child. Research has corroborated the interactional-stress pattern by documenting the presence of child characteristics, deficits in parents' skills, and negative parent-child interactions (Bousha & Twentyman, 1984; Department of Health and Human Services, 1993).

Attachment Problems. Evidence from several sources suggests interpersonal interaction difficulties in abusive and neglecting families in the form of disturbed patterns of attachment (Egeland, Sroufe, & Erickson, 1983; Kolko, 1992). Attachment is an enduring emotional bond that develops progressively over the first year of an infant's life while the infant is completely dependent on his or her caretaker for survival. This enduring bond serves an important function, because through the caretaker-child relationship, the infant develops a sense of trust and security, a sense of self, and an ability to learn and explore (Ainsworth, 1973; Bowlby, 1980). Failure to form a secure attachment early in life, on the other hand, may be related to an inability to develop close personal relationships in adulthood (Ainsworth & Bowlby, 1991; Bowlby, 1980; Corvo, 1992; Frankel & Bates, 1990).

Using a specially designed observation procedure (Strange Situation format; Ainsworth, 1973), researchers have been able to accurately classify infants as either securely or insecurely attached. Securely attached infants display several unique characteristics such as good-quality play behaviors and the ability to be comforted by their caregiver. Insecurely attached infants (i.e., anxiously attached), in contrast, exhibit poor-quality play behaviors and are not easily comforted by their caregivers (avoid or resist the caregiver). Research has consistently observed insecure patterns of attachment in physically abused, neglected, and psychologically maltreated children (Crittenden, 1992; Erickson & Egeland, 1987; Kolko, 1992).

Researchers have only recently used attachment theory to account for abusive behavior in adults (Goldner, Penn, Sheinberg, & Walker, 1990). Insecurely attached adults suffer renewed anxiety and anger when faced with a partner who threatens to leave. It is these intense feelings that fuel an assault against that partner (Dutton, Saunders, Starzomski, & Batholomew, 1994; Mayseless, 1991). Attachment theory deals with the unexpected finding that love and violence do not seem to be opposite forces as one might expect, but coexist (e.g., Billingham, 1987; Dutton & Painter, 1981).

Social Exchange Theory. Social exchange theory explores interactions between victim and perpetrator from a cost-benefit point of view. Exchange theory assumes that humans will only enter into relationships, and only stay in relationships, when they perceive that the benefits (money, love, self-esteem, security, recognition, admiration, etc.) outweigh the costs (Gelles, 1983). Social exchange principles, of course, are applicable to marriage. Marriage partners assume the benefits (e.g., companionship) will outweigh the costs (e.g., added responsibilities). When these expectations are not met, one partner may perceive the relationship as inequitable.

Social exchange theorists argue that inequitable relationships will be terminated, when possible (Brinkerhoff & Lupri, 1988). When a marriage seems inequitable, however, it cannot easily be dissolved. When a spouse does not receive the benefit he or she expects, and cannot easily terminate the relationship, he or she may experience frustration and become aggressive (frustration-aggression hypothesis; Gelles, 1983). Although social exchange theory cannot specify why such spouses choose violence (as opposed to another response), it has identified some probable antecedents to violence (Gelles & Straus, 1979).

The social exchange formulation can apply to other forms of abuse, such as elder abuse or child abuse. Not all parents, for example, perceive the benefits of parenthood as outweighing the costs, yet the parent-child relationship is next to impossible to legally terminate, although some parents do abandon their children (Gelles & Straus, 1988). Lacking attractive alternatives, a parent may deal with the dissatisfaction of parenthood with violence. This theoretical perspective might help explain the evidence that rates of abuse are higher for sick, handicapped, premature, ugly, and demanding children (Gelles, 1983; Sullivan, Brookhouser, Scanlan, Knutson, & Schulte, 1992).

Symbolic Interactionism. Symbolic interactionism emphasizes the symbolic communication between humans. Within the ongoing process of social interactions, the actors construct and reconstruct their own social reality. From this viewpoint, it is simplistic to assume that human behavior can be understood merely on the basis of objectively specifiable variables, such as the actors' background characteristics or external stimuli.

As it relates to family violence, the theory focuses on perpetrator-victim interactions from the subjective viewpoint of an actor's meanings or definitions of these interactions. The key to understanding violent family interactions is understanding the meanings that family members attach to various family interactions. As a particular example, the personal meaning of an elder's biological aging for his caregiver may affect whether the caregiver is abusive. If the elder's aging evokes unpleasant thoughts in the caregiver about his or her own aging, the caregiver might avoid the elder, thus behaving in a neglectful way toward the elder. Alternatively, if a caregiver is dependent on the elder, he or she may feel powerless and, in turn, become abusive (see Finkelhor, 1983).

Multidimensional Theories

Overall, the problem of family violence has such complexity and so many dimensions that social scientists continue to be challenged in positing an inclusive model (see Shotland, 1992). Suppose that a very hostile man (pathology) who was abused as a child (socialization or learning) and is currently unhappily married (interpersonal interaction) uses male privilege (patriarchy) as a justification for assaulting his wife. Clearly, no singular etiological theory fully explains his violence. The need for multidimensional models is especially true when examining other cultures (Perilla, Bakeman, & Norris, 1994). Multidimensional models are the logical extension of the failure of a single theory to account for family violence. These theories attempt to integrate several of the unidimensional theories.

Intermediate Chapter Summary

Microtheories are narrower in scope than macrotheories. Microtheories explain family violence through the behaviors of specific individuals rather than through whole segments of the society.

Socialization or learning explanations are often extrapolations of laboratory findings theoretically applied to individuals involved in family violence. For example, classical and operant conditioning principles are useful in explaining how a victim's compliance reinforces (rewards) a perpetrator's use of violence. The failure to use punishment effectively allows children to practice violent acts. Other learning theories, such as learned helplessness, may help account for battered women's reactions to violence. An abusive male partner's loving behavior interspersed with beatings could be conceptualized as a form of intermittent reinforcement.

Social learning theory (modeling) is an especially well recognized explanation. **Modeling,** or imitation of observed social and cognitive behaviors, is at the core of this theory. Presumably, a child becomes violent by watching other violent people. Expanded formulations include modeling of behaviors like conflict resolution and inclusion of specific features of the family-of-origin's violence.

Individual (Intrapersonal) explanations include the assumption that the psychopathology (i.e., mental illness) of perpetrators is the basic cause of family violence. **Psychological traits theories** attribute family violence to individual variation in personality traits. Individuals who are more hostile, for example, tend to be more violent. **Biological theories** posit that certain physiological, genetic, or neurological abnormalities contribute to family violence. Factors such as head injuries seem to prompt violence.

Interpersonal interaction theories, such as **dyadic stress conceptions,** presuppose that interpartner dysfunction provokes violence. This viewpoint suggests that it is the behaviors of both partners that promote violence, not just one violent individual. Unsatisfactory **parent-child relationships** also increase the chances of child abuse. **Attachment theory** suggests that children who have been unable to bond with a caregiver (i.e., are insecurely attached) are at risk for abuse and that these patterns are related to later adult behaviors. This theory accounts for the intermingling of both love and violence so characteristic of abusive family members. **Social exchange theory** contends that when the costs of maintaining a relationship outweigh the benefits, the person who feels he or she is getting the "short end of the bargain" may become violent. Behavior can be understood by how individuals construct their social reality through **symbolic interactionism.** In this perspective, violent family interactions are seen as a result of the meanings various members attach to family interactions.

Because of the complexity of family violence, many researchers have speculated about the need for **multidimensional theories.** A few multidimensional models have recently begun to appear.

Methodology: How Researchers Try to Answer Questions

Conducting research on family violence has proven especially difficult. Several problems have complicated research efforts. First, the predicaments of victims are so compelling that an unwieldy number of people from myriad specialties and viewpoints (e.g., social scientists, clinical practitioners, activists, government agencies, and media talk show hosts) have become involved. Second, the genesis of concentrated academic exploration is so recent, no more than 30 years, that time has not permitted sufficient scholarship. Early researchers in the area of marital violence, for example, "swept with a wide broom," desperately searching for commonalities that might offer insight into the phenomenon. Partially as an outcome of the emotional climate, a number of leaders in the field used flawed research designs and small, handy samples. These endeavors, in turn, led to a proliferation of what were essentially pilot studies that failed to produce the crucial information so eagerly sought (see Rosenbaum, 1988).

According to Weis (1989), two interconnected methodological impediments have jeopardized the comparability, generalizability, and reliability of research findings on family violence—inadequate theory construction and imprecise nominal and operational definitions. It is also true that gathering data is especially problematic because of the delicate and private nature of the subject matter. Many aspects of family violence, such as sexual assault, are extremely sensitive. Reporting such material generates fear of reprisal and could lead to legal sanctions, stigmatization, and shame. These problems and others contribute to the vast underreporting of family violence (Weis, 1989).

Sources of Data

There are several sources of data on family violence. One system delineates five major, alternative sources: *official records* come from the FBI or social service agencies and reflect the amount of officially reported family violence; *self-reports* are mail, phone, or face-to-face surveys of the general public concerning violence in the family; *victimization surveys* are mail, phone, or face-to-face surveys of victims of family violence; *informant reports* are mail, phone, or face-to-face surveys of observers (e.g., parents) of behavior (e.g., fights between siblings) that do not inquire directly of the individual agents involved (e.g., siblings); and *direct observations* are empirical observations (e.g., measurement of physiological responses during a quarrel) made by social scientists in a laboratory (Weis, 1989). No data source is inherently superior to the others; rather, each has its own strengths and weaknesses.

Official Estimates. Official statistics reflect rates of reported intimate violence, for example, the number of cases reported to the police or to public social service agencies. The Uniform Crime Report (UCR) is the most commonly cited official data source. It is an annual compilation by the FBI of all reported crimes and arrests made for those crimes. Other government protection agencies, such as adult protective services (APS) or child protective services (CPS), accumulate reports of specific forms of family violence (e.g., child abuse).

Official statistics are plagued by a number of flaws. The most glaring is that only a small proportion of family violence is reported. The violence that is reported, furthermore, tends to be the most serious and therefore not representative of family violence as a whole. Other problems include the failure of government agencies to track criminal acts against children under the age of 12. Occasionally, justice agencies have mismanaged record-keeping by categorizing certain kinds of family violence under other types of crime (Steinman, 1991). Specific information on offender-victim relationships (e.g., boyfriend, spouse, ex-spouse) is often merged into two imprecise offender categories, stranger and nonstranger. Gradually, however, the UCR has modified its crime classifications and has improved its coverage, reliability, and detail (Jensen & Karpos, 1993; Ohlin & Tonry, 1989).

Self-Report Perpetration Surveys. Self-report perpetration surveys ask respondents about their own violent behavior directed toward another intimate (i.e., child, spouse, partner, parent). The obvious advantage of self-report surveys is that they provide access to information about violence that is not reported to official agencies. They are especially useful for information on subabusive behavior (e.g., corporal punishment, marital pushes).

Some of the problems inherent in these reports, such as memory lapses or distortions, arise because of their retrospective nature. Other complications may include differential interpretations of questions and motivated or unconscious response errors. There are also a number of other potential problems, including the possibility that perpetrators might lie, underreport, or minimize the severity of the violence (see Dutton & Hemphill, 1992; Edleson & Brygger, 1986; Riggs, Murphy, & O'Leary, 1989). In addition, a number of reporting biases exist, such as perceiving one's own violence as justified and therefore not reportable (see Baumeister, Stillwell, & Wotman, 1990; Kruttschnitt & Dornfeld, 1992).

Self-Report Victimization Surveys. Victimization surveys are especially useful for crimes like spouse abuse or date rape, where victims may be reluctant to talk to the police but may be willing to reveal the crime in an anonymous survey. The most commonly cited victim survey is the National Crime Victimization Survey, a semiannual survey of 60,000 households conducted by the Bureau of the Census.

Because victimization surveys ask respondents about specific time periods (e.g., the previous 6 months), they generally fail to tap the chronic and repetitive nature of victimization so typical of family violence (Weis, 1989). Moreover, like self-report perpetration surveys, victim surveys also suffer from underreporting. Even though respondents are promised anonymity and confidentiality, they may not tell the truth about an incident because they "thought it was a private matter," had already "reported it to another official," or "feared retaliation" (BJS, 1992). The relationship between the perpetrator and victim strongly influences reporting. Victims do not often want to report violence by other family members (Harris, 1991). In addition, the gender of the interviewer has very strong effects. Women reveal sexual assault more readily to female interviewers (Sorenson, Stein, Siegel, Golding, & Burnam, 1987). Some underreporting by male respondents may arise from a "wimp effect," a desire not to report their own victimization (Browning & Dutton, 1986).

Informant Methods. Informant data require individuals, such as children, to report the use of violence by someone else, such as parents (e.g. Cronin, 1995; Kenning et al., 1991; Kruttschnitt & Dornfeld, 1992). Although seemingly valid at first glance, informant methods may lack validity because informants (e.g., teachers) may not always know the extent of the behavior (e.g., sexualized behaviors with peers). In fact, researchers in the area of exposure to parental violence more frequently ask parents to report on their children's behaviors than they ask children to provide self-report data (Peled & Davis, 1995). These reports may also be biased for reasons such as informants' defensiveness and level of psychological distress

(Hughes & Barad, 1983; Wolfe, Zak, Wilson, & Jaffe, 1986).

Direct Observation. Direct observation of violent acts is a rarely used mode of data collection, but it may provide unusual insight into the dynamics of interpersonal violence (Weis, 1989). An illustration of this approach is direct observation of couples quarreling in their home (Margolin, Burman, & John, 1989). Another example would be the monitoring of physiological responses of couples quarreling in the laboratory (Jacobson & Gottman, 1993).

The Conflict Tactics Scales

The Conflict Tactics Scales (CTS; Straus, 1979) are the most widely used scales in family violence research. The construction of these scales represented an impressive leap forward in the identification and quantification of specific, violent behaviors.

Participants responding to the CTS indicate how many times in a given time period (e.g., the previous year) they used *reasoning and argument, verbal and symbolic aggression,* or *physical aggression* during disagreements and fights. In marital violence, researchers assess methods of conflict resolution by interviewing one or both members of a randomly selected couple. In child abuse, researchers ask a parent to describe his or her interactions with a child. Researchers have also used the CTS to estimate adolescent violence, dating violence, and elder violence. A number of studies have found evidence corroborating the reliability and validity of the scales (Barling, O'Leary, Jouriles, Vivian, & MacEwen, 1987; Herzberger, 1991; Straus, 1990a).

Straus and his colleagues have conducted two large national surveys using the CTS. The 1975 National Family Violence Survey was a face-to-face survey of 2,143 individuals (see Straus et al., 1980). The 1985 replication of this study, the National Family Violence Re-Survey, was a phone survey of 6,002 respondents. These two surveys remain the only nationally representative studies of family violence (see Straus & Gelles, 1986).

Despite the general impetus to the field provided by the CTS, their use has generated concern that seems to represent a microcosm of the many problems inherent in family violence research. Much of the disagreement hinges directly on the perceived limitations of the CTS themselves—what they do *not* measure and how this affects perceptions of family violence (see Fantuzzo & Lindquist, 1989; Koss et al., 1994a, for reviews). According to Fantuzzo and Lindquist (1989), for example, the CTS restrict acts of violence to those that occur in a conflict, not those that might be unprovoked. Furthermore, the CTS do not provide any data on the antecedents or consequences of violence. Although reference to the CTS included in this text relates to the original CTS, it is important to point out that Straus and his colleagues (Straus, Hamby, Boney-McCoy, & Sugarman, 1995) have very recently modified the CTS. The revised CTS2 includes five scales: physical assault, psychological aggression, negotiation, injury, and sexual coercion. All but the negotiation scale include minor and severe subscales.

CTS couples' data indicate only that women are as *frequently* violent as men with spouses (Straus & Gelles, 1986) and dating partners (see Sugarman & Hotaling, 1989, for a review). The problem is that this "gender-neutral" approach fails to take into account many important gender context dissimilarities: (a) strength, severity, and injury differentials; (b) repetitiveness and offender rates; (c) motivation (e.g., self-defense); and (d) fear, dependency, and female devaluation (see Koss et al., 1994a, for a review). There is a danger that gender equivalence of participation *rates* can become transposed to gender equivalence of marital *violence*. A further discussion of this important topic appears later in this volume (see Chapter 8).

Methodological Issues in Family Violence Research

Family violence research tends to be methodologically weak (see Rosenbaum, 1988). Because of overreliance on small, selective samples without comparison groups, many experts find the clinical literature on family violence "extensive but not definitive" (Ohlin & Tonry, 1989).

Definitional Ambiguity. As pointed out previously, the most problematic issue plaguing family violence research is definitional ambiguity. Definitions of terms, such as child neglect, date rape, spouse abuse, and elder abuse, are inherently subjective and have

sparked considerable controversy. Definitional ambiguity has struck at the very heart of the field, undermining every aspect of scientific inquiry. This lack of consensus has significantly impeded understanding about the very meaning of family violence. It has limited interpretations of the findings and restricted generalizations across studies. In the final analysis, it has played a key role in preventing development of effective interventions and solutions (Ohlin & Tonry, 1989).

Populations Sampled. Researchers have used widely divergent samples: (a) random samples of the population, (b) volunteers recruited from clinics and emergency rooms, (c) volunteers recruited through advertisement and door-to-door solicitation, and (d) individuals referred by agencies and police reports. Obviously, systematic differences between these samples are very likely, and their noncomparability hampers cross-comparisons of the findings (Gelles, 1976).

The representativeness of samples is another issue in family violence research. *Representative* samples are those that are similar to the population from which they were drawn. When samples are representative, such as in the National Family Violence Surveys and the National Crime Victimization Surveys, they can be used to make inferences about the population. National representative surveys provide the only kind of data that allow an examination of patterns of family violence in the United States as a whole.

So-called representative samples, however, may still exclude people who have no telephones or fall into restricted categories (e.g., gay men, homeless people, non-English-speaking individuals) (Koss et al., 1994a). Furthermore, because of time and cost constraints, large surveys usually have to limit the number of questions asked. Nonresponse is also a problem. Sensitive topics, like marital violence, child abuse, or date rape, may make people hesitant to participate in surveys. A high nonresponse rate raises questions about why people choose not to respond and whether their nonparticipation limits the representativeness of the sample (Koss et al., 1994a).

Another type of sample is referred to as a clinical sample. *Clinical* samples can come from any number of sources: group homes for abused children, shelters for battered women, prisons, criminal justice records, or social service agencies (Bridges & Weis, 1985). They are small, nonrepresentative, purposive, or convenience ("handy") samples that provide little information about the general patterns of behavior in a broader population. Data derived from clinical samples often lack generalizability even within small subgroups of the population. Data from women living in battered women's shelters, for example, cannot be generalized to battered women residing elsewhere. Despite these serious limitations, studies based on clinical samples provide useful information on the dynamics and causes of abuse and often provide preliminary notions about prevention and treatment (Weis, 1989).

Some researchers have been inclined to misapply findings derived from one type of sample to the other (Straus, 1993). Specifically, Straus (1991b) describes the problem in terms of the "clinical fallacy" and the "representative sample fallacy." The clinical fallacy refers to inappropriate generalization of clinical samples to the entire population. Generalizations may not hold because persons who seek or receive treatment are often not representative of the entire population. On the other hand, automatically assuming that large population samples are superior to smaller clinical samples (the representative sample fallacy) is unwarranted if the two groups are quite different. Clinicians, for example, often need information about specific groups of people, such as male sex offenders. In this case, clinicians would like to obtain a representative sample of male sex offenders, not just a representative sample of males.

Comparison Groups. Most studies have suffered from a failure to include satisfactory comparison groups of subjects (see Rosenbaum, 1988). In fact, Bolton, Laner, Gai, and Kane (1981) found that less than 5% of studies in the field of family violence included comparison groups (also see Frieze & Browne, 1989). Comparison groups allow researchers to determine how perpetrators or abuse victims might be different from or similar to other people. When comparison groups have been used, moreover, they have often been insufficient (Wolfe & Mosk, 1983). The best way to evaluate the success of a sexual abuse treatment plan, for example, is to compare a randomly selected treatment group with a nontreatment control group (see Plotkin, Azar, Twentyman, & Perri, 1981). Researchers, however, seldom conduct research of this kind.

Conceptualization of appropriate comparison groups is another ongoing problem. Rosen-

baum (1988) proposed, for example, that a suitable comparison group for studying maritally violent men is not just maritally nonviolent men, but unhappily married, maritally nonviolent men (see Holtzworth-Munroe et al., 1992).

When comparison group data cannot be obtained easily, researchers sometimes use normative data (i.e., published standards). As an illustration, researchers might initially obtain mothers' ratings of abused children on the Child Behavior Checklist (CBCL), a standardized checklist of a variety of behavior problems (Achenbach & Edelbrock, 1983). The investigators could then compare this sample of mothers' ratings with those obtained previously from a large sample of mothers from the general population (the normative sample) who had also rated their children using the CBCL.

The advantage to researchers in using the normative data from the CBCL is the ability to compare participants' scores without recruiting a comparison group of mothers who would be willing to rate their children. The disadvantage is that a researcher cannot generally control for confounding variables (e.g., prenatal drug exposure) with normative data. As a result, establishing cause-and-effect relationships is difficult. If the abused children in the above illustration, for instance, are rated as displaying more behavioral problems than children rated for the published norms, there is no way of determining what caused this difference.

Longitudinal and Outcome Studies. Ideally, investigations of family violence should be longitudinal. Longitudinal studies, however, are expensive, participants are difficult to obtain, and attrition rates for participants are high. In addition, researchers are under pressure to produce immediate results (Azar, 1988). As a result, most research designs are cross-sectional designs with retrospective, self-report survey data (e.g., Hoshmond, 1987). Only a few researchers have conducted longitudinal studies (e.g., O'Leary et al., 1989). It is also true that academic training for execution of large-scale longitudinal studies is inadequate (Stouthamer-Loeber, van Kammen, & Loeber, 1992). On the other hand, investigators are beginning to fashion newer procedures for tracking highly mobile participants (e.g., designated contacts, return visits, letters) (Rumptz, Sullivan, Davidson, & Basta, 1991).

Estimating Rates of Family Violence. Scientists typically report rates of family violence in either *incidence* or *prevalence* rates. Incidence is the "frequency with which a condition or event occurs within a given time and population" (Wolman, 1973, p. 190). Prevalence is the "percentage of the population that is affected with a particular disease [i.e., condition] at a given time" (*Merriam-Webster's Collegiate Dictionary*, 1993, p. 924). Family violence researchers appear to have commonly used incidence to describe frequency of a behavior over the past year and prevalence to describe frequency of a behavior over the lifetime of a relationship (see Hotaling & Sugarman, 1986; Rosenbaum, 1988).

Ethical Considerations

Informed Consent. Ethical considerations necessary to protect vulnerable research participants place many restrictions on researchers. What is the researcher's responsibility, for example, if he or she learns about abuse of the participants during the course of a research study? Having guaranteed confidentiality and anonymity, does the researcher honor the pledge or report the abuse to appropriate authorities? Most reporting laws mandate researchers to report certain forms of family violence (e.g., child abuse and neglect). One solution adopted by investigators is to inform research participants in advance of the limits of confidentiality and to specify how they plan to address disclosures of abuse (Monahan, Appelbaum, Mulvey, Robbins, & Lidz, 1993; Ohlin & Tonry, 1989).

Ensuring Victims' Safety. Also important in conducting family violence research is the issue of victims' physical and psychological safety. One possibility is that interviews or questionnaires will arouse disturbing memories (e.g., of incest). Interviewing child sexual abuse victims about their abuse experiences, for example, might have negative effects. In this circumstance, researchers need to be prepared to offer clinical referrals. Another possibility is that an abusive spouse will threaten the person to coerce certain responses. If the person's safety is being threatened in this way, the researcher has to abandon the research protocol and help the threatened person find protection (Margolin, 1979).

Disclosure of Research Findings. Researchers should carefully disclose the conclusions and limitations of their research, especially when their work affects social policy. Battered women's advocates have accused researchers, for example, of misconstruing the true problem of wife battering by emphasizing the mutuality of marital violence (Dobash, Dobash, Wilson, & Daly, 1992). Critics charge that such interpretations have adversely affected funding of programs for battered women (see Schechter, 1988).

Statistical and Evaluation Matters

One could characterize past research efforts as "diffuse, fragmented, specific, and narrow" because of the overreliance on single-variable analysis (reported by Michaelson, 1993). Within the field of marital violence, for example, an analysis of a single variable (e.g., self-esteem), rather than multiple variables (e.g., age, self-esteem, and childhood socialization), has failed to provide the comprehensive picture needed for accurate understanding (Williams, 1992). Fortunately, studies have increasingly used multivariate statistical methods to examine the effects of several independent variables.

Dependency on correlational analysis has raised the usual problem of confusing correlational relationships with causal relationships. Social scientists have more recently attempted to obtain a broader view by using a statistical strategy called *meta-analysis*. Meta-analysis is a set of "quantitative procedures for summarizing or integrating the findings obtained from a literature review of a subject" (Vogt, 1993, p. 138). By combining the findings from a large number of studies and thus going beyond the limitations of many univariate studies, meta-analysis brings clarity to areas where there are conflicting results.

Hotaling and Sugarman (1986) have conducted several meta-analyses to obtain a reliable overview or pattern of results on the topics of marital violence and courtship violence. These analyses permitted them to designate several *risk markers* (e.g., alcohol use) for marital violence and courtship violence. Hotaling and Sugarman use the term *risk marker* to describe an attribute, exposure, or factor or characteristic that is associated with an increased probability of the reception and/or expression of another condition (e.g., family violence).

Summary

Diverse segments of society, such as academicians, professionals, and activists, have embraced the issue of family violence, some more zealously than others. Social scientists tutored in different academic disciplines have used their expertise to ascertain the reality of family violence but have provided a fragmented, disorganized appraisal in need of an overarching framework. Although social scientists have promulgated numerous theories to explain and integrate disparate research findings, they have met with little success. One practical organization classifies theories into two groupings: macrotheories and microtheories.

Macrotheories are broad-based conceptions, such as cultural acceptance of violence, patriarchal influences, and the subculture of violence. Family structural factors (e.g., family stress), deterrence theory (i.e., low cost of family violence), and social structural factors (e.g., poverty) are other useful explanations. Microtheories are anchored on more individual behavior. Learning explanations, the most empirically grounded of the group, rest primarily on conditioning and social learning (modeling). Individual intrapersonal theories (psychopathology, psychological traits, biological traits) and interpersonal interaction (dyadic stress, parent/child stress, insecure attachment, and social exchange perspectives) complete this elementary category. Macrotheories are often too broad to account for individual differences, and microtheories are too narrow. Even current multidimensional theories are lacking.

Early research on family violence has been methodologically weak and suboptimal along several dimensions. It is too new, unformed, fervid, and rushed. Researchers in various subfields began by collecting data from a wide variety of sources compatible with their expertise. These include official records, self-reports, victimization surveys, informant reports, and direct observation.

The Conflict Tactics Scales (CTS) have been the most widely used test of family-violent behaviors. They contain 18 questions that assess conflict resolution behaviors in three areas: reasoning, verbal statements, and physical actions (mild and severe). They assess violent behaviors through self-reports or perpetrators, vicitimization reports, and informant reports. Researchers frequently use the CTS to establish incidence or prevalence estimates of abusive behaviors. Despite their extensive use, a number of experts in the field have criticized the scales because of the scales' failure to incorporate questions about the context (e.g., motives) of the violence. The spark that ignited the debate was their use in national surveys indicating gender parity in marital violence. This unusual finding rallied activists and spawned a "battle of the sexes."

At the core of criticisms of research across the whole field is a lack of clearly defined, operational definitions. Populations sampled have generally been either representative or small clinical samples. Neither sampling procedure has proved to be optimal. Whereas national surveys have failed to provide sufficient contextual information about violence, small clinical samples have had limited generalizability. Comparison (control) groups have been so rare as to be almost nonexistent, and their absence has circumscribed assumptions about cause-and-effect relationships.

Nonetheless, early efforts laid the groundwork for later procurement of more adequate samples, specification of appropriate comparison groups, and execution of long-term and outcome studies. Research designs and statistical manipulations have slowly improved over the past 20 years. Ethical considerations are extensive and necessary but tend to be restrictive. They impel serious consideration of participant safety but pose limitations on sample procurement. Statistical questions have arisen about reliance on univariate designs. Although statistical methods have sometimes lacked sufficient refinement, newer meta-analytic procedures have garnered respect and have added useful synthesis of disparate research findings.

In the final analysis, it is important to note that despite the many methodological limitations of research on family violence, there is still a large body of research worthy of academic consideration and a modest core of principles that have met with general acceptance.

3

Physical Child Abuse

CHAPTER OUTLINE

An Interview With Murray Straus

"We can diminish family violence if churches get involved. When was the last time you heard a sermon saying that spanking is violence and we should stop bringing up our kids violently?"

MURRAY STRAUS is the world's preeminent family violence researcher. He can be credited with organizing the field after the initial impetus provided by medical research on child abuse. He is currently Professor of Sociology and Codirector of the interdisciplinary Family Research Laboratory at the University of New Hampshire. He has authored or coauthored over 200 articles and 15 books related to the family. An early and significant book, published in 1980 and coauthored with Richard Gelles and Suzanne Steinmetz, is Behind Closed Doors: Violence in the American Family. *His latest book is* Beating the Devil out of Them: Corporal Punishment in American Families *(1994). He has served as President of several professional organizations, such as the National Council on Family Relations, and has received one prestigious honor after another, including the 1992 Distinguished Contribution Award from the New Hampshire Psychological Association. Dr. Straus received both his B.A. in international relations and his Ph.D. in sociology (1956) from the University of Wisconsin.*

Q: What sparked your interest in family violence?

A: It was the old scientific principle: If you come across something interesting, drop everything else and study it. In my case, it was the discovery in 1979 that one quarter of my students had been hit by their parents during their senior year in high school, and another quarter had been threatened with being hit. Somehow, it clicked with me that this kind of parental violence might be one of the roots of the violence that came to national attention during the Vietnam War era, a period of riots and assassinations, and the rising murder rate.

Q: Why did your work meet with such wide acceptance?

A: I think it was because my research on wife beating coincided with the establishment of battered women's shelters. They needed data

on how pervasive the problem was, and our National Family Violence Surveys provided the statistics. A major accomplishment of the shelter movement was to create consciousness of and concern about wife beating.

Q: What has been your most influential article in the field?

A: The article on the Conflict Tactics Scales [CTS]. The CTS was a technological breakthrough. Up until then, psychologists and sociologists tended to think that they had to rely on official statistics or case studies to get data on family violence. The CTS showed that it was possible to get valid data from questionnaires in an ordinary clinical or research interview.

Q: What is your current research focus?

A: After more than 20 years of studying wife beating, I returned to just where I started in family violence 27 years ago—research on spanking and other legal forms of corporal punishment. I'm also developing new measures for use in family violence research. We have just finished a major revision of the CTS, and we are well along on developing another test. It is going to be called the Violence Risk Marker Inventory.

Q: What would you like to do if you had a large grant?

A: I would do a community experiment on corporal punishment. Corporal punishment will take a long time to end if we deal only with parents. Convincing them that they are more likely to have well-behaved children if they *never* spank tends to get undone when the inevitable misbehaviors occur and their friends and relatives say that what that child needs is a good spanking. So we have to change the culture of communities before parents will feel free to bring up children without violence.

Q: What research would you like to see others undertake?

A: I think it is important to study violence *by women* against their partners. Almost everyone is afraid to deal with this issue despite data showing that women strike out physically against their partners as often as do men, and they also hit first just as often as men. My concern with the issue is partly because I think the evidence is clear that when women engage in what they call "harmless" violence, it is not. True, the man is rarely harmed, but it tremendously increases the risk that the woman will be.

Q: What social institutions must get involved to end family violence?

A: Unless churches get involved, things are going to progress much more slowly. When was the last time you heard a sermon saying that spanking is violence and we should stop bringing up our kids violently?

Introduction

They cry in the dark so you can't see their tears.
They hide in the light so you can't see their fears.
Forgive and forget.
All the while, love and pain become one in [*sic*]
    the same
in the eyes of a wounded child.

Because hell, hell is for children.
And you know that their little lives can become
    such a mess.
Hell! Hell is for children.
And you shouldn't have to pay for your love with
your bones and your flesh.

It's all so confusing this brutal abusing.
They blacken your eyes and then apologize.
Be Daddy's little girl and don't tell Mommy a
    thing.
Be a good little boy and you'll get a new toy.
Tell Grandma you fell off the swing.

Benatar, Geraldo, and Capps (1981)

In 1980, Pat Benatar recorded the lyrics to the song titled *Hell Is for Children* to describe the world of an abused child. Until the 1960s, society was relatively unaware of the "hell"

characteristic of abused children's lives. Child abuse was considered a mythical or rare phenomenon that occurred only in individuals' imaginations or at best in "sick" families from lower-social-class groups. As will be evident in this chapter and the two that follow, child abuse is an ugly reality for millions of children each year. The U.S. Advisory Board on Child Abuse and Neglect (ABCAN; 1990) recently proclaimed that child abuse and neglect are a national emergency.

This chapter focuses on one form of child maltreatment: physical child abuse (PCA). The first part of the chapter examines issues related to defining the physical abuse of children and determining the magnitude of the problem in terms of official estimates and self-report surveys. Attention then shifts to the typical characteristics of physically abused children and the adults who abuse them in terms of age, gender, and additional characteristics. The short-term as well as long-term consequences of PCA are also evaluated. The chapter concludes with a discussion of the major theories proposing causes of PCA and recommendations for addressing the problem.

Scope of the Problem

What Is Physical Child Abuse?

One of the most significant issues in attempting to understand the problem of PCA is defining the term *physical child abuse*. Consider the following situations:

Three-year-old Jimmy was playing with his puppy near a pond in his backyard. He tried to make his puppy drink from the pond by roughly holding his face to the water. Jimmy's father saw him forcing the puppy to drink and yelled at him to stop. After Jimmy did not respond, his father pulled Jimmy away from the dog and began holding his head under water to "teach him a lesson" about the appropriate way to treat his dog.

Angela's baby, Maria, had colic from the day she was born. This meant that from 4:00 in the afternoon until 8:00 p.m., every day, Maria would cry inconsolably. No matter what Angela did, nothing would help Maria to stop crying. One evening, after Maria had been crying for 3 straight hours, Angela began shaking Maria out of frustration. The shaking caused Maria to cry more loudly, which, in turn, caused Angela to shake the 5-month-old more vigorously. Angela shook Maria until she lost consciousness.

Ryan and his brother Matthew were playing with their Power Rangers when they got into a disagreement. Both boys began hitting each other and calling one another names. Alice, the mother of the boys, came running into the room and pulled the boys apart. She then took each boy, pulled down his trousers, put him over her knee, and spanked him several times.

These vignettes portray a range of behaviors, some of which are clearly abusive, others that may or may not be considered abusive. Acts of violence by adults against children and adolescents range from mild slaps to extremely injurious attacks. Researchers and practitioners are also discovering that violence against children, in rare instances, can take significantly unusual forms (see boxed insert: "Unusual Manifestations of Physical Child Abuse"). Prior to the 1960s, however, few, if any, of these situations would have been labeled abusive.

With the "discovery" of child abuse during the 1960s (Kempe, Silverman, Steele, Droegemueller, & Silver, 1962), and the increased interest in child protection that followed, child abuse definitions changed rapidly. For the most part, the definitions that emerged during this time focused on acts of violence that caused some form of observable harm. Therefore, although recognition of PCA was increasing, the definition of physical abuse was still restrictive. As Gelles and Cornell (1990) point out, "If a father takes a gun and shoots at his child and misses, there is no physical injury. There is, of course, harm in a father's shooting and missing, but the act itself does not qualify as abuse" (p. 21). If physical injury or harm is not a necessary criterion for a definition of abuse, what range of behaviors should be included under the umbrella of PCA?

Physical Punishment and Child Rearing. As discussed previously, most experts and researchers in the field define *violence* as an act carried out intentionally (or nonaccidentally) to cause physical pain or injury to another person (Gelles & Cornell, 1990). *Physical pain* and *injury*, however, can range from the sting of a slap to the excruciating pain and injury of a burn to death. In Chapter 1, a distinction was made between legitimate and illegitimate violence. At one extreme of the continuum are those practices considered to be "normal" violence, including commonplace physical acts such as slapping, pushing, or spanking. Many people consider such acts to be an acceptable part of punishment and child rearing. Should such behavior be considered normal or labeled as abusive?

Survey data suggest that such behaviors are not labeled as abusive by most and are actually quite common. Surveys of parents, for example, show that 90% use some form of physical punishment on their children (Straus, 1983; Wauchope & Straus, 1990a). Surveys of young adults show comparable rates, and 93% to 95% report experiencing some physical punishment as children or adolescents (Bryan & Freed, 1982; Graziano & Namaste, 1990). As Graziano and Namaste (1990) state,

Slapping, spanking, paddling, and, generally, hitting children for purposes of discipline are accepted, pervasive, adult behaviors in U.S. families. In these instances, although anger, physical attack, and pain are involved between two people of vastly different size, weight, and strength, such behavior is commonly accepted as a proper exercise of adult authority over children. (pp. 459-460)

For many who study family violence, the level of acceptance of this "normal" violence is appalling. Perhaps the most significant critic of the cultural acceptance of corporal punishment is Murray Straus, who in recent years has attracted considerable attention for his research and views on spanking (e.g., Straus, 1991c, 1994). Spanking is harmful, Straus argues, for two reasons. First, it legitimizes violence. When authority figures spank, they are, in essence, condoning the use of violence as a way to deal with frustration and to settle disputes. Second, the implicit message of acceptance contributes to violence in other aspects of society. To explain this extension of violence, Straus (1991c) employs a "cultural spillover theory," arguing that violence "in one sphere of life tends to engender violence in other spheres" (p. 137).

The research evidence tends to support this perspective that spanking is positively correlated with other forms of family violence, including sibling abuse and spouse assault. Based on the first Family Violence Survey, Straus (1991c) estimated that children who had been physically punished during the previous year were 3 times more likely to have assaulted a sibling during that year.

UNUSUAL MANIFESTATIONS OF PHYSICAL CHILD ABUSE

Many unusual forms of PCA have been described and documented in the literature on child maltreatment. One atypical form of PCA is fatal pepper aspiration. The first report of fatal pepper aspiration was documented by Adelson in 1964 and involved a 3½-year-old girl whose mother punished her by pouring black pepper into her mouth, causing her death (as cited in Reece, 1990). Intentional microwave burns to small infants have also been reported. Alexander, Surrell, and Cohle (1987), for example, reported on a 14-month-old boy whose teenage baby-sitter placed him in a microwave oven for 60 seconds. Other unusual manifestations of child abuse reported in the literature include poisoning and smothering (Myers, 1992; Zumwalt & Hirsch, 1987).

An increasing amount of attention has focused on an additional unusual manifestation of PCA termed *Munchausen syndrome by proxy*. Munchausen syndrome by proxy, also commonly referred to as factitious disorder, is a condition in adults characterized by repeated presentation for medical treatment for no apparent purpose other than to assume the role of a patient. The term *Munchausen syndrome by proxy* was first described by Meadow (1977) and is used to characterize adults who use a child as the vehicle for fabricated illness. The most recent version of the *Diagnostic and Statistical Manual of Mental Disorders* (American Psychiatric Association, 1994) defines the essential features of the condition as the "deliberate production or feigning of physical or psychological signs or symptoms in another person who is under the individual's care" motivated by "a psychological need to assume the sick role by proxy" (p. 725).

Typically, the children are "paraded before the medical profession with a fantastic range of illnesses" (D. A. Rosenberg, 1987, p. 548). Jones (1994) recently described the principal routes taken by caregivers to produce or feign illness including the fabrication of symptoms by caregivers, alteration of laboratory specimens (e.g., urine or blood), and the direct production of physical symptoms or disease in the child. Reports in the literature abound that describe the bizarre manifestations of this condition. Caregivers have been noted, for example, to contaminate children's urine specimens with their own blood and present the specimen to their doctor, claiming that the child had been urinating blood (D. A. Rosenberg, 1987). One mother repeatedly administered laxatives to her child, causing severe diarrhea, blood infection, and dehydration (Peters, 1989). In another case, a mother injected feces into her child's IV line to produce illness in the child (D. A. Rosenberg, 1987).

Until relatively recently, virtually nothing was known about Munchausen syndrome by proxy outside of anecdotal case reports. Recognition of the condition has been followed by an increasing number of empirical investigations directed at assessing the characteristics of victims and perpetrators. Victims are typically young children in their preschool years (D. A. Rosenberg, 1987). The perpetrator is most often the child's mother, and these women often have considerable experience or knowledge in health-related areas (Meadow, 1990). Recent evidence suggests that such individuals frequently suffer from psychiatric and personality disturbances such as Munchausen syndrome and personality disorders (Bools, Neale, & Meadow, 1994). The majority of conditions inflicted on these children involve the gastrointestinal, genitourinary, and central nervous systems (American Psychiatric Association, 1994). Recent studies also suggest that another characteristic of these families are unusual circumstances surrounding the deaths of siblings (e.g., multiple sibling deaths) (Meadow, 1990). Although Munchausen syndrome by proxy is believed to be relatively uncommon, recent reports suggest that it may be more common than once believed (Schreier & Libow, 1993).

The production or feigning of illness in dependent children is considered abusive, in large part, as a result of the consequences of such behavior to the child. The procedures used by caregivers to produce illness often cause physical discomfort or pain for the child. McClung, Murray, and Braden (1988), for example, describe the intentional administration of ipecac to produce symptoms in children (e.g., recurrent and chronic vomiting and diarrhea). Such behavior on the part of caregivers can also result in the death of a child. In one review of cases between 1966 and 1987, the authors concluded that 9% of children died as a result of the procedures inflicted on them by their parents (D. A. Rosenberg, 1987). Children are also often subjected to unnecessary and sometimes painful and potentially harmful medical procedures, such as surgery, X rays, and medications, as physicians unwittingly attempt to diagnosis and treat the symptoms described by caregivers (Malatack, Wiener, Gartner, Zitelli, & Brunetti, 1985; Meadow, 1977). Such children are also at risk for both short- and long-term physical illness and dysfunction (D. A. Rosenberg, 1987) as well as psychological problems (McGuire & Feldman, 1989).

Spanking is also correlated with crime outside the home, including self-reported delinquency, arrest, and homicide (Straus, 1991c).

As Straus (1994) himself recognizes, however, it is important to remember that two variables can be correlated without necessarily being causally connected. Perhaps, for example, children with problem behaviors tend to be spanked and then these same children go on to a life of crime. It is also possible that the main reason spanking and other forms of violence are correlated is because PCA and violence are correlated. Because children who are physically abused are presumably likely to be spanked, spanking might appear to be a causal contributor when it is not.

Although many accept the notion that spanking is harmful, it remains a common practice and is certainly not considered a behavior worthy of the abuse label in the minds of the general public. In fact, as will become clear in the next section, many states explicitly exclude corporal punishment from child abuse statutes (see Chapter 12 for a discussion of the problems associated with spanking and corporal punishment).

Legal Perspectives. Legal definitions of PCA are different from conceptual definitions but come with their own set of difficulties. Daro (1988) has identified several problems involved in developing and operationalizing state statutes, including but not limited to the following: (a) defining abuse in as objective a manner as possible; (b) balancing children's rights with parental rights, and (c) applying the legal system to the solution of such a complex human problem.

Unfortunately, there is no uniform law that defines PCA for all jurisdictions within the United States. Instead, each of the 50 different states has its own legal definition of PCA and corresponding reporting responsibilities. All states acknowledge that PCA, in general, is physical injury caused by other than accidental means that results in a substantial risk of physical harm. Other key features of definitions, however, vary according to the specificity of the acts included as physically abusive (Myers & Peters, 1987; Stein, 1993). Most emphasize the overt consequences of abuse such as bruises or broken bones (Wolfe, 1987). In addition, most states generally allow parents to use "reasonable" corporal punishment with children (Myers, 1992). The California state statute, as outlined by Westat in 1991, for example, indicates that

PCA "does not include reasonable and age appropriate spanking to the buttocks where there is no evidence of serious physical injury" (cited in Myers, 1992, p. 141).

How Common Is Physical Child Abuse?

Despite problems in defining PCA, researchers have made numerous efforts to determine the scope of the problem. Within the United States, researchers generally use one of two different methods of estimation.

Legal definitions of physical child abuse are different from conceptual definitions.

In the first method, *official estimates* represent the number of cases of physical abuse *reported* to governmental social service agencies. In the second method, *self-report surveys* analyze the proportion of PCA in a population.

Official Estimates. The number of children who are officially reported to child protection agencies because of child abuse has increased each year. The National Center on Child Abuse and Neglect conducted two surveys (the National Incidence Studies: NIS-1 and NIS-2) designed to measure the number of cases of PCA reported to investigatory agencies, schools, hospitals, and other social service agencies. The first of these surveys, published in 1981, estimated that there were 199,100 reported cases of PCA (Department of Health and Human Services [DHHS], 1981). The second survey found that the figure had risen to approximately 311,500 children in 1986 (Sedlak, 1990).

Since 1976, the American Association for Protecting Children (AAPC), a division of the American Humane Association (AHA), has conducted an annual National Study of Child Neglect and Abuse Reporting. This study, which is an annual survey of official reports of child maltreatment documented by child protective services agencies, similarly estimated that between the years 1976 and 1987, there was a threefold increase in child maltreatment reporting overall (AAPC, 1989). In the majority of cases, caseworkers classified injuries as minor (e.g., minor cuts, bruises, and welts) rather than major (e.g., brain damage, bone fracture, internal injuries, poisonings, and burns and scalds) (e.g., AAPC, 1988).

The most recent figures available estimate that social service agencies received 3,140,000 reports of child maltreatment (including physical and sexual abuse, neglect, and psychological maltreatment) in 1994, about 47 children out of every 1,000 children in the United States (Weise & Daro, 1995). Almost 1 million of these cases (e.g., 816,400) were specific instances of PCA. Additionally, the National Committee to Prevent Child Abuse (NCPCA) estimated that in 1993, approximately 715 children died as a result of PCA, and another 520 children died as a result of physical neglect (McCurdy & Daro, 1994b).

Self-Report Surveys. Estimates based on nationwide surveys of families across the United States provide another source of information on the rates of PCA. The self-report surveys discussed in this chapter are self-report estimates from surveys of parents in the general population who report using some form of physical violence on their children. The most significant study of this kind is the second National Family Violence Survey, conducted in 1985 (Gelles & Straus, 1987, 1988). In this telephone survey, which uses the CTS to measure abuse, parents report on the "conflict tactics techniques" they used with their children in the past year. The techniques respondents could select ranged from mild forms of violence (e.g., slapped or spanked child) to severe forms of violence (e.g., beat up child, burned or scalded child, or used a knife or gun).

Results indicated that as many as 75% of the reporting sample admitted at least one violent act in the course of rearing their children. Approximately 2% of parents engaged in one act of abusive violence (a high probability of injuring the child) during the year prior to the survey. The most frequent type of violence in either case was slapping or spanking the child. Thirty-nine percent of respondents reported slapping or spanking their children more than two times in the past year.

Is the Rate of Physical Child Abuse Increasing?

There are several problems in estimating PCA. Perhaps the most significant problem is the lack of definitional consensus. Depending on the definition of abuse employed, for example, the rate of abuse could range from nearly all children (i.e., those who are spanked) to very few children (i.e., those who are threatened with a gun). With specific regard to official estimates, there is the obvious problem that PCA is a hidden crime and often goes unreported. There is also a problem in the way cases of abuse are counted. Some states, for instance, use the family as the unit of analysis, which underestimates abuse because more than one child may be maltreated per family. Other states count individual children. In addition, the retrospective nature of self-report studies and the possibility that parents may not admit their abusive behavior limit their validity.

These methodological problems contribute to the difficulty in determining whether PCA is increasing, a matter of considerable debate among scholars (e.g., Besharov, 1990; Finkelhor, 1990). The answer to the question seems to depend on whether one examines evidence from official or self-report studies. Official estimates indicate that rates of PCA are increasing. Gelles and Straus (1987) suggest that official rates of PCA have increased because the attention focused on the problem of child abuse has resulted in higher rates of reporting in recent years. Changes such as broader definitions of abuse, mandatory reporting laws, 24-hour hotlines, and state and national media campaigns have all contributed to increases in reported violence.

Although official reports of PCA increased dramatically between 1976 and 1987, in recent years, the *rate* of increase has declined (Gelles & Cornell, 1990). In addition, statistics from self-report studies have not shown increases in parental reports of violence directed at children. Gelles and Straus (1987), for example, replicated their 1975 nationwide survey 10 years later and found the estimated rate of violence toward children actually declined from 1975 to 1985. The most substantial decline was in the use of severe and very severe violence, which was 47% lower in 1985. Severe violence, defined as "kicking, biting, punching," "hitting or trying to hit with an object," "beating, threatening with a knife or a gun," or "using a knife or a gun over the past 12 months," declined from 1975 to 1985.

It is unclear, however, to what degree *reporting* rates reflect *true* rates of PCA. Are decreasing rates the result of an actual decline in PCA or decreased willingness on the part of respondents to admit participating in such violence? Gelles and Straus (1987) suggest several reasons why the true rate of child abuse may actually be declining: (a) family organization has changed, as reflected in the increase in the average age at first marriage and having a first child, as well as the decrease in the number of children per family and the number of unwanted children; (b) the economic climate in 1985 improved over that of 1975, as shown by a reduction in the unemployment and inflation rate; (c) there was a massive increase in public awareness of child abuse over this period; and (d) innovative prevention and treatment programs have been implemented.

Intermediate Chapter Summary

Society has not always recognized physical violence directed at children as abusive. Despite delays in recognizing that violence toward children is wrong, today PCA is illegal in every state. Most state statutes and experts in the field recognize that PCA includes a range of acts carried out with the intention of harm that puts a child at considerable **risk for physical injury.** Disagreement continues to exist, however, in regard to behaviors that do not result in any physical signs of injury (e.g., spanking) or that lie in the borderland between "normal" corporal punishment and that which is excessive (e.g., resulting in broken bones). Effective **legal statutes** depend on objective definitions, balancing children's rights with parental rights, and enforcement of workable solutions for such a complex human problem.

Protective services receive hundreds of thousands of reports of PCA each year, and the number of reports has steadily increased over the past two decades. **Official estimates** as well as **self-report surveys** indicate that violence toward children in the home occurs frequently. As many as 75% of Americans, for example, report using at least one violent act toward their children at some point during child rearing. Debate over whether the rate of PCA is increasing has focused on official reporting statistics, which show a yearly increase in reports of PCA, compared with self-report survey data, which generally show stable, or declining, rates of PCA.

Searching for Patterns: Characteristics of Victims and Perpetrators

Are girls or boys more likely to be the victims of PCA? Are children with particular behavioral characteristics or from specific ethnic backgrounds more vulnerable to physical abuse? What are the specific characteristics and traits of the adults who perpetrate violent acts against children? Agencies that receive official reports of abuse, or survey data collected from representative samples of the population, have provided much of the information on the sociodemographic characteristics of victims and perpetrators of PCA. Clinical as well as empirical studies have also provided information relevant to the psychological characteristics of PCA perpetrators. Although these sources of information are limited by the biases discussed in the previous section, they nonetheless provide some insight into the characteristics of child victims and adult perpetrators of PCA.

Characteristics of Victims of Physical Child Abuse

Age. Research findings reflect the effect of age on reported rates of PCA. Much evidence suggests that the risk of physical maltreatment generally declines with age (AAPC, 1989; DHHS, 1994). Statistics from the AAPC (1985), for example, indicate that for all types of officially reported physical abuse, the majority of child victims fall between the ages of 0 and 5 years (51%), followed by children aged 6 to 11 (26%), and then children aged 12 to 17 (23%).

Although young children are the most frequently reported victims of PCA, experts in the field have increasingly recognized that adolescents are often the victims of family violence as well. The highest rates of physical injury, for example, occur in infants and toddlers and in adolescents—the two extreme age groups (AHA, 1984; DHHS, 1981, 1988). AHA reported that adolescents consistently represented about 25% of officially reported victims of maltreatment for most years between 1976 and 1982 (Trainor, 1984). The most recent information from the AAPC (1988) indicates that 35% of all maltreatment reports are for adolescents between 12 and 17 years.

Gelles and Cornell (1990) suggest that the absence of attention toward adolescent victims, until recently, may result from societal perceptions that adolescents share some complicity in their abuse due to their size, strength, or difficult behaviors that may provoke the violence they receive. Consequently, such violent interactions may not be viewed as abusive but rather as legitimate methods of parental control. In addition, adolescents may appear to be less physically vulnerable or in danger of bodily harm (Powers & Eckenrode, 1988).

Gender. In regard to gender, results are mixed. Some studies have determined that boys receive more physical abuse than girls, whereas others have found relatively equal proportions of abuse across gender. Results from the second National Family Violence Survey found that for both minor and major forms of violence, males were at greater risk (Wolfner & Gelles, 1993). In contrast, the most recent statistics from the AAPC (1988) indicate that for minor acts of physical abuse, males and females are equally at risk. For major acts of physical abuse, however, boys (54%) are slightly more at risk than are females (46%). According to official reports from 1992 data summarized by the National Center on Child Abuse and Neglect (DHHS, 1994), for children under 12, males are more likely to be victims of PCA, whereas for ages 13 and above females are more likely to be victims of PCA.

Socioeconomic Status. Although maltreatment occurs in all socioeconomic groups, official reporting statistics have consistently shown that PCA occurs disproportionately more often among economically and socially disadvantaged families (DHHS, 1981, 1988; Sedlak, 1991; Zuravin, 1989). Official reporting rates of physical abuse, for example, were $3\frac{1}{2}$ times higher among children from families with annual incomes less than $15,000 (Sedlak, 1991). According to the most recent data from the AAPC (1988), 49% of all families

reported for maltreatment were receiving public assistance in the form of Aid to Families With Dependent Children (AFDC) such as food stamps or Medicaid. Low income also appears to be related to the severity of abuse, with serious or fatal injuries being more likely among families whose annual income is below the poverty level (e.g., Gil, 1970; Pelton, 1994; Wolfner & Gelles, 1993). Studies on the representativeness of epidemiological data indicate that this finding does not appear to be a consequence of bias in reporting, especially because it has consistently emerged over the past 20 years (DHHS, 1981).

Race. Studies attempting to determine racial differences in rates of PCA are fraught with methodological difficulties (Asbury, 1993) and, as a result, should be interpreted cautiously. According to the most recent official reporting statistics from the AAPC (1988), 68.2% of PCA reports involved Caucasian children, 16.1% involved African American children, and 11.5% involved Hispanic children. Hampton (1987) evaluated percentages of substantiated reports and found that 77.4% involved Caucasian families, 15.8% involved African American families, and 4.2% involved Hispanic families. According to 1991 census data, 84.1% of the U.S. population is Caucasian, 12.4% is African American, and 3.5% is "other" (U.S. Bureau of the Census, 1991). These figures suggest that African Americans appear to be slightly overrepresented and Caucasians slightly underrepresented in PCA reports. Some experts, however, have suggested that children from minority groups are simply more likely to be labeled abused than other children (Hampton, 1987).

Findings from national self-report studies of PCA are mixed. The first National Family Violence Survey found, for example, that rates of PCA for Caucasians and African Americans were consistent with their rates in the U.S. population at large (Straus et al., 1980). Native American and Asian heritage, however, were risk factors. In the second National Family Violence Survey, African American families were at greatest risk for PCA (Wolfner & Gelles, 1993).

Additional Risk Factors. Many researchers in the field of PCA have argued that special characteristics of children may put them at increased risk for abuse and neglect (e.g., Kirkham, Schinke, Schilling, Meltzer, & Norelius, 1986). Several studies, for example, suggest an association between PCA and birth complications such as low birth weight and premature birth (Parke & Collmer, 1975). Studies have also implicated physical, mental, and developmental disabilities as risk factors for PCA (e.g., Ammerman, Van Hasselt, Hersen, McGonigle, & Lubetsky, 1989; Friedrich & Boriskin, 1976). Other research, however, has failed to find prematurity and disabilities as risk factors for abuse (e.g., Benedict, White, Wulff, & Hall, 1990).

The National Center on Child Abuse and Neglect (DHHS, 1993) addressed the incidence of child abuse among children with disabilities (e.g., mental retardation, physical impairments such as deafness and blindness, serious emotional disturbance) by collecting data from a nationally representative sample of 35 child protective services agencies. Results indicated that the incidence of child maltreatment was almost twice as high (1.7 times higher) among children with disabilities compared to the incidence among children without disabilities. For children who were physically abused, the rate of disability was 2.1 times the rate for maltreated children without disabilities (vs. 1.8 for sexually abused and 1.6 for neglected children). The most common disabilities noted included emotional disturbance, learning disability, physical health problems, and speech or language delay or impairment.

A major difficulty in interpreting these data hinges on the specification of the sequence of these events. Were children disabled before the abuse or is the disability the result of abuse? Child protective services caseworkers reported that for 47% of the maltreated children with disabilities, the disabilities directly led to or contributed to child maltreatment (DHHS, 1993). For 37% of children, abuse presumably caused the maltreatment-related injuries.

Characteristics of Perpetrators of Physical Child Abuse

Age. The mean age for perpetrators of physical abuse is 32 (AAPC, 1988). Another descriptive finding is that abusive parents often begin their families at a younger age than do families in the general population, with many being in their teens at the birth of their first child (AHA, 1984; DHHS, 1981).

Gender. Authorities receive slightly more PCA reports for females than males (53% female, 47% male; AAPC, 1988). When the severity of injury is taken into account, data from the AAPC indicated that female offenders are associated with more major forms of physical abuse, and males are associated with more minor physical injury (AAPC, 1988). Some have suggested that the disproportionate level of child-rearing responsibilities assigned to women might be the primary cause of gender disparity found in official reporting statistics (Gelles & Cornell, 1990). Self-report studies have also found results contrary to official estimates. In the second National Survey on Family Violence, for example, female caretakers reported a higher rate of minor violence compared to men, and gender differences for severe violence were nonexistent (Wolfner & Gelles, 1993).

Relationship to the Victim. The child's parents are the perpetrators of physical abuse in the majority of cases (82%; AAPC, 1988). Cases involving strangers or outsiders involve only a small minority of cases (14%; AAPC, 1988). New research, however, suggests that violence perpetrated by siblings may be an unrecognized form of PCA (see boxed insert: "Sibling Violence").

Speculation about whether single parents and stepparents are at particular risk of abusing their children has prompted several investigations. Official report data and survey data show that single parents are overrepresented among abusers (AHA, 1984; Gelles, 1989). Gelles (1989), however, has argued that the greater risk among single parents is not a function of raising children alone but rather a function of the high rate of poverty in such families. Societal stereotypes also suggest that stepparents are more likely to abuse their nonbiological children. The fairy tale about Cinderella is a prime example of the evils of stepparenting. Official report data from the AHA tend to support the risk of PCA associated with stepparents (AHA, 1976). Self-report surveys, on the other hand, do not indicate that stepparents are more likely to physically abuse than biological parents (Gelles & Harrop, 1989a).

Psychological Characteristics. Many studies have evaluated the psychological characteristics of adults who abuse children. Early studies of perpetrators identified several characteristics of abusive adults such as emotional and behavioral difficulties, interpersonal problems,

SIBLING VIOLENCE

Public views of family violence reflect the perception that violence between adults and children or between husbands and wives is the most common form of violence. The most common form of violence, however, may occur between siblings (Straus et al., 1980). Consider the following example:

> I can't remember a time when my brother didn't taunt me, usually trying to get me to respond so he would be justified in hitting me. Usually he would be saying I was a crybaby or a sissy or stupid or ugly and that no one would like me, want to be around me, or whatever. Sometimes he would accuse me of doing something, and if I denied it, he would call me a liar. I usually felt overwhelmingly helpless because nothing I said or did would stop him. If no one else was around, he would start beating on me, after which he would stop and go away. (Wiehe, 1990)

Most individuals who have a brother or sister can undoubtedly remember a time when they engaged in some altercation with their sibling: pulling hair, name-calling, pinching, pushing, and so on. In fact, some have argued that because such behaviors are so common, they are rarely defined as family violence (Gelles & Cornell, 1990; Wiehe, 1990). Such interactions may be rationalized as sibling rivalry and considered a normal part of development between siblings.

Based on research from the first National Family Violence Survey, Straus and his colleagues (1980) found that 82% of American children with siblings between the ages of 3 and 17 engaged in at least one violent act toward a sibling during a 1-year period. In addition, Steinmetz (1982) found that between 63% and 68% of adolescent siblings in the families she studied used physical violence to resolve conflicts with brothers or sisters. Roscoe, Goodwin, and Kennedy (1987) studied 244 junior high students who completed an anonymous questionnaire examining negative interactions and conflict resolution strategies between siblings. Results indicated that 88% of males and 94% of females reported that they were victims of sibling violence some time in the past year. Likewise, 85% of males and 96% of females admitted they were the perpetrators of sibling violence.

Critics have argued, however, that much of the aggression that occurs between siblings is not serious and therefore should not be considered abusive. Research supports this contention and indicates that the majority of violence between siblings would be classified as nonabusive. This fact does not negate, however, the high frequency of violence occurring between siblings that would be categorized as abusive. When Straus et al. (1980) viewed only severe forms of violence, for example, results continued to indicate a high incidence of violence between siblings: 42% of parents reported kicking, biting, and punching between siblings; 40% reported hitting or attempted hitting with an object; and 16% reported siblings "beating up" one another. Roscoe et al. (1987) found similar results in their sample of junior high students: 46% reported being kicked, 38% reported being hit with an object, 37% reported being hit with a fist.

Although the majority of research has investigated physical abuse between siblings, there is also evidence that sibling abuse involves other forms of maltreatment including emotional and sexual abuse (e.g., Wiehe, 1990; Worling, 1995). In a self-report survey, Wiehe (1990) found a significant amount of overlap between the various forms of abuse, with emotional abuse between siblings most common (78% of respondents) followed by sexual (67%) and physical abuse (64%). Research evaluating gender characteristics has found that males and females perform these behaviors to a nearly equal degree (Roscoe et al., 1987; Straus et al., 1980). In regard to age differences, research suggests that as children grow older, sibling violence becomes less common (Steinmetz, 1982; Straus et al., 1980).

low levels of intelligence, and a lack of child development knowledge (e.g., Hunter, Kilstrom, Kraybill, & Loda, 1978; Smith, Hansen, & Noble, 1974; Steele & Pollock, 1968). These early studies were primarily descriptive in nature, based on the observations of clinicians. As a result, such studies provided little information about whether these characteristics were unique to physically abusive parents. Later studies were more scientifically sound and included control groups of nonabusive parents as well as standardized measurement instruments. Although the use of more sophisticated methodology cannot

Table 3.1 Characteristics of Adults Who Physically Abuse Children

Emotional and behavioral difficulties	Parenting difficulties
Self-expressed anger	Unrealistic expectations of children
Depression	Disregard for child's needs/abilities
Low frustration tolerance	Deficits in child management skills
Low self-esteem	Viewing parenting role as stressful
Rigidity	Negative bias/perceptions regarding child
Anger control problems	Poor problem-solving ability with regard to child rearing
Deficits in empathy	Intrusive/inconsistent parenting
Anxiety	Less communication, interaction, stimulation
Family and interpersonal difficulties	**Other**
Marital difficulties	Physical health problems
History of abuse in childhood	Perceived life stress
Deficits in positive interactions with child and other family members	Substance abuse/dependence
	Physiological overreactivity
Isolated from family and friends	

SOURCE: Information for this table was obtained from the following references, which are representative but not exhaustive: Azar, Barnes, and Twentyman (1988); Bousha and Twentyman (1984); Cappell and Heiner (1990); Friedrich and Wheeler (1982); Milner and Wimberly (1980); Mitchel (1989); Teteur, Ewigman, Peterson, and Hosokawa (1995); Whipple and Webster-Stratton (1991); and Wolfe (1991).

definitively establish whether parental characteristics *cause* a parent to physically abuse a child, such information can be helpful in guiding treatment efforts. Table 3.1 lists the most common characteristics of physically abusing adults described by researchers.

Studies comparing nonabusive parents to physically abusive parents have confirmed several characteristics typical of abusive parents that were noted in earlier clinical studies, such as anger control problems, low frustration tolerance, depression, low self-esteem, deficits in empathy, and rigidity (e.g., Friedrich & Wheeler, 1982; Lahey, Conger, Atkeson, & Treiber, 1984; Milner & Wimberly, 1980). Physically abusive adults are also more likely to exhibit family and interpersonal difficulties, high rates of perceived life stress, substance abuse or dependence, and a childhood history of PCA (e.g., Cappell & Heiner, 1990; Dore, Doris, & Wright, 1995; Whipple & Webster-Stratton, 1991).

These more sophisticated studies have also evaluated other variables such as the context of the abusive family and characteristics of parenting. Compared to nonabusive adults, for example, abusive individuals have unrealistic expectations and negative perceptions regarding their children (Azar, Barnes, & Twentyman, 1988; Bauer & Twentyman, 1985; Larrance & Twentyman, 1983). Such parents often regard their child as bad, slow, or difficult to discipline and view the child's behavior as if it were intended to annoy them. A parent may expect a child to be toilet trained

at an extremely early age (e.g., 7 months), for instance, and then interpret the child's continual lack of training as deliberate misbehavior. Abusive parents also tend to view the parenting role as stressful, and they exhibit numerous deficits in child management skills (Mash, Johnston, & Kovitz, 1983; Trickett & Kuczynski, 1986).

Physically abusive parent-child interactions also involve a lower rate of interaction; a higher rate of directive, critical, and controlling behavior; and a higher frequency of verbal and physical aggression (Bousha & Twentyman, 1984; Mash et al., 1983; Whipple & Webster-Stratton, 1991). Tuteur, Ewigman, Peterson, and Hosokawa (1995), for example, observed mother-child dyads for 10 minutes in a private room of a public health clinic equipped with toys, a table, and paper and crayons. Mothers sat at the table with their child, who was allowed to use the paper and crayons but was not permitted to play with the toys. Tuteur and his colleagues found that abusive mothers, when compared to nonabusive mothers, used more negative and rigid control (e.g., chased child under the table) rather than positive (e.g., comfortably directed child), and requests were either neutral (e.g., Keep going) or negative (e.g., Draw a circle right now) rather than positive (e.g., Can you please draw a circle for Mommy?).

Biological Factors. Biological factors associated with PCA perpetrators are a final area receiving attention. Several reports, for example, demonstrate that adults who abuse children have more health problems and physical disabilities than nonabusing adults (e.g., Conger, Burgess, & Barrett, 1979; Lahey et al., 1984). The biological area receiving the most empirical attention and support, however, is physiological reactivity. Evaluations examining physiological reactivity in perpetrators of PCA are abundant and consistently demonstrate that perpetrators of PCA are hyperresponsive to positive and negative child stimuli (e.g., Disbrow, Doerr, & Caulfield, 1977; Frodi & Lamb, 1980; Milner & Chilamkurti, 1991). Frodi and Lamb (1980), for example, found that abusive mothers showed increases in heart rate and skin conductance to videotapes of both a crying and smiling infant relative to control mothers. These results suggest that abusive parents may view their children as aversive regardless of the child's emotional state.

Intermediate Chapter Summary

Sociodemographic characteristics of children who are victims of PCA do not suggest that any particular subpopulation of children is the sole target of violence. Girls as well as boys are reportedly maltreated, and all age groups are represented in the literature. A diversity of ethnic backgrounds also characterizes the victims of PCA. There is evidence, however, that some characteristics place certain individuals at more risk than others. Young children, for example, between 0 and 5 years of age are at particularly high risk for PCA. Victims of physical abuse are also disproportionately represented among economically disadvantaged groups. Children with special needs such as those with physical or mental disabilities also appear to be at higher risk for abuse. With regard to race, most studies show that African American children are more frequently reported for PCA, although a cautious interpretation of such data is warranted.

A relatively large volume of literature is available that addresses the **characteristics of perpetrators** of PCA. Although no single profile of PCA perpetrators exists, research supports several attributes that represent elevated risk for PCA. The average age for perpetrators is 32 years, although high rates of abuse are also found in individuals who begin their families at a young age. In the overwhelming majority of reported cases, perpetrators are the parents of the victim. Single parenthood is also associated with abuse; the contribution of stepparenting as a risk factor is less clear. Data regarding perpetrator gender are mixed, although it is clear that PCA is committed by males as well as by females. Studies evaluating personality characteristics and biological factors associated with perpetrators have found numerous factors that differentiate abusive parents from nonabusive parents such as depression and anger control problems, parenting difficulties, family difficulties, and physiological overreactivity. Although many characteristics of perpetrators have been identified, it is important to note that not every individual possessing such risk factors is abusive.

Consequences of Physical Child Abuse

Children who experience physical maltreatment are more likely to be physically, behaviorally, and/or emotionally impaired, compared to their nonabused counterparts (for reviews, see Ammerman, 1991; Fantuzzo, 1990; Kolko, 1992). In some cases, the negative consequences of abuse continue to affect the individual well into adulthood (for reviews, see Gold, 1993; Malinosky-Rummell & Hansen, 1993). Table 3.2 displays the most frequently reported effects of PCA for children as well as for adolescents and adults.

Effects of Abuse on Children

Research examining the effects of PCA on children has been limited to physical harm until relatively recently. The more subtle, yet significant, social and psychological effects were ignored in evaluations that focused only on visible signs of trauma such as physical injuries. More recent research indicates that PCA is also associated with detrimental ef-

Table 3.2 Possible Effects Associated With Physical Child Abuse for Children, Adolescents, and Adults

Children
Medical complications: bruises; head, chest, and abdominal injuries; burns; fractures
Cognitive difficulties: decreased intellectual and cognitive functioning; deficits in verbal facility, memory,
   perceptual-motor skills, and verbal abilities; decreased reading and math skills; poor school achievement;
   increase in special education services
Behavioral problems: aggression, fighting, noncompliance, defiance, property offenses, arrests
Socioemotional deficits: delayed play skills, infant attachment problems, poor social interaction skills, deficits in
   social competence with peers, avoidance of adults, difficulty making friends, deficits in prosocial behaviors,
   hopelessness, depression, low self-esteem

Adolescents
Antisocial behavior: violent interpersonal behavior, delinquency, violent offenses, substance abuse
Other: attentional problems, depressed school performance, increased daily stress, low self-esteem, homosexuality

Adults
Criminal/violent behavior: arrests for delinquency, adult criminal behavior, violent criminal behavior, marital
   violence (for adult males), received and inflicted dating violence, physical abuse of own children
Substance abuse: abuse of alcohol and other substances
Socioemotional problems: self-destructive behavior, suicidal ideation and behavior, anxiety, hostility, dissociation,
   depression, unusual thoughts, interpersonal difficulties

SOURCE: Information for this table was obtained from the following references, which are representative but not exhaustive: Ammerman (1991); Chu and Dill (1990); Cicchetti and Barnett (1991); Eckenrode and Doris (1991); Fantuzzo (1990); Gold (1993); Kaufman and Cicchetti (1989); Kolko (1992); Malinosky-Rummell and Hansen (1993); Marshall and Rose (1990); Myers (1992); Smith (1994); Widom (1989); Williamson, Borduin, and Howe (1991); and Wodarski, Kurtz, Gaudin, and Howing (1990).

fects on the child's emotional, social, and intellectual functioning.

Medical Problems. The medical consequences of PCA are numerous and can range from minor physical injuries (e.g., bruising) to serious physical disfigurements and disabilities. In extreme cases, abuse can result in the death of a child (see boxed insert: "Killing Our Children"). Bruises are one of the most common types of physical injuries associated with PCA. Nonabused children, however, also incur bruises. Physically abused children, however, have bruises in uncommon sites (e.g., buttocks, back, abdomen, and thighs) (Schmitt, 1987). Other markings can result from grabbing, squeezing, or using belts, switches, or cords (Myers, 1992). A series of unusual injuries is often an indication of nonaccidental injury or PCA (Myers, 1992).

One of the most dangerous and life-threatening types of injury is head injury, which is the most common cause of death in abused children (e.g., Smith, 1994). Various actions can result in head injury, including a blow to the head by an object, punching the head with a fist, or throwing a child against a hard surface. Another dangerous form of abuse that can result in head injury is grasping the child and vigorously shaking the child back and forth. This type of injury, known as shaken

baby syndrome or shaken impact syndrome, can result in the child's brain moving within the skull, causing blood vessels to stretch and tear (Bruce & Zimmerman, 1989). The end result can be severe injury, coma, or death. Commonly, parents who bring their children into emergency rooms with nonaccidental head injury report that the child's injury was caused by a fall from an item of furniture (crib, couch, bed, etc.). Research evaluating injury from accidental falls, however, disputes such parental claims because accidental events typically result in minor injuries such as bruises or cuts or no injury at all (Lyons & Oates, 1993).

Other common injuries include chest and abdominal injuries, burns, and fractures (Myers, 1992; Schmitt, 1987). Abdominal injuries can be caused by hitting a child with objects, grabbing children tightly, or punching or kicking children in the chest or abdominal areas, resulting in organ ruptures or compressions. Burns, which are often inflicted as punishment, can include immersion in scalding water or contact burns with objects such as irons, cigarettes, stove burners, or heaters. Finally, fractures of bones in various areas of the body often result from PCA. Fractures can be caused by any of a number of actions, including punching, kicking, twisting, shaking, and squeezing.

KILLING OUR CHILDREN

On October 25, 1994, Susan Smith loaded her two small boys into the back seat of her Mazda. As Susan drove along county roads in South Carolina, Michael, age 3 years, and his brother, Alexander, age 14 months, fell asleep. Susan Smith pulled the car up to a boat ramp by a lake and got out of the car. The mother of the two children then watched as the car rolled into the lake, floated for a few minutes, and then sank beneath the surface with the boys still strapped into their car seats (Adler, Carroll, Smith, & Rogers, 1994). Susan Smith murdered her two children and shocked the nation, once again, by demonstrating that parents are capable of killing their own children.

Roughly 1,271 children were killed as a result of child abuse or neglect in 1994 (Wiese & Daro, 1995). The rates of fatalities reported to child protective services, furthermore, have steadily increased over the past several years. Between 1985 and 1994, for example, the rate of child deaths increased by 48% (Wiese & Daro, 1995). These statistics in and of themselves are cause for concern and become even more alarming in light of the belief that such figures represent underestimates of actual fatality rates. These numbers do not reflect, for example, child deaths due to maltreatment reported to other authorities such as law enforcement agencies, hospitals, or coroners (Wells, 1994b). Also excluded are cases that are improperly classified as accidental deaths or as sudden infant death syndrome rather than as maltreatment (Ewigman, Kivlahan, & Land, 1993).

Characteristics of child maltreatment deaths have been evaluated, and some consistencies have emerged. According to data derived from reporting agencies, approximately half of child fatalities result from physical abuse (McCurdy & Daro, 1994b). These deaths might result from cumulative beatings or single violent episodes. The other half of victims die as a result of neglect when parents fail to provide for a child's basic needs (e.g., medical care or adequate supervision) (AAPC, 1986). The leading cause of death among physically abused children is death associated with some type of injury to the head (Smith, 1994). The large majority of these children are also under the age of 5 years, with close to half of these children under the age of 1 year at the time of their death (McCurdy & Daro, 1994b).

Children dying at the hands of their parents or other caregivers seems to represent the ultimate failure of child protective services. Although Susan Smith had not been previously identified by child protective services, many cases of fatal child maltreatment had prior or current contact with child protective services agencies. Approximately 30% to 50% of children killed by parents or caretakers are killed after they have been identified by child welfare agencies and have been involved in interventions and were either left in their homes or returned home after a short-term removal (Besharov, 1991; Mitchel, 1989). Just because a child dies in a community, however, is not evidence of a faulty child protective services system. As Carroll and Haase (1987) note, "Even in the best of social service departments and with the best of services, children, most tragically, will die. In this field of protective services, human judgments are being made; and being human, mistakes are inevitable" (p. 138). Carroll and Haase (1987) believe that the important determination in such cases is whether the child's death or injury resulted from a lack of response by child protective services or as a result of an incorrect human judgment. Recent evidence suggests that the majority of fatal maltreatment cases have not had prior contact with protective service agencies (Wells, 1994b).

What can be done to help prevent child maltreatment fatalities? One response to the problem of child maltreatment fatalities that is receiving increasing support is the concept of child death review teams. Child death review teams are typically composed of a board of community professionals representing multiple agencies (Durfee, 1994). Child death review teams are forming across the United States, Canada, and other countries. Although the functions of such teams vary, most review child death cases to identify the prevalence of deaths due to abuse and neglect and to improve the policies and procedures of child protective services to prevent future abuse (Cavaliere, 1995; Thigpen & Bonner, 1994). Other prevention efforts have focused on the investigation of risk factors associated with child maltreatment fatalities. One study, for example, compared maltreatment fatality cases with nonfatal maltreatment cases and found several factors to be associated with fatality such as paternal drug use, absence of a maternal grandmother in the home, ethnicity, young age of the child, presence in the home of a father or father substitute, a sibling with medical problems, and prior removal of the child from the home (Fontana & Alfaro, 1987). A recent review concluded that a child's young age was the best predictor of severe and fatal physical abuse (Hegar, Zuravin, & Orme, 1994).

Finally, Daro and Alexander (1994) have called for a broad public health approach to preventing childhood maltreatment deaths. They recommend efforts directed at federal, state, and local levels such as expanding available funding for programs and research, reforming judicial and child welfare policy, increasing professional and community education, and providing community-based support for at-risk families. Many believe that a comprehensive approach will be necessary to realize an actual reduction in child maltreatment fatalities. As Attorney General Janet Reno (1994) recently stated, "The problem of child maltreatment-related deaths is not a simple one, and the solutions require the coordinated efforts of many agencies and professionals as well as the commitment of the entire community" (p. 1).

Cognitive Problems. Studies have documented that physically abused children exhibit lower intellectual and cognitive functioning relative to control group children on general intellectual measures as well as specific measures of verbal facility, memory, verbal language, communication abilities, and perceptual motor skills (e.g., Fantuzzo, 1990; Friedrich, Enbender, & Luecke, 1983; Hoffman-Plotkin & Twentyman, 1984).

Academic performance is another area of substantiated difficulty in physically abused children. Relative to controls, physically abused children display poor school achievement and adjustment, receive more special education services, score lower on reading and math tests, exhibit more learning disabilities, and are more likely to repeat a grade (de Paul & Arruabarrena, 1995; Eckenrode & Doris, 1991; Salzinger, Kaplan, Pelcovitz, Samit, & Krieger, 1984).

Behavioral Problems. Physical aggression and antisocial behavior are among the most common correlates of PCA (Wolfe, 1987). In most studies, abused children show more aggression, even after statistical correction for the poverty, family instability, and wife battering that often accompany abuse (e.g., Fantuzzo, 1990). In other words, abuse seems to have an effect on behavior independent of the potential contribution of other factors. This negative behavioral pattern has appeared across a wide variety of settings, such as summer camp (Kaufman & Cicchetti, 1989) and preschool and day care programs (Alessandri, 1991), using a variety of data collection procedures (i.e., adult ratings: Hoffman-Plotkin & Twentyman, 1984; observations: Bousha & Twentyman, 1984). Other behavioral difficulties include drinking and drug use, noncompliance, defiance, fighting in and out of the home, property offenses, and arrests (e.g., Hotaling, Straus, & Lincoln, 1990).

Socioemotional Difficulties. Some researchers argue that victims of PCA suffer from problems related to attachment to caregivers and social interactions (Cicchetti & Barnett, 1991; Conaway & Hansen, 1989; Youngblade & Belsky, 1990). The quality of the parent-child bond, for example, consistently reflects insecure attachments (e.g., increased avoidance of and resistance to the parent) in infants exposed to PCA (Cicchetti, Toth, & Bush, 1988; Kolko, 1992).

These early patterns of parent-child interaction may also lay the foundation for subsequent difficulties in social interactions for older children (Kolko, 1992). Physically abused children exhibit poor social interactions with peers as well as adults (e.g., Fantuzzo, 1990; Kinard, 1982; Salzinger, Feldman, Hammer, & Rosario, 1993). Difficulties include trouble making friends, deficits in prosocial behavior (e.g., smiling) with peers, and delays in a number of interactive play skills (Alessandri, 1991; Howes & Eldredge, 1985; Prino & Peyrot, 1994).

Studies have also demonstrated a higher incidence of emotional difficulties in physically abused children relative to controls. School-aged children, for example, have been found to display lower levels of self-esteem relative to controls (Allen & Tarnowski, 1989; Kaufman & Cicchetti, 1989). Finally, evidence suggests that victims of PCA exhibit feelings of hopelessness, depression, and low self-worth (Allen & Tarnowski, 1989; Fantuzzo, 1990).

Effects of Abuse on Adolescents

Although the consequences of PCA for young children have received extensive interest in the empirical literature, much less attention has focused on the physical, social, and psychological effects of PCA on adolescents. The fact that some cases of adolescent PCA began in adolescence, whereas others began in childhood, also contributes to the difficulty in understanding the effect of PCA on adolescents. Nonetheless, some have argued that the effects of PCA may be expressed somewhat differently in adolescents (e.g., Williamson, Borduin, & Howe, 1991).

The few reports that have examined the consequences of maltreatment in adolescents suggest that deviant or problematic behavior is often found among adolescents who were abused in childhood. Such individuals often display antisocial as well as violent interpersonal behavior such as dating violence (Dodge, Bates, & Pettit, 1990; Reuterman & Burcky, 1989) and aggression toward parents and siblings (Kratcoski, 1984). Abused children also have higher rates of delinquency compared to general population as well as to poverty samples (e.g., Alfaro, 1981; Kratcoski, 1984; Zingraff, Leiter, Myers, & Johnsen, 1993). One study found higher rates of homosexuality in individuals who experienced abuse during adolescence compared to nonabused adolescents (Harry, 1989). Consequences of PCA in adolescents also include externalizing behavior problems, attention problems, poor self-esteem, substance abuse, depressed school performance, and more daily stress (Cavaiola & Schiff, 1988; Truscott, 1992; Williamson et al., 1991; Wodarski, Kurtz, Gaudin, & Howing, 1990).

Long-Term Effects

Understanding the effects of abuse on children is important because such problems may lead to long-term difficulties. It is evident, in fact, that many of the psychological and social difficulties that emerge in childhood are also evident in adults who have a history of PCA (Malinosky-Rummell & Hansen, 1993). It is further believed that many of the social and behavioral impairments that begin in childhood and persist in adulthood may contribute to the intergenerational transmission of abuse (Wolfe, 1987). Unfortunately, only a few studies have empirically examined the long-term sequelae of PCA.

Criminal and Violent Behavior. One of the most frequently discussed long-term consequences of PCA is criminal behavior. Widom (1989), for example, compared a sample of validated cases of child abuse and neglect (identified 20 years earlier by social service agencies) to a sample of matched controls. She evaluated juvenile court and probation department records to establish occurrences of delinquency, criminal behavior, and violent criminal behavior. Although the study did not distinguish between various forms of maltreatment, results indicated that the abused-neglected group had a higher likelihood of arrests for delinquency, adult criminality, and violent criminal behavior than did the control group. Importantly, however, 74% to 90% of individuals with a history of PCA did not have any offenses or violations, suggesting that the link between abuse and criminality is far from perfect.

Other research suggests that adults with a childhood history of physical abuse are more likely to both receive and inflict dating violence (Marshall & Rose, 1990; Riggs, O'Leary, & Breslin, 1990). In addition, male adults who were physically abused as children are more likely to physically abuse their marital partners (Rosenbaum & O'Leary, 1981b).

Researchers have also found that adults who were victims of physical abuse as children are more likely to be perpetrators of PCA as adults. The percentage of adults who later go on to abuse their own children ranges from 7% to 70% (Kaufman & Zigler, 1987; Widom, 1989). Once again, it is important to remember that childhood abuse is neither a necessary nor sufficient cause of adult perpetration.

Substance Abuse. The rate of substance abuse in adults with a history of physical abuse has also attracted scientific attention. Examination of substance abuse, however, has focused on alcohol abuse in men, which limits its generalizability. In a recent review of the literature linking substance abuse with a history of PCA, Malinosky-Rummell and Hansen (1993) reached the following conclusions: (a) Adults who abuse substances report a higher incidence of childhood physical abuse compared to the general population; (b) Physically abused male alcoholics, relative to nonabused alcoholics, report more problematic drinking and associated lifestyle behaviors, social, and medical difficulties; and (c) Physically abused inpatients tend to experience more alcoholism and substance abuse compared to nonabused inpatients.

Socioemotional Difficulties. Less information is available on the long-term socioemotional consequences of physical maltreatment compared to other forms of abuse (e.g., sexual). Nonetheless, some recent research suggests a relationship between PCA and psychological adjustment in adults. Evidence to date indicates that adults with a history of PCA exhibit more significant emotional problems (e.g., higher incidence of self-destructive behavior, suicidal thoughts and behavior, anxiety, hostility, depression) compared with nonabused controls (Bryer, Nelson, Miller, & Krol, 1987; Chu & Dill, 1990; Kroll, Stock, & James, 1985; Yesavage & Widrow, 1985). Reports also confirm that a history of PCA is associated with greater dissociation, suicidal ideation, and negative feelings about interpersonal interactions (e.g., Briere & Runtz, 1988).

Mediators of Abuse Effects

Data from studies evaluating the consequences of PCA on children, adolescents, and adults abused as children require cautious interpretation. The way in which PCA affects its victims is not well understood, in large part, because of the difficulties associated with studying such a complicated problem. Physical abuse, for example, often occurs in association with other problems within the family or in the environment such as marital violence, alcohol or drug use by family members, parental depression, psychological maltreatment, or low socioeconomic status. It is therefore difficult to conclude with any certainty that the psychological problems associated with PCA result solely, or even primarily, from the violent interactions between parent and child.

To add to the uncertainty in understanding the effects of PCA, it is also true that the experience of PCA does not affect each victim in a consistent or predictable way (Cicchetti & Rizley, 1981). For some, the effect of PCA may be pervasive and long-standing, whereas for others the experience may not be invariably negative or disruptive. Researchers are examining a number of factors that might be influential in mediating the effect of PCA.

One mediating factor is the severity and duration of the abuse. The assumption is that more severe and/or chronic maltreatment will lead to more severe outcomes.

Although empirical support is sparse, some evidence supports this contention (e.g., Erickson, Egeland, & Pianta, 1989; Kinard, 1982; Wind & Silvern, 1992). In addition, some researchers have suggested that the greater the number of subtypes of maltreatment (e.g., physical abuse, sexual abuse, neglect), the more negative the outcome will be for the child as well as the adult with a history of PCA (Kurtz, Gaudin, Howing, & Wodarski, 1993; Wind & Silvern, 1992).

Other research suggests that the negative effects of abuse are greatest for children in families where there are high levels of stress and parental psychopathology (e.g., schizophrenia) or depression (Kurtz et al., 1993; Walker, Downey, & Bergman, 1989). Reports are also beginning to appear that demonstrate the influence of sociocultural and family variables (e.g., socioeconomic status and the quality of the parent-child interaction) on negative outcome (Herrenkohl, Herrenkohl, Rupert, Egolf, & Lutz, 1995). Finally, recent studies have implicated the protective influence of certain factors such as high intellectual functioning (Herrenkohl, Herrenkohl, Egolf, & Wu, 1991) and the presence of a supportive parent figure (Herrenkohl et al., 1995).

Intermediate Chapter Summary

The problems associated with PCA are multiple and far reaching and include negative physical and psychological effects for child and adolescent victims as well as adults who report a childhood history of PCA. The negative **effects for children** include medical (e.g., head injury), cognitive (e.g., school problems), behavioral (e.g., aggression), and socioemotional (e.g., poor social skills) problems. Although less is known about the negative consequences of abuse for adolescents, available research indicates that the **effects for adolescents** range from antisocial and violent behavior to poor self-esteem and substance abuse. Many of the same social and behavioral impairments found in childhood are also **effects for adults,** including criminal and violent behavior, substance abuse, and socioemotional difficulties. The experience of PCA, however, does not affect each individual in a consistent or predictable way. Specific characteristics of victims' families or their abuse experiences can serve to **mediate the effects** of abuse. Victims whose families are characterized by high stress and whose abuse experiences are more severe, for example, tend to exhibit greater levels of psychological distress. On the other hand, victims who benefit from high levels of intelligence and a supportive parent figure appear to be protected in some way and demonstrate fewer psychological symptoms.

Explaining Physical Child Abuse

Unfortunately, it is impossible at this point in time to specify the exact circumstances that lead to PCA. Several factors have contributed to the dearth of knowledge about the causes of physical abuse. First, PCA is not a simple behavior but a very complex set of interacting behaviors and factors. Second, methodological problems have plagued the research in this area. Most studies are retrospective, for example, relying on information that could be biased by the memory or perceptions of individuals. In addition, sample sizes are often small and nonrandom, calling into question the validity and generalizability of findings. The definition of what

---

Physical child abuse is not a simple behavior but a very complex set of interacting behaviors.

---

constitutes abuse has also varied across studies, contributing to difficulties in interpreting results. In addition, ethical issues prohibit the implementation of experimental studies that might establish cause-and-effect relationships between variables under study. Finally, it is clear that the population of abusers and victims are heterogeneous groups in terms of psychological, social, and demographic characteristics, limiting any widespread application of the causes of abuse that could account for all, or even most, cases of PCA.

Despite such qualifications, several models have attempted to explain the causes of PCA. Since the early 1960s, views on the primary causes of child abuse have expanded to move beyond disturbed adults or children to include the more pervasive influences of parent-child relationships, the family environment, socioeconomic disadvantage, and cultural sanctioning of violence and corporal punishment (e.g., Wolfe, 1991). Table 3.3 displays the multiple risk factors implicated in the empirical literature as playing a role in the physical abuse of children.

The Individual Pathology Model

When PCA was viewed as a rare social problem, it was easy to assume that perpetrators were disturbed individuals who must be "crazy" or "sick." The earliest models of abuse thus asserted that child abusers were seriously disturbed individuals with significant psychopathology (e.g., Kempe, Silverman, Steele, Droegemueller, et al., 1962). The psychiatric model associates PCA with an adult who is suffering from mental illness, personality disorder, alcohol or drug abuse, or some other individual defect. Some research, in

fact, has identified a subgroup of severely disturbed individuals who abuse children (Berger, 1985; Walker, Bonner, & Kaufman, 1988), although only a small proportion of abusive parents (less than 10%) are significantly psychiatrically disturbed (Kempe & Helfer, 1972; Straus, 1980a). As noted previously, however, perpetrators of PCA often do exhibit specific "nonpsychiatric" psychological characteristics and behaviors that distinguish them from nonabusive parents, such as anger control problems, depression, and substance abuse.

Parent-Child Interaction

The legal statutes governing adult behavior do not grant adults the right to inflict physical injury on children. When an adult does inflict injury, he or she is legally responsible for his or her behavior. As a result, children cannot be held responsible for their own victimization. As noted previously, however, there are certain characteristics of the child that place him or her at risk for abuse. Difficult behaviors, young age, and physical and mental disabilities, for example, are all child characteristics associated with abuse. Although some of these traits could be the result of abuse rather than a precipitant of abuse, common to all of them is their association with child care that is more demanding and difficult than in the absence of such factors. At the same time, it is also true that there are specific characteristics of parents that are linked with an increased risk of abuse such as deficits in parenting skills, lack of knowledge regarding normal childhood behavior, and unrealistic expectations for children.

Parent-child interaction theories suggest that difficult child behaviors interact with specific parental behaviors to result in physical abuse. It is the behavior of both the parent and the child, rather than either of them alone, that promotes violence. Studies have repeatedly demonstrated, for example, that punitive parenting is associated with negative child behavior and outcomes (e.g., Denham, Renwick, & Holt, 1991; Dowdney & Pickles, 1991). Such findings raise what is known as the "directionality question": Who affects whom? Clearly, parenting practices have direct effects on children. A child's behavior, however, also contributes to a parent's response to that child (Bell & Chapman, 1986).

Table 3.3 Risk Factors Associated With Physical Child Abuse

Factors associated with individual pathology
Perpetrator characteristics
  Self-expressed anger and anger control problems
  Depression
  Low frustration tolerance
  Low self-esteem
  Rigidity
  Deficits in empathy
  Substance abuse/dependence
  Physical health problems
  Physiological reactivity

Factors associated with parent-child relationship
Characteristics of the child
  Difficult child behaviors
  Young age
  Physical and mental disabilities
Characteristics of the adult
  Deficits in parenting skills
  Unrealistic expectations of children
  Viewing the parenting role as stressful
  Negative bias/perceptions regarding child

Factors associated with family environment
Characteristics of the family
  Current abusive family practices (e.g., spouse abuse)
  Intergenerational abusive family practices (e.g., child abuse)
  Marital discord
  Few positive family interactions

Factors associated with situational and societal conditions
Situational
  Low socioeconomic status
  Single-parent household
  Public assistance
  Blue-collar employment
  Unemployment or part-time work
  Situational stress (e.g., large family size)
  Social isolation
Societal
  Cultural approval of violence in society, generally
  Cultural approval of corporal punishment
  Power differentials in society and the family

Anderson, Lytton, and Romney (1986) examined parent-child interactions in a study in which mothers of boys with conduct problems (e.g., antisocial and aggressive behavior problems) and mothers of boys with normal behavior interacted one at a time with three children: their own child, a child of like diagnostic classification, and a child of different diagnostic classification. Conduct-disordered children complied less regardless of the mother with whom they were interacting, and they elicited more negative feedback and requests from all mothers than did normal children. The authors concluded that the child's behavior influenced negative maternal behaviors. It would appear that both parent and child characteristics interact to fuel a parent's sense of frustration, stress, and impatience, resulting in an increased risk for abuse (e.g., Bell, 1977; Parke & Collmer, 1975; Wolfe, 1987).

Social Learning Theory

Many retrospective studies have demonstrated that a significant percentage of adults who abuse children were abused themselves as children (e.g., Cappell & Heiner, 1990; Gelles, 1973; Hunter et al., 1978). These adults presumably learned, through experiences with their own parents, that violence is an acceptable method of child rearing. Being raised in such an environment might also preclude the opportunity for PCA victims to learn more appropriate and nurturing methods of adult-child interaction.

Mounting evidence also suggests that a child may not need to experience abuse directly to learn violent interpersonal interaction styles. Through witnessing the negative interactions between the significant adults in their lives, for example, children also learn maladaptive or violent methods of expressing anger, reacting to stress, or coping with conflict (Jaffe, Wolfe, & Wilson, 1990; Kalmuss, 1984; see Chapter 6 for a discussion of children who observe marital violence). Studies of adults who abuse children indicate that such individuals are more likely to come from homes characterized by considerable marital discord and violence (Gelles, 1980; Hotaling & Sugarman, 1986; Kalmuss, 1984).

As stated previously, however, the cycle of violence is not a universal law, and many abused children do not become abusive adults. Kaufman and Zigler (1987) recently reviewed the empirical literature on this question and concluded that the rate of intergenerational transmission is 30% ± 5%, which means that approximately 70% of those who were abused as children do not go on to become abusive adults. Because not all parents who experience childhood physical abuse become physically abusive, there may be factors that mediate the effects of this relationship. Egeland, Jacobvitz, and Sroufe (1988), for example, found that those mothers who were physically abused, but did not abuse their own children, were significantly more likely to have received emotional support from a nonabusive adult during childhood, have participated in therapy during some period in their lives, and been involved in a nonabusive, stable, and emotionally supportive and satisfying relationship with a mate. Nonabusive mothers with a history of PCA are also reportedly less anxious, dependent, immature, depressed, and are more flexible in how they view their children (e.g., Caliso & Milner, 1994; Egeland et al., 1988). Hunter and Kilstrom (1979) also found that parents who did not repeat child maltreatment were more likely to report childhood social support, such as a positive relationship with one parent.

Situational and Social Conditions

During the 1970s, a radical shift occurred in the theoretical orientation related to the causes of PCA. Interest in the *context* of abusive behavior led to research examining situational, social, and cultural factors that might foster abuse. Sociological models of abuse were developed that focused on sociological factors such as economic conditions, societal and cultural values, and social systems (e.g., Gelles & Straus, 1988; Gil, 1970).

Gil (1970) was one of the first to point out the high proportion of abused children coming from poor and socially disadvantaged families. As mentioned previously, recent research supports these earlier findings by indicating that PCA is more common among low-income families and families supported by public assistance (AAPC, 1988; Sedlak, 1991). Additional measures of socioeconomic disadvantage also indicate disproportionate representation from physically abusive families. Children whose fathers are unemployed or work part-time, for example, are more at risk for abuse compared with children of fathers with full-time employment (AAPC, 1988; McCurdy & Daro, 1994b; Wolfner & Gelles, 1993). A study by Mills in 1982 compared the changes in county unemployment rates during 1981 with the annual child abuse and neglect official report figures during that same year (cited in Pelton, 1994). Of the 51 counties in the study that showed increased unemployment rates, approximately 69% had increases in child abuse and neglect reporting compared to 19% of the 21 counties with unemployment rate decreases. A person's occupation is also related to the occurrence of abuse. Blue-collar workers, for example, are more likely to engage in physical punishment and abuse than white-collar workers (Straus et al., 1980; Wolfner & Gelles, 1993).

Social isolation, including a lack of extended family or peer support network, has also been a social factor associated with abuse (Gil, 1970). Research suggests that abusive parents have fewer contacts with peer networks, as well as with immediate family and other relatives (Disbrow et al., 1977; Whipple & Webster-Stratton, 1991; Zuravin & Grief, 1989). Increased social isolation has also been suggested by the finding that abusive parents are less likely to have a phone in the household (Dubowitz, Hampton, Bithoney, & Newberger, 1987).

Zuravin (1989), using official reporting statistics, measured social isolation by evaluating community variables associated with maltreating families. Results indicated a significant relationship between physically abusive families and communities with high proportions of single-family dwellings and vacant housing. According to Garbarino and Crouter (1978), these variables serve as physical impediments to social networks by isolating families from one another and decreasing the number of social supports available. Other researchers have found that maltreating families engage in few social or recreational activities and do not use available community resources (e.g., Corse, Schmid, & Trickett, 1990; Smith, 1975).

Situational variables, particularly as they affect the level of stress within a family, have also been associated with PCA. Stressful situations such as a new baby, illness, death of a family member, poor housing conditions, and larger than average family size are also risk factors in maltreatment (Gil, 1970; Johnson & Morse, 1968; Straus et al., 1980). Wolfner and Gelles (1993), for example, found that households with two to four children at home were at increased risk for both minor and abusive violence. Other situational variables associated with PCA include high levels of stress from work-related problems and pressures, marital discord, conflicts over school performance, illness, and a crying or fussy child (Barton & Baglio, 1993; Gelles, 1973).

Cultural Approval of Physical Child Abuse

Specific cultural factors have also been suggested as playing a role in conditions leading to PCA. The general pervasiveness of violence in America, as discussed previously, is a good example of an aspect of American culture that might create a cultural context that fosters the physical abuse of children. The general acceptance, and sometimes support, of corporal punishment as a method of discipline is another aspect of American culture conducive to violence in general and to PCA more specifically. The Supreme Court, for example, has ruled that schools have the right to corporally punish disobedient children, the only individuals in American society whom it is legally permissible to strike (Zigler, 1977; Zigler & Hall, 1989). Unequal power differentials in the structure of society, particularly the family, might also contribute to PCA (Gelles & Cornell, 1990). Children are abused, in part, because they are unable to defend themselves against stronger and more powerful adults (e.g., financially, emotionally, and physically). Some evidence consistent with this idea is found in official estimates of physical abuse that suggest that the rates of PCA decrease with child age, as the child becomes older and stronger and more capable of self-defense (Gelles & Hargreaves, 1981).

Intermediate Chapter Summary

Views on the primary causes of PCA have included a **variety of models,** such as those that focus on the psychiatric disturbance of abusers (e.g., mental illness, personality disorder, substance abuse) and those that suggest that the problem is rooted in dysfunctional parent-child interactions (i.e., increased risk of abuse because of parental frustration, stress, and impatience).

In addition, evidence suggests children **learn to model violent behavior** by merely witnessing negative interactions, perpetuating a cycle of violence. Nevertheless, qualifications regarding the **reliability of information** about the causes of PCA (e.g., methodological problems, sample sizes, definitions of abuse, ethical issues, heterogeneous groups) have affected research in the field.

A significant shift in the conceptualization of the causes of PCA occurred with the birth of **sociological models** of abuse that focused on the situational and social context of abuse. These models emphasized the possible implications of socioeconomic disadvantage (e.g., physical abuse), social isolation (e.g., less peer support), situational stressors (e.g., illness or poor housing), and cultural approval of violence (e.g., acceptance of corporal punishment) in contributing to PCA.

Currently, PCA is conceptualized as a complex problem resulting from **multiple interacting factors** from many different domains including the adult perpetrator, parent-child interactions, family environment, and situational and social conditions.

Responding to
Physical Child Abuse

Solutions to the PCA problem have paralleled the etiological frameworks described in the previous sections. Some have considered psychological treatment interventions focusing on the individual child or adult, disturbed marital relationships, or the parent-child interaction. Others have emphasized situational variables. Interventions directed at ameliorating PCA and its associated sequelae include the protection of children, psychological treatment, and community interventions.

Protecting the Child

Federal and state laws provide for the protection of children who are at risk for child abuse or neglect. In most states, such responsibility falls on the local department of social services. In different states, this department may be called the department of public welfare, the department of human resources, or the department of human services (Carroll & Haase, 1987). Regardless of the label, the de-

---

The role of child protective services is to attempt to prevent child abuse and neglect in the child's own home.

---

partment of social services has a division responsible for the protection of children, usually referred to as child protective services. Protection may be implemented on either a voluntary or involuntary basis and may result in a child's remaining at home or being placed in some type of out-of-home care.

Child Protective Services. The role of child protective services is to protect children via four services: investigation of reports of maltreatment, provision of treatment services, coordination of services with other agencies in the community, and implementation of preventive services (Carroll & Haase, 1987; Wells, 1994a). In all cases, the role of child protective services is to attempt to prevent child abuse and neglect in the child's own home through various crisis intervention and treatment services. These services include

crisis nursery or respite care, community-based family resource centers, counseling for children and parents, parenting education, lay therapy, home visitor services, and self-help or volunteer programs such as Big Brothers/Big Sisters, Parents Anonymous, and Parents United (Daro, 1988; Wells, 1994a).

In recent years, child protective services agencies across the country have come under fire because of concern over the seeming inability of the system to provide adequate protection for those children reported for maltreatment (see boxed insert: "Killing Our Children"). This criticism reflects a growing number of problems faced by protective services agencies: the consistent increase in child abuse reports and resulting increases in workloads, low budgets, and a high turnover rate of well-trained social workers who are leaving the field (Carroll & Haase, 1987; McCurdy & Daro, 1994a). The recommended maximum workload for acceptable treatment services, for example, is 17 families per social worker (Smolowe, 1995). Reports of current caseloads are often between 30 and 50 families per caseworker (Gelles & Cornell, 1990). Under these conditions, it is not difficult to understand why approximately one third of the state administrators contacted by the Child Welfare League of America (1986) do not routinely investigate reports within the 24 to 48 hours mandated by child welfare legislation.

Melton and Barry (1994) have pointed to another reason for the failure of the system, arguing that "the system responds to allegations, not needs" (p. 5). Historically, child protective services has narrowly focused on reporting and investigation to the exclusion of efforts directed at prevention and treatment. At the present time, approximately 40% of the families in which maltreatment has been substantiated do not receive any "service" other than investigation (McCurdy & Daro, 1994a).

In reaction to the problems with the system and its response to abused and neglected children, ABCAN (1993) formulated a new national strategy for the protection of children in 1993. Melton and Barry (1994) summarized this strategy, which includes the following elements:

1. Strengthening neighborhoods as environments for children and families
2. Refocusing the delivery of human services so that efforts are focused on services to prevent child maltreatment rather than almost exclusively on services provided after abuse has occurred

3. Reorienting the role of government in child protection so that incentives are offered for prevention and treatment rather than investigation

4. Targeting societal values that may contribute to child maltreatment such as cultural acceptance of violence and exploitation of children

5. Increasing the knowledge base about child maltreatment through federal research programs

Out-of-Home Care. Federal law mandates that the primary goal of social service agencies is to preserve or reunite the family. Although all states have programs to prevent the dissolution of the family when desirable and possible (Stein, 1993), state laws also permit placement in out-of-home care to protect children. When danger to the child is imminent or when prevention attempts are unlikely to be effective, a judicial determination can be made to place the child outside of the home. Most states require that a custody hearing be initiated within 24 to 48 hours (Stein, 1993). Out-of-home care is then used to ensure the child's safety until services are able to alter parental behavior or environmental conditions so that the child can return home without further risk of abuse. If reasonable efforts to produce change are ineffective, the child remains in out-of-home placement on a permanent basis until he or she reaches adult age or parental rights are terminated and the child is adopted.

In 1985, there were 276,000 children in out-of-home care settings, primarily as a result of child abuse, physical neglect, parental incompetency, or abandonment (Sudia, 1986). Out-of-home care includes foster care placements, court placements to relatives, residential treatment centers, and institutions. The number of children placed in such settings currently has escalated to more than 400,000, with approximately 75% of these children placed in foster care (George, Wulczyn, & Fanshel, 1994; Morganthau et al., 1994). In addition to criticisms leveled at the child protective system in general, placement decisions have also become a topic of considerable debate in recent years (see boxed insert: "Out-of-Home Placement Dilemmas").

Psychological Treatment

The psychopathology-based view of PCA led to treatment efforts directed primarily at individual parents. Such methods were criticized for being too narrow in scope, ignoring the other serious contributors to and consequences of PCA. Current approaches are broader and include not only adult interventions but also child-focused and family interventions (Oates & Bross, 1995; Walker et al., 1988; Wolfe & Wekerle, 1993).

Adult Interventions. Since the 1970s, adult interventions have increasingly used behavioral approaches including some form of skills training that focuses on anger-, child-, or stress-management skills (Azar & Wolfe, 1989; Walker et al., 1988). The most frequently used behavioral approach is to train parents in child management skills. Such training involves educating parents about the effects of reinforcement and punishment on behavior and the importance of consistency in discipline (e.g., Wolfe & Sandler, 1981). Parents also learn how to appropriately deliver both reinforcement and punishment for child behaviors (e.g., Walker et al., 1988). Programs achieve these goals by providing appropriate parenting models through demonstration (video or live) and problem-solving approaches for increasing child compliance (e.g., Crimmins, Bradlyn, St. Lawrence, & Kelly, 1984). Parent programs also attempt to guide parental behavior by providing opportunities for role-play to practice skills and feedback about performance (e.g., Wolfe, St. Lawrence, Graves, Brehony, Bradlyn, & Kelly, 1982).

Anger control techniques attempt to reduce negative emotional responses and thoughts and enhance coping ability. These programs achieve these goals by assisting parents in identifying events that increase negative emotions and helping parents to replace anger-producing thoughts with more appropriate ones. Anger control programs also attempt to teach self-control skills in an effort to reduce uncontrolled expressions of anger (e.g., Nomellini & Katz, 1983; Whiteman, Fanshel, & Grundy, 1987). Stress management techniques typically involve education and training of parents with regard to relaxation techniques, ways to reduce psychological stress, and methods for coping with stressful interactions with their child (e.g., Egan, 1983).

In their review of empirical studies evaluating the effectiveness of interventions for adults who abuse children, Wolfe and Wekerle (1993) concluded that parent-focused approaches consistently demonstrate improvements in parenting skills such as positive interactions with their children; effective control of unwanted behavior; and decreases in nega-

OUT-OF-HOME PLACEMENT DILEMMAS

The U.S. Advisory Board on Child Abuse and Neglect recently concluded that "the *system* the nation has devised to respond to child abuse and neglect is *failing*" (ABCAN, 1993, p. 2). One component of that system receiving increasingly more and more criticism is out-of-home placement. One problem is that there are decreasing numbers of families participating as foster parents, which limits the number of placements available for children (Morganthau et al., 1994). Other concerns focus on the potential negative psychological effects that might result from out-of-home placement such as emotional and behavioral problems. Critics also argue that the system is harmful for children because it puts them at increased risk for abuse in out-of-home settings.

Concerns voiced about out-of-home placement create a dilemma about what to do with children without homes—those who are abused, neglected, or unwanted. Reform of this system has been the topic of recent debate in Washington (Morganthau et al., 1994). Republicans are proposing to end welfare, which would mean drastic reductions in AFDC and concomitant disruption in the system's ability to provide adequate living conditions for children. House Speaker Newt Gingrich has recommended bringing back orphanages as one solution to this problem (Fornek & O'Donnell, 1994).

Public perceptions of orphanages are generally negative and conjure up images of lonely and emotionally starved children. Orphanages have been likened to prisons, useful for warehousing large numbers of children unable, for whatever reason, to live at home (Blankenhorn, 1994). In addition to distasteful images, the notion of resurrecting the orphanage has also raised concern over the resulting effect on the physical, social, and emotional well-being of children living in such arrangements. Gates (1994), for example, reviewed the history of the orphanage, describing the overcrowded conditions, poor nutrition, and unreasonable labor characteristic of orphanages of the 1800s. The orphanages of today, however, are group homes or residential treatment centers that include smaller living quarters with higher staff-child ratios.

What, then, is the best alternative for maltreated children? In arriving at the best alternative, the costs and benefits of leaving the child in the home versus foster care versus residential living must be evaluated. An analysis of the financial costs of each alternative indicates that the least expensive alternative is to keep the child in the home, followed by placing the child in foster care. The maximum monthly AFDC payments to parents range from $253 in Alaska to $192 in Vermont (Green, 1994, cited in Morganthau, 1994). These figures translate into approximately $6 to $8 a day per child. Foster care placement ranges from $12 to $16 a day per child (Spencer & Knudsen, 1992). The most expensive alternative is institutional care. Boys Town, a residential group home, spends approximately $111 to $133 a day per child (Morganthau et al., 1994).

Financial expenses are not the only consideration, however. What about the other potential costs associated with various alternatives such as the potential for negative socioemotional consequences

---

tive, coercive, or physically punitive management techniques. These techniques are also effective in enhancing anger control and stress management techniques by increasing coping and problem-solving skills. Parent-focused programs also exhibit some collateral effects by decreasing aggressive or negative behavior in the children of abusive parents and by increasing social skills and networks (Oates & Bross, 1995; Wolfe & Wekerle, 1993).

Child Interventions. In extreme cases, physically abused children may be exhibiting such severe psychological and behavioral difficulties that hospitalization is required. Most child interventions, however, involve therapeutic day treatment programs, individual therapy, and play sessions. Therapeutic day treatment programs typically provide group activities, opportunities for peer interactions, and learning experiences to address developmental delays (Culp, Little, Letts, & Lawrence, 1991; Parish, Myers, Brandner, & Templin, 1985). Individual therapy often incorporates relaxation skills, problem-solving strategies, anger management techniques, and efforts to improve self-esteem (Walker et al., 1988). Play sessions often include opportunities for play interaction between abused children and adults and/or peers (e.g., Davis & Fantuzzo, 1989).

Studies evaluating the effectiveness of child-focused treatment interventions indicate that

and the risk for further maltreatment? Some experts have argued that the social and emotional damage created by out-of-home placement may outweigh the potential harm a child faces by remaining in the home (Besharov, 1990). Others believe that the doctrine of family reunification should be abandoned for programs that focus on child protection and intervention aimed at the child's needs (Gelles, 1993c).

The research evidence evaluating these issues, unfortunately, is inconclusive. With regard to the potential psychological damage resulting from out-of-home placement, some studies have found better outcomes for children in foster care (Hensey, Williams, & Rosenbloom, 1983), whereas others have found better outcomes for children who remain at home (Lynch & Roberts, 1982). In a recent study, Kurtz et al. (1993) found no effect on child outcome for length of time spent in foster care, but they did find that greater numbers of foster care placements were associated with more negative child outcomes.

Research evaluating the risk for further maltreatment associated with in-home and out-of-home placement is also inconclusive. Cohn and Daro (1987), for example, found that 30% to 47% of parents continued to abuse their children while receiving treatment services. Abuse, however, also occurs in out-of-home placements (Rosenthal, Motz, Edmonson, & Groze, 1991; Spencer & Knudsen, 1992). Some reports suggest that such abuse is uncommon, constituting less than 1% of confirmed abuse cases (McCurdy & Daro, 1994b), whereas other research suggests that abuse in out-of-home settings is more common than in-home abuse (Rabb & Rindfleisch, 1985). Spencer and Knudsen (1992) compared relative risk for maltreatment among a variety of out-of-home facilities and found that children in day care and school facilities were less likely to be maltreated than those in foster homes, residential homes, or state institutions and hospitals.

The best placement alternative for any given child will likely depend on the particular circumstances of that individual. Placement decisions must involve a flexible and comprehensive approach that respects the potential contributions of many types of interventions. In some instances, keeping the child in the home while the family receives intensive intervention has proven cost-effective (Daro, 1988; Walton, Fraser, Lewis, & Pecora, 1993). On the other hand, there is no question that out-of-home care will be necessary for some children. Ultimately, the solution to the placement dilemma will involve many challenges:

> Increased risk to children and families occurs when either protection or preservation is emphasized to the exclusion of the other. If prevention of placement or reunification is framed as the primary "success," we introduce an incentive which may endanger children. Conversely, an emphasis on protection, without providing parents in-home services at the level they need, may harm children. (Lloyd & Sallee, 1994, p. 3)

these programs are successful in decreasing aggressive and coercive behaviors and in improving social behavior, cognitive development, and self-esteem in abused children relative to controls (Oates & Bross, 1995; Wolfe & Wekerle, 1993). Unfortunately, however, most of the studies evaluating treatment interventions directed at the child victim of PCA focus on preschool or young children to the exclusion of school-age and adolescent victims and do not make distinctions between various forms of maltreatment (Wolfe & Wekerle, 1993).

Family Interventions. Very limited information is available regarding interventions that target the family such as marital or family therapy approaches. One exception is the study conducted by Brunk, Henggeler, and Whelan (1987), which compared 33 maltreating families randomly assigned to either parent training or family therapy. Results indicated that both treatments were associated with decreases in psychological complaints, perceived stress, and overall severity of identified problems.

Intensive family preservation programs (IFPP) are another family-oriented approach that offers some promise for physically abusive families. IFPP were developed in an effort to prevent out-of-home placement of abused and neglected children by providing short-term, intensive therapeutic and supportive interventions including a range of in-home services such as behavior modification, crisis intervention therapy, and assertiveness training (Haapala & Kinney, 1988). Several evaluations of IFPP demonstrate their success in preventing out-of-home placement of children (e.g., Bath & Haapala, 1993; Schwartz, AuClaire, & Harris, 1991).

Community Interventions

Several community interventions commonly serve as adjuncts to some of the other intervention methods reported in this section. The idea behind such interventions is twofold: (a) to directly address some of the factors believed to contribute to PCA (e.g., social isolation) (see Walker et al., 1988) and (b) to alleviate the general stress level of abusive families to allow parents to work on therapeutic issues (Azar & Wolfe, 1989).

Social Networks. Because many abusive parents are socially isolated, researchers have suggested providing them assistance in developing a social network (Gaudin, Wodarski, Arkinson, & Avery, 1990; Walker et al., 1988). These networks would include personal friends as well as community contacts. Community contacts would vary depending on a particular family's needs but might include crisis hotlines, support groups (e.g., Parents Anonymous), or educational classes (e.g., Wolfe, Edwards, Manion, & Koverola, 1988). Home visitation programs offer another avenue of support to abusive parents. Such programs involve professionals or community volunteers who provide a variety of intervention approaches during regular visits to abusive parents. Home visits not only serve as a source of social support for parents but also provide parents with knowledge about child development and management (see Amundson, 1989; Roberts, Wasik, Casto, & Ramey, 1991). Home visitation programs are also recommended for the prevention of PCA (ABCAN, 1993) and are discussed further in Chapter 12.

Economic Assistance. Abusive families often need assistance to establish basic necessities such as food and shelter. Unfortunately, programs aimed at macrolevel concerns, such as poverty, are almost nonexistent (Hay & Jones, 1994). Local service organizations, the family's caseworker, or the Salvation Army might be able to provide such assistance. Professionals might also make job and educational referrals, although additional support may be necessary to combat the economic difficulties faced by these families (Hay & Jones, 1994). Parents may also need assistance completing government forms to obtain state funds for AFDC, food stamps, and child support (Walker et al., 1988).

Child Care Programs. Because abusive parents often find the parenting role challenging and have fewer child care options, child care programs can provide relief for overly burdened parents who need a break (Hay & Jones, 1994). Therapeutic child day care centers, for example, provide an environment similar to traditional day care programs but additionally provide services to target developmental delays and behavioral disorders associated with child maltreatment. Children can also be enrolled in preschool programs, Head Start centers, or families can take advantage of respite care services (e.g., home aides). Research has shown that such programs are successful in enhancing abused children's functioning (Daro & McCurdy, 1994).

Summary

The physical abuse of children is a complex problem that is not well understood despite nearly four decades of research efforts. The complexity of PCA is evident in attempts at defining what specific circumstances constitute abuse. Although most experts recognize that PCA includes a range of behaviors that cause observable harm to children, the boundary between PCA and "normal" parenting practices, or behaviors that do not result in observable harm, is less clear. Despite definitional ambiguities, however, it is clear that thousands of children are subjected to the harm associated with PCA each year. The majority of Americans report using at least one violent act toward their children at some point during child rearing.

Research examining the characteristics of the victims and perpetrators of PCA demonstrates the heterogeneity of victim and offender populations. Child victims, as well as adults who perpetrate PCA, represent all gender, age, race, and socioeconomic groups. A number of risk factors, however, have been consistently associated with PCA. Victims, for example, are often young children between 0 and 5 years of age. Children with special needs such as those with physical or mental disabilities also appear to be at higher risk for abuse. Perpetrators of PCA are disproportionately represented among economically disadvantaged groups, and their environments include a number of additional stressors such as having children at a young age and single parenthood. Adults who inflict violence against children also display a number of other psychological characteristics including depression and anger control problems, parenting difficulties, family difficulties, and physiological overreactivity.

PCA has been associated with a number of negative effects including both negative physical and psychological effects for child and adolescent victims as well as for adults who report a childhood history of PCA. Such negative consequences affect a variety of areas of functioning including the physical, emotional, cognitive, behavioral, and social domains. The experience of PCA, however, does not affect each individual in a consistent or predictable way. Specific factors can mediate the effects of PCA, either increasing or decreasing its detrimental effects. Factors associated with an increased effect of PCA include the severity of abuse, the duration, and the number of forms of abuse experienced.

The causes of PCA are not well understood, although a number of models have been proposed in an attempt to understand the violence that occurs between adults and children. Early theories focused on psychiatric disturbances in abusers, whereas later theories have implicated dysfunctional parent-child interactions. A significant shift in the conceptualization of PCA occurred with the birth of sociological models of abuse, which focused on the situational and social factors associated with abuse, including the role of socioeconomic disadvantage, social isolation, situational stressors, and cultural approval of violence.

Early solutions to the PCA problem focused on the abusing parent to the exclusion of other potentially helpful interventions. More recently, child protective services, under the administration of both federal and state systems, have provided assistance (e.g., child care, community centers, counseling and education, visitor and self-help programs) for children who are at risk for child abuse or neglect. Because of the complexity of PCA, any single intervention or treatment is not likely to be successful, particularly with high-risk families. Psychological approaches for children and their families target parenting skills; anger control and stress management; social and developmental skills; and child-centered, marital, and family interactions. Some families may also need additional treatment interventions that focus on psychiatric disorders or substance abuse problems or provide in-home services (e.g., crisis intervention, assertiveness training). Furthermore, community interventions have expanded to address situational and social factors that might contribute to PCA, namely, social isolation and economic stressors. In such cases, home visits, hotlines, support groups, local service organizations, family caseworkers, and government programs such as Aid to Families With Dependent Children (AFDC) or distribution of food stamps are called on for support. Although evaluation studies suggest that these interventions appear promising, additional research is needed to enhance efforts directed at solving the PCA problem.

4

Child Sexual Abuse

C H A P T E R   O U T L I N E

An Interview With David Finkelhor

"I'd like to see a bit of redress in the balance between the interest in children as perpetrators of crime and children as victims of crime."

DAVID FINKELHOR is a renowned family violence researcher with wide-ranging interests. He is currently Research Professor of Sociology and Codirector of the Family Violence Laboratory at the University of New Hampshire. Here, he recently served on the conference committee to host the 4th International Family Violence Research Conference. He has written extensively on topics such as sexual abuse of children and marital rape. Of the 11 books he has edited or written, the latest are Nursery Crimes: Sexual Abuse in Daycare *(1989), coauthored with Linda Williams and Nanci Burns, and* Missing, Abducted, Runaway, and Thrownaway Children in America *(1990), coauthored with Gerald Hotaling and Andrea Sedlak. He also serves as an associate editor of three family violence journals. One of the many research grants he has received is the 1991-1994 grant from the Boy Scouts of America titled* A National Study of Youth Victimization Prevention. *Dr. Finkelhor received his B.A. in social relations, his Ed.M. in sociology (from Harvard), and his Ph.D. in sociology (from the University of New Hampshire).*

Q: How did you become interested in family violence?

A: There were two factors involved. First, I was influenced by some people doing work in this area who impressed me with the kinds of research questions they were asking. Second, I felt I could combine my scientific orientation with an opportunity to solve a pressing social problem. What has kept me involved is the continuing need for valid scientific information.

I've studied a number of different, interrelated topics within the field partially out of my own curiosity. From the beginning, I've espoused the point of view that we should be interested in more than one aspect of these problems. In fact, I've tried to model this approach in my own research.

Q: What has shaped your approach to the field?

A: Practitioners have been very important for me in specifying issues that needed atten-

tion. Some heated public controversies have also been influential in making me think that someone ought to be looking at these ideas more objectively. Also, my disciplinary training as a sociologist has affected my work. I've been very impressed with the ability of contemporary survey research to talk to people candidly about sensitive subjects. There have been a number of recent breakthroughs in methodology, and I feel that these methods can be applied in the area of family violence.

Q: What is your current research focus?

A: My current research interest is in child victimization, in general, and all the different kinds of ways that children get victimized inside and outside the family.

Q: What would you do if you had a large research grant?

A: If I had a large amount of money, I would do some studies that extend the National Crime Victimization Survey to include children of all ages, that is, below age 12. This would help us get a better understanding, or picture, of child victimization even at very early ages.

Q: What other types of research or advocacy should be done?

A: I'd like to see a bit of redress in the balance between the interest in children as perpetrators of crime and the interest in children as victims of crime. We spend far more time discussing juvenile delinquency than we spend on discussing juvenile victimization.

Q: What can society do to diminish family violence?

A: I would recommend home visitation and other programs that support parents. One way to prevent child abuse, and possibly reduce spouse abuse, is to provide parents with more support. One avenue of approach is to offer these programs within a comprehensive health care system.

Q: What is the biggest problem in trying to eliminate family violence?

A: The greatest problem is at the sociological level. The American public is not able to "swear off" violence. We tolerate violence. We believe that it is an effective method for solving problems. Violence is a part of male identity. We tend to romanticize violence. We need to discourage the use of corporal punishment, eliminate exposure to violence in the media, and help teenagers learn nonviolent, problem-resolution skills.

Q: What should the government do to combat family violence?

A: The federal government ought to fund more demonstration programs to stimulate new ideas about dealing with family violence. I'd also like to see the government establish clearinghouses for dissemination of scholarly articles and a resource bank of statistics from survey data. I'd also like to see more money for training of specialists.

Introduction

CASE HISTORY: SASHIM'S SECRET

Sashim was 6 years old and an only child when her parents divorced. Her father had been physically violent with both Sashim and her mother, and all subsequent ties with him were eliminated after the divorce. The next 3 years were difficult for Sashim because she rarely saw her mother, who worked two jobs in an attempt to make ends meet. When Sashim was 9 years old, her mother met a man named Bhagwan, a 39-year-old construction foreman. Shortly after Sashim's mother met him, Bhagwan moved in with the family and took a serious interest in Sashim. He took her to movies, bought her new clothes, and listened to the difficulties she was having at school. He seemed to provide her with the parental attention that she had missed for so many years.

After several months, Bhagwan's behavior toward Sashim began to change. He became much more physical with her, putting his arm around her when they were at the movies, stroking her hair, and kissing her on the lips when he said

good night. He began to come into her bedroom or the bathroom without knocking (e.g., when she was changing or bathing). Bhagwan then began "checking on her" in the middle of the night. During his visits, he would stroke and caress her body. In the beginning, he only touched her nonprivate areas (e.g., shoulders, arms, legs), but after several visits he began to touch her breasts and genitals. Eventually, he began to kiss her sexually during his touching, all the while telling her how much he loved her and enjoyed being her father. He warned her that she should not tell anyone about their time together because others would not understand their "special" relationship.

One night, Bhagwan attempted to have sexual intercourse with Sashim and she refused. A few days later, one of Sashim's favorite teachers asked if something was bothering her. Sashim began crying and told her teacher everything that had happened. Sashim's teacher reassured her that she believed her and would help her. Sashim's teacher called child protective services and reported her conversation with Sashim. Two social workers came to school and listened to Sashim as she told her story. Bhagwan was arrested. Sashim's mother was incredulous and could not believe that Bhagwan could do such a thing or that such a thing could occur without her knowing about it. She refused to believe Sashim, calling her a liar and a "home-wrecker." As a result, Sashim was placed in a foster home. Shortly thereafter, Sashim was diagnosed with leukemia and was told that she had only 6 months to live. Her only request was that she be able to die at "home" with her foster parents, to whom she had become quite attached. The hospital required that Sashim have parental consent before they could grant her request. Her biological mother still had legal custody of Sashim, however, and refused to grant the request unless Sashim agreed to recant her story about Bhagwan. (Author's case history)

* * *

As this case history demonstrates, child sexual abuse (CSA) is a multifaceted problem, which is extraordinarily complex in terms of its characteristics, dynamics, causes, and consequences. This chapter examines the major issues that contribute to this complexity. The chapter opens by addressing issues related to defining the scope of CSA, including definitions and rates of the problem. Attention then focuses on the typical characteristics of CSA victims as well as perpetrators in terms of age, gender, the relationship between perpetrator and victim, and additional factors. Next, a discussion follows of the dynamics of CSA and the consequences of this form of maltreatment for the victim. Finally, the chapter concludes with an analysis of potential causes of CSA and responses to the problem. It is important to note at the outset that although the discussion focuses on CSA in the broader context of family violence, attention will not be limited to intrafamilial (i.e., incestuous) sexual abuse because a significant proportion of sexual abuse is extrafamilial.

Scope of the Problem

What Is Child Sexual Abuse?

As discussed previously, one of the greatest barriers to understanding different forms of child maltreatment is the difficulty inherent in defining the problem. The issue is no less problematic with CSA. Which of the following case examples, for instance, deserve the label *CSA*?

Jamie, a 15-year-old adolescent, frequently babysat his neighbor, 4-year-old Naomi. Each time Jamie baby-sat Naomi, he had her stroke his exposed penis while they watched her favorite video.

Manuel and Maria frequently walked around nude at home, in front of their 5-year-old son, Ernesto.

Matt, a 10-year-old boy, was repeatedly forced to have anal intercourse with his uncle when Matt was between the ages of 5 and 9 years. After his abuse stopped, Matt frequently sneaked into his 6-year-old sister's room and had anal intercourse with her.

Sally was a 16-year-old, self-proclaimed "nymphomaniac." Sally had numerous boyfriends from school with whom she had physical relationships (e.g., kissing, fondling, sexual intercourse). One evening while Sally was home alone with her 45-year-old stepfather, he asked her if she would like to "mess around." Sally willingly agreed to have sexual intercourse with him.

Dexter, a 30-year-old man, invited 7-year-old Jimmy to his house frequently for an after-school snack. After their snacks, Dexter had Jimmy undress and assume various sexual poses while he made videotapes, which he distributed for profit.

The interactions described in each of these vignettes raise several important questions about defining CSA. First, what behaviors are defined as *sexual*? Second, under what circumstances do sexual interactions become *abusive*?

Cultural Context. In Chapter 1, a review of the discovery of CSA indicated that sexual interactions between children and adults have occurred throughout history, beginning in ancient times. It is only recently that CSA has been recognized as a social problem. It is thus apparent that any definition of CSA is dependent on the historical period in question, the cultural context of the behavior, and the values and orientations of specific social groups (Wurtele & Miller-Perrin, 1992). To define CSA today, it is essential to know something about what types of behavior are generally regarded as acceptable in American families. Is it abusive for Manuel and Maria to walk around nude in front of their 5-year-old son? What if their son were 13 years of age? How much variation in terms of nudity, touching various body parts, or kissing on the lips is socially acceptable?

Unfortunately, researchers have conducted few studies on normal patterns of touching and physical contact. One exception is the research of Rosenfeld and colleagues, which examined typical family patterns of bathing and touching (Rosenfeld, Bailey, Siegel, & Bailey, 1986; Rosenfeld, Siegel, & Bailey, 1987). Survey responses of 576 parents revealed that parents rarely bathed with their children at any age, particularly with the opposite sex (e.g., mothers with sons), after the children were 3 to 4 years of age. The touching of mothers and fathers (e.g., genitals or breasts) by children was relatively common among preschoolers, but declined as the children became older. Additional research is necessary to determine the frequency of other family behaviors such as sleeping patterns, nudity, privacy, or other types of touching (e.g., kissing, hugging) as well as cultural differences in such behaviors.

Conceptual Issues. The National Center on Child Abuse and Neglect (NCCAN; 1978) defined child sexual abuse as

contacts or interactions between a child and an adult when the child is being used for the sexual stimulation of the perpetrator or another person. Sexual abuse may also be committed by a person under the age of 18 when that person is either significantly older than the victim or when the perpetrator is in a position of power or control over another child. (p. 2)

This definition is consistent with most legal and research definitions of CSA and incorporates four key components that are generally regarded today as essential in defining CSA. First, definitions of CSA are typically broad enough to include not only cases of intrafamilial abuse (i.e., incest) but also cases of extrafamilial abuse. Second, definitions of CSA often include sexual experiences with a child involving both physical contact and noncontact activities. CSA, for example, may include physical contact such as fondling or intercourse as described in the vignette in-

---

One way to distinguish between abusive and nonabusive behaviors is to evaluate the intent of the perpetrator.

---

teractions involving Jamie, Matt, and Sally. Sexual abuse can also include noncontact forms as illustrated in the last scenario depicting Dexter making a pornographic video of Jimmy.

Controversy continues to exist, however, regarding the specific behaviors deemed abusive, regardless of whether those behaviors are classified as contact or noncontact experiences. Parental nudity, for example, is clearly a noncontact behavior, but is it an abusive behavior? One way to distinguish between abusive and nonabusive behaviors is to evaluate the intent of the perpetrator. Many definitions of CSA, for example, define abuse as sexual activities that are intended for sexual stimulation, thus excluding normal family or caregiving interactions (e.g., nudity, bathing, displays of affection). In practice, however, determining whether a behavioral intention is sexual or nonsexual can be difficult. How can one determine, for example, whether a grandfather's kiss to his granddaughter is innocent affection or sexual contact meant for his sexual gratification? Furthermore, some experts argue that caregiving behaviors can go beyond normal experiences and become abusive, such as when children are repeatedly exposed to genital examinations or cleanings (Berson & Herman-Giddens, 1994).

A third important component of CSA definitions emphasizes the exploitation of adult

authority and power to achieve the adult's sexual ends. Implicit in this definition is the assumption that children are incapable of providing informed consent to sexual interactions with adults for two reasons. First, because of their developmental status, children cannot give informed consent because they are not capable of fully understanding what they are consenting to and what the consequences of their consent might be. Second, children's ability to provide informed consent is limited because they might not be in a position to decline involvement due to the adult's authority status. The incident between Sally and her stepfather is abusive because, despite Sally's sexual experience and "consent" in this situation, she is not mature enough to understand the ramifications of having sexual intercourse with her stepfather. As Haugaard and Reppucci (1988) point out, "The total legal and moral responsibility for any sexual behavior between an adult and a child is the adult's; it is the responsibility of the adult not to respond to the child" (p. 193).

A final component of CSA definitions addresses the age or maturational advantage of the perpetrator over the child. Although many definitions limit abuse to situations involving an age discrepancy of 5 years or more between perpetrator and victim (e.g., Conte, 1993), others include children and adolescents as potential perpetrators if a situation involves the exploitation of a child by virtue of the perpetrator's size, age, sex, or status. Broader definitions of CSA include circumstances such as those described in the second scenario between 10-year-old Matt and his 6-year-old sister. An increasing number of reports involving both adolescent offenders and children victimizing children younger than themselves are beginning to appear (e.g., Abel & Rouleau, 1990; Gomes-Schwartz, Horowitz, & Cardarelli, 1990; Johnson, 1989).

Estimates of Child Sexual Abuse

Despite problems in defining CSA, researchers have made numerous efforts to determine the scope of the problem. In the United States, researchers generally use one of two different methods of estimation: official estimates based on reported cases and self-report surveys of adults who report having experienced sexual victimization during childhood.

Official Estimates. Most studies of official reporting statistics evaluate the number of new cases of CSA reported over the course of a year. Two National Incidence Studies (NIS-1 and NIS-2) evaluated the frequency of CSA in the United States (Department of Health and Human Services [DHHS], 1981, 1988; Sedlak, 1990). NIS-1 counted cases that came to the attention of community professionals and child protection agencies in a national probability sample of 26 counties in 10 states. The study arrived at a figure of 42,900 children under the age of 18 who were abused in 1980. NIS-2 used a probability sample of 29 counties and estimated that 133,600 children nationwide had been sexually abused in 1986.

Another source of information about official estimates of CSA comes from annual surveys conducted to assess the number of official reports of CSA documented by child protective services in the United States (American Association for Protecting Children [AAPC], 1988; Weise & Daro, 1995). Data from 1986 indicate that approximately 50,714 children were reported to child protective services for CSA (AAPC, 1988). The most recent estimate of CSA nationally found that in 1994, 11% of all child abuse and neglect reports involved CSA, representing approximately 330,000 children (Weise & Daro, 1995).

Official estimates are difficult to interpret for several reasons. First, any type of child abuse tends to be underreported by professionals as well as by the victims and families themselves (e.g., Kalichman, Craig, & Follingstad, 1989; Russell, 1983a). Professionals across the country, for example, failed to report approximately half of the maltreatment cases they identified (Sedlak, 1990). Wurtele and Miller-Perrin (1992) outlined several reasons for underreporting such as (a) failure to report because the reporter feels there is insufficient evidence (e.g., physical or laboratory evidence); (b) reluctance by professionals to report when statutory definitions are vague; (c) nondisclosure by victims because of ignorance, embarrassment, or threats of harm; and (d) underreporting by social service workers who may define less serious cases as unsubstantiated due to a lack of resources in managing cases.

Other factors, such as the definition of CSA employed, also contribute to the difficulties in interpreting reporting statistics. In the second National Incidence Study (DHHS, 1988), for example, rates were higher when teenagers, in addition to adults, were considered perpetrators of abuse. Official statistics also often include duplicate reports or reports made only to child protective services, contributing to the difficulty in interpreting findings.

Self-Report Surveys. Self-report surveys examine the proportion of a population that acknowledges having experienced sexual victimization during childhood. Self-report surveys include samples of college students, clinical or special groups (e.g., psychiatric inpatients, runaway youths), and community members (e.g., Finkelhor, 1979; Finkelhor, Hotaling, Lewis, & Smith, 1990; Powers, Eckenrode, & Jaklitsch, 1990). Estimates from self-report surveys vary dramatically depending on the population sampled. In their review of college student and community studies, for example, Wurtele and Miller-Perrin (1992) indicated that the prevalence of sexual abuse in these samples ranged from 7% to 62% for females and from 3% to 16% for males. When nonrandom clinical and special groups are used (e.g., psychiatric patients, prostitutes), self-report estimates are even higher. Briere and Zaidi (1989), for example, noted that 70% of women who sought treatment at a psychiatric emergency room reported a history of CSA.

Although variability in samples as well as definitions of abuse can account for some of the discrepancy in rates of CSA between self-report surveys, other factors also play a role. Underreporting, for instance, contributes to another portion of the disparity: Some men and women who were victimized as children may not remember their experiences or may be reluctant to report them as adults (see Williams, 1994). One review of self-report surveys, however, suggested that the most important factor in explaining variations in self-report estimates is the number of questions used to elicit an abuse history, with multiple questions resulting in increased disclosures of abuse (Peters, Wyatt, & Finkelhor, 1986). A recent review of the most representative and methodologically sound self-report surveys concluded that at least 20% of women and between 5% and 10% of men in North America have experienced some form of sexual abuse as children (Finkelhor, 1994a).

Is Sexual Abuse Increasing? Official estimates indicate that reports of CSA have increased dramatically since 1980. Does this increase in official reports indicate a true rise in the rate of CSA? It is certainly possible that sexual abuse could be increasing because of changes taking place within the family such as divorce, mothers working outside the home, and the greater presence of stepfathers and baby-sitters. Others argue that official reports are inflated as a result of false allegations and social hysteria (Rabinowitz, 1990). There has been considerable controversy among researchers and in the media surrounding the issue of fabricated reports of CSA, although the research evidence suggests that false allegations by children are rare (e.g., Jones & McGraw, 1987; Romer, 1990) (see boxed insert: "Do Children Fabricate Reports of Child Sexual Abuse?").

It seems likely that the actual occurrence of CSA is not increasing but rather CSA is reported more often as a result of legislative changes and increases in public and professional awareness. A study conducted by Feldman and colleagues (1991), for example, examined self-report estimates by comparing English-language studies from the 1970s and 1980s with those of the 1940s. When the variations in methodology across studies were controlled (e.g., definitions of abuse, upper age limits used for victims), results indicated that prevalence figures in 1940 were not significantly different from prevalence estimates of the 1970s and 1980s (e.g., 12% vs. 10% to 12%, respectively, of females younger than

14 years of age). Another study surveyed various age cohorts regarding childhood experiences of CSA and found that the 18- to 19-year-olds recalled proportionately less sexual abuse than the 20- to 27-year-olds, suggesting that in recent years there has been a significant decline in CSA (Bagley, 1990).

Sexual Abuse in Other Cultures. The view that CSA is a social problem of significant magnitude has largely been an American phenomenon. Until recently, CSA has received a great deal more attention in the United States than in other countries, particularly relative to other forms of maltreatment. Studies from other countries that address the problem of CSA internationally, however, are beginning to appear (e.g., Ho & Kwok, 1991; Krugman, Mata, & Krugman, 1992; Sariola & Uutela, 1994). Finkelhor (1994b) summarized the international rate of CSA in a review of 21 nonclinical population studies primarily from English-speaking and northern European countries, but also included studies from Costa Rica, the Dominican Republic, Spain, and Greece. Finkelhor's analysis revealed international rates of CSA comparable to North American studies including Canada and the United States. Prevalence estimates ranged from 7% to 36% for women and 3% to 29% for men.

Intermediate Chapter Summary

Sexual interactions between children and adults have existed throughout history. Society has not recognized these types of interactions, however, as abusive and harmful until relatively recently. Although any definition of CSA is time- and culture-bound, today's definition focuses on the **types of behaviors** and the **intent** involved, as well as the **age and/or power discrepancy** between offender and victim. Legally, it is assumed that children are incapable of or limited in providing **informed consent** to sexual interactions with adults. CSA includes both contact (e.g., fondling, intercourse) and noncontact (e.g., taking a pornographic video) experiences; events that occur within and outside the family; and behaviors that involve the exploitation of authority, status, and physical size to achieve the perpetrator's sexual interests.

Although the true number of children victimized by CSA is unknown, it is apparent that sexual victimization in childhood is a common experience. Indeed, there is good reason to speculate that official and self-report estimates **underestimate** the extent of the problem. Underreporting by professionals may occur due to insufficient evidence; vague statutory definitions; nondisclosure by victims because of ignorance, fear, or embarrassment; and lack of resources for managing less serious cases, for example. The **variability** of self-report survey samples and **difficulties in interpreting** official statistics are two more reasons for discrepancies in estimates of CSA incidents. Research over the past several years has documented significant increases in reporting rates; nevertheless, it is likely that increasing rates, both in the United States and elsewhere, are the result of social factors rather than of an increase in the actual incidence of abuse.

DO CHILDREN FABRICATE REPORTS
OF CHILD SEXUAL ABUSE?

Each year, there are persons who go to jail and lose their life savings, their homes, their reputations, and their jobs because social workers, psychologists, prosecutors, jurors, and judges believe what young children tell them about being sexually molested. Hundreds of thousands of individuals each year are accused falsely of child abuse. (Emans, 1988, p. 1000)

The origin of the statement that "hundreds of thousands of individuals each year are accused falsely" is typically attributed to Douglas Besharov, the first director of the National Center on Child Abuse and Neglect and keynote speaker at the first Victim of Child Abuse Laws (VOCAL) conference (Hechler, 1988). Besharov attributes the large number of false allegations to massive publicity surrounding child abuse accompanied by a dramatic increase in reporting (Besharov, 1985). Is there an epidemic of false allegations? Do parents and other individuals who interact with children need to be concerned that they may be accused of CSA?

After watching the television news or reading the newspaper, it might be easy to conclude that the answer to both questions is a resounding yes. A number of well-publicized cases have contributed to the perception among many that there is an epidemic of false allegations. Celebrities Woody Allen and Michael Jackson, for example, have recently argued that they were falsely accused of CSA. Another case that has received a great deal of attention involved Dale Akiki, a mentally and physically disabled child care worker in San Diego. Akiki was recently acquitted of sexually abusing, torturing, and kidnapping nine preschool-age children. In their report, the grand jury rebuked therapists, parents, and prosecutors for being "overzealous" and using improper investigation procedures. "Lawyers should try cases, not causes" (Mydans, 1994, p. A7).

A few years earlier, one of the longest and most costly criminal trials in U.S. history, the McMartin Preschool case, similarly ended without convictions. In the 1983 McMartin case, Ray Buckey, his mother Peggy McMartin Buckey, and five other child care workers were accused of sexually abusing some 360 children over several years (Victor, 1993). As in the Akiki case, the defendants were said to be "devil worshipers" and were accused of many bizarre and unspeakable acts. The district attorney's office, citing the "leading questions" of many of the social workers who counseled the children, eventually dropped the charges on everyone except Ray and Peggy Buckey. In January 1990, the Buckeys were acquitted on 52 of the 65 counts against them. Later that year, the prosecution dropped the remaining charges against Ray Buckey.

Although highly publicized cases like these might suggest that most accusations of CSA made by children are fabricated, a more accurate appraisal results from evaluating the research evidence relevant to false allegations. One line of research has examined whether children have the general capacity to lie. Current research suggests that children under age 7 are unlikely to be successful at telling a lie (Morency & Krauss, 1982). Other experts have examined the capacity of children to lie about CSA specifically and have concluded that nonsexually abused prepubescent children simply do not have the sexual knowledge or vocabulary to describe many of the explicit sexual acts experienced during abuse. Another line of research has evaluated whether children have the capacity to form and recall detailed memories of events. Current research and theory regarding memory in children indicate that children's memory ability depends on their language skills and ability to order and interpret events, skills that are particularly difficult for young children (Perry, 1992). However, in some situations, younger children can provide more accurate recall than adults (e.g., for a particularly salient event; Lindberg, 1991). In addition, children as young as 2 or 3 years of age can reconstruct events with 75% accuracy when they mentally re-create a scene to be remembered (reported in Perry, 1992).

Critics suggest, however, that children are not *intentionally fabricating* stories or memories, but that false reports result from parents and professionals who *create* such memories in children. Studies have examined the suggestibility of children by exposing them to some event and questioning the child about it. Most studies find that young children, especially preschoolers, are more suggestible than older children and adults (Ceci & Bruck, 1993). By age 10 to 11 years, however, children are no more suggestible than adults (Saywitz & Snyder, 1993).

(continued)

The memory of young children, as a result, can be contaminated by misleading information. Loftus and Ketcham (1991), for example, described research whereby preschool and kindergarten children were shown 1-minute films and subsequently interviewed. Children were asked suggestive questions such as "Did you see a boat?" and "Didn't you see a bear?" and responded affirmatively that they had seen these objects in the film. Because there was no boat or bear in the films, the researchers concluded that they were able to alter the children's responses or possibly create a memory simply by asking a suggestive question. Others have criticized the connection between this research and false allegations of sexual abuse, arguing that the circumstances in such experimental situations are quite different from an actual event of sexual abuse.

Investigators have also evaluated interview techniques relevant to sexual abuse investigations and found that in general, the techniques are not unduly suggestive. The majority of children, for example, do not disclose sensitive material in response to open-ended questions about a medical exam (Saywitz, Goodman, Nicholas, & Moan, 1991). Studies evaluating the use of anatomically correct dolls indicate that they are unlikely to elicit erroneous information (Everson & Boat, 1990). Other research has shown that the use of reinforcement during the course of an interview does not affect accuracy of recall negatively (Goodman, Bottoms, Schwartz-Kenney, & Rudy, 1991). Evaluating an interview technique for research purposes, however, may not reflect the way in which some interviews are conducted in the "real world." Asking a child the same question repeatedly, for example, could make the child feel pressure to respond affirmatively (e.g., "Did he touch any of your private parts?"). Making reference to the responses of other children potentially involved in sexual exploitation might also unduly influence a child's response and result in a false allegation (e.g., "Jose said that Jimmy touched his penis, did anything like that happen to you?").

The most direct research evidence associated with false allegations comes from studies that have examined samples of cases reported to child protection agencies or other professionals. Most studies of official estimates of CSA indicate that approximately 50% of CSA cases are unsubstantiated (Wiese & Daro, 1995). Confusion continues to exist, however, regarding what kind of case constitutes an unsubstantiated case. Some have equated "unsubstantiated" with false allegations. This definition, however, is misleading because there are several reasons why a case may be labeled unsubstantiated. Unsubstantiated cases include reports that are fabricated (false) as well as those involving insufficient evidence. Unsubstantiated cases theoretically include true reports with insufficient evidence as well as false allegations of abuse.

Current estimates of false allegations of abuse range from 3% to 8% of sexual abuse reports (Everson & Boat, 1989; Jones & McGraw, 1987). For example, Jones and McGraw (1987) reviewed 576 reports of alleged sexual abuse made to the Denver Department of Social Services in 1983. Of those 576 reports, 53% were confirmed as substantiated reports of abuse. Seventeen percent were unsubstantiated but categorized as representing a legitimate suspicion by the reporter. Another 24% were categorized as having insufficient information to make a determination about the abuse. The remaining 6% of reports were categorized as false allegations. Of the false allegations, 26 were reports from adults, and 8 were made by children or adolescents (5 of these 8 reports were made by disturbed adolescents who had been sexually victimized by an adult in the past). Of the adult cases, the large majority were allegations that arose in the context of custody or visitation disputes, although other studies have indicated that the overwhelming majority of custody disputes do not involve sexual abuse allegations (Faller, 1993).

There are several reasons to be cautious about results from such studies, because rates of false allegations vary depending on the type of population sampled (Everson & Boat, 1989). In addition, whether a report is considered to be true or false depends on the criteria used, which can vary from the consensus of clinicians to the disposition of child protective services to a judge's opinion. Such judgments are fallible, and as a result, the "true" rate of false allegations could be either somewhat higher or lower. Despite these methodological limitations, the rate of false allegations across studies is consistently low, representing a minority of reports. Even the smallest percentage of false positives, however, warrants continued research focusing on the methods of validating sexual abuse such as increasing the accuracy of validation attempts, improving interview techniques, and enhancing training for evaluators. By preventing false allegations, we not only avoid harming those falsely accused but refocus attention on identified victims of abuse.

Searching for Patterns: Characteristics of Victims and Perpetrators

Characteristics of the Victims of Child Sexual Abuse

Research evaluating demographic characteristics associated with CSA addresses several questions about the victims and perpetrators of this form of abuse. Studies focus on the age and gender of the adults and children involved in abuse, the relationship between perpetrator and victim, and specific risk factors associated with CSA.

Age. Definitional restrictions limit the upper age range typically to 16 to 18 years, but at the lower age range, children as young as $3^1/_2$ months have been reported for CSA (Ellerstein & Canavan, 1980). Cases on the extreme ends of this continuum are less common, however, and most clinical studies and official estimates indicate the mean age of children reporting abuse as 9 to 11 years (e.g., AAPC, 1988; Gomes-Schwartz et al., 1990). Retrospective studies of adults support the findings that prepubescence (approximately 7 to 12 years of age) is the most vulnerable period for CSA (Finkelhor, 1993; Finkelhor et al., 1990). It is likely, however, that abuse of young children goes undetected because young children are less likely than older children to report abuse, and adults in self-report surveys may not remember abuse that occurred early in childhood (Williams, 1994).

Gender. Official estimates and self-report surveys indicate that the majority of CSA victims are female (DHHS, 1988; Finkelhor, 1993; Finkelhor et al., 1990). Many experts, however, believe that males are simply less likely to report abuse. Some self-report surveys of adult males, for example, indicate that male victims are less likely to disclose abuse (e.g., Finkelhor, 1981). Several societal norms may contribute to the underreporting of males, including (a) the expectation for boys to be dominant and self-reliant, (b) the notion that early sexual experiences are a normal part of boys' lives, (c) fears of being considered homosexual because most boys who are abused are abused by men, and (d) pressure on males not to express helplessness or vulnerability (Nas-

jleti, 1980; Rew & Esparza, 1990). New evidence suggests that a higher proportion of males are being abused than previously thought. The rates of abuse for males appearing in self-report surveys of adults, for example, are higher than rates obtained from official reporting statistics (Larson, Terman, Gomby, Quinn, & Behrman, 1994).

Additional Risk Factors. In an effort to identify and describe other risk factors associated with CSA, several researchers have compared victims and nonvictims on additional characteristics (e.g., Finkelhor, 1984; Finkelhor et al., 1990; Gruber & Jones, 1983). A number of family and social characteristics such as the presence of a stepfather or living without one's natural parents for extended periods have been associated with an increased risk for CSA (Finkelhor, 1984; Finkelhor et al., 1990; Paveza, 1988). Other risk factors include having a mother who was employed outside the home or who was disabled or ill; living with parents whose relationship was conflicted; living with parents having alcohol, drug abuse, or emotional problems; having few close friends; and having a poor relationship with one or both parents (Finkelhor, 1984; Gruber & Jones, 1983).

Other variables have been linked to an increased risk of CSA in some studies but not others. Some studies, for example, have evaluated whether social isolation is a risk factor. Rural residence is associated with increased CSA in some studies (e.g., Finkelhor, 1984) and decreased CSA in others (e.g., Wyatt, 1985). Studies of ethnicity are also variable and inconclusive (e.g., Doll, Joy, & Bartholow, 1992; Finkelhor et al., 1990; Kercher & McShane, 1984). Research on socioeconomic status suggests that low socioeconomic status is often associated with increased CSA in samples of student populations and officially reported cases (DHHS, 1988; Finkelhor & Baron, 1986). In contrast, self-report surveys of community samples have found small or no differences in CSA among various socioeconomic groups (Bagley, 1991).

Characteristics of the Perpetrators of Child Sexual Abuse

When contemplating an image of a CSA perpetrator, many people picture a stranger or "dirty old man." Research examining the demographic characteristics of CSA perpetrators, however, suggests that these stereotypes are rarely accurate.

Age. Research shows that offenders vary widely in age, although the AAPC (1988) reported $32\frac{1}{2}$ years as the mean age of reported perpetrators. A growing amount of research evidence, however, is suggesting that juvenile perpetrators may be underestimated among reported cases and constitute a significant segment of the CSA offender population (Barbaree, Marshall, & Hudson, 1993; Ryan & Lane, 1991). Finkelhor (1979), for example, estimated from self-report surveys that one third of all offenders are under age 18. Clinical data from victims also suggest that a substantial proportion of their offenders are adolescents (Gomes-Schwartz et al., 1990). Other studies of perpetrator samples suggest that most sexual offenders *develop* deviant sexual interests prior to age 18 (e.g., Abel & Rouleau, 1990). Furthermore, increasingly large numbers of adolescents are being referred for treatment for sexual offenses against children (Ryan & Lane, 1991). For the most part, the characteristics of the juvenile offender are similar to the adult offender. The juvenile offender, for example, is primarily male and represented by all ethnic, racial, and socioeconomic groups (Margolin & Craft, 1990; Ryan & Lane, 1991).

Gender. Most perpetrators are male. Most studies indicate, for example, that among reported perpetrators, 90% or more are male (Finkelhor, 1984; Russell, 1983a). In addition, there is evidence that a significant minority of the general male population has committed this type of sexual offense. In their nationwide random sample survey, Finkelhor and Lewis (1988) found that between 4% and 17% of the male population acknowledged having molested a child. Similarly, Briere and Runtz (1989) found that 21% of male undergraduate students reported

having experienced sexual attraction to children, and 7% indicated some likelihood of having sex with a child if they could avoid detection and punishment.

Female perpetration, however, may be more common than surveys suggest. Females may go unnoticed because inappropriate sexual contact may occur more subtly, for example, during culturally prescribed and routine child care (Lawson, 1993; Schetky & Green, 1988). Studies are beginning to evaluate the characteristics of the female perpetrator of CSA, and preliminary results suggest that female offenders are often accomplices to males, lonely and isolated single parents, adolescent baby-sitters, or women who develop romantic relationships with adolescent boys (Elliott, 1993; Finkelhor, Williams, & Burns, 1988; Margolin & Craft, 1990).

Relationship to the Victim. The most comprehensive information regarding the victim-perpetrator relationship in sexually abusive encounters comes from large-scale community surveys of women reporting childhood histories of abuse (e.g., Finkelhor et al., 1990; Russell, 1983a). In Russell's (1983a) survey, for example, 11% of victimizations involved experiences with fathers or stepfathers; 45% involved acquaintances, friends, or family friends; 20% involved other relatives; and 11% involved strangers. In the first national survey of adults reporting histories of CSA (Finkelhor et al., 1990), percentages for victim-perpetrator relationships for both female and male victims, respectively, were as follows: strangers (21%, 40%), friend or acquaintance (41%, 44%), and family member (29%, 11%). In this sample, males were more likely to have been abused by a stranger, whereas females were more likely to have been abused by a family member. These data suggest that the perpetrator is a person familiar to the child in the majority of cases.

Intermediate Chapter Summary

Research suggests it is unwise to stereotype the demographic characteristics of CSA perpetrators. One of the most consistent findings from research evaluating risk factors associated with CSA, however, is **gender differences.** Females are more likely to be victims of CSA, and males are more likely to be perpetrators of CSA. On the other hand, new research suggests that the female perpetrator, and the male victim in particular, may represent a significant proportion of these populations but go undetected by researchers, practitioners, and reporting agencies. CSA perpetrators vary by age, but they consistently develop a trusting relationship with their victims and commonly include acquaintances or friends, fathers or other parental figures, as well as other family members. **Family and social variables** that increase the risk of CSA include such factors as a victim's age (i.e., 7 to 12 years old), family composition (e.g., presence of a stepfather), maternal availability, and family conflict (e.g., parents with emotional or drug- related problems).

In reviewing these findings, it is important to remember that the populations of victims and offenders are **heterogeneous,** suggesting that sexual abuse occurs in virtually all demographic, social, and family circumstances. Furthermore, the majority of research has focused on female victims and male perpetrators, and as a result, most research findings do not pertain to male victims or female perpetrators. As a final caveat, it is important to acknowledge the difficulty in determining whether these variables are actual risk factors for abuse, consequences of abuse, or correlates of abuse history.

Dynamics of Child Sexual Abuse and Consequences for the Victims

Dynamics of Child Sexual Abuse

To develop a comprehensive understanding of CSA, it is also necessary to examine the characteristics of the victimization experience itself. Much of what is known about the victimization experience comes from cases reported to protective services or studies of CSA victims and perpetrators.

Type of Sexual Activity. Both adults and children have provided descriptions of the types of sexual behavior they encountered in abusive situations. Although the range of sexual activities theoretically extends from exhibitionism to intercourse, the questions posed by researchers have influenced the variability in the types of activities actually reported. In addition, the procedures employed (e.g., face-to-face vs. anonymous interviews or surveys) and the type of sample studied (e.g., community samples of adults or children reported for abuse; clinical populations vs. college students) can affect the proportion of victims reporting various types of abuse.

Russell (1983a) distinguished between three types of sexual activity: *very serious* abuse (e.g., completed or attempted vaginal, oral, or anal intercourse, cunnilingus, analingus), *serious* abuse (e.g., completed and attempted genital fondling, simulated intercourse, and digital penetration), and *least serious* abuse (e.g., completed and attempted acts of sexual touching of buttocks, thighs, legs or other body parts, clothed breasts, or genitals; or kissing). Of the sample of 930 women, 38% reported a childhood experience involving one of these forms of sexual abuse. Of these women reporting a childhood experience of abuse, 38% experienced very serious abuse, 34% serious abuse, and 28% less serious abuse. In another study of 156 sexually abused children, Gomes-Schwartz et al. (1990) assessed specific sexual behaviors and found that 28% experienced either vaginal or anal intercourse; 38% experienced oral-genital contact or object penetration; 23% experienced fondling or mutual stimulation; and 6% experienced some form of attempted sexual contact (i.e., the offender requesting that the child touch his genitals), touching, or voyeurism.

Organized Exploitation. Sexual abuse also encompasses the exploitation of children for sexual stimulation or commercial gain in the form of four related activities: sex rings, pornography, prostitution, and ritualistic abuse. Knowledge regarding the dynamics of organized exploitation is limited because it has been the topic of only a small number of scientific studies (e.g., Lanning & Burgess, 1984; Wild, 1989). Despite the limited scientific knowledge about organized exploitation, the sensationalistic nature of sex rings, pornography, and ritualistic abuse have made these topics popular in the media. At the same time, these media accounts have often contributed to public misperception about the *extent* of organized exploitation.

One form of organized exploitation receiving increasing attention is ritualistic abuse. Ritualistic abuse has been defined as "abuse that occurs in a context linked to some symbols or group activities that have a religious, magical, or supernatural connotation, and where the invocation of these symbols or activities are [*sic*] repeated over time, and used to frighten and intimidate the children" (Finkelhor et al., 1988, p. 59). Ritual abuse is often associated with sexual abuse and is reported to involve forced drug usage, cannibalism, impregnation, witnessing and receiving physical abuse or torture (e.g., biting, burning, whipping, animal mutilation), being buried alive, death threats, witnessing or forced participation in infant "sacrifice"

Perpetrators do not molest every child but instead select children who are vulnerable in some way.

---

and adult murder, "marriage" to Satan, and acts involving feces, urine, and blood. The source of this information comes primarily from reports of children attending day care centers and from the memories of adults reporting a history of childhood abuse. The existence of ritualistic abuse has been a controversial topic in both the popular media and the scientific literature (Jones, 1991; Putnam, 1991), and many issues remain unresolved (see boxed insert: "The Satanic Ritual Abuse Controversy").

Initiation of the Abuse. Preliminary reports have provided some information about the techniques perpetrators use to identify and recruit child victims (e.g., Budin & Johnson, 1989; Conte, Wolf, & Smith, 1989; Elliott, Browne, & Kilcoyne, 1995). Perpetrators do not molest every child to whom they have access but instead select children who are vulnerable in some way. Vulnerable children include those who are passive, quiet, trusting, young, unhappy in appearance, needy, or live in a divorced home.

Once the perpetrator has identified the child, he or she desensitizes the child to sexual activity through a "grooming" process that involves a progression from nonsexual to sexual touch in the context of a gradually developing relationship. The typical scenario, for example, begins with seemingly accidental or affectionate touches and then proceeds to sexual touches. Offenders tend to misrepresent moral standards or misuse their authority or adult sophistication to seduce children (e.g., "It's okay, you're my daughter"). Additionally, perpetrators report employing a range of coercive tactics to initiate the relationship such as separating children from other protective adults, conditioning children through reward (e.g., money, toys,

candy, or clothes) and punishment (e.g., threatening to hit the child or to hurt loved ones), forcing children to observe violence against their mothers, or using physical force or threatening gestures.

This information originated from interview and survey data from men incarcerated for CSA or participating in treatment programs for CSA offenders. To avoid overreliance on data derived solely from acknowledged perpetrators, researchers have also asked victims directly about their abuse experiences. Berliner and Conte (1990), for example, interviewed child victims (10 to 18 years or age) about the process of their own sexual victimization. The children's accounts closely resembled those provided by the perpetrators. The children reported that their perpetrators initiated sexual activity by gradually shifting from normal affectionate contact or physical activities (e.g., bathing, hugging, massaging, wrestling, tickling) to more sexual behaviors (e.g., genital touching). The children also reported that their perpetrators made statements attempting to justify the sexual contact. The most common themes of such statements were to suggest that the behavior was not really sexual or to acknowledge that the behavior was sexual but that it was acceptable (e.g., "I'm just going to look, I won't touch"; "I'm teaching you about sex").

Maintenance of the Abuse. Studies evaluating victim and perpetrator perspectives on the process of abuse also shed light on strategies used to maintain children in sexual activities for prolonged periods. Central to maintaining ongoing sexual activities with children is the ability to convince the child that the activities should be kept secret so that other adults cannot intervene to terminate the abuse. Studies of child victims as well as adults victimized as children indicate that the majority of victims do not disclose their abuse immediately, and a significant number do not disclose for a period of years (Gomes-Schwartz et al., 1990; Timnick, 1985).

Perpetrators report a range of coercive activities used to maintain the abusive relationship including bribes, threats, and physical aggression. The child may maintain silence about the abuse, for example, because the offender has offered the child attention, money, or purchases of special toys in exchange for his or her silence (e.g., Elliott et al., 1995). Threats such as harming or killing the child, a significant other, or a pet; sending the victim to a frightening place; or show-

THE SATANIC RITUAL ABUSE CONTROVERSY

Patti was 32 and her sister, Bonnie, was 45 when they began seeing Huntington Beach therapist Timothy Maas in 1988. Soon after the treatment began, both reached the conclusion that they suffered from a severe and unusual form of mental disorder called multiple personality disorder. The multiple personalities, they concluded, allowed them to repress three decades of abuse by their mother, 78-year-old Ellen Roe. As their therapy progressed, they uncovered increasingly bizarre memories—black-robed satanists performing bloody rituals, animal mutilations, satanic orgies, and infant sacrifices (Weber, 1991). Eventually, the two sisters brought a civil suit against their mother. In a 10 to 2 compromise vote, the jury ruled that although the women may well have been abused by someone, at worst Ellen Roe was guilty of negligence. The sisters were awarded no money (Lachnit, 1991).

Since the 1980s, stories like this have increasingly appeared. More and more adults are reporting recovered repressed satanic memories. Children have also begun to tell stories of satanic rituals. The term *satanic ritual abuse* (SRA) was introduced to describe this "new" form of child abuse. SRA refers to the systematic emotional, physical, and sexual abuse of children as part of satanic worship. Proponents of the reality of SRA believe that thousands of children each year are being victimized in satanic rituals involving cannibalism, sexual torture, incest, and murder. Are there large numbers of satanists preying on our children, or is the so-called satanism scare merely rumor and mass hysteria?

Many trace interest in SRA to the book *Michelle Remembers,* by psychiatrist Lawrence Pazder and his patient (and later, wife) Michelle Smith (Smith & Pazder, 1980). Smith was being treated by Pazder when she suddenly began to remember being victimized by a satanic cult during the 1950s. Among the many claims made by Smith is that she witnessed numerous ritualistic murders by the satanists. She was also force-fed the ashes of a cremated victim. On another occasion, a fetus was butchered in front of her and the bloody remains were smeared across her body (Victor, 1993).

Michelle Smith's story attracted considerable attention. Pazder and Smith were featured in *People Weekly* and the *National Enquirer.* They made numerous television and radio appearances and became nationally known "experts" on SRA (Victor, 1993). It was Pazder, in fact, who coined the term *satanic ritual abuse* in a presentation to the American Psychiatric Association in 1980. Despite the considerable attention, however, there is no evidence that Michelle's stories are true. In fact, her family, including two sisters who were not mentioned in the book, claim none of it happened (Victor, 1993).

Another survivor story that attracted national attention was *Satan's Underground,* by Lauren Stratford (1988). Like Michelle Smith, Stratford appeared on many television shows and used notoriety from her book to launch a career as an SRA therapist. When three writers for the evangelical magazine *Cornerstone* decided to investigate her story, however, they concluded that it was a "gruesome fantasy" (Passantino, Passantino, & Trott, 1990). Perhaps the most outrageous claim made by Stratford was that she was impregnated by satanists on three separate occasions, and each of the children was taken from her and killed. Because Stratford claims to have led a fairly normal public life, Passantino and his colleagues found her claims easy to investigate. They found several people who knew Stratford in high school and college (when she claims to have had the children), but each witness denied that she was ever pregnant. Stratford could produce no witness to her pregnancy. According to Passantino and his colleagues, no one from Harvest House (the publisher) ever bothered to check her story.

Proponents of SRA admit that some stories might be fabricated but continue to maintain that SRA is a real threat to children. Those who have been charged with investigating this threat, however, are skeptical. FBI agent Kenneth Lanning, for example, a well-respected authority on child abuse, confesses that

> in 1983 when I first began to hear victims' stories of bizarre cults and human sacrifice, I tended to believe them. I had been dealing with bizarre, deviant behavior for many years and had long since realized that almost anything is possible. The idea that there are a few cunning, secretive individuals in positions of power somewhere in this country regularly killing a few people as part of some ritual or ceremony and getting away with it is certainly within the realm of possibility. But the number of alleged cases began to grow and grow. We now have hundreds of victims alleging that thousands of offenders are murdering tens of thousands of people, and there is little or no corroborative evidence.

(continued)

Until hard evidence is obtained and corroborated, the public should not be frightened into believing that babies are being bred and eaten, that 50,000 missing children are being murdered in human sacrifices, or that satanists are taking over America's day care centers. (Lanning, 1991, pp. 172, 173)

If there is so little evidence confirming the existence of SRA, why do so many perceive the SRA threat to be real? One reason is that many of the major daytime talk shows (e.g., "The Oprah Winfrey Show," "Geraldo," "Donahue"), and some prime-time shows (e.g., "20/20"), have aired programs on satanism and SRA. The 1988 Geraldo Rivera special, "Exposing Satan's Underground," which featured Lauren Stratford and her story, attracted one of the largest audiences for an NBC documentary in history. Unfortunately, it is hard to imagine that many of the 19.8 million people who saw Stratford on "Geraldo" in 1988 were aware of the *Cornerstone* investigation or would later know that the book's publisher, Harvest House, pulled the book from store shelves in 1990 (Richardson, Best, & Bromley, 1991; Victor, 1993).

Another reason for misperceptions about SRA is that many helping professionals also believe SRA is real. Therapists, police officers, and child protection authorities, who are often required to attend seminars on current developments in their field, are exposed to SRA "experts." Although advertised as training workshops, these seminars tend to employ proselytizing techniques characteristic of organizations seeking recruits (Mulhurn, 1991). Many well-meaning helping professionals, who are generally motivated by the desire to help abused clients, become convinced of the existence of SRA through these seminars. These professionals, in turn, have influenced state and county governments to respond to the SRA problem. In Los Angeles County, for example, a Ritual Abuse Task Force was formed in 1988 to deal with the perceived increase in SRA. The task force received front-page attention in the *Los Angeles Times* in 1992 when many of its members claimed that satanists were attempting to silence them by pumping the pesticide Diazinon into the air-conditioning vents of their offices, homes, and cars. Despite the fact that Diazinon poisoning is easy to detect, according to the epidemiologist assigned to the case, none of the 43 alleged victims of the poisoning could provide any evidence (Curtis, 1992).

These factors help explain why so much of the general public believes the SRA threat is real. Can these factors also explain why so many people believe they were personally exposed to satanic abuse? Imagine an individual who is suffering in some way. That person might turn to a therapist to help alleviate this suffering. Recognize that therapists have been trained to suspect childhood histories of abuse in a large percentage of their clients. They are also trained to listen and accept victim accounts of abuse. Add to this situation a societal fascination with satanism, and distortions are possible, maybe even likely. In some situations, SRA may provide a therapist and client a believable explanatory framework for psychological symptoms and problems. This may be especially likely with highly disturbed clients, who may be more susceptible to explanations and interpretations offered by therapists who probe for SRA patterns.

The fact that clients (through the popular media) and therapists (through training seminars) are often exposed to the same theories of SRA may also explain why survivor stories, although independently offered, are often similar in detail. Proponents often cite this pattern as evidence that SRA must exist. According to Frank W. Putnam of the National Institute of Mental Health (1991), however, such reasoning represents a "naive and simplistic model of contagion" (p. 177). "The child abuse community," he continues, "is particularly susceptible to such a rumor process as there are multiple, interconnected communication/educational networks shared by therapists and patients alike." Satanist experts, talk show hosts, movies, and news magazine shows all share the same stories. Given that both therapists and potential clients are exposed to the same SRA stories, it is not surprising that survivor accounts are often quite similar.

Those who accept claims of SRA often maintain that society is simply unwilling to believe the "unbelievable." Proponents accurately remind us that sometimes the unbelievable is real. Until relatively recently, "outrageous" stories of sexual abuse and incest were dismissed as fantasy. At the same time, however, there is danger in accepting at face value accounts provided by "cult survivors," no matter how credible the witnesses might appear. Plausibility is not evidence. Lots of things are possible. The more outrageous the claims, the more the burden of proof must lie with those who are making the claims. Skeptics continue to raise several questions for which there appears to be no answer (see Richardson et al., 1991; Victor, 1993). If the number of satanists is increasing, they ask, where are they all? Where are the defectors who could so easily expose the satanists? Where are the dead bodies the satanists have supposedly used for sacrifices? Where are the animal carcasses that have supposedly been used to threaten children into silence?

Understandably, therapists do not see their clinical responsibility as one of corroborating client accounts of abuse. At the same time, it is important that they recognize that unfounded claims of SRA probably hurt the goals of child protection. There can be little question that fabricated SRA stories have "fueled the fire" for skeptics who believe that children are not really abused. For example, despite the fact that many recovered memories may be real, fabricated SRA memories feed those skeptics who question the validity of all repressed memories. Similarly, although most childhood disclosures of abuse are substantiated, the fact that in a few highly publicized cases children have told improbable stories also feeds skepticism. Attention to SRA appears to be creating additional problems rather than providing much-needed solutions to child sexual abuse.

ing pictures of the child involved in sexual acts to the parents might also maintain a child's silence. Finally, overt acts of aggression, such as physically overpowering the child, may be used to reinforce secrecy (Budin & Johnson, 1989; Conte et al., 1989; Lang & Frenzel, 1988). Until recently, sexual offenses against children were largely characterized as nonviolent, with most experts estimating that physical violence accompanies approximately 20% of incidents (e.g., Timnick, 1985). Newer studies, however, suggest that offenders are more frequently aggressive (Becker, 1994; Stermac, Hall, & Henskens, 1989).

Effects of Child Sexual Abuse

Authorities have debated the effects of adult-child sexual interactions in the context of a secret relationship since the initial recognition of CSA. Some have suggested that children who are sexually exploited by adults do not suffer mental harm—either while children or later as adults (e.g., Yorukoglu & Kemph, 1966). The majority of research evidence, however, suggests that a variety of negative psychological, behavioral, and interpersonal problems are more prevalent among CSA victims compared to individuals without such a history (see reviews by Beichtman et al., 1992; Beichtman, Zucker, Hood, daCosta, & Akman, 1991; Briere & Elliott, 1994; Kendall-Tackett, Williams, & Finkelhor, 1993). The consequences of CSA can be clas-

sified as either initial effects (occurring within 2 years following the abuse) or long-term effects (consequences beyond 2 years subsequent to the abuse).

Initial Effects. In terms of initial effects, investigators have identified a wide range of emotional, cognitive, physical, and behavioral problems. The specific manifestations of symptomatology appear to depend on the developmental level of the victim (Beichtman et al., 1991; Kendall-Tackett et al., 1993; Wurtele & Miller-Perrin, 1992). Table 4.1 displays the most common symptoms associated with CSA for preschool, school-age, and adolescent children.

In a review of 45 of the most recent empirical studies on initial effects, Kendall-Tackett et al. (1993) concluded that one of the two most common symptoms identified in sexually abused children is sexualized behavior (e.g., overt sexual acting-out toward adults or other children, compulsive masturbation, excessive sexual curiosity, sexual promiscuity, and precocious sexual play and knowledge). Sexualized behavior is also believed to be one of the most predictive consequences of sexual abuse (Friedrich, 1993). The other most frequent problem is posttraumatic stress disorder (PTSD) symptomatology, which includes a number of difficulties such as nightmares, fears, feelings of isolation and an inability to enjoy usual activities, somatic complaints, symptoms of autonomic arousal (e.g., easily startled), and guilt feelings.

Table 4.1 Short-Term Effects Associated With Sexual Abuse in Preschool, School-Age, and Adolescent Children

Behavioral	Emotional	Cognitive	Physical
Preschool			
Regression/immaturity	Anxiety[a]	Learning difficulties	Bruises
Social withdrawal	Clinging		Genital bleeding
Sexualized behavior[a]	Nightmares[a]		Genital pain
Sexual preoccupation[a]	Fears		Genital itching
Precocious sexual	Depression		Genital odors
knowledge[a]	Guilt		Problems walking
Seductive behavior[a]	Hostility/anger		Problems sitting
Excessive masturbation[a]	Tantrums		Sleep disturbance
Sex play with others[a]	Aggression		Eating disturbance
Sexual language[a]			Enuresis
Genital exposure[a]			Encopresis
Sexual victimization of			Stomachache
others[a]			Headache
Family/peer conflicts			
Difficulty separating			
Hyperactivity			
School age			
Regression/immaturity[a]	Anxiety	Learning difficulties[a]	Stomachache
Social withdrawal	Phobias	Poor concentration	Headache
Sexualized behavior	Nightmares[a]	Poor attention	Genital pain
Sexual preoccupation	Fears[a]	Declining grades	Genital itching
Precocious sexual	Obsessions		Genital odors
knowledge	Tics		Problems walking
Seductive behavior	Hostility/anger		Problems sitting
Excessive masturbation	Aggression[a]		Sleep disturbance
Sex play with others	Family/peer conflicts		Eating disturbance
Sexual language	Depression		Enuresis
Genital exposure	Guilt		Encopresis
Sexual victimization of	Suicidal		
others	Low self-esteem		
Delinquency			
Stealing			
Poor peer relations			
Hyperactivity[a]			
Adolescent			
Social withdrawal[a]	Anxiety	Learning difficulties	Stomachache
Self-injurious behavior[a]	Phobias	Poor concentration	Headache
Sexualized behavior	Nightmares	Poor attention	Genital pain
Sexual preoccupation	Obsessions	Declining grades	Genital itching
Precocious sexual	Hostility/anger		Genital odors
knowledge	Depression[a]		Problems walking
Seductive behavior	Guilt		Problems sitting
Promiscuity	Suicidal[a]		Pregnancy
Prostitution	Low Self-Esteem		Eating disturbance[a]
Sexual language			Sleep disturbance[a]
Sexual victimization of			
others			
Delinquency[a]			
Running away[a]			
Early marriage			
Substance abuse[a]			
Truancy			
Dropping out of school			
Stealing			
Poor peer relations			

SOURCE: Information for this table was obtained from the following references, which are representative but not exhaustive: Beitchman, Zucker, Hood, daCosta, and Akman (1991); Dubowitz, Black, Harrington, and Verschoore (1993); Everson, Hunter, Runyon, and Edelson (1990); Friedrich, Grambusch, and Damon (1992); Friedrich, Urquiza, and Beilke (1986); Gil and Johnson (1993); Gomes-Schwartz et al. (1990); Lanktree, Briere, and Zaidi (1991); Mannarino, Cohen, Smith, and Moore-Motily (1991); Mennen and Meadow (1994); Wells, McCann, Adams, Voris, and Ensign (1995); and Wozencraft, Wagner, and Pellegrin (1991).
a. Indicates most common symptoms for age group.

In addition to the myriad symptoms documented in sexual abuse victims, CSA has been associated with a wide range of psychopathology. Of the victimized children studied by Gomes-Schwartz et al. (1990), 17% of the preschool group (4 to 6 years of age) evidenced "clinically significant pathology," 40% of the school-aged group (7 to 13 years of age) scored in the seriously disturbed range, and 8% of adolescent victims (14 to 18 years of age) exhibited severe psychopathology. Dubowitz, Black, Harrington, and Verschoore (1993), using a checklist of parent-reported behaviors to assess the effects of sexual abuse on 93 prepubertal children, found that 36% had significantly elevated scores on the Internalizing Scale (e.g., depression, withdrawn behavior), and 38% had elevated scores on the Externalizing Scale (e.g., acting-out behaviors). Similar levels of dysfunction would be expected in only 10% of the general population of children.

Overall, evidence to date strongly suggests that CSA results in disturbing psychological sequelae in a significant portion of child victims. In their review, Browne and Finkelhor (1986) concluded that from 20% to 40% of abused children seen by clinicians manifest pathological disturbance. Most of the types of symptoms demonstrated in victims of CSA, however, are no different than the difficulties seen in clinical samples of children and adolescents more generally. In addition, in terms of the degree of symptomatology, sexually abused children generally exhibit significantly more psychological symptoms than nonabused children, but fewer symptoms than clinical children. The only exceptions to this pattern are the findings that indicate that sexually abused children exhibit more sexualized behavior and PTSD symptomatology than both nonabused and clinical groups of children (Beichtman et al., 1991; Kendall-Tackett et al., 1993).

Long-Term Effects. The psychological consequences of childhood sexual victimization can extend into adulthood and affect victims over a lifetime. A history of CSA has been associated with a variety of symptoms, such as emotional reactions including depression and anxiety (e.g., Chu & Dill, 1990; Elliott & Briere, 1992; Swett, Surrey, & Cohen, 1990). According to Browne and Finkelhor (1986), depression is the most common symptom reported by adults sexually abused as children. Additional effects include problems with interpersonal relationships, PTSD symp-

tomatology (i.e., reexperiencing traumatic events through intrusive thoughts, flashbacks, or nightmares), sexual adjustment, and behavioral dysfunction (i.e., substance abuse, eating disorders, self-mutilation) (e.g., Briere & Conte, 1993; Elliott, 1994; Springs & Friedrich, 1992; Steiger & Zanko, 1990). Table 4.2 summarizes the long-term symptoms found in adult victims of CSA.

Although investigators of the long-term effects of CSA have generally obtained data from clinical populations, they have also conducted studies using nonclinical populations, such as college students (e.g., Briere & Runtz, 1990; Fromuth, 1986) and randomly selected subsamples of adults abused as children (e.g., Burnam et al., 1988; Siegel, Sorenson, Golding, Burnam, & Stein, 1987), and detected significant negative effects. In their review, Browne and Finkelhor (1986) concluded that approximately 20% of adults who were sexually abused as children evidence serious psychopathology as adults.

Explaining the Variability in Effects. Perusal of these research findings reveals the heterogeneity in the symptoms, as well as the degree of psychopathology, characteristic of sexual abuse victims. It is clear that no single symptom or pattern of symptoms is present in all victims of CSA. In addition, some CSA victims exhibit no symptoms at all. In their review of CSA effects, for example, Kendall-Tackett et al. (1993) concluded that approximately 20% to 50% of children are asymptomatic at initial assessment, and only 10% to 25% become symptomatically worse over the 2-year period following victimization. Why is it that some victims are severely affected, others moderately, and still others are left relatively unscathed? Furthermore, why do some victims manifest anxiety in response to their abuse and others show physical symptoms or depression?

One difficulty in determining the effects of CSA is that methodological weaknesses have plagued the research in this area (see Briere, 1992b). The definition of sexual abuse, for example, varies across studies. In addition, several studies have failed to include comparison groups, whereas others have employed subjective, unstandardized interviews and assessment devices. The samples used in research on the effects of CSA are also problematic. College student samples, for example, tend to be biased in terms of intelligence, social class, and motivational aspects. Clinical samples of CSA victims are also bi-

Table 4.2 Long-Term Effects Associated With Child Sexual Abuse

Type of Effect	Specific Problem	Specific Symptoms
Emotional	Depression	Depressed affect
		Suicidality
		Low self-esteem
		Guilt
		Poor self-image
		Self-blame
	Anxiety	Anxiety attacks
		Fears
		Phobias
		Somatic symptoms
		Migraine
		Stomach problems
		Aches and pains
		Skin disorders
Interpersonal		Difficulty trusting others
		Poor social adjustment
		Social isolation
		Feelings of isolation, alienation, insecurity
		Difficulty forming/maintaining relationships
		Parenting difficulties
		Sexual revictimization
		Physical victimization
Posttraumatic stress disorder symptomatology	Reexperiencing	Intrusive thoughts
		Flashbacks
		Nightmares
	Numbing/avoidance	Dissociation
		Amnesia for abuse events
		Disengagement ("spacing out")
		Emotional numbing
		Out-of-body experiences
	Associated symptoms	Poor concentration
Sexual adjustment		Anorgasmia
		Arousal/desire dysfunction
		Sexual phobia/aversion
		Sexual anxiety
		Sexual guilt
		Promiscuity
		Prostitution
		Dissatisfaction in sexual relationships
Behavior dysfunction	Eating disorders	Binging
		Purging
		Overeating
	Substance abuse	Alcoholism
		Illicit drugs
	Self-mutilation	Cutting body parts
		Carving body areas
		Hitting head or body with or against objects

SOURCE: Information for this table was obtained from the following references, which are representative but not exhaustive: Briere (1992a); Brier and Conte (1993); Briere and Runtz (1987, 1990); Chu and Dill (1990); Elliott (1994); Elliott and Briere (1992); Morrison (1989); Springs and Friedrich (1992); Steiger and Zanko (1990); Swett, Surrey, and Cohen (1990); Urquiza and Goodlin-Jones (1994); and Widom (1995).

ased because they include only CSA cases referred for treatment services and therefore may not be generalizable to all cases of CSA (e.g., such samples may not include less symptomatic children or undisclosed victims). Finally, studying the psychological effects of adolescents or adults abused as children does not allow the establishment of a definitive

Table 4.3 Potential Mediators of the Effects of Child Sexual Abuse

Potential Mediators	*Influence on Child Sexual Abuse Effects*
Abuse characteristics	
Duration and frequency	Results are mixed for research evaluating child victims; increased duration is associated with more negative effect for adults abused as children
Type of sexual activity	More severe forms of sexual activity (e.g., penetration) are associated with more negative effect
Age at onset	Results are mixed
Child/perpetrator relationship	More negative effect is associated with fathers, father figures, or intense emotional relationships
Number of perpetrators	Results are mixed for research evaluating child victims; a greater number of perpetrators are associated with more negative effect for adults abused as children
Victim gender	Results are mixed, with some findings showing similarities between genders and some suggesting more externalizing symptoms for males and internalizing symptoms for females
Force or physical injury	Presence of force or physical injury is associated with greater negative effect
Multiple forms of abuse	Different combinations of child maltreatment are associated with more negative effect
Postabuse characteristics	
Response toward the victim	Negative reactions are associated with greater negative effect
Court involvement	Results are mixed
Out-of-home placement	Results are mixed
Available social support	Increased social support is associated with less severe effect
Perceptions of abuse	
Perceived severity	Increased perceived severity of abuse is associated with greater negative effect

SOURCE: Information for this table was obtained from the following references, which are representative but not exhaustive: Bagley and Ramsay (1986); Beichtman et al. (1991, 1992); Conte and Schuerman (1987); Feinauer (1989); Browne and Finkelhor (1986); Gomes-Schwartz et al. (1990); Kendall-Tackett et al. (1993); Mennen and Meadow (1995); Williams (1993); and Young, Bergandi, and Titus (1994).

causal relationship between symptoms and a history of CSA. In the absence of longitudinal studies, it is difficult to determine whether the observed characteristics result from early sexual abuse or some other variable such as family dysfunction. Although studies conducted within the past 10 years are achieving greater empirical precision by using larger numbers of participants, multiple measures, comparison groups, and longitudinal designs (e.g., Briere & Runtz, 1987; Erickson, Egeland, & Pianta, 1989; Gomes-Schwartz et al., 1990), more research is needed to clarify the specific effects of CSA for a given individual victim.

Researchers attempting to understand the effects of childhood sexual victimization have explored the association between characteristics of the sexually abusive situation or its aftermath and differential psychological effects. Are the psychological effects of CSA, for example, more severe when a child is abused

by a father figure versus an uncle? Are the effects more severe when the child's disclosure is met with disbelief? Researchers have evaluated the relationship between CSA effects and a number of factors, including the circumstances of the abuse, postabuse characteristics, and victim perceptions of the abuse. Table 4.3 lists the variables that have been examined and their influence on the effects of CSA.

Several aspects of the abuse situation are associated with increased symptomatology in both child victims and adult survivors. Perhaps the most consistent finding is that threats, force, or violence by the perpetrator are linked with increased negative outcome (Beichtman et al., 1992; Browne & Finkelhor, 1986; Gomes-Schwartz et al., 1990). Studies have also demonstrated that the least serious forms of sexual contact (e.g., unwanted kissing or touching of clothed body parts) are associated with less trauma compared to more serious forms of genital contact (e.g., vaginal or anal intercourse) (Bagley & Ramsay, 1986; Elwell & Ephross, 1987; Mennen & Meadow, 1995). Researchers have also investigated the nature of the relationship between the child victim and his or her perpetrator and its relationship to sexual abuse effects. Most studies indicate that abuse perpetrated by fathers, father figures, or individuals having an intense emotional relationship with the victim is associated with more severe consequences (Beitchman et al., 1991; Beichtman et al., 1992; Feinauer, 1989). In addition, when victims are exposed to multiple forms of child maltreatment (e.g., sexual and physical abuse), they exhibit increased symptomatology (e.g., Egeland & Sroufe, 1981; Ney, Fung, & Wickett, 1994).

Specific postabuse events (i.e., how family and institutions respond) have also shown a relationship to the effects of CSA. It is well established that responses toward the victim by parents, relatives, teachers, and other adults have a significant effect on the trauma and recovery associated with CSA. Studies have consistently found that negative responses tend to aggravate the trauma experienced by children (e.g., Gomes-Schwartz et al., 1990). In contrast, the availability of social supports following the disclosure of abuse, such as maternal support or a supportive relationship with an adult, appears to mitigate negative effects and plays a protective role (e.g., Conte & Schuerman, 1987; Gomes-Schwartz et al., 1990).

New areas of research are also examining other potential mediators of abuse such as the victim's subjective perceptions of the event (e.g., Hazzard, 1993; Miller-Perrin, 1996; Williams, 1993). For example, Williams (1993) found in her sample of 531 adult victims that victims' perceived severity of the abuse was the major determinant of subsequent adjustment or maladjustment. Future research should examine additional potential mediators, particularly those that might decrease the negative effects of CSA.

Intermediate Chapter Summary

Greater numbers of empirical studies evaluating the dynamics of CSA victimization are beginning to appear that describe the **types of sexual activity** involved, forms of organized exploitation, and how the abuse is initiated and maintained. Specific sexual activities (e.g., categorized as *least serious* to *very serious*) range from exhibitionism to various forms of penetration. Various **types of abuse** include a single perpetrator paired with one child, sex rings that include multiple children and one or more perpetrators, pornography, prostitution, and ritualistic abuse. Perpetrators appear to **target children who are vulnerable** in some way and **initiate the abuse** by desensitizing children to increasingly more sexual types of contact. To both initiate and **maintain the abuse,** perpetrators may use any of a number of coercive tactics such as verbal threats or overt aggression.

Numerous empirical studies have documented the myriad psychological consequences associated with childhood sexual victimization. Difficulties of an emotional, physical, cognitive, and behavioral nature can result in the **short term** (e.g., sexualized behavior) as well as the **long term** (e.g., troubled interpersonal relationship, PTSD symptomatology). There is a wide range of psychopathology (e.g., acting out, depression, withdrawn behavior) among victims, with some exhibiting few problems and others experiencing significant psychopathology. This heterogeneity in symptomology of CSA victims and degree of psychopathology plus methodological weaknesses in the field (e.g., lack of standard definitions, comparison groups, adequate samples, longitudinal studies) have led researchers to **equivocal findings.** Nevertheless, it appears that the factors most likely to increase trauma include increased duration and multiple forms of abuse, the presence of force and/or violence during the abuse, abuse by someone who is a father figure or emotionally close to the victim, abuse that involves more invasive forms of sexual activity, and negative reactions by significant others once the abuse has been revealed. Recent research has also examined **potential mediators** of abuse such as the victim's subjective perceptions of the events and the availability of social support following disclosure.

Explaining Child Sexual Abuse

The victims and perpetrators of CSA are characterized by a great deal of diversity, and the dynamics and consequences of abuse show similar variability. Such heterogeneity contributes to the difficulty in answering one of the central questions in understanding CSA: Why do some individuals sexually abuse children? Experts have developed theoretical formulations that focus on different individuals or systems that are involved in CSA, including the victim, the perpetrator, an abusive family, and society. Table 4.4 displays the risk factors associated with each of these systems.

Focus on the Victim

Early explanations for the occurrence of CSA focused on the role of the victim and his or her culpability in encouraging or "allowing" the sexual abuse to occur. Researchers described victims as seductively encouraging the perpetrator or as enjoying the abuse (Faller, 1988). Little evidence, however, exists to support these positions. Admittedly, many CSA victims exhibit sexualized behavior, but most experts believe that such behavior is the result rather than the cause of abuse. In addition, the idea that children encourage or "want" the abuse experience is contradicted by research evidence suggesting that only a minority of victims report that their abuse had pleasurable or positive characteristics (e.g., victims reporting that they felt loved during the abuse) (Faller, 1988). Whether the victim in CSA is viewed as culpable also depends on how the definition of sexual abuse is conceptualized. As previously discussed, current perspectives of CSA preclude victim culpability because children are viewed as developmentally incapable of allowing or permitting the abuse to occur.

Culpability, however, can be distinguished from vulnerability, and as previously described, more recent research has focused on attributes of children that might make them special targets for molesters. Young, female children who have few close friends or who have many unmet needs appear to be particularly susceptible to the attention and affection of a potential molester. At particular risk are children described as passive, quiet, trusting, young, unhappy or depressed, and needy. CSA victims also appear to have strong needs for attention, affection, and approval (Berliner & Conte, 1990; Erickson et al., 1989; Finkelhor et al., 1990).

Focus on the Offender

Theorists also implicate the perpetrator in their efforts to determine the roots of CSA. Researchers attempting to delineate traits of perpetrators initially relied on the psychiatric model, assuming that the causes of abuse stem from the individual psychopathology of abusers. Later attempts additionally focused on deviant patterns of sexual arousal and childhood history.

Offender Pathology. Early theories viewed abusers as psychotic, brain-damaged, senile, or mentally retarded individuals who could not control their own behavior (Weinberg, 1955). Subsequent research, however, suggests that psychiatric, intellectual, and neurological problems characterize only a small minority of offenders (National Center for Prosecution of Child Abuse, 1978; Williams & Finkelhor, 1990).

A variety of less severe forms of psychopathology, however, do typify sexual abusers, including antisocial tendencies such as disregard for the interests and concerns of others or lack of impulse control (Bresee, Stearns, Bess, & Packer, 1986; Groth, Hobson, & Gary, 1982; Yanagida & Ching, 1993). Such findings suggest that offenders have a willingness to exploit others and to violate social norms (Williams & Finkelhor, 1990). Other studies describe molesters as passive, having feelings of vulnerability, inadequacy, and loneliness; being overly sensitive about their sexual performance with women; and as exhibiting deficits in heterosocial skills (Hayashino, Wurtele, & Klebe, 1995; Katz, 1990; Milner & Robertson, 1990; Seidman, Marshall, Hudson, & Robertson, 1994). Presumably, these problems may lead offenders to turn to children to have their social and relationship needs met while avoiding the demands of adult relationships.

Deviant Sexual Arousal. Other theories propose that perpetrators seek out sexual encounters with children primarily because they are sexually attracted to children (Abel, Becker, & Cunningham-Rathner, 1984; Marshall, Barbaree, & Butt, 1988). The origins of such deviant sexual arousal, however, are undeter-

Table 4.4 Risk Factors Associated With Child Sexual Abuse

System Level	Risk Factor
Child	Female gender
	Prepubescent age
	Few close friends
	Passivity
	Quiet
	Trusting
	Unhappy appearance
	Depressed affect
	Needy
Perpetrator	Male gender
	Childhood history of sexual and physical victimization
	Antisocial disregard for concerns of others
	Poor impulse control
	Passive
	Sensitive about performance with women
	Deficient heterosocial skills
	Feelings of dependency, inadequacy, vulnerability, loneliness
	Sexually attracted to children
	Use of alcohol/drugs
	Use of cognitive distortions to justify behavior
	Fantasizing about sexual activity with children
Family	Spouse abuse
	Divorced home
	Unhappy family life
	Poor relationship with parents
	Parents in conflict
	Living in a family with a stepfather or without natural father
	Mother employed outside of home
	Mother has not completed high school
	Mother disabled or ill
	History of sexual abuse in mother
Sociocultural	Sanctioning sexual relations between adults and children
	Neglecting children's sexual development
	Male-dominated household
	Oversexualization of normal emotional needs
	Socializing men to be attracted to younger, smaller, more vulnerable sexual partners
	Blocking the development of empathy in males
	Socializing stoicism in males
	Objectifying sexual partners
	Child pornography

mined. Some researchers have suggested that deviant sexual arousal is the result of biological factors such as abnormal levels of male hormones called *androgens* (Bradford, 1990). Learning theorists, on the other hand, have proposed that deviant sexual arousal develops when it is reinforced through fantasies of sexual activity with children and masturbating to those fantasies (Laws & Marshall, 1990; Marshall & Eccles, 1993). Although some support exists for each of these theo-

ries, other studies have yielded inconsistent results (e.g., Bradford, 1990; Hunter, Goodwin, & Becker, 1994; Salter, 1988).

Regardless of the cause of deviant sexual arousal, the procedure most often used to determine whether CSA perpetrators have an unusual sexual arousal to children is penile plethysmography. This procedure involves the placement of a gauge around the base of the penis, in the privacy of a lab or clinic. The participant then views slides or videotapes of different types of sexual partners (e.g., same-age opposite-sex partners, young male children, adolescent females) or listens to audio-taped descriptions of different kinds of sexual encounters (e.g., consenting nonviolent sex with a same-age opposite-sex partner, non-consenting violent sex with a male child). The penile gauge is sensitive to small increases in the circumference of the penis, and the percentage of arousal is recorded by the plethysmograph.

Investigators have compared the sexual responses of child molesters, incest offenders, and nonoffending men with mixed results. Freund and his colleagues (e.g., Freund & Langevin, 1976) conducted some of the first studies and found that molesters were significantly more aroused by slides of both female and male children interacting with adults than were nonoffending males. Subsequent studies examining sexual arousal in specific categories of perpetrators, however, have yielded conflicting results. Quinsey, Chaplin, and Carrigan (1979), for example, found that incestuous fathers exhibited more appropriate adult sexual arousal than nonincestuous child molesters. In contrast, Marshall, Barbaree, and Christophie (1986) found that although incest offenders paralleled normals by showing low arousal to children, they showed no dramatic arousal increase to adult females. Indeed, the incest offenders exhibited less arousal to adult females than did the control group. The non-incestuous offenders, on the other hand, showed considerable arousal to children up to age 9, minimal arousal for 11- to 13-year-olds, and increased arousal again to adult females. Taken together, these findings suggest that compared to control group males, some subgroup of CSA perpetrators, primarily extrafamilial child molesters, exhibit deviant sexual arousal toward children. The pattern of sexual arousal exhibited by incestuous offenders is less clear.

Complicating the role of deviant sexual arousal in CSA even further is evidence that nonoffenders also exhibit some level of sexual arousal toward children. Freund, McKnight, Langevin, and Cibiri (1972), for example, found that nonoffending adult males had higher arousal to pictures of nude pubescent and younger girls than to landscapes or pictures of nude boys. Because not all individuals who are sexually aroused by children act on their feelings, researchers have hypothesized that other factors, usually referred to as *disinhibitors,* must be operating.

One possible disinhibitor is alcohol, which may affect the perpetrator's ability to maintain self-control over sexual impulses toward children (Abel et al., 1984; Finkelhor, 1984). Other possible disinhibitors are cognitive distortions. From this viewpoint, perpetrators rationalize and defend their behavior through distorted ideas or thoughts. "Having sex with children," for example, "is a good way to teach them about sex," or "Children need to be liberated from the sexually repressive bonds of society" (Abel et al., 1984; Abel et al., 1989; Segal & Stermac, 1990). Research evidence is accumulating that supports the presence of cognitive distortions in CSA perpetrators (Hayashino et al., 1995; Segal & Stermac, 1990).

In evaluating research on deviant sexual arousal, it is important to view such studies within the confines of their conceptual and methodological limitations. Many studies, for example, have mixed the types of perpetrators within groups (e.g., natural fathers, stepfathers, and adoptive fathers into a single incest sample) (Marshall et al., 1986). Other limitations include the use of small and unrepresentative samples. The penile plethysmography procedure itself has also been questioned due to false positives and false negatives and the ability of some molesters to inhibit sexual arousal in the lab (Conte, 1993). In examining the role of deviant sexual arousal, alcohol and drug use, and cognitive distortions, it is important to note that these factors may not play a role in all cases of CSA. It is also unclear to what degree such variables cause, rather than result from, the abuse.

Childhood History of Victimization. Many researchers have suggested that childhood sexual victimization contributes to adult perpetration. The sexual abuse may have been directly experienced by the perpetrator in the past or may have occurred to another family member while the perpetrator observed or was aware. Overholser and Beck (1989), for example, noted that 58% of their sample of child molesters reported being molested as children, compared with 25% of the rapist group, and only 5% of matched controls. The relationship between perpetration and a history of previous sexual victimization holds for adolescent sexual offenders as well (Becker, Kaplan, Cunningham-Rathner, & Kovoussi, 1986; Johnson, 1989; Katz, 1990). Several studies have also demonstrated frequent reports of sexual abuse against some other family member in the offender's family of origin (Williams & Finkelhor, 1990). Others have noted a relationship between sexual perpetration of children and high rates of physical abuse in the backgrounds of offenders (Williams & Finkelhor, 1990).

Why would a history of victimization lead to perpetrating sexual offenses? One possible explanation is that subsequent abuse is an effort to resolve, assimilate, or master the anxiety resulting from the perpetrator's previous abuse (Groth, 1979; Hartman & Burgess, 1988). Another interpretation refers to the lack of a nurturing parental relationship, betrayal as a child, and the subordination of one's own needs to those of an abuser, factors that preclude the development of empathy or sensitivity toward others (Ginsburg, Wright, Harrell, & Hill, 1989). Still others have suggested that repeatedly having one's needs subordinated and having one's body invaded or manipulated may result in feelings of powerlessness and a later need to exploit others to regain personal power and control (Wurtele & Miller-Perrin, 1992). A final possibility is that by experiencing victimization, the offender learns through modeling that children can be used for sexual gratification (Laws & Marshall, 1990).

Research on the intergenerational transmission of sexual abuse has been questioned on methodological grounds, such as overreliance on retrospective designs, self-report data, and correlational studies. Lack of appropriate comparison groups and the possibility that perpetrators report histories of abuse as rationalizations for their behaviors are also factors that contribute to difficulty in interpreting findings. It is likely that although some association exists, most children who are sexually abused do not grow up to abuse other children, and some individuals without a history of abuse become CSA perpetrators.

Focus on the Family

Family dysfunction models view CSA as a symptom of a dysfunctional family system. These theories hold that the family in general, or one of its members (e.g., typically the perpetrator or nonoffending adult), contributes to an environment that permits and possibly encourages the sexual victimization of children.

A number of family theories focus on how a mother's behavior may contribute in some way to her child's victimization. Early theories held mothers responsible for the abuse by blaming them for poor marital relationships or infrequent marital sex. In this view, infrequent marital sex increased a husband's sexual frustration, thus "driving" him to seek satisfaction elsewhere in the family (e.g., Justice & Justice, 1979). Other theories viewed mothers as culpable for the abuse because of their inability to protect the victim from the offender. As noted previously, maternal employment outside of the home and maternal disability or illness are risk factors for CSA. Such theories, however, have often relied on clinical impressions or retrospective data or have not been supported by research. In addition, many of the so-called contributing characteristics ascribed to mothers could be the result of living with a perpetrator.

Contemporary theories view the mother's role in the context of contributing to a child's vulnerability, rather than as being responsible for the abuse. Research suggests, for example, that mothers may actually be co-victims rather than coconspirators. Mothers from incestuous families are often physically and emotionally abused by the perpetrator themselves and also frequently have a childhood history of CSA (e.g., Faller, 1989; Gomes-Schwartz et al., 1990; Truesdell, McNeil, & Deschner, 1986). According to this view, mothers may contribute to their children's vulnerability by withdrawing from their children or being unavailable to them (either emotionally or physically) because they lacked an adequate representation of a secure mother-child relationship themselves (Friedrich, 1990). Faller (1988, 1989) also suggested that these women may gravitate toward men who are similar to their own abusers or who will not make sexual demands on them because they are sexually attracted to children.

Other family systems theorists have focused on general characteristics of the family as a unit rather than on individual members and have identified significant levels of dysfunction in families of CSA victims. As previously noted, several risk factors are associated with abusive families, including parental conflict in the home, poor relationships between children and parents, and divorce in the home. There is also evidence that sexual abuse victims are more likely to come from homes characterized by other types of family violence, such as spouse abuse (e.g., Paveza, 1988; Sirles & Franke, 1989). Other research has confirmed that CSA families are frequently inflexible and controlled, disorganized, lacking cohesion and involvement between members, and deficient in community involvement (e.g., Jackson, Calhoun, Amick, Maddever, & Habif, 1990; Ray, Jackson, & Townsley, 1991).

Experts have proposed several explanations for how poor family relations might be related to CSA. To reduce the tension that exists within the marital relationship, for example, a father might distance himself from his wife by turning his sexual and emotional attention to his daughter. This distancing stabilizes the marital conflict and reduces the likelihood of a breakup. Gruber and Jones (1983) attempted to explain the role of marital conflict in extrafamilial abuse by suggesting that victims living in an unstable home may seek some sense of emotional stability through relationships outside of the home, such as with a potential offender. Others have suggested that families that lack cohesion, concern between members, and organization may fail to supervise children adequately, thus exposing them to more opportunities for sexual abuse (Ray et al., 1991; Sgroi, 1982).

Focus on Society and Culture

Social and cultural factors focus on the broad context of society and community forces that play an etiological role in CSA. Current theories target social attitudes, male socialization factors, and child pornography. Most sociocultural theories remain speculative, unconfirmed by empirical investigation.

Social Attitudes. One theory views CSA as a problem stemming from the inequality between men and women that has been perpetuated throughout history by the patriarchal social system (e.g., Birns & Meyer, 1993). Rush (1980) extends the boundaries of inequality to include children by pointing out that, traditionally, both women and children have shared the same minority status, and as a result, both have been subject to sexual abuse by men. Some limited support for the feminist theory of CSA comes from a study

conducted by Alexander and Lupfer (1987). These researchers found that female university students with a history of incest rated their family structure as having greater power differences in male-female relationships than female university students with a history of extrafamilial sexual abuse or those with no history of abuse.

Male Socialization. Some experts suggest that processes associated with the socialization of masculine traits may explain greater male involvement in CSA (e.g., Finkelhor & Lewis, 1988; Gilgun, 1988). Finkelhor and Lewis (1988) proposed several problems associated with masculine sexualization that may contribute to CSA. Men, for example, may be more likely to commit sexual offenses against children because they are socialized to be attracted to sexual partners who are younger, smaller, and more vulnerable than themselves. Females, in turn, are socialized to be attracted to sexual partners who are older, larger, and more powerful. Others have claimed that socialization processes for men emphasize sexual gratification as an end in itself and promote an orientation in which males see sexual partners as objects to be used for their sexual gratification (Armstrong, 1978). Some evidence exists to support the role of male socialization processes in CSA, including the work of Gilgun and Connor (1989), who found that perpetrators perceived children not as persons, but as objects, during the sexual act.

Child Pornography. Other sociocultural theories of CSA implicate media portrayals of children as a factor in CSA (e.g., Rush, 1980; Wurtele & Miller-Perrin, 1992). Child pornography is one type of media that may stimulate sexual interest in children and ranges from photographs to films or videotapes to magazines and books that depict children in sexually explicit acts. Research evaluating the relationship between child pornography and CSA is mixed, with some studies failing to support the hypothesized relationship and others finding that child molesters do use pornography (see review by Murrin & Laws, 1990).

Intermediate Chapter Summary

Despite the work of numerous researchers in the field of CSA, it is still unclear what causes an individual to sexually abuse a child. Some theories **focus on the child** and characteristics that may make a child more vulnerable (e.g., being passive, quiet, trusting, young, unhappy, and needy). Other theories **focus on the perpetrator** and describe him or her as having psychological dysfunction, deviant sexual arousal patterns, or a childhood history of victimization (e.g., physical, emotional, social) that leads to adult perpetration. Numerous **family characteristics** are also associated with CSA, including family conflict (from poor relationships to divorce), dysfunction (e.g., use of violence, alcohol, withdrawal behaviors), and families with a mother who has a history of childhood sexual abuse. Recent theories further suggest that mothers may be co-victims as well. A final group of theories proposes that sociocultural forces such as **social attitudes** (e.g., inequality between men and women), **male socialization** (resulting in attraction to vulnerable partners), and **child pornography** (that tends to objectify the sexual partner) are responsible for CSA. No one theory by itself or in combination with other theories can effectively explain CSA.

Responding to Child Sexual Abuse

Throughout the chapter, descriptions about what is known about CSA have been provided in an attempt to explore the relevant issues more thoroughly. A comprehensive understanding of any problem is a necessary

---

There are symptoms of abuse that are so common that therapists should expect to address them in the majority of victims.

---

first step in attempting to intervene in that problem. Once authorities receive a report of CSA, several systems become involved in the responses and interventions directed at the problem including the mental health and criminal justice systems.

Treatment Interventions

One of the earliest responses to the CSA problem was to provide therapeutic services to victims and offenders, as well as to their families. Several programs originated in the early 1970s, although they were restricted in number and focus. More recently, there has been a renewed interest in the treatment of sexual abuse victims as well as perpetrators that better reflects an understanding of the complexity of the CSA problem.

Basic Issues in Treatment. Whether treatment centers on the child victim, the adult survivor, or the perpetrator of abuse, there are several basic treatment issues. First, victims and perpetrators of CSA are diverse in terms of their preabuse history, the nature of the abuse experience, and available social supports and coping resources. As a result, any treatment program needs to be tailored to meet the particular needs of each individual (Chaffin, 1994; Courtois & Watts, 1982). There is no "canned" treatment program that will be effective for all victims or for all perpetrators or for all families.

Second, therapists and others working in the area of CSA need to be aware of issues associated with countertransference (their own personal reactions) toward victims, perpetrators, and their families. Individuals working with a child's perpetrator, for example, may have feelings of anger or hatred toward him or her that make it difficult to respond in a therapeutic manner. Or as Haugaard and Reppucci (1988) put it, "The image of a 5-year-old girl performing fellatio on her father in submission to his parental authority does not engender compassion" (p. 191). Clinicians may also feel uncomfortable when working with child victims who sometimes behave sexually toward their therapists. In addition, studies have revealed that a significant number of professionals who work with victims have a history of child abuse themselves (Feldman-Summers & Pope, 1994; Nuttall & Jackson, 1994). These experiences might affect practitioners' views of CSA and its victims, contributing to distorted perceptions of patients and also possibly to therapy-induced memories (Beutler, Williams, & Zetzer, 1994). (For further discussion, see boxed insert: "The Repressed Memory Controversy.")

Therapy for Child Victims and Adult Survivors. A number of professionals, including master's-level therapists, clinical social workers, psychologists, and psychiatrists, conduct therapy for child victims and adult survivors of CSA.

THE REPRESSED MEMORY CONTROVERSY

1989   The California Court of Appeal extended the statute of limitations under the doctrine of "delayed discovery," allowing individuals claiming a history of CSA during childhood to sue their parents. Individuals must be able to demonstrate that memories of the event were repressed (by providing certification by a licensed mental health professional).

1990   Nineteen-year-old Holly Ramona accused her father, Gary Ramona, of repeatedly raping her between the ages of 5 and 8. Holly's memories of the abuse surfaced while she was a college student receiving therapy for depression and bulimia. Over the course of several months of therapy, Holly experienced flashback memories of her father sexually molesting her. Just before accusing her father, Holly received the hypnotic drug sodium amytal and recounted multiple episodes of abuse by her father. After the allegations surfaced, Gary Ramona lost his $400,000-a-year job, his daughters refused to interact with him, and his wife divorced him.

1992   The False Memory Syndrome (FMS) Foundation was established to provide information and support to more than 2,300 families. The group contends that there is a "rash" of individuals who have been falsely accused of sexual abuse.

1994   The Napa Valley Superior Court jury ruled that Holly Ramona's memories were "probably false" and that although her therapists had not implanted the memories, they had negligently reinforced them (Butler, 1994). Gary Ramona was awarded $500,000 of the $8 million he sought in damages.

This chronology of events effectively illustrates some of the dilemmas associated with the repressed memory debate. Are Holly and others like her victims of CSA? Or are the adults being accused the victims of false memories? There is little consensus regarding these questions among legal, medical, and mental health professionals. In one camp, there are experts who believe that repressed memories are quite common and result from either repression of negative feelings associated with the abuse or amnesia associated with dissociative defenses (i.e., multiple personality disorder) of a traumatic event (Briere & Conte, 1993). In the other camp are the critics of repressed memories who claim that such memories may be due to fantasy, illusion, subsequent contextual cues, or the result of implantation by a therapist or other perceived authority figure (Ganaway, 1989; Loftus, 1993).

In support of the argument that repressed memories exist, Herman and Schatzow (1987) found that 64% of female incest survivor patients did not have full recall of their sexual abuse and reported some degree of amnesia. One fourth of these women reported severe memory deficits or complete amnesia for the event. Approximately 75% of the women obtained evidence to corroborate their abuse reports such as confirmation from other family members, discovering that a sibling had also been abused, or a confession by the perpetrator. A more recent study conducted by Briere and Conte (1993) also showed a substantial rate of repressed memories in a clinical sample of sexual abuse victims (59%). Such studies, however, are limited due to the retrospective and self-report nature of the data and the fact that the individuals were in therapy. An additional study, however, followed a community sample of 100 victims of CSA who reported abuse in their childhood and found that 17 years later, 38% did not recall the previously reported incident (Williams, 1992).

Critics of repressed memories, on the other hand, emphasize the limitations of such studies: specifically, the problem that participants in clinical samples are attempting to remember "a memory for forgetting a memory" (Loftus, 1993, p. 522). Other potential sources of repressed memories have been suggested. For example, some claim that popular writings exaggerate sexual abuse as "nearly universal" (Bower, 1993b) and contain unvalidated claims such as "If you are unable to remember any specific instances but still have a feeling that something abusive happened to you, it probably did" (Bass & Davis, 1988, p. 21). Proponents of false memories claim that such statements are dangerous given the malleability of memory. Research has shown that memory is subject to distortion from stress, incentives to keep secrets, and suggestion (Loftus, 1993; Perry, 1992).

Others contend that popular writings encourage emotional confrontations with alleged perpetrators (Loftus, 1993) and in general are written as part of a "sexual abuse industry" to create victims (Travis, 1993). Since 1989, a total of 19 states have passed legislation allowing people to sue for recovery of damages for injury suffered as a result of CSA remembered for the first time during adulthood, and an estimated 300 lawsuits involving formerly repressed memories had been filed as of September 1993 (Bower, 1993a). Some have suggested that the motivation behind these lawsuits is fame and fortune (Davis, 1991; Lachnit, 1991) rather than justice.

(continued)

The final argument offered by critics of repressed memories is the notion that therapists may "implant" memories through either overt or covert suggestions. Therapists may inadvertently communicate to their clients their own belief that repressed memories are common, and clients might subsequently assume that it is likely to have happened to them (Loftus, 1993). Others have suggested that therapists may overtly implant a memory of CSA by diagnosing abuse after too brief an evaluation, the use of leading questions, or the use of questionable assessment or therapeutic techniques such as hypnosis and sodium amytal (Butler, 1994; Loftus, 1993).

Unfortunately, the debate over whether memories of CSA are repressed or false remains unresolved, and it is unlikely that the question will receive a clear answer in the near future. To date, there is no definitive way of knowing whether a given memory is true or false. Both sides do agree, however, in the importance of improving methods to assess and treat victims of CSA and to continue seeking empirical knowledge to uncover the realities regarding repressed memories. An APA task force was recently appointed to examine what is known about repressed memories and included a panel of both skeptics and believers. A preliminary report from the group indicated that they had reached a consensus regarding the extremes of the debate: "Both ends of the continuum on people's memories of abuse are possible. . . . It is possible that under some cue conditions, early memories may be retrievable. At the other extreme, it is possible under some conditions for memories to be implanted or embedded" (DeAngelis, 1993).

Treatment can take a variety of forms, such as individual counseling, family treatment, group therapy, or marital counseling and often includes various combinations (e.g., individual counseling and group therapy).

Despite the diversity of treatment modalities, there are several goals of therapy that are common to most approaches. One goal of therapy is to alleviate any significant symptoms presented by the individual child or adult (Courtois & Watts, 1982; Lipovsky & Elliott, 1993; Rust & Troupe, 1991). The variability of responses to CSA dictates the development of specialized treatment strategies to meet each individual's needs. A child victim might present with self-injurious behavior, for example, and will need a behavior modification program tailored specifically to help alleviate such behaviors. Or an adult might present with a specific sexual dysfunction that requires a modified sex therapy technique.

There are other symptoms of abuse that are so common that therapists should expect to address them in the majority of child victims and adult survivors. The guilt, shame, and stigmatization experienced by the victim, for example, need to be addressed by helping the victim to change his or her perception about being "different" as well as somehow to blame for the abuse. Here, therapists often undertake some form of cognitive restructuring to appropriately relocate the responsibility of the abuse to the offender

(Cahill, Llewelyn, & Pearson, 1991; Jehu, Klassen, & Gazan, 1986). Many experts believe that group therapy is a particularly effective modality in which to counter self-denigrating beliefs and to confront issues of secrecy and stigmatization as participants are able to discuss their experiences with peers who have also been abused (Cahill et al., 1991; Celano, 1990).

Anxiety and fear are also common symptoms, and one task of therapy is to give victims the opportunity to diffuse these feelings by talking about their abuse experience in the safety of a supportive therapeutic relationship (Berliner, 1991; Courtois & Watts, 1982). Adults are often able to process the abusive experience simply by discussing it with their therapist. For children, however, other avenues may be necessary such as reenacting the abuse through play. For both the adult survivor and child victim, it is necessary to teach strategies for managing the fear and anxiety that may accompany the processing of the abuse such as relaxation training, problem-solving skills, the use of positive coping statements, and the use of imagery (Berliner, 1991; Meichenbaum, 1977).

Another goal of therapy is to teach the client to express his or her anger in appropriate ways (Blake-White & Kline, 1985; Jones, 1986). To combat depression and low self-esteem, many experts use cognitive and interpersonal exercises and role-plays and emphasize the victim's survival skills and personal strengths (e.g., Corder, Haizlip, & De-Boer, 1990; Courtois & Watts, 1982). In addition, providing the victim with sex education and self-protection skills may lead to a sense of empowerment or serve to prevent any further victimization (Berliner, 1991; Damon, Todd, & MacFarlane, 1987).

To date, relatively little is known about the success of victim-oriented interventions for CSA because of the dearth of systematic evaluations. Most reports of therapy outcome consist of descriptive data and nonstandardized approaches that show only modestly positive or nonsignificant results (Beutler et al., 1994; Kolko, 1987). Some outcome studies have evaluated self-reported behavioral change and found that participants report increased self-esteem and feelings of self-efficacy and decreasing feelings of isolation, guilt, and shame (Tsai & Wagner, 1978). Others have demonstrated improvement in social, emotional, and behavioral functioning on standardized measures (e.g., Cohen & Mannarino, 1993; Friedrich, Luecke, Beilke, & Place, 1992; Rust & Troupe, 1991). Researchers have also begun to evaluate variables that enhance or inhibit treatment efficacy and have found that therapist and victim gender, as well as the victim's relationship to his or her perpetrator, affect treatment outcome (Fowler & Wagner, 1993; Friedrich, Berliner, Urquiza, & Beilke, 1988; Friedrich, Luecke, et al., 1992).

Offender Treatment. The primary treatment goal in working with CSA offenders is to reduce the likelihood of recidivism or repeated offenses. Studying treatment outcome and measuring recidivism, however, are difficult tasks. It is often difficult, for example, for a researcher to determine whether convicted offenders commit a subsequent offense unless long-term follow-ups to monitor reoffenses are extended indefinitely. In one study, 27% of offenders did not reoffend for at least 4 or more years after release (Romero & Williams, 1995). There are also numerous methodological problems that characterize the research examining treatment outcome with CSA offenders, including nonrandom assignment to treatment conditions, biased samples, and attrition among treatment participants (see Becker, 1994; Marshall & Pithers, 1994). Despite these difficulties, one recent review of the treatment literature concluded that recent advances in treatment approaches "provide definite grounds for optimism about the responsiveness of some segments of the

offender population to existing treatment modalities" (Becker, 1994, p. 188).

A variety of treatment approaches exist for CSA offenders, including physiological approaches, insight-oriented therapy, family systems, and cognitive-behavioral approaches (e.g., Becker, 1994; Marshall, Jones, Ward, Johnston, & Barbaree, 1991). Physiological approaches include castration (surgical removal of the testicles), brain surgery, and drug therapy (e.g., Bradford, 1990; Heim & Hursch, 1979; Marshall et al., 1991). Most physiological treatments are based on the notion that there is some sort of biological mechanism affecting the offender's sex drive and causing the abusive behavior. Early approaches focused on castration and removal of certain brain areas (e.g., hypothalamus) in an attempt to control sexual behavior. Although some outcome studies show a reduction in sex offenses, the presence of methodological problems, ethical concerns, and negative side effects casts doubt on the usefulness of these techniques (Heim & Hursch, 1979; Marshall et al., 1991).

Newer approaches focus on the use of drugs to treat child molesters in an attempt to reduce sexual-offending behavior (Marshall et al., 1991). These treatments have largely employed drugs called antiandrogens, agents that reduce sexual drive. Outcome studies have revealed contradictory results (e.g., Berlin & Meinecke, 1981; Wincze, Bansal, & Malamud, 1986). In a review of the literature, Marshall et al. (1991) concluded that drug therapy may be beneficial for some offenders but should be used conservatively in conjunction with other treatments or as a temporary method until psychological treatments can begin.

Insight-oriented therapy is another approach designed to treat CSA offenders that primarily involves psychoanalytic or psychodynamic individual counseling for the offender. The general purpose of this therapy is to assist the perpetrator in understanding the role sexual abuse plays in his or her life. Outcome studies evaluating various insight-oriented approaches have been mixed (Prendergast, 1979; Sturgeon & Taylor, 1980), probably as a result of methodological differences across studies. According to a recent survey of sex offender treatment programs, individual counseling techniques are only used in approximately 2% of treatment programs (Knopp, Freeman-Longo, & Stevenson, 1992).

Other treatment programs for offenders emphasize family systems approaches. Giarretto

(1982) pioneered the Child Sexual Abuse Treatment Program, a comprehensive program that uses a sequence of therapies for incest families including individual counseling for the child victim, mother, and perpetrator; mother-daughter counseling; marital counseling; perpetrator-victim counseling; group counseling; and family counseling. Typical themes addressed in family therapy include parents' failure to protect the victim from abuse, feelings of guilt and depression resulting from the abuse, the victim's anger toward parents, the perpetrator's responsibility for the abuse, confusion over blurred role boundaries, poor communication patterns, and the effect the abuse has had on the child (Giarretto, 1982; Sgroi, 1982; Wolfe, Wolfe, & Best, 1988). Family therapy may also address the needs of family members indirectly affected by the abuse, such as those of nonoffending parents and siblings, as well as disruptions caused by the disclosure of abuse, such as incarceration, financial hardship, and parental separation (Wolfe, Wolfe, & Best, 1988). Whenever victims and abusers are seen together in therapy, however, special attention should be paid to protecting the victim from intimidation. Although the research evaluating the outcome of the family therapy approach is scant and does not include long-term follow-up, available reports do demonstrate the effectiveness of the approach (Giarretto, 1982).

Cognitive-behavioral approaches represent an additional method of treatment and are the most widely available and actively researched forms of therapy for CSA offenders (for a review, see Marshall et al., 1991). Behavioral interventions primarily emphasize deviant sexual arousal patterns of CSA perpetrators and attempt to alter them. Most behavioral approaches have used some form of aversive therapy. Abel, Becker, and Skinner (1986), for example, report on a process called masturbatory satiation. In this technique, the perpetrator is instructed to reach orgasm through masturbation as quickly as possible using *appropriate* sexual fantasies (e.g., sexual encounters between two mutually consenting adults). Once he has ejaculated, the offender is to switch his fantasies to images involving children and continue to masturbate until the total masturbation time is 1 hour. This technique supposedly reinforces the appropriate fantasies through the pleasurable feelings of orgasm and diminishes the fantasies involving children because they are associated with nonpleasurable masturba-

tion that occurs after ejaculation. Cognitive therapies, in contrast, are designed to teach offenders how to recognize and change their inaccurate beliefs (e.g., that the perpetrator is simply "teaching" the victim about sex) (Abel et al., 1986).

Many treatment programs combine both cognitive and behavioral techniques with other components (e.g., improving social and life skills) to create a multidimensional approach (e.g., Marshall & Barbaree, 1988). Consistent with a multidimensional approach, some experts advocate that treatment should focus on additional nonsexual difficulties, such as antisocial behavior and a history of sexual victimization (e.g., Chaffin, 1994; Scavo, 1989). One final treatment component that is gaining increasing support is relapse prevention. Programs that include a relapse prevention component include assisting perpetrators in identifying patterns in their behavior that are precursors to abuse and providing long-term, community-based supervision (Marques, Nelson, West, & Day, 1994; Miner, Marques, Day, & Nelson, 1990; Pithers & Kafka, 1990). In a recent review of the treatment literature, Marshall and Pithers (1994) endorsed multidimensional treatment programs by stating that "implementation of a single therapeutic intervention, even by the most high skilled practitioners, cannot be considered sufficient treatment for most sex offenders" (p. 25).

Most experts agree that the therapeutic value of cognitive-behavioral approaches has been clearly demonstrated (Marshall et al., 1991; Marshall & Pithers, 1994). Others, however, have argued that such a conclusion is premature given the methodological limitations of studies (Quinsey, Harris, Rice, & Lalumiere, 1993). One criticism of outcome studies is that although some treatment approaches have been shown to alter arousal patterns to pictures and/or stories of children, such changes do not necessarily apply to actual children. Other methodological limitations include limited follow-up information, overreliance on self-report data, and lack of appropriate comparison groups. In his recent review of the treatment outcome literature, Chaffin (1994) concluded,

Despite previous skepticism regarding the efficacy of offender treatment, there are good data to support its effectiveness with the kinds of patients often seen in outpatient settings. This suggests that practitioners can justify favorable prognoses for less severe patients. The data are less optimistic regarding the outlook for severe populations. (p. 233)

The Criminal Justice System

The criminal justice system primarily centers on the punishment of perpetrators of CSA. Researchers and practitioners, however, have also focused on the effect of the criminal justice system on the victim and methods to assist the child victim or witness.

Perpetrators. The criminal justice response toward the perpetrator who is accused or convicted of CSA can take many forms, including prison sentences, plea bargaining, diversion programs, or probation. Although there are no national statistics on the number of CSA prosecutions or the number of perpetrators who receive diversion programs or probation, research on selected jurisdictions provides some information about the criminal justice system response to CSA.

Criminal prosecutions for CSA offenders are not always initiated. In 1987, for example, Chapman and Smith found that approximately 42% of sexual abuse allegations substantiated by child protective services or reported to the police were forwarded for prosecution (cited in Finkelhor, 1994a). Many factors influence whether prosecution is initiated (e.g., Tjaden & Thoennes, 1992). Cases involving victims younger than age 7 are less likely to be prosecuted, for example, whereas cases of abuse that are severe, involve force, and include perpetrators with a prior criminal record are more likely to be prosecuted (e.g., Myers, 1994; Tjaden & Thoennes, 1992).

As is true of other crimes, plea bargaining is common in cases of CSA. Approximately two thirds of cases, for example, result in the perpetrator pleading guilty in exchange for reduced charges (e.g., Tjaden & Thoennes, 1992). Diversion or probation programs are also often used, which include agreements between prosecutors and defendants whereby the defendant participates in some form of counseling or treatment with the understanding that charges will be dismissed if the defendant complies (Myers, 1993). In Smith, Hillenbrand, and Govestsky (1990), for example, 80% of convicted child molesters were sentenced to probation, which usually included court-mandated treatment as a condition for probation.

Some have suggested that a failure to prosecute and jail CSA offenders reflects a lack of social recognition and commitment to the problem (Wurtele & Miller-Perrin, 1992). There are many reasons, however, why CSA cases are not prosecuted. In 1987, the U.S. Supreme Court, for example, stated that "child abuse is one of the most difficult crimes to detect and prosecute because there often are no witnesses except the victim" (quoted in Myers, 1993, p. 573). In addition, physical evidence in cases of CSA is rarely available (Bays & Chadwick, 1993). The child's testimony is often the only evidence in the case, and the public, prosecutors, and judges are often concerned about the credibility of the child witness (Finkelhor, 1994a; Myers, 1993, 1994).

Despite the difficulty in prosecuting cases of CSA, there is some evidence that child abuse is treated much like other crimes within the criminal justice system. The percentage of CSA cases that proceed to trial, for example, is approximately 10%, which is similar to criminal cases in general (Goodman et al., 1992; Tjaden & Thoennes, 1992). A strong criminal justice system response is also evidenced by the fact that the majority of CSA prosecutions that go to trial result in convictions (Gray, 1993). Research has also demonstrated that the percentage of child maltreatment cases where criminal prosecutions are

---

The percentage of cases where criminal prosecutions are initiated is higher for child sexual abuse cases than for other types of maltreatment.

---

initiated is higher for CSA cases than for other types of maltreatment (e.g., Tjaden & Thoennes, 1992).

The criminal justice system has also responded to CSA offenders in other ways. Thirty-eight states have laws requiring convicted sex offenders to register with local law enforcement agencies subsequent to conviction and following any geographical move ("Justice Department Announces Plans," 1995; National Center for Prosecution of Child Abuse, 1993). Steps are also being taken to form a national child abuse registry. In 1993, for example, President Bill Clinton signed the National Child Protection Act, requiring states to report information on child abuse arrests and convictions to the national criminal history record system of the Federal Bureau of Investigation. In addition, some states require that registered sex offenders submit specimens of body fluids that can be genetically compared with specimens taken from victims (Myers, 1994). Although the law allows law enforcement agencies to release information to the general public, notification of sex offenders' addresses is rare ("Justice Department Announces Plans," 1995). Some legal experts argue that such laws are unconstitutional although the courts have upheld the constitutionality of such registration laws (Myers, 1994).

There is considerable debate regarding the punitive role of the criminal justice system in responding to CSA. Some argue that prevention and therapy rather than litigation and sentencing are what is ultimately important in responding to the problem (U.S. Advisory Board on Child Abuse and Neglect, 1993). Advocating prosecution of offenders, however, is not necessarily inconsistent with prevention and treatment efforts and has the added value of validating the victim's innocence and society's view that CSA is unacceptable (Myers, 1994; Peters, Dinsmore, & Toth, 1989; Wurtele & Miller-Perrin, 1992). Unfortunately, systematic research studies examining the effects of various criminal justice system responses (e.g., incarceration vs. plea bargaining vs. mandated treatment) on rates of recidivism are rare.

Child Victims. Another concern associated with the criminal justice system has centered around how to protect child victims from the stress associated with case investigation and court proceedings. Several experts have suggested that stress results from activities that the child must endure such as multiple interviews and face-to-face confrontations with the perpetrator (Goodman et al., 1992; Montoya, 1993). Imagine the fear of a 4-year-old, for example, who must sit on the witness stand, in a strange courtroom in front of strangers, and describe an event as potentially upsetting as sexual abuse. Or imagine the 7-year-old child who is expected to testify against the perpetrator who happens to be the child's parent. In addition, child witnesses must often endure cross-examination from the defense that is often directed at destroying the child's credibility. Most adults might find such an experience significantly distressing.

In addition to increasing the discomfort of the victim, stress associated with the criminal justice system response is also believed to decrease a child's attention, reduce his or her motivation, and possibly interfere with memory recall (Saywitz & Snyder, 1993). In a study of child witnesses of CSA, for example, Saywitz and Nathanson (1993) found that a courtroom environment impaired memory performance and was associated with increased child reports of stress. Legal professionals and mental health experts have suggested a number of approaches designed to minimize the stress and discomfort experienced by CSA victims.

One positive development has been the practice of minimizing both the number of interviews that a child experiences and the number of interviewers. One method that accomplishes this task is the use of videotaped investigative interviews with children (see Montoya, 1993). This practice is effective because the numerous professionals involved can view the tape rather than subjecting the child victim to multiple interviews by different professionals. The use of multidisciplinary teams may also be helpful in reducing the number of interviews that a child is subjected to, thus reducing additional stress to the child victim (Pence & Wilson, 1994). Multidisciplinary teams consist of various professionals involved in the investigation and adjudication of CSA cases, including law enforcement officials, health professionals, and child protective services workers, who work together to pool and coordinate resources. Children are typically interviewed by only one highly trained professional while other members of the team observe from behind a one-way mirror. Most states have laws authorizing or mandating the use of such teams (Pence & Wilson, 1994).

The practice of courtroom accommodations for child witnesses is another positive development designed to reduce criminal justice system-related stress. Some courts, for example, have allowed the child witness to testify outside the direct presence of the offender by permitting videotapes at trial in lieu of the child's testimony (Montoya, 1993; Perry & McAuliff, 1993). The Sixth Amendment of the Constitution, however, protects the defendant's right to confront his or her accuser, in this case, the child witness. As a result, most states do not categorically allow the admissibility of videotaped testimony (Pence & Wilson, 1994). As an alternative, some courts allow children to testify in the judge's chambers via a closed-circuit television monitor (Myers, 1992).

Another positive development is the use of preparation and support for the victim of CSA as he or she experiences criminal justice proceedings. Many practices, for example, can be implemented to help make the courtroom a less frightening place for children such as familiarizing the child ahead of time with the courtroom (e.g., through tours of the courtroom, or court schools), closing the courtroom to the public and press, and allowing a trusted adult to remain in the courtroom while the child testifies (Myers, 1994; Regehr, 1990; Saywitz & Snyder, 1993). Accumulating evidence suggests that such approaches are helpful in improving the completeness of children's reports, their ability to answer questions, and the consistency of their responses (Goodman et al., 1992; Saywitz & Snyder, 1993).

Summary

No one knows the specific number of children who are victimized by child sexual abuse each year. The confusion in determining accurate rates of CSA is largely due to the difficulty inherent in defining and studying such a complex social problem. Although no precise estimates are available, it is clear that large numbers of children are sexually exploited by adults. Conservative estimates derived from the most methodologically sound studies suggest that 20% of women and between 5% and 10% of men experience some form of CSA during childhood.

Research examining the characteristics of CSA demonstrates the heterogeneity of victim and offender populations. Victims, for example, can be male or female, range in age from infancy to 18, and come from a variety of racial and socioeconomic backgrounds. Perpetrators are also heterogeneous and represent all possible demographic and psychological profiles. A number of risk factors, however, have been consistently associated with CSA. Victims, for example, are often female, have few close friends, and live in families characterized by poor family relations and the absence or unavailability of natural parents. Perpetrators of CSA are most often male and someone who is familiar to the child, such as a relative or an acquaintance.

The dynamics that characterize CSA situations are consistently described by both perpetrators and victims. Perpetrators usually target children who are vulnerable or needy in some way, such as those who are unhappy or come from a divorced home. Perpetrators typically involve the child in a grooming process that involves desensitizing the child to sexual abuse by gradually progressing from nonsexual to sexual touch. Perpetrators also use a variety of coercive tactics to initiate and maintain the abuse such as threats, bribes, and physical force.

The psychological sequelae for victims associated with CSA are variable and consist of short-term as well as long-term effects. Difficulties associated with CSA include a variety of symptoms that affect emotional well-being (e.g., depression), interpersonal functioning (e.g., social withdrawal), behavior (e.g., substance abuse), sexual functioning (e.g., sexualized behavior), physical health (e.g., headaches), and cognitive functioning (e.g., poor concentration). Variability in outcome for victims is associated with a number of factors including the severity of the sexual behavior, the degree of physical force used by the perpetrator, the response the victim received following disclosure, and the identity of the perpetrator.

The heterogeneity of victim and perpetrator populations has contributed to the difficulty in establishing a single explanation for why sexual abuse occurs. One perpetrator may abuse a certain type of child for one reason, and another may abuse a different type of child for a completely different reason. Etiological theories have focused on different individuals and systems involved in CSA. Some theories have centered on the role of the victim or the mother, whereas the majority emphasize some form of offender dysfunction associated with personality, deviant sexual arousal, or childhood history. Some family theories have also proposed a set of specific characteristics of the family system (e.g., parental conflict, family disorganization) that might contribute to CSA. Finally, several theories have implicated sociocultural factors (e.g., male socialization practices, child pornography) that might play a contributory role.

In recognition of the significance of the CSA problem, a number of professionals have been involved in the response toward victims and perpetrators. Criminal justice system responses directed at the problem of CSA include punitive responses for the perpetrators of CSA as well as interventions designed to alleviate the stress associated with victim involvement in the investigatory and legal processes. Researchers and practitioners have also developed an array of treatment interventions in an effort to address the multiple causes and far-reaching consequences of CSA. Regardless of the type of approach that is used, the therapeutic goals for child victims and adult survivors generally include addressing significant symptomatology as well as common emotions associated with abuse such as guilt, shame, anger, depression, and anxiety. Group therapy has also been recommended as a beneficial intervention for victims to reduce self-denigrating beliefs, secrecy, and stigmatization. Treatment programs for offenders include a variety of approaches but most typically incorporate cognitive and behavioral components to reduce deviant sexual arousal and cognitive distortions associated with abuse. These approaches demonstrate some promise although further studies are needed to address the limitations of extant research methodologies, the consequences of system responses on recidivism, mediators to minimize victims' stress, and alternative treatments (e.g., improving social and life skills) to accompany therapeutic interventions.

5

Child Neglect and Psychological Maltreatment

CHAPTER OUTLINE

An Interview With Mildred Daley Pagelow

"As a society, we should begin to actively work to turn around our popular culture of violence."

MILDRED DALEY PAGELOW, clinical sociologist, is Adjunct Research Professor of Sociology at California State University, Fullerton, and Director of Educational Consulting Services. Dr. Pagelow received her B.A. in sociology from California State University, Long Beach, in 1975 and her Ph.D. in sociology from the University of California, Riverside, in 1980. Dr. Pagelow has done extensive research on family violence and has written two books, Woman-Battering: Victims and Their Experiences *and* Family Violence.

Dr. Pagelow is a legal consultant and expert witness and offers training on domestic violence identification and prevention. She served as consultant to the California Commission on Crime Control and Violence Prevention and testified before both houses of Congress and the California State Legislature on domestic violence legislation. She also testified at hearings of the California Commission on Gender Bias in the Courts. She was one of the founding members of WomenShelter in Long Beach and Laura's House and Women's Transitional Living Center in Orange County. She is on the advisory boards of the latter two shelters.

Q: What sparked your interest in family violence?

A: In the spring of 1976, I saw a National Organization for Women publication featuring a cover photo of a badly bruised face and an article inside calling for research into the newly discovered problem of battered wives. The disturbing article led me to search my library of textbooks on the family and deviance (my areas of specialization as a graduate student), but nowhere did I find a reference to the topic. Here and there were a few paragraphs on child abuse, but nothing at all about wife abuse. It was then I knew the topic of my dissertation research, and the experts who would give me some answers were battered women themselves.

Q: What are your research and advocacy interests?

A: Traditional sociology holds that this is a "values-free" science, and research is conducted by neutral social scientists who stay within the ivy-covered walls of academia. Research is for others to interpret and set policy. Within the profession, another group calls for the formation of "clinical sociology" and "applied sociology," which basically insists that what researchers learn can better be applied by those who are most closely familiar with the data and findings. I am aligned with the latter ideology.

Because I conducted my research face to face with my respondents and used a variety of methodologies, I have greater understanding of the experiences, fears, needs, and hopes of hundreds of women who were beaten by the men they had loved. In the process of doing the research, learning from victims and their children what their lives were like, testifying, and speaking before many groups, I discovered I had become an advocate as well as a researcher. Neither role was compromised by my participation in the other.

Q: Looking back over the area of family violence, what policy recommendations would you make?

A: My concerns are that we, as a society, should begin to actively work to turn around our popular culture of violence. We must begin with parenting education that will stress the importance of equal rights and responsibilities in the home and the elimination of gender-role expectations of children. Schools must rid themselves of all remnants of gender-role stereotyping and promote equal educational opportunities. All children should be educated to become as strong, assertive, and self-supportive adults as possible.

Q: What sort of research do you think is most needed?

A: There are a number of areas that urgently concern me, but I'm most concerned about women who are attempting to free themselves from abusive spouses, only to face the formidable task of fighting the legal system for child custody. Although some research has examined the relatively few cases where battered women kill their abusers, very little attention has been paid to the struggles of the many women who merely want to "break free" of the violence. Additionally, some research is needed on batterers who turn killers, with the goal of saving lives, perhaps through prediction.

Q: What are your future advocacy interests?

A: It gives me great satisfaction when I can be of service in civil and criminal cases involving victims. I plan to continue to help whenever expert assistance is requested. In a sense, my advocacy work is repayment to the many women who shared with me their most painful memories and intimate thoughts, which they did in the selfless hope that their experiences would help other women avoid the pain they had endured.

Introduction

CASE HISTORY: WILL AND MARK— "WHERE ARE THE PARENTS?"

Will and Mark arrived at the psychiatric unit of the county hospital after being apprehended by the police the night before. Their clothes were covered with dirt, and the odor emanating from their bodies indicated that they had not bathed in quite some time. Both were thin and immediately asked the nursing staff for some food. An interview revealed that they were brothers and part of a family of seven, although many other "friends of the family" often stayed in their house. Neither parent worked, and Will and Mark stated that they often had the responsibility to bring home money for their parents. Their father had taught them how to beg for money on various street corners around the city. After the interview, the events of the previous evening were clear. Mark and Will had been out "killing time" by wandering around the neighborhood. They had decided to "get some fresh air" when their father began swearing at them, as he frequently did, for failing to have his dinner ready on time. After roaming the city for hours, Mark and Will spotted a pickup truck and took it for a ride. After a short drive, they stopped at a local furniture store,

broke in, and began to vandalize the merchandise by ripping the furniture with Will's knife. A woman from the community spotted the intruders and called the police. She told the police that two young boys, probably somewhere between 7 and 9 years of age, had broken into a local business. (Author's case history)

* * *

The events depicted in this vignette clearly reflect parenting practices that are less than ideal. Such behaviors, however, would not be characterized as physically or sexually abusive as previously defined. The interactions described in this vignette may not be labeled abusive at all, but do illustrate two additional proposed forms of child maltreatment: child neglect and psychological maltreatment. The present chapter addresses these final two forms of child maltreatment, although much less is known about them. Child neglect, for example, has been referred to as the "most forgotten" form of maltreatment (Daro, 1988). In addition, Wolock and Horowitz (1984) coined the phrase "the neglect of neglect" to describe the veritable disinterest in the topic reflected by professionals as well as society. Likewise, psychological maltreatment was not recognized as a distinct form of child maltreatment until recently.

Why has most research focused on physical and sexual child abuse (PCA and CSA) with less emphasis on child neglect and psychological maltreatment? The most obvious answer is that physical abuse and, to a lesser degree, sexual abuse result in immediate and observable harm. Child neglect and psychological maltreatment are much more elusive, in terms of their negative consequences. In cases of child neglect or psychological maltreatment, for example, a single act is unlikely to result in significant and immediate harm. The cumulative effects of these forms of abuse, however, are insidious and often require repeated occurrences before negative effects may become apparent.

Child neglect and psychological maltreatment are also evasive in terms of definitional issues. Although defining PCA and CSA involves some ambiguities, particularly at the less extreme ends of the continuum, understanding what comprises child neglect and psychological maltreatment poses even greater problems. Where should the line be drawn between less than adequate parenting or parental error and negligence or psychological maltreatment? Many of the specific behaviors used to define child neglect or psychological maltreatment are less "deviant," that is, they are committed by many parents at one time or another. Ignoring or criticizing a child, for example, or being unsupportive, are behaviors that most parents engage in during the normal course of parenting. As a result, it is also necessary to consider under what circumstances these behaviors might constitute child neglect or psychological maltreatment.

Related to definitional ambiguities is the problem of overlap between child neglect and psychological maltreatment with other forms of child abuse. Child neglect and psychological maltreatment rarely occur in isolation as "pure" forms of maltreatment but rather often coexist with one another, as well as with other forms of child abuse (e.g., Claussen & Crittenden, 1991; Ney, Fung, & Wickett, 1994). Coexistence with other forms of maltreatment is particularly characteristic of psychological maltreatment, which in the broadest sense (e.g., parental actions that damage a child's self-worth and esteem) occurs as a component of all forms of maltreatment (e.g., Hart & Brassard, 1991).

The complex nature of child neglect and psychological maltreatment has contributed to a serious lack of information about the characteristics, consequences, and causes of these forms of child maltreatment. The realization, however, that child neglect and psychological maltreatment may be the most pervasive and damaging forms of child maltreatment has spurred research interests in these topics. The first part of the chapter addresses what is currently known about child neglect; the latter half of the chapter focuses on psychological maltreatment. Much of the literature for both forms of maltreatment aims to clarify definitional issues, and each section reflects this emphasis accordingly. Because research evaluating these forms of abuse is in its infancy, discussion of causes, solutions, and interventions for each form of maltreatment is addressed simultaneously.

Child Neglect

As is true of all forms of child maltreatment, child neglect is not new. It was not until the early 20th century, however, that the neglect of children's basic needs was acknowledged or defined as a social problem (Wolock & Horowitz, 1984). In more recent times, widespread recognition of this form of child maltreatment, and subsequent empirical attention directed at it, has taken a back seat to physical and sexual forms of child abuse (Berliner, 1994; Dubowitz, 1994; Wolock & Horowitz, 1984). Historically, professionals have viewed child neglect as a less significant appendage of the more tangible forms of maltreatment, as a stepchild of PCA.

There may be several reasons for inattention to child neglect:

1. Some believe that neglect does not result in serious consequences.
2. Many may feel that it is inappropriate to judge parents involved in poverty-related neglect.
3. Many may be reluctant to become involved in child neglect because the problem seems insurmountable.
4. Some may find other forms of maltreatment more compelling.
5. Ambiguity and vagueness regarding what constitutes neglect causes confusion.
6. Child neglect provokes negative feelings (Dubowitz, 1994).

The realization, however, that child neglect is the most frequently reported form of child maltreatment (Daro & McCurdy, 1991; Sedlak, 1990; U.S. Department of Health and Human Services [DHHS], 1988) has increased clinical and research efforts directed at the problem.

Scope of the Problem

In response to increased interest in child neglect, professionals have focused on defining the parameters of child neglect and determining the magnitude of the problem. As is true of other forms of child maltreatment, reaching a consensus regarding conceptual and operational definitions as well as determining the rates of the problem are two of the greatest challenges to the field.

WHAT IS CHILD NEGLECT?

Current Definitions. The way child neglect is defined is critical because such definitions influence the way that the problem is conceptualized for purposes of conducting research, reporting neglect, understanding the causes of neglect, and formulating interventions as well as prevention strategies for the problem. Most experts generally agree that child neglect refers to deficits in the provision of a child's basic needs (e.g., Dubowitz, Black, Starr, & Zuravin, 1993; Munkel, 1994). Gaudin (1993), for example, recently defined child neglect as follows: "Child neglect is the term used most often to encompass parents' or caretakers' failure to provide basic physical health care, supervision, nutrition, personal hygiene, emotional nurturing, education, or safe housing" (p. 67). This definition emphasizes parental blame, parental responsibility, or both, in child neglect. Such a narrow focus on the role of the caretaker in child neglect is inadequate because it might limit understanding of the problem. By focusing exclusively on the failures of the parent, for example, professionals might confine intervention strategies to improving of parental behaviors, thereby excluding some other important contributors to neglect such as poverty.

In response to this criticism, other researchers have called for a more comprehensive definition of child neglect that incorporates a variety of factors that might lead to neglect (e.g., Dubowitz, Black, Starr, et al., 1993; Helfer, 1990; Paget, Philp, & Abramczyk, 1993). The definition used in the second National Incidence Study (DHHS, 1988), for instance, defined child neglect to include various forms of physical neglect such as refusal of health care, abandonment, inadequate supervision, and inadequate nutrition, clothing, and hygiene. In addition, this definition distinguished between parental failure to provide when options are available and failure to provide when options are not available by excluding certain situations where parents or caretakers were involved in acts of omission because of financial limitations (e.g., an inability to afford health care). This definition calls attention to additional social factors potentially involved in neglectful behaviors and thus encourages awareness about the complexity of child neglect. Understanding the multidimensional nature of child neglect may, in turn, be more effective in directing research and intervention efforts.

Variability also exists regarding exactly what constitutes a child's "basic needs." Are a mother and father negligent, for example, if they leave their 8-year-old son, Mark, to care for his 3-year-old sister, Maria? Obviously, it would depend on the specific circumstances. What if Mark were responsible for Maria's care for 5 minutes while she is playing on the floor? For 5 minutes while she is playing in the bathtub? For one evening between 9 p.m. and 1 a.m.? For every evening between 9 p.m. and 1 a.m.? What if Mark were responsible for Maria's care while her parents take a 2-week vacation? A given behavior can be interpreted as neglectful or not depending on the severity of the consequences to the child, the duration and frequency of neglect, as well as the cultural context in which the behavior occurs.

Severity. Many experts have argued that the severity of child neglect is an important but overlooked variable in defining child neglect (Crouch & Milner, 1993). Child neglect severity can be conceptualized along a continuum ranging from optimal care to that which is grossly inadequate. Severity is typically assessed according to the magnitude of outcomes to children or the degree of demonstrable harm (DHHS, 1981; Dubowitz, Black, Starr, et al., 1993). A case in which a child dies from bleach poisoning, for example, might rank as more severe than a case in which a child receives a minor burn from an iron, even though the same parental behavior contributed to both injuries (i.e., lack of supervision).

One problem with the criterion of demonstrable harm is that some negative outcomes of child neglect are difficult to measure (e.g., emotional consequences). In addition, for some forms of neglect, the consequences are neither immediate nor short term. Zuravin (1988a), for example, found that only 25% of neglected children reported to a protective services agency suffered immediate, physical harm. In recognition of this dilemma, the DHHS (1988), in the second National Incidence Study, added a category titled "endangered." This new category allowed for reporting children who demonstrated no actual harm (i.e., present evidence of injury) but for whom it was reasonable to suspect potential harm (i.e., future risk of injury). The laws in most states include risk of harm or endangerment in their definitions of neglect (Myers & Peters, 1987).

One difficulty in considering potential harm, as articulated by Dubowitz and colleagues (1993), is predicting the likelihood that harm will actually occur and whether that potential harm is significant. An illustration is the potential for harm present each time a person gets into a car, crosses a street, or consumes food with a high cholesterol content. In each case, there is uncertainty about whether actual harm will result and whether such harm will be significant. Professionals are faced with a continuum of behaviors that require human judgment in making child neglect determinations, resulting in a definitional process that may be even more subjective than other forms of family violence discussed in this book. We agree with Dubowitz and colleagues (1993) that potential harm that is probable and severe in its consequences should be considered in definitions of neglect. Leaving a 10-month-old unattended in a bathtub full of water, for example, could very likely result in severe injury or even death if the infant is left for a significant amount of time.

Frequency and Duration. The frequency and duration of neglecting behavior is also an important definitional consideration (Claussen & Crittenden, 1991; Dubowitz, Black, Starr, et al., 1993; Zuravin & Taylor, 1987). Single incidents of neglectful behavior or occasional lapses in adequate care usually qualify as a normal characteristic of parenting or as parental error, rather than as an indication of serious child neglect. If a child occasionally misses a bath or skips a meal, for example, few would identify such a child as neglected. In contrast, a pattern of frequent and repeated deficits in child care (e.g., very few baths, numerous skipped meals) would more likely be considered neglectful (Daro, 1988; Dubowitz, Black, Starr, et al., 1993).

Furthermore, some have argued that frequency and chronicity should be evaluated in the context of the severity of harm involved in a particular act (DHHS, 1988; Dubowitz, Black, Starr, et al., 1993; Zuravin, 1991). Some isolated incidents or brief omissions in care can result in serious consequences, for example, when a caretaker leaves a young child or infant alone near a swimming pool, or when a parent fails to use a seatbelt or car seat for a young child who dies in a car accident. Serious omissions of this nature have led some to argue that "an omission in care that harms or endangers a child constitutes neglect, whether it occurs once or a hundred times" (Dubowitz, Black, Starr, et al., 1993, p. 18).

Distinctions based on frequency and chronicity are helpful not only in defining child neglect but also in understanding characteristics and causes of child neglect. Research conducted by Nelson, Saunders, and Landsman (1990), for example, found differences between chronic and nonchronic neglectful families. Chronically neglectful families were characterized by multiple problems

and deficits including lack of knowledge, skills, and tangible resources. Nonchronically neglectful or "new neglect" families had experienced recent significant crises (e.g., parental divorce or illness) that appeared to presently overwhelm normally sufficient coping abilities. Nelson et al. (1990) concluded that the characteristics of nonchronically neglectful families suggested short-term crisis, stress-management, and support group in-

---

Some argue that "an omission in care that harms or endangers a child constitutes neglect, whether it occurs once or a hundred times."

---

tervention, whereas characteristics of chronically neglectful families suggested the need for multiple treatment interventions over a long duration.

Cultural Issues. The point at which child care moves from the adequate to the inadequate is largely determined by cultural and community values. The acceptable age, for example, for a minor to be responsible for preparing his or her own meals might be different for various cultural groups. Some groups might condemn the notion of a 12-year-old taking on this responsibility, whereas other groups might approve of it. Ultimately, community or cultural standards dictate the societal reactions that define adequate from inadequate care.

Research, however, indicates that community and cultural views of what constitutes household cleanliness, appropriate medical and dental care, and adequate supervision vary little across sociodemographic variables. Polansky and colleagues (Polansky, Ammons, & Weathersby, 1983; Polansky, Chalmers, & Williams, 1987; Polansky & Williams, 1978), for example, have evaluated nonmaltreating mothers with various sociodemographic backgrounds using the Childhood Level of Living (CLL) scale. The CLL scale is designed to assess the importance of basic standards of child care, including cognitive, emotional, and physical care. Results have consistently indicated that there is strong agreement about the basic elements of child care, with similar standards of care found for rural, urban, working-class, and middle-class individuals. When socioeconomic status (SES) is controlled, however, gender and race differences have emerged. Ringwalt and Caye (1989), for example, found that African Americans as well as females were more likely than Caucasians or males to perceive child neglect situations as severe. These findings suggest the importance of examining cultural and community standards of child care in defining child neglect.

Forms of Neglect. Additional efforts aimed at defining the precise nature of child neglect have led researchers to propose numerous typologies clarifying the various situations that constitute child neglect. Most authors agree that child neglect exists in many forms such as physical neglect, educational neglect, developmental neglect, and emotional neglect (e.g., DHHS, 1988; Hegar & Yungman, 1989; Wolock & Horowitz, 1984). Some experts in the field have also proposed an additional category termed *prenatal neglect* that occurs even before a child is born (see boxed insert: "Neglecting the Unborn Child").

Although general agreement exists regarding these broad categories of neglect, there is disagreement regarding the precise behaviors or subtypes included under physical, educational, developmental, and emotional neglect. The strongest consensus exists for *physical neglect,* generally defined as a deficit in basic necessities such as food, clothing, and shelter. The DHHS (1988) broadened the concept of physical neglect to also include "refusal or delay in seeking health care, abandonment, expulsion from home or not allowing a runaway to return home, and inadequate supervision" (p. 6). *Educational* or *developmental neglect* generally refers to deprivation of experiences necessary for growth and development such as intellectual and educational opportunities. The greatest disagreement exists in determining situations consistent with *emotional neglect.* Although most experts agree on broad conceptual parameters of emotional neglect that include failure to provide support, security, and encouragement, they disagree on the operationalization of such behaviors. Current attempts to delineate the behaviors that constitute emotional neglect include situations that others have traditionally viewed as physical, educational, or developmental neglect (e.g., DHHS, 1988; Hegar & Yungman, 1989). There is also considerable overlap between definitions of emotional neglect and psychological maltreatment (Paget et al., 1993).

Despite the disagreement and overlap in organizational frameworks, several subtypes of neglect are repeatedly reported in the literature and are summarized in Table 5.1. At least 11 subtypes of child neglect have been consistently described: (a) health care neglect, (b) personal hygiene neglect, (c) nutritional neglect, (d) neglect of household safety, (e) neglect of household sanitation, (f) inadequate shelter, (g) abandonment, (h) supervisory neglect, (i) educational neglect, (j) emotional neglect, and (k) fostering delinquency.

ESTIMATES OF CHILD NEGLECT

Over the past 15 years, child neglect has emerged as the most frequently reported and substantiated form of child maltreatment (Weise & Daro, 1995). The American Association for Protecting Children (AAPC; 1988) reported that child neglect cases (i.e., deprivation of necessities) accounted for approximately 55% of all child maltreatment cases reported to child protective services in 1986. Data from the National Center on Child Abuse and Neglect (NCCAN) indicated that child neglect cases, including medical as well as other forms of neglect, accounted for 52% of reported cases (DHHS, 1994). Data from the National Committee to Prevent Child Abuse (NCPCA), consisting of the most recent statistics available, revealed that child neglect accounted for approximately 45% of reported cases (Weise & Daro, 1995).

Although child neglect is consistently the mostly frequently reported form of child maltreatment, these studies indicate that specific estimates of the problem vary and are influenced by definitional and methodological differences across studies. The National Incidence Studies (NIS-1 and NIS-2), which have attempted to evaluate the incidence of child neglect, are illustrative of the problems inherent in estimating child neglect. In the NIS-1, the number of children reported for physical neglect was 103,600 and for educational neglect, 174,000 (DHHS, 1981). In the NIS-2, the number of children reported for physical neglect was 507,700 and for educational neglect, 285,900 (DHHS, 1988; Sedlak, 1990). This increase reflects, in part, the broadening of the definition of child neglect in the NIS-2 to include children at risk for harm in addition to those actually harmed. The NIS-2 also included reports from agencies in addition to those connected with child protective

NEGLECTING THE UNBORN CHILD

Prenatal neglect generally includes actions that occur during the prenatal period that can potentially harm the unborn child. Most conceptualizations of prenatal neglect, however, focus on women who abuse illicit drugs and alcohol during pregnancy, exposing infants to their harmful effects in utero. National estimates of the number of drug-exposed infants vary widely because no state requires the uniform testing of infants for drug exposure. In its annual national survey, the National Committee to Prevent Child Abuse found that 6,922 infants were reported for drug exposure in 1993 (McCurdy & Daro, 1994b). The figure increased to 7,469 drug-exposed infants in 1994 (Wiese & Daro, 1995). It is estimated that approximately 20% of babies born in California have been exposed to drugs prenatally (Atkins, 1992).

Most of the concern over prenatal drug exposure has been generated as a result of the increasing numbers of studies demonstrating a relationship between prenatal drug exposure and negative developmental outcomes for the fetus (see reviews by Chiriboga, 1993; Zuckerman & Bresnahan, 1991). Fetal alcohol syndrome (FAS), for example, is a well-recognized consequence of alcohol abuse during pregnancy. Babies born to mothers consuming large quantities during pregnancy suffer from numerous difficulties including growth deficiency, anomalies of brain structure and function, and abnormalities of the head and face (Sokol & Clarren, 1989). Research has also linked prenatal use of illicit drugs such as heroin, cocaine, and marijuana to fetal harm, including growth retardation, microcephaly, and increased rates of organ anomalies (e.g., Bays, 1990; Hadeed & Siegel, 1989).

In light of these research findings, many advocate for mandatory drug testing of newborns and criminal liability for substance-abusing pregnant women (e.g., Garrity-Rokous, 1994). There are many methodological constraints to such research, however, that limit the establishment of definitive cause-effect relationships between prenatal drug exposure and negative developmental outcome. Maternal drug use, for example, often occurs in association with poor maternal nutrition, and as a result, it is difficult to determine which variable is responsible for negative developmental outcome (Chiriboga, 1993). The results of such studies are also difficult to interpret when the influence of the parenting environment subsequent to birth is not considered, a factor demonstrated to influence the developmental outcome of drug-exposed infants (Black, Schuler, & Nair, 1993).

Despite these limitations, legal responses to the problem of prenatal neglect are appearing. Many states, for example, have mandated that professionals report drug-exposed infants or substance-abusing pregnant women to child protective services. As of 1994, 27 states required the reporting of drug-exposed babies, an increase from 19 states in 1993 (Daro & McCurdy, 1994; Wiese & Daro, 1995). Although some states explicitly include infants born with a positive drug toxicology as abused or neglected children, most do not (Clearinghouse on Child Abuse and Neglect Information, 1992). In addition, successful criminal prosecutions under child abuse and neglect statutes are rare (Garrity-Rokous, 1994). Civil proceedings, however, which result in removal of the child from the home rather than prison sentences, are a more likely outcome for substance-abusing pregnant women. Several recent cases, for example, have supported court intervention to protect drug-exposed newborns on the basis that such circumstances were probative of child neglect (Myers, 1992). Prosecutors have also sometimes used related state statutes (e.g., involuntary manslaughter, prohibitions against delivering drugs to minors) to charge women who abuse substances during pregnancy, although this approach has been generally unsuccessful in obtaining criminal convictions (Garrity-Rokous, 1994).

One reason for the lack of uniformity in response to prenatal neglect may involve the disagreement surrounding the relative significance of the rights of the unborn child versus the rights of the pregnant woman (Fleisher, 1987; Garrity-Rokous, 1994). Another source of confusion is the ambiguity of state statutes, which often leaves considerable room for variability in interpreting what circumstances can be legally sanctioned. In addition, punitive responses toward substance-abusing pregnant women have been questioned on practical, constitutional, therapeutic, and empirical grounds (e.g., Garrity-Rokous, 1994). Although the problem of prenatal neglect continues to be the focus of much theoretical discussion and empirical research, solutions will likely remain elusive for some time.

Table 5.1 Subtypes of Child Neglect

Type	Description	Examples
Health care neglect	Refusal to, or delay in, providing physical or mental health care	Failing to obtain a child's immunizations Prescriptions not filled and provider's instructions not followed Dental needs left untreated Prescribed psychological help not obtained
Personal hygiene neglect	Standards of personal care and cleanliness are not met	Infrequent bathing Poor dental hygiene Clothing inadequate for weather conditions or size Sleeping arrangements that prohibit a child from obtaining adequate sleep
Nutritional neglect	Failure to provide a diet of quality and nutritional balance	Insufficient calories Meals do not represent the basic food groups Food is stale or spoiled
Neglect of household safety	Safety hazards in or around the house pose a danger	Structural hazards within the home, such as broken stairs or railings, broken windows, holes in floors or ceilings Fire hazards, such as frayed wiring, the presence of combustible materials, objects too close to heat sources and therefore pose a burn threat Chemicals or drugs accessible to children
Neglect of household sanitation	Standards of housekeeping care and cleanliness are not met	Excess accumulation of garbage and trash in home Vermin and insects are uncontrolled Surfaces are covered with dirt and filth Bedding is unclean
Inadequate shelter	A physical shelter and/or stable "home" is not provided or is inadequate	Refusing custody responsibilities of one's child Not allowing a runaway to return home Inability to provide a stable and permanent home (i.e., homelessness) Overcrowded living conditions (e.g., 25 people living in a four-bedroom home) "Throwing" an adolescent out of the home
Abandonment	Physical desertion of one's child, including potentially fatal or nonfatal abandonment	Placing children in dumpsters, parks, and so on Abandoning children while in the care of others (e.g., baby-sitters, hospitals, relatives)
Supervisory neglect	Deficits in parental supervision that can lead to injury	Children are left in the home alone for prolonged periods Children are allowed to roam the streets at night

Table 5.1 Continued

Type	Description	Examples
Educational neglect	Parents do not provide necessary care and supervision to promote education	Children of mandatory age are not enrolled in school
		Frequent and chronic truancy are permitted
		Inattention to special education needs
Emotional neglect	Child's need for emotional support, security, and encouragement are not provided	Caretaker is unavailable emotionally
		Caretaker is indifferent or rejects child
Fostering delinquency	Encouraging the development of illegal behaviors	Rewarding children for stealing

SOURCE: Information for this table was obtained from the following references, which are representative but not exhaustive: U.S. Department of Health and Human Services (1988), Hegar and Yungman (1989), Munkel (1994), Wolock and Horowitz (1984), and Zuravin (1991).

services, such as mental health agencies, public schools, and police departments.

Searching for Patterns: Characteristics of Victims

Agencies that receive official reports of neglect provide information on the sociodemographic characteristics of victims such as age, gender, race, and SES. These official estimates, despite their limitations, provide most of the available information on the characteristics of neglected children.

Age. The average age of neglected children is 6 years (AAPC, 1988). Several sources of estimates for child neglect indicate that the risk for child neglect generally declines with age (AAPC, 1988; DHHS, 1994). The most recent data from the NCCAN, for example, indicate that 51% of reported child neglect victims are under 5 years of age and that 34% of those reports are for children under 1 year of age (DHHS, 1994). Serious injuries and fatalities due to neglect are also more common for younger children (DHHS, 1988). This general pattern, however, varies for different subtypes of neglect. In the NIS-2 (DHHS, 1988), for example, older children were more likely to be victims of educational neglect, which is obviously a reflection of the greater educational needs of older children.

Gender. In regard to gender, few differences have been associated with rates of child neglect (Claussen & Crittenden, 1991; DHHS, 1988, 1994). The NCCAN (DHHS, 1994) found, for example, that 52% of reported

cases were males and 48% were females. Research findings also support an absence of gender findings associated with subtypes of neglect (e.g., DHHS, 1988).

Race. Studies attempting to determine racial differences in rates of child neglect are fraught with methodological difficulties and, as a result, should be interpreted cautiously (Asbury, 1993). According to the most recent official reporting statistics from the AAPC (1988), 63% of child neglect reports involved Caucasian children, 20% involved African American children, and 12% involved Hispanic children. Because census data indicate that 12.4% of the population are African American and less than 3.5% are Hispanic, the risk of neglect appears to be higher for African American and Hispanic children. The significance of this pattern, however, is unclear because race is also associated with SES.

Socioeconomic Status. Although child neglect occurs at all levels of society, rates of neglect are higher in families characterized by very low income, unemployment, and dependence on social assistance (AAPC, 1988; DHHS, 1988). SES, in fact, is a stronger predictor of child neglect than physical abuse (Crittenden, 1988; Zuravin, 1986, 1989). The median income of neglectful families is significantly lower than the national average (American Humane Association [AHA], 1984). In addition, approximately 51% of the children reported for neglect reside in single-female-headed households, and approximately 42% of the primary caretakers are unemployed (AAPC, 1988). These percentages are considerably higher than rates of physical abuse in single-female-headed households and households where the primary caretaker is unemployed (25% and 29%, respectively). Income level has also been associated with severity of neglect, with higher-income families generally associated with less severe forms of neglect (see Claussen & Crittenden, 1991).

Consequences for Victims of Child Neglect

Although there has been considerable research evaluating the negative consequences associated with other forms of child maltreatment, there is relatively little research available that examines the unique effects of child neglect on children's functioning. This state of affairs is somewhat of a paradox given the suggestion that the effect of child neglect can be both significant and long lasting and may be associated with more serious harm than physical or sexual abuse (e.g., Crittenden, 1992; Egeland, Sroufe, & Erickson, 1983; McCord, 1983; Ney et al., 1994).

In addition to the paucity of research on the effects of child neglect, what studies are available are marred by methodological problems (see Crouch & Milner, 1993, for a review). Some of the same difficulties that characterize studies of other child maltreatment groups also plague studies of victims of child neglect. Limited sample sizes, the use of unstandardized measures, definitional variability, and the lack of comparison groups, for example, are also limitations of research on the effects associated with child neglect. An additional problem is that samples are heterogeneous, consisting of victims not only of child neglect but also of other forms of abuse (e.g., Vondra, Barnett, & Cicchetti, 1990).

The limited number and quality of research investigations examining the effects associated with child neglect make the interpretation of findings difficult. When samples are composed of children who are victims of physical child abuse and child neglect, for example, it is impossible to sort out the effects of one form of child maltreatment from the other. An increasing number of sound investigations that focus specifically on child neglect victims, however, is beginning to appear (see Crouch & Milner, 1993, for a review). Collectively, these studies have consistently uncovered several problems associated with child neglect including social difficul-

ties, intellectual deficits, emotional and behavioral problems, and physical consequences. Refer to Table 5.2 for a summary of the negative effects associated with neglected children.

Social Difficulties. One of the most often cited problems associated with neglect is difficulty in social skills and adjustment. As evidence of social difficulties, a number of studies have revealed a relationship between neglect and disturbed patterns of infant-caretaker attachment (e.g., Bousha & Twentyman, 1984; Crittenden, 1992; Egeland & Sroufe, 1981). Egeland and colleagues (Egeland & Sroufe, 1981; Egeland et al., 1983), for example, are conducting a longitudinal study in which 267 women (and their children) are periodically assessed beginning in the last trimester of pregnancy and continuing through the preschool period. Four maltreatment groups of maltreating mothers, including physically abusive, hostile or verbally abusive, psychologically unavailable, and neglecting, as well as a control group of nonmaltreating mothers, participated in a series of situations to assess the developmental consequences of maltreatment. Evaluation during the first 2 years of life focused on the quality of attachment between the mother and child. Investigators observed the mother-infant pairs during several interactions including feeding and play situations, a stressful situation where a stranger was introduced into the environment, and a problem-solving task. Results indicated that a significantly higher proportion of neglected children were anxiously attached (e.g., overly dependent, clingy, prone to crying) at both 12 and 18 months than children in the control group.

Other indications of disturbed parent-child interactions have appeared, demonstrating the deficits in communication, increased aggression, and poor involvement characteristic of the interactions between neglecting mothers and their children (Bousha & Twentyman, 1984; Christopoulos, Bonvillian, & Crittenden, 1988; Crittenden, 1992). Additional research has also revealed other areas of social maladjustment in victims of child neglect such as socially withdrawn behavior and decreased prosocial behavior (Allen & Oliver, 1982; Crittenden, 1992; Prino & Peyrot, 1994).

Intellectual Deficits. An additional area of functioning affected by neglect is intellectual ability. A large group of studies comparing neglected children and adolescents to matched

Table 5.2 Negative Effects Associated With Child Neglect

Social difficulties
    Disturbed parent-child attachment
    Disturbed parent-child interactions
       Child is passive, shows deficits in prosocial behaviors and communication, and displays physical aggression
       Parent exhibits less sensitivity, appears more withdrawn and uninvolved, uses less general speech and phrases
          of acceptance, uses more direct imperatives, has or displays low rates of social interaction and verbal
          instruction
    Disturbed peer interactions such as deficits in prosocial behavior, social withdrawal, and isolation

Intellectual deficits
    Receptive and expressive language deficits
    Academic problems
    Intellectual delays
    Lower levels of overall intelligence
    Less creative and flexible in problem solving
    Deficits in language comprehension and verbal abilities

Emotional and behavioral problems
    Apathy and withdrawal
    Low self-esteem
    Ineffective coping
    Physical and verbal aggression
    General behavior problems
    Negative affect (e.g., anger, frustration)
    Conduct disorder
    Psychiatric symptoms

Physical consequences
    Death
    Failure to thrive

SOURCE: Information for this table was obtained from the following references, which are representative but not exhaustive: Bousha and Twentyman (1984); Christopoulos, Bonvillian, and Crittenden (1988); Crittenden (1992); de Paul and Arruabarrena (1995); Egeland and Sroufe (1981); Egeland, Sroufe, and Erickson (1983); Prino and Peyrot (1994); Williamson, Bordui, and Howe (1991); and Wodarski, Kurtz, Gaudin, and Howing (1990).

comparison groups have indicated that neglect victims show deficits in language abilities, academic skills, intelligence, and problem-solving skills (e.g., Egeland et al., 1983; Hoffman-Plotkin & Twentyman, 1984; Wodarski, Kurtz, Gaudin, & Howing, 1990). Wodarski and colleagues (1990), for example, evaluated 139 school-age and adolescent physically abused, neglected, and nonmaltreated children and found that neglected children evidenced significantly more academic problems, including overall school performance and tests of language, reading, and math skills, than the control group of nonmaltreated children.

Emotional and Behavioral Problems. Emotional and behavioral difficulties are an additional area of maladjustment frequently found in neglect victims. Studies have demonstrated that neglectful mothers rate their children as having more behavior problems in general compared to nonmaltreating mothers (Rohr-

beck & Twentyman, 1986; Williamson, Borduin, & Howe, 1991). Researchers have also documented differences in specific behavioral and emotional problems in neglected preschool and school-age children compared to controls (e.g., Bousha & Twentyman, 1984; de Paul & Arruabarrena, 1995; Williamson et al., 1991). Egeland et al. (1983), in summarizing the findings of their longitudinal research on physically and emotionally abused and neglected children, made the following conclusion about the neglect group: "This is an unhappy group of children, presenting the least positive and the most negative affect of all groups . . . and in general did not have the skills necessary to cope with various situations" (p. 469).

In contrast, other researchers have failed to find differences in adjustment between neglected and nonmaltreated children when evaluating other types of behavioral and emotional difficulties (e.g., Rohrbeck & Twentyman, 1986; Wodarski et al., 1990). Specific

FAILURE TO THRIVE

One consequence of child maltreatment is a clinical disorder known as failure to thrive (FTT). The term was initially coined to describe infants and young children hospitalized or living in institutions in the early 1900s. Such children were described as exhibiting marked deficits in growth as well as abnormal behaviors such as withdrawal, apathy, excessive sleep, unhappy facial expressions, and self-stimulatory behaviors including body rocking or head banging (e.g., Bakwin, 1949; Kempe & Goldbloom, 1987; Spitz, 1945). Some cases of FTT are organic in nature, resulting from diseases such as kidney or heart disease. More controversial are FTT cases believed to be nonorganic in nature, resulting from "psychosocial diseases" such as physical neglect and psychological maltreatment.

Although most experts agree that nonorganic FTT results from psychosocial difficulties that reduce caloric intake, the nature of the psychosocial difficulties has been the subject of considerable debate. Some focus on the physical aspects of the syndrome, such as the lack of nutrients, and therefore view FTT as primarily a medical condition due to physical child neglect (e.g., inadequate food and nutrition). The physical aspects of FTT have been operationalized as height and weight gain below the third percentile on standardized growth charts of expected development (e.g., Lacey & Parkin, 1974). FTT has traditionally been viewed as a physical or medical condition because the physical problems associated with the syndrome (e.g., malnutrition) often bring the child to the attention of medical professionals.

Others, however, focus on the psychological aspects of FTT, such as isolation and the lack of stimulation in the child's environment, and therefore view FTT as primarily a psychological condition due to psychological neglect. The psychological aspects of FTT have been operationalized in the *Diagnostic and Statistical Manual of Mental Disorders (DSM-IV;* American Psychiatric Association, 1994), which uses the term *reactive attachment disorder of infancy or early childhood* to describe the behavioral consequences associated with FTT. Reactive attachment disorder is defined as follows:

> The essential feature of Reactive Attachment Disorder is markedly disturbed and developmentally inappropriate social relatedness in most contexts that begins before the age of 5 and is associated with grossly pathological care. The child shows a pattern of excessively inhibited, hypervigilant, or ambivalent responses (e.g., frozen watchfulness, resistance to comfort, or a mixture of approach and avoidance). (p. 116)

Numerous studies have appeared demonstrating a relationship between nonorganic FTT and maternal deprivation or disturbed mother-infant interactions. Studies evaluating differences between nonorganic FTT infants and normally developing infants, for example, have found that the interactions between FTT children and their mothers are characterized by deficits in attachment, sensitivity toward the child, and degree of comfort between mother and child (Ayoub & Milner, 1985; Haynes, Cutler, Gray, O'Keefe, & Kempe, 1983; Hegar & Yungman, 1989). Drotar, Eckerle, Satola, Pallotta, and Wyatt (1990) also found that mothers of nonorganic FTT infants demonstrated less adaptive social interactional behavior, less positive affect, and more arbitrary terminations of feedings. Kempe and Goldbloom (1987) have described additional characteristics of FTT parent-child dyads. In feeding situations, for example, mothers may ignore the child's hunger and instead initiate play. In addition, mothers may misinterpret the child's refusal of food as defiance rather than as a sign of satiation. During play situations, mothers may be socially withdrawn (e.g., failing to look at or smile at the child) or refuse to interact with the child (e.g., placing the child in his or her crib).

Theoretical and research advances in the field have broadened conceptual understanding of nonorganic FTT. Kempe and Goldbloom (1987), for example, have argued that the term *nonorganic FTT* should be dropped and replaced with *malnutrition due to neglect* to direct professionals to "more precise descriptions of deficits in nutrition and growth, weight and height levels, and the individual developmental and behavioral characteristics of a given child" (p. 312). Others have likewise argued the importance of a diversity of interacting factors in nonorganic FTT including environmental variables related to feeding and nurturance in addition to organic factors (Ayoub & Milner, 1985; Hathaway, 1989; Lachenmeyer & Davidovicz, 1987). In addition, although most studies investigating FTT have focused on mothers as parents, additional research suggests that fathers also play a significant role and that parental deprivation characterizes the family dynamics of nonorganic FTT (Gagan, Cupoli, & Watkins, 1984). A broader conceptual perspective should focus treatment efforts not only on enhancing a child's nutritional status and improving the parent-child relationship but on additional environmental variables as well.

behaviors and areas of adjustment such as levels of hyperactivity, distractibility, and impulsivity; observed as well as fantasy aggression; and levels of depression do not distinguish neglected from nonmaltreated children (Egeland et al., 1983; Kaufman, 1991; Reidy, 1977; Rohrbeck & Twentyman, 1986). In addition, Wodarski and colleagues (1990) found few differences in adaptive behavior between neglected and nonmaltreated children, suggesting that neglected children demonstrate competence in the area of life skills.

Physical Consequences. A final consequence associated with child neglect includes physical effects. The most serious physical conse-

quence of child neglect, of course, is death. In 1994, an estimated 1,271 children died from child abuse and neglect. Of these, approximately 45% died from child neglect (Weise & Daro, 1995). An additional physical consequence often associated with neglect is failure to thrive (FTT). FTT is a syndrome characterized by marked retardation or cessation of growth during the first 3 years of life (Kempe, Culter, & Dean, 1980). Because FTT also includes nonphysical components, its designation as a consequence of physical neglect versus psychological maltreatment is controversial (see boxed insert: "Failure to Thrive").

Intermediate Chapter Summary

Although child neglect is not a new form of child maltreatment, traditionally it has not received as much attention, socially or empirically, as sexual and physical child abuse. Reasons for this disinterest might be because **neglect issues "seem less deviant"** than PCA or CSA and because of **reluctance by professionals to judge or blame** parents (especially in cases of poverty).

Current research efforts concentrate on defining the problem, both conceptually and operationally. Most experts agree that, conceptually, child neglect refers to deficits in the provision of a child's **basic needs** (e.g., health care, nutrition, supervision). Many experts have formulated a number of typologies of neglect in an effort to operationalize precisely what is meant by basic needs. Current typologies include physical, educational, developmental, and emotional neglect. Researchers have also emphasized the need to incorporate several characteristics of neglect into current definitions, such as the severity, frequency and duration, and community and cultural (e.g., socioeconomic) aspects of the neglecting situation. Despite considerable efforts, little consensus exists regarding the best definition for child neglect.

The true incidence of child neglect is not known because of the many **inherent methodological problems** in trying to study rates of child maltreatment (e.g., reporting biases, definitional variability, failure to differentiate among subtypes of neglect). Despite these difficulties, it is clear that hundreds of thousands of children are reported for child neglect each year—so many children, in fact, that child neglect is the most frequently reported form of child maltreatment, accounting for 45% to 55% of reported maltreatment cases.

Official estimates of child neglect, despite their limitations, provide most of the available information on the subject. Research has demonstrated that the majority of children reported for neglect are under the age of 5 and that the risk for child neglect and severity of neglect generally decreases with age. The importance of gender differences is not now supported by the research nor is there a clear pattern of the role of racial differences because of the existence of confounding factors such as SES and methodological difficulties. The strongest predictor of child neglect is, in fact, **economic disadvantage,** because low-income children, unemployed parents, and children residing in a single-female-headed household are at greatest risk.

Relative to other forms of maltreatment, less research has examined the unique effects of child neglect on children's functioning, although an increasing number of methodologically sound investigations are appearing. Available research to date suggests that child neglect is associated with a variety of problems including **social difficulties** (e.g., disturbed parent-child interactions, socially withdrawn behavior), **intellectual deficits** (e.g., in language abilities, problem-solving skills, academic skills), **behavioral and emotional problems** (e.g., low self-esteem, aggression), and **physical dysfunction** (e.g., failure to thrive, or FTT). Specifically, studies have shown that very young children are adversely affected by maltreating mothers who are physically abusive, hostile or verbally abusive, or psychologically unavailable. Future studies should attend to additional variables potentially associated with child neglect outcome, such as the victim's age and gender, the severity of neglect, and various subtypes of neglect (Crouch & Milner, 1993). Research is also needed to evaluate the potential long-term effects of child neglect.

Psychological Maltreatment

John, get your fat ass over here right now.

Pilar, if you do that again, I am going to knock your f——g head right off your shoulders.

Amy, you are the most stupid, lazy kid on earth. I can't believe you're my child. They must have switched babies on me at the hospital.

Most individuals have witnessed interactions between a parent and a child that seem inappropriate. John, Pilar, and Amy may not be physically or sexually abused. They may not be neglected. Despite the lack of overt physical aggression, sexual behavior, or physical signs of maltreatment, however, most peo-

---

Psychological maltreatment may be the "most ambiguous form of maltreatment."

---

ple would probably view this behavior as wrong or, at the very least, less than optimal. Examples like these have led researchers into a discussion of an additional form of child maltreatment: psychological maltreatment.

Several authors are now suggesting that psychological maltreatment may be the most destructive and pervasive form of maltreatment (Brassard, Germain, & Hart, 1987b; Garbarino, Guttman, & Seely, 1986). Imagine the potential consequences to children who grow up hearing that they are worthless or stupid or ugly. The social psychologist W. I. Thomas once said: "When men define situations as real, they are real in their consequences." In other words, a child who is told that he or she is worthless, stupid, or ugly will begin to believe it. Perhaps even more tragic, the child may *act* worthless, stupid, or ugly.

Historically, professionals have tended to marginalize psychological maltreatment in much the same way as they marginalized neglect. They viewed psychological maltreatment as a side effect of other forms of abuse and neglect, rather than as a unique form of child maltreatment. Some reasons why psychological maltreatment may often be overlooked were recently articulated by O'Hagan (1993), who stated that psychological maltreatment is "slow and protracted, will create no stir, pose no threat of scandal nor media scrutiny, and has little political significance for the managers of child care bureaucracies" (p. 15).

Within the past decade, however, psychological maltreatment has been increasingly recognized as worthy of scientific study as a form of child maltreatment existing in its own discrete form (see Hart & Brassard, 1993; Loring, 1994; Wiehe, 1990). Community surveys also indicate that the public is concerned about this type of maltreatment. The NCPCA, for example, conducted a nationally representative public opinion poll between 1987 and 1992 and found that approximately 75% of adults who were surveyed over this 6-year period viewed "repeated yelling and swearing" at children as harmful to their well-being (Daro & Gelles, 1992).

Scope of the Problem

WHAT IS PSYCHOLOGICAL MALTREATMENT?

Psychological maltreatment may be the "most ambiguous form of maltreatment" (Daro, 1988). Nearly all parents, at some level, psychologically mistreat their children at some time. Most parents, for instance, say and do hurtful things they wish they had not. Such mistakes are a characteristic of most intimate relationships. Few would assert, however, that most children are victims of psychological maltreatment. How, then, does one determine when psychological maltreatment has occurred? Which verbal interactions are abusive, which behaviors are psychologically ne-

Table 5.3 Conceptual Perspectives on Psychological Maltreatment

	Parent Behaviors	
	Physical	*Nonphysical*
Consequences to the child		
Physical	Physical abuse	Psychological maltreatment
Nonphysical	Psychological maltreatment	Psychological maltreatment

SOURCE: Modified from "Psychological Maltreatment: Toward an Operational Definition," by R. A. McGee and D. A. Wolfe, 1991, *Development and Psychology, 3.* Copyright 1991 by Cambridge University Press. Reprinted with the permission of Cambridge University Press.

glecting, and which interactions are a necessary part of parenting?

Conceptual Issues. Professionals have proposed many conceptual definitions for psychological maltreatment to guide research, clinical practice, and social policy. Indeed, the disagreement over how to define psychological maltreatment, in part, stems from the variety of purposes for using definitions (e.g., to make legal decisions, for conducting interventions with victims, to determine incidence figures). As a result, there is much debate and confusion in the literature regarding what exactly constitutes psychological maltreatment.

Some researchers offer very broad definitions and argue that psychological maltreatment is pervasive. Authors, for example, have suggested that psychological maltreatment is embedded in all major forms of child abuse and neglect (Garbarino et al., 1986; Hart, Germain, & Brassard, 1987). Others have suggested even broader definitions to include ecological factors such as racism, sexism, and war zone environments (Hart et al., 1987; Jones & Jones, 1987). Such broad definitions are clearly problematic because, in the worst case, everyone is a victim of psychological maltreatment and, at best, such definitions fail to distinguish psychological maltreatment as a unique form of child maltreatment. Other authors define psychological maltreatment more narrowly, focusing on specific abusive behaviors on the part of adults (e.g., repeatedly swearing at a child), which naturally leads to the identification of less abuse in society (e.g., AHA, 1981).

At the core of conceptual problems in defining psychological maltreatment is a lack of clarity in what is meant by the term *psychological*. There has been a great deal of confusion in the literature regarding whether this word refers to behavior on the part of perpetrators or to the consequences that result for

the child victim. McGee and Wolfe (1991) proposed a matrix to explain the multiple conceptual perspectives emphasized by experts about psychological maltreatment. Table 5.3 displays a modified version of the matrix, which displays various combinations and possibilities depending on the type of parent behavior and the consequences to the child.

Using this matrix, parent behaviors can be physical or nonphysical and can result in either physical or nonphysical (e.g., psychological) consequences to the child. When parent behaviors are physical and result in physical consequences (e.g., touching a child with a cigarette that results in a burn), such a scenario illustrates a commonly accepted conceptualization of physical child abuse (McGee & Wolfe, 1991). According to McGee and Wolfe (1991), researchers have defined psychological maltreatment using the remaining combinations of parenting behaviors and psychological outcomes. When a parent engages in physical behavior (e.g., touching a child with a cigarette) that results in physical as well as nonphysical outcomes (e.g., anxiety and fear), some have included this situation as psychological maltreatment (e.g., Garbarino et al., 1986). Based on this model, additional physical behaviors carried out by parents, such as sexual abuse or physical neglect that results in negative psychological outcomes, would also be considered psychological maltreatment.

In contrast, some parental behaviors can be nonphysical in nature and result in either physical or nonphysical harm to the child. Insensitive parenting (e.g., not responding to a child's needs for nurturance and attention), for example, has been linked to both physical (e.g., malnutrition; Lacey & Parkin, 1974) and nonphysical (e.g., cognitive development; Egeland et al., 1983) outcomes. The combination of nonphysical parental behavior (e.g., swearing at a child) and nonphysical outcomes (e.g., decreased self-esteem) reflects the conceptualization of psychological maltreatment as a distinct or "pure" form of child maltreatment (Garbarino et al., 1986; McGee & Wolfe, 1991).

McGee and Wolfe (1991) argue that psychological maltreatment should be defined primarily based on specific parental behaviors rather than on the effects these behaviors may produce. Others have supported this approach but emphasize the need to consider secondarily the effect of maltreatment (Hart & Brassard, 1991). It might be difficult to define psychological maltreatment, for example, in the absence of its effects on the child victim given that parental behaviors lie on a continuum. Although not all parental behaviors consisting of criticism are abusive, for instance, some may be. One way to distinguish between abusive and nonabusive behaviors might be to consider the behavior's negative effect on development. Effects on child functioning, however, need to be determined by research, as do additional variables such as the specific characteristics of neglecting behaviors (e.g., frequency, intensity, duration) (Hart & Brassard, 1991; McGee & Wolfe, 1991).

Subtypes of Psychological Maltreatment. In an effort to define specific parental behaviors more precisely, several authors have developed organizational frameworks that identify various subtypes of psychological maltreatment (e.g., Baily & Baily, 1986; Garbarino et al., 1986; Hart & Brassard, 1991; O'Hagan, 1995). Table 5.4 summarizes the various subtypes of psychological maltreatment reported in the literature. Eight forms of psychological maltreatment have been consistently identified: (a) rejecting, (b) degrading (i.e., verbal abuse), (c) terrorizing, (d) isolating, (e) missocializing (i.e., corrupting), (f) exploiting, (g) denying emotional responsiveness (i.e., ignoring), and (h) close confinement.

An example of an organizational framework is the typological system provided in NIS-2 (DHHS, 1988), which distinguished between forms of psychological abuse and psychological neglect. Psychological abuse included a variety of behaviors such as close confinement and verbal or emotional assault, as well as miscellaneous behaviors. Close confinement referred to "torturous" restriction of movement such as tying a child's limbs together or tying a child to an object, such as furniture. Verbal or emotional assault included

such behaviors as belittling, denigrating, threatening harm, and other forms of hostile or rejecting treatment. Other miscellaneous behaviors included extreme forms of punishment (e.g., withholding food or sleep) and economic exploitation (e.g., prostitution).

Psychological neglect in NIS-2 included both educational neglect and emotional neglect. Educational neglect consisted of permitted chronic truancy, failure to enroll a child of mandatory school age, and inattention to a child's special education needs (e.g., failure to obtain recommended remedial educational services or treatment for a diagnosed learning disorder). Emotional neglect included a variety of behaviors ranging from inadequate nurturance and affection to permitted drug and/or alcohol abuse. In addition, emotional neglect was also defined as witnessing extreme or chronic domestic violence, permitting maladaptive behavior (e.g., chronic delinquency), and refusal or delay in obtaining needed psychological treatment.

The typologies in Table 5.4 illustrate the subjective nature of definitions of psychological maltreatment. Definitions and typological systems represent a compilation of the various behaviors and circumstances that have been identified by researchers in the field. As such, these conceptualizations reflect the values of those who created them, with various advocates and researchers determining the kinds of parent-child interactions that "should be" considered inappropriate. For example, "refusing to help a child" may be abusive in the eyes of a particular researcher but may be seen as important in helping a child gain independence from a parent's perspective.

McGee and Wolfe (1991) recently outlined several other criticisms of current typological systems. Psychological maltreatment subtypes, they argue, are not inclusive of all potentially psychologically abusive and neglectful behavior. Inconsistent parenting practices, for example, have not been included in typologies of psychological maltreatment despite their detrimental effects on a child's development (McGee & Wolfe, 1991). Another problem with classification systems is that the subtypes are not mutually exclusive: One behavior can be considered under more than one subtype. Insulting a child by shouting, "You're nothing but a fat, lazy pig!" for example, could be considered not only as an act of degrading but also as an act of rejecting. A final criticism levied against typologi-

Table 5.4 Subtypes of Psychological Maltreatment

Type	Description	Examples
Rejecting	Verbal or symbolic acts that express feelings of rejection toward the child	Singling out a specific child for criticism and/or punishment Refusing to help a child Routinely rejecting a child's ideas
Degrading (i.e., verbal abuse)	Actions that deprecate a child	Insulting a child (calling a child names) Publicly humiliating a child Constantly criticizing a child Continually yelling or swearing at a child
Terrorizing	Actions or threats that cause extreme fear and/or anxiety in a child	Threatening to harm a child Threatening to harm a loved one Setting unrealistic expectations with threat of loss and harm Punishing child by playing on normal childhood fears Threatening suicide or to leave child
Isolating	Preventing the child from engaging in normal social activities	Locking a child in a closet or room Refusing interactions with individuals outside of family Refusing interactions with other relatives
Missocializing (i.e., corrupting)	Modeling, permitting, or encouraging antisocial behavior	Encouraging criminal or delinquent behavior Encouraging alcohol or substance abuse Indoctrinating racist values
Exploiting	Using a child for the needs, advantages, or profits of the caretaker	Treating a child as a surrogate parent Using a child for child pornography or prostitution Using a child to live the parent's unfulfilled dreams
Denying emotional responsiveness (i.e., ignoring)	Acts of omission whereby caretaker does not provide necessary stimulation and responsiveness	Caretaker is detached and uninvolved with child Caretaker interacts with child only if absolutely necessary Failing to express affection, caring, and love toward child Does not look at child or call by name
Close confinement	Restricting a child's movement by binding limbs	Tying a child's arms and legs together Tying a child to a chair, bed, or other object
Other	Types of emotional maltreatment not specified under other categories	Withholding food, shelter, sleep, or other necessities as a form of punishment Chronically applying developmentally inappropriate expectations (sometimes referred to as overpressuring)

SOURCE: Information for this table was obtained from the following references, which are representative but not exhaustive: Baily and Baily (1986); U.S. Department of Health and Human Services (1988); Garbarino, Guttman, and Seely (1986); Hart and Brassard (1991); and Hart, Germain, and Brassard (1987).

cal systems is that these subtypes are sometimes defined in terms of their outcomes. *Corrupting,* for example, is defined as stimulating the child to engage in destructive and antisocial behavior.

Research is beginning to appear that addresses some of the problems associated with typological systems. Hart and Brassard (1991), for example, have described five distinct subtypes of psychological maltreatment that have been empirically validated: spurning (verbal statements of rejection and hostile degradation), terrorizing, isolating, exploiting or corrupting, and denying emotional responsiveness. Other research has demonstrated empirical distinctions between broader subtypes of maltreatment (e.g., psychological abuse vs. psychological neglect; Brassard, Hart, & Hardy, 1993; Crittenden, 1990). In addition, some research has failed to confirm specific subtypes as distinct categories of psychological maltreatment. Hart and Brassard (1991), for example, reported that rejection is a component of both spurning and denying emotional responsiveness rather than a unique form of psychological maltreatment.

Legal Issues. State reporting statutes do not always specifically cover psychological maltreatment, although most state statutes include some reference to the concept (Hart et al., 1987). Public Law 93-247 refers to psychological maltreatment as "mental injury" and delegates the responsibility of more specific definitions to each individual state.

Most state definitions emphasize harm to the child rather than focusing on parental actions. Pennsylvania, for example, provides a very specific and narrow definition for its category of "serious mental injury": "a psychological condition . . . caused by acts of omission . . . which render the child chronically sick and severely anxious, agitated, depressed, socially withdrawn, psychotic, or in fear that his/her life is threatened" (quoted in Garbarino et al., 1986). The state of Oregon added mental injury, more broadly defined, to its child abuse reporting law in 1985. This law states that any mental injury to a child shall include only observable and substantial impairment of the child's mental or psychological ability to function caused by cruelty to the child, with due regard to the culture of the child (ORS 418.740).

These legal statutes further illustrate the problems associated with defining psychological maltreatment, because the law generally requires that a given act result in identifiable harm. "It will not suffice for a reporter to imagine a child might possibly be injured later by a particular course of parental behavior" (State of Oregon Children's Services Division, 1991, p. 4). The effects of psychological maltreatment, however, may only rarely be identifiable, or they may be identifiable only after years of maltreatment.

ESTIMATES OF PSYCHOLOGICAL MALTREATMENT

As is true of child neglect, the actual rate of psychological maltreatment is unknown because of difficulties associated with definitional and methodological issues. Lack of nationally standardized and operational definitions has been central to measurement difficulties. Despite these problems, however, several studies have investigated the scope of the problem.

Official Estimates. Studies attempting to determine the official rates of psychological maltreatment through national reporting statistics have consistently demonstrated that psychological maltreatment is the least common form of reported and substantiated maltreatment. Estimates vary, however, and are influenced by definitional and methodological variability across studies. These rates suggest that psychological maltreatment accounts for anywhere from 3% to 28% of all officially reported cases of child maltreatment. The AAPC (1988), for example, found that psychological maltreatment (defined as *emotional maltreatment*) accounted for approximately 8% of all official reports of child maltreatment in 1986. Data from the NCCAN indicated that psychological maltreatment accounted for 5% of reported child maltreatment cases (DHHS, 1994). The most recent statistics available indicate that 3% of reported cases consist of psychological maltreatment as the primary (e.g., distinct from physical abuse, child neglect, etc.) form of abuse (Weise & Daro, 1995).

The National Incidence Studies (DHHS, 1981, 1988) have obtained the highest rates for psychological maltreatment. In NIS-2, the 391,100 reported cases of psychological maltreatment (including psychological abuse and emotional neglect) accounted for 28% of all cases of child maltreatment (Sedlak, 1990). National Incidence Study data indicate that between 1980 and 1986, the rate of psychological abuse increased by 43%, and the rate of emotional neglect more than doubled. As is true for child neglect reports, rates of psychological maltreatment are higher when definitions are broadened to include potential harm.

As with other forms of child maltreatment, many professionals believe that psychological maltreatment is underreported. Although psychological maltreatment is the most uncommon form of child maltreatment reported to protective service agencies, it is the most commonly reported form of child maltreatment among families involved in therapeutic treatment programs for child abuse and neglect (Daro, 1988). One reason that psychological maltreatment may be underreported is because its effects are rarely visible or immediate. In addition, recognition that psychological maltreatment is a reportable form of child maltreatment is relatively recent. As a result, many individuals in a position to report it may fail to do so because they do not realize that specific parental behaviors constitute psychological maltreatment. Another reason to suspect underreporting is due to evidence suggesting that psychological maltreatment often co-occurs with other forms of abuse (Claussen & Crittenden, 1991). The fact that psychological maltreatment is the least reported form may actually reflect the fact that it is not usually the primary form of abuse experienced by a particular child.

Self-Report Surveys. Daro and Gelles (1992) reported on the parenting practices of a nationally representative sample of 1,250 parents surveyed each year between 1988 and 1992. Although rates fluctuated over the 6-year period of data collection, 45% of parents reported insulting or swearing at their children in 1992 (Daro & Gelles, 1992).

Analysis of data from the second National Family Violence Survey provides additional information on self-report estimates of psychological maltreatment (Vissing, Straus, Gelles, & Harrop, 1991). Psychological maltreatment included both verbal (e.g., insulting or swearing) and nonverbal (e.g., sulking or refusing to talk) forms of interaction with a child. Results indicated that approximately 63% of parents reported using one of these forms of interaction with their children at least once over the past year. These authors also attempted to determine the frequency of these types of interactions and found that the average number of instances was 12.6 per year, with approximately 21% reporting more than 20 instances.

Searching for Patterns: Characteristics of Victims

Most of the available information about sociodemographic characteristics of psychological maltreatment victims comes from official reports made to child protective services agencies. However, because only a small percentage of psychological maltreatment cases are reported, knowledge about sociodemographic characteristics of psychological maltreatment victims is tentative at best.

Age and Gender. Findings from the second National Incidence Study, with its broad definition of psychological maltreatment, found no association between psychological maltreatment and age (DHHS, 1988). The average age of reported psychologically maltreated children is 8 to 8 ½ years (AAPC, 1988; Daro, 1988). Official estimates also indicate few gender differences associated with rates of psychological maltreatment (DHHS, 1988, 1994) as do some clinical reports (e.g., Claussen & Crittenden, 1991). The NCCAN (DHHS, 1994) found, for example, that 47% of reported cases were males and 53% were females. When gender and age are considered together, however, studies have found age and gender effects. Female adolescents, for example, appear to be at greater risk for psychological maltreatment than their male counterparts (DHHS, 1994).

Other Risk Factors. Researchers have also demonstrated a link between psychological maltreatment and other risk factors, such as the child's race or ethnicity and his or her family's income (AAPC, 1988; Jones & McCurdy, 1992). Contrasted with other forms of abuse, for example, Caucasian children are more likely than African American or Hispanic children to be victims of psychological maltreatment. Caucasians account for 77% of psychological maltreatment cases and 67% of other forms of abuse (AAPC, 1988). In terms of family income level, the AAPC (1988) indicated that 34% of psychological maltreatment reports include families headed by a single female, and in 33% of reported cases the primary caretaker is unemployed. The NIS-2 also found an association between economic factors and psychological maltreatment. Lower-income families (i.e., yearly income less than $15,000) were more than 5 times as likely to be characterized by psychological maltreatment (defined as *emotional abuse*) than higher-income families (DHHS, 1988).

Consequences for Victims of Psychological Maltreatment

Both researchers and clinical practitioners have speculated about the potential short-

Table 5.5 Negative Effects Associated With Psychological Maltreatment

---

Interpersonal maladjustment
  Insecure attachment to caregiver
  Low social competence and adjustment
  Few friends
  Difficulties with peers

Intellectual deficits
  Academic problems
  Lower educational achievement
  Deficits in cognitive ability
  Deficits in problem solving
  Lack of creativity

Affective-behavioral problems
  Aggression
  Disruptive classroom behavior
  Self-abusive behavior
  Anxiety
  Hostility and anger
  Pessimism and negativity
  Dependent on adults for help, support, and nurturance

SOURCE: Information for this table was obtained from the following references, which are representative but not exhaustive: Brassard, Hart, and Hardy (1991); Claussen and Crittenden (1991); Crittenden and Ainsworth (1989); Egeland (1991); Erickson and Egeland (1987); Erickson, Egeland, and Pianta (1989); and Vissing, Straus, Gelles, and Harrop (1991).

and long-term consequences of psychological maltreatment, such as antisocial behaviors, depression, withdrawal, and low self-esteem (e.g., Gross & Keller, 1992). Descriptive clinical and case study research appears to confirm many of these difficulties, although methodologically sound research in this area is lacking (Cabrino, 1978; Kavanagh, 1982).

Many of the same methodological problems encountered in studying the effects of other forms of child maltreatment (e.g., lack of standardized definitions) also plague the research investigating the negative effects of psychological maltreatment. The use of samples of individuals experiencing multiple forms of abuse has also contributed to confusion in interpreting results. Despite these problems, however, some progress has been made in assessing the negative initial and long-term effects associated with psychological maltreatment.

Initial Effects. The short-term effects associated with psychological maltreatment receiving consistent empirical support are listed in Table 5.5 and include interpersonal maladjustment, intellectual deficits, and affective-behavioral problems.

In the interpersonal realm, researchers have documented maladjustment in psychologically maltreated children in the areas of attachment, social adjustment, and peer relationships. Psychologically maltreated children, for example, are significantly more likely than their nonmaltreated peers to be insecurely attached to a parent (e.g., Crittenden & Ainsworth, 1989; Egeland, 1991). Several investigators have also found that psychologically maltreated children exhibit lower levels of social competence and adjustment (e.g., have trouble making friends) relative to their nonmaltreated counterparts (e.g., Brassard, Hart, & Hardy, 1991; Claussen & Crittenden, 1991; Vissing et al., 1991).

Intellectual deficits also distinguish psychologically maltreated children from controls (e.g., Erickson & Egeland, 1987; Erickson, Egeland, & Pianta, 1989; Hart & Brassard, 1989). In a longitudinal study of educational achievement, for example, researchers found lower achievement in psychologically maltreated children compared to matched controls (Erickson & Egeland, 1987). Other studies have uncovered academic problems and deficits in cognitive ability and problem solving (e.g., Erickson & Egeland, 1987; Erickson et al., 1989).

A final effect of psychological maltreatment includes a variety of affective and behavioral problems. Several studies, for example, have substantiated that psychologically maltreated children exhibit significantly more general behavior problems relative to control children (e.g., Hart & Brassard, 1989; Hickox & Furnell, 1989; Vissing et al., 1991). Psychologically maltreated children also demonstrate more specific problems such as aggression, delinquency, disruptive classroom behavior, self-abusive behavior, hostility and anger, and anxiety when compared to control children (e.g., Egeland & Erickson, 1987; Vissing et al., 1991).

Long-Term Effects. A very limited number of studies have evaluated the potential long-term effects of psychological maltreatment. The available information, however, indicates that adults who report a childhood history of psychological maltreatment exhibit psychological difficulties (e.g., Briere & Runtz, 1988, 1990). Gross and Keller (1992), for example, evaluated 260 university students identified as physically abused, psychologically abused,

both physically and psychologically abused, or nonabused. On standardized instruments, psychologically abused respondents had lower self-esteem scores than nonabused respondents but did not differ significantly on measures of depression and attributional style. Respondents experiencing both physical and psychological abuse, however, exhibited higher levels of depression than nonabused college students or college students with a history of only one type of abuse. Regression analysis also revealed that psychological abuse was a more powerful predictor of depression, self-esteem, and attributional style (attributing outcomes for events to external, unstable, or specific causes) than was physical abuse. Other studies have confirmed the presence of low self-esteem, anxiety, depression, dissociation, and interpersonal sensitivity in adults with a history of psychological maltreatment (e.g., Briere & Runtz, 1988, 1990).

Intermediate Chapter Summary

Authors have described psychological maltreatment as the most difficult form of child maltreatment to define. Disagreement originates in determining what is meant by the term *psychological.* Some experts emphasize **nonphysical behaviors on the part of adults,** such as failing to respond to a child's needs for nurturance and attention, terrorizing a child, or insulting or swearing at a child. Others focus on the **nonphysical consequences to the child victim** (e.g., "mental injury"), including a variety of emotional and cognitive symptoms such as anxiety and fear. Still other experts define psychological maltreatment broadly, including a combination of physical (e.g., physical neglect or sexual abuse) and nonphysical parental actions that result in negative psychological consequences. Although researchers have devised **numerous subtypes** of psychological maltreatment, significant variability in definitions continues to exist in the field, with little consensus regarding the most appropriate definition.

The **true rate** of psychological maltreatment is difficult to determine and largely unknown. Official estimates derived from reporting agencies indicate that between 3% and 28% of reported cases of child maltreatment are for psychological maltreatment, distinguishing psychological maltreatment as the least reported form of child maltreatment. There is some evidence, however, to suggest that psychological maltreatment is **underreported.** Self-report surveys also suggest that parents frequently engage in negative behaviors consistent with psychological maltreatment. Researchers have used official reports to study risk factors, with early findings showing no age correlation to psychological maltreatment and few gender differences, yet a significant race, ethnicity, and family income link. The frequency, intensity, duration, and context of maltreating and neglecting behaviors need additional study.

Results from studies evaluating the negative effect of psychological maltreatment should be considered tentative at best. This is an emerging research area, and many of the same methodological problems already discussed (e.g., lack of standardized definitions) apply here also. To date, studies have indicated that psychological maltreatment may result in a variety of problems for the victim that may extend into adulthood.

Negative effects associated with psychological maltreatment in children include difficulties in interpersonal, intellectual, and affective and behavioral realms of functioning. For example, these children demonstrate more problems (e.g., aggression, delinquency, self-abuse, anxiety, hostility, and anger) when compared to control children. Researchers have found similar problems in adults who report a childhood history of psychological maltreatment (e.g., low self-esteem, depression, interpersonal sensitivity). Future research should attempt to examine the effect of development on the consequences of psychological maltreatment, the effects of psychological maltreatment alone or in combination with other forms of maltreatment, and the distinctive effects associated with various subtypes of psychological maltreatment.

Explaining Child Neglect and Psychological Maltreatment

Experts have applied many of the same theories proposed to explain the physical and sexual abuse of children in their attempts to specify the causes of child neglect and psychological maltreatment. Researchers, for example, have applied ecological and transactional models (e.g., Belsky, 1980; Hickox & Furnell, 1989; Zigler & Hall, 1989; Zuravin, 1989) and social learning and intergenerational transmission theories (e.g., Crittenden, 1982; Hickox & Furnell, 1989; Ney, 1989) to child neglect and psychological maltreatment. Causal models have also incorporated characteristics of neglecting and psychologically maltreating parents, as well as parent-

---

Females are significantly more likely than males to be reported for neglect.

---

child relationships (e.g., Carlson, Barnett, Cicchetti, & Braumwald, 1989; Kneisl, 1991; Pearl, 1994). Because the fields of child neglect and psychological maltreatment are in the beginning stages of research inquiry, limited empirical evidence is available to support specific factors or causal models involved in producing neglectful or psychologically maltreating circumstances. To date, most research in this area has focused on parental characteristics of child neglecting and psychologically maltreating families.

Characteristics of Neglecting Parents

Studies evaluating the characteristics of neglecting parents have examined demographic as well as psychosocial characteristics. With regard to demographic characteristics, the majority of information has been obtained from official reporting statistics. The AAPC (1988), for example, found that parents are the primary perpetrators of child neglect, accounting for 92% of reported cases. The average age of neglecting parents is 31 years, and the gender distribution indicates that females (70%) are significantly more likely than males (30%) to be reported for neglect. The higher proportion of females reported for neglect may reflect social attitudes that mothers, rather than fathers, are responsible for meeting the needs of children.

Other researchers have examined the psychosocial characteristics of neglecting parents. Most research in this area has attempted to distinguish characteristics of neglectful parents compared to physically abusive parents and nonmaltreating parents. Several studies, for example, have evaluated social factors such as the mother's age, the number of children in the family, and educational achievement (e.g., Lujan, DeBruyn, May, & Bird, 1989; Zuravin, 1988b; Zuravin & DiBlasio, 1992). Studies conducted by Zuravin and her colleagues (e.g., Zuravin, 1988b; Zuravin & DiBlasio, 1992) have consistently found that lower educational achievement is associated with neglect. In addition, mothers who have a greater number of children during their teen years or who are younger at the birth of their first child are at increased risk for neglect. Furthermore, teenage mothers whose first child was premature or low birth weight were more likely to neglect their children than older mothers whose infants were healthier (Zuravin & DiBlasio, 1992).

Other social factors, including the level of community integration and social support, may play a role in child neglect. Polansky, Ammons, and Gaudin (1985), for example, found that compared to a control group, neglecting mothers were less involved in informal helping networks, exhibited less participation in social activities, and described themselves as more "lonely." Polansky, Gaudin, Ammons, and Davis (1985) investigated the level of social support for neglecting families by interviewing 152 neglecting and 154 nonneglecting families receiving Aid to Families With Dependent Children (AFDC). The investigators compared responses of families officially designated as neglecting, a control group of nonneglecting AFDC families, and a group of adults who were the next-door neighbors of the neglecting families. Results indicated that neglectful mothers viewed their neighborhood as less supportive than both controls and their next-door neighbors.

Researchers have also investigated the psychological characteristics of neglecting parents compared to abusive parents and non-abusive/nonneglectful parents. Neglectful parents exhibit poor problem-solving skills, intellectual deficits, and inappropriate developmental expectations for their children (Crittenden, 1988; Hansen, Pallotta, Tishelman, Conaway, & MacMillan, 1989; Twentyman & Plotkin, 1982). Twentyman and Plotkin (1982), for example, found that neglectful parents' expectations of their children are either too high or too low compared to their nonneglectful counterparts. Additional studies comparing neglecting mothers to controls indicate that neglecting mothers report more depressive symptoms and levels of parental stress (Culp, Culp, Soulis, & Letts, 1989; Ethier, Lacharite, & Couture, 1995).

Other studies have investigated the hypothesis that neglecting parents are neglectful because during their childhood they themselves received inadequate parenting. Several studies have reported a childhood history of both neglect and abuse in adults who neglect their children (e.g., Widom, 1989). It is difficult to determine, however, which form of maltreatment is the likely contributor to the current neglecting behavior. Few studies have examined the intergenerational transmission hypothesis with subject groups who have experienced child neglect only. One exception is a recent study conducted by Ethier (1991) in which she compared the childhood histories of physically abusive mothers to neglectful mothers (cited in Ethier, Palacio-Quintin, & Jourdan-Ionescu, 1992). Results indicated that neglectful mothers were more likely to have been victims of neglect, both physical and emotional. Zuravin and DiBlasio (1992) found contradictory findings in their sample of teenage mothers. Neglecting mothers were no more likely to have been poorly attached to their caregivers growing up, physically abused, or neglected than nonneglecting mothers. Instead, neglecting teenage mothers were more likely to have been sexually abused.

Characteristics of Psychologically Maltreating Parents

Research examining the characteristics of psychologically maltreating parents includes demographic and psychological variables but is extremely sparse. As is true for neglecting parents, most of the available demographic information comes from studies evaluating official reporting statistics. The AAPC (1988), for example, found that parents are the primary perpetrators of psychological maltreatment, accounting for 90% of reported cases.

Psychologically maltreating parents exhibit more difficulty coping with stress.

The average age of psychologically maltreating parents was 33 years. The gender distribution of reported cases indicated that females (58%) were slightly more likely to be reported for psychological maltreatment than males (42%). With regard to race, the parents of psychologically maltreated children are more likely to be Caucasian than in other forms of child maltreatment.

A few researchers have also examined the psychological characteristics of psychologically maltreating parents. Such parents exhibit more psychosocial problems, more difficulty coping with stress, more difficulty building relationships, and more social isolation compared to nonabusive parents (Pemberton & Benady, 1973). Researchers found similar characteristics in a study evaluating a group of parents legally established as emotionally abusive (Hickox & Furnell, 1989). Hickox and Furnell (1989), for example, found that emotionally abusive parents were characterized by more problem psychosocial and background factors compared to a matched comparison group of parents identified as needing assistance with child care and management. Emotionally abusive parents had more difficulty building relationships, exhibited poor coping skills, and displayed deficits in child management techniques. In addition, emotionally abusive mothers demonstrated a lack of support networks (both personal and community) as well as greater levels of perceived stress, marital discord, and alcohol and drug use.

Intermediate Chapter Summary

Findings from official statistics that evaluate demographic and psychosocial characteristics of parents in neglecting and emotionally maltreating parents are preliminary and, as a result, should be viewed cautiously. The most consistent findings have been observed in **neglecting mothers,** who are characterized as having low educational achievement, increased levels of stress (e.g., greater numbers of children), inappropriate developmental expectations for their children, and low levels of community involvement and social support. Although fewer studies are available that evaluate psychologically maltreating parents, results suggest that **psychologically maltreating mothers** are more likely to be characterized by a number of problems such as high levels of stress, psychosocial problems, social isolation, and deficits in child management skills. Future studies should attempt to replicate current findings while improving methodology and should also evaluate the characteristics of fathers in neglecting and psychologically maltreating families.

Responding to Child Neglect and Psychological Maltreatment

Researchers and practitioners have proposed few interventions that are unique to child neglect and psychological maltreatment versus other forms of abuse. Indeed, many of the previously described interventions (e.g., child protective services, out-of-home placement, economic assistance, therapeutic day care) also apply to child neglect and psychological maltreatment. The paucity of unique research efforts directed at solutions and interventions is particularly true for the field of psychological maltreatment. Some experts have even questioned whether the addition of specific interventions for psychological maltreatment is feasible given the limited success of the already overwhelmed child protective services system in meeting the needs of other maltreated groups (Claussen & Crittenden, 1991). As a result, research evaluating intervention approaches unique to psychological maltreatment is nearly nonexistent.

Research directed at interventions specifically for neglected children and their families is less limited, although available studies suffer from a variety of methodological limitations, including single-subject research designs, exceedingly small sample sizes (e.g., one participant in Sarber, Halasz, Messmer, Bickett, & Lutzker, 1983), nonstandardized assessment methods, and biased samples (Gaudin, 1993). In addition, most intervention programs directed at neglect include services for parents, with few direct services for children (Cohn & Daro, 1987). The in-

terventions for children that are available primarily focus on improving social interaction and skills (e.g., Davis & Fantuzzo, 1989; Fantuzzo, Stovall, Schachtel, Goins, & Hall, 1987). There appears to be general consensus among researchers and clinicians in the field that currently available interventions for addressing child neglect are ineffective (Daro, 1988; Gaudin, 1993).

One form of intervention that has shown promise with neglecting families are the parent-directed approaches that take advantage of behavioral techniques to teach neglecting parents specific skills. Lutzker, Lutzker, Braunling-McMorrow, and Eddleman (1987), for example, investigated the use of simple prompts to increase the appropriate affective responses by mothers during parent-child interactions. Mothers who received prompts to increase affective responses demonstrated more affective responses with their children than mothers who received no prompting. Other studies have demonstrated skills improvements in neglecting mothers, including problem-solving skills (Dawson, DeArmas, McGrath, & Kelly, 1986), personal hygiene skills (Lutzker, Campbell, & Watson-Perczel, 1984; Rosenfield-Schlichter, Sarber, Bueno, Greene, & Lutzker, 1983), nutrition skills (Sarber et al., 1983), and infant stimulation skills (Lutzker, Megson, Dachman, & Webb, 1985). Neglecting mothers have also learned to reduce the number of hazards in their home (Barone, Greene, & Lutzker, 1986).

Experts have also recommended multiservice intervention approaches for both psychologically maltreating and neglecting families because they are designed to target the multiproblem nature of such families

(Daro, 1988; Fortin & Chamberland, 1995; Lujan et al., 1989). Multiservice interventions typically include the delivery of a broad range of services including combinations of the following: individual, family, and group therapies; behavioral methods to eliminate problematic behavior; and parenting education. Evaluation studies of such programs have demonstrated some positive results. The NCCAN, for example, has recently funded a series of multiservice projects directed at chronically neglectful families. Evaluations of these projects have indicated that a combination of parenting groups, intensive in-home counseling, and supportive interventions (e.g., paraprofessional aides) has been effective in improving neglectful parenting practices (Landsman, Nelson, Allen, & Tyler, 1992). Other researchers have also found family-focused, multiservice projects to be effective interventions for neglecting families (e.g., Daro, 1988; Lutzker, 1990; Wesch & Lutzker, 1991). Two recent studies suggest, however, that outcomes for neglecting families are less positive than for abusive families or families of delinquents (Berry, 1991; Yuan & Struckman-Johnson, 1991).

Summary

Child neglect and psychological maltreatment are the two most elusive forms of maltreatment and, as a result, have received less attention. The vague nature of these forms of maltreatment is evident by the observation that a significant proportion of the research directed toward them focuses on definitional issues. At the present time, there is no single definition of child neglect or psychological maltreatment that is universally accepted. Although experts generally agree on conceptual definitions of child neglect (i.e., deficits in the provision of a child's basic needs), little consensus exists regarding operational definitions. Establishing the parameters of psychological maltreatment has proven even more difficult and confusing. Researchers disagree about whether definitions should be broad or narrow, for example, and about the relative importance of parental behaviors (e.g., swearing at or denigrating a child) versus child outcomes (e.g., mental injury).

The true incidence of these forms of maltreatment is also largely undetermined as are the victim characteristics associated with child neglect and psychological maltreatment. Researchers have obtained much of the information about rates and correlates of child neglect and psychological maltreatment from official reports made to child protective services. Although such reports are limited (e.g., lack of definitional consensus among researchers), it is clear that hundreds of thousands of children are reported for child neglect and psychological maltreatment each year. Child neglect, in fact, is the most frequently reported form of child maltreatment, accounting for approximately 45% to 55% of reported cases. Least commonly reported is psychological maltreatment, which accounts for 3% to 28% of reported cases. The majority of child neglect victims are under age 5, with the risk for neglect declining as children become older. Available research does not support an association between age and psychological maltreatment, suggesting that all children are equally vulnerable to this form of maltreatment. Child neglect and psychological maltreatment are similar in that both genders appear to be at equal risk as are children who come from families experiencing a variety of financial stressors (e.g., low income, unemployment).

Studies examining the negative effects associated with child neglect and psychological maltreatment are limited in both number and quality, making the interpretations of findings difficult. Available research, however, has consistently uncovered a variety of associated problems that are similar for both child neglect and psychological maltreatment. Child victims often demonstrate social difficulties, intellectual deficits, and emotional and behavioral problems. Although many experts believe that the negative effects of child neglect and psychological maltreatment extend into adulthood, more research is needed to establish the relationship between a childhood history of neglect and psychological maltreatment and adjustment problems in adulthood.

In attempting to establish the causes of child neglect and psychological maltreatment, researchers have often applied many of the same theories proposed to explain the physical and sexual abuse of children (e.g., environmental factors, parent-child interaction, intergenerational transmission). Several studies are appearing that distinguish maltreating from nonmaltreating parents on various characteristics. For both forms of maltreatment, the parent-child interactions are disturbed and parents have increased levels of stress, with few social supports and limited integration into the community. Neglecting parents are also characterized by low educational achievement and tend to become parents at a young age. Further research is needed, however, to determine additional contributing factors given that not all parents with these characteristics maltreat their children.

Few interventions are available to address the unique aspects of child neglect and psychological maltreatment, and as a result, research evaluating the effectiveness of therapy, protective services, and community interven-

tions for victims of these forms of maltreatment is limited. Preliminary efforts directed at neglecting parents have been effective in teaching such parents specific skills such as increasing positive parent-child interactions, improving problem-solving abilities, and enhancing personal hygiene and nutrition skills. Although few direct services are implemented for children, available programs have been successful in improving social interaction and developmental skills. Multiservice intervention approaches designed to target the multiproblem nature of these families are also appearing and demonstrate some effectiveness.

6

Children Exposed to Marital Violence

CHAPTER OUTLINE

An Interview
With David Wolfe

"The outdated views of politicians is one of the biggest stumbling blocks to action. The existing political paradigm can be summed up as, 'If it ain't broke, don't fix it.' "

DAVID WOLFE is one of North America's foremost researchers in the area of children exposed to marital violence. Currently, he is Professor of Psychology and Psychiatry at the University of Western Ontario. He has a diplomate in clinical psychology from the American Board of Professional Psychology. He serves on the boards of several organizations, such as the Child Witness Preparation Program. He authored a significant book titled Child Abuse: Implications for Child Development and Psychopathology. *Along with Peter Jaffe and Susan Wilson, he coauthored a best-selling family violence book titled* Children of Battered Women. *With K. Kaufman, J. Aragona, and J. Sandler, he coauthored* The Child Management Program for Abusive Parents. *He is a member of the editorial boards of several journals, such as* Child Abuse & Neglect, Journal of Family Violence, Delinquencia, *and* Journal of Interpersonal Violence. *He received his B.A. in psychology from the University of Rochester and his Ph.D. in clinical psychology (with an emphasis in child psychology) from the University of South Florida.*

Q: What shaped your approach to the field of children exposed to marital violence?

A: In 1980, I met Peter Jaffe and became active in prevention of child abuse. With grant money, we designed group education and abuse prevention programs for children of battered women. We were interested in the similarities between children who witness violence and those who are abused themselves.

Q: What are your future personal goals?

A: For the next 10 years, at 6-month intervals, I would like to follow the progress of the adolescents we have been treating. We need to evaluate the effectiveness of the education and treatment we have given them. We would then be in a position to specify what changes are needed in education programs to prevent adolescents from becom-

ing the next generation of abusive parents or partners.

Another interest I have is in prenatal education. The roots of child abuse and neglect are often visible before having children. We need to use prenatal screening as a method for identifying parents at high risk for child abuse. We then need to apply a public health model by adopting a referral system to help these at-risk parents obtain medical services and abuse prevention education. Screening could be the first step in starting the referral service.

Q: How can society diminish family violence?

A: We need to focus on cultural values. Family privacy is such a strongly held value that society fails to intervene sufficiently. Abuse is hidden behind closed doors. While we need to maintain family privacy, we also need to get out the message about the prevalence of abuse in particular neighborhoods and to offer support to parents.

Communities need to establish abuse prevention panels made up of volunteer citizens. These groups could establish community centers to assist violent families and recruit volunteers who are willing to go out and talk with their neighbors about abuse. Frequently, women's groups spearhead campaigns to raise community awareness. The media can contribute by providing information about abuse and the locations of agencies where families can get help. The approach needs to be inclusionary rather than punitive. Isolation of parents and lack of support for parents play key roles in allowing child abuse to continue. Citizen support networks play a crucial role in preventing child abuse by offering a help-ing hand to abusive parents.

Q: Why can't we as a society seem to elimi-nate child abuse?

A: It would cost a lot of money and all of our money is tied up in responding to casualties. We spend millions of dollars on the crises caused by abuse—on crime and health costs. It would take a concerted effort to reach and educate those who will repeat the cycle across generations. As a society, we need to begin the prevention process by educating adoles-cents. A proactive approach to abuse pre-vention would be very costly initially, but very cost effective in the long run.

Q: How have governmental policies failed to prevent abuse?

A: The outdated views of politicians is one of the biggest stumbling blocks to action. The existing political paradigm can be summed up as, "If it ain't broke, don't fix it." Politicians work in a crisis mode. They allocate funds only for disasters. Politicians do not take the lead in long-range planning.

Introduction

CASE HISTORY: BRIAN AND HIS "STUPID" SON, MIKIE

Seven-year-old Mikie and 2-year-old Melanie were the children of Brian and Colleen. Brian was a batterer who was completing a court-mandated counseling program for assaulting Colleen. He was 26 years old, married for 5 years, and a semi-employed roofer by trade. Although he loved Colleen, she caused him a lot of trouble by quar-reling with the neighbors over the neighbor's dog. The dog kept coming over into his yard and Mikie was always throwing rocks at it. Because Colleen wasn't punishing Mikie enough, Brian had little choice but to "shape her up." He locked her out of the house and "slapped some sense into her" every now and again.

Brian was puzzled and alarmed that Mikie had nightmares and often "peed in his pants." Worst of all, he was failing in school. Brian loved little Mikie a lot, but Mikie was dumb, just like him. According to Brian, a lot of the problem was Colleen's poor parenting. She didn't know how to discipline the children, cook well, or even keep the house clean. She couldn't even get Mikie to stop hitting the baby. As a lesson to Mikie and

baby Melanie, who "might just as well learn early," Brian had the children watch the way he repri-manded Colleen. Usually, only a screaming match ensued, but now and then Colleen wouldn't shut up, so Brian had to "show her who was boss" by pushing her around "some."

Brian tried to help Mikie do better in school, just like his own father had tried to help him, by telling Mikie he was dumb. He also thrashed Mikie, when he came home with any failing grades, "to make him work harder." He occasionally threat-ened Mikie by saying he would lock him out of the house "just like he had to lock his mother out" if he didn't study harder. On the positive side, Brian bought Mikie a little school desk, but he made Mikie sit at it for 2 hours every night. Brian was puzzled over Mikie's poor performance de-spite all the "discipline" he gave him.

The group counselor asked Brian whether his own father had actually called him "dumb." "Oh yes, nearly every day," Brian replied. "Sometimes he put a dunce cap on me and had me sit at the table without any dinner." The therapist asked Brian how he felt when his own father said he was dumb. Suddenly, tears welled up in Brian's eyes and he couldn't say a word. He just sat there, racked with emotion. His shoulders sort of shook on the outside in rhythm with his weeping on the inside. He did not speak for the remaining 30 minutes of the group session.

At the next weekly meeting, Brian proudly reported that he hadn't told Mikie that he was dumb once all week! The group beamed smiles of approval toward him. Perhaps it was not too late to change Brian's behavior. He had already quit hitting Colleen. Maybe Mikie could be saved too. (Author's case history)

Throughout history, children have not only been abused directly themselves, but they have also suffered indirectly by observing violence between their parents (e.g., Pleck, 1987). Recognition that children exposed to interparental abuse, as a group, are in need of services grew out of the work of advocates, clinicians, and researchers in the late 1970s. During this era, there also was a growing aware-ness that the consequences of child abuse posed a serious problem for the individual later in life (e.g., Dobash & Dobash, 1979; Hilberman & Munson, 1978; Straus, Gelles, & Steinmetz, 1980). Up until this time, the public and the scientific community seemed to be-lieve that children were oblivious to marital violence or that it had no effect (Rossman, 1994). This belief has turned out to be totally false. As Roy (1988) observed, "Children from violent homes are human time-bombs set to explode when they assume the role of husband or wife in adulthood" (p. 14).

Given the historical indifference to this problem, it is not surprising that research on children exposed to marital violence lags behind most other areas of domestic violence research. In approaching the area, professionals have borrowed from studies on child abuse and child psychological maltreatment (see Brassard, Germain, & Hart, 1987a; Nelson, 1984). Available empirical information about these "hidden," "unintended," "silent," or "forgotten" victims of marital violence (see Dembo, Williams, Wothke, Schmeidler, & Brown, 1992) is typically rudimentary. Even an acceptable designation for these children is tenuous. Although most researchers have referred to them as *child witnesses to marital violence*, others have questioned this terminology because of its possible confusion with children who testify in court. As an alternative, Geffner and Pagelow (1990a) suggested the use of *child observers of marital violence*, but now this nomenclature has given way to *children exposed to marital violence*.

So far, the text has explored the effects on children of direct physical, sexual, and psychological mistreatment, as well as the effects of neglect. This chapter moves forward to include exposure to marital violence as a form of abuse. Children, of course, frequently suffer from direct and indirect forms of abuse simultaneously. Of particular significance in understanding children exposed to marital violence is the manifold nature of the threats they face. Children in these violent homes are traumatized by fear for themselves and their mothers, and they experience a painful sense of helplessness (Silvern, Karyl, & Landis, 1995). They may also blame themselves for not preventing the violence or for causing it. Finally, they themselves are likely to experience abuse, neglect, or injury. Cumulatively, they receive a powerful lesson that people who love each other also hurt each other (Jaffe, Wolfe, & Wilson, 1990).

Scope of the Problem

Estimates of the number of children aged 3 to 17 in the United States exposed to marital violence range from 3.3 million (Carlson, 1984) to nearly 10 million (Straus, 1991a). In a retrospective study of college students, 16% reported exposure to at least one incident during the past year in which one of their parents had physically abused the other. Nearly half of these parents had used physical force against their children as well (Bowker, Arbitell, & McFerron, 1988).

There is also some uncertainty about how much marital violence children have actually observed. Some parents seem to think that their children were unaware of the violence because they were occupied elsewhere (e.g., playing outside, watching television, or in their rooms) during most of the violent episodes. In contrast, there have been some reports of male batterers who insisted that their children observe the violence (Dobash & Dobash, 1979).

Incidence and Prevalence of Exposure to Marital Violence

How much marital violence children observe depends on whom one asks. A recent study based on data from multiple informants (both parents and children) found that mothers' reports of children's exposure agreed with fathers' fairly well. Parents' and children's reports, however, agreed much less closely (O'Brien, John, Margolin, & Erel, 1994).

In a national survey of battered women residing in shelters, fewer than 25% thought their children had been exposed to the marital violence within their home (Tomkins et al., 1994). Another inquiry of battered women suggested that 87% of children living in violent homes actually observed the violence (Walker, 1984). Based on data using a different measurement strategy in which children provided self-reports of their attempts to intervene in marital conflicts, at least 71% of a sample of English children living in maritally violent homes were exposed (Jenkins, Smith, & Graham, 1989). Yet another type of evaluation, an analysis of police calls, disclosed that children were present 41% of the time police went on domestic calls (Bard, 1970). The implication of these findings is that battered women underestimate their children's exposure (Hilton, 1992), perhaps from shame or guilt, stress or trauma (Elbow, 1982).

Defining Exposure to Marital Violence

When referring to the effects of exposure to marital violence on children, most specialists in the field concentrate on the consequences of recurrent male-to-female violence (Jaffe et al., 1990). The children most frequently recruited by researchers, those temporarily residing in shelters, have probably observed repeated assaults. One study of shelter residents, for example, indicated that half of the women had been battered at least once a week for more than 5 years (Layzer, Goodson, & DeLange, 1986).

Conceptualization. Many experts conceptualize exposure to marital violence, having to live in a violent and unstable environment or being influenced by negative and limiting role models, as a form of psychological maltreatment or emotional abuse (Brassard et al., 1987a). Others surmise that exposure to marital violence is a form of trauma that terrorizes the children by forcing them to observe a loved one being physically or verbally assaulted. Legally, courts have rarely grappled with problems related to children exposed to marital violence, but when they have, they have subsumed these cases under the rubric of child neglect and maltreatment (see Tomkins et al., 1994).

Forms of Exposure. The wide range of experiences that might qualify as exposure to marital violence also complicates specification of a definition. Children may actually observe a violent act, overhear some form of violent behavior, or see the results of the assaults (e.g., bruises). The outcome of such ambiguity has been to hinder agreement about which behaviors constitute exposure and which tests best measure these effects.

Effects of Marital Violence on the Family and Children

Added to the general lack of clarity in the entire field is the uncertainty about how the negative effect of exposure to marital violence compares with other negative childhood experiences. Anecdotal observations have prompted researchers generally to presume that the consequences of negative childhood experiences lie on a continuum: The more violent the behavior and the more directly related it is to the child, the more detrimental it is to the child. Experts, for example, have proposed that exposure to marital vio-

lence is more detrimental to children than exposure to marital discord (Forsstrom-Cohen & Rosenbaum, 1985; Jouriles, Murphy, & O'Leary, 1989). Another supposition is that the effects of exposure to marital violence are similar to those caused by exposure to parental alcoholism or to witnessing a homicide (Rutter, 1979). It is also probable that exposure outcomes are somewhat less severe than experiencing physical abuse directly (Hughes, 1988; Jouriles et al., 1989; cf. Jaffe, Wolfe, Wilson, & Zak, 1986b, and Tomkins et al., 1994). To measure the consequences of exposure to marital violence, researchers have most frequently selected the reliable and valid Child Behavior Checklist (CBCL; Achenbach & Edelbrock, 1983), a 120-item test of behavior problems and social competence to be completed by mothers. Its age range is limited to children 4 to 16 years, and it is therefore inappropriate for use with some age groups (e.g., toddlers). It yields ratings of three broad-band factors: *internalizing behaviors* (anxiety, depression, withdrawal), *externalizing behaviors* (aggression, delinquency, hyperactivity), and *social competence* (school performance), as well as *total problem behavior.* The manual provides age- and sex-based normative data.

Effects of Exposure to Marital Violence on Family Functioning—Stress Factors

One likely repercussion of marital violence is a general poisoning of the family environment, which in turn, may indirectly generate the adverse outcomes noted in children exposed to family violence. As levels of marital violence increase, levels of family strengths, marital satisfaction, and parental satisfaction decrease (Meredith, Abbot, & Adams, 1986). Looking at the relationship in reverse, one investigation found that the more effectively the family functioned, the less likely it was that intrafamily violence occurred (Kratcoski, 1984). With maritally violent couples, children may suffer from becoming the focal point of arguments that culminate in battering (Hilton, 1992). Imagine how a child might feel if his father slapped his mother during a quarrel about the child's punishment for not cleaning his room. One comparison revealed that physically violent families exhibit a dominance hierarchy, conflict, and lack of organization and openly express anger. In contrast, nonviolent families are emotionally spontaneous, share pleasurable activities and goals, and emphasize personal rights and freedoms (Resick & Reese, 1986). Such findings support a violence-induced family stress explanation of the repercussions of marital violence on children. Parents who cannot cope effectively because of stress are handicapped in their efforts to fulfill their parental roles. In fact, their inadequate coping might be more detrimental to children than the actual observation of violence. Maternal stress and paternal irritability are two recognized violence-related variables that engender harm to children exposed to marital violence (also see Hershorn & Rosenbaum, 1985).

Effects on Mothers. Mothers in violent relationships commonly have their psychological energy absorbed by feelings of guilt, depression, low self-esteem, or fear for their own safety (see Aguilar & Nightingale, 1994; Sato & Heiby, 1992; Trimpey, 1989). In addition to these typical victimization effects, women living in these circumstances also report feeling much less able to cope with the ordinary demands of parenting than nonvictimized mothers. One comparison of abused and nonabused mothers' reports, for example, uncovered significant differences in parenting styles (parental inconsistencies) between mothers and fathers and in the mothers' changes or modifications in parenting (e.g., became more lenient or more harsh in the presence of father). As one illustration, a mother who would ordinarily punish her child for taking away a sibling's toy might take no action just to avoid any possible irritation of the father (Holden & Ritchie, 1991). The results of this study, however, failed to identify significant differences in positive parenting practices (e.g., reasoning) or negative parenting practices (e.g., power tactics), as reported by the mothers. The most probable explanation for this unexpected outcome was the narrow choice of maternal parenting practices measured (i.e., hypothetical parenting responses to vignettes of children's misbehaviors). Assessment did not tap variables such as empathic responding, emotional availability, and ability to set and enforce limits. Future research exploring the consequences of these variables should eventually pinpoint differences in parenting practices, such as an empathy deficit, that might account for the link between maternal stress and children's behavior problems (Holden & Ritchie, 1991).

Paternal Irritability. Fathers in violent households suffer from a number of adverse personality characteristics that also have the potential to interact with the effects of exposure to violence on children. Some commonly noted traits are poor problem-solving skills, hostility, high stress levels, depression, and psychopathology (see Barnett, Fagan, & Booker,

---

> ## Maternal stress and paternal irritability are two recognized violence-related variables.

1991; Hamberger & Hastings, 1986b; Hastings & Hamberger, 1988; Kishur, 1989; Maiuro, Cahn, & Vitaliano, 1988).

These fathers are also frequently irritable for no explicit reason. Illustrative of fathers' increased irritability is their behavior on being awakened from a nap. Of a group of battered women, 67% reported that their husbands would respond with power-assertive responses, whereas only 30% of a nonbattered group of women typified their husbands' behavior as power assertive. A measure of paternal irritability, including frequent anger and fault finding, was significantly linked with maternal ratings of children's behavior problems (Holden & Ritchie, 1991). Men who assault their wives are also likely to be emotionally distant from their children and use power tactics to control them. In one inquiry, battered women rated their assaultive husbands as uninvolved, inconsistent, and in conflict with their own parenting styles. Abusive husbands shared child-rearing tasks with their wives only 21% of the time, compared with nonabusive husbands, who shared child-rearing tasks 41% of the time (Holden & Ritchie, 1991). Men who batter their wives also appear to be even more inclined than women to physically abuse their children. In one analysis of 116 battered women and their abused children, the father abused approximately 50% of the children, the mother abused 35%, and both parents abused the remaining 15% (Stark & Flitcraft, 1988).

Effects of Exposure to Marital Violence on Children

Since the late 1970s, researchers have made progress in documenting a number of profoundly negative psychosocial and physical consequences of exposure to marital violence on children (e.g., Hershorn & Rosenbaum, 1985; Jaffe, Hastings, & Reitzel, 1992; Mertin, 1992). Attempts to sort through this tangle of differing findings, however, underscores the array of methodological problems plaguing research in this area.

Classifying Findings. Researchers summarize the effects of exposure to marital violence along several dimensions: (a) short- and long-term effects; (b) emotional, cognitive, and behavioral effects; and (c) internalized symptoms (e.g., sadness, withdrawal, somatic complaints, fear, anxiety), externalized symptoms (e.g., aggression, cruelty to animals, disobedience, destructiveness), or both. They also classify the outcomes according to a group of broad parameters expected to mediate the effect of observation: age, sex, stage of development, role in the family, and type of violence experienced. Finally, they categorize exposure effects as direct (e.g., modeling) or indirect (parent-child relationship) (see Hughes, 1992).

Overall Findings. A summary of research findings on the effects of exposure to marital violence on children reveals that children are prone to suffer psychological damage in four general areas: (a) immediate trauma; (b) adverse affects on development; (c) living under high levels of stress, particularly fear of injury to themselves and their mother; and (d) exposure to violent role models. Results from the 1985 National Violence Re-

---

Children exposed to marital violence tend to exhibit many more behavior problems than nonexposed children.

Survey of adults who had been exposed to parental violence identified a host of risk factors: (a) health and mental health problems, (b) drinking and drug use, (c) marital conflict and violence, (d) physical abuse of children, and (e) assaults and crime outside the family (Straus, 1991a).

Children exposed to marital violence tend to exhibit many more behavior problems than nonexposed children, and symptoma-

tology frequently overlaps (Gleason, 1995). That is, a behavior such as truancy occurs as well as a problem such as frequent headaches (Fantuzzo & Lindquist, 1989; Rossman, 1994; Rossman et al., 1993). Across studies, approximately 35% to 45% of shelter children receive scores above the cutoff score designating a clinical problem (see Hughes, 1992; McKay, 1987; Sternberg et al., 1993; Wildin, Williamson, & Wilson, 1991). In a recent shelter study of 185 children, 22% fell within the 98th percentile on a checklist for externalizing behavior problems (e.g., aggression), and 31% fell within the 98th percentile on internalizing problems (e.g., depression; O'Keefe, 1994a). In particular, children exposed to marital violence suffer elevated levels of physical symptoms such as colds, sore throats, and bed-wetting, and they experience more hospitalizations (Alessi & Hearn, 1984; Davidson, 1978). Refer to Table 6.1 for a synopsis of more precise outcomes on children exposed to marital violence (also see Pfouts, Schopler, & Henley, 1982; Ulbrich & Huber, 1981).

Long-Term Effects. Some of the most striking recent findings are that childhood exposure to parental abuse is correlated with a number of psychological problems in college students. For women, significant associations emerged between childhood exposure and three other variables: (a) higher levels of depression, (b) higher levels of trauma-related symptoms, and (c) lower levels of self-esteem (also see Henning, Leitenberg, Coffey, Turner, & Bennett, 1996). For men, the primary relationship was between childhood exposure to marital violence and higher levels of current trauma-related symptoms (e.g., anxiety and sleep disturbance; Silvern, Karyl, Waelde, et al., 1995).

Two recent inquiries show additional negative results from exposure to marital violence in childhood. In a sample of 617 community women aged 19 to 87 in Vermont, those who had witnessed father-to-mother or mutual parental violence exhibited higher levels of current psychological distress and lower levels of social adjustment than their counterparts (Henning et al., 1996). Another recent study of 1,836 men interviewed in the second National Violence Survey linked exposure to marital violence with ineffective conflict resolution strategies in adulthood (Choice, Lamke, & Pittman, 1995).

Table 6.1 Reported Effects of Observing Interparental Violence on Children

Internalizing and emotional effects

Anxiety/temperament	Holden and Ritchie (1991)
	Hughes (1988)
	McKay (1987, 1994)
	Randolf and Conkle (1993)
Low self-esteem	Elbow (1982)
	Hughes (1988)
	McKay (1987, 1994)
Shyness	Hershorn and Rosenbaum (1985)
Depression	Christopoulos et al. (1987)
	Hershorn and Rosenbaum (1985)
	O'Keefe (1994a)
Suicide attempts	Hershorn and Rosenbaum (1985)
	Hughes (1986)
	Koski (1987)
Withdrawn	Hughes (1986)
Trauma/stress reactions	Jaffe, Wolfe, and Wilson (1990)
	Rossman et al. (1993)
	Silvern and Kaersvang (1989)
	Terr (1991)
Feeling of loss/anger/sadness/confusion	Alessi and Hearn (1984)
	Carlson (1984)
	Cassady, Allen, Lyon, and McGeehan (1987)
	Jaffe et al. (1990)
	Layzer, Goodson, and DeLange (1986)
Self-blame	Ericksen and Henderson (1992)
	Jaffe et al. (1990)
Physical problems	Fantuzzo and Lindquist (1989)
	Keronac, Taggart, Lescop, and Fortin (1986)
	Layzer et al. (1986)
	Mertin (1992)
	Reid, Kavanaugh, and Baldwin (1987)

School and social competence

School problems	Hilberman and Munson (1978)
	Layzer et al. (1986)
	Pfouts, Schopler, and Henley (1982)
	Westra and Martin (1981)
	Wildin, Williamson, and Wilson (1991)
Social incompetence	Hughes (1988)
	Layzer et al. (1986)
	Rossman et al. (1993)
	Wolfe, Zak, Wilson, and Jaffe (1986)
Low empathy	Hinchey and Gavelek (1982)
	M. S. Rosenberg (1987)
Poor problem-solving, nonviolent resolution, and conflict resolution skills	Grossier (1986)
	Jaffe et al. (1990)
	Moore, Pepler, Mae, and Kates (1989)
	M. S. Rosenberg (1987)
	Straus, Gelles, and Steinmetz (1980)
Acceptance/legitimization	Hanson, Sawyer, Hilton, and Davis (1992)
	Jaffe et al. (1990)
	Ulbrich and Huber (1981)
Poor cognition	Hart and Brassard (1990)
	Westra and Martin (1981)

(continued)

Table 6.1 Continued

Externalizing behavioral problems

Aggression	Holden and Ritchie (1991)
	O'Keefe (1994)
	Randolf and Conkle (1993)
	Rutter and Giller (1983)
	Sternberg et al. (1993)
	Straus, Gelles, and Steinmetz (1980)
	Westra and Martin (1981)
Alcohol/drug use	Dembo, Williams, Wothke, Schmeidler, and Brown (1992)
	Fantuzzo and Lindquist (1989)
	Keronac et al. (1986)
	Layzer et al. (1986)

Effects of Mediating and Confounding Variables

First, the parameters of exposure to marital violence (i.e., frequency of exposure, severity of violence observed, recency of exposure, multiplicity of types of exposures) are dissimilar for specific children. Second, these diverse exposure effects are mediated by the individual characteristics (e.g., age, gender, race, ethnicity) of the children exposed. Some other salient mediators are general life stress and inadequate maternal functioning. Research on the effects of such mediators has often produced mixed results (see Fantuzzo et al., 1991; Holden & Ritchie, 1991; Jaffe, Wolfe, Wilson, & Zak, 1986a; O'Keefe, 1994a).

Age. Available data reveal no consistent age differences among exposed children (Gyrch & Fincham, 1990). Although several studies have found evidence for more behavioral problems in young as compared with older children (Hughes, 1988; Hughes & Barad, 1983), others have found the reverse (Gleason, 1995; Holden & Ritchie, 1991; Hughes, Parkinson, & Vargo, 1989). One multifactor analysis indicated that younger exposed children had more externalizing problems than older children, but not more internalizing problems (O'Keefe, 1994a).

Gender. Gender analyses have also yielded mixed results. Surveys seem to suggest that boys may be more negatively affected than girls (Carlson, 1990; Rosenbaum & O'Leary, 1981a; Wolfe, Zak, Wilson, & Jaffe, 1986). Several controlled studies, for example, that relied on maternal reports of behavior problems, determined that boys' externalizing (e.g., aggression) problems are more severe than

girls' (Porter & O'Leary, 1980; Rosenbaum & O'Leary, 1981a; Wolfe, Jaffe, Wilson, & Zak, 1985; Wolfe et al., 1986). One investigation showed that preschool boys also display more internalizing symptoms than girls (Stagg, Wills, & Howell, 1989), but others found that girls exhibit more internalizing symptoms (Christopoulos et al., 1987; Holden & Ritchie, 1991; Hughes, Vargo, Ito, & Skinner, 1991). Another account demonstrated that differences were inconsistent and were related to the choice of informant (child, mother, father; Sternberg et al., 1993). Two other studies used normative comparison data from a subsection of the CBCL and data provided by both maternal reports and child self-reports. Both of these, a shelter sample (Randolf & Conkle, 1993) and a sample from a community with low socioeconomic status (Spaccarelli, Sandler, & Roosa, 1994), found that girls' self-report scores of conduct problems are higher than those of boys. A large shelter sample using maternal reports detected no gender differences (O'Keefe, 1994a). Another account of shelter children using maternal, teacher, and child specialist responses to three valid and reliable questionnaires also found no gender difference (Gleason, 1995). Collectively, the extreme noncomparability of these findings across divergent data sources, samples, measurements, and type of comparison data obtained leaves the issue of gender effects unsettled (also see Carlson, 1990).

Race and Ethnic Variation. A particularly notable shortcoming of the research in the field is the dearth of knowledge about the cultural effects of race and ethnicity as mediating variables (Fantuzzo & Lindquist, 1989). Three studies found that European American children scored higher on externalizing behavior problems than African American children (O'Keefe, 1994b; Stagg et al., 1989; Westra & Martin, 1981).

Maternal Impairment. One of the most important factors affecting the repercussions of exposure to marital violence on children is the mother's reactions to the violence (Jouriles et al., 1989). Margaret Elbow (1982) posits that the greater the level of maternal stress caused by the violence, the lower the level of effective maternal parenting. Studies consistently indicate that maternal stress from violence or other sources has significant detrimental effects on children. In one investigation of life event stresses, for example, poor health and housing crises accounted for 19% of the variance in explaining child behavior problems (Wolfe et al., 1985).

A subsequent study that compared maternal parenting stress in battered and nonbattered women, rather than life event stress, was able to account for 33% of the variance in children's behavior problems (e.g., difficult temperaments, internalizing problems, and aggression). Maternal stress levels were positively and significantly correlated with paternal irritability and the degree to which mothers changed their behavior in the presence of the father (Holden & Ritchie, 1991).

Another repercussion of marital violence for exposed children is the mother's psychological unavailability or inability to offer safety and nurturance (Elbow, 1982; Hart & Brassard, 1987; van der Kolk, 1987). In addition to lack of adequate parenting, a mother's unavailability may place a child at greater risk for other abuses, like severe physical violence or sexual abuse (see Finkelhor, 1986; Straus et al., 1980).

Exposure to Multiple Forms of Violence. As might be expected, studies have also generally revealed that observation of marital violence coupled with either direct physical or sexual abuse increases the adverse psychological consequences on children (Davis & Carlson, 1987; Hughes et al., 1989). In one controlled study, children who had both observed marital violence and experienced direct physical abuse had higher problem behavior scores on a behavior inventory than children who were observers only. These two groups had higher scores than a comparison group of children who were neither directly abused nor exposed to marital violence (Hughes, 1988). In another survey, both the amount of marital violence exposure and mother-child aggres-

sion were significantly related to child behavior problems (O'Keefe, 1994b).

Other Stressors. In all probability, children living in maritally violent homes experience many risk factors simultaneously: marital conflict, exposure to marital violence, parental alcoholism, low income, stress, maternal impairment, and direct physical abuse and neglect (Hughes et al., 1989). Children exposed to marital violence, for example, have a 40% to 60% chance of also being physically abused (see Gibson & Gutierrez, 1991; Hughes, 1988; Rosenbaum & O'Leary, 1981a; Straus et al., 1980; Suh & Abel, 1990). The overlap is so high, in fact, that professionals are beginning to recommend routine child abuse screening of children of battered women (Petchers, 1995). This multiplicity of situational factors, of course, complicates specification of unique effects or patterns of effects attributable only to observation of abuse (e.g., Forehand, Long, & Brody, 1988; Sternberg et al., 1993). Nonetheless, one recent study that controlled for the effects of a large number of variables (e.g., amount of mother-child and father-child violence, the quality of the parent-child relationships, parental marital satisfaction level, family cohesion and adaptability, stressful life events, family size, socioeconomic status, and formal and informal social support systems) still found that a child's adjustment was related to the amount of violence observed by the child (O'Keefe, 1994a).

Accounts such as these point out that children living in violent families presumably suffer from an accumulation or compounding of stressors (Jaffe et al., 1986b). In fact, it may be the total amount of stress from combined sources that debilitates children. The consequences may be additive rather than synergistic (Jouriles et al., 1989). Despite their importance, researchers have failed to rank on a routine basis the effects of stressors like parental alcoholism, divorce, or incarceration (see Spaccarelli et al., 1994).

Protective and Vulnerability Factors. Other factors that play a crucial role in children's resilience to exposure to marital violence are individual attributes of the child, social support somewhere within the family system, and social support from figures outside the family (Garmezy, 1983). In one investigation of protective factors, positive child temperament (low emotionality and high sociability), positive feelings of self-worth, school competence, and a positive relationship with the mother all served to mitigate the deleterious effects of exposure to marital violence. Vulnerability factors that exacerbated exposure to violence were numerous exposures, high mother-child violence, and frequent stressful life events in the child's life (O'Keefe, 1994a). In a highly unusual study based on physiological measures, 5-year-old children's inability to regulate their emotions, as indexed by certain cardiac rhythms, was related to high levels of externalizing behavior 3 years later (Katz & Gottman, 1995). Results like these underscore the need to appraise situational and personality variables that mediate the effects of exposure to marital violence.

Evaluation of the Research on Exposure to Marital Violence

Research in the field of children exposed to marital violence is exceptionally challenging. Reliance on maternal reports as the major source of data; near exclusive employment of small, shelter samples; failure to ascertain adequately exposure to marital violence; failure to evaluate multiple types of stress; and insufficient use of comparison groups are the most obvious problems. Although research designs have steadily improved over the years, their findings still require cautious interpretation (see Fantuzzo & Lindquist, 1989, for a review).

Data Source. By far, the most common source of data about children exposed to marital violence is maternal report. Only one available study included data about children's behavior problems from fathers (Sternberg et al., 1993). In this analysis, mothers', fathers', and children's reports showed little correspondence (Sternberg et al., 1993; cf. Rossman, 1994). Parents (primarily mothers), for example, were more cognizant of externalizing problems, whereas children acknowledged more internalizing problems. Fathers' ratings (perhaps awareness) of children's problem behaviors were extremely low (Sternberg et al., 1993). One credible explanation for such discrepancies between reports of externalizing versus internalizing problems is the level of observability. Also, disparity between parents' accounts is positively correlated with level of conflict (Christensen, Margolin, & Sullaway, 1992).

Occasionally, researchers extend data collection efforts beyond mothers to encompass other professional observers like teachers or shelter staff (Keronac, Taggart, Lescop, & Fortin, 1986), or to collect self-report data from exposed children themselves (O'Brien, Margolin, John, & Krueger, 1991; Peled & Davis, 1995; Randolf & Conkle, 1993; Spaccarelli et al., 1994; Sternberg et al., 1993). In all these cases, protecting children's confidentiality poses special problems (Ericksen & Henderson, 1992). Furthermore, reports of this nature may be especially susceptible to inaccuracy. Some evidence suggests problems in underreporting related to various face-saving maneuvers or response styles. Even children may be unwilling or unable to report all the violence they have observed (O'Brien et al., 1994).

Although maternal reports are the most frequent source of information, researchers have nevertheless raised questions about their precision. One issue is that mothers' reports rest on their perceptions of the child's exposure. Mothers might be mistaken or insensitive to the child's exposure (O'Brien et al., 1994). Mothers, after all, are not in an ideal reporting state, because of the problems they are experiencing. Those in shelters are likely to be in a crisis situation brought on by factors such as injuries, insufficient funds, departure from their homes, depression, and posttraumatic stress disorder (PTSD) (see Pagelow, 1981a; Saunders, 1994; Walker, 1977).

One study, for example, disclosed that mothers reported adverse consequences of domestic violence on their children only when they themselves were victims. That is, mothers did not report high levels of behavior problems in children who were the sole victims of abuse (Sternberg et al., 1993). Similarly, research on mothers and sons exposed to marital violence indicated that the type (physical, verbal only, low conflict) and level (low to high) of conflict exposure significantly alters appraisals of family and marital interactions (O'Brien et al., 1991).

One common finding across studies is that mothers, as a group, offer more negative behavioral ratings of their own children than other observers do (e.g., Christensen et al., 1992; Sternberg et al., 1993). It is possible that mothers' greater knowledge produces greater accuracy (higher ratings of behavioral problems) compared with ratings provided by other observers (Hughes & Barad, 1983). Alternatively, mothers' evaluations may be higher as a reflection of negative bias.

Some mothers may associate their sons with their fathers, the violent men who are battering them (see Jaffe et al., 1986a). A third hypothesis is that mothers' judgments of the child's behavioral problems mirror their own level of psychological distress (Hughes, 1988). A final possibility is that mothers exaggerate the child's behavior problems as a way of justifying their own harsh physical punishment of the child (Jouriles et al., 1989). Without other sources of validation, such as those of shelter staff or teachers, mothers' evaluations provide only one perspective on the child's functioning and should be accepted with caution.

One recent investigation examined the general reliability and diagnostic efficacy of parental reports of their children's exposure to marital violence by using advanced statistical methods that account for individual variations in perception (O'Brien et al., 1994). A multiple-informant method (each parent and child) indicated that interparental agreement was moderate, whereas agreement between parents and children was only fair. A trade-off occurred between estimating true positives and false positives of exposure. Requiring both parents to agree that marital violence occurred and that children were exposed led to an identification of fewer than 25% of the children who also reported the exposure, but falsely categorized 3% as being exposed. Requiring a report of only one parent elicited identification of about 80% of the children who also reported marital violence. A second question falsely classified 40% of the children as exposed.

Samples. Another defect of the studies is their restrictive sampling. Probably the most commonly tested group of children exposed to violence are those 7 to 13 years of age residing in shelters. These samples vary greatly from general population samples in many important ways such as family income. Their nonrepresentativeness has almost precluded generalization (see Peled & Davis, 1995). An exception is an Israeli sample of children residing at home with both biological parents (Sternberg et al., 1993).

Measurement Problems. Compounding all of these problems are the numerous problems inherent in measurement. One particularly acute problem is the effect of a crisis setting (e.g., shelter) on measurements. It is not only difficult for family members to participate in research in the midst of a crisis, but it is also difficult for investigators to rule out the wide variety of outcomes caused by family disruption. In addition, researchers have failed to assess the level of possible confounding variables such as mental health, abuse status (e.g., severity of observed abuse), or maternal stress levels.

There is also the problem of defining exposure to abuse (i.e., observing, overhearing, seeing the consequences of) (Fantuzzo & Lindquist, 1989). Most studies have not directly measured children's exposure to marital violence, but have classified children's exposure simply by their residence with maritally violent parents (Peled & Davis, 1995).

Next, there is the customary problem of defining violent or traumatic events. The marital violence level of the parents is most often quantified solely by the mothers' reports on the Conflict Tactics Scales (CTS; Straus, 1979), yet investigators in the field have complained of the scales' limitations (Fantuzzo & Lindquist, 1989).

Failure to Collect Comparison Group Data. Finally, most studies have failed to use comparison groups (see Fantuzzo & Lindquist, 1989; Peled & Davis, 1995). Comparison groups would allow researchers to determine how exposed children or abuse victims might be different from or similar to children not exposed to marital violence. Without comparison groups, establishing cause-and-effect relationships is less clear.

Analysis. The complexity of conducting research about children exposed to marital violence has left investigators with considerable uncertainty about their generalizability. The inconsistency of research findings across the area has prompted a number of questions, such as the following: Did the results occur because mothers, instead of children, provided the data? If so, are mothers prone to overreporting? Would a follow-up or longitudinal study make disparate results more similar? Why do gender differences arise? When girls appear to have greater symptomatology, is it because they have identified with a battered mother? What unique variation in effects is attributable to exposure to violence as opposed to exposure to other variables or to combinations of other variables, such as maternal alcoholism coupled with paternal incarceration? These questions are just a few of the many that remain unanswered.

Variability of the Effects of Exposure to Marital Violence

The summary of effects of exposure to marital violence in Table 6.1 reflects extreme variability in outcomes. Although many children are adversely affected, some are not. Scientists do not have a clear understanding of why this variability occurs.

Direct and Indirect Effects. In the noteworthy analysis of Israeli children's self-reports of problem behavior on the Childhood Depression Inventory (Kovacs, 1981) and the Youth Self-Report (Achenbach & Edelbrock, 1987), only direct abuse (abuse alone or abuse plus exposure, not exposure alone) was associated with elevated scores on internalizing behaviors (Sternberg et al., 1993). In terms of indirect effects, one study uncovered a strong link between children's internalizing behavior problems and maternal parenting stress in battered mothers but was unable to specify how mothers' parenting was impaired by the added stress (Holden & Ritchie, 1991).

Problems in Research Methodology. The research methodology applied to assess the effects of exposure to marital violence has not been optimal. First, measurement of children's actual exposure is rarely obtained. Studies that have documented the presence of exposure may not have additionally considered chronicity of exposure. As a result, the described results are not clearly related to exposure.

Along the same lines, the choice of samples and lack of comparison groups have jeopardized assumptions about causality and generalizability of the findings. Whether the effects summarized in Table 6.1 are actually the consequences of exposure to marital violence is indeterminate. The effects of exposure to marital violence listed may be confounded with those stemming from other more direct parent-to-child forms of physical violence or familial stress.

Furthermore, variability in the nature of research outcomes underscores the issue of validity. At issue is the excessive dependency of the data on the selection of informants. Validity estimates of data provided by various kinds of informants are unavailable. It cannot be determined a priori that mothers' reports are more or less valid than teachers', clinicians', or children's. It may be fair, however, to question the accuracy of fathers' reports, given that they are less correlated with children's self-reports, that fathers in violent households spend so little time with their children, and that abusive men are known to underreport their own aggression (see Holden & Ritchie, 1991; Riggs, Murphy, & O'Leary, 1989; Sternberg et al., 1993).

Interaction Effects of Key Mediating Variables. Cataloging the consequences of exposure to marital violence is further hampered by the variety of key variables that influence its effects. Although age is an essential factor that is uniformly reported, researchers appear not to have adopted any classification guidelines demarcating younger from older children that would help consolidate findings. Gender is uniformly reported also but rarely integrated into meaningful theoretical explanations.

Another understudied critical element that moderates the effects of exposure to marital violence is the child's personality. Children's protective and vulnerability factors may vary across samples and contribute to the variability of reported outcomes, but remain largely unrecognized (Rossman, 1994). Finally, parenting styles, as noted by Holden and Ritchie (1991), surely affect the results of exposure but, again, are rarely quantified. Future research that accounts for the effects of the multitude of mediating and confounding variables should go a long way in simplifying and reducing the variability of effects of exposure to marital violence as condensed in Table 6.1.

Intermediate Chapter Summary

Marital violence is associated with many forms of family dysfunction. *Families* where marital violence is occurring are generally experiencing **high levels of stress.** *Children* in such families are subject to self-blame, feelings of helplessness, neglect, abuse, and injury. Most likely, *mothers* in these families are **psychologically unavailable** for their children and are **inconsistent in their parenting style.** *Fathers* in maritally violent families appear **more irritable** than other fathers and **less likely to be involved in parenting.** The children are traumatized by the threat of either observing violence or becoming the object of physical assault.

Whether the effects of exposure to marital violence (i.e., repeated male-to-female violence) are less severe or more severe than the effects of other forms of family dysfunction or abuse is unknown. For the most part, child observers of marital violence (e.g., observing, overhearing, seeing the results such as bruises) have a strong probability of also **experiencing many concurrent forms of maltreatment,** such as parental alcoholism or physical abuse.

The literature on the outcomes of exposure to marital violence lacks generalizability and must be considered tentative. Exposure to marital violence, nevertheless, is related to significant short- and long-term **adjustment problems** in children: emotional distress (e.g., anxiety and depression), cognitive impairments (e.g., lowered academic performance), behavioral effects (e.g., aggression, drug use, truancy), and health and mental effects (e.g., low self-esteem, physical problems such as colds, headaches, bed-wetting, hospitalizations), and social effects (e.g., exposure to violent role models).

Many factors mediate these effects, so finding the unique variation attributable to observing abuse is a little like looking for a needle in a haystack. Research has failed to establish strong age- and gender-related patterns of influence among the different and often contrasting findings. Likewise, the link between such variables as race, a mother's stress-induced impairment, the father's irritability, life-events stress, and the child's behavioral maladjustment is inexact. Several kinds of family violence commonly accompany observation of marital violence and tend to heighten the negative effect of a single type of abuse. Fortunately, some children have **protective factors** (e.g., a positive temperament, school competence, high sociability) that make them less vulnerable to the consequences of exposure to marital violence.

Conducting research in the field has posed **serious challenges to investigators.** The most commonly used assessment of effects is the reliable and valid **Child Behavior Checklist,** which examines internalizing behaviors, externalizing behaviors, social competence, and total problem behavior. Sources of information about the effects, however, rely too heavily on reports of mothers living in shelters, leading to an observed "shelter bias." There is **little correspondence between the accounts** of mothers, fathers, and children. Samples are usually small, ill defined, and probably nonrepresentative. For example, conclusions are hampered by the problem of defining *exposure* to abuse as well as by the **lack of exact measurements** of actual exposure. Also, quantification of exposure effects occurs too infrequently, and there is overreliance on normative data because of the paucity of comparison groups. Long-term follow-up studies are almost nonexistent as well.

Collectively, the methodological problems typifying the research and the correlational nature of the analyses provide **inconsistent findings** that lack sufficient validity about the outcomes of exposure to marital violence. Finally, the overlapping of numerous forms of abuse and multiple life stresses may promote researcher misidentification of the causes of child behavior problems in these homes.

Explaining the Effects of Exposure to Marital Violence on Children

Researchers have proposed four main theories to account for the translation of exposure to marital violence into behavioral outcomes. The first is social learning theory. Another is family disruption (stress) theory. Newer theoretical formulations consist of posttraumatic stress disorder (PTSD) and attachment theory.

Social Learning Theories. Social learning theory holds that children learn directly to be violent by observing their violent parent(s). Observation leads to imitation of behavioral aggression and cognitive incorporation of proviolence attitudes. Failure to punish children's aggressive behavior further provides ample opportunity to adopt and practice violent interpersonal skills (Patterson, 1982). A cognitive model assumes that children adopt parental beliefs that violence is an acceptable means of expressing anger, of reacting to stress, or controlling others (Kalmuss, 1984). Children also imitate inept problem-solving styles. Last, children can fail to learn valuable skills, such as nonviolent conflict resolution, because they lack appropriate parental models (M. S. Rosenberg, 1987).

Children's elevated scores on behavioral problem checklists or their social incompetence, therefore, simply represent learned behaviors. Put simply, children exposed to marital violence use violence in their own interpersonal interactions. Those exposed to inept problem-solving methods are poor problem solvers. The types of difficulties reported in children exposed to marital violence (e.g., aggression), in fact, are similar to the types of problems seen in adult batterers (e.g., anger control deficit) (MacEwen & Barling, 1988). Educating battered women in shelters about the emotional needs of their children should reduce intergenerational transmission of violent behavior patterns (Webersinn, Hollinger, & DeLamatre, 1991).

Family Disruption (Stress) Hypothesis. Family disruption theory holds that negative events related to violence (e.g., frequent moves, erratic school attendance, parental separation or loss, and economic hardship) indirectly account for the heightened emergence of behavioral symptoms. Not only do such events challenge children's personal abilities to cope, but they also diminish parents' ability to comprehend and respond to their children's needs (see Jouriles, Barling, & O'Leary, 1987).

Posttraumatic Stress Disorder. A newer explanation for the effects of exposure to marital violence is PTSD. This theory assumes that traumatic experiences (e.g., an earthquake, observing homicide) elicit a cluster of violence-related stress reactions that affects children's mental health (Pynoos & Eth, 1985; Terr, 1991). Common PTSD reactions in children are physical symptoms, anxiety and fear, guilt and denial, behavioral disturbances, and behavioral regression (Mowbray, 1988). Because mothers of children exposed to marital violence report that their children exhibit many of these symptoms (e.g., Jaffe et al., 1986a), observing battering may qualify as a terrorizing or traumatizing event that evokes PTSD (Kenning, Merchant, & Tomkins, 1991). Consequences of exposure to marital violence, then, are actually PTSD effects (Hart & Brassard, 1990).

Attachment Theory (Emotional Insecurity). An emotional insecurity hypothesis may help explain the consequences of exposure to marital violence on children (Davies & Cummings, 1994). Presented in a simplified form, this theory suggests that marital conflict and violence have the potential of making children feel insecure by interfering with parent-child bonding. Insecure attachment, in turn, places children at risk for behavior problems. One avenue of effect occurs by increasing the negativity of parent-child interactions. Another is by decreasing parental involvement and emotional availability. Other pathways occur through the distressed parents' seeking of emotional support from their children or by their pressuring the children to "take their side." Children exposed to marital violence become emotionally aroused (i.e., fearful of the implications) and, when combined with certain parenting styles, may feel insecure (DeLozier, 1992). It is even possible that there is an intergenerational transmission of insecurity in close family relationships (Zeanah & Zeanah, 1989).

Intermediate Chapter Summary

The solid, scientific foundation of **learning theory,** coupled with evidence that the types of problems characterizing children who observe marital violence (e.g., aggression, anger control deficit) parallel those of adult batterers, makes this theory a powerful explanation for behavioral outcomes related to marital violence. **Family disruption theory** attempts to explain the consequences of observation of marital violence *indirectly* through effects of maternal impairment brought on by both life stress (e.g., economic hardship, frequent moves, a change in marital status) and violence-induced stress.

Newer **posttraumatic stress disorder (PTSD)** formulations suggest that perceived effects are almost indistinguishable from those of trauma victims. From this perspective, exposure to marital violence is a traumatizing event that elicits a cluster of violence-related stress reactions such as fear, guilt, denial, and behavioral regression. Critics of stress and PTSD explanations generally point out the wide variation in individual stress reactions (vulnerability factors) among children (O'Keefe, 1994a).

Attachment theory (emotional insecurity) provides a framework for incorporating a number of ideas about how marital conflict (e.g., physical violence) makes children feel insecure—afraid of what might happen. Children become physically aroused by the conflict, may encounter parents who are less available, may become involved in the conflict through parental needs, and eventually display behavioral problems.

Intervention and Prevention for Children Exposed to Marital Violence

Although involvement of professional groups in helping children exposed to marital violence should be beneficial, almost none of them has taken much responsibility—not the legal profession nor law enforcement, and not social service agencies. Furthermore, elected officials have tended to turn their backs on this group of victims (Tomkins et al., 1994). Intervention on behalf of children exposed to marital violence is most closely linked with the battered women's movement and with the child welfare system (Peled, 1993). Almost no child receives treatment unless the child's mother seeks help at a shelter (Jaffe, Wilson, & Wolfe, 1989).

Clinical Assessment

Even though a substantial minority of children exposed to marital violence develop symptoms in the clinical range, a significant proportion does not and may even demonstrate above-average strengths in social competence and adjustment (Wolfe et al., 1985). Because of such diversity, a decision about appropriate intervention needs to begin with careful assessment and diagnosis. Some issues to consider are the length of intervention required and which members of the family need treatment (Rossman, 1994).

Diagnosis is not straightforward because symptomatology overlaps. It is important to know, for example, if the symptoms are connected with trauma, depression, conduct, or attention deficit disorder (Silvern & Kaersvang, 1989). A study comparing 30 child observers with a cohort of 42 matched controls indicated a surprising overlap of symptoms within the exposed-child group, such as behavioral maladjustment, trauma symptoms,

and dissociative disorders (Rossman et al., 1993). A single child, for example, might have a history of conduct disorders and trauma symptoms. On the other hand, a heterogeneous diagnostic picture could easily result from exposure to multiple stressors (e.g., observation of violence, sexual abuse, parental alcoholism) and differential levels of resilience (Rossman, 1994).

Safety Assessments. Before consideration of other issues, practitioners need to evaluate and plan for the child's physical and psychological safety. It is too easy for children to get caught in the cross fire. The four issues involved are (a) keeping the child's whereabouts confidential, (b) working out a safety plan for the child if marital violence recurs, (c) helping the child avoid becoming an intermediary in stopping the violence, and (d) conducting a lethality estimate to avoid revictimizing the child when it seems essential to bring abusive family members together (Rossman, 1994).

Family History. Examination of family history or other types of pretrauma information is useful. Ascertaining the presence of risk factors such as depression among the child's family members, for instance, provides clues about depressive symptoms in the child. Other useful background material consists of knowledge about possible antisocial behavior among family members. This approach may help separate out symptoms that are unrelated to the symptoms brought about by exposure to parental violence (Rossman, 1994). Finally, possible constraints placed on families because of their cultural or ethnic background need elucidation (Fantuzzo & Lindquist, 1989).

Child's Developmental Level. A major consideration in assessment is the child's development level. Obviously, an infant's or a preschooler's needs are different from those of teenagers, and there are individual differences in reactions to trauma within age groups.

Chronological age, however, may not be the best indicator of functional level because traumatized children may be developmentally delayed (Rossman, 1994).

Interventions

As in other areas of family violence, practitioners most frequently dichotomize their treatment approaches to fit either victims or perpetrators. Within the area of children exposed to marital violence, most mental health workers have focused their counseling efforts on either psychopathologies and developmental impairments of the exposed children or on the inadequacies of the parents who are involved in the violent marital relationships (Peled & Davis, 1995). A variety of new services for children of battered women have come into fruition, but the two most typical types of treatment afforded are crisis intervention and group counseling (Jaffe et al., 1990; Peled, Jaffe, & Edleson, 1994). Some therapists use strategies designed for individual treatment (Arroyo & Eth, 1995; Black & Kaplan, 1988; Silvern, Karyl, & Landis, 1995). In addition, there are a number of programs for mothers and a few for families.

Children exposed to marital violence can be difficult to treat for several reasons. They may have trouble in accurately processing information (Dodge, 1991; Fish-Murray, Koby, & van der Kolk, 1987). Their arousal and emotional levels are likely to be high, and their abilities to calm themselves may not be adequate (O'Brien et al., 1991). Short, 10-week programs are not a panacea for the myriad problems characterizing these children (Wilson, Cameron, Jaffe, & Wolfe, 1989). In fact, such brief programs may be inappropriate for any family violence intervention program.

Children's Group Counseling. Customarily, children receive treatment in a group situation (e.g., Alessi & Hearn, 1984; Gibson & Gutierrez, 1991; Gruszinski, Brink, & Edleson, 1988; Ragg & Webb, 1992). In addition to shelters, children receive group treatment in safe homes, family court clinics, and outpatient social service agencies. Hughes (1992) summarizes the goals of group treatment as follows: (a) labeling feelings, (b) dealing with anger, (c) developing safety skills, (d) obtaining social support, (e) developing social competence and a good self-concept, (f) recognizing one's lack of responsibility for a parent or for the violence, (g) understanding family violence, and (h) specifying personal wishes about family relationships (also see Jaffe et al., 1990).

Data about the effectiveness of these programs are limited and inconsistent (Jaffe et al., 1989). Preliminary results of one pilot program indicated that in a sample of 33 children between the ages of 2 months and 12 years, the children exhibited better social skills, screamed less, and reported fewer physical complaints (Cassady, Allen, Lyon, & McGeehan, 1987). Other studies suggested that treatment resulted in an increase in self-esteem, ability to trust, and conflict resolution skills, as well as a decrease in physical symptoms, feelings of blame, acceptance of violence, and victimization proneness (see Gentry & Eaddy, 1980; Grusznski et al., 1988; Peled & Edleson, 1992). A recent controlled study of 8- to 13-year-old children referred by a social agency has probably provided the most encouraging evidence of positive treatment effects. The pre- and posttreatment difference scores of the 38 children who received a 10-week counseling program (see Wilson, Cameron, et al., 1989) and the 16 comparison children showed significant changes. The counseled children evidenced a favorable change in their attitudes and responses to anger and a diminished sense of responsibility for their parents' violence as assessed by the Child Witness to Violence Interview (Jaffe et al., 1990). The treatment did not succeed, however, in increasing children's knowledge of support and safety skills; thus, more modification of the program is proposed (Wagar & Rodway, 1995).

Mothers' Counseling. A different approach is to help mothers learn how to respond effectively and supportively to their children's needs. Although this is a worthy goal, it is important that counseling the mother does not imply that she is to blame for the violence and therefore a poor parent in need of mandated counseling (Bograd, 1990). Parent management programs have also been successful with antisocial children by helping parents to discipline their children more effectively (Kazdin, 1987).

Conjoint Family Therapy. Parents need to become sensitive to the harmful effects their violence has on children and to take more responsibility (see Jouriles et al., 1989). Whether families involved in violence should undergo conjoint family therapy, however, is highly controversial. Feminist advocates argue against this approach because of safety concerns and because they view the abuser as responsible for the violence, not the whole family. The family systems position supports conjoint therapy on the grounds that the violence is maintained by reciprocal processes in the family. Because everyone presumably contributes to the violence, everyone needs treatment.

Modifications of the systems approach include the reconstructionist approach, which suggests a progression in treatment from individual counseling to mother-child counseling and finally to conjoint therapy. Lethality assessments are particularly warranted before recommending conjoint family therapy (see Rossman, 1994, for a review). A related approach is conjoint mother-child therapy in which a therapist works with a mother-child pair to improve attachment.

Other Programs. Having a trained shelter volunteer accompany police on domestic disturbance calls may be a very effective means of reducing a child's initial distress and perhaps subsequent trauma symptomatology (Rossman et al., 1993). Terr (1991) notes the usefulness of behavioral desensitization, medication, or both, as additional treatment for trauma-related fears and anxiety.

Training of Professionals

One of the biggest stumbling blocks in helping children exposed to marital violence is mental health professionals' lack of awareness. Because training rarely covers the difficulties faced by these children (Tomkins et al., 1994), professionals may fail to ask children about marital violence and hence fail to identify the problem of exposure (Jaffe et al., 1990; Kenning et al., 1991). Even if told about a child's exposure, they may feel too overloaded with children who are physically and sexually abused to offer assistance (Carlson, 1984).

Enhancing Shelter Services

To clarify the extent of shelter services for children exposed to marital violence, one team of investigators conducted two surveys: (a) a structured interview study with 59 caregivers (professionals and volunteers) and five agency administrators, (b) a mail survey of 350 social service professionals and adminis-

---

Whether families involved in violence should undergo conjoint family therapy is highly controversial.

---

trators from crises and treatment centers. Altogether, over 400 persons responded to questions such as the following: Does the caregiver [e.g., shelter worker] question the mother about whether her children have observed the violence when woman battering is suspected or known? What are agency policies?

Shelter personnel infrequently reported child exposure to the police. Not reporting was related to the perceived lack of services for such children and the pervasive attitude of many authorities that abuse was not a real problem (Tomkins et al., 1994). Shelter staff customarily intervened through referrals to other treatment agencies or the police, but rarely to child protective services agencies. Referral agencies, however, were so inundated with direct abuse victims that they gave exposed children very low priority. Referrals appear to have been made pro forma, without any expectation that the child would actually receive services. About two thirds of the respondents in the national mail survey indicated that they offered some form of in-house treatment (also see Alessi & Hearn, 1984; Jaffe, Wilson, & Wolfe, 1986).

Intermediate Chapter Summary

There are **no standard policies and practices** in regard to intervention with children who observe marital violence. Diagnosis of **safety needs** is paramount but is not secured because of a dearth of organizational leadership within the professions and because of the variability and overlapping of symptomology.

The preliminary focus of clinicians treating children exposed to marital violence should be **assessment.** Although it is a complex task, it is important to know how problems are interrelated (e.g., from trauma, depression, conduct, attention deficit, sexual abuse, parental alcoholism). Practitioners need to consider carefully the child's family history, developmental level, and the type and length of treatment (e.g., crisis or long-term, group or individual) best suited to the child's needs.

Despite the lack of empirical information guiding mental health workers, they have forged ahead with several **recommendations.** Primarily, exposed children need to label and deal with their emotions related to the violence, and probably with the father, in particular. They need to develop safety skills and learn how to develop social support networks. From another perspective, they need to understand family violence and to understand that they are not responsible for it. Unfortunately, treatment amounts to helping children be "sane in an insane place" (Grusznski et al., 1988).

The most common form of clinical intervention with children exposed to marital violence is **group counseling** within a shelter setting. Preliminary research has indicated that this approach may lessen both the short- and long-term negative psychological outcomes. A very frequent adjunct to group counseling for children is **counseling for mothers.** Educating mothers about the emotional needs of their children and providing them with emotional support is a common goal. Whether practitioners should attempt conjoint family therapy is uncertain (e.g., family systems theory supports, feminist advocates argue against). Shelter workers, for example, voice grave concerns for mothers' and children's safety in confrontations with batterers. Some advocate a graduated family approach only after safety concerns have dwindled (i.e., reconstructionist approach).

Professionals such as mental health workers not only need **more resources,** but they also need **additional training** to sensitize them to the problems of children exposed to marital violence. Communities should expand their efforts to develop crisis teams to intervene when police make domestic disturbance calls. Shelters offer a variety of services to victims of family violence, but they may have a tendency to let children get lost in the shuffle when their mothers are in crisis. They most frequently make pro forma referrals to mental health agencies.

Policy Implications

Child exposure to marital violence remains virtually hidden from public debate. It was not until 1984 that the federal government officially recognized it as a problem (U.S. Department of Justice, 1984). One reason that child exposure has not evoked public consternation is because it has not undergone sufficient construction as a social problem (Peled, 1993; Tomkins et al., 1994). Neither mental health agencies nor the legal system has adequately addressed the problem. How a problem is construed and defined influences policy decisions. A 1987 survey of southwestern Pennsylvania human service agencies that dealt with family violence by Grantsmakers (cited in Stagg et al., 1989), for example, revealed that 85% of the agencies contacted had no program for children exposed to marital violence. Similarly, the American Bar Association states that despite its obligation to protect children living in violent households, the law has generally failed to even recognize their exposure as a problem (H. Davidson, 1994). Agencies of the government, the mental health profession, and the legal system all need to examine this issue and respond as agents of change.

Ideally, a community needs to intervene at several levels. Various home and community role models can begin the process at a primary level by offering general prevention programs, perhaps in the schools. Professionals need to design secondary intervention programs for children identified at high risk but who are not yet "acting out," and tertiary intervention programs for children who are already showing symptoms, perhaps children in shelters (Jaffe et al., 1990).

Custody, Mediation, and Visitation Issues

Custody and financial support are two of the most critical issues for battered women and their children (Jaffe, Austin, Lescheid, & Sas, 1981). Although laws should protect the children and victim-parents from continued exposure to domestic violence, a number of recent laws governing mediation during divorce, child custody, or visitation have backfired against battered women (Sonkin, 1989). Barbara Hart (1990) of the Pennsylvania Coalition Against Domestic Violence, in fact, flatly states that neither joint custodial solutions nor mediation will produce good outcomes for battered women and children (cf. Erickson & McKnight, 1990).

Custody. A fight over custody of children is a common, and often successful, threat that abusive husbands make to prevent battered women from leaving (Nicarthy, 1982). Critics complain that abusive behavior toward the mother is frequently considered irrelevant in custody disputes and that violence toward the mother does not necessarily pose a danger to the child (Chesler, 1986; Walker & Edwall, 1987). By 1992, only 14 states had passed laws requiring consideration of a batterer's violence as a factor in intrafamily custody cases (National Center on Women and Family Law, Inc., 1994). By comparison, courts have all too often labeled battered mothers as unfit because of their violence-induced parental inadequacies (i.e., PTSD symptoms) and then removed the children from the mothers' care (Pagelow, 1992). The American Bar Association, however, says that where there is proof of abuse, batterers should be presumed by law to be unfit custodians for their children (H. Davidson, 1994). Similarly, documentation of woman battering should be a trigger to require mental health professionals to conduct an evaluation of the family and issue a report (Kenning et al., 1991).

Confusion has occurred about whether joint custody is in the best interests of the children. Battered women themselves frequently remain in violent relationships because they have come to believe that their children are better off with a father in the home (Barnett & Lopez-Real, 1985; Hilton, 1992). Past legalization of joint custody led to such a strong, false assumption that it was superior to sole custody that some states had to amend their statutes to indicate that no preference in custody arrangements should automatically apply (Bruch, 1988). Evidence does not indicate, for example, that children are better off when kept in contact with a father while strong marital conflict is ongoing (Furstenberg, Morgan, & Allison, 1987).

Mediation. Although mediation is an ever-growing and popular alternative to court proceedings involving divorce, custody, and visitation, it can be an inappropriate and dangerous alternative when used for children from homes marked by marital violence ("Domestic Violence," 1989). Forced mediation may subject an abused adult or child to a psychologically harmful confrontation with the abuser and can be physically

---

A number of recent laws governing mediation during divorce, child custody, or visitation have backfired against battered women.

---

dangerous as well (Geffner & Pagelow, 1990b). A number of situations have occurred in which an abuser has used mediation sessions to continue his threats, and a few abusers have used their access to the mother as an opportunity for murder. One potential pitfall for mediators is to presume an equal power balance between parents (Lerman, 1984) or to assume that both can speak freely at mediation sessions ("Domestic Violence," 1989). Johnston and Campbell (1993) suggest that an appraisal of individuals involved in mediation should be a requirement, because some are unsuitable for mediation (e.g., male batterers and psychotic-paranoid individuals) (Thoennes, Salem, & Pearson, 1995).

Mandatory Visitation. It is difficult for women to discontinue contact with an abusive partner (e.g., leave the city) if the court mandates paternal visitation rights. Many battered women and children are terrified because batterers often use visitation as an opportunity to continue their abuse (Geffner & Pagelow, 1990b; Sonkin, Martin, & Walker, 1985). In a 1989 Toronto study by Leighton (cited in Jaffe et al., 1990), for example, 25% of 235 women with children reported that their husbands continued to make threats against their lives during visitation, and 5% reported threats of kidnapping. Another analysis of interviews with 20 battered women indicated that 90% of the children became involved in the psychological or physical abuse in some way even after separation (Hilton, 1992). If the court refuses to terminate the parental visitation rights of the batterer, prosecutors need to advocate strongly for supervised visitation and for mandatory batterer counseling (H. Davidson, 1994). The entire area of supervised visitation, however, requires fine-tuning. Although the Supervised Visitation Network has undertaken the task of preparing guidelines and standards for supervised visitation programs, none currently exist. Finally, any set of guidelines will be of little use unless state and federal funding of supervised visitation services is made available (Straus, 1995).

Many courts have held that a batterer's murder of the child's mother renders him an unfit parent. Oddly, others have judged the violence to be a problem "only to the extent of analyzing the impact of the act on the abusers' parenting abilities" (National Center on Women and Family Law, Inc., 1994, p. 45)! The case of Betty and Henry illustrates the dangers women face in legal disputes with batterers.

CASE HISTORY: BETTY AND HENRY— "IF I DON'T COME BACK"

Betty and Henry were married and had a 14-month-old daughter, Melissa. Henry was self-employed but unmotivated. He was also possessive, controlling, and insecure. When Betty's independence got the better of him, he became abusive. Betty had gone to work on numerous occasions with bruises on her face and arms. For the most part, nobody talked about what was happening. (It is often easier for friends and family to deny abuse, to minimize the severity of discord, and to ignore evidence.)

Betty's friends and financial security were a threat to Henry. He became more controlling, and he threatened to kill her if she tried to leave. His obsession culminated in Betty's 2-week "confinement." He stayed at home to watch her. Eventually, he needed money and took her to the bank to make a withdrawal from her savings account. Betty and Melissa escaped to the Long Beach Battered Women's Shelter.

Henry threatened to sue Betty for custody of the baby unless he was allowed to visit her. A third-party visitation was set up by the shelter through her attorney. No one at the shelter felt good about this arrangement, but everyone felt compelled to go ahead with the plan because of the legal ramifications of noncompliance. Betty and the baby were to go to her attorney's office accompanied by a male friend of Betty's (the father of one of her friends). While they were in the parking lot, Henry grabbed the baby and told

Betty to get into his car or she would never see Melissa again.

Betty's body was not discovered for several months. Henry was charged with murder. He had taken Betty to an isolated spot in the desert where he beat and shot her. Melissa was in the car. Betty's body had to be identified by her dental records. At Henry's trial, one of his previous wives admitted to the abuse she had experienced at his hands. She was still afraid of him. Henry was eventually convicted of second-degree murder. Betty's last words to one of the authors of this case (A. L.) as she left to meet Henry were, "If I don't come back, it is because he killed me" (cited in Barnett & LaViolette, 1993, pp. 49-50).

Policy Recommendations

Trial courts have shown considerable reluctance in recognizing that domestic violence is harmful to children (National Center on Women and Family Law, Inc., 1994). Substantiated instances of woman battering should be prima facie evidence that one or both parents have overstepped permissible parental behaviors by creating a milieu that is inappropriate for children's healthy development (Kenning et al., 1991). Children who are exposed to severe or very frequent battering of their mothers are at risk of developing behavioral and psychological problems and may also be in physical danger (Kenning et al., 1991). Documented abuse of children should justify intrusion into family "privacy" and interference with parents' constitutional rights.

Judges and Prosecutors. Judges clearly need education about the topic, but experts have not provided it. One of the few professional books on custody evaluations, for example, ignored the problem of family violence except to warn professionals to be cautious about exaggerated reports of violence by women (Parry, Broder, Schmitt, Saunders, & Hood, 1986). Prosecutors also need training in custody and visitation matters. Children are more directly involved in legal issues than one might imagine. In one study of 1,014 witnesses who testified in 928 wife assault cases, for instance, 50% were children (Bowker et al., 1988). Although it is apparent that child witnesses suffer emotional distress from testifying, very little research on the exact effects is available (see Goodman, Levine, Melton, & Ogden, 1991). Prosecutors could render better services to children by enlisting community mental health professionals to sponsor support groups for children to familiarize them with the court process (Gwinn, 1994).

Police. Police need training about what questions to ask children and when to ask them. Police also need standards to help them determine when to make a report to child protective services (Gwinn, 1994). Stubbing (1990), a police trainer and advocate for battered women, has tried to raise police sensitivity toward and empathy for battered women by using children to describe how they "pray" that the police will come and remove the batterer. This approach could be slightly modified to focus police attention on the plight of the children themselves. One novel way to awaken not only the police but the community at large is to play tapes of children's desperate 9-1-1 calls in training sessions or in a public forum (Gwinn, 1994).

Nursing Personnel. Another proposal is that nursing personnel should form support groups for children (Ericksen & Henderson, 1992). Very frequently, the first outside contact battered women make is in an emergency room. It would be very helpful if health care personnel would ask about family violence and assist children who accompany their mothers (Wildin et al., 1991).

Research Recommendations

Researchers have encountered perplexing research design problems brought on by the myriad confounding variables. Investigators need to strengthen their research efforts in a number of ways. First, there is a need for epidemiological surveys to provide basic information about the lifetime prevalence of exposure to violence in representative samples. Researchers also need to move away from shelter-based samples and attempt to identify and test high-risk children or community samples (as in Sternberg et al., 1993). When using shelter-based samples, however, researchers should conduct follow-up assessments to rule out crisis effects (Spaccarelli et al., 1994).

Moreover, researchers need to document and quantify more carefully the timing, severity, and frequency of marital violence exposure. It would also be valuable, if possible, to specify the extent to which exposure to marital violence was composed of father-to-mother episodes, mother-to-father episodes, or was mutual. Similarly, it is essential to understand more about exposure to concurrent risks (e.g., parental alcoholism, direct child abuse) associated with exposure variables. No investigations featured an ideal employment of five groups of respondents: physical abuse only, exposure to marital violence only, exposure to both physical and marital violence, no exposure, and exposure only to nonviolent forms of stresses such as parental alcoholism.

Some remediation of the problem of informants and the validity of their protocols is essential. Application of research from other fields might help clarify issues about children's abilities to report, mothers' tendencies to report higher levels of problems, and fathers' seeming lack of awareness of children's problems.

Finally, government agencies should fund demonstration projects as a fundamental step toward shaping public policy (Stagg et al., 1989). Demonstration projects allow selected agencies with different approaches to gather basic kinds of scientific data for comparative purposes. Funding ordinarily allows researchers to gather more comprehensive sets of measurements on numerous variables (e.g., child's exposure to violence, child's personality, parental alcoholism), thus enabling subsequent analyses to substantiate important relationships.

Summary

At least 3.3 million children are exposed to marital violence annually. Although exposure to marital violence is a historical problem, it did not receive much scientific scrutiny until the late 1970s, and society as a whole lacked awareness of it as a problem. Exposure to marital violence, consisting of a violent and unstable home environment and violent and ineffective role models, is an adverse situation that is very likely to cause psychological damage to the child and increase his or her risk of physical abuse. Exposure effects are probably best conceptualized as a form of psychological maltreatment.

Children observe direct assaults, overhear violent behaviors and words, and see resultant bruises and injuries. To measure the consequences of exposure on children, researchers usually rely on maternal reports of children's behavioral problems on the Child Behavior Checklist (CBCL). Other informants such as fathers, however, provide accounts that often disagree with maternal accounts. Observing battering can have a direct negative effect on children or an indirect effect mediated by factors such as the mother's violence-induced psychological impairment. Basically, exposure to marital violence is related to a number of emotional outcomes (e.g., increased anxiety), cognitive effects (e.g., school problems), behavioral effects (e.g., aggression), and health problems (e.g., illness, alcohol use).

There are a number of variables that mediate and confound the consequences of exposure to marital violence. The relationships between age and gender and effects of exposure to marital violence, for example, are extremely unclear. In addition, children growing up in these families are frequently exposed to other negative circumstances, such as parental alcoholism and direct physical or sexual abuse. These problems tend to coexist in families. The extent to which mothers' violence-related impairment or other stressors (e.g., frequent school changes) play a role in these exposure-related outcomes is also unclear. Although children may be equally exposed, they exhibit individual differences in certain protective factors or vulnerability factors.

The number of variables simultaneously influencing children's behavior makes ferreting out the effects attributable only to observation of marital violence a truly challenging research task. Failure to take all these variables and risk factors into account, however, greatly undermines the validity of child-observer research overall. Consequently, any synthesis of research findings of the effects of marital violence must be regarded as tentative. Research in the field is relatively new, exceptionally difficult to conduct, and limited so far. Much more systematic research is needed.

In addition, methodological limitations (e.g., overreliance on maternal reports as the primary data source; small, nonrepresentative samples; overreliance on normative data) and the dearth of longitudinal studies have compromised the integrity and generalization of available findings. In reality, there is little known with certainty about the effects of observing marital violence.

Theoretical speculations are sparse but include learning theory, family disruption (e.g., stress formulations), trauma explanations, and attachment models. None of these theories is totally adequate in explaining the complexity of exposure and its consequences.

Clinical intervention must start with careful assessment because children exposed to marital violence customarily have overlapping symptoms caused by exposure to multiple, overlapping kinds of problems and abuses. Nonetheless, mental health workers have developed broad programs, generally offered within a group shelter setting, that focus on emotional labeling, safety enhancement, growth in competence, procurement of social support, and understanding of family violence. These programs place special emphasis on helping children to reduce feelings of self-blame. Many shelter programs also offer parenting training to resident mothers. These programs focus on supporting the mother so that she can be psychologically available, educating her about the harmful consequences of observation of marital violence on children, and advising her of specific parenting skills.

Children who live in violent home environments need more protection and assistance than they have received in the past. The overriding problem in providing aid is society's near total lack of awareness and sensitivity to the issue. Efforts have begun to construe exposure to marital violence as a social problem needing social attention.

Various kinds of legal intervention have the potential for placing victims of marital violence in renewed danger (e.g., mandatory mediation). Fortunately, the legal profession is a primary group actively working to protect children from the adverse consequences of exposure to marital violence. Professionals in this field have spearheaded efforts to educate attorneys and judges about the need for legislation and about the seriousness of custody and visitation decisions. It is important for legal professionals to avoid blaming the mother for her inability to protect herself and her children from a violent husband and father. Judges, prosecutors, and the police need more training about specific actions to take or to avoid.

Mental health professionals need more training in recognizing exposed children and more funding before they can contribute to the solution. Medical personnel and the police generally have no programs in place to combat the problem. Nursing personnel, like the police, are likely to be a battered woman's first line of defense. Acknowledgment by nurses and other medical personnel of the problem of children who are exposed to marital violence would also serve as a beginning step in assisting children.

Finally, researchers need to enhance their research strategies to provide more accurate information, and government agencies should fund their efforts. An initial approach is to devise methods of identifying child observers of marital violence. In the final analysis, it is society that remains blind to the problems of children exposed to parental violence. Advocacy efforts need to begin with awakening public concern.

7

Courtship Violence and Date Rape

An Interview With
K. Daniel O'Leary

"We may have to alter our sights to reasonable treatment and change goals—accepting the very clear possibility that not all aggressive individuals may be amenable to treatment."

K. DANIEL O'LEARY is a prolific researcher in courtship and marital violence. He is Distinguished Professor of Psychology at the State University of New York at Stony Brook, where he has supervised the dissertations and postdoctoral training of a large number of clinical psychology students whose subsequent careers have been quite noteworthy. He serves on the editorial boards of the following journals: Journal of Interpersonal Violence, Journal of Family Violence, Journal of Abnormal Child Psychology, *and* Behavior Therapy. *He has a National Institute of Mental Health (NIMH) research training grant for pre- and postdoctoral fellows conducting research on the etiology and treatment of spouse abuse, an NIMH grant evaluating treatments for men and women in physically violent relationships, and an NIMH grant evaluating a high school curriculum to prevent dating violence. He received his B.A. in psychology from Pennsylvania State University and his Ph.D. in clinical psychology from the University of Illinois in 1967.*

Q: What has shaped your approach to the field?

A: Much of my early training included a mixture of cognitive and behavioral methodologies with professors like Wesley Becker, Leonard Ullmann, and Donald Dulaney. Jerry Wiggins taught a course in personality that was one of the best courses I have ever had. This diverse instruction provided the broad base of my training and probably my ultimate development.

Q: What is your current research focus?

A: Currently, my research focus is on the etiology and treatment of physical aggression in relationships (the etiology of wife abuse). I have now become interested in personality variables as predictors of physical aggression in marriage. Indeed, we published research documenting the role of impulsivity, defendence, and aggression (as personality traits) in the etiology of physical aggression.

Over the past 3 years, we have been documenting the effectiveness of two different types of treatment for men and women in physically aggressive relationships where the aggression was at moderate levels and where the wife did not fear being in treatment with a partner. Both the gender-specific treatment for men and women and the couple treatment resulted in significant reductions in physical and psychological aggression.

Q: Which of the many articles that you have written in the past 10 years has attracted the most attention?

A: A longitudinal study of physical aggression in marriage coauthored with Julian Barling, Ileana Arias, Alan Rosenbaum, Jean Malone, and Andrea Tyree. A sequel to that article will probably also have a significant impact ultimately.

Q: What are your future research goals?

A: I would like to be able to classify types of men and women who might respond to different types of treatment, and to classify those who might not respond to any psychological intervention. Aggression is a very stable phenomenon in both children and adults, in fact, as documented in a 1979 article by Daniel Olweus, almost as stable as intelligence. Thus, we may have to alter our sights to reasonable treatment and change goals— accepting the very clear possibility that not all aggressive individuals may be amenable to treatment.

Q: What policy recommendation would you make?

A: To reduce levels of physical aggression in our society, of which partner aggression is simply one facet, we need to take broad preventive approaches. Like the approaches to alcohol and smoking, the prevention efforts have to start early. Furthermore, advocacy research needs to be more community oriented and broad based. Given the intractability of the problem, prevention efforts need to be given much greater priority, as is beginning to be the case at the federal level. Psychological treatments should be evaluated for what they can and cannot do, and legal punishments should receive continuing evaluations.

We also need to address gender issues in a straightforward manner with less volatility. We know that teens and young adult females engage in high levels of interpartner aggression, in fact, higher than those for males, and it appears that self-defense is not the main issue in young couples. We also know that fear and injury are higher for young women than for men. We do not understand all of the contextual reasons for the aggression, and we need to know. We are attempting some contextual analyses based on Dina Vivian's work.

Introduction

CASE HISTORY: IVANA AND BRUCE— "TEACHING HER A LESSON"

Ivana and Bruce met during their senior year in high school. After a few dates, they fell madly in love, and by the end of high school they began talking about marriage. Most of the time, Ivana felt very proud and lucky to have "landed" Bruce. Occasionally, however, Bruce seemed to be unexpectedly moody and jealous. He voiced numerous suspicions about whether Ivana was lying to him. Eventually, he secretly began to follow Ivana. He liked to follow her unobtrusively in his car while she walked home, and then he would ask her detailed questions about her trip home. In time, Ivana noted his car parked here and there on the route. Although Bruce's angry outbursts were unpleasant, Ivana felt that his possessiveness was a sign of true love. His constant watchfulness actually made her feel more secure.

On one occasion, Bruce accused Ivana of being insensitive to his feelings. After thinking it over, Ivana began to think that Bruce probably was right, so she decided to be very careful about how she treated him. It didn't seem to help Bruce feel more relaxed, though, because he began complaining about Ivana's many friends "who

took up all her time." Ivana felt somewhat confused, so she discussed the situation with her best friend, who urged her to work it out if she really loved him. Ivana decided to try even harder to please Bruce because they had been dating for nearly a year and a half and she believed that Bruce really loved her.

Next, Bruce started to call Ivana several times a day "just to check in and see how she was doing." Although his calls were pressuring, Ivana thought that Bruce was just insecure and that he surely would feel loved when he could finally believe that she loved him and no one else. She still had a lot of hope that Bruce would change.

One evening when Bruce came to pick her up for a date, he was angry because she was wearing a tight sweater. He wanted to know "why she was trying to turn on other guys"; wasn't he enough for her? Ivana was shocked, but she assured Bruce that she loved only him and she would be glad to change clothes. After all, changing into a loose blouse wasn't too much to ask, she thought. Bruce appreciated her effort and was very attentive and loving during the date, but for the first time, Ivana felt vaguely disturbed by Bruce's requests. She also felt disappointed that he couldn't seem to trust her.

When it came time to go on an annual vacation with her family to Tahiti, Bruce forbade Ivana to go. Ivana stopped talking about the trip, but one day when Bruce came over while Ivana was packing, he searched her suitcases and removed all her bathing suits. Ivana still loved him, but she felt burdened, restricted, and uneasy. Bruce seemed to be watching her every move. She hoped that a break from school and a break from Bruce might help her relax and clear her mind. It didn't.

When Ivana returned home, she put together an album of snapshots from the family's trip. When Bruce visited, he decided to look through the album. When he saw snapshots of Ivana in a bikini, he "went ballistic," screaming, shaking Ivana, and finally tearing out sections of the album. Ivana broke off her relationship with Bruce with a heavy heart. She felt she had failed somehow to convince him that she really loved him.

After a few weeks, Ivana decided to accept a date with Bruce and to try again to work out their relationship. After all, he had apologized and promised never to act that way again. In the car after the date, Bruce seemed nonchalant until they drove out to the beach; then his mood turned ugly. A fight broke out. Bruce yelled at Ivana, saying that she had never loved him. He called her a "no-good, f——g bitch." Although Ivana was upset and furious, she did everything she could think of to calm Bruce down. Saying that she loved him simply enraged him further. Suddenly, Bruce grabbed Ivana by the throat. He slapped her and choked her. She tried to fight back by scratching him and pulling his hair, but she was no match for him. She could hardly believe what was happening. Bruce ripped off her clothes and raped her, all the time screaming and cursing at her, "I'll teach you to fool around behind my back!" Finally, he pushed Ivana out of the car and left her sobbing on the beach.

Ivana did not call the police or tell anyone what had happened to her for over 2 years. Although Bruce apologized when he saw her again, she refused ever to see him again. (Author's case history)

* * *

The story of Bruce and Ivana illustrates another form of intimate violence that is sometimes included in discussion of family violence—courtship violence and date rape. Because interest in courtship and dating violence grew out of research on marital violence, there are a number of similarities in topics covered, research methods used, explanations offered, and constructs applied. One major difference is the greater inclusion of sexual assault factors in courtship violence compared with marital violence. A second major difference exists in the amount and kind of information available. Official estimates of the frequency of courtship violence and its injurious outcomes and date rape are quite sparse because government agencies have only recently begun to classify violence by boyfriends and girlfriends as a separate category of crime.

Courtship violence and date rape research have vigorously examined proviolence attitudes, especially in terms of sex-role attitudes, male peer-group support, and gender dissimilarities in acceptance of rape myths. Researchers have made some headway in understanding individual psychological and dyadic factors that promote aggression. Experts do not agree on what causes courtship violence, although many offer a social learning explanation. Finally, advocates working in the field of courtship violence and date rape have actively pursued programs of education and prevention.

Scope of the Problem

Defining Courtship Violence and Date Rape

What Is Courtship Violence? The term *court-ship* refers to a dyadic interaction with emo-

tional commitment with or without sexual intimacy. One usable definition of courtship or dating violence maintains that "dating violence involves the perpetration or threat of an act of physical violence by at least one member of an unmarried dyad on the other within the context of the dating process" (Sugarman & Hotaling, 1989, p. 5). Operational definitions used on self-report questionnaires of courtship violence are quite

---

At the center of the debate over date rape is the issue of consent.

---

similar to those constructed for marital violence. They vary along the same dimensions, such as whether to include nonphysical acts of aggression, and they most frequently are anchored on the Conflict Tactics Scales (CTS; Straus, 1979). Official estimates rest solely on physical assault assessments. Most research samples consist of college students. Other samples are composed of high school students, but samples rarely contain unmarried individuals older than college age. Behaviors assessed most frequently include physical and psychological aggression, as well as sexual assault.

What Is Date Rape? Because rape is such a controversial topic, it has provoked strong disputes about definition and measurement. At the center of the debate is the issue of consent. Claims-makers differ dramatically in the definitions of consent they offer. Must she grant consent verbally, or can her actions or dress communicate consent? Are there certain situations (e.g., drunkenness) when a woman cannot give consent? Some experts propose very broad definitions of rape, whereas others offer relatively narrow definitions. Issues of consent have proved especially problematic, and proponents of particular viewpoints are frequently split along gender lines (Lonsway & Fitzgerald, 1994).

For purposes of data gathering, government statisticians within the Bureau of Justice Statistics (BJS) have until recently defined rape from a narrow, legal perspective as "sexual intercourse or attempted sexual intercourse with a female against her will by force or threat of force" (Flanagan & Maguire, 1991, p. 779). Note, for example, that males cannot be raped according to this restricted legal definition. Adding to the confusion are variations among states in defining rape. Many states, whose rape statistics form the basis of reports to the federal government, have not employed precisely the same narrow BJS definition (see Sorenson & White, 1992).

Social scientists, especially those who are also women's advocates, have frequently moved away from these narrow, legally phrased definitions. They have often used broader assessment techniques that rest on a large number of nonlegally phrased questions that are fairly easy to understand. From this more inclusive perspective, researchers have found that the definition of rape is not clear-cut, but seems to fall on a continuum. The point at which individuals are likely to define sexual aggression as date rape is strongly influenced by factors such as age, sex, race, socioeconomic status, and relationship status (Koss, 1985). Victims who are acquainted with or romantically involved with an assailant, for example, are much less likely to characterize a sexual experience as rape (see Bourque, 1989). Obviously, variations in definitions affect statistical accounts.

Costs of Courtship Violence and Date Rape

Women, more than men, appear to bear the brunt of courtship violence. The most important negative outcome of dating aggression is injury, and studies consistently show that it is women who are disproportionately likely to sustain serious injuries (e.g., Makepeace, 1986; Sugarman & Hotaling, 1989). Other significant negative consequences are emotional harm, feelings of victimization, and fear of further violence; all are more likely to be experienced by women (Bernard & Bernard, 1983; Stets & Pirog-Good, 1989).

One reason that sexual assault and date rape are such important issues is that research routinely shows that sexual crimes have the potential to evoke a large number of severe psychological symptoms: fear and anxiety, posttraumatic stress disorder (PTSD), lowered self-esteem, social adjustment problems, and sexual dysfunctions (Jones & Muehlenhard, 1994; Resick, 1993; Santello & Leitenberg, 1993). These distressing reactions frequently occur in a cluster, as a group of rape-related PTSD symptoms (American Psychiatric Association, 1994), and are subsumed under the nomenclature of "rape trauma syndrome" (Burgess, 1995).

Estimates of Courtship Violence

Like other forms of intimate violence, when dating violence does occur, it usually takes place in private and is therefore hidden (Roscoe & Benaske, 1985). It also tends to be highly repetitive (e.g., Arias, Samios, & O'Leary, 1987; Stets & Straus, 1989). Furthermore, several investigations have called attention to the problem of nonparticipation of high school and college students in courtship violence surveys and have thereby questioned the representativeness of the samples used in such studies (Bernard & Bernard, 1983; Carlson, 1996; Showalter & Bevill, 1996).

Official Estimates. Federal offender-victim classification systems have made it difficult to determine murder and assault rates for dating partners. Information about dating partners (or cohabitants) as a separate group is very limited because it has only recently been quantified. Estimates most applicable to dating violence fall under the newer heading of violence against intimates, a category that includes family members, spouses, ex-spouses, boyfriends/girlfriends, and other relatives. Even homicide data are quite insufficient and ambiguous because victim-offender relationships are unknown in 41% of male homicides and 31% of female homicides. What is known is that of 3,454 women murdered in 1992 in which the victim-offender relationship was identified, 10.3% were killed by a boyfriend/ex-boyfriend. Of the 10,351 murdered men, 1.4% were killed by a girlfriend/ex-girlfriend (Bachman & Saltzman, 1995).

Only a few additional official estimates of courtship violence are available. In one examination of official reports of 1,764 violent incidents, 22.7% involved boyfriends/girlfriends (Erez, 1986). There is some evidence that rates of courtship violence are actually higher than rates of marital violence but that marital violence may be more severe. In a study of 1,870 cases of domestic assault reports filed over a year's time, 51.5% were classified as boyfriend/girlfriend, 44.6% as spouse, and 3.9% as ex-spouse. Of those actually arrested, however, 39.0% were in the category of boyfriend/girlfriend, 58.7% were spouses, and 2.2% were ex-spouses (Bourg & Stock, 1994).

Self-Report Surveys. Self-report estimates, as usual, diverge sharply from official estimates. National Crime Victimization Survey (NCVS) data for 1992-1993 revealed that boyfriends/ex-boyfriends perpetrate approximately 16% of aggravated and simple assaults against women, and girlfriends/ex-girlfriends perpetrate about 2% of assaults against men (Bachman & Saltzman, 1995). Because the 1992-1993 survey was the first to categorize assaults by dating and ex-dating partners, no trend data over years are available. It is important to keep in mind that NCVS data reflect information provided by a national, random sample of women aged 12 and over, regardless of their marital or dating status. The NCVS data allow an examination of the percentage of assaults that are committed by dating partners. Other surveys estimate the percentage of dating relationships that are characterized by violence.

Stets and Henderson (1991), for example, conducted a telephone survey of 272 dating men and women aged 18 to 30 randomly selected from a national sample of dating couples. CTS data indicated that 21.9% of men and 40.0% of women reported *perpetrating* severe aggression against an intimate partner in the last year. Comparable *victimization* rates were 32.2% for men and 29.6% for women.

A nationally representative sample of 4,704 college students responded to the CTS twice, once to assess their own aggression (perpetration) against a dating partner and a second time to assess aggression experiences as a victim (victimization). Responding to questions about the previous year, 37% of men and 35% of women reported inflicting aggression, and 39% of men and 32% of women reported having sustained aggression (White & Koss, 1991).

There are no national or representative estimates of courtship violence in high school-aged students. One recent study of victimization prevalence rates in three high school samples found a *lifetime* rate of 15.5% for women and 7.8% for men (Bergman, 1992).

Estimates of Date Rape

Reported rape rates are strikingly dissimilar depending on how a particular researcher or agency operationally defines rape. Clearly, broad definitions contribute to high rates, and narrow definitions lead to low rates. The narrow definitions previously used by government statisticians, for example, differ substantially from the broader definitions used by social scientists (see Sorenson & White, 1992). Until 1992, government agencies dichotomized rape into stranger and nonstranger (acquaintance) categories. Hence, there was no separate grouping for intimates such as boyfriends or girlfriends. This unsatisfactory classification strategy made it impossible to determine whether the victim simply knew the perpetrator (e.g., lived in the same building), was dating the perpetrator, or was sexually intimate with the offender.

Definitional ambiguity also influences whether a particular perpetrator or victim will label a given sexual encounter as rape. Selection of questions, context of questions, confidentiality concerns, and method of data collection have all combined to increase nondisclosure (Koss, 1993). Finally, even when victims realize they have been raped, they are ordinarily hesitant to report it to official agencies because of privacy concerns and fears of stigmatization (Bachman & Saltzman, 1995; Russell, 1983b). Despite these substantial limitations, it has become increasingly clear that rape is not the crazed behavior of a few deranged strangers; rather, it most frequently occurs between acquaintances.

Koss's 1989 Self-Report Survey of College Students.
Koss (1989) conducted a landmark study of 3,187 female and 2,972 male college students. Using a carefully worded questionnaire that avoided legal terminology, students responded to a graduated series of sexual aggression items that appraised the incidence of rape. The content of Koss's test items covered topics such as sexual contact by misuse of authority; intercourse by alcohol/drugs; and oral/anal penetration by threat of force. Koss's data yielded a rate of 38 rapes per 1,000 for women aged 18 to 24. In stark contrast, the 1984 NCVS data that relied on legal definitions of rape (cited in Koss, 1989) indicate an annual victimization rate of 3.9 per 1,000 for women aged 16 to 19 and 2.5 per 1,000 for women aged 20 to 24. Furthermore, men's admission of rape was 2 to 3 times higher on Koss's survey. Recent evidence further shows that both male and female college students tend to coerce their dating partners into sexual activity. The gender patterns of techniques used differ, and males use more coercive tactics than women (Waldner-Haugrud & Magruder, 1995).

DEBATING THE SCOPE OF DATE RAPE

Neil Gilbert, Professor of Social Welfare at the University of California at Berkeley, critiqued so-called advocacy statistics provided by Mary Koss, Professor of Family and Community Medicine, Psychiatry, and Psychology at the University of Arizona in Tucson. This debate began with Gilbert's emphasis on the huge gap between National Crime Victimization Survey statistics and Koss's. He criticized Koss's inclusion of the 73% of rape "victims" who did not label what happened to them as rape and her inclusion of "verbal coercion" as a form of threat or force (Gilbert, 1993). Koss and Cook's (1993) rebuttal was that the experiences of the women met the legal definition of rape, even if they failed to label the assault accurately or did not report it to authorities. Koss asserted that the women may have miscategorized their experience as some form of serious sexual abuse.

Gilbert (1993) also observed that 40% of rape victims in Koss, Gidycz, and Wisniewski's (1987) survey had a subsequent sexual encounter with the men who supposedly raped them. Gilbert essentially argued that if the women had "really" been raped, they would not have remained sexually involved with the perpetrator. Koss (1992), however, offered several interpretations for these interactions. One explanation was that many of the women were romantically involved with their rapists and had subsequent nonforced sexual encounters. Of victims in Koss's study, however, 87% did eventually terminate the relationship with the men who raped them.

The vast disparity in data appears primarily to result from important wording differences in test questions. Koss's (1985) inventory did not require respondents to label their experience as a criminal act of rape. According to Koss (1989), the very brief and legally worded questions used in the NCVS (often asked by a male interviewer) undermined full disclosure (see boxed insert: "Debating the Scope of Date Rape").

Revised NCVS Data. In response to criticisms of their procedures, the BJS undertook a 10-year project to redesign its questionnaires (Bachman & Taylor, 1994). New NCVS methods of cuing respondents about potential experiences with victimizations and new behavior-specific wording, rather than legal word-

---

Of the approximately 500,200 annual rapes and sexual assaults reported yearly, three fourths of the perpetrators were known to the victims.

---

ing, dramatically increased rape rates to 4.6 per 1,000 women (not just college students). Of the approximately 500,200 annual rapes and sexual assaults reported yearly (1992-1993) to NCVS interviewers, three fourths of

the perpetrators were known to the victims: Intimates committed 26%; acquaintances, 53%; relatives, 3%; and complete strangers, only 18%. The boxed insert titled "Comparison of New and Old Screener Questions" lists the questions used by NCVS interviewers (Bachman & Saltzman, 1995).

Cross-Cultural Courtship Violence and Sexual Aggression

Although cross-cultural data broaden our view on courtship violence and sexual aggression, they are so sparse that they must be viewed very cautiously. Survey data of courtship violence and sexual assault in other countries seem comparable with those in the United States but exhibit some dissimilarities. A Canadian study of 1,307 male and 1,835 female college students, for example, yielded dating violence rates that were somewhat lower than those obtained in the United States. Using the CTS, the male perpetration (males' reports) prevalence rate since high school was 17.8%, and the female victimization (females' reports) was almost 35.0% (DeKeseredy & Kelly, 1993).

Canadian high school students, responding to the London Family Court Clinic Questionnaire on Violence in Intimate Relationships (Jaffe, Sudermann, Reitzel, & Killip, 1992), reported lifetime prevalence levels of dating

---

COMPARISON OF NEW AND OLD SCREENER QUESTIONS

Violent Crimes—New (beginning January 1992)

1. Has anyone attacked or threatened you in any of these ways—
   a. with any weapon, for instance a gun or knife;
   b. with anything like a baseball bat, frying pan, scissors, or stick;
   c. by something thrown, such as a rock or bottle;
   d. include any grabbing, punching, or choking;
   e. any rape, attempted rape, or other type of sexual assault;
   f. any face-to-face threats;
      or
   g. any attack or threat or use of force by anyone at all? (Please mention it even if you were not certain it was a crime.)
2. Incidents involving forced or unwanted sexual acts are often difficult to talk about. Have you been forced or coerced to engage in unwanted sexual activity by—
   a. someone you didn't know before,
   b. a casual acquaintance, or
   c. someone you know well?

Violent Crimes—Old (1972-1992)

1. Did anyone take something directly from you by using force, such as by a stickup, mugging, or threat?
2. Did anyone *try* to rob you by using force or threatening to harm you?
3. Did anyone beat you up, attack you, or hit you with something, such as a rock or bottle?
4. Were you knifed, shot at, or attacked with some other weapon by anyone at all?
5. Did anyone *threaten* to beat you up or *threaten* you with a knife, gun, or some other weapon, *not* including telephone threats?
6. Did anyone *try* to attack you in some other way?

---

violence by Grade 12 that are somewhat lower than those reported in American studies. Out of a sample of 1,547 students, 9.2% had suffered physical abuse and 9.0% had been sexually abused. Female students reported significantly more abuse in each category than male students (Sudermann & Jaffe, 1993).

In a survey of 434 Arab-Palestinian engaged men, percentages of men who used CTS physical aggression tactics against their fiancées were as follows: 7.1% threw something at her; 8.0% pushed, grabbed, or shoved her; 7.5% kicked, bit, or hit her; 6.4% hit (or tried to hit) her with something; 4.5% beat her up; 3.8% threatened her with a gun or knife; and 4.0% used a knife or gun (Haj-Yahia & Edleson, 1994).

Intermediate Chapter Summary

The interest in courtship violence and date rape grew out of **research on marital violence,** and experts have uncovered similarities in topics, methodologies, conclusions, and suggestions for education and intervention. The major differences in this area of research are the inclusion of sexual assault factors, as well as the limited nature of the information available.

Experts have rarely relied on past estimates of courtship violence supplied by state and federal governments because classification strategies have been so circumscribed. There is an ongoing **controversy about definitions of consent and the measurement of rape,** for example, and social scientists and women's advocates increasingly seek broader assessment techniques that incorporate a nonlegal, easy-to-understand basis of questioning. Newer, 1992-1993 **official**

records suggest that women more than men bear the consequences of courtship violence, that is, far more boyfriends/ex-boyfriends (10.3%) murder girlfriends/ex-girlfriends than the reverse (1.4%). Of assaults, 22.7% of boyfriends and girlfriends have assaulted their dating partners.

The revised NCVS data for 1992-1993 (for individuals over age 12) disclosed that boyfriends/ex-boyfriends commit 16% of the aggravated and simple assaults against women and girlfriends/ex-girlfriends commit 2% against men. Estimates based on CTS data vary in respect to the nature of the sample. Roughly, 20% to 50% of both men and women in college-age dating relationships have physically abused a dating partner at least once over a lifetime. The lifetime prevalence rate for high school students appears to fall within the range of 9% to 27%. Collectively, these **vast differences** in both overall rates and gender-specific rates arising from different populations and information based on different questionnaires are perplexing.

Rape and sexual assault rate estimates anchored on early NCVSs yielded a rate of 3.9 per 1,000 women between the ages of 16 and 19 and 2.5 per 1,000 for women aged 20 to 24. In contrast, Koss's (1985) pioneering work, using modified questions, suggested the level of behaviors that would qualify as date rape emerged at a staggering 15.4% over a lifetime or 38 per 1,000 women for women aged 18 to 24 (Koss & Gidycz, 1985). Such sweeping divergence not only sparked a heated controversy over so-called advocacy statistics but prompted the BJS to recast its questionnaire. Newer estimates place annual rape and sexual assault rates of women over age 12 (not limited to college women) at 4.6 women per 1,000. Although NCVS researchers have **expanded offender classifications** to differentiate between intimates, other relatives, acquaintances, and strangers, they have not included a separate grouping for date rape. For a review of rape statistics, see Koss (1993).

Limited accounts from other countries suggest that the prevalence of dating violence and date rape are much the same or lower than those in the United States.

Searching for Patterns: Characteristics of Victims and Perpetrators

In searching for patterns of traits that typify perpetrators and victims of courtship violence and date rape, it is useful to examine the customary social structural variables such as age, gender, and cohabitation status, as well as other variables such as level of commitment.

Social Structural Variables

Age and Gender. A sampling of different studies indicates that it is impossible at this point in time to specify age variation. Data on gender differences, however, are more definitive. NCVS categorization of boyfriend/girlfriend assaults by individuals over age 12 was not available until 1995 (Bachman & Saltzman, 1995). These data show that serious aggravated and simple assaults by boyfriends/ex-boyfriends were disproportionately higher than assaults by girlfriends/ex-girlfriends. Similarly, an analysis of restraining orders against 757 teen batterers in Massachusetts revealed that 80.8% were against boys (Adams, Isaac, Cochran, & Brown, 1996).

In contrast, 11 surveys based primarily on CTS data (both minor and severe aggression) using college and high school samples revealed no marked gender differences in frequency of violence (Sugarman & Hotaling, 1989). Similar to the studies on marital violence, many studies found that women are actually more likely than men to report committing courtship violence and slightly more likely to report having sustained courtship violence (see Stets & Henderson, 1991; Stets & Straus, 1990). Women seem also to more often initiate the violence (DeMaris, 1992). Based on these results, many experts have characterized courtship violence as largely reciprocal (Cate, Henton, Koval, Christopher, & Lloyd, 1982; Worth, Matthews, & Coleman, 1990).

Explanations for reciprocal courtship violence correspond to those offered for reciprocal marital violence. Some gender differences in CTS self-reported perpetration in college and high school samples may be symptomatic of a general underreporting style of men (Riggs, Murphy, & O'Leary, 1989), or a social desirability bias in which women tend to see themselves as victims and therefore underreport their own violence (Makepeace, 1981). Males may be more likely than females to perceive aggression as mutual (Laner & Thompson, 1982; White, 1983) and to judge themselves as less culpable and females as more culpable for relationship violence (Le-Jeune & Follette, 1994). Furthermore, Foo and Margolin (1995) speculate that women's aggression may have more emotional salience than men's, thus contributing to better memory of such events and hence higher self-report rates.

Perhaps most important, as is discussed in the marital violence chapters, the CTS may effectively measure the frequency of violent interactions, but they do not consider the motivations or consequences of the violence. Similarly, few details about the antecedents of dating violence are available. As an example of the importance of contextual factors, consider the case of Tiffany that follows.

CASE HISTORY: TIFFANY— A VIOLENT DATE?

Tiffany was a beautiful 22-year-old manicurist working in Beverly Hills, where she hoped to launch a modeling career. She started dating Ralph, a 28-year-old fashion photographer. After two casual luncheon dates and a movie, Ralph offered to shoot a layout of Tiffany as a gift for her birthday.

During the shoot, Ralph frequently approached Tiffany to tilt her chin, adjust her hair, and reposition her pose. Without warning, Ralph walked over, tugged on Tiffany's blouse, and asked her to remove it. She jokingly replied, "Oh, you haven't got enough money to pay me for that." After trying for a while to convince her that he really wanted a topless photo, Ralph became menacing. When Tiffany decided to leave, Ralph blocked the exit. Tiffany became frightened. She suddenly hit him as hard as she could before running out onto the street. (Author's case history)

* * *

If a researcher were to question Tiffany and Ralph about who inflicted courtship violence and who was a victim of physical assault, both of these dating partners would probably have said that Tiffany was the perpetrator of dating violence. She struck Ralph, so he was the victim. The case would then become one more statistic suggesting that females aggress more than males. Without

information about rationales, such as need for control or self-defense, which the CTS do not supply, it is difficult to place these findings in context (see Stets & Pirog-Good, 1990).

Cohabitation. There is some evidence that the rate of severe violence, as defined by the CTS, is higher among cohabitants (22%) than for either dating partners (10.6%) or married couples (10.5%) (Stets & Straus, 1989).

Other Variables. In terms of socioeconomic status, dating violence and rape have been generally higher in lower socioeconomic groups (Belknap, 1989). Individuals of African American ethnicity also show a higher rate than other groups (e.g., McLaughlin, Leonard, & Senchak, 1992). Evidence is mixed about whether religious affiliation or church attendance differentiates individuals involved in dating violence from those who are not (e.g., Makepeace, 1987; McLaughlin et al., 1992). The use of alcohol and drugs appears to be a risk factor for courtship violence or date rape but does not imply inevitable causation (e.g., Harrington & Leitenberg, 1994; Laner, 1983; Makepeace, 1981; Roscoe & Benaske, 1985). One study, for example, found that 55% of one sample of victims of sexual aggression considered themselves at least "somewhat drunk" at the time of the assault.

Level of Commitment and Leaving a Violent Relationship

One of the most interesting findings in the literature is that interpartner aggression does not seem to occur frequently in dating relationships until the relationship has been sustained for an extensive period of time (Arias et al., 1987; Sigelman, Berry, & Wiles, 1984). Indeed, research has shown that both the length of the relationship and the commitment level are positively correlated with both physical and sexual abuse (Arias et al., 1987; Belknap, 1989; Stets & Pirog-Good, 1990). This circumstance may explain, at least in part, why roughly 30% to 50% of dating couples have not terminated their relationship despite interpartner aggression (see Cate et al., 1982; Makepeace, 1981; Roscoe & Benaske, 1985). Flynn (1990), for example, noted that the longer the period of dating prior to the first violent incident, the longer the woman remained in the relationship afterward.

These results are surprising because it seems logical to expect unmarried persons victimized by interpartner violence or rape simply to break off their relationship. In fact, recent evidence indicates that college students predict that in the long run, dating violence will lead to a breakup of the relationship (Carlson, 1996). Possibly, violence continues because the partners have accepted it very early as a legitimate form of conflict resolution. Among those who do not leave, roughly 60% say the violence either had no effect or even improved their relationship (e.g., Cate et al., 1982; Makepeace, 1981; Roscoe & Benaske, 1985). In fact, 33.8% of the women involved in violent dating relationships, in one analysis, expected to marry their abuser (Lo & Sporakowski, 1989).

Others have interpreted these unexpected findings to suggest that level of commitment is a precursor to dating violence (e.g., Burke, Stets, & Pirog-Good, 1989; Cate et al., 1982; Laner & Thompson, 1982) or that violence somehow solidifies the attachment of the couple (Billingham, 1987). About 30% of those who do not leave explain the violence as an act of love (see Cate et al., 1982; Makepeace, 1981; Pape & Arias, 1995; Roscoe & Benaske, 1985). Flynn (1990), for instance, found that there is a positive correlation between repeated violence and feelings of love for the partner (also see Follingstad, Rutledge, Polek, & McNeill-Hawkins, 1988). In fact, women who stay with a violent dating partner may resolve the cognitive dissonance evoked by the violence by convincing themselves that they are in love. Another explanation is that abused women stay because they believe that they can persuade their violent partner to change and thereby "save" the relationship (Lloyd, Koval, & Cate, 1989). Table 7.1 summarizes relevant sociodemographic factors and their relationships to courtship violence and date rape.

Intermediate Chapter Summary

Whether age is related to courtship violence is equivocal, but women under age 30 are more likely to be raped than older women. In college and high school samples, with CTS data, female students frequently report both higher perpetration and victimization rates than male students. Reciprocity estimates of dating violence vary from 50% to 70%. NCVS serious assault victimization data for dating individuals over age 12 reveal much **higher male-to-female rates** than the reverse. Higher CTS rates for female college and high school dating partners and reciprocity levels are surprising given that women are disproportionately injured. **Male underreporting** may be one causal factor. The surprisingly high level of CTS female-to-male violence reported has not only emphasized the need for a more thorough analysis of multiple variables such as gender effects but has also fueled a number of scientific debates.

Data indicate that rates of violence between cohabitants and dating partners are **higher than between married couples.** Individuals with lower incomes, of African American ethnicity, and who use alcohol or drugs seem more likely to be involved with courtship violence and date rape (both as victims and as perpetrators) than their counterparts. The link between religion and courtship violence is unclear. For a summary of these variables, see Sugarman and Hotaling (1989).

As one might expect, **level of commitment** and **length of the relationship** are interrelated. What is not so expected is that both these variables are positively correlated with high levels of courtship violence and sexual assault. Higher cohabitation rates, in fact, might be a reflection of these variables. Because it is not obvious why dating partners would remain in a violent relationship, researchers have advanced a number of explanations. One speculation is that dating partners have accepted interpartner aggression as a **legitimate conflict resolution tactic.** Some have conjectured that level of commitment is an antecedent to violence. Another speculation is that women remain because they are in love and believe that they can change their partner and/or save the relationship.

Table 7.1 Sociodemographic and Individual Risk Factors Associated With Courtship Violence and Date Rape

Factor	*Risk Factor for Abuse*	*Short Listing of Supporting Research*
Age	Indeterminant	Arias et al. (1987)
		Marshall and Rose (1987)
Gender		
Physical abuse perpetration	Indeterminant	Sugarman and Hotaling (1989)
		White and Koss (1991)
National Crime Victimization Survey assault data		
Males	Increased	Bachman and Saltzman (1995)
Rape perpetration		
Males	Increased	Koss and Gidycz (1985)
Females	Decreased	Bachman and Saltzman (1995)
Cohabitation	Increased	Stets and Straus (1989)
Low socioeconomic status	Increased	Belknap (1989)
African American ethnicity	Increased	Makepeace (1987)
Religious beliefs/background	Indeterminant	McLaughlin, Leonard, and Senchak (1992)
		McLaughlin et al. (1992)
Alcohol/drug use	Increased	Laner (1983)
		Harrington and Leitenberg (1994)
		Roscoe and Benaske (1985)
Level of emotional commitment and length of relationship	Increased	Arias et al. (1987)
		Belknap (1989)
		Flynn (1990)
		Sigelman, Berry, and Wiles (1985)
		Stets and Pirog-Good (1990)

Explaining Courtship Violence and Date Rape

In addition to a variety of social and relationship commitment variables, some cultural variables, socialization practices, and individual psychological factors also seem to differentially promote courtship violence and sexual assault. Although factors like the gender of the perpetrator and the circumstances of the date modify opinions elicited by surveys, people do not uniformly condemn courtship violence and forced sex.

Cultural Variables

As is common in the other subareas of family violence literature, experts have hypothesized that patriarchal beliefs and attitudes affect levels of violence and sexual assault. Generally, the results within the courtship violence and sexual assault area have been positive but weak. A survey of 1,307 Canadian college males, for example, examined respondents' patriarchal beliefs (e.g., "A man has the right to decide whether or not his wife or partner should go out in the evening with her friends") and patriarchal attitudes (e.g., "It is all right for a man to slap his girlfriend if she won't do what he tells her to do"). Statistical analyses revealed that both measures helped account for variation in physical and sexual abuse, but only to a slight extent (DeKeseredy & Kelly, 1993).

Peer-Group Support and Attitudes. A number of experts have proposed that adolescent peer-group support for aggressive behavior plays a key role in courtship violence. In their survey of Canadian male college students, DeKeseredy and Kelly (1993) found that both informational peer support (e.g., "Did any of your male friends tell you that you should respond to your dates' or girlfriends' challenges to your authority by using physical force, such as hitting or slapping?") and peers' patriarchal attitudes (e.g., "Would your male friends approve of a man slapping his girlfriend if she won't do what he tells her to do?") contributed a small portion to variation in male-to-female physical dating violence and sexual abuse.

A number of investigators have found that adolescents who have sexually aggressive friends are more likely than their counterparts to accept and engage in such behaviors themselves (e.g., Ageton, 1983; Kanin, 1957;

Schwendinger & Schwendinger, 1985). Those who have been either victims or aggressors themselves tend to have friends who are either victims or aggressors, whereas those without personal experience have friends also without experience (see Burcky & Reuterman, 1989; Tontodonato & Crew, 1992). Worth and her collaborators (1990) also found evidence suggestive of a relationship between dating violence and athletic and fraternity associations. This pattern is confirmed by Martin and Hummer (1995), who suggest that fraternity norms and practices often view sexual coercion of female acquaintances (a felony crime) as a sport, a contest, or a game.

CASE HISTORY: MARY AND HER DATE, DAN—A FRATERNITY BASH

Mary, a freshman at Florida State, had been drinking tequila before attending a fraternity party as the date of 23-year-old Dan, a junior and member of Pi Kappa Alpha. When she arrived, already intoxicated, he gave her wine and left her alone in his room. Police lab tests later placed her blood-alcohol level at over .349, which under some circumstances is enough to cause death.

Later Dan returned, forced sex on her, and then took her to the fraternity shower room where at least two other fraternity brothers raped her in a group and further used a toothpaste pump as a means of penetration. Afterward, the fraternity brothers dumped her in the hallway of a second fraternity house, the Thetas, where members of yet a third fraternity came over and etched their initials on her thigh with a ballpoint pen.

As news got out and gossip pervaded the campus, Mary started to believe she might have been to blame for her own rape, perhaps an accessory of some sort. Countermeasures such as changing her hair color did not prevent her notoriety. Mary was unable to cope with her life any longer and checked into a psychiatric hospital for treatment of alcoholism, bulimia, and depression. Dan pleaded no contest to forcible rape and received a sentence of 1 year, a stiff sentence by most standards. The fraternity brothers were allowed to plea-bargain to a lesser charge.

Mary, now working as a bookkeeper, said it had been therapeutic to see her assailants convicted. "These men robbed me of any pride or hope or self-esteem that I had and replaced it with anger and self-hate and fear. To see their lives affected is some vindication" (Bane et al., 1990).

* * *

The case history of Mary and her date underscores the seriousness of date rape and illustrates the widespread nature and acceptability of this type of male-to-female violence. At least three men in one fraternity participated in the rape; men in another house partook in initialing her thigh; and men in a third seemed willing to play host to still other indignities that befell Mary. It is this kind of behavior that so clearly sounds a cultural alarm.

Romanticism. Other cultural influences may also contribute to understanding of courtship aggression. Lloyd (1991) has proposed that two major cultural factors increase the likelihood of courtship and sexual aggression: romanticism and gender-related themes (i.e., control and relationship status). Romanticism, the idea that "love conquers all," may encourage dating partners to believe that their dyadic problems are mainly situational (e.g., just an angry outburst) and will dissolve upon marriage. A dominant relationship theme (or motivation) for men is control of dyadic intimacy (closeness-distance) and an analogous theme for women is dependency on a relationship. Whereas men may select violence as a means of controlling commitment levels, women may accept violence as part of the price of maintaining the relationship (see Henton, Cate, Koval, Lloyd, & Christopher, 1983). The following case history represents a situation in which a young girl wants a romantic relationship no matter what the cost.

CASE HISTORY: CLAUDIA AND ROBERTO—THEIR LAST DANCE AT THE PROM

Claudia met Roberto when she was a junior in high school. It was love at first sight. All Claudia ever wanted was a boyfriend who loved her and made her feel special. One problem Claudia and Roberto had was that they fought "like cats and dogs." It didn't matter what the situation was, what movie to see, where to get a hamburger, or whether to go out on Friday or Saturday.

Sitting in the car one night, Claudia accused Roberto of flirting with an old girlfriend. When the argument got heated, Roberto leaned over and slapped Claudia across the face. She slapped him back. They always fought like this, just like a couple of kids, the way they thought most couples do. After all, didn't all couples fight and hit each other?

Over the next 10 months, Claudia and Roberto continued fighting, and Claudia got bruised from time to time. One time, she got a black eye. The next morning, she told her parents that the bruises on her face came from a minor car accident. She wore a long-sleeved turtleneck shirt to hide her other bruises. A month later, she got another set of bruises. In fact, Roberto bit her arm several times and pulled her hair. She tried to bite him back.

Claudia loved Roberto, and she knew he loved her. In fact, she believed that he would not have hit her if he didn't love her. One thing she did to please him was give up her participation on the debate team, because Roberto hated it if she stayed after school once a week for practice. In fact, she stopped seeing nearly all of her old friends. Roberto told her that it was her "nagging" that set him off, and he had to get her to stop. She tried harder and harder to please him and thought that their quarrels would cease, especially if she stopped provoking him.

Her greatest fear was not that she would get seriously injured but that Roberto would never call her again. He was her whole world. She worried that if her parents found out about Roberto's violence, they would forbid her to ever see him again and that her two brothers might decide to beat him up. Every time she got hurt, Claudia renewed her efforts to hide her injuries.

On the night of their senior prom, Claudia was ecstatic. High school was over. She thought that she and Roberto would get married, and she would finally have everything she always wanted, but it didn't work out that way. As usual, Claudia and Roberto got into a quarrel, but this time Roberto's buddies could overhear the argument, and he felt humiliated because he "couldn't keep Claudia in line." Roberto decided that they should leave the prom. On the way to the car, however, the quarrel turned violent, and Roberto got out of control. He punched and kicked Claudia over and over again, letting out all of his rage about everything in his whole life. He was so infuriated that he left Claudia in the parking lot, bleeding and unconscious.

Another couple found Claudia and called the paramedics, who took her to the hospital. When Claudia revived the next morning, her parents were in a state of shock. They could not believe that Roberto had ever hit her. Her brothers vowed to beat him up, and the police were out looking to arrest him. Claudia was worried when the doctors told her she might lose the vision in one of her eyes. She was even more worried that she would never see Roberto again, that he would never call her again, and that he might stop loving her. Without Roberto, her life would be over. (Author's case history)

* * *

Initiation of Date and Who Pays. Additional cultural variables, such as the dating activity or who pays for a date, may influence students' acceptance of sexual aggression (see Makepeace, 1981; Stets & Henderson, 1991). Slightly over a fifth of students in one study said that under certain circumstances (e.g., church or movie date), it was allowable for "John" to have sex with "Mary" against her will (Muehlenhard, 1989). These variables, in turn, affected the respondents' other ratings. Women who initiate or pay for dates, as an example, are perceived to be more responsible for sexual aggression.

Male Misperceptions of Female Consent. Men often think women are more willing to have sex and that rape is more justifiable than women do. In fact, men's proclivity to sexualize women's behavior may constitute a form of miscommunication. That is, men may think women are more interested in sex and willing to engage in intercourse than women claim they are. No matter who initiates a date, who pays, or where a couple goes, men are more likely than women to interpret the woman's behavior as representing her desire for sex (Muehlenhard, 1989).

Gender constitutes an especially important organizing variable in explaining interpersonal violence (see Bookwala, Frieze, Smith, & Ryan, 1992; Fenstermaker, 1989). On balance, when a man feels "led on" by a woman's behavior, people are inclined to believe that rape is allowable (Goodchilds & Zellman, 1984). On actual dates that became aggressive, men in one survey reported believing that women wanted more sexual contact, but the women maintained that they wanted less (Muehlenhard & Linton, 1987). Such misreading of social cues, proviolence attitudes, rape myths, rape fantasies, and negative attitudes toward a woman's right to say no promote sexual assault (see Burt, 1980; Koss, 1985).

Attitudinal Factors

Despite long-standing interest in the issues, questions about the socialization of sexist attitudes in courtship violence and sexual assault remain unresolved (e.g., Bernard, Bernard, & Bernard, 1985). The specificity of the findings on these topics defies summarization, and the level of theoretical support for these variables is in a state of transition (also see Bookwala et al., 1992).

Male Sex-Role Traditional Beliefs. Men who accept traditional sex roles, that is, who assume a dominant role during the date, who hold adversarial attitudes regarding relationships, and who accept rape myths are more likely to be sexually aggressive than men without these attributes (Muehlenhard & Linton, 1987). Worth et al. (1990) demonstrated that college men who lacked so-called feminine qualities (e.g., being sensitive to others, affectionate, and understanding) were more apt to abuse their partners than men who possessed those qualities (also see Beaver, Gold, & Prisco, 1992; Makepeace, 1981; Marshall, 1987).

Female Sex-Role Contemporary Beliefs. Sex-role attitudes seem to exhibit potential for predicting a woman's response to violence as well (Flynn, 1990). One inquiry revealed that the more contemporary a college woman's attitudes are on the Attitude Toward Women Scale (Spence, Helmreich, & Stapp, 1973), the less likely she is to tolerate dating violence (also see Bookwala et al., 1992; Follingstad et al., 1988).

Individual Trait and Interpersonal Interaction Factors

In addition to sociocultural factors, certain kinds of personality traits, such as need for interpersonal control or hostility, seem to precipitate abusive events (Laner, 1983; Makepeace, 1981; Stets & Pirog-Good, 1987). "Hypermasculinity" in men may also play a role in anger, aggression, and lack of empathy (Vass & Gold, 1995).

Trait and Relationship Issues. The complexity of measurement issues in assessment of individual traits and relationship factors contributes to the difficulty in understanding the possible role of such issues in dating aggression. Whether dating aggression stems primarily from the presence of a violent person (individual personality trait; e.g., Burke et al., 1989; Matthews, 1984; Roscoe & Benaske, 1985) or more from a violent relationship (interpersonal factors; Cate & Lloyd, 1992) remains unresolved. Follingstad, Kalichman, Cafferty, and Vormbrock (1992), for instance, showed that a laboratory situation with ag-

gressive components is likely to stimulate abusive men (high trait violence) to be more aggressive but to inhibit aggression in nonabusive men (the situation). Hence, it may be the violent trait rather than situational cues (e.g., interpersonal relationships) that directly instigates high levels of aggression (also see Bookwala et al., 1992; Riggs, 1993). In fact, a cluster of traits may distinguish male sexual abusers from nonabusers. Male sexual abusers tend to view their courtship relationships as adversarial, to be hostile toward women, and to believe in rape-supportive myths (e.g., Garrett-Gooding & Senter, 1987; Lundberg-Love & Geffner, 1989).

Need for Interpersonal Control. Theoretically, need for interpersonal control might lead an anxious or ambivalent dating partner to use a dominating conflict resolution style, violence, or psychological aggression to equalize what is perceived to be an unbalanced relationship (see Kasian & Painter, 1992; Mayseless, 1991; Pistole, 1989). Using a six-item, experimenter-designed interpersonal control scale (e.g., "I keep my partner in line"), Stets (1991), for example, found that control needs were an important predictor of psychological aggression (e.g., "insulted him or her") both in perpetration and victimization of courtship violence. This account suggested that individual control variables (personality traits) offer a more valid explanation for aggression than do structural control factors (i.e., the patriarchy).

Reactance. In a different sort of inquiry, still within the framework of control issues, investigators assessed *psychological reactance*. Psychological reactance is the feeling of threat one experiences to his or her personal sense of freedom (Hong & Page, 1989). Typical questions include such items as "When something is prohibited, I usually think that's exactly what I am going to do" and "I resist the attempts of others to influence me." Hockenberry and Billingham (1993) found strong support for their thesis that college men and women who were courtship abusive, as assessed by the nonviolent items on the CTS (e.g., "stomped out of the room"), had higher psychological reactance scores than courtship-nonabusive students. These findings suggest that dating violence is connected to feelings of threat to one's sense of personal freedom and autonomy.

Need for Independence. In another inquiry, both men and women who were more instrumental (e.g., independent, self-confident, holding up well under pressure) were less likely to be recipients of dating violence (Stets & Pirog-Good, 1987).

Childhood Socialization

Social learning theory implies that childhood socialization factors such as direct physical victimization, direct sexual victimization, or indirect victimization via exposure to interparental violence are associated with later involvement in dating aggression, as either perpetrator or victim. Testing this relationship has been difficult for customary reasons, such as limitations of assessment and samples. The probability that childhood socialization variables have a differential gender effect has further complicated interpretation.

Direct Physical Abuse and Exposure to Interparental Violence. Several studies have found that childhood socialization factors are related to involvement in dating aggression for males. In terms of direct physical abuse during childhood, data from one analysis indicated a positive association with perpetration of later dating violence (Follingstad, Kalichman, et al., 1992). Data from two other studies revealed that physical abuse during childhood was linked with later victimization in dating relationships (Marshall & Rose, 1988; Stets & Pirog-Good, 1987). In regard to childhood exposure to interparental violence, two of four studies found a positive relationship with later dating aggression (see Carlson, 1990; Foo & Margolin, 1995; Marshall & Rose, 1988; O'Keefe, Brockopp, & Chew, 1986; Stets & Pirog-Good, 1987). The relationship between these childhood variables and female involvement in dating violence is especially inconsistent (see Foo & Margolin, 1995, for a review).

Sexual Abuse. Two studies have found that being a direct female victim of child sexual abuse is related to later sexual victimization by a dating partner (Koss & Dinero, 1989; Lundberg-Love & Geffner, 1989). Childhood sexual victimization may lower a woman's ability to resist assault (Lundberg-Love & Geffner, 1989) or create greater vulnerability with respect to factors such as negative self-identity (Koss & Dinero, 1989).

Other Related Variables. Other research has uncovered associations between observation of interparental aggression or child-to-parent abuse and later dating violence (Cornell & Gelles, 1982; Foo & Margolin, 1995). An interesting tangential inquiry disclosed a strong association between previous violent sexual victimization (not during childhood) and later dating aggression in both men and women (Foo & Margolin, 1995).

Social Learning Theory. Despite the complexity and discrepancies in the findings regarding the relationship between childhood experiences and later dating violence, theorists have attempted to fit them into social learning theory. From this stance, dating violence may be located on a continuum extending from childhood victimization experiences to adult violence (perpetration and/or victimization) (e.g., Burcky & Reuterman, 1989; Kelsey & Roscoe, 1986). Hence, involvement in courtship violence is the mediating link or stepping stone between childhood experiences in an abusive home and later involvement in a maritally violent relationship (Bernard & Bernard, 1983; Makepeace, 1981).

Other Viewpoints. Without taking childhood experiences into consideration, it is possible to view dating violence and marital violence as either overlapping or separate. Interpersonal violence may begin at a low level in courtship and simply carry over or overlap with later marital violence (Alexander & Follette, 1992; Cate et al., 1982; Roscoe & Benaske, 1985). Retrospective reports from battered women reveal this progression (Star, Clark, Goetz, & O'Malia, 1979).

Some experts maintain, however, that there is a separation, rather than an overlap, between courtship and marital violence. Levy (1991), for instance, proposed that certain aspects of adolescence such as inexperience, intensity, romanticism in intimate relationships, and the pressure to have a boyfriend separate teenage dating violence from marital abuse. Others (e.g., DeMaris, 1987) view premarital and marital violence as dissimilar because courtship violence occurs most frequently at a low level of severity, whereas marital battering occurs at a very high level of severity (Rouse, Breen, & Howell, 1988). Still others object to differentiations of this sort altogether, not only because they appear artificial but also because they may minimize the seriousness of some dating violence (e.g., Hamberger & Arnold, 1989; also see Adams

Table 7.2 Cultural, Attitudinal, and Socialization Risk Factors Associated With Courtship Violence and Date Rape

Factor	Risk Factor for Abuse	Short Listing of Supporting Research
Cultural		
Patriarchal attitudes	Increased	DeKeseredy and Kelly (1993)
Peer-group acceptance	Increased	DeKeseredy and Kelly (1993)
Friends		
Aggressive friends	Increased	Burcky and Reuterman (1989)
		Gwartney-Gibbs, Stockard, and Bohmer (1987)
		Tontodonato and Crew (1992)
Fraternity member	Increased	Martin and Hummer (1995)
		Worth et al. (1990)
Romanticism	Increased	Lloyd (1991)
Female initiation of or pay for date	Increased sex aggression	Muehlenhard (1989)
Male misperceptions of social cues	Increased sex aggression	Muehlenhard and Linton (1987)
Cultural and attitudinal		
Male sex role		
Traditional beliefs	Increased	Muehlenhard and Linton (1987)
Interpersonal insensitivity	Increased	Beaver, Gold, and Prisco (1992)
		Worth et al. (1990)
Female sex role		
Contemporary beliefs	Decreased	Flynn (1990)
Male trait violence	Increased	Burke, Stets, and Pirog-Good (1989)
		Follingstad, Kalichman, et al. (1992)
		Matthews (1984)
		Roscoe and Benaske (1985)
Dyadic (couple) factors	Increased	Cate and Lloyd (1992)
Male/female control needs	Increased	Stets (1991)
Male/female psychological reactance	Increased	Hockenberry and Billingham (1993)
Male/female independence	Decreased	Stets and Pirog-Good (1987)
Childhood socialization		
Male direct abuse		
Perpetration	Increased	Follingstad, Kalichman, et al. (1992)
Victimization	Increased	Marshall and Rose (1988)
		Stets and Pirog-Good (1987)
	Indeterminant	Foo and Margolin (1995)
Female direct abuse	Indeterminant	Foo and Margolin (1995)
		Marshall and Rose (1988)
		Stets and Pirog-Good (1987)
Male/female exposure to parental violence	Indeterminant	Carlson (1990)
		Marshall and Rose (1988)
		Stets and Pirog-Good (1987)
Male exposure only	Increased	Foo and Margolin (1995)
Male/female child sexual abuse	Indeterminant	Foo and Margolin (1995)
Female only child sexual abuse	Increased	Koss and Dinero (1989)
		Lundberg-Love and Geffner (1989)
Male/female violent sexual victimization	Increased	Foo and Margolin (1995)
Parent-to-child aggression	Increased	Foo and Margolin (1995)

et al., 1996). See Table 7.2 for a summary of risk factors associated with socialization and attitudinal factors.

Models of Courtship Violence and Date Rape

Despite the inconsistency of research findings, investigators have proposed several theo-

1 **Factors that enhance motivation to sexually abuse**	2 **Factors that reduce internal inhibitions**	3 **Factors that reduce external inhibitions**	4 **Factors that reduce victim resistance**

a. power and control needs
b. miscommunication about sex
c. sexual arousal
d. emotional incongruance
e. imbalance in power differential
	a. attitudes:
	  1. traditional sex roles
	  2. acceptance of violence
	  3. endorsement of rape myths
	  4. adversarial relationships
	b. prior abusive acts
		a. date location
		b. mode of transportation
		c. date activity
		d. alcohol or substance use
			a. passivity
			b. poor self-defense techniques/strategies
			c. history of sexual abuse
			d. traditional attitudes
			e. poor sexual knowledge

1 + 2 + 3 + 4 = DATE RAPE

Figure 7.1. Four-Preconditions Model of Date Rape

SOURCE: From "Date Rape: Prevalence, Risk Factors, and a Proposed Model," by P. Lundberg-Love and R. Geffner, 1989, in M. A. Pirog-Good and J. E. Stets, *Violence in Dating Relationships: Emerging Social Issues*, p. 179. Copyright 1989 by Praeger Publications. Reprinted with permission of Greenwood Publishing Group, Inc., Westport, CT.

ries of courtship violence or date rape. Models rest on varying levels of established evidence, but none has undergone sufficient analysis to be widely accepted.

Riggs and O'Leary (1989) proposed a plausible social learning model of courtship aggression that incorporates several elements. The first component includes individual factors such as exposure to models of aggression in intimate relationships and acceptance of aggression as a suitable response to conflict. The second component includes situational factors such as stress and relationship conflict. These two closely connected groups of factors interact with each other to instigate dating violence.

Attachment Theory. Attachment theory (Bowlby, 1980), as recently revived to accommodate dating aggression, posits that in adult intimate relationships, responses learned in childhood such as anxiety and anger over fear of abandonment erupt again to fuel an assault against a partner who threatens to leave (Mayseless, 1991). A primary advantage of this theory is its ability to explain not only the co-occurrence of love and violence but also to account for variability in commitment to a relationship, a partner's "on-again, off-

again" romantic behavior, and the stress it generates.

Model-Testing Study. The only study of courtship violence conducted principally to test theoretical assumptions examined which of three models (patriarchy, intergenerational learning, interpersonal skill deficit) best predicted the use of conflict resolution tactics (i.e., level of CTS scores). Haj-Yahia and Edleson (1994) tested an Israeli sample of 434 engaged Arab-Palestinian men on eight different inventories. Results supported an explanatory framework that encompassed all three theoretical models. The only consistent predictor of courtship violence across all three subscales of the CTS, however, was the presence of direct childhood abuse (intergenerational theory).

Model of Date Rape. A summary and application of information on date rape has led to one model that emphasizes the preconditions for date rape (Lundberg-Love & Geffner, 1989). This model begins with factors that enhance motivation to sexually abuse, adds factors that reduce both internal and external inhibitions, and ends with factors that reduce victim resistance. Refer to Figure 7.1 for a more detailed description of this model.

Intermediate Chapter Summary

A variety of factors have been examined by researchers to explain courtship violence and date rape. Although certain cultural beliefs and male peer pressure are supportive of patriarchy, the evidence is not strong. On the other hand, incidence of **peer support of male-to-female violence, beliefs of one's friends,** and **fraternity association** may be influential. Although the "birds of a feather flock together" doctrine seems to hold, more research is needed to specify the precise nature of these variables.

Romanticism may prompt some individuals to accept courtship violence on the grounds that a dating partner may change because "love conquers all." The location of the date (e.g., a church party), the nature of the preassault behaviors (e.g., petting), and which dating partner, if either, had been drinking altered college students' **perceptions of liability.** Many people also seem to believe that male sexual exploitation of women is almost inevitable and even tolerable under certain conditions. The most powerful determinant of judgments is the gender of the rater. Males are generally more likely than females to both perceive a female dating partner's behavior as giving consent and as sexual. The greatest area of **gender disparity** pertains to which partner is most responsible for a sexual assault.

Although current evidence is inconclusive, endorsing traditional **gender attitudes** may propel some men toward interpartner aggression, whereas accepting more modern sex-role attitudes may encourage women not to tolerate courtship violence. Although **trait research** has only just begun, several studies have shown that certain intraindividual or interpersonal traits are related to courtship violence and sexual assault. Clusters of traits describing "types" of abusers have proved valid only for male sexual abusers. What meager information is available suggests that individuals with a high need to control others, to protect their own personal freedom, and to be dependent on others are more likely to be involved in courtship violence and date rape than are other individuals.

Retrospective data and correlative analyses have been unable to provide conclusive evidence about the effects of direct abuse and exposure to interparental violence on dating aggression. What evidence is available suggests differential gender effects on both perpetration and victimization rates. Questioning the extent to which **intergenerational patterns** of abuse are explanatory has evoked intense discussion but no conclusive answers. Whereas some experts propose a link between being abused as a child and later interpartner aggression, others espouse a connection limited to courtship violence and later marital violence.

Theory construction in the area of dating aggression and sexual assault essentially remains at a primitive level despite recent efforts. Models of courtship violence or date rape most frequently rely on **social learning theory** for determinants of aggression (i.e., individual background characteristics, situational variables). A promising new application of **attachment theory** to dating aggression ties feelings of anger and insecurity learned in childhood with later fears of abandonment that subsequently elicit male-to-female dating violence. One study that examined three theoretical positions found that the only consistent predictor of interpartner aggression was direct childhood abuse (intergenerational theory). No theory has proved entirely adequate, thus calling attention to the need for a **multidimensional model.**

A model of date rape attempted to link several precipitating individual traits of perpetrators with intervening situational factors that reduce internal or external inhibitions that, in turn, are associated with individual victimization traits. This model, although not directly tested, incorporates much of what is currently known about date rape. Table 7.1 summarizes **risk factors** associated with courtship violence and date rape.

Responding to Courtship Violence and Date Rape

Community professionals may have little opportunity to respond appropriately to court-ship violence and rape because they receive comparatively few reports. Among a sample of high school students, for instance, only 22% told anyone about their victimization (Bergman, 1992). Pirog-Good and Stets (1989) found very low reporting rates among a sample of 714 female and 532 male college students involved in dating violence as assessed by CTS scores: 3.4% of women and 1.5% of men told a parent; 14.0% of women and 6.4% of men told a friend; 0.4% of women and 0.0% of men told a counselor or physician; and 1.1% of women and 0.6% of men told a criminal justice authority. The most significant determinant of reporting was the student's perception (i.e., labeling) of having been physically abused (also see LeJeune & Follette, 1994). It is also probable that women do not believe that their complaints will receive consideration (Goldberg-Ambrose, 1992) and that men simply have a decided proclivity for underreporting (Riggs et al., 1989).

Rape is generally one of the most unreported crimes by any standards (Koss, 1993; Russell, 1983b). Given the difficulty women face in recognizing their victimization as a crime of rape, their inclination for self-blame (Frazier, 1991), and the lack of support they receive (Davis & Brickman, 1991), it is understandable that so little date rape is reported (Koss, 1993).

CASE HISTORY: DOMINIQUE'S BLIND DATE AND CAMPUS REGULATIONS

Dominique decided to go out on a group blind date with a guy who was a buddy of her girlfriend, Carol. Later, Dominique let the whole group into her dorm room to cap off their fun evening at a rock concert. After Carol and her boyfriend left, Dominique and her date, Greg, started kissing and petting. When Dominique eventually tried to stop Greg's advances, he wouldn't stop, and he forced Dominique to have sex.

Because Dominique felt so guilty and ashamed, she did not report the incident to campus authorities. Indeed, she initially tried to keep the whole incident a secret. She was afraid authorities would discover that she had broken school rules about allowing dates into the dorm past 11:00 p.m. With a counselor's support, Dominique finally did report the rape to both the local police department and campus police.

On further examination and reflection, campus authorities changed the school's rules. Although they maintained the same curfew, they announced that they would no longer pursue sanctions against women caught in situations like Dominique's. Instead, they encouraged women to come forward so that they might apprehend date rapists. They even went so far as to install alarms throughout the buildings and grounds so that women in danger would have a better opportunity to call for help. In addition, the Inter-Greek council met and inaugurated a rape awareness program on campus even though the date rapist came from another campus and was not in a fraternity. (Author's case history)

The Criminal Justice System

Caringella-MacDonald (1988) has offered a number of vital analyses of the aftermath of legal reforms for sexual assault, marital rape, and domestic violence victims. Her research, as well as that of others, has continued to point out the inadequacy of laws in achieving the positive outcomes envisioned by reformers (e.g., Jeffords, 1984; Spohn & Horney, 1991). It is still true, for example, that only a few states extend orders of protection and other safeguards to individuals in dating relationships who have been threatened with an assault (see Koss et al., 1994b). The major obstacle in obtaining restraining orders is the difficulty teens face in meeting statutory relationship requirements (i.e., married, related by blood, a child in common, living together; Brustin, 1995). One exception, perhaps, is in cases of "stalking" (Anderson, 1993; also see Adams et al., 1996).

One particular obstacle in securing justice for victims has been the failure to eliminate juror misconceptions about rape and its victims. Despite reforms in admissibility of evidence and changes in jury instructions, for example, juries continue to include extralegal information (e.g., the victim's conformity to conservative gender-role behaviors) as a basis for their judgments (Goldberg-Ambrose, 1992). It is also important to point out that jurors' subjective interpretations of whether rape has occurred can be incredibly different from legalistic definitions of rape (Churchill, 1993). Illustrative of this problem is that jurors may fail to define nonconsensual intercourse as rape if the victim had formerly consented to sex, but on the occasion in question said no. The effects of jurors' perceptions came to light in one study showing that defendants convicted of acquaintance rape were less than half as likely to go to prison as those convicted of stranger rape (Candell, Frazier, Arikan, & Tofteland, 1993).

Treatment and Interventions

Many believe that intervention in violent premarital relationships is crucial because patterns of conflict and violence may carry over into marriage (e.g., Lloyd et al., 1989; Roscoe & Benaske, 1985). Others express concern about the long-lasting effects of sexual aggression on victims (e.g., Burgess, 1995). Educators must emphasize that courtship violence cannot be tolerated, just as violence between others (e.g., two coworkers) cannot be permitted (Laner, 1990). Even when dating violence happens publicly, for example, onlookers do not uniformly intervene (Laner, 1983).

Counseling for Courtship Violence. A very relevant problem in counseling is to help dating partners label their own or their partners' behavior as a form of violence and to help them modify their beliefs about the legitimacy of physical aggression (e.g., Pirog-Good & Stets, 1989). Another goal should be to encourage and empower people to leave a violent relationship (O'Leary, Curley, Rosenbaum, & Clarke, 1985). Qualitative research has shown, however, that leaving a battering relationship is a process, not a single event (Rosen & Stith, 1995). An additional goal for counseling might be to alert college women to the inherent dangers of allowing themselves to be controlled by their male partners (Follingstad et al., 1988). Counseling must also deal with issues of sexist attitudes and problems of peer-group support for aggression.

Many prescribe programs that target students who have grown up in violent homes. Bringing the problem into the open and discussing how family violence has affected them might decrease the likelihood of future violence. In general, the problems experienced by college students with a background of family violence do not call for new approaches but a commitment to known treatments (Rouse, 1991).

Counseling for Rape. The most traditional intervention for rape recovery is counseling at a rape crisis center, but crisis intervention is far from sufficient (Kilpatrick & Veronen, 1983). One of the most debilitating effects of sexual assault is the development of PTSD. Although therapists have devised and applied numerous rape interventions, researchers have conducted little systematic investigation of their effectiveness. In general, only a few well-controlled studies have appeared in the literature. Available studies show that cognitive-behavioral treatments focusing on fear reduction and provision of specific coping mechanisms have resulted in a reduction or remission of PTSD sequelae (Foa, Rothbaum, & Steketee, 1993).

In some circumstances, counselors should be cautious in applying research results to treatment strategies. Although it is possible that women who initiate or pay for dates are more at risk of date rape than women who do not, it may be imprudent to forewarn single women to avoid asking men for dates under any circumstances (Muehlenhard, 1989).

Summary

This chapter has attempted to define the meaning of courtship violence and date rape and to present what statistical information is known about its prevalence. For the most part, police departments and government agencies, such as the Bureau of Justice Statistics, have procured little accurate information, partially because dating partners and rape victims do not often make formal complaints and partially because government agencies have failed to clearly categorize offender-victim relationships. In addition, self-report surveys have only recently employed sensitive questionnaires. The dearth of accurate information in the United States is paralleled in other countries.

Self-report questionnaires administered by researchers have ascertained that dating violence is very common. Whereas National Crime Victimization Survey (NCVS) data estimate male serious-assault rates at 16% and female assault rates at 2%, other studies based on Conflict Tactics Scales (CTS) data with college and high school samples provide estimates of 20% to 50% for couples over their dating lifetime. Date rape occurs less frequently, but lifetime prevalence rates indicate a female victimization rate of 15%. Courtship violence and sexual assault are common in other countries as well.

A possible association of courtship violence with age may be difficult to ascertain because of the limited age range of individuals involved in dating relationships. In terms of gender, NCVS data suggest higher male assault rates and, of course, higher male rape perpetration. Although gender differences, if any, in perpetration rates of courtship violence seldom emerge with CTS data, women report more frequent victimizations and more frequent physical injuries and emotional traumas. The surprisingly high frequency of female-to-male CTS-reported violence has prompted additional research and speculation.

Given other findings in family violence, it is not surprising that some social structural variables like income, ethnicity, cohabitation status, and alcohol and drug use are linked with courtship violence. It is also interesting to note that religious beliefs and background seem not to play a role.

One of the most noteworthy findings in the area is that level of commitment and length of relationship are two key variables that are strongly and positively related to the occurrence of courtship violence. Several researchers have suggested that commitment is an antecedent to courtship violence. Others have proposed that some dating women, like married women, remain in a violent relationship because they love their partner and believe that they can change him or save the relationship.

Some cultural variables like differential weighting of male-to-female violence may work to decrease male-initiated violence. Other variables such as patriarchy, peer support, and proviolence attitudes of peers may be related to courtship violence. Sex-role attitudes seem likely to be related to some forms of courtship violence and rape, but evidence is weak and inconsistent. Factors such as romanticism and gender differences about issues of consent and attributions about responsibility for violence and rape have provided very useful information. Educators and therapists, in fact, should increasingly put this knowledge to use in program designs.

Although findings should be accepted tentatively, certain attitudinal factors such as male sex-role traditionality may also fuel courtship abuse. Individual traits, such as need for control, personal freedom, and emotional dependence, seem more related to violence and sexual assault than dyadic factors, but more research is needed to establish such generalizations. One of the most puzzling issues is the extent to which courtship violence and sexual assault result from experiences of direct childhood abuse or exposure to violence. On the whole, evidence shows several links between these factors, but cautions against premature assumptions of causality. Closely aligned is the question of whether courtship violence is either a stepping stone or training ground for marital violence.

By and large, dating partners who are involved in courtship violence or date rape do not inform either helping professionals or criminal justice agencies about their encounters. Consequently, these potential sources of community support have little opportunity to offer assistance. Bringing courtship and date rape into the open, therefore, may be a first step in motivating disclosure. Reformers envision changing the criminal justice system so that victims will find their interactions more satisfactory.

Counselors have addressed treatment for courtship violence and have pinpointed issues like the need to modify attitudes or the need to avoid control by others. Sexual assault has attracted extensive attention to both treatment and research. Cognitive-behavioral approaches have yielded some positive outcomes in decreasing trauma symptoms that have occurred in the aftermath of sexual assault.

Collectively, studies on courtship violence have shed light on the general problems of interpartner aggression. First, the high level of violence and CTS-based studies of gender mutuality of the violence seem to underscore cultural acceptance of violence. One ominous speculation is that for many young adults, interpersonal violence may be just "one relationship away." Another ramification of this review is the recognition that courtship relationships embody both violence and love. Finally, violence between intimates is not evoked solely by marital stresses and strains but is far more complex than previously envisioned.

8

Marital Violence

An Overview

C H A P T E R   O U T L I N E

An Interview With Lawrence W. Sherman

"My policy recommendation is to treat domestic violence like AIDS and to invest in research to find the best prevention and remedies that we can identify."

LAWRENCE W. SHERMAN is currently Professor and Chair of the Department of Criminology at the University of Maryland. He is an experimental criminologist who has evaluated crime control strategies for 25 years in over 30 police agencies, including those in New York, Washington, Chicago, Kansas City, Minneapolis, and Milwaukee and the Australian Federal Police. He conducted the first controlled experiment in the use of arrest for domestically violent men. His 1992 book Policing Domestic Violence: Experiments and Dilemmas *received the 1993-1994 American Sociological Association Distinguished Scholarship Award in Crime, Law, and Deviance. He is the author of four other books and over 100 other scholarly publications. He earned his diploma in criminology from Cambridge University (1973) and his Ph.D. from Yale University (1976).*

Q: What are your interests in the field of domestic violence?

A: My interests are in attempting to discover the most effective ways that police can help victims of domestic violence, given that there are many different kinds of domestic violence patterns to which the police must respond.

Q: How did you become interested in the role of police in domestic violence?

A: This question first struck me while I was a graduate student riding in police cars in New York City. I discovered that there were no evaluation data that could guide police policies about whether to arrest a batterer in the same way that doctors are guided in their choice of treatments for dealing with different kinds of diseases.

Q: In addition to your research on predicting homicide and serious injury from domestic violence in the United States and Australia, do you have any other future goals?

A: One goal that I would like to work on in the future is the testing of the radio emergency alarm that some jurisdictions are now starting to issue to women when they get

orders of protection. I think we need a controlled experiment to show whether this is an effective way to protect women who have already been seriously injured and may be at risk for murder.

Emergency alarms have been used in Liverpool, England, for years now and the cost is relatively low. This is not unlike the elderly panic alarm for people who fall and cannot get up. If the alarm is directly connected to police headquarters, the police can be dispatched to the home that the batterer is ordered not to visit. If the police get there quickly, it can lead to the batterer's being apprehended and, more important, to the prevention of serious injury.

Q: Do you have any policy recommendations?

A: My policy recommendation is to treat domestic violence like a complex phenomenon that is not amenable to ideological solution. My policy recommendation is to treat domestic violence like AIDS and to invest in research and development to find the best prevention and remedies that we can identify. We as a nation spend approximately 5% as much on violence reduction research as we spend on disease treatment research. That is, we spend 20 times more on diseases, many of which don't affect people until the end of their lives, rather than on domestic violence that can be a lifetime affliction.

This is a resource question. Regardless of whether violence is a "disease," we are not treating it as a researchable problem. AIDS victims are out on the streets of cities protesting that there is not enough research being invested in AIDS. So far, I've never seen any victims' groups protest for lack of research on domestic violence.

Q: Your research seems to have been centered on the problem of how the police respond to domestic violence.

A: Yes, and I've been criticized for that as being too narrow a perspective, but I think that if the field is to advance we need to explore various viewpoints in depth. It's clear to me that there is a great lack of understanding about how the police experience these events and what options that they really have within their own constraints. I make no apologies for looking at the policy choices from a police perspective simply because the police are doing more about this than anybody else.

Q: How does your ideological approach contrast with those of others in the field of domestic violence?

A: Victims' advocates tend to be ideological in their approach. Those who protest public and police policies assume that we have the answers and all that we lack is the will to implement them. My policy recommendation is to admit our ignorance, to admit the fact that we don't have the answers. The first thing we need is to get better understanding of this problem.

Introduction

CASE HISTORY: MR. K.— GETTING EVEN WITH THE WOMAN HE NO LONGER LOVED

On learning that his wife had begun divorce proceedings, Mr. K. of Enumclaw, Washington, got a demolition permit and bulldozed his wife's home into shambles.

The city's police dispatcher reported getting calls from men across the nation offering to set up a defense fund for Mr. K. "He's got a real cheering section out there," the dispatcher noted (p. 108). An informal tally of opinions offered by men frequenting a bar in a nearby working-class neighborhood showed that the men thought it was "just wonderful; he really got even with her!"

They seemed to ignore information that Mr. K. had told his wife that he no longer loved her and that the couple had agreed jointly to a separation. The predominant feeling seemed to be that this type of violence is not only permissible but also "macho" and praiseworthy (Brower & Sackett, 1985).

* * *

When people talk about marital violence, they are talking about slaps, assaults, rapes, and murders between intimate partners. Although marital violence as a social problem provokes more and more public outrage, on a more personal level its acceptance remains at surprisingly high levels. "It is sometimes easier to get your point across with a slap," we are told. "When you put a man and a woman together, sometimes sparks are going to fly—ain't no way around it." One has to wonder how violence between people who love each other came to be so acceptable.

This chapter presents information about all forms of marital violence, extending from mild verbal abuse to severe physical abuse. A section on marital violence statistics tries to answer questions about the frequencies of minor slaps, injury-producing assaults, and homicides. A comparison of official statistics with self-report data emphasizes two National Family Violence Surveys. Another section considers the ongoing debate about whether female-to-male violence is a serious problem. A final part describes some of the social costs of marital violence, such as use of medical services, an increase in homelessness, and an escalation in marital dissatisfaction.

An examination of the causes of marital violence centers on social structural dimensions such as age and gender, cultural factors, and socialization. A discussion of these causes and two well-known correlates of marital violence—alcohol use and marital dissatisfaction—help to explain how marital violence occurs within a larger social context that serves to promote or inhibit its occurrence. Next, we summarize responses from several community professional groups, such as the clergy, the medical field, and shelter services. The last section explains the role of the criminal justice system in combating marital violence.

Scope of the Problem

As can be seen throughout the book, defining *violence, abuse,* and *battering* is far more difficult than it appears on the surface. Compounding the problem is the fact that labeling interpersonal interactions as abusive is a very subjective matter (Marshall, 1994). It is important to place marital violence within the context of a serious social problem, however, because of its grave consequences. According to C. Everett Koop, former U.S. Surgeon General, domestic violence causes more injuries to women than automobile accidents, muggings, and rapes combined (Koop, 1989).

Defining *Marital Violence* and *Marital Rape*

It is obvious that marital violence lies on a continuum, but the exact nature of the continuum remains in debate. Some experts place all physically violent acts on a continuum ranging from mild to severe. Others propose a separate classification for the more serious, repetitive, and controlling forms of physical violence termed battering. Marital sexual assault deserves special recognition. Other experts debate whether certain nonphysical forms of abuse such as humiliation or evocation of fear are not actually more abusive than physical forms such as slapping (e.g., Walker, 1979).

What Is Marital Violence? One approach to defining marital violence has been to delineate categories of marital violence, using statistical methods such as factor analysis. However, these approaches, based on diverse questionnaire data, have failed to identify uniform violence categories. In 1992, for example, Pan, Neidig, and O'Leary (cited in O'Leary, 1993) conducted one such study notable for its large database of Conflict Tactics Scales (CTS; Straus, 1979) scores. These investigators isolated three correlated but separate types of marital violence: verbal aggression, mild physical aggression, and severe physical aggression. Rodenburg and Fantuzzo (1993) developed a different measure of wife abuse that grouped items into four abuse dimensions: physical, sexual, psychological, and verbal. Aguilar and Nightingale (1994) uncovered four somewhat divergent clusters designated as emotional/controlling, physical, sexual/emotional, and miscellaneous.

Another approach that has failed to yield positive results has been to delimit the terminology used to define marital violence. Straus (1991b), for instance, distinguishes *abuse* and *battering* from *violence* on the basis of distinct levels of intentionality. He states that in abuse and battering, there need be no intention to do harm. In contrast, violence assumes a purposeful inflicting of physical pain or injury. *Assault,* on the other hand, reflects a legal connotation that the violence was unlawful. Marshall (1994) argues that the term *violence* is best suited for physically forceful acts modified by appropriate terms such as *mild* or *severe*. Still another stance has been the insistence that *interpartner violence* (i.e., physical violence) be differentiated from *battering* (e.g., Pagelow, 1981a). Basically, battering relationships are characterized by fear, oppression, and control (Adams, 1986; Tinsley, Critelli, & Ee, 1992), as well as by cyclical patterns and increasing levels of violence (e.g., Walker, 1979).

What Is Marital Rape? Defining *marital rape,* at least theoretically, has been an easier task. It is just one of several forms of sexual assault. Findings from one study indicated that anal intercourse (52.8%) actually occurred more frequently than vaginal rape (Campbell, 1989b). Battered women in this study suffered from other forms of extreme sexually related degradation, such as having objects inserted (28.6%) or being sexually abused in front of their children (17.8%); 46% had been coerced into having sex immediately after discharge from a hospital (usually after giving birth).

Estimates of Marital Violence

Contrary to what one might expect, attempts to assess marital violence have not only failed to provide clear-cut results, they have also sparked an ongoing debate about gender dissimilarity involved in the use of such behaviors. There are several methods for categorizing reports of marital violence: (a) homicides as derived from official accounts, and (b) assaults as derived from both official and self-reports. Because marital violence data depend on factors such as the selection of crime categories used in various jurisdictions, the classification of data in terms of offender-victim relationships, the validity of survey respondents' memories, and the representativeness of the samples tested, the resultant statistics remain only estimates.

OFFICIAL ESTIMATES

Although the Uniform Crime Reports (UCR) gather data on offender-victim relationships for the crime of homicide, investigations fail to identify the offender in approximately 40% of cases. Consequently, it is impossible to know exactly how many murders are committed by intimates. Even conservative estimates, however, lead to the con-

---

The percentage of homicides committed by intimates is somewhere between 9% and 15%.

---

clusion that a surprisingly large percentage of U.S. murders are intrafamilial. According to the UCR, of the 22,636 homicides committed in the United States in 1992, 1,288 (6%) were committed by a spouse or ex-spouse and 762 (3%) were committed by a boyfriend or girlfriend. These figures obviously are underestimates, because no doubt some of the homicides in which the offender was not identified involved spouses or boyfriends or girlfriends. If one examines only those homicides in which the relationship between the victim and offender was identified, then 9% were committed by a spouse or ex-spouse, and 6% were committed by a boyfriend or girlfriend. The actual percentage of homicides committed by intimates, therefore, is probably somewhere between 9% and 15% (see Bachman & Saltzman, 1995; U.S. Department of Justice [FBI], 1992).

Further examination of these data debunks the popular myth that men are especially vulnerable in intimate relationships. Among intimate homicides (i.e., spouses, ex-spouses, boyfriends, or girlfriends), 69% were perpetrated by men against women. This means that there were more than twice as many husbands or boyfriends who killed their wives or girlfriends than the converse. This is an important observation because for homicide cases in general, men are the most likely victims. Indeed, 78% of all victims of homicide are males, and 90% of all perpetrators of homicide are male (U.S. Department of Justice [FBI], 1992). Taken collectively, these figures suggest that although relatively few women kill, when they do kill, they often do so in intimate settings (Goetting, 1991; Jurik & Winn, 1990).

Similarly, when women are killed, they are often killed in an intimate setting. In fact, in 1992 husbands or boyfriends were the known assailant in 28% of all female homicides and 41% of the female homicides in which the

offender was identified (Bachman & Saltzman, 1995). Plass and Straus (1987) estimate that one third of all female homicides are perpetrated by husbands or boyfriends. In contrast, between 3% and 5% of male homicide victims are killed by wives or girlfriends (Bachman & Saltzman, 1995).

In terms of marital assaults, UCR data are of limited usefulness because they do not compile information about offender-victim relationships. For 1991, the Bureau of Justice Statistics (BJS) (Flanagan & Maguire, 1992) recorded 133,028 assaults by spouses and 64,808 by ex-spouses. The value of these data is further reduced by extreme underreporting. Kaufman and Straus (1990), for example, believe that less than 7% of marital assaults are officially reported.

SELF-REPORT SURVEYS

Because approximately 90% of marital violence never becomes part of official UCR records (Schulman, 1979; Teske & Parker, 1983), many experts have turned to self-report estimates as more accurate estimates of the frequency of marital violence. As a measure of marital violence, however, self-report data still underestimate the amount and seriousness of marital violence. Of the variety of factors contributing to underreporting, some of which have been described previously, the observation that violent men tend to minimize the frequency and severity of their actions is particularly relevant (e.g., Riggs, Murphy, & O'Leary, 1989; Szinovacz, 1983). Adding to the uncertainty caused by underreporting is the doubt raised by contrasts in survey results.

National Family Violence Surveys. The two National Family Violence Surveys are the only nationally representative studies that estimate marital violence (Straus, 1990b). When data from the first Family Violence Survey were published (Straus, Gelles, & Steinmetz, 1980), one point stood out clearly: Marital violence is very common. In fact, the rate of violence among married couples was high enough that Straus and his colleagues concluded that the marriage license might in many ways be considered a "hitting license." Data from both surveys revealed that approximately 16% of American couples (married and cohabiting couples) experienced at least one act of violence during the year prior to the survey.

Table 8.1   Rates of Marital Violence: 1975 Family Violence Survey and 1985 Family Violence Re-Survey (in percentages)

	Husband-to-Wife		Wife-to-Husband	
Type of Violence	*1975* (N = 2,143)	*1985* (N = 3,520)	*1975* (N = 2,143)	*1985* (N = 3,520)
Minor violence acts				
1. Threw something	2.8	2.8	5.2	4.2
2. Pushed, grabbed, or shoved	10.7	9.3	8.3	8.9
3. Slapped	5.1	2.9	4.6	4.1
Severe violence acts				
4. Kicked, bit, or hit with a fist	2.4	1.5	3.1	2.4
5. Hit or tried to hit	2.2	1.7	3.0	3.0
6. Beat up	1.1	0.8	0.6	0.4
7. Threatened with a gun or knife	0.4	0.4	0.6	0.6
8. Used a gun or knife	0.3	0.2	0.2	0.2
Violence indexes				
Overall violence (Items 1-8) (used any violence act in the previous year)	12.1	11.3	11.6	12.1
Severe violence (Items 4-8) ("wife beating")	3.8	3.0	4.6	4.4

SOURCE: From "Societal Change and Change in Family Violence From 1975 to 1985 as Revealed by Two National Surveys," by M. A. Straus and R. J. Gelles, 1986, *Journal of Marriage and the Family, 48*, p. 477. Copyrighted 1986 by the National Council on Family Relations, 3989 Central Ave. NE, Suite 550, Minneapolis, MN 55421. Reprinted by permission.
NOTE: This table has been modified to give the percentage of spouses who used any one act of violence from the Conflict Tactics Scales for a given year.

Rates of more serious violence were considerably lower, with slightly more than 6% of the couples experiencing *severe* violence (Items 4-8 from the CTS) (Straus & Gelles, 1986).

Table 8.1 presents rates of violence from the 1975 and the 1985 surveys for both husbands and wives. These data indicate that wives hit husbands as frequently as husbands hit wives. More specifically, rates of overall marital violence during 1985 (Items 1-8 in Table 8.1) are actually higher for wives (12.1%) than they are for husbands (11.3%). The rate of severe violence is also higher for wives (4.4%) than for husbands (3.0%).

National Crime Victimization Surveys. Vastly different estimates of the rate of family violence, especially gender-specific violence, originate from analyses of the National Crime Victimization Surveys (NCVS) data (see Feld & Straus, 1989). According to a 1984 NCVS report, 91% of spousal violent crimes were attacks on women by their husbands or ex-husbands (Klaus & Rand, 1984). NCVS data also disclosed that assaulted wives had a very high revictimization rate; 32% were assaulted again in a 6-month period (Langan & Innes, 1986). Furthermore, popular assumptions that women's safety is increased by leaving

assaultive males also proved to be erroneous. In 1992, the victimization rate of women separated from their husbands was about 3 times higher than that of divorced women and about 25 times higher than that of married women (Bachman & Saltzman, 1995).

Nonrepresentative Sample Surveys. Estimates based on nonrandom sample survey data, although limited in generalizability, have still served to broaden conceptions about marital violence. In an early study of 600 American applicants for divorce, for example, Levinger (1966) found that 36.8% of wives and 3.3% of husbands complained that their partner had physically hurt them (also see Newmark, Harrell, & Salem, 1995). Longitudinal data from 272 couples 18 months before and 30 months after their marriage indicated that 44% of females versus 31% of males self-reported physical aggression before marriage. After marriage, the figures dropped to 32% for women and 25% for men. Thus, for some couples, aggression begins before marriage and continues, but then it may diminish with increasing age (O'Leary et al., 1989). Another analysis found that military men reported higher levels of marital violence than comparable civilian men (Cronin, 1995).

Cross-Cultural Surveys. Although very little evidence has accumulated about marital violence rates in other countries (Chester, Robin, Koss, Lopez, & Goldman, 1994), available information tends to underscore the universal nature of marital violence. Data from Canadian and Australian studies have tended to replicate findings of the U.S. National Family Violence Surveys, or sometimes have indicated even higher levels of marital violence (Brinkerhoff & Lupri, 1988; Knight & Hatty, 1992; Scutt, 1983). A Korean account

---

The rate of violence for gay or lesbian couples is about the same as that for heterosexual couples.

---

of marital violence revealed exceptionally high rates, 37.5% for wives in the year prior to the survey and 23.2% for husbands (Kim & Cho, 1992). Cross-cultural examinations of gender differences in injury-causing assaults detected a consistent pattern of male-to-female violence, whether in Austria (Bernard & Schlaffer, 1992), Nigeria (Kalu, 1993), or Japan (Yoshihama & Sorenson, 1994).

Gay and Lesbian Surveys. In addition to heterosexual comparisons of interpartner aggression, researchers have more recently broadened the scope of investigations to include gay and lesbian populations (see Lockhart, White, Causby, & Isaac, 1994). For gay male couples, Island and Letellier (1991) estimated the rate at between 10.9% and 20.0% (also see Bourg & Stock, 1994). In a sample of 1,566 lesbians, Loulan (1987) found a rate of interpartner violence of 17%, and in another analysis, Lie, Schlitt, Bush, Montagne, and Reyes (1991) found a rate of 26%. These data suggest that the rate of violence for gay or lesbian couples is about the same as that for heterosexual couples.

Estimates of Marital Rape

Because government agencies do not separate marital rape from rape by other intimates in their collection and analysis of data (see Bachman & Saltzman, 1995), researchers have surveyed community or clinical samples of women to obtain estimates. Data from these nonrandom surveys suggest that sex-

ual assault and rape occur rather frequently in violent marital relationships, but not in isolation from other physical assaults (e.g., Frieze, 1983).

Data indicate that from 10% to 14% of all married women and at least 40% of assaulted wives have been raped by their husbands (Finkelhor & Yllö, 1987; Russell, 1983b). Experts have also concluded that approximately twice as many women are raped by their husbands as by other men (Finkelhor & Yllö, 1987; Russell, 1983b). As with other forms of physical violence, leaving a sexually assaultive partner provides little protection against continued sexual violations (Campbell & Alford, 1989). In one clinical study, for example, 55.0% of raped wives were no longer living with their partners; 35.8% were legally separated or divorced (Hanneke, Shields, & McCall, 1986). Apparently, the marriage license is not only a hitting license but also a "license to rape."

Gender Perspectives on Marital Violence

Marital violence survey data suggesting that men and women are equally violent have fueled a continuing debate between some mainstream sociologists (Straus, 1993) and feminists (Kurz, 1993). At issue is whether family violence is most accurately conceptualized as "mutual and family-based" or "male-based" (Schwartz & DeKeseredy, 1993). Feminist researchers perceive the "real" marital violence problem to be wife battering, not mutual marital violence. In particular, studies showing that women are more frequently injured than men in domestic disputes (Brush, 1990; Saltzman et al., 1990; Stets & Straus, 1990) seem indicative of women's greater victimization.

In 1977, however, Suzanne Steinmetz argued that some men suffer from a "battered husband syndrome" comparable to the "battered woman syndrome." In a strong response, Pleck (1978) referred to Steinmetz's work on the battered husband syndrome as the "battered data syndrome." The phrase, the "myth of sexual symmetry in marital violence," captures the fervor and antagonism expressed by some advocates (Dobash, Dobash, Wilson, & Daly, 1992). For his part, Straus (1993) reaffirmed his position that assaults by women (e.g., slapping) are still a serious social problem, just as slapping a coworker would be a problem. Furthermore, female-to-male violence has the potential of increasing male-to-female violence in that men will respond by escalating their use of violence (Feld & Straus, 1989). Within the framework of social learning theory, women's violence provides a model of violence that "teaches" exposed children to be violent. As Straus (1993) has emphasized, overlooking women's violence as inconsequential helps to perpetuate cultural norms that accept or permit marital violence.

In line with a gender-neutral approach, CTS data from a broad spectrum of community-based (nonclinical) marital violence surveys have almost uniformly revealed little gender disparity in frequency of marital violence (Straus, 1993). In contrast, data from a number of other sources have disclosed large gender differences. Males, for example, accounted for 88% of all violent crime arrests (U.S. Department of Justice [FBI], 1992), and the NCVS data disclosed that women are about 6 times more likely than men to experience intimate violence (Bachman & Saltzman, 1995). Along with injury rate disparity, other data sources, such as calls to the police, calls to shelters, and emergency room visits, also suggested differential gender effects (see Bachman & Saltzman, 1995; Stark et al., 1981; Steinman, 1991).

As attention finally turned to issues of defining and measuring interpartner violence, skeptics of the mutual violence theory increasingly indicted the CTS for its perceived limitations. Some experts held that a simple counting of violent acts between couples on the CTS places too much emphasis on frequency and not enough on its motivations (e.g., self-defense) or outcomes (i.e., interpersonal control; Browne, 1990). From a diametrically opposed position, Straus (1993) countered that separating assaultive acts from their contexts is generally the better approach and that researchers interested in assessing contextual factors should simply use additional tests along with the CTS. In the end, a number of researchers either modified the CTS or developed alternative scales (see, e.g., Barnett, Lee, & Thelen, 1995; Shepard & Campbell, 1992; Tolman, 1989), and Straus and his colleagues revised the CTS to include injury outcomes and sexual assaults (CTS2; Straus, Hamby, Boney-McCoy, & Sugarman, 1995).

Injuries. According to most surveys, physical acts of marital violence are most often in the less severe range and appear gender neutral (Aldarondo, 1996; Holtzworth-Munroe & Stuart, 1994; Straus, 1993). These episodes include hitting, throwing things, slapping, and pushing, and the resultant cuts and bruises rarely require hospitalization. Whether initiation of marital violence is gender neutral remains unresolved (see Emery, Lloyd, & Castleton, 1989; Saunders, 1989b; Straus, 1993). In terms of severity of marital violence, men appear to use more severe forms of violence than women (Browning & Dutton, 1986; Saunders, 1989b) and to use a greater amount of force than women (Straus, 1980b).

Serious injury-related marital violence is clearly and consistently associated with male-to-female violence (Saltzman et al., 1990). Based on data from two different studies (Brush, 1990; Stets & Straus, 1990), Straus (1993) concluded that the annual rate of injury-producing assaults by husbands was 3.7 per thousand and by wives was 0.6 per thousand. Using the new version of the CTS (CTS2; Straus et al., 1995), Cantos, Neidig, and O'Leary (1994) convincingly demonstrated that topographically similar behaviors (e.g., slapping) cause far more injuries, especially severe injuries, for women than for men.

In a survey of marital rape victims, the most common injury-related outcome was pain (72%). Some of the other injuries included anal or vaginal stretching (36.1%), bladder infections (50.9%), vaginal bleeding (29.6%), leakage of urine (32.4%), missed menstrual periods (25%), miscarriages and stillbirths (20.4%), unwanted pregnancies (17.5%), infertility (7.4%), and sexually transmitted diseases (6.5%). Posttrauma symptoms are particularly common in battered women who have been raped (Russell, 1982; Walker, 1984), and the symptoms can be long lasting (Riggs, Kilpatrick, & Resnick, 1992).

Fear. What little information is available suggests that strong gender differences also occur in the level of fear generated by marital violence. Whereas battered women report being very afraid of their violent partners (Russell, Lipov, Phillips, & White, 1989), batterers report little fear of physical assault from their female partners and almost no fear of adverse consequences from the criminal justice system (Carmody & Williams, 1987). Similarly, compared with responses by battered women, batterers report that their violence more frequently "frightens their partner" and it helps them "get their own way" (Barnett, Lee, & Thelen, 1995).

Self-Defensive Aggression. The degree to which women's violence is self-defensive is particularly controversial. A major drawback in interpreting data gathered to assess self-defensive behaviors hinges on the specification of the sequence of the violent events. The story of Mark and Cher makes vivid the contextual nature of some battered women's violence and the confluence of their emotions: fear, desperation, and anger. It also highlights the problems of determining the extent to which Cher's violent behaviors can be classified as self-defensive.

CASE HISTORY: CHER AND MARK— RUNNING FOR THEIR LIVES

Mark suddenly jumped on me from behind, knocking me to the living room floor. He started choking me and calling me a "bitch." Then he forced sex on me right in front of my 12-year-old son, Danny. Danny grabbed the poker near the fireplace and hit his dad on the head. Mark was stunned. I got up and hit him on the head as hard as I could with a dining room chair. Then I began to kick him as hard as I could anywhere that I could. I knew he would come after me again when he came to, so I grabbed Danny with one hand and my purse with the other, and we ran for our lives. (Author's case history)

* * *

As in the case of Mark and Cher, clinical studies typically reveal that when assaulted wives are violent, they are often reacting to what is done to them, rather than initiating a confrontation (Cascardi, Langhinrichsen, & Vivian, 1992). That is, their marital aggression is often a matter of self-defense (e.g., Browne, 1987; Hamberger & Arnold, 1991; Saunders, 1988) or fear (Laner & Thompson, 1982; Marshall & Rose, 1990). Interview data from 1,000 abused wives in one inquiry indicated that 665 used self-defensive violence at least once over the lifetime of the relationship (Bowker, 1993). Even so, an analysis of 9,919 crisis calls to a battered women's shelter indicated that only 5% of the women had attempted any self-defensive counterattacks during their most recent battering. All of these attempts were unsuccessful and resulted in even more physical injury (Murty & Roebuck, 1992). Straus (1993), however, claims that assaults by wives are not necessarily self-defensive or "preemptive strikes." New evidence from a small 1989 study by Jurik and Gregware (cited in Straus, 1993), for example, ascertained that only 21% of male homicides occurred in response to men's prior abuse or women's threats. Furthermore, analysis of the 1985 National Family Violence Survey revealed that at least 25% of wives were the only member of a couple to have used violence during the previous year (also see Brush, 1990).

In the final analysis, it may be best not to view marital violence victimization as an either-or proposition but as a problem of "dissimilar proportions." Both genders can be violent, but women appear to be more frequently victimized (see boxed insert: "Debating Female-to-Male Violence: Does It Really Matter Who Wins?").

Monetary Costs of Marital Violence

In many respects, the costs of marital violence are immeasurable. Because battering has been thought of as a private matter for so long, society has hardly begun to calculate the price it must pay. One approach researchers have used is to estimate injuries. Another has been to investigate the costs of homelessness and welfare that are related to battering. Finally, agencies within the criminal justice system are more closely scrutinizing the costs of processing battery cases.

Medical Costs. Although it is clear that injuries and illness caused by marital violence increase health care costs, no one has been able to estimate accurately the actual monetary amounts. Based on a Kentucky survey of women (Schulman, 1979), Straus (1986) estimated that women make 1,453,437 medical visits per year for treatment of injuries resulting from an assault by a spouse. Approximately 20% to 50% of all female emergency patients are there to receive treatment for marital assault (Campbell & Sheridan, 1989). Costs for hospital emergency room care for battered women in New York City may be as high as $506 million annually ("The Billion-Dollar Epidemic," 1992).

Homelessness and Welfare Costs. Homelessness and welfare costs are another cost of battering. Studies indicate that domestic violence is the main reason for homelessness among women and children (Zorza, 1991). A 1988 study funded by Victim Services identified 21% of the homeless as battered women (cited in Friedman, 1991). In 1992, Senator Roy Goodman of the New York State Com-

DEBATING FEMALE-TO-MALE VIOLENCE: DOES IT REALLY MATTER WHO WINS?

The issue of female-to-male marital violence is very controversial. No doubt both sides are right to some degree. Gelles and Straus (1988) are right when they condemn all family violence: men hitting women, women hitting men, parents hitting children. Critics of Gelles and Straus are also right. Past research has failed to emphasize sufficiently the contextual factors surrounding marital violence. It is women who are more likely to show up in emergency rooms, shelters, and the morgue. It may be appropriate for them to use self-protective violence, given the objective nature of the external threat facing them (e.g. Bograd, 1990).

How important is it to resolve this type of academic controversy? Does it really matter who wins? From a sociological point of view, the debate cannot be easily dismissed as insignificant. It is important because whoever wins this battle earns the right to define the nature of the problem. As mentioned previously, sociologists refer to the combatants in debates such as these as claims-makers. Claims-makers view their cause as a moral cause, and their ultimate goal is persuasion. Feminist Demie Kurz (1993) summarizes the consequences like this:

> This debate over men's and women's use of violence has significant consequences for popular and academic conceptions of battered women, and for social policy. How a problem is framed determines the amount of concern that is generated for that problem as well as the solutions that are proposed. Research findings influence whether the media and the public take battered women seriously, or whether they view them as equally blameworthy partners in family violence. Feminists fear that framing the problem as spouse abuse will lead to decreased funding for shelters, a diversion of resources to battered men, and/or increased arrests of women in domestic disputes under mandatory arrest policies. More generally, feminists fear that a focus on "spouse abuse" diverts attention from the causes of violence against women—inequality and male dominance. (p. 89)

According to Schwartz and DeKeseredy (1993), Straus (1990b) seems to have won the ear of government and policymakers. Furthermore, the work of Straus and Gelles, "at least in the popular press and some mainstream sociological quarters, is approaching status as the standard canon in the field" (Schwartz & DeKeseredy, 1993, p. 250). On the other hand, Senator Joseph Biden (1993) has succeeded in passing the Violence Against Women bill ("Model Law," 1994), and the O.J. Simpson case has focused the entire nation's attention on the plight of battered women. Neither side's viewpoints have prevailed unilaterally, and the battle of the claims-makers is likely to continue.

mittee on Investigations, Taxation, and Governmental Operations (cited in Zorza, 1994) estimated that New York State spends $30 to $40 million annually to house homeless women. One study of court orders from women seeking protection orders revealed that the court awarded support to only 13% of women (Rowe & Lown, 1990).

Costs of Criminal Justice System Processing. Police, court, probation, and prison costs associated with battering are also difficult to estimate. Some authorities suggest that domestic violence calls are the largest category of calls to the police each year (Gelles & Cornell, 1990). According to the same New York State committee that investigated medical costs, New York City made 12,724 domestic violence arrests at an average cost of $3,241 per arrest. Including these police costs and those for the court and detention, the city paid at least $41 million (see Zorza, 1994).

Intermediate Chapter Summary

It has become increasingly clear that **no consensus** has been reached about the differential meaning of words such as *violence, assault,* and *abuse,* coupled with concepts such as intention, consequence, and degree of repetition. In the final analysis, marital violence may be like the elephant studied by the three blind men. Everyone may have a distinct point of view. The most common form of sexual assault in marriage is forced anal sex, and the most common outcome of sexual assault is pain.

Estimates of the amount of physical violence experienced by marital partners varies according to the **type of data collected** and the **samples surveyed.** In 1992, official records indicated that 1,288 homicides (6%) were committed by a spouse or ex-spouse (U.S. Department of Justice [FBI], 1992). For 1991, the Bureau of Justice Statistics (Flanagan & Maguire, 1992) recorded 133,028 assaults by spouses and 64,808 by ex-spouses. Analyses of these data clearly show that women are the most likely victims of lethal intimate aggression. National victimization surveys reveal that over 90% of violent crimes committed by spouses are attacks on women by their **husbands or ex-husbands.**

The **National Family Violence Surveys,** using self-report data, found that 16% of married partners suffered an episode of violence during the year prior to the survey and that men and women reported near equal rates of marital violence (Straus & Gelles, 1986). Nonrandom **community surveys** often showed even higher rates of interpartner aggression. Survey data from **different countries** and from **gay and lesbian partners** generally paralleled those obtained from other populations. Data derived from self-reports, of course, are fraught with problems such as underreporting and even intentional falsification. In the last analysis, the amount of marital violence remains only an estimate.

The meaning of frequency data based on the CTS has led to a serious and **long-lasting debate** in the field. Some mainstream sociologists hold that marital violence is most accurately conceptualized as mutual and family based. Feminist researchers, in contrast, strongly contend that marital violence is male based (Schwartz & DeKeseredy, 1993). Although individuals such as Straus emphasize the inappropriateness of any marital violence and hold open the option of the battered husband, feminists emphasize the necessity of viewing marital violence in terms of contextual features such as motivations and outcomes and placing blame on the perpetrator (usually a male) (Koss et al., 1994a).

Reaching a conclusion about gender differences, of course, rests on the type of findings one accepts, such as self-reports or emergency room records. Research has consistently indicated that women are far **more likely to be injured** during episodes of marital violence, and they are **more likely to experience fear.** Some experts contend that women's marital violence is primarily self-defensive in nature. Finally, who wins the battle between **mainstream sociologists and feminist scholars** does make a difference in terms of how the problem is conceptualized in the public eye. Until now, the ideas of mainstream sociologists have been predominant (Schwartz & DeKeseredy, 1993).

Marital violence has a number of **societal costs.** Injuries have increased medical costs. The need for women and children to flee from their homes has increased homelessness, and criminal justice processing of marital violence cases has increased criminal justice costs.

Explaining Marital Violence

There are several macrolevel theories (e.g., cultural explanations, structural characteristics of the family, deterrence, external stressors) that help explain marital violence, as well as several microlevel theories (e.g., socialization, intrapersonal, interpersonal). The following section provides more detail for some of the more traditional explanations: structural characteristics (e.g., age, gender, socioeconomic status [SES], race), cultural (e.g., social acceptance of violence, patriarchy), socialization, and interpersonal interaction patterns (marital conflict). Also included is a discussion of the role of alcohol and drug use in marital violence.

Social Structural Variables

Structural factors such as age, sex, SES, and race and ethnicity are all used to predict family violence. It is important to remember, however, that these factors explain patterns and variation in the rates of marital violence but not precisely who will or will not become a perpetrator or victim. Indeed, as the following case history suggests, batterers come in all shapes and sizes.

CASE HISTORY: JOHN FEDDERS— HIS JOINT CAREER AS WIFE BEATER AND CHAIRMAN OF THE SECURITIES AND EXCHANGE COMMISSION

In a divorce hearing, Charlene Fedders accused her husband, John, of blackening her eyes, punching her, breaking her eardrum with a blow to the head, and permanently injuring her neck by trying to throw her over a balcony. He also attacked her while she was pregnant, saying that he did not care if he killed her and the baby.

Fedders, chief enforcement officer of the Securities and Exchange Commission, expressed remorse but said in his own defense that he had been suffering from financial duress. His lucrative salary of $161,000 per annum from his private law practice had decreased as a government employee to only $72,000. He was having difficulty paying the tuition for a private education for his sons. Mr. Fedders described his upbringing as "very strict Catholic" and said that he and his siblings described both their parents as "General Patton."

Because Mr. Fedders was undergoing psychiatric treatment and was awaiting "divine intervention" from God, the judge granted John a 4-month postponement of the divorce so that he would have time to win back his wife (Jackson, 1985).

* * *

The case of John Fedders contradicts every stereotype that exists about wife batterers. He is White, he is educated, and he is rich. Stereotypes can have some serious consequences. What if judges, for example, were to form an impression of "prototypical" battering as occurring only in certain racial and economic groups (Schuller & Vidmar, 1992)? They might ignore cases like that of John Fedders. Therefore, although it is important to recognize patterns of abuse, it is equally important that these patterns not contribute to stereotypes.

Age. Marital violence, a crime in the family, occurs most frequently between ages 18 and 30, just as it does in nonfamily crime (Straus et al., 1980).

Gender. As already discussed, official estimates suggest that males are more assaultive than females, and they clearly commit a greater proportion of intimate homicides (Bachman

& Saltzman, 1995; U.S. Department of Justice [FBI], 1992). Large representative samples using self-report data indicate that wives are as frequently violent as husbands and as likely as males to initiate the violence (Straus & Gelles, 1986). Wives, however, are not as severely violent (Browning & Dutton, 1986; Saunders, 1989b; Straus, 1980b). In contrast with large representative samples, nearly all clinical research indicates that men usually initiate the violence and are more likely to engage in multiple acts of assault (Emery et al., 1989; Saunders, 1989b).

Socioeconomic Status. The National Family Violence Surveys provide self-report evidence that battering is more prevalent in bluecollar and lower-class families. Straus and his colleagues (1980) estimate that families living at or below the poverty line have a marital violence rate that is 500% greater than in the wealthiest families (also see Hutchison, Hirschel, & Pesackis, 1994; Klaus & Rand, 1984). An investigation of Thai couples provided very strong support for the importance of SES in the level of physical wife abuse (Hoffman, Demo, & Edwards, 1994).

Race and Ethnicity. Studies exploring race and ethnicity prevalence rates should be taken as speculative. Some studies (e.g., Goetting, 1989; Neff, Holamon, & Schluter, 1995) suggest that minority families tend to be more violent, especially when the violence is severe (as in Barnett & Planeaux, 1989; Stets, 1990). Others question the marital violence-race relationship, arguing that when demographic and socioeconomic factors are controlled, minorities are no more likely than nonminorities to be violent (Hutchison et al., 1994; Straus & Smith, 1990). Statistics based on police arrest records may overrepresent minorities and the poor because of differential arrest policies (Black, 1980).

The latest evidence shows that more minorities call the police, and those who do are treated similarly in terms of arrests (Hutchison et al., 1994). Another analysis of telephone calls to a shelter uncovered a disproportionate number of help-seeking calls placed by minorities (cf. Gondolf, Fisher, & McFerron, 1988). Two other studies, one of Caucasian women, Mexican American women born in Mexico, and Hispanic women born in this country (Sorenson & Telles, 1991), failed to find a racial distinction, as did an account of marital violence by African American and European American men in the military

(Cronin, 1995) (also see Kantor, Jasinski, & Aldarondo, 1994).

Cultural Variables

Cultural factors can also be useful in explaining marital violence. In some cultures, violence is accepted; in others, it is condemned. In this country, many authorities blame marital violence on widespread cultural acceptance of violence, as reflected in television, movies, sports, toys, and video games (see Eron, Huesmann, Lefkowitz, & Walder, 1987). Others cite approval of violence within the home as a contributing factor. For some, the most crucial element is cultural recognition of male dominance.

Acceptance of Marital Violence. Many couples accept a certain amount of marital aggression. More than one third of younger couples may engage in "normative" aggression in which neither partner typifies the violence as abusive or self-defensive (O'Leary et al., 1989).

CASE HISTORY: BEN AND LORI— MAKING UP IS NOT HARD TO DO

At an after-theater party that Ben and Lori attended on their vacation, Ben struck up a conversation with Vanessa, a 20-year-old ingenue from the Dominican Republic. When Lori took note of Ben's interest in Vanessa, she began flirting with one of the young male dancers, Danny. Lori made a game of "kicking back" with Danny, requesting slow music, rubbing up against him while they danced, and asking him to bring her several glasses of wine. Next thing Lori knew, Ben was out of sight and so was Vanessa. Lori stormed out of the party, with Danny in hot pursuit.

As Lori walked down Broadway on foot at midnight, Ben came out of nowhere and pleaded with her to come back. Lori slapped his face, screamed that he was a "cheat," and marched on toward their hotel. Ben tried to stop Lori by pinning her to the wall of a building. Ben accused Lori of being "turned on" by Danny, so Lori taunted Ben with quips like, "Young guys in tight pants look good to me!" When Ben couldn't shut Lori up, he slapped her once and twisted her arm behind her back. When he let go, Lori ran crying into their hotel.

Inside their room, Lori slammed things around, insisting that Ben no longer loved her. She threw Ben's jacket to the floor and stomped all over it. Ben said that Lori ought to know that he loved her. Didn't she know that he thought she was the "sexiest woman at the party, so blond, so cool, so beautiful"? Lori burst into tears, saying that she wanted only him. Ben grabbed Lori and began kissing her passionately. The "real" party lasted until 3:00 a.m. Lori and Ben had learned long ago that a few slaps "here and there" were just part of their relationship. After all, they weren't really violent, Lori said, because they loved each other and no one ever got hurt. (Author's case history)

* * *

The relationship between Ben and Lori is far from unusual. Dibble and Straus (1980) estimate that 28% of Americans believe that hitting a spouse is sometimes necessary, normal, or good and that one third had actually slapped a spouse. Similarly, Briere (1987) found that 79% of a sample of college males rated themselves as having some hypothetical likelihood of hitting a woman in a variety of situations. Although almost everyone believes that strangers should not hurt one another, many do not apply the same standard to married couples (Shotland & Straw, 1976). Unfortunately, community standards have not changed much despite the spate of publicity and condemnation regarding intimate violence over the past decade (1982-1992) (Grasmick, Blackwell, Bursik, & Mitchell, 1993).

Patriarchy. The acceptability of marital violence may have its roots in patriarchy: a form of social organization in which males enjoy power and the right of decision making (Tiff, 1993). Batterers, for example, might think that they have the right to control and punish a partner (Gamache, 1991). Husbands who espouse patriarchal beliefs and attitudes tend to be more violent toward their wives than men who do not accept patriarchy (Coleman & Straus, 1986; Smith, 1990). Historically, women have had to accept the violence directed toward them because they have been considered the property of males. According to Dobash and Dobash (1978), early marriage laws literally dictated male ownership of women:

The man was the absolute patriarch who owned and controlled all properties and people within the family. A wife was obligated to obey her husband, and he was given the legal right and moral obligation to control and punish her for any "misbehavior," including adultery, drinking wine, attending public games without his permission or appearing unveiled in public. (p. 428)

The degree to which patriarchy can be used to explain marital violence, however, is especially controversial. Variability in attributing marital violence to patriarchy originates both from the type of information used and the aspect of patriarchy examined (male dominance, status, privilege, or power and female dependence). Some contend that patriarchal theories are inadequate accounts of marital violence. Dutton (1994), for example, contends that if patriarchy were the predominant cause of wife beating, nearly all men socialized in male dominance would be involved. At the very least, because only 30% of men in the United States have ever physically abused their female partners even once over the lifetime of the marriage, it seems clear that patriarchy is not the only cause of marital violence. Studies on gay and lesbian populations have further disputed the link between gender power differentials and violence, because they have uncovered no clear status differentials (e.g., income, education) between perpetrators and victims in these relationships (see Bologna, Waterman, & Dawson, 1987; Claes & Rosenthal, 1990; Kelly & Warshafsky, 1987; Renzetti, 1992).

On the other hand, accounts based on female dependence seem to support patriarchal explanations of wife abuse. Rates of violence are higher among couples when women have little work experience, few financial resources, and few alternatives to marriage. Specifically, women whose "objective dependence" on marriage is high (women who do not work outside the home, earn 25% or less of the family income, and have young children at home) and women whose "subjective dependence" on marriage is high (women who perceive that compared to their husbands, they would suffer more from divorce) tend to experience more violence than women whose dependence is low (Kalmuss & Straus, 1990).

Cross-Cultural Studies. Investigations of the status of women and children in other cultures have strongly contributed to a conceptualization of family violence as an outgrowth of patriarchy, male privilege, and devaluation of females as a human rights issue (Gondolf, 1990; Menon, 1990). Worldwide, potentially deadly customs such as female circumcision illustrate the powerlessness of women. Only recently have government officials begun to prohibit such rituals (see Heise, 1989; Holloway, 1994, for reviews).

Broude and Greene (1983) documented wife beating in 57 of 71 societies, thus revealing how common and unexceptional wife beating is throughout the world. In Finland, 44% of people do not support legal interference in family violence (Peltoniemi, 1982). Cultural acceptance of marital violence, however, is not uniform in these countries. Singaporeans, for example, support police intervention in cases of wife assault and expect judges to treat such cases as seriously or more seriously than similar crimes (Choi & Edleson, 1995).

In societies where women are treated equally, they are much less likely to be abused (Levinson, 1988). Wife assault is more likely to be permitted in societies where men control family economic resources, where conflicts are solved by means of physical force, and where women do not have an equal option to divorce (Brown, 1992). An analysis of cross-cultural violence, however, disclosed no consistent links with any macrolevel factors such as patriarchal beliefs (Gartner, 1993).

Socialization

Socialization plays a pivotal role in explanations derived from studies documenting the occurrence of marital violence in successive generations. Researchers consistently find that men exposed to parental violence are substantially more likely to be violent toward their spouse than are men not exposed to parental violence (Hotaling & Sugarman, 1986; Kalmuss, 1984). A more sophisticated analysis across three generations replicated these findings but also showed that females exposed to parental aggression were somewhat more likely to become victims (Doumas, Margolin, & John, 1994). The role of socialization in women's violence, however, is especially controversial (Foo & Margolin, 1995; Hotaling & Sugarman, 1990). Socialization can neither account for the large number of people who are maritally violent, but did not come from abusive homes, nor for the large number of people from abusive households who do not engage in adult violence (Bennett, Tolman, Rogalski, & Srinivasaraghavan, 1994; Smith & Williams, 1992).

Studies are beginning to evaluate the role of socialization as it applies to the learning of cognitive or attitudinal variables (Barnett, Fagan, & Booker, 1991). One team of investigators, for example, proposed that ineffective problem-solving strategies learned in childhood carried over into adult relationships and precipitated male-to-female marital violence (Choice, Lamke, & Pittman, 1995). Another group found evidence linking shame proneness learned in childhood with adult marital male-to-female violence (Dutton, Van Ginkel, & Starzomski, 1995). Fear of abandonment and emotional dependency stemming from childhood experiences may also mediate interpartner aggression (Barnett, Martinez, & Bleustein, 1995; Murphy, Meyer, & O'Leary, 1994).

Other Correlates of Marital Violence

In addition to cultural acceptance of marital violence and exposure to parental violence during childhood, other factors such as alcohol abuse and marital dissatisfaction are associated with marital violence.

Alcohol and Drugs. Research is somewhat mixed on the role drugs and alcohol play in marital violence. Certainly, society has historically placed much of the blame for marital violence on alcohol. Alcohol can facilitate aggressive behavior (Bushman & Cooper, 1990), and recently Flanzer (1993, p. 171) flatly stated that "alcoholism causes family violence."

Men who batter when they are drinking may also batter when they are sober.

Evidence supporting this view reveals that alcohol is present in many marital violence situations. Estimates vary from less than 20% (e.g., Coleman & Straus, 1983) to over 80% (Leonard & Jacob, 1988).

In terms of abusive husbands, 60% to 70% assault their partners while drunk, and 13% to 20% do so while high on other substances (Gorney, 1989). In addition, marital assaults by men with alcohol problems tend to be more frequent and serious than those of men free of alcohol problems (Browne, 1987; Walker, 1984). Alcohol, however, is probably not the causal agent it is assumed to be (LaBell, 1979; Zubretsky & Digirolamo, 1994). One contradiction is that men who batter when they are drinking may also batter when they are sober (Nisonoff & Bitman, 1979). Stress, however, may be the antecedent to

both drinking and spouse abuse (see Barnett & Fagan, 1993; Barnett et al., 1991). Drinking rates among maritally violent men may be no higher than rates found in other groups where stress levels are inordinately high (Finn, 1985; MacEwen & Barling, 1988).

In regard to battered women, evidence suggests that they also drink more heavily than nonbattered women (e.g., Telch & Lindquist, 1984). Data from hospital injury records tend to corroborated this view (Stark et al., 1981). On the other hand, several investigators have contended that battered women do not drink more than nonbattered women (e.g., Rosenbaum & O'Leary, 1981a; Van Hasselt, Morrison, & Bellack, 1985). One study shed light on the problem by examining the timing of the drinking. The female incidence of drinking during abuse was 17.8%, and the male incidence was 30%. Following abuse, 48.1% of the female partners drank contrasted with 24.2% of the abusers (Barnett & Fagan, 1993). In summary, a review abstracting data from all available controlled studies indicated that alcohol use by battered women was an inconsistent risk factor (Hotaling & Sugarman, 1986, 1990).

Police behavior also plays a role in perceptions about the role of alcohol in spouse abuse. Drinking by battered women, for example, makes them seem especially blameworthy in the eyes of many police officers (see Downs, Miller, & Panek, 1993; Waaland & Keeley, 1985). Police officers' greater likelihood of arresting an abusive spouse or victim who also is drunk increases the probability of finding a link between alcohol use and family violence. Correlational data indicating a link between alcohol use and spouse abuse, therefore, may be spurious (Bard & Zacker, 1974).

One reasonable assumption about alcohol-related violence is that it occurs because of expectancy (Collins & Schlenger, 1988). People learn it is acceptable to have a "time out" from normal behavior when drinking (MacAndrew & Edgerton, 1969). From this perspective, alcohol offers a socially acceptable rationale for partners to leave and return (Gelles, 1993a). Misunderstanding of the alcohol misuse-spouse abuse connection contributes to inappropriate reactions by agents of society like the police, or to suboptimal treatment approaches (Zubretsky & Digirolamo, 1994). In the final analysis, "alcohol is neither a necessary nor a sufficient explanation for family violence, but is one important factor often associated with it" (Yegidis, 1992, p. 522).

By themselves, other drugs, such as marijuana, LSD, heroin, or cocaine, are equally unlikely to prompt aggression (Bennett et al., 1994). One exception is the finding that amphetamine use can instigate aggression in monkeys (Smith & Byrd, 1987). A credible hypothesis, therefore, is that human amphetamine users might become more violent toward their marital partner.

Interpersonal Marital Interaction Patterns. One framework for understanding marital violence considers violence to be a product of the interactions of the spouses in a marital system, rather than the result of the individual behavior of only one assaultive spouse (Giles-Sims, 1983). Within the realm of couple interactions, several patterns related to marital violence, in fact, have emerged (Yegidis, 1992). As one example, studies have revealed high rates of marital discord in maritally violent couples (e.g., Rosenbaum & O'Leary, 1981b).

Inadequate communication also plays a role in marital violence. In one study, for example, violence increased in husband-abusive marriages when both partners had poor communication skills (Babcock, Waltz, Jacobson, & Gottman, 1993). According to Burman, Margolin, and John (1993), communication difficulties in the form of arguments or conflicts between abusive couples are exceptionally hostile and reciprocal (also see Eisikovits, Guttmann, Sela-Amit, & Edleson, 1993). If one member of the couple makes an angry statement, the partner is very likely to respond in kind. Members showed a high level of contempt for one another, which lasted for a considerable length of time. Wives in violent relationships were especially likely to make comments with aggressive content. In contrast, when members of nonviolent couples made angry comments, their partners were much less likely to reciprocate with angry or contemptuous remarks. Instead, partners might respond with nonhostile negative, neutral, or even positive comments. In fact, they frequently found ways to exit arguments altogether (Burman et al., 1993).

There is also evidence to suggest that violent couples, especially male partners, are manipulative, predominantly in sexual or romantic matters. Partners in violent relationships tend to see each other as a "means toward an end," rather than as a unique person (Seawell, 1984). Partners fail to express their love, for example, by asking such ordinary questions as, "How did your day go?" or "What did the doctor say about your headaches?" Instead, they may only concern themselves with what their partners have done or not done to make them feel better.

Although many researchers and practitioners are willing to acknowledge the negative effect that angry, inadequate communication patterns or marital dissatisfaction might have on a couple, they are less willing to blame marital violence on these factors (see Margolin & Burman, 1993; Murphy & Cascardi, 1993). Feminist researchers, in particular, express outrage at formulations of marital violence that place any responsibility on victims (Bograd, 1992). They further emphasize how attributing violence to the "couple" instead of the "perpetrator" may create a dangerous situation for victims by influencing other decisions, such as the police decision to arrest.

Intermediate Chapter Summary

Several **macro- and microlevel theories** help explain marital violence. Social structural variables present patterns and rates of marital violence but cannot predict precisely who will a perpetrator or a victim. At the same time, available information plainly shows that younger people are the most frequent perpetrators of intimate violence. Gender differences remain unresolved in the minds of some experts. Although findings are far from uniform, marital violence probably occurs more frequently in lower classes. Least certain is whether marital violence occurs more frequently or with greater severity in any particular ethnic minority. Reasons for the greater documented preponderance of cases in lower-socioeconomic-status groups and possibly some minority groups may originate in other correlates of marital violence such as the higher stress associated with poverty.

Criminologists, sociologists, and anthropologists have uncovered a number of cultural factors conducive to marital violence. First, **American culture** accepts a certain amount of relationship violence as normative, and standards are not changing rapidly. Second, **patriarchal**

attitudes have made it possible for men to control women through force. Note, however, that **research on lesbian couples** implies that patriarchy may not totally account for power imbalances between couples. Although patriarchy contributes to wife beating, it is probably not the sole cause. The **cross-cultural relationship** between male dominance-female dependence and wife beating may offer some support to patriarchal theory.

Certain **socialization** practices during childhood are significantly related to marital violence in adulthood, but social learning theory appears inadequate as a complete explanation. Although male batterers have more frequently been abused or witnessed abuse compared with nonbatterers, most individuals raised in abusive homes do not become abusive later. New approaches suggest that **behaviors learned in childhood,** such as inadequate problem-solving skills, shame proneness, and fear of abandonment, function as cognitive mediators of aggression and may therefore lend support to social learning theory models.

A number of behaviors, such as **alcohol abuse, inadequate interpartner communication styles,** and **marital dissatisfaction,** may characterize either one or both members of maritally violent couples. Partners in violent relationships may also fail to demonstrate affection in relationship-enhancing ways. A systems viewpoint of attributing marital violence to a couple's marital dissatisfaction or inadequate interaction rankles those who strongly believe individuals must be held accountable. Although marital violence experts are normally cautious in assigning causality to these factors, the lay public is not. **Misattributions** about the causes of marital violence misdirect efforts made by social agents and couples themselves to end the violence by assigning responsibility for the violence to the wrong behavior or to the wrong spouse.

Responding to Marital Violence

Motivated community professionals can promote the reduction or elimination of marital violence. Battered women's advocates believe that to prevent family violence, it is crucial that all levels of society (e.g., the police, churches, schools, hospitals, counselors) start with the credo that family violence is unacceptable. Research on the availability, the attitudes, and the effectiveness of community professionals, however, indicates that progress in changing attitudes is slow.

The Clergy

Bowker and Mauer (1986) reported that after the first battering incident, wives are more likely to contact the clergy than any other helping group except the police. Many feminist writers, however, believe that the clergy may be the wrong place to turn. They contend that traditional theologies have contributed to the victimization of wives by supplying Biblical evidence that God ordains patriarchy (Dobash & Dobash, 1979; Martin, 1978; Walker, 1979). The 19th-century suffragette Mathilda Gage (Stanton, Anthony, & Gage, 1881/1889) asserted that "the most grievous wound ever inflicted upon women

has been in the teaching that she was not created equal with man, and the consequent denial of her rightful place and position in Church and State" (p. 754).

Alsdurf (1985) mailed a two-page questionnaire to 5,700 ministers from Protestant churches in the United States and Canada. Responses indicated that 26% of the surveyed pastors agreed that a wife should submit to her husband and trust that God would honor her action by either stopping the abuse or giving her the strength to endure it. About 50% of the pastors expressed concern that the husband's aggression not be overemphasized and used as a justification to break up the marriage. Results also revealed that 33% of the ministers felt that abuse would have to be severe to justify a Christian wife's leaving her husband. According to 21% of these clergy, no amount of abuse would justify a separation. Only 17% believed that mild physical violence was compelling enough to allow a woman to separate from her husband.

Even though clergy, as a group, strongly support preservation of marriages, some research has disclosed that more recently, clergy have begun to furnish information about treatment programs, provide extended counseling, or suggest that the victim obtain professional therapy. Half of the surveyed clergy relay information about shelters. Much less frequently, they advise women to call police, obtain a civil protection order, or separate from the abuser (Martin, 1989).

The Medical Field

Health care providers, like other segments of society, have tended to view spouse abuse as a private matter. Barbara Seaman of the National Council on Women's Health ("Focus—Call for Help," 1994), however, contends that the health care system should be the first entry point for societal intervention. In response to such appeals, the American Medical Association now makes use of a booklet for doctors' use in detecting family violence (Children's Safety Network, 1992).

Emergency Room Responses. For some assaulted spouses, the emergency room staff may be the first contact they have regarding the abuse. In 1992, the Joint Commission for the Accreditation of Health Care Organizations passed regulations saying that emergency rooms "had to identify" battered women ("Focus—Call for Help," 1994). If staff respond appropriately by helping the victim identify the problem as abuse, they may help the victim begin the long road to recovery.

In a 1988 study of emergency room personnel, only 11% made a positive response (e.g., discussed the abuse, provided helpful information) to battered women (Kurz & Stark, 1988). McLeer and Anwar (1989) found that on development of an emergency room protocol for asking how injuries occurred, identification of victims rose from 5.6% of cases to 30.0%. Medical personnel should routinely ask about sexual assault (Campbell & Alford, 1989). One general improvement would be to integrate emergency room personnel with victim support services (Shepherd, 1990).

Doctors' Responses. Sugg and Inui (1992) interviewed 38 primary care physicians about their responses to domestic violence. Qualitative analysis revealed that most physicians did not want to discuss domestic violence with patients for fear of opening a Pandora's box, of intruding on their patients' privacy, or because they felt powerless to intervene. About 70% of the doctors identified time constraints as a major barrier and felt primarily able to offer only medical assistance. Hamberger (1991) noted that physicians need training in such skills as understanding the dynamics of domestic violence and in safety planning.

As a final note, education of health care workers is crucial to intervention (Burge, 1995). According to the Family Violence Prevention Fund and Injury Center for Research and Prevention, 20% of California hospitals neither train physicians and nurses to recognize family violence victims nor are they well equipped to assist them. A law requiring health practitioners to report domestic violence took effect in California on January 1, 1994. A second California law being phased in over 2 years will oblige medical and social work professionals to be trained in how to detect evidence of domestic abuse (cited in Brommer, 1993).

Insurance Companies' Responses. Some American insurance companies are denying health, life, or disability coverage to abused women. In recognition of the repetitive nature of spouse abuse and its high probability of causing injury, illness, or death, these companies have categorized battered women as having a "preexisting medical condition." Battered women are too risky to insure; the cost to insurance companies is too high. Fortunately, legislators have introduced bills into both houses of Congress that would prohibit discrimination against battered women seeking insurance coverage (see Parker, 1996; Zorza, 1994).

The Counseling Field

Psychologists and psychiatrists, as a group, have frequently failed to recognize the existence of spouse abuse in the clients they treat. Hansen, Harway, and Cervantes (1991, p. 235) used two hypothetical cases to study the abilities of family therapists to recognize marital violence and recommend appropriate protection strategies. In one of two test stories, Carol told her therapist privately that she had sought an order of protection because James "grabbed her and threw her on the floor in a violent manner and then struck her." In the other vignette, Beth claimed that Tony "punched her in the back and stomach and caused her to miscarry." Tony asserted that Beth tried to hit him and punched herself in the back.

Of the 362 therapists, 22% identified the problem as violence and 17% as an abusive relationship. Others classified the problem as conflict (8%), anger (5%), a power struggle (4%), lack of control (1%), or other type of conflict (4%). The remaining 39% selected nonconflict options, such as lack of communication, lack of trust, or secrecy. Only 45% of the therapists advised crisis intervention; 48% called for further assessment, 60% suggested work on a nonviolent marital problem, and 28% recommended couples counseling. Only 10% addressed the need for protection.

Gondolf (1992) cited the neglect of violence as a subject in psychiatric hospitals as yet another failure of the counseling and medical communities to recognize spouse abuse. Even after violence has been identified in the emergency room, there is a progressive decrease in discussion about violence as a case moves from clinician-patient to clinician-psychiatrist, and finally to psychiatrist-patient. To offset such serious oversights, Poteat, Grossnickle, Cope, and Wynne (1990) have advocated the use of a spouse abuse screening questionnaire, and Herman (1986) and Gondolf (1992) both highlighted the need to explore histories of violence in outpatient psychiatric patients. Geffner (1990) has proposed the establishment of minimum standards and credentials for practitioners in the family abuse field.

Shelters and Safe Homes

Because battered women are frequently destitute and homeless, advocates have insti-

gated the development of shelters and safe homes.

Shelters. Less than half of the women who are battered seek emergency housing in shelters for battered women. Those who do are likely to have experienced the more serious battering and lack of family supports (Berk, Newton, & Berk, 1986). Many battered women are unaware of the existence of emergency shelters, and those who know about them frequently encounter difficulty finding space available (Frisch & MacKenzie, 1991; Irvine, 1990). In Los Angeles County, there are 411 beds and cribs in 18 shelters to serve 3.5 million women over the age of 14. The shelters turned down requests from 8,840 families in 1994 (Burke, 1995). Lesbian victims of battering have an especially difficult time finding shelter (Irvine, 1990) as do African American women (Asbury, 1987).

Safe Homes. One less expensive innovation has been the provision of safe home services to battered women and to their children. A safe home network relocates women with host families in their own neighborhoods who can shelter a woman and her children for up to 3 months. In addition to crisis intervention, support groups, and children's treatment groups, some programs provide services such as photographic documentation of injuries and help with obtaining protection orders from the courts (Gibson & Gutierrez, 1991).

Intermediate Chapter Summary

Community professionals such as clergy, medical doctors, and mental health professionals have been slow to recognize the plight of battered women and to obtain the requisite knowledge about how to help. One possible point for social intervention occurs when battered women interact with emergency room personnel. In 1992, the American Medical Association began distributing a booklet to help doctors recognize and handle domestic violence cases appropriately. New legislation is currently implementing **requirements for training health professionals** in detecting and reporting abuse. An unfortunate countermovement has been the **efforts of insurance companies** to deny health, life, and disability coverage to women identified as battered.

Much assistance for battered women has accrued from the **work of advocates** who have spearheaded efforts to establish **shelters and safe homes.** Shelter space is so woefully inadequate that large numbers of families fleeing domestic assault cannot find refuge. Very likely, at least one fifth of the homeless are battered women and their children.

Intervention by the Criminal Justice System

According to Jaffe, Wolfe, and Wilson (1990), a battered woman's safety is "ultimately a community responsibility and [ensuring her safety is] a role of the police officers and courts" (p. 88; also see Francis, 1993).

The Police

Because of their gatekeeping role, police response to marital violence is crucial (Steinman, 1991). In addition to the legal requirements of the law, some of the variables that influence police decision making and ensuing action are their experiences, their attitudes, and their training (Saunders & Size, 1986). Contextual and demographic factors, such as victim injury, the perpetrator's nonhistory of abuse, and the minority status of both perpetrators and victims (e.g., African American) are also predictors of arrest. These same factors play a significant role in victims' willingness to report their abuse to police in the first place (Bachman & Coker, 1995).

Past Police Behaviors. Historically, police have been underinvolved in combating spouse abuse. Until the late 1970s, they could arrest a batterer only if they had reason to suspect the batterer had committed a felony or actually committed a misdemeanor in the presence of the officer (Buzawa & Buzawa, 1990; Zorza, 1992). When called to the scene of a domestic complaint, police typically delayed their response for several hours, and on investigation seldom arrested the abuser (e.g., Chadhuri & Daly, 1991). Furthermore, training procedures customarily instructed police to intervene by taking a "mediational" role, removing the abuser from the home to "cool off" or removing the victim from his or her home, rather than to arrest the perpetrator. The police also discouraged the victim from pressing charges (Eigenberg & Moriarty, 1991).

Police attitudes appeared to be at the foundation of police inaction (Ferraro, 1989; Saunders & Size, 1986). Police departments traditionally trivialized family violence as noncriminal, noninjurious, inconsequential, and primarily verbal (Berk, Fenstermaker, & Newton, 1990; Fields, 1978; Waaland & Keeley, 1985). They seemed also to have held the contradictory and erroneous opinion that intervention is one of the most dangerous actions that police are called on to undertake (Garner & Clemmer, 1986). Police have been reluctant to get involved for several other reasons as well. They presumed that violence is a private, "family" matter. Some assumed that if he beats her and she stays, there are no real victims (see Waaland & Keeley, 1985). Others saw the violence as her fault or justified (Saunders, 1995). Still others believed that police action, which treats the symptoms rather than the causes, cannot effect long-term changes in domestic violence (see Hirschel & Hutchison, 1991, for a review).

In one study, Pagelow (1981b) maintained that police ignored 61% of the requests to arrest made by battered women (also see Hutchison et al., 1994; Yegidis & Renzy, 1994). Dutton (1988) similarly estimated that police in Canada arrested suspected batterers in only 21.2% of the cases, even with prima facie evidence of assault. In the United States, a study of 1,870 reports of domestic violence filed in a 12-month period indicated that only 28.8% of all cases and only 37.4% of the most serious charges resulted in arrest (Bourg & Stock, 1994).

Challenges to Police Policies. As awareness of marital violence increased, the laissez-faire approach of the police gave way to calls for "get tough" police policies. In the early 1980s, victim rights and women's organizations exerted public pressure on police and courts. Of particular consequence was a battered woman's successful suit against a police department that failed to arrest her violent husband (*Thurman v. City of Torrington*, 1984). In addition, early research on the deterrent effects of arrest by Sherman and Berk (1984) showed the effectiveness of arrest compared to other alternatives (see boxed insert: "Mandatory Arrest Policies"). Finally, battered women won a few landmark cases against

---

In one survey, only 1% of the batterers received jail time beyond time served at arrest.

---

police who failed to execute orders of protection (see Zorza & Woods, 1994b, for a review). Slowly, mandatory and pro-arrest policies evolved in many jurisdictions. Currently, 27 states have laws that mandate ar-

MANDATORY ARREST POLICIES

The police community has increasingly emphasized treating marital violence as a serious crime. "Arresting an offender," writes police officer Tony Bouza (1991), "is a societal statement that his behavior is a crime, that it must stop, that punishment will follow, and that it is sensible to secure treatment to avoid repeating the behavior" (p. 195). Arresting an assaultive spouse also offers support to the victim and makes it clear that violence will not be tolerated.

In 1984, sociologists Lawrence Sherman and Richard Berk published initial results of a study that tested the deterrent effects of arrest in domestic violence cases. With the help of the Minneapolis Police Department, they devised a system of randomly assigning suspects to one of three police responses: mediation (counseling the parties involved), separation (suspects were told to leave the residence), and arrest. They assessed deterrent effects in two ways. First, researchers interviewed the victims 6 months after initial contact. Second, they examined police records to see if suspects had been rearrested for domestic violence. Analysis of the data showed that suspects who had been arrested were less likely to reoffend than suspects in either of the other intervention groups. Subsequent studies also confirmed the deterrent effects of arrest (Berk & Newton, 1985; Jaffe, Wolfe, Telford, & Austin, 1986; Langan & Innes, 1986).

The results of the Minneapolis experiment had an immediate effect on public policy. By the late 1980s, many state and local governments were strongly encouraging or, in some cases, requiring police to make arrests when probable cause existed (Ferraro, 1989). Some police officers resented the loss of discretion in making arrests (see Balos & Trotzky, 1988). Most researchers and battered women's advocates, although expressing concern that many police were ignoring the pro-arrest policies (see Bourg & Stock, 1994), nevertheless applauded the change in philosophy.

The social scientific community watched as policy changed, all along expressing caution that more research would be needed before definitive conclusions could be reached (Sherman & Berk, 1984). The National Institute of Justice responded to the call for more research by funding a series of six "replications" (various experimental designs) in U.S. cities, five of which have been released. Unfortunately, the replications of the research proved generally disappointing (Berk, Campbell, Klap, & Western, 1992; Dunford, Huizinga, & Elliott, 1990; Pate & Hamilton, 1992; Sherman, Smith, Schmidt, & Rogan, 1992).

According to Sherman (1992), three showed some deterrent effects and three did not. Findings from a replication in Milwaukee showed that although arrest seemed to deter offenders who had a lot to lose (e.g., marriage, employment), it seemed to increase the rate for those who had little to lose

---

rest. More than 40 have laws that either mandate arrest or have pro-arrest policies (Zorza & Woods, 1994b).

Renewed Calls for a Get-Tough Policy. The equivocal nature of mandatory arrest outcomes spawned additional inquiry. Studies uncovered continuing police resistance, if not a backlash effect, presumably tied to removal of police discretions. The studies also identified more clearly the problem of dual arrests of perpetrator and victim. Surveys further pinpointed a severe lack of prosecutorial follow-through (Zorza & Woods, 1994b). In one survey, for instance, only 1% of the batterers received jail time beyond time served at arrest (often just a few hours) (Hirschel et al., 1992).

Development of a Model Law. The need to revamp policies is reflected in a recent model law on family violence developed by a task force of judges, law enforcement officers, attorneys, advocates, and legislators (see "Model Law," 1994). The model law code calls for mandatory arrest in misdemeanor as well as felony cases of marital violence. A written explanation would be required in cases where the police officer did not make an arrest. The code forbids officers from basing their decisions on perceptions of the victim's willingness to testify or from threatening to arrest all parties to discourage future calls for police intervention. The code also requires the officer to determine if there is a primary aggressor in cases where both parties com-

(Sherman et al., 1992). On the other hand, criminal sanctions did not appear to increase the risk of new violence (through retaliation) (Buzawa & Buzawa, 1993; Ford, 1991). Because the effects in various cities and on different kinds of individuals were not uniform, Sherman (1992) has argued against a federal policy that requires arrest.

Interpretations of the studies as showing that mandatory arrest has no deterrent effect are contested. Zorza and Woods (1994a), for example, point out that the studies failed to take into account the potential effect of postarrest outcomes, such as whether prosecution or conviction ensued. As an illustration, in the Milwaukee analysis, prosecutors charged only 5% of those arrested for violence, and the conviction rate was 1%. In the absence of prosecution and conviction, the costs of arrest remain minimal, thus severely limiting the potential deterrent effect of police action. Using results such as these as the foundation for claims about the general ineffectiveness of legal sanctions seems unwarranted.

Other experimental design features also restrict confidence in their generalizability. As a group, the studies assessed only misdemeanor arrests, not felonies or violations of orders of protection. Factors such as data source (police reports vs. victims' reports, injuries), length of follow-up (e.g., 3 weeks, 12 months), offenders' employment status, marital or separation status of the victim and perpetrator, selection of excluded cases, and postarrest outcomes proved to be powerful sources of variation affecting the results. In fact, Zorza and Woods (1994a) interpreted the findings as supporting assumptions of some general deterrence, rather than of no deterrence.

From a different perspective, other experts denounced the implementation of mandatory arrest policies, rather than the actual findings of the replication studies. These experts reported that mandatory arrest policies not only failed to protect battered women as expected, but they also led to an increase in arrest of victims (Saunders, 1995; Stafne, 1989; Zorza & Woods, 1994b). In one midsized community of 85,000, for example, there was a twelvefold increase in arrests of women and a twofold increase in arrests of men in the year following the institution of mandatory arrest policies. On further investigation, two thirds of the women arrested acted in self-defense (Hamberger & Arnold, 1991). At the very least, it is apparent that mandatory arrest policies are not the panacea they were once thought to be.

From yet a different point of view, many believe that it should not matter whether arrest deters marital violence. Assault is assault, whether it occurs inside or outside the family. Policymakers do not "require" that all arrests deter. Spouse abuse, in fact, "is probably the only area of criminal behavior in which it has been considered necessary to justify arrest of offenders on the grounds that such arrests will serve as a deterrent" (Hirschel, Hutchison, Dean, & Mills, 1992, p. 276).

plain, and it allows the officer discretion in arresting only the primary aggressor.

Revised Police Training. There is also growing pressure on police departments to treat spouse abuse as a unique problem requiring unique training. Some have proposed development of a police manual and enhanced language clarity in legislation. In fact, involvement of the police at all stages of changes affecting police is crucial for success (see Zorza & Woods, 1994a, 1994b, for a review). Lydia Bodin ("Focus—Call for Help," 1994) reported that some police departments, such as the Los Angeles Police Department, have created special units trained to deal with domestic violence, including special teams of prosecutors. Lack of funding of police departments can be another serious problem in both officer availability and in training, according to James Hahn (1994), city attorney of Los Angeles.

Other Legal Remedies for Spouse Abuse

Historically, the courts have treated the family as a single entity and have consequently established differential prosecutorial practices for family-related crimes (Straus, 1974). Today, every state in the United States condemns spouse abuse in theory and has at least one statute pertaining to battered women (Myers, Tikosh, & Paxson, 1992). Nonetheless, these laws have not adequately protected women from continued assault and injury (Klein, 1995; Zorza, 1995). This is particularly true for battered immigrant women (Orloff, Jang, & Klein, 1995). Consequently, legal innovations have continued, especially in the areas of restraining orders and court reforms (see Finn, 1991, for a review).

Restraining Orders. A common approach has been to recommend that a battered spouse obtain a civil order of protection (Horton, Simonidis, & Simonidis, 1987). A protection order empowers police to evict an abusive person from a common residence and to arrest him (or her) for violation. Concomitant petitions for "relief" may apply in areas such as child custody and visitation orders, financial support, property allocation, attorney fees, and counseling for the respondent. A battered woman may not be able to obtain a restraining order or keep it in effect, however, and obtaining one does not guarantee her safety ("Domestic Violence," 1989; Keilitz, 1994). To better understand the types of protection orders provided, their effectiveness, and how to improve them, the Bureau of Justice Assistance and the Department of Justice sponsored 11 demonstration programs (Hofford & Harrell, 1993). Unfortunately, attitudes unfavorable to battered women and ultraconservative attitudes of police hamper their enforcement of protection orders (Rigakos, 1995).

An Urban Institute study of 350 civil protection orders issued in Boulder and Denver, Colorado, followed petitioners' progress in procuring a final protection order for a period of 1 year. This analysis revealed a number of important outcomes: (a) Only 13% of the women who had obtained protection orders reconciled with the abuser during the first 3 months; (b) violent reoffending occurred in 29% of the cases; and (c) of the women who obtained temporary orders, 40% did not apply for permanent orders, usually because the perpetrator had stopped his offenses or because he could not be found (Harrell, Smith, & Newmark, 1993). In another survey of 200 randomly selected court petitions in one Pennsylvania county, approximately 76% of the petitioners were able to obtain a final protection order (Gondolf, McWilliams, Hart, & Stuehling, 1994).

When protection orders are too limited, they are usually inadequate (Gondolf et al., 1994). An unemployed woman denied financial support by the court and ordered to allow visitation by the abuser, for example, cannot easily extricate herself from an abuser. Furthermore, orders that force women into mediation or couples counseling intimidate and endanger battered women (Hansen et al., 1991; Hart, 1990). Of course, police failure to enforce protection orders is yet another unresolved problem (e.g., Holmes, 1993), and in some cases, mutual restraining orders have been issued against both spouses, causing unwarranted complications (Asher, 1990; Myers et al., 1992). The primary indicators of effectiveness in the Colorado cities were specificity of the restraining order, comprehensiveness of the terms of the order, and enforcement of the order (Chadhuri & Daly, 1991).

Prosecutors and the Courts. Stopping marital violence requires a vigorous, affirmative effort from the courts, the police, prosecutors, and other criminal justice officials, as well as provisions of treatment services for batterers and shelters for victims (see Cahn & Lerman, 1991, for a review). The attitudes of many judges reflect "a man's home is his castle," which often results in a "hands-off" policy. Judges also are inclined to believe men's accounts of the violence more than women's, if the two versions differ. Various groups, in fact, have documented considerable gender bias in the courtroom (National Center on Women and Family Law, Inc., 1994). Prosecutors frequently accuse women who tried to defend themselves physically as being "mutual combatants" (Hofford & Harrell, 1993).

One solution is to have specially trained clerks, victim advocates, or volunteers located at intake points within criminal justice agencies to help victims file complaints, request protection orders, or obtain other aid (Hofford & Harrell, 1993). In Bouza's (1991) opinion, advocates should advise women to testify because the probability of conviction is greater. Others believe that advising battered women, as a support technique, is counterproductive to their recovery. Instead, the best course of action is to empower battered women by proposing that they make their own decisions about testifying (e.g., Dutton-Douglas & Dione, 1991).

Others, such as Michael Dowd of Pace University's Battered Women's Center in New York State ("Focus—Call for Help," 1994), have called attention to the dearth of affordable legal services for battered women. In many cases, a poor woman might have to wait 2 years to obtain legal services to assist with a divorce or custody issues. In the interim, she is forced to remain connected to a batterer. According to Dowd, society neither trains lawyers how to help nor encourages lawyers to do much pro bono work.

Summary

This chapter has revealed the widespread nature of interpartner aggression, thus verifying the notion of the "marriage license as a hitting license" (Gelles & Straus, 1979). Defining and measuring marital violence are of pivotal importance in understanding marital violence but remain a challenge to researchers. The bulk of information advances the position that women are the major victims of battering and that the supposition of a comparable battered husband syndrome is of marginal significance. Nonetheless, female-to-male violence is common and should not be ignored. A strong debate between mainstream sociologists advancing a "gender mutual" approach and feminist researchers promoting a "gendered" approach has resulted. Marital violence exacts personal costs for those involved and social costs in terms of medical expenses, additional welfare benefits, and costs for the legal justice system.

An examination of social structural variables reveals that younger males are the most frequent perpetrators, and although marital abuse occurs in all segments of society, it seems to be more common in lower socioeconomic groups. Cultural forces that endow men with unequal power over women promote spousal violence but are not the sole cause of wife beating. Although male socialization teaches young boys that a crucial aspect of masculinity is male dominance and men raised in abusive childhood homes tend to be partner-abusive husbands, evidence for a relationship between socialization and wife abuse is not clear-cut. High levels of alcohol abuse and marital dissatisfaction are associated with high levels of marital violence, but these correlates appear not to be causally related.

Some of the community professionals most likely asked to help are clergy, doctors, and counselors. The responses of all these community agents generally reflect insufficient knowledge and a concomitant need for training. Some of the problems rest in sexist attitudes. Collectively, social systems have been ineffective in protecting spouses (usually women) from assault.

The criminal justice system is the major social institution involved in combating spouse abuse. The first "line of defense" against marital violence is police intervention. Historically and in the present, however, the police have been unwilling to intervene. The nonsupportive attitudes of police toward battered women and their failure to respond to calls for protection have led to strong political action. Advocates have successfully lobbied for enactment of more mandatory and pro-arrest laws, but evidence remains inconclusive about the effectiveness of these new policies. They may not have uniformly strong deterrent effects on further assaultive behaviors.

Once perpetrators are arrested, the criminal justice system fails to hold them accountable. Both prosecution and conviction rates are very low. Many advocate policy changes within the entire criminal justice system. Judges need training, and court support services need fine tuning to be more supportive of battered women. The police also need a different type of training. Finally, society needs to address the difficulty faced by battered women who lack sufficient funds or other resources but who desperately need to obtain vital legal services. Although remarkable headway has been made over the past decade, much remains to be done.

9

Marital Violence

Battered Women

CHAPTER OUTLINE

An Interview With Angela Browne

"We have virtually no appropriate measures to tap and document the strengths of women who are in or have been in violent and threatening relationships."

ANGELA BROWNE is a highly regarded researcher and expert in the area of battered women. She has published widely, especially in the areas of assault and threat in adult intimate relationships and posttrauma effects of physical and sexual assault. She served as the founding editor of the journal Violence and Victims. *She authored both the AMA's review and policy statement titled "Violence Against Women" and the American Psychological Association's review titled "Violence Against Women by Male Partners." She graduated from the University of Colorado in 1980 and received her Ph.D. in social psychology from the Union Institute in 1983.*

Q: What is your current position?

A: Currently, I devote 100% of my time to government-funded research and writing. In Massachusetts, I am involved in a National Institute of Mental Health-funded study of the life histories of 500 very poor, housed and homeless single mothers. This study examines the relationship between experiences with traumatic victimization and poverty across the lifespan and mental health outcomes such as posttraumatic stress disorder. I also am Coinvestigator on a National Institute of Drug Abuse study of 600 women at Bedford Hills maximum-security prison. This study explores the relationship of victimization in childhood and adulthood with development of alcohol and other drug abuse.

Q: What has shaped your approach to the field?

A: Listening to and learning from women and their life experiences shaped my approach to the field. Survivors' strength, courage, insight, and experience remain the well from which I draw both knowledge and the energy to keep pursuing understanding and social change. Women's stories—and the research statistics that verified them—were the core of my book *When Battered Women Kill.* The realities of their lives and the hard choices

with which they are confronted still form the context within which I view empirical findings.

In addition, I began this work at the end of the 1970s in close association with the first researchers and activists to write in depth about violence against women by male partners: Lenore Walker, Del Martin, Irene Frieze, Ginny NiCarthy, Millie Pagelow, Diana Russell. I will always treasure their commitment and passion.

Q: What are some of your current concerns?

A: In working with extremely poor and incarcerated populations in recent years, I have become increasingly concerned with the nexus of poverty and violence in women's and children's lives and with the continuing neglect of minority populations and issues—in research and in the feminist movement, as well as in social policy.

Q: What governmental policies seem most related to family violence?

A: We cannot ignore our increasing levels of poverty and reduce violence at the same time. Poverty has consistently been found to constitute a serious risk factor for child abuse and neglect as well as for partner violence. Current policies threaten to force even more families and individuals far below normal subsistence levels, further extending the sense of despair now contributing to violence in our society.

Q: What topics have attracted your research interest?

A: Since 1979, I have specialized in topics of violence between adult partners; partner homicide and battered women's self-defense; patterns of courtship, onset of abuse, and violence by abusive male partners; and the short- and long-term effects of physical and sexual abuse on women and children.

Although we know that poverty is highly correlated with all forms of violence, our concerns for poverty and early intervention consistently take a back seat to our national attraction toward punishment. The special irony of this approach comes when we add cost savings to the discussion, since the cost of crime and punishment, including incarceration—carried on the backs of the taxpayers—is far greater than the costs of prevention and community-based interventions could ever be.

Q: What types of new research are needed in the field of family violence?

A: I would like to help promote more explicit discourse on the strengths of women survivors of physical and sexual assault and molestation. Although we have a multitude of measures with which to assess the negative outcomes of trauma, and tend to focus research and interventions around them, we have virtually no appropriate measures to tap and document the strengths of women who are in or have been in violent and threatening relationships. Even our labels limit women to the abusive situation (victim of, survivor of), when, as whole individuals, they are much more complex.

Introduction

CASE HISTORY: LISA—STAYING FOR BETTER OR FOR WORSE

I believe that you stay with your partner for better or for worse. I didn't know what "worse" was when I made that promise, but I promised. I believe my husband loves me, and I'm starting to believe he could kill me. I'm not sure how long I should stay and how "bad" is "too bad." I know I don't believe I should be hit. But I do believe if my relationship is a mess, I should stay to help make it better. (quoted in Barnett & LaViolette, 1993, p. 2)

* * *

The preceding chapter discussed many of the patterns and explanations of marital violence—the slaps and physical assaults between married couples, and even the sexual assaults that sometimes occur. It should be clear from that chapter that although both males and females are sometimes violent,

women are the more likely victims of severe abuse. In this chapter, the effect of marital violence (physical, sexual, verbal, and psychological) as it is experienced by women becomes clearer. People tend to have strong, and frequently "gendered," opinions about marital abuse. Some wonder how men can "behave like animals," whereas others may be thinking women "ask for it." Most people believe that they could never become involved in an abusive relationship themselves or stay in the relationship. Those who have firsthand experience say that it can happen to anybody.

This chapter begins by discussing the myths about battered women that have contributed to the propensity of others to blame battered women for being victimized. Next is a consideration of the reasons why women stay in abusive relationships. Finally, the discussion focuses on how women attempt to stop the violence and how counseling support may help women cope with the violence directed at them by intimate male partners.

Blaming Battered Women

Some argue that society provides women little protection because women are consenting adults, responsible for their own behavior (Tilden & Shepherd, 1987). Indeed, unlike children and elders, women are often blamed for their own victimization. Importantly, women often accept the blame that society places on them.

Societal Blaming

One of the most crucial issues surrounding the topic of marital violence is the propensity of society to blame the victim. In one such demonstration, Ewing and Aubrey (1987) surveyed a random sample of 216 community members regarding attitudes and attribution of responsibility in violent relationships. Adults completed a questionnaire after reading a scenario about a violent couple. More than 40% reported that the woman in the scenario must have been at least partly to blame for her husband's assaults, even though the story provided no rationale for such a belief. Over 60% of the respondents agreed that if a battered woman were really afraid, she would simply leave. There was also some tendency for respondents to believe that the woman must have been emotionally disturbed or that if she would enter counseling, she could prevent the beatings (also see Frieze & Browne, 1989; Muldary, 1983).

Lesbian victims have an even more difficult time in being perceived as "worthy" victims. There appears to be a strong reluctance within the lesbian community to acknowledge interpartner aggression. Some of the problem stems from a strong belief that intimate partners in lesbian relationships should be equal and that interpartner violence arises from patriarchal practices (Renzetti, 1992). A related problem is connected to the greater willingness to attach the label "mutual combat" to lesbian abuse compared with heterosexual violence (Hart, 1986).

Blaming by Professionals

The extent to which battered women are perceived to be at fault for the violence in their marriage has a profound effect on the treatment they receive in a number of settings, such as in the clinic or in the courtroom. It is clear that mental health professionals, medical personnel, and the police are likely to assume that the victim was an accomplice or at least indirectly responsible for the violence (see Hansen, Harway, & Cervantes, 1991; Kurz, 1990; McKeel & Sporakowski, 1993; Waaland & Keeley, 1985). In a 1991 Kentucky survey of service providers (mental health, social services, corrections, shelters, law enforcement courts, prosecution, and coroners), 13.9% agreed or strongly agreed with the statement "Victims 'ask' for it" (Wilson & Wilson, 1991). By and large, community agents, as well as individual community members, seem reluctant to place all the blame on the perpetrators (Frieze, Hymer, & Greenberg, 1984; Whatley & Riggio, 1991).

Holding False Beliefs About Battered Women

Not only do members of society tend to blame battered women, but they also seem to have selected specific areas in which to fault battered women. As mentioned in the first chapter, one of the common myths about battered women is that they "ask for it." They either drink too much (as described in the previous chapter), come from the wrong family, or suffer from low self-esteem. People also find it hard to believe that sex within marriage can actually be a sexual assault. To explore these assumptions more fully, researchers have searched for factors that make some women especially vulnerable to becoming battered. Some of the research that has centered on victim characteristics, in particular, seems to place blame on battered women.

Childhood History. Women may appear blameworthy because of their family background. Women who either experienced physical abuse themselves or observed excessive amounts of parental violence during childhood might be inclined to accept violence as the norm in their own marriages (Kalmuss, 1984; Owens & Straus, 1975). Although victims more generally become perpetrators (Finkelhor & Dziuba-Leatherman, 1994), a few studies have found a modest relationship between being exposed to violence as a child and being a victim of violence as an adult (Kalmuss, 1984; Rosenbaum & O'Leary, 1981a; Sedlak, 1988a). Most research, however, suggests that battered women are no more likely to have been exposed to violence as children than nonbattered women (Astin, Lawrence, & Foy, 1993; Bergman, Larsson, Brismar, & Klang, 1988; Hamberger, 1991; Hotaling & Sugarman, 1990). Nevertheless, "typical" cases of an abused child later becoming a battered woman are easy to find. Consider, for example, the following case history of Juanita and Miguel.

CASE HISTORY: JUANITA— "JUST THE SAME OLD THING"

When I was a child, my father switched my legs when I failed to clean my room right, and he used a belt if I got "sassy." When he was really mad, he slapped me across the mouth. He also hit anyone else in the family who "got in his way," including my mother.

When I met Miguel, he transformed my world. Everything was just perfect. Miguel told me that I was beautiful and that he couldn't live without me. He was always so gentle and kind. I knew that I was finally going to have a home of my own where I would be loved. It was the happiest time of my life.

The week after the wedding, Miguel slapped me for the first time. I felt heartbroken. I just couldn't believe it. I couldn't figure it out. I wanted something better; I was hoping for something normal. I thought about leaving, but I just felt stunned. One thing I did know was that going back home wouldn't help. (Author's case history)

* * *

Despite the perfect "fit" between Juanita's childhood history and her subsequent marital abuse, there is no evidence that Juanita, or women like Juanita, like being beaten and purposely choose abusive men to marry. Juanita's background of abuse may have been simply coincidental with her later marriage to a batterer. Straus (1991a) argues that so many American children are exposed to corporal punishment and parent-to-parent violence during childhood that pinpointing specific effects of childhood abuse that carry over into adulthood is a little like "looking for a needle in a haystack."

Low Self-Esteem. Another popular assertion has been that battered women suffer from the "fault" of having low self-esteem (see Mills, 1985). Presumably, their low self-esteem, in turn, renders them more willing to tolerate abuse. Certainly, there is some research indicating a link between the severity of the abuse experienced and low self-esteem (Bowker, 1993; Cascardi, Langhinrichsen, & Vivian, 1992). Researchers have concluded, however, that low self-esteem is an outcome of victimization rather than a precursor (Stark et al., 1981; Telch & Lindquist, 1984). Aguilar and Nightingale (1994), for example, established an association between low self-esteem in battered women and their experiences of a specific kind of abuse (emotional/controlling) by the abuser. Stark et al. (1981) have alleged that abuse by an intimate, in and of itself, is apt to lower self-esteem by creating or adding to a sense of personal defectiveness. Findings like these should not be surprising, because previous research has demonstrated a nearly universal tendency of crime victims to suffer simultaneously from self-blame and low self-esteem (Miller & Porter, 1983; Trimpey, 1989).

A Man Cannot Rape His Own Wife. Diane Russell (1982) can be credited with drawing attention to the problem of marital rape. Her work has dispelled some of the most common myths. Marital rape is one of the most prevalent (not least common) kinds of rape, and it has grave repercussions. Many individuals appear to believe that as "couples progress from a first date to marriage, men gain support to violate their partner's consent, and to a lesser degree, women lose support to assert their rights" (Margolin, Moran, & Miller, 1989, p. 45). In one group of 115 battered women, for example, 87.4% reported that their husbands thought it was their right to have sex with their wives whether the wives want to or not (Campbell & Alford, 1989). In addition to medical consequences previously described, raped wives suffer grave harm to their sexuality and sense of self (Campbell & Alford, 1989). Sexually assaulted wives are just as traumatized as victims of stranger rape (Riggs, Kilpatrick, & Resnick, 1992). According to Browne (1987), one raped wife said, "It was as though he wanted to annihilate me. More than the slapping, or the kicks . . . as though he wanted to tear me apart from the inside out and simply leave nothing there" (p. 103). By and large, battered women have greater frequency of sexual intercourse accompanied by lower levels of sexual assertiveness, arousability, and satisfaction than nonbattered women (Apt & Hurlbert, 1993). Their attitudes toward sex are more negative or erotophobic, and they more strongly avoid sex.

Sexual assault occurs in other countries, as well as in the United States. Of a group of Japanese battered women, for example, 81% reported unwanted sex, and 25% reported high levels of forced, violent sex (Yoshihama & Sorenson, 1994). An interesting cultural difference was that having to share living quarters increased the amount of forced sex during a time when the woman was "concerned about having other family members around."

Intermediate Chapter Summary

People seem willing to **blame battered women** without any evidence, and the longer the woman remains after abuse, the more likely it is that people will find her blameworthy. Lesbian battered women elicit even less sympathy from the public. Even individuals "trained" to help others in critical situations, like mental health professionals, seem inclined to hold victims responsible.

Research debunks most of the **commonly held myths** about battered women. The implications of the studies are that battered women do not come from substantially more abusive homes than those of nonbattered women (Hotaling & Sugarman, 1990). Research on self-esteem is difficult to interpret, because the studies finding low self-esteem in battered women cannot rule out the probability that its occurrence is a consequence of the beatings rather than a precipitating factor. People are also prone to believe that battered women have consented to any and all marital sex and have no right to decline.

Sexual assault results in **trauma** that may last a very long time (Campbell & Alford, 1989). Women's sexual pleasure is generally reduced (Apt & Hurlbert, 1993). Sexual assault is very **prominent in other cultures** as well. In one survey of Japanese battered women, for instance, 25% reported being violently sexually assaulted by their husbands (Yoshihama & Sorenson, 1994).

Consequences of Being a Battered Woman

Violence is perhaps the most powerful element in producing behaviors that characterize victims in general and battered women specifically. Violence has a number of negative outcomes for victims, such as recurrent fear, feelings of helplessness, and stress. Although battering relationships are nonviolent some of the time, women caught in them rarely feel safe. First and foremost, battered women fear another beating.

Violence and Fear

Using comparison groups of nonabused women, Russell, Lipov, Phillips, and White (1989) noted that abused women were more fearful than other women on a mood state scale (McNair, Lorr, & Doppleman, 1981). In the Barnett and Lopez-Real (1985) study, battered women offered some of the following descriptions of their fears: "He was suicidal; I feared he would come after me" and "I remember feeling many times afraid to go and afraid to stay. That very real fear of revenge is a powerful deterrent to doing anything constructive."

Violence and Learned Helplessness

The fear, anger, and frustration experienced by assault victims also evokes feelings of helplessness. Research has established that helplessness is the most immediate feeling that crime victims experience following an assault; depression and anxiety usually set in

later (Shepherd, 1990). Among battered women, these feelings of helplessness are often referred to as *learned helplessness* (Walker, 1977). Gerow (1989) defines learned helplessness as "a condition in which a subject does not attempt to escape from a painful or noxious situation after learning in a previous,

---

Helplessness is the most immediate feeling that crime victims experience following an assault.

---

similar situation that escape is not possible" (p. 193). During the 1970s, Lenore Walker (1977) popularized the term by using it to explain why women stay in abusive relationships. She argued that abused women who have tried unsuccessfully to end the violence may eventually resign themselves to the inevitability of the abuse, to simply give up the struggle to be free of violence. Research on learned helplessness in dogs (Seligman, 1975) became the cornerstone for Walker's (1977) theories. Researchers subjected one of three groups of dogs to inescapable shock trials (Maier & Seligman, 1976). A second group could escape, and a third comparison group received no shocks at all. Later, the experimenters tried to teach the dogs a new task, how to jump over a barrier to avoid a shock. The dogs given inescapable shocks were almost entirely unable to learn the new task. The other two groups of dogs learned to avoid shocks in the new task quickly. The shocked dogs had apparently learned that nothing they do makes a difference (learned helplessness).

Research on learned helplessness in battered women has focused primarily on three components: (a) emotional trauma (increased feelings of helplessness, frustration, and depression), (b) intellectual impairment (e.g., poor problem-solving ability), and (c) motivational impairment (e.g., passivity).

Emotional Trauma. Congruent with learned helplessness theory, a number of researchers have documented the outcome of clinical depression in battered women (e.g., Riggs et al., 1992; Sato & Heiby, 1992). In the 1985 National Re-Survey, Straus and Smith (1990) found that depression and suicide attempts were 4 times more likely in female victims of severe assault than among women who were not victims of violence. These results have been so uniform that little debate has emerged.

Intellectual Impairment. Learned helplessness may also be at the root of the poor problem-solving abilities manifested in battered women (see Claerhout, Elder, & Janes, 1982). Launius and Jensen (1987), for example, studied problem solving in three different groups of women: (a) battered women, (b) nonbattered women in therapy for anxiety and depression, and (c) women who were neither battered nor in therapy. All three groups received everyday problems to solve (Getter & Nowinski, 1981), such as "You are in a long line in the theater and two people cut in ahead of you. You don't appreciate this. What can you do?" To analyze the data, the researchers used special statistical techniques that accounted for the identified differences in depression and anxiety. The results indicated that battered women chose fewer effective solutions to the situations presented than did the other groups, and they generated fewer total problem-solving options. The researchers concluded that treatment for battered women should include problem-solving skills. In a different investigation involving a hypothetical abuse situation, however, battered women exhibited no deficit in problem-solving ability (Campbell, 1989a). Thus, some controversy has arisen about the level of problem-solving deficits in battered women (see Orava, McLeod, & Sharpe, 1996).

Motivational Impairment. Perhaps the most controversial aspect of Walker's (1977) theory is her assertion that learned helplessness produces motivational impairment (i.e., passivity) in battered women. Because it appears that battered women could "obviously" escape the violence if they were motivated to do so, outside observers ask, "Why don't they just leave?" Walker (1977) answered the question by invoking learned helplessness. From this perspective, battered women feel so trapped that they become immobilized; they come to believe that they cannot take the actions necessary to escape the abuse.

Studies exploring battered women's attempts to cope with their violent male partners have produced diametrically opposed results. On the one hand, there is evidence that battered women are less inclined to use active coping strategies (e.g., obtaining social support, reframing stressful events, and seeking spiritual support) and are more likely to use passive strategies (e.g., fantasizing about a better relationship) (Emery, Lloyd, & Castleton, 1989; Finn, 1985; Nurius, Furrey, & Berliner, 1992). Critics of learned helplessness argue, however, that battered women's help-seeking efforts illustrate that they are actively struggling for survival and control (Bograd, 1990; Emery et al., 1989). In fact, Gondolf (1988a) formulated a "survivor theory" based on data showing that battered women averaged six helpseeking behaviors (e.g., calling the police or contacting a member of the clergy) before they entered a shelter. Finally, although "the research literature describes the battered woman as 'feeling helpless,' or having 'learned helplessness,' such feelings may be less a reflection of a personal attribute or characteristic than an accurate reflection of reality" (Webersinn, Hollinger, & DeLamatre, 1991, p. 238). Evidence showing that women who had previously experienced intimate assaults were less likely to notify police of subsequent assaults, for example, may be indicative of these victims' belief that nothing could or would be done to stop the violence (Bachman & Coker, 1995). Many battered women have no money, no job skills, a scant education, and little perceived social support. They also may have had little experience in other arenas of life such as counseling.

Violence and Stress

Battering, like other forms of violence, is especially likely to produce environmental stress that, in turn, manifests itself in a vast array of symptoms. The stress associated with prolonged physical and emotional victimization has many overlapping symptoms. Psychological reactions to stress include cognitive impairment (e.g., confusion and poor test performance), emotional responses (e.g., anxiety, anger, aggression, and depression), and physical illness (e.g., headaches and gastrointestinal problems). Not only do individuals differ in their ability to handle stress, but also environments differ dramatically in the amount of stress they produce.

Stress and Physical Illness. There is mounting evidence that battered women suffer from stress-related physical illnesses and mental problems (Koss, Koss, & Woodruff, 1991; McLeer & Anwar, 1989). A task force sponsored by the American Psychological Association identified physical and sexual assault as an underdiagnosed precursor to many women's mental health problems (Russo, 1985), a finding validated by subsequent studies (e.g., Follingstad, Brennan, Hause, Polek, & Rutledge, 1991). Using a number of measures such as the Cornell Medical Index (Abramson, Terespolsky, Brook, & Kark, 1965), Koss et al. (1991) established that battered women needed substantially more medical care than nonvictimized women.

Posttraumatic Stress Disorder. When a traumatic event, such as losing a family member in a house fire, causes an acute and prolonged emotional reaction, psychologists and psychiatrists have designated the reaction posttraumatic stress disorder (PTSD). PTSD is a common reaction to trauma and terror. Doctors first applied the PTSD diagnosis to Vietnam veterans (American Psychiatric Association, 1987). Of course, individuals' pretrauma experiences play a significant role in the severity and duration of the symptoms experienced (Solomon, Mikulincer, & Flum, 1988).

PTSD is an anxiety disorder produced by an extremely stressful event (e.g., assault, rape, military combat, death camp) and characterized by a number of adverse reactions: (a) reexperiencing the trauma in painful recollections or recurrent dreams; (b) diminished responsiveness (numbing), with disinterest in significant activities and with feelings of detachment and estrangement from others; and (c) such symptoms as exaggerated startle response, disturbed sleep, difficulty in concentrating or remembering, guilt about surviving when others did not, and avoidance of activities that call the traumatic event to mind (Goldenson, 1984). The definition of the disorder is comparatively recent and is evolving (Herman, 1992). PTSD in battered women represents a configuration of factors: high arousal, high avoidance, intrusive memories, memory loss, and cognitive confusion. Over 60% of battered women

in two samples of women seeking treatment experienced PTSD symptoms (Saunders, 1994). In another sample of battered women, Houskamp and Foy (1991) found that 45% met full criteria on the *DSM-III-R* for PTSD (American Psychiatric Association, 1987). Houskamp and Foy established that the extent and severity of exposure to violence, as judged by the revised Conflict Tactics Scales (CTS; Straus, 1979), were significantly correlated with severity of PTSD symptomatology in battered women. Sustained contact with the batterer through such events as court appearances "is likely to have significant influence on symptomatology" (p. 374). The following case history illustrates an experience very likely to elicit PTSD symptoms in the battered woman involved.

CASE HISTORY: SOPHIA AND BORIS— LOCKDOWN

Boris seemed to get angrier every day. He was convinced that Sophia was having an affair, even though she was 8 months pregnant. He brought some lumber home from work one day and began boarding up all the windows in the house. He also removed the telephone. When he left for work in the mornings, he locked the front door from the outside with a new lock he had installed. One day, he just never came back.

Boris went to work every day and stayed with a girlfriend at night. Boris felt sad a lot of the time, so he went out to bars after work. Although he drove by the house every night, he never checked on Sophia's situation because "she deserved what she got; she never cared how he felt about anything. Probably the baby wasn't his because she was such a whore."

Apparently, Sophia could not get out even though she screamed and tried to break through a window. There was almost no food in the house. Sixty days later and 20 pounds lighter, Sophia was finally rescued. A man from the gas company making a meter repair found her and called the police and the paramedics.

In the hospital, Sophia lay in a state of emotional and medical shock. Boris was her first visitor. He brought her flowers and apologized. When he tried to "make love" to Sophia in the hospital, a nurse caught him and called the police. Boris was arrested. Although the judge did not sentence Boris to any jail time because he "was working," the judge did order him into a 10-week counseling program for batterers. One reason Boris is attending the counseling "class" is that he wants Sophia to come back. (Author's case history)

* * *

DEFENDING BATTERED WOMEN WHO KILL

On March 9, 1977, Francine Hughes poured gasoline over her sleeping husband and dropped a lighted match. She then drove herself and her children to the Sheriff's Department in Danville, Michigan, and turned herself in. As the facts in the case unfolded, it became apparent that this was not a simple case of first-degree murder. As the prosecution would later argue, Francine "premeditated" the murder; she had killed her husband while he slept.

When he wasn't sleeping, Mickey Hughes was a violent man. For many years, he had beaten and tormented his wife. Francine had children and few job skills and few options. Over the years, Mickey's pleas for forgiveness, alternating with threats to harm her, neutralized her efforts to leave (cited in Gelles & Straus, 1988).

Francine's defense attorney, Aryon Greydanus, did not believe that Francine was guilty of murder. Because she was not in immediate danger, however, a plea of self-defense seemed inapplicable. Instead, he entered a plea of innocent by reason of temporary insanity. In the end, after hours of evidence about her brutal existence, Francine was acquitted (cited in Gelles & Straus, 1988).

The plight of Francine Hughes attracted considerable attention. She appeared on the "Donahue" show twice, and the television movie based on her life, *The Burning Bed,* drew a large viewing audience. Despite increasing awareness about the predicament of battered women during the 1980s, it was still difficult to win an acquittal on an insanity plea. Many battered women who killed were convicted (see Ewing, 1990b). In addition, feminist legal scholars expressed concern that the insanity defense was inappropriate for battered women. Claims of insanity placed battered women in an untenable position and further contributed to general discrimination against women in society and in the courtroom (see Schneider, 1986). Why should women be put in a position of pleading insanity, advocates argued, when they had little choice but to kill?

During the 1980s, feminist clinicians began to argue that battered women often suffer from a trauma-induced condition they labeled battered woman syndrome (BWS; Walker, 1983). This mental disorder is distinguished by a subset of stress symptoms similar to those found in victims of posttraumatic stress disorder (Gleason, 1993). BWS essentially expands the concept of legal self-defense to take into account the specific "state of mind" of a battered woman who kills. This defense holds that a battered woman is virtually held hostage in a violent household by a man who isolates and terrorizes her, convincing her that if she leaves, he will track her down and kill her. DePaul (1992) describes the syndrome as "the situation of a long-time victim of physical, sexual, and psychological abuse who loses self-confidence, feels trapped, and eventually strikes back, assaulting or killing the abuser" (p. 5).

Some sociologists view BWS as an example of the "medicalization" of deviant behavior (Conrad & Schneider, 1992). The medical model assumes that certain behaviors are symptomatic of an underlying disease process, just as certain red spots on the skin indicate the underlying disease of chicken pox. By analogy, the BWS defense suggests that killing one's husband is "caused" by an underlying, unseen mental disorder. It is impossible to prove empirically that this nonobservable state of mind exists. Proponents of BWS argue that abuse causes battered women to believe that escape is impossible, but opponents point out that such a belief is not empirically identifiable. Many battered women do, in fact, get away (e.g., Gondolf, 1988b). Obviously, these problems make BWS a controversial legal defense. Where the prosecution sees the evidence of abuse as motivation for revenge ("Why didn't she just leave?"), the defense sees it as evidence for BWS ("She was psychologically trapped and could not leave.").

(continued)

The Battered Woman Syndrome. One disagreement has arisen over whether the effects of PTSD and learned helplessness may eventually culminate in a cluster of cognitions, feelings, and behaviors that constitute a special type of PTSD, the battered woman syndrome (BWS) (Bowker, 1993; Walker, 1993). (For more on the controversy over BWS, see boxed insert: "Defending Battered Women Who Kill.") According to several experts (Douglas, 1987; Herman, 1992; Walker, 1983), the pattern of symptoms found in BWS is sufficiently similar to those listed as posttraumatic symptoms (*DSM-III-R*; American Psychiatric Association, 1987) that it can be considered a subcategory of PTSD. Recent

For conservatives like Rush Limbaugh, a national radio talk-show host, BWS is little more than "legalized revenge." "Until recently, the law on self-defense has been clear: If someone attacks you, you have the right to use force to protect yourself. You do not have the right to kill or maim someone you claim assaulted you an hour ago. That's not legal self-defense. That's revenge" (Limbaugh, 1994, p. 56). Many judges and lawyers agree. Los Angeles Superior Court Judge Lillian Stevens is concerned about authorizing "preventive murder." "The only thing that really matters is whether there was an immediate danger. There can't be an old grievance" (quoted in Gibbs, 1993, p. 42).

Feminist legal scholars, however, counter that the self-defense justification to which Stevens refers is gender biased. As originally written into law, self-defense seems to have applied to two strangers of approximately equal fighting ability (see Schneider, 1986). The law required that the user of deadly force must have acted to avert what "reasonably" appeared to be "imminent danger" of serious bodily harm brought about by an action of the victim. Would it have been more "reasonable," for example, for the user of deadly force to "retreat" and thus avoid a killing altogether? The experiences of a battered woman, however, are very unlike those of two men fighting in a bar. She may have few options for escape (e.g., no money, no car). She may fear for her life and realize that she cannot hope to win a physical fight against her stronger male partner (Avni, 1991). In fact, many battered women who leave are hunted down and killed by their abusers (Lehnen & Skogan, 1981). Moreover, the medical model is used in a number of situations both psychological and legal. Legal insanity itself, the inability to distinguish right from wrong, is also an "unseen mental disorder." A battered woman may perceive homicide to be her only option for escape. "Morally and legally," argues defense attorney Leslie Abramson, "she should not be expected to wait until his hands are around her neck" (quoted in Gibbs, 1993, p. 43). Abramson finds it disturbing that historically no one decried the "heat of passion" defense used by men who killed their wives and their lovers when found in flagrante delicto (in the very act of sexual intercourse). She believes that whereas men may kill out of wounded pride, women most often kill out of fear (Abramson, 1994). The "reasonable man" standard needs extension to a "reasonable woman" standard (Schneider, 1986).

For some, the controversy surrounding BWS is part of a larger debate over the degree to which mitigating circumstances like poverty, marital abuse, child abuse, drugs, and alcohol should be relevant in a court of law. In the minds of many, these and other "abuse excuses" are getting out of hand. Lorena Bobbitt was acquitted for cutting off the penis of her sleeping husband. Although a second jury convicted them, a jury could not agree on the guilt of Lyle and Erik Menendez, who had "no choice but to gun down their wealthy parents, fake a burglary and go on a spending spree with their victims' money" (Limbaugh, 1994, p. 56). Someone shoots a ghetto youth because of "urban survival syndrome." One teenager kills another for her coat because of "cultural psychosis." "Black rage" presumably explains Colin Ferguson's mass murder of White passengers on a New York subway (cited in Bonfante, Cole, Gwynne, & Kamlani, 1994).

Feminist legal scholars and battered women's advocates, however, argue that the experiences of battered women are unique and should be explained to a jury (Dodge & Greene, 1991). Increasingly, this viewpoint is being heard, and the result is a national movement toward clemency for women who have been convicted of killing abusive husbands. Many states have reexamined cases where abused women were convicted of homicide, and several governors have commuted their sentences, partially because the court did not allow BWS testimony (Gibbs, 1993). In the final analysis, society continues the struggle to find a balance between expressing compassion and concern for victims of abuse without condoning violent responses.

research has, in fact, demonstrated elevated levels of psychosexual dysfunction, major depression, PTSD, generalized anxiety disorder, and obsessive-compulsive disorder in battered women (Gleason, 1993). Although the American Psychological Association has endorsed the validity of the syndrome (cited in Schuller & Vidmar, 1992), the *DSM-IV* (American Psychiatric Association, 1994) has not recognized this distinctive BWS classification.

Intermediate Chapter Summary

The controversy surrounding **learned helplessness** (see Bowker, 1993; Walker, 1993) is difficult to resolve empirically. The most reasonable conclusion seems to be that some women respond to violence with learned helplessness (e.g., emotional trauma, intellectual impairment, motivational impairment) and some women respond with helpseeking efforts. Their level of motivational impairment probably depends on the factors specific to their own situation, such as the number of options available (see Carlisle-Frank, 1991, for a review). Studies show that many battered women are lacking in money, job skills, education, and social support.

Stress is a very potent element in the lives of battered women. Evidence indicates that the stress experienced by battered women frequently results in physical illness. For many women, stress becomes severe enough to be labeled posttraumatic stress disorder (PTSD). Not everyone, however, has accepted the appropriateness of categorizing the symptoms (e.g., psychosexual dysfunction, major depression, obsessive-compulsive disorder) suffered by battered women as PTSD. The subcategorization of these symptoms into a separate **battered woman syndrome (BWS)** classification is quite debatable. Currently, courts almost uniformly allow experts to inform juries about BWS in cases of legal claims of self-defense in homicide cases.

Remaining With an Abuser

"Why does she stay?" is often the first question people ask when confronted with the issue of battered women. The problem with this question is that it implicitly places emphasis on the actions of the victimized woman rather than on the perpetrator. Some commentators believe that the first questions should be "Why does he do it?" and "How can society stop him?" When a liquor store clerk is robbed and shot at point-blank range, they point out, the first question is not "Why didn't he do something to stop it?"

For battered women who do leave, the decision-making process may be painstakingly slow. Most women, in fact, do not want to leave; rather, they want the battering to stop, and "just leaving" does not guarantee either physical or emotional health to a woman (Horton & Johnson, 1993; see Ellis, 1992, for a review). The weight of evidence has shown that women in violent relationships often do leave and return several times (an average of six times) before making their departure permanent (Gondolf, 1988b; Okun, 1986; Snyder & Scheer, 1981).

One of the reasons women stay, then, is that leaving may make things worse. This is, of course, not the only reason. Women's response to violence is shaped by their own diverse cultural, racial, ethnic, class, and sexual orientation experiences and expectations (Miller, 1989; Rasche, 1988). Moreover, there is a complex web of social causes (e.g., marital

dependency) interacting with psychological factors (e.g., fear and hope) that challenge battered women's ability to cope (Kalmuss & Straus, 1982; Strube & Barbour, 1983). Some authorities refer to the psychological changes brought about by these conflicts as *entrapment* (Landenburger, 1989; Walker, 1979).

The use of the word *entrapment* is bothersome to some observers because the word implies that battered women are unable to exercise choice. The fact that many women do leave violent relationships provides those who are perhaps less sensitive to the pressures put on battered women with "proof" that battered women are not really trapped. It may be better to conceptualize the problem in terms of the factors that sometimes make it difficult for women to leave. Of the many reasons why women stay, some of the most important are society's tendency to blame the victim, economic dependence, and relationship issues like commitment and fear of loneliness. Others include the effects of trying to escape but not succeeding, gradual adaptation to living in a violent relationship, and the effects of extreme isolation.

Economic Dependency

Many researchers have noted the economic-dependency/failure-to-leave connection (e.g., Pagelow, 1981a). In fact, studies frequently cite economic dependence as the primary reason that battered women remain with their abusers (e.g., Strube & Barbour, 1983). Divorce tends to make matters worse. Newer no-fault divorce laws and equitable distribution of property laws, originally thought to remedy a host of maladies, have had a very negative financial effect on women in general. Women and children's postdivorce incomes, for example, have declined substantially under these laws (Garrison, 1991; Rowe & Lown, 1990).

In a study of 426 shelter residents (Johnson, 1988) and in another of over 1,000 women (Aguirre, 1985), the probability of staying in their violent relationships was highest for women whose husbands were the sole breadwinners. When women reentered a shelter, their reasons for returning resembled those for entering in the first place (i.e., economic dependency) (Wilson, Baglioni, & Downing, 1989). That is, women who worked outside the home were far more likely to leave if violence recurred.

Although they did not discuss causative factors, Hotaling and Sugarman (1990) concluded in their meta-analysis that battered women tended to be employed less frequently than nonbattered women. One partial explanation for the low employment of battered women is that batterers may use physical force or threats to control the woman's ability to participate in the workplace (Pence & Paymar, 1986). In one analysis, battering resulted in absenteeism from work in 55% of battered women, lateness or leaving early in 62%, job loss in 24%, and batterer harassments at work in 56%. Additionally, 33% of the battered women in this sample reported being prohibited from working, 21% were prevented from finding work, 59% were discouraged from working, 24% were not allowed to attend school, and 50% were discouraged from attending school. Ending the abuse, however, enabled 48% to change their employment or school status (Shepard & Pence, 1988).

These studies clarify why many battered women feel forced to choose between having a home and financial security (with an abuser) and having no home and little income (without the abuser) (Frisch & MacKenzie, 1991; Johnson, 1988). Ferraro's (1981) study vividly described the obstacles facing unemployed battered women. Most of the women in her study were young high school graduates with relatively few job skills and with one or more small children to support. They generally had no cars, no access to public transportation, faced a wait of up to 2 years for a vacancy in a small number of subsidized housing units, and were unable to find affordable child care.

Relationship Issues

Beliefs about the value of relationships, coupled with emotions such as hope and loneliness, propel many battered women into staying with an assaultive male partner despite his violence (Johnson, Crowley, & Sigler,

---

Studies frequently cite economic dependence as the primary reason that battered women remain.

1992). In many cultures, battered and nonbattered women alike agree that women should marry, take responsibility for the quality of their marital relationships, provide a home for their children, and remain with their husbands. Ferguson (1980) proposed that "women's identity is forthrightly and consistently defined in terms of the contexts of social relationships" (pp. 159-160). "A woman's very sense of herself becomes organized around being able to make and then maintain affiliations and relationships" (Miller, 1976, p. 83).

Relationship Commitment. One reason that battered women remain is to honor their relationship commitments. A battered woman may perceive her choice as either to leave and abandon her commitments or to stay and be beaten. Society praises marital partners who are "committed" to a relationship and criticizes those who "give up too easily." Sayings like "sticking together through thick and thin" or "I married him for better or worse" capture these social tenets. Vaughn (1987) has argued that both abusive and nonabusive couples devise plausible reasons for preserving unhappy relationships. Couples may believe in commitment and may not want to quit. They may believe that they can make the relationship better. They may feel a religious conviction to make the relationship work. They may feel legally bound together.

Alternatively, they may want to avoid hurting their partner or may want to protect their children and parents. Extended family members may pressure them with "You made your bed, now lie in it." They may worry that if they leave the relationship, they will not be able to find a new one, especially when told routinely that they are "stupid and ugly and no one else would ever want you." In general, couples hide their troubled relationships from others and develop rationalizations, such as "all relationships have trouble."

Believing that they should stay together "no matter what" is significantly related to battered women's decision to stay (Ferraro & Johnson, 1984; Frisch & MacKenzie, 1991; Strube & Barbour, 1984). In one study, Bauserman and Arias (1992) showed that battered women's commitment was related to their level of failed investment. That is, battered women may have stayed and worked harder to make the relationship work to justify the time and effort already expended on the relationship. These findings were congruent with an entrapment explanation of battered women's behavior.

Relationship Hope. Relationship hope is an especially powerful influence on battered women. Procci (1990) has noted that the failure of a marriage to meet one's expectation causes bitter disappointment. Both men and women generally want marriages to succeed. Battered women will often stay in the marriage because they hope and need to believe that their abuser will stop the violence, a need Muldary (1983) termed *learned hopefulness.* The women in Muldary's study of shelter residents listed several reasons for staying or returning to a battering relationship. They "wanted to save the relationship" or "thought we could solve our problems." Despite the abuse, many claimed that they loved their partners. In another study, Barnett and Lopez-Real (1985) found that the primary reason women said they remained with their abusive partners was "hoped partner would change." Learned hopefulness fits in well with being trapped in a premarital situation as well (Cate, Henton, Koval, Christopher, & Lloyd, 1982). Pagelow (1981a) found that 73% of one shelter sample returned home because the batterer repented and they believed he would change. Both Okun (1983) and Thompson (1989) discovered that the hopes of battered women were rekindled by the male partner's attendance at even one counseling session, even before he had made any real changes in his behavior. Hope also springs from the fact that an abusive male's behavior is intermittently rewarding rather than continuously abusive. Batterers can be kind, romantic, and intimate (Dr.

Jekyll) as well as intimidating and assaultive (Mr. Hyde) (Hastings & Hamberger, 1988). The periods of kindness interspersed with sporadic violence not only create hope but also allow the battered woman to deny the side of the abuser that terrifies her (Graham, Rawlings, & Rimini, 1988).

Fear of Loneliness. Like widows, battered women mourn the loss of the relationships they have come to value. Seventy percent of the battered women interviewed by Turner and Shapiro (1986) returned to their husbands because of feelings of loneliness and loss generated by the separation. Varvaro (1991) identified 12 losses encountered by battered women that exacerbated their feelings of loneliness: safety, everyday routine, living in a home, personal possessions, self-esteem, a father figure for the children, love and caring from a spouse, success in marriage, hopes and dreams, trust in mate, view of the world as a safe place, and status and support systems.

Lack of Perceived Social Support. Unlike widows, however, battered women who leave their spouses may not receive sufficient social support to offset their losses, and the "support" given may be of doubtful value (Mills, 1985; Nurius et al., 1992; Shepherd, 1990). Ieda (1986), for example, noted that friends tend to support a battered woman by encouraging her to tolerate the abuse rather than by ending the relationship. In addition, battered women may need more social support than other victims of violence to restore their faith in people (Janoff-Bulman, 1985). Overall, the perceived lack of support, both personal (e.g., Aguirre, 1985; Barnett, Martinez, & Keyson, 1996) and social (Alsdurf, 1985; Gelles & Harrop, 1989b), tends to impede battered women's attempts to leave (Tan, Basta, Sullivan, & Davidson, 1995).

Attempts to Stop the Violence

In situations where battered women kill their abusers to "stop the violence," their own use of violence has necessarily become the paramount issue. One fundamental reason for the use of severe violence by many battered women is self-defense (e.g., Barnett, Lee, & Thelen, 1995; Browne, 1987; Hamberger & Arnold, 1991; Saunders, 1988).

In addition to studies of battered women's counterviolence, researchers have cataloged a host of other nonviolent methods for ending marital violence. Bowker (1993) found that women employ a variety of strategies in their attempt to end the battering. Of the 1,000 women interviewed, a majority of women used at least one of seven strategies to end the battering: (a) 868 avoided the men physically or avoided certain topics of conversation, (b) 855 covered their faces and vital organs with their hands or used other passive defenses, (c) 758 threatened to call the police or file for divorce, (d) 752 attempted to extract promises that the men would never batter them again, (e) 716 attempted to talk the men out of battering them, (f) 665 fought back physically, and (g) 651 hid or ran away when attacked. According to McLeer (cited in "The Battered Woman," 1989), "early on, she [the battered woman] may be trying to figure out how to decrease the violence but keep her relationship intact. It can take a long time for her to recognize that she can't do anything about his violence—he's a violent man—all she can do is get out" (p. 108).

Adaptation to Violence

Another reason that battered women remain with abusers is that they have learned to make numerous accommodations to their battering relationships. A prerequisite to learning how to live with an abusive person is finding a way to make his (or her) violence acceptable. Basic psychological defense mechanisms of rationalization and denial achieve this goal. By denying that their mates harmed them or even intended to, battered women can negate the danger they confront (Dutton-Douglas, 1991; Ferraro & Johnson, 1984). In fact, people generally have come to believe that in families, a certain amount of physical force is not a repudiation of love but can even be tangible proof of it. Women in relationships may state, "If he didn't love me so much, he wouldn't be so jealous." Walker (1985) cites several modern myths about battering relationships; for example, it is impossible to love someone who hits you. The commonly heard phrase "If he ever lays a hand on me, I'll leave" does not mirror reality. Physical aggression does not herald the demise of a marriage (Lloyd, 1988; Margolin & Fernandez, 1987).

Another way to deal with violence is to assign blame to oneself (Kaner, Bulik, & Sul-

livan, 1993; Overholser & Moll, 1990). A common attribution made by battered women about themselves is that they somehow provoked the violence or that they should have been able to prevent it by changing their own behavior (Prange, 1985). Raped wives are especially prone to blame themselves for the assault (Frieze, 1983). Male batterers contribute to battered women's self-blame by holding them responsible for the relationship abuse (Bennett, Tolman, Rogalski, & Srinivasaraghavan, 1994). Battered women in the Barnett and Lopez-Real (1985) study reported feeling blame more than any other feeling listed in a survey (e.g., anxious, angry, powerful). In a British study of 286 victims of violence, Andrews and Brewin (1990) found that 53% of assaulted women still involved with the perpetrator experienced self-blame for causing the violence, compared with 35% of those who were no longer in the relationship. Most researchers have relied on one or two questions about self-blame and concluded that battered women do not blame themselves for the violence in their relationships (Campbell, 1990; Holtzworth-Munroe, 1988; Langhinrichsen-Rohling, Neidig, & Thorn, 1995). Other researchers have observed a decrease in the level of battered women's self-blame over time as they realize that nothing they do makes a difference (e.g., Walker, 1984).

Relying on a 61-item test and two comparison groups of nonbattered women, however, Barnett et al. (1996) found significantly higher levels of self-blame in battered women. The test used in this study asked such questions as "Was I to blame because I did not listen to him?" Their self-blame even encompassed contradictory sorts of actions exemplifying a kind of "damned if I do, damned if I don't" predicament. As a group, for example, they blamed themselves for either "tolerating the abuse" or for being "too afraid to leave." Clearly, more research is needed to determine the extent to which battered women experience self-blame.

Psychological Entrapment Theories

Research on battered women's rationales for remaining with abusers such as fear, economic dependency, and self-blame seem quite understandable. Battered women who stay are not necessarily irrational. In the words of

Bowker (1993, p. 158), there may well be "worse things than battering" (e.g., homelessness). Some experts, however, find social and cultural explanations incomplete or inapplicable to certain groups of battered women. Proponents of more psychological explanations, such as learned helplessness and BWS (Walker, 1993), contend that conditions like anxiety, poor problem-solving skills, fear, and depression render battered women psychologically trapped.

Animal research has provided a number of useful analogs that, when taken together, more fully explain entrapment (see Barnett & LaViolette, 1993, for a review). Early animal research, for example, showed that an infant could be classically conditioned to fear a white rat (Watson & Raynor, 1920). Animal research on intermittently reinforced behavior (Skinner, 1938) and intermittent punishment (Azrin, Holz, & Hake, 1963) led researchers to speculate that an abusive partner's sporadic loving behavior along with occasional battering might help explain battered women's persistence in abusive relationships (Long & McNamara, 1989; Wetzel & Ross, 1983). In examining the cyclical nature of violence (e.g., Walker, 1979), for example, researchers reinterpreted "punishment followed by reinforcement" as analogous to "battering followed by contrition," and they conjectured that abuse followed by loving contrition actually increases the female partner's tendency to remain in the relationship (see Serra, 1993).

Taken one step further, some have hypothesized that in unusual instances, violence can actually increase a woman's attachment to her abusive mate (see Graham et al., 1995)! In the words of Dutton and Painter (1981), a battered woman can form a "traumatic bond" to a man who alternately assaults and rewards her with love and attention. Learning theory supports the notion that intermittent reward along with intermittent punishment increases persistence of responses (see Barnett & LaViolette, 1993, for a review). More recently, Dutton and Painter (1993b) have empirically demonstrated that extreme abuse intermittency, in combination with other dynamic factors such as power differences, does contribute to long-term feelings of attachment. Many questions about whether "typical" marital violence is cyclical and about its possible consequences remain unresolved (Aldarondo, 1996; Follingstad, Hause, Rutledge, & Polek, 1992; O'Leary et al., 1989).

Do Battered Women Stay?

The most common method of stopping domestic violence is the physical and legal termination of the relationship (Bowker, 1983; NiCarthy, 1987). Despite this fact, laws fail to protect women who wish to leave (e.g., Klein, 1995; Zorza, 1995). The ultimate reason for leaving for many women is because of risks to their children (Barnett & Lopez-Real, 1985; Hilton, 1992). Battered women also have grave concerns about maintaining custody of their children (Geffner & Pagelow, 1990b). Lehnen and Skogan's (1981) analysis of the National Crime Survey revealed that most female victims of abuse were, at the time of their interview, divorced or separated. These data imply that "many or even most women leave abusive relationships" (p. 239).

Although clinical studies typically find that about a third of battered women fleeing to shelters return to their partners, the figure may run as high as 70% (Johnson et al., 1992). Gondolf (1988b) discovered that 24% of shelter women planned to return, with an additional 7% undecided. Snyder and Scheer (1981) found a 33% return rate. In a study of 512 abused women living in a shelter, 74.2% had separated from their mates at least once, and some had separated more than 10 times (LaBell, 1979). Dutton-Douglas (1991) points out, however, that the most relevant measure is not whether a woman returns but whether she continues to be battered.

Newer research has finally provided some information about the variables that make it possible for women to stay. In a national sample of 185 postabuse survivors, Horton and Johnson (1993) found only 27 who were able to retain their relationship, and, of these, only 16 rated themselves as feeling "satisfied" or "very satisfied" with the relationship. On average, the survivors had endured abuse for 10 years before finding ways to end it. The successful victims tended to be younger, had been more severely abused, pursued more methods for ending the abuse, had abusive partners who became involved in the change process and sought drug and alcohol treatment more readily, were more committed to their partners, and felt more hopeful about their relationship. Dissatisfied survivors were more trapped by fewer job opportunities, had a strong fear of failure, had more children, had husbands who were more likely to sexually abuse them, and had husbands who were more likely to physically abuse their child. Dissatisfied women were more than 3 times as likely as successful victims to have been forced to have sex. Both successful and dissatisfied victims noted the importance of acknowledging the problem and of seeking professional counseling. Without appropriate intervention, battered women may remain mired in an abusive relationship for a considerable length of time.

Intermediate Chapter Summary

The **reasons battered women remain** with abusers are almost too numerous to mention. Research pinpoints **economic necessity** as the primary reason. In addition to traditional problems faced by nearly all working women, like inadequate child care, battered women face obstacles in holding down a job caused more directly by their batterer. Many batterers, for example, attempt to prevent their wives from working through intimidation and harassment.

Relationship issues provide extremely compelling reasons for battered women to remain with their abusive partners. Most battered women, like other women, feel committed to their relationship and want to maintain their homes. They love the abuser and keep hoping that he will "change back" to the man they married. They also fear they will be lonely if their relationship ends. Last, they receive very little social support from family and friends that would make it easier for them to leave. Another reason that battered women stay is that their attempts to leave did not work out. Battered women ordinarily make a number of both violent and nonviolent attempts to leave, including avoiding the batterer and fighting back. Other reasons that battered women stay is that they gradually adjust to the battering. It becomes a way of life.

The implications of some research suggest that violence alternated with love may prompt a number of battered women to form a "traumatic bond" with their abusers and thus become emotionally trapped in the relationship. Animal research using **intermittent reward and punishment** offers some interesting analogs about how inconsistent treatment evokes persistence in behavior (i.e., remaining in abusive situations). Although **psychological entrapment theories** "explain" the puzzling fact that some battered women do not leave, their acceptance remains limited.

Actually, most battered women do not stay. Only about one third of women in shelters seem to return to their abusive partners. Of those who return, some are much more satisfied with their relationships than others. A number of variables, such as sexual assault, are related to dissatisfaction with remaining with an abuser.

Treatment of Battered Women

It was grassroots organizations that defined the range of services needed by battered women: shelter, transportation, counseling, legal assistance, and child care (Schwendinger & Schwendinger, 1981). Perhaps Sullivan (1991) is correct: The solution to battering does not lie totally with the battered woman (see Zorza, 1995). Those interested in helping battered women should center their efforts mainly on community-based strategies such as building a shelter (Johnson et al., 1992). Nonetheless, there are a number of individual, therapy-oriented approaches that might help battered women escape the violence (Dutton-Douglas, 1991).

Shelter Treatment

The temporary separation from a batterer offered by a shelter can assist women by helping them feel safe and by providing them with people who will listen to their concerns.

> *Probably the most important aspect of any shelter program is to help residents make plans for their safety.*

Probably the most important aspect of any shelter program is to help residents make plans for their safety (Dutton-Douglas, 1991).

A DAY IN THE LIFE OF A SHELTER MANAGER/ CASE MANAGER, BY ALICE SOWTER

INTERFACE CHILDREN FAMILY SERVICES OF VENTURA COUNTY

8:05 a.m. Monday

I arrive and start reading the transition (weekend) notes. I have been off over the weekend, but the weekend staff called me on Saturday about placing Jane, a new woman with two children, one of whom is severely handicapped and needs frequent medication.

8:20 a.m.

Before I can finish the transition notes, I receive a crisis call from a 75-year-old woman whose husband of 40 years has hit her on the head with a pan. In retaliation, she tried to kick him, but slipped and fell. She wants the shelter to provide a ride to a local hospital. Unfortunately, we do not offer that particular service. I give her a few referrals to other agencies that could help her. I feel bad about not helping her, especially as I begin to realize she had been in our shelter once in 1982 and has been in two others since then. I reluctantly accept the fact that she probably is not going to make any changes in her life. This *is* her life.

8:30 a.m.

Jane, the new client, is pacing about, anxiously waiting to speak with me. She says she cannot wait around for the 72-hour hold. (We have a shelter rule that for the first 72 hours, a woman may not leave, make phone calls, or receive phone calls. The rule helps the woman know she is safe and that she will get support, and it gives her a chance to acclimate to her new surroundings.) Jane is so nervous and anxious that I begin to suspect she is on drugs. When I ask her she says, yes, but she claims that she has been clean for 2 weeks. We talk. I try to convince her to stay because I feel she needs our program and our services. Although she has no place to go, she refuses to stay. She makes some phone calls to try to get help from her friends, but no one will take her in. She says again that she has to leave, that she can just be dropped off on a corner. I express my concern about her safety and the children's needs. She gets hostile and says she will walk to the corner on her own. At this point, I begin to get angry because she shows no concern about her children's welfare. I arrange a ride and she leaves. As she walks out the front door, I get on the phone to make a report to Child Protective Services, stating my concern about child endangerment. The report is taken, and I get on with the day.

Planning for safety includes foresight, such as knowing the location of a safe place to go and having money hidden or in a separate account. Gelles (1976) states that a shelter counseling program helps end a battered woman's feelings of isolation, which in turn allows her to evaluate her own situation differently. (For a glimpse into the daily work of a shelter manager, see the boxed insert: "A Day in the Life of a Shelter Manager/Case Manager, by Alice Sowter.")

Economic Independence

Achieving economic independence for battered women often plays a decisive role in their freedom from victimization. Wilson, Baglioni, et al. (1989) concluded that working away from home appears to be a crucial survival strategy, possibly because it lessens the battered woman's economic, social, and emotional dependence on her husband.

11:30 a.m.

Debbie, a former client, drops by to pick up some mail, to give us her new address, and to update us on her situation—how she is doing and the status of her husband. She has moved out of her old neighborhood and has taken a new, but lower-paying job. So far, her husband has not found her nor tried to see her. She feels that she is starting to get on with her life. Her visit reminds me that many of our clients keep in touch for years after they leave the shelter.

11:40 a.m.

I get another crisis call from a woman in a very violent situation. We accept her as a client, but tell her we have to place her in our other shelter, a 45-minute drive away. Because her residence is within a mile of the shelter, it is too dangerous to keep her here. After we talk more, she says she will get a restraining order and call us back to find out where to go. When she phones, she says she has decided to stay with friends because of the logistics of getting to her job and to child care. I caution her that she is at risk even with a restraining order. I end the conversation, disappointed that she will not be in shelter. I feel that counseling and support for her and her two children could make a real difference in her life.

12:10 p.m.

A Spanish-speaking client calls, but there isn't anyone available at the moment to speak with her at our shelter. I call our new bilingual shelter (Puerto De Paz), where she speaks with a Spanish counselor. She is placed there.

1:00 p.m.

The Parenting Group at the shelter is starting. The children are not down for their quiet time, and there is still a lot of crying and fussing. Finally, things settle down and the group starts late, as usual. As the moms talk about their children, it is clear that many of them have a hard time with scheduling and setting boundaries.

2:00 p.m.

The evening manager arrives, and we talk about the events of the day to make the transition between shifts. (Our time overlaps for 2 hours.) I can now take an hour or so to do case management. I speak with Gloria about the status of a restraining order she has been trying to get. Her husband cannot be found. He is hiding out because there is a warrant out for his arrest. Gloria has a job and child care, but she is in too much danger to leave the shelter before she obtains the restraining order. Gloria will have to go back to court again and wait another week to see if her husband can be served. She is in limbo, and we are all frustrated.

(continued)

Gelles (1976) contends that holding down a job also helps diminish a battered woman's isolation, thus giving her a different perspective on the world. Helping battered women obtain temporary welfare benefits and helping them prepare for employment (e.g., referral to training programs) must be a top priority for shelter programs (Dutton-Douglas, 1991).

Counseling

People who have never experienced the beneficial effects of counseling may be hesitant to seek help. Battered women who are aware of their need for support may still not know whom to call or what sort of assistance they might receive. To make matters worse,

2:15 p.m.

Another crisis call from a homeless woman comes in. I realize that she has been drinking, which she admits when asked. I refer her to an alcohol program.

2:30 p.m.

I return a number of phone calls from volunteers, shelter workers, and others who want to make donations to the shelter. I feel so rushed that as I hang up, I wonder whether I have come across as disinterested or ungrateful. I continue making other calls, as an advocate for a client. I call other agencies, such as welfare or housing. Today, I also called the police and the jail to find out the status of a batterer.

3:50 p.m.

I make my regular call to Angie, a former client who is now residing in our new transition home with her two children. She has made excellent progress, and I feel positive about her success. She is paying a percentage of the rent, and she is saving money as she is obligated to do. She is a hard worker and very motivated. I make plans to visit her for my weekly visit to discuss any problems or issues that may have come up, to see what advocacy work I need to do for her. When I hang up the phone, I feel a sense of satisfaction about working with her.

4:00 p.m.

My day has "officially" ended. Before I leave, the evening manager and I talk about getting groceries for the clients and getting a room cleaned up where Jane had stayed earlier in the day. Jane left without fulfilling her responsibility of leaving the room as she found it. We plan to ask the volunteers for help. We transition a bit more.

4:30 p.m.

I say good-bye to the clients, close the door, and try to close out the events of the day. I don't succeed. I drive home worried about the little handicapped girl. I wanted to be able to put her in a warm and loving place, out of harm's way. "At least Angie is going to make it," I say to myself.

SOURCE: Used by permission of Alice Sowter and the Interface Children Family Services, Ventura County, California.

some counseling techniques geared to ameliorate spouse abuse have been detrimental for battered women (Davis, 1984; Dutton-Douglas, 1991; Hansen et al., 1991). Finally, a general lack of knowledge about resources available to battered women has inspired some advocates to mount community enlightenment campaigns.

CASE HISTORY: WENDY CALLS A HOTLINE

The third time the police arrested Wendy's husband for beating her, they handed Wendy a card with the name and phone number of a battered women's hotline. The next day, while her cut lip was still hurting and she felt afraid and alone, she called the hotline and spoke with Judy. Judy provided her with a lot of information and told her about the battered women's outreach group that met Wednesday mornings at 11:00. Although Wendy did not see how sitting around talking and listening to other battered women could possibly help her personally, she attended her first group meeting. Wendy was amazed to hear about the experiences of other women, how some were trying to get jobs, others were making plans to move in together to share expenses, and still others were seeking civil damages against their abusers in court. For the first time in 10 years, Wendy felt that maybe she really could do something to stop her husband's assaults, and she began to think more carefully about her safety needs. (Author's case history)

A battered woman may look to counseling for any number of reasons. Most likely, she wants the counselor to help her find ways to end the violence, rather than to find ways to leave the relationship (Landenburger, 1989). Battered women may need to undergo a metamorphosis in what Heppner (1978) calls the "wishing and hoping" complex (i.e., giving up learned hopefulness). Whatever the outcome, counseling is a crucial element of helping battered women make decisions.

Dealing With Loss. Most battered women feel great deprivation and loss when their relationships end (Walker, 1984). Varvaro (1991) found that assessing battered women's losses and dealing with them in a support group enabled the women to avoid the immobilizing effects of grief and to develop a new sense of self-determination.

Changing Beliefs. Wetzel and Ross (1983) contend that some of the most important work with battered women is the remaking of their belief systems to help them stop believing that they cause or can stop the abuse. Douglas (1987) alleges that therapy can help a battered woman accept personal responsibility for her safety while rejecting personal responsibility for the violence. Painter and Dutton (1985) surmise that as long as a battered woman "continues to believe that she causes the violence, and that changes in her behavior might prevent the violent behavior from occurring, she is locked into the battering relationship" (p. 373). Walker (1984) conjectures that the battered woman may misinterpret her own focus on her batterer's happiness and her own use of coping strategies as actually being in control of the violence in her relationship. Under this "illusion of control," she may come to believe that she can induce her abuser to stop his abuse if only she could find the right "key." A battered woman who ceases blaming herself will feel better and begin to see alternatives whether or not she decides to leave.

Providing Social Support. Inclusion of a support group will enhance coping capacity in battered women (Rubin, 1991; Tan et al., 1995). Social supports should help by emboldening a battered woman to redefine marriage as a relationship in which violence in not allowed (Bagarozzi & Giddings, 1983). Chang (1989) has theorized that supportive involvement with others is critical in the transformation of a battered woman into a self-

saver, rather than a wife who concentrates on either saving the relationship or helping her abuser change. For African American women, groups should include a focus on racial stereotypes of Black women as a means of reducing isolation and providing social support (Brice-Baker, 1994).

Indeed, Johnson (1988) found that 63% of battered women who had little or no support returned to their abusers, whereas only 19% of those who had strong support systems returned. Along the same lines, Dalto (1983) found that battered women who formed close relationships with other shelter residents or staff were more likely to leave their abusive relationships than those who did not.

Problem Solving and Coping Capacity. Training in problem-solving skills (D'Zurilla, 1986) and developing the ability to make self-directed decisions (Bowen, 1982) is pivotal in helping battered women mobilize their coping capacity. An initial step may be anxiety reduction to enhance concentration (Trimpey, 1989). Similarly, therapists need to be alert to the strong probability that their battered clients are suffering from PTSD, with its attendant anxiety-related symptoms. Listening to other battered women in a group setting describe their trauma-related symptoms and how these symptoms interfere with functioning validates a woman's experiences and tends to reassure her that she is not "crazy" (Saunders, 1994).

At a practical level, counselors can role-play job interviewing techniques, assertion skills, parenting skills, and even basic apartment- or house-hunting proficiency (Holiman & Schilit, 1991). Along with other types of competency training, Cummings (1990) believes that self-defense training for women is critical.

Couples Counseling. Seeking the help an abuser needs to stop the violence may eventuate in couples counseling (Bagarozzi & Giddings, 1983). Therapists who recommend couples therapy believe that violence may be a product of the interactions of the spouses in a specific marital system, rather than the individual behavior of one spouse (Giles-Sims, 1983). Others think that because couples so frequently wish to stay together despite the violence, it may be best to treat them together, especially if the violence is not severe (Lane & Russell, 1989). Generally, however, the rationale underlying conjoint approaches is that the presence of both partners expedites the goal of ending the violence (see Margolin & Burman, 1993).

Many experts believe that couples counseling places battered women in danger (Davis, 1984; Dutton-Douglas, 1991; Hansen et al., 1991) just at a time when the first duty of

---

It is critical to recognize that a battering problem belongs to the person who batters.

---

clinicians is to ensure women's safety (Hamberger & Barnett, 1995). Forced mediation before a divorce, for example, may subject a battered woman to physically dangerous confrontation with her violent partner (Geffner & Pagelow, 1990b). Some criticize the systems approach as simply a way to make violence seem more manageable than it really is (Bograd, 1992). Others condemn it because an individual issue (e.g., violence) may become confused with a family issue (e.g., communication). It is critical to recognize that a battering problem belongs to the person who batters. Nowhere is this admonition needed more than in treating lesbian victims of interpartner battering (Renzetti, 1992).

Alcoholism Programs. Experts working jointly in the fields of substance abuse and family violence have called attention to the dangers inherent in substituting typical Alcoholics Anonymous or Al-Anon methods for typical shelter programs. The codependency strategy of encouraging battered women to become self-focused or to set limits is the direct opposite of the life-saving skills that battered women have developed. Likewise, the "sobriety first" model applied to chemically dependent women is almost doomed to failure, because it both disregards the requisite "safety first" approach and the recognition of alcohol use as a method for coping with unremitting danger and fear (Zubretsky & Digirolamo, 1994).

Summary

Society's tendency to blame victims is reflected in the acceptance of myths about battered women—that they come primarily from abusive homes or drink too much. Findings of low self-esteem in abused women indicate that the problem stems from being battered rather than from inherent personality flaws. In general, women entering relationships that eventually become abusive do not initially differ from their nonbattered counterparts. Sexual assault in marriage is all too common, but it is finally being recognized as a serious problem with long-lasting repercussions.

The violence endured by battered women has profound effects on them. Most apparent is their development of high levels of fear and depression. More controversial is whether battered women suffer from "learned helplessness" as exemplified in poor problem-solving abilities and in passivity. The extreme stress generated by exposure to violence evokes a posttraumatic stress disorder (PTSD) in substantial numbers of battered women. Whether a special PTSD subcategory of battered woman syndrome (BWS) is warranted, however, has generated debate. In particular, application of BWS as the foundation for a self-defense plea in spousal murder cases has evoked both strong support and fierce criticism.

Battered women typically try a number of nonviolent strategies (e.g., threaten divorce or leave temporarily) as well as counterviolence to end the violence. Leaving, however, does not ensure a battered woman's safety. In fact, leaving may increase her chances of being assaulted. Researchers have searched for explanations as to why many battered women remain in abusive relationships despite the violence. In addition to economic dependence (e.g., need for shelter, transportation, child care, counseling), battered women feel committed to their marriages and seem to experience a type of "learned hopefulness" that their partner will change. They can easily envision the losses they will undergo without a husband or father in the home, and they receive little social support for the decision to leave.

Women who remain with abusers, whether in traditional or lesbian relationships, seem to find a way to tolerate the violence by accepting it as normal, denying that it is a serious problem, or by accepting the blame themselves. Factors such as the intermittent nature of both the abuse and the positive rewards of the relationship have led some investigators to propose psychological entrapment theories to characterize the effects of victimization. In reality, most battered women do leave their abusers despite the difficulties they must overcome.

Shelters can effectively offer battered women a safe place to begin the decision-making process. Whereas treatment initially focuses on safety needs (e.g., knowing where to go, hiding money), it eventually incorporates components such as economic stability, dealing with loss, and changing one's beliefs about responsibility for the violence. Counseling is often a critical component of change—for both individuals and couples. Finally, providing social support and teaching battered women practical problem-solving skills are methods geared to begin the process of undoing the overwhelming problems engendered by marital assault.

10

Marital Violence

Batterers

CHAPTER OUTLINE

An Interview With
L. Kevin Hamberger

"Responding adequately to battered victims is a quality of life issue as well as a cost-benefit issue that concerns all health care providers."

KEVIN HAMBERGER is one of the most productive researchers in the area of male batterers in the United States. In Kenosha County, Wisconsin, he is President of the Board of Directors of Women's Horizons Inc., a battered women's shelter. He also is a member of the Kenosha Domestic Abuse Intervention Project, a multidisciplinary task force that develops policy and monitors abuse intervention programming in the community. A licensed psychologist, he chairs a committee of the Wisconsin Governor's Council on Domestic Violence to develop standards of treatment for court-ordered male batterers. He chairs the Society of Teachers of Family Medicine's Group on Violence Education. He also serves on the editorial boards of two journals. He is coeditor (with Lynn Caesar) of Treating Men Who Batter and (with Claire Renzetti) Domestic Partner Abuse. He is editing a third book, Violence Issues for Health Care Educators. This book broadens the scope of violence to elder abuse, teen violence, and professional misconduct.

Q: What are your current research interests?

A: I have three major foci. Violence education is my first interest. I am surveying battered women about their direct experiences with physicians when seeking health care for their injuries. We inquire about which kinds of physician behaviors are useful and helpful and which are not. We are using this information to develop a curriculum for physicians that is particularly sensitive to battered women's needs.

A second major interest is a study of the personality characteristics of batterers. We have collected a large database of 830 men who have received treatment for wife abuse, and are currently analyzing the data. We hope to be able to develop more fine-grained pictures of different types of male batterers and their relevance to treatment.

My last area of interest is examining gender differences in men's and women's use of violence in intimate relationships. Men and women frequently have different reasons for being violent, and it is important to understand these differences.

Q: What are your future research and advocacy goals?

A: I would like to extend my efforts to help refocus attention on health care provider education. I want to continue to help push for the development of fairly well-developed, if not standardized, curricular pieces for inclusion in both medical schools and psychology programs.

Q: Why do you view violence education as such an important issue in the field of family violence?

A: Some evidence indicates that battered victims make more frequent visits for medical care, not just for acute injuries but for general health care as well. Victims are often left with psychological sequelae that lower their sense of well-being and self-perceived health status. Responding adequately to these victims, therefore, is a quality of life issue that concerns all health care providers.

Responding appropriately to battered victims and survivors is also a cost-benefit issue. When victims are seeking care but not getting appropriate assistance, they remain locked into the health care system pursuing symptoms. It is the health care provider's job to offer a more complete package of care.

The health care system is ideally suited to identify a maximum number of victims of violence (or injured perpetrators) to begin intervening with them and funneling them into appropriate resources. Without this intervention, victims of violence will go unrecognized and may languish without appropriate help. Generally speaking, we have to help partners involved in a violent relationship to "stop the violence" or "get away."

Q: What do you think communities need to do assist victims?

A: Dovetailing my work on our local task force with my involvement in the health care system reinforces my belief in the importance of improving and strengthening the safety net for battered victims. It is important to focus on providing health care, not just for its own sake, but as one more part of a community's response that, as a whole, tells battered women that there is safety for them and that they do not deserve to be assaulted. Part of this community response is also to tell men they must stop the violence, and that they alone are responsible for it. These bits and pieces of community intervention add to the total set of resources that are available to victims as well as perpetrators.

Introduction

CASE HISTORY: BERNADETTE AND ARI— WHEN A LITTLE SLAP IS A KNOCKOUT PUNCH

Ari came into group counseling like so many other men arrested and ordered into counseling. He seemed calm and collected, dressed nicely from his day's work as a department store manager where he worked on commission. He protested his arrest, claiming that it was "all a mistake." All he did was give Bernadette a little push in the car because she wouldn't "shut up."

Ari's story was that he came home exhausted from a long day at work to find Bernadette all dressed up, saying that she "had to get out of the house"; she wanted to go out to dinner. Ari said he was too tired, but Bernadette got angry and started screaming that he only "thought of himself." Ari gave in.

It was already 8:30 by the time they pulled into the parking lot. The restaurant was crowded and noisy and Ari was angry and sullen as they waited for their dinner. He and Bernadette each had several drinks, but Ari could not calm down. "No one ever cares about my feelings," he thought. When they returned to the car, Bernadette launched into a diatribe about Ari's "failure" to accept her 6-year-old son by a previous marriage. She kept "mouthing off as usual," and Ari's driving became

erratic. As they arrived home, Ari reached over and slapped her because he "had to do something to get her attention." When he went around to open Bernadette's door, she "fell out and hit her head on the pavement."

The paramedics and the police were called by the neighbors and Ari was arrested. Bernadette's medical report said that she had been "knocked out"; she did not fall and hit her head. It took over 10 weeks of group counseling before Ari would admit that his little slap was really a knockout punch. (Author's case history)

* * *

The actions typified in Ari's case are quite typical of spouse-abusive behaviors. Through the remainder of the chapter, some of the components of this case history will be illustrative of specific problems of batterers. Note, for example, that Ari dismissed the incident as a mistake. He was tired and probably stressed after a day of work. To him, Bernadette did not seem understanding or compromising. Ari's anger and stress contributed to his assault on his wife, which he minimized. In fact, according to Ari, she provoked his physical attack.

This chapter examines the behavior of batterers, men who abuse and control women through threats and physical, psychological, verbal, and sexual aggression. The focus is on men, not because women are never violent and not because their violence should be overlooked. Research suggests, however, that in a majority of battering cases, men are the primary injury-producing perpetrators and women are the more truly victimized partners for a number of reasons. Nonetheless, other research calls attention to the fact that marital violence is often mutual.

Topics include descriptions of batterers by their partners and themselves and similarities between family-only violent men and men who are violent both within and outside the family. A discussion of etiological theories including socialization, biological traits, relationship factors, and personality traits and psychopathology compose another section. The chapter concludes with a synopsis of counseling approaches used in treatment. Despite heightened attention from researchers and clinicians, batterers' behavior remains a poorly understood phenomenon. There are disagreements about the major causes of battering, the characteristics of male spouse abusers, and the appropriateness of treatments.

Descriptions of Batterers

One subject that has prompted diverse solutions is how best to investigate batterers. Should information be derived from victims, perpetrators, or other informants? Allied with this question is whether batterers should be characterized as a unique group of men whose violence targets family members only or whether batterers are simply run-of-the-mill, violent criminals.

Battered Women's Descriptions of Batterers

The first attempts by psychologists to examine wife abuse generally consisted of descriptions provided by battered women in counseling. Premised on her discussions with battered women, Elbow (1977), for example, attempted to group maritally violent men into four categories: *controller, defender, approval seeker,* and *incorporator.* Briefly summed up, the controller envisions his wife as an object of control, and she symbolizes the parent who controlled him. The defender, on the other hand, thinks of his mate as both a seductress and hostile other. The value of the approval-seeker's mate is her ability to reinforce his self-image. She represents the conditional love of the parent. For the incorporator, the mate signifies parental love, and doing without her as a complete loss of the self.

Lenore Walker's (1979) research with battered women enabled her to delineate a sequence of male spouses' battering that she termed the "cycle of violence." The cycle of violence describes interpersonal aggression that intensifies in degree and frequency over time and holds the people involved in an established pattern of behavior. The cycle of violence consists of three phases:

1. *Tension building.* In this phase, minor incidents of violence may occur along with a buildup of anger. This phase may include verbal put-downs, jealousy, threats, and breaking things and can eventually escalate to the second phase.
2. *Acute or battering.* In this phase, the major violent outburst occurs. This violence can be seen as the major earthquake. Following the second phase, the couple sometimes enters Phase 3.
3. *The honeymoon or loving respite.* In this phase, the batterer is remorseful and afraid of losing his partner. He may promise anything, beg forgiveness, buy gifts, and basically be "the man she fell in love with."

Batterers' Descriptions of Themselves

When researchers or practitioners ask men accused of wife beating about their own behavior, the responses provided reveal batterers' tendencies to blame others for their assaults, most especially their female partners, and to downplay the significance and seriousness of their violence.

The "Blame Game." The role of blame in a battering relationship is a critical issue because men who blame their female partners are likely to be even more violent than those who do not (Byrne, Arias, & Lyons, 1993). Dutton (1986b) coded wife assaulters' free-form accounts of the causes of their battering and isolated three general classifications: (a) victim provocation, (b) self-blame with denial and minimization of its effects, and (c) self-blame with attributions to some aspect of themselves such as a drinking problem.

Probably the most common explanation given by batterers runs something like this: "I told her not to do it [e.g., staying late after work, mouthing off]. She knew what would happen. She did it anyway. She got what she asked for" (see Barrera, Palmer, Brown, & Kalaher, 1994). This scenario illustrates batterers' propensities to formulate and externalize blame (Sapiente, 1988) and to justify their violence by pronouncing that it is warranted, given the situation (Ptacek, 1988).

Denial and Minimization. Batterers also deny the abusive nature of their behavior (Edleson & Brygger, 1986; Wetzel & Ross, 1983). Sonkin, Martin, and Walker's (1985) interpretation of this proclivity is that batterers minimize and deny their assaultive behavior because they themselves disapprove of it. Other research indicates that batterers may be unaware of the true reasons for their abusive behaviors (Barnett, Lee, & Thelen, 1995).

Similarities and Differences Between Maritally Only Violent and Generally Violent (Panviolent) Men

Another avenue of approach in understanding wife assault has been to contrast batterers' behavior (maritally only violent) with that of violent criminals (generally violent or panviolent men, violent inside and outside the family). Perhaps the tendency to view wife assault as a private matter has obscured the true continuities between maritally only violent and generally violent men.

Proportion of Family-Only Crime. Several studies have explored the question of whether spouse abusers are also violent with nonfamily members. In an early inquiry based on interviews with 270 domestic violence victims, Fagan, Stewart, and Hansen (1983) showed that almost half of all spouse abusers had been arrested previously for other violence and that violence in the home was positively correlated with violence toward strangers (also see Shields, McCall, & Hanneke, 1988). Another survey presented consistent data by showing that husbands of women living in shelters tended to have criminal records (Dunford, Huizinga, & Elliott, 1990).

Using a larger sample of 2,291 males from the 1985 National Family Violence Survey data of 6,002 households (Straus & Gelles, 1990), Kandel-Englander (1992) identified 311 men (15%) who had been violent during the previous 12-month period. From the violent group,

208 (67%) had been violent only toward a wife (family), 71 (23%) had been violent only toward a nonfamily member, and 32 (10%) had been violent toward both a wife and a nonfamily individual (panviolent). Thus, the selection of the target (assaulted person) most clearly differentiated the groups.

Social and Behavioral Differences. Other surveys have sought to unravel social and behavioral dissimilarities between subsamples of violent men. One study found that men charged with domestic homicide experienced more behavioral problems in childhood (e.g., truancy) than men charged with nondomestic homicide. Both groups were more likely than nonviolent men to have disturbed childhoods, such as a missing parent (Anasseril & Holcomb, 1985). Another account of 85 violent men indicated that generally violent men (panviolent—both wives and nonfamily individuals) and men violent only toward nonfamily individuals were comparable in terms of background characteristics but very dissimilar in terms of other attributes, such as socioeconomic status, drug use, and prior conviction rates (Shields et al., 1988).

Intermediate Chapter Summary

Battered women provided clinicians with some of the first **anecdotal reports** of batterers. Investigators, such as Walker (1979), provided some provisional information about batterers' tendencies to blame others and to minimize the seriousness of their own behavior. This early work set the stage for the proliferation of empirical studies that followed.

In **queries of batterers** themselves about their behavior, they offered accounts consistent with those outlined by Walker. Batterers most often blame the female partner—"She didn't do what she was supposed to do." They further deny their violence or tend to minimize it—"I didn't really hurt her; I just pushed her."

Although incomplete, available information has shown that **subsamples of violent men** (family only, nonfamily only, or both family and nonfamily) vary in important ways, they also share some important attributes (e.g., disturbed childhoods). Data based on samples of wife assaulters indicate frequent arrests for nonfamily violent crime. Data from larger, more representative samples suggest that the major difference between these groups may be in their selection of targets of violence. Only 10% of a large sample of men were violent toward both their wives (family) and strangers (nonfamily).

Becoming and Remaining a Batterer

The next section of this chapter summarizes some of the socialization practices that contribute to battering and some of the biological forces that generally support male aggression. Socialization forces are paramount in discussing battering behavior because violence may be a learned behavior. Biological support for male aggression, a frequently overlooked topic, needs further elucidation to help provide a more complete understanding of male violence. Research on dyadic or interpersonal relationship variables has generated a relatively large amount of data on topics such as marital dissatisfaction, communication styles, stress, and control issues.

Socialization

A number of researchers have carefully thought about socialization variables that might promote spouse abuse by males. There may be generalized modeling that conveys approval of violence and specific modeling that teaches that certain behaviors are acceptable and certain people are the proper targets (e.g., Kalmuss, 1984).

Childhood Socialization. The finding that exposure to violence during childhood is associated with later male-to-female violence is almost universal (e.g., Howell & Pugliesi, 1988; Roberts, 1987; Rouse, 1984; cf. Bennett, Tolman, Rogalski, & Srinivasaraghavan, 1994). In a sample of college students, Briere (1987) was able to link male students' childhood abuse experiences with their likelihood of battering a spouse. Observations of abuse, according to Hotaling and Sugarman (1986), may be a more powerful indicator of future marital violence than experiencing abuse directly, and paternal violence may be a better predictor than maternal violence (see also Barnett, Fagan, & Booker, 1991; Caesar & Hamberger, 1989; Choice, Lamke, & Pittman, 1995; Seltzer & Kalmuss, 1988; Widom, 1989).

Researchers are now beginning to examine other variables related to intergenerational abuse. Harsh treatment as a child, for example, may lead to the development of an antisocial orientation, which, in turn, is associated with chronic (repeated) spousal aggression (Simons, Wu, & Conger, 1995). Most recently, researchers have suggested that anxious attachment during childhood is related to shame in adult batterers (Wallace & Nosko, 1993). In one study, level of male-to-female marital violence was strongly associated with two childhood factors that would be expected to interfere with attachment: (a) the number of separation and loss events experienced, and (b) the presence of paternal substance abuse (i.e., possible erratic caregiving; Corvo, 1992).

Furthermore, a new study has linked parent-to-child shaming and guilt inducement during childhood with chronic adult anger, trauma symptoms, male-to-female marital abusiveness, and borderline personality disorder in adult perpetrators of physical abuse (Dutton, Van Ginkel, & Starzomski, 1995). Although replication studies are needed, these findings provide an important account of the relationship between variability in childhood experiences of abuse and adult individual differences in battering (Dutton et al., 1995).

Male Socialization and Cultural Factors. Men can also be socialized to expect their wives to treat them with deference. Male entitlement to power and the use of dominance in marital conflicts to control female partners hinge on sex-role socialization (Birns, Cascardi, & Meyer, 1994).

Influences such as television, movies, magazines, dating partners, and peer groups promote aggression (Kruttschnitt, Heath, & Ward, 1986; Seltzer & Kalmuss, 1988). Men receive a number of messages that encourage them to be tough, aggressive, competitive, and emotionally distant (Scher, 1980; Watts & Courtois, 1981). Some information teaches them to confuse violence with sexuality (Stevens & Gebhart, 1985) and to tune out feelings (except anger; Heppner & Gonzales, 1987). As Breines and Gordon (1983) maintain, however, cultural antecedents should not be accepted as the sole explanation for wife abuse. Not all men who have been socialized to be dominant beat their wives. Indeed, wife beating is not universal in our society. It is used only by some men in some relationships (Maertz, 1990).

Because patriarchal beliefs presumably contribute to spouse abuse, researchers have questioned whether batterers hold more sexist views toward women than nonbatterers. Results seem to depend, however, on the type of scale used. In a controlled study of male spouse abusers, sex-role scores were inconsistent and primarily depended on the test instruments selected (Barnett & Ryska, 1986). Tests assessing masculinity and femininity as separate personality dimensions yielded significant differences between maritally violent and nonviolent men (Rosenbaum, 1986). In contrast, questionnaires combining masculinity and femininity into a single score (e.g., low scores representing masculinity and high scores representing femininity) failed to discriminate between groups (e.g., Caesar, 1988). In this case, a meta-analysis revealed that batterers scored significantly lower on both masculinity and femininity (Sugarman & Frankel, 1993).

Sommer (1990) compared batterers and nonbatterers on four sex-role attitude inventories. An analysis of all the scales combined and individually indicated that the groups varied significantly. She found that batterers do have misogynist attitudes and are more tolerant of interpersonal violence than are nonbatterers.

Violence, Biology, and Genetics

One question that is receiving increasing research scrutiny is whether the male violence observed in spouse abuse might have some biological basis, rather than being simply a consequence of socialization. Recent discoveries on the relationships between biology and violence raise the age-old "nature-nurture" controversy. Evidence suggests that biological determinants, such as hormones, may influence male violence. Furthermore, there may be a gene-crime relationship and a birth trauma-crime relationship.

Biological Sex Differences. It is not surprising that a meta-analysis determined that men are generally more aggressive than women (Eagly & Steffen, 1986). With continued sci-

---

Comparing children's behavior with both their biological fathers and their adoptive fathers constitutes an excellent test of the gene-crime relationship.

---

entific advances, researchers have reported that the major male hormone testosterone forms part of a configuration of components contributing to a general latent predisposition toward aggression but that social factors moderate its influence. Although hormonal distinctiveness might, in part, explain why men are more violent than women, hormone levels do not explain individual variations among men (Booth & Osgood, 1993).

One way to appraise biological contrasts is with genetic studies. In a controversial approach, several investigators have attempted to identify a gene-crime association. Some criminologists, for example, have posited that social factors alone, like poverty, cannot account for certain types of observed differences in rates of crime and have pointed to genetics as a possible explanation (e.g., Wilson & Herrnstein, 1985).

One of the most accurate ways to isolate genetic from environmental contributions to criminality is with adoption studies (Walters, 1992). Children share 50% of their genetic inheritance with each biological parent and none with genetically unrelated persons, such as adoptive parents. Comparing children's behavior with both their biological fathers and their adoptive fathers constitutes an excellent test of the gene-crime relationship. The question is whether the behavior of the adopted boys corresponds more to that of the biological parents or to the adoptive parents.

In a series of analyses conducted in Denmark, Mednick and his colleagues (Mednick, Gabrielli, & Hutchings, 1987) reported that boys whose biological parent had a criminal record were more likely to have been convicted of a crime than were boys whose adoptive parent had been convicted. In other words, the biological parents' genetic contribution had a greater effect on behavior than did the adoptive parents' rearing. In a meta-analysis, Walters (1992) concluded that despite methodological problems with many of the studies, a low-moderate, but significant, association exists between heredity variables and indexes of crime. Based on the analysis of 13 adoption studies, Walters suggests that the individual genetic inheritance of criminal behavior is 11% to 17%.

Birth Complications and Head Injuries. There is also evidence that birth complications and head injuries contribute to crime ("Biology and Family," 1996). In a Danish investigation, Kandel and Mednick (1991) examined longitudinal data from a birth cohort study. Adult data included records of violent crimes and property crimes. Background information included factors like the mental health classification of the parents (e.g., character disorder) and pregnancy and birth complications of the individuals. The three comparison groups consisted of 15 violent criminals, 24 property criminals, and 177 nonoffenders. Birth complications did predict adult violent offending but not property crimes, especially in high-risk individuals and repeat violent offenders. Thus, the results suggest a link between birth complications and adult violence. In an analysis of trauma effects in adult males, Rosenbaum and Hoge (1989) uncovered a history of head injury in 61% of the abusers in their sample (see also Warnken, Rosenbaum, Fletcher, Hoge, & Adelman, 1994). Future research might attempt to link physical abuse of males during childhood with the head injuries noted in wife abusers.

Relationship Factors and Problems in Living

Some of the most striking problems batterers exhibit are those occurring in their personal relationships: hostility, jealousy, insecurity, and emotional dependence. Some batterers experience intemperate levels of stress as a result of events like the wife's "poor" housekeeping. They frequently misperceive such behaviors as a sign of the wife's disregard. In some cases, batterers seem unable to make their needs known verbally, and they may resort to violence as a means of control. These kinds of marital interactions are so intolerable that they precipitate the dissolution of the marriage, the very relationship that the man is fighting to keep.

CASE HISTORY: KIM AND KEVIN— "SHE DIDN'T CLEAN THE LINT TRAP"

Kevin was a handsome, 32-year-old cameraman for a local television station. He frequently was called out of town to cover a story and even went overseas occasionally. His beautiful wife, Kim, who earned money modeling, went with him if she wasn't working. They had no children.

On the job, Kevin felt fearful from time to time when he had to shoot at a location in a ghetto neighborhood. He was afraid that local hoods would try to beat him up, and he wouldn't be able to defend himself because he was so *small*. He was anxious about Kim's behavior as well. Other guys were always flirting with her, and she saw nothing wrong with "just being friends" with them. Kevin saw a lot wrong with it, and he warned her to watch her step. Kim also was very sloppy around the house. No matter what he said, she was always forgetting to empty the lint trap on the clothes dryer. It was clear to him that Kim didn't care how he felt, and he felt desperate about doing something to make her "treat him better."

The night Kevin got arrested for beating Kim up (for the first time, we were told) he had come home around 6:30 after several weeks in Australia. He had caught an early flight back to surprise Kim with an expensive pearl ring and some champagne that he bought on the way home from the airport. He really loved her, and he was looking forward to a romantic reunion.

The first thing that went wrong was that Kim was not home. He was both disappointed and suspicious. Perhaps she wasn't at work but was out having a drink with some guy who had picked her up at a bar. He had never actually caught her doing this, but he thought she probably did it a lot when he was

out of town. The second thing that happened was that there were some dirty dishes on the counter near the sink, and when he decided to do his laundry, the lint trap had not been emptied again!

At 7:30, he saw Kim coming out of the neighbor's house. He grabbed a shotgun, and ran up and down the side yard, shooting into the air over the neighbor's house. He took a sharp tool out of the garage and sliced his neighbor's tires. By the time the police arrived, Kim was on the living room floor with a broken nose and two broken ribs. Our *6-foot-5-inch* batterer was sitting on the couch, sobbing. Kim was threatening to leave him. He hadn't meant to hurt her, but what other options did he have? (Author's case history)

*   *   *

Kevin's behavior represents a number of problems that many batterers have. He seems to be extremely insecure and jealous. He probably misperceives Kim's behavior as being flirtatious and insensitive to his needs. He also is very stressed and does not seem to

---

About half of the men who assault their wives highly value their relationships and score above the median on marital satisfaction tests.

---

know how to handle his feelings. His reaction is to strike out impulsively and violently and then to regret his actions.

Marital Dissatisfaction. One of the most common assumptions people make is that happily married men would not hit their wives. Such a belief is intrinsically appealing, of course, but as the case of Kim and Kevin illustrates, it is not always true. On the whole, research on marital satisfaction does show that many maritally violent men score below published normative data on marital satisfaction levels and below that of comparison groups of nonviolent men (e.g., Rosenbaum & O'Leary, 1981b).

Only a handful of experts, however, attribute battering to marital dissatisfaction (see Barnett & Hamberger, 1992; Rosenbaum & O'Leary, 1981b). First, about half of the men who assault their wives highly value their relationships and score above the median on marital satisfaction tests (Locke & Wallace, 1957; Spanier, 1976). Second, men who score very low on marital satisfaction do not necessarily batter their wives. Last, longitudinal data from early marriages reveal that relationship discord is not an antecedent of marital abuse. Repeated abuse, however, may result in relationship dissatisfaction (Riggs & O'Leary, 1989).

Lack of Verbal Skills and Poor Communication. Inept communication appears to be another typical problem for some maritally violent men. Many batterers suffer from assertion deficits (e.g., inadequacy in stating one's views forcefully or in making requests appropriately; Dutton & Strachan, 1987; Maiuro, Cahn, & Vitaliano, 1986; Rosenbaum & O'Leary, 1981b), and these deficits are associated with greater verbal hostility (Maiuro, Cahn, & Vitaliano, 1988). Assertion deficits, however, may be more representative of marital dissatisfaction levels than of marital assault levels (O'Leary & Curley, 1986). Across studies, most research indicates that lack of assertiveness is a risk marker for wife assault (Hotaling & Sugarman, 1986).

Misperception of communication is yet another difficulty experienced by violent men (Margolin, John, & Gleberman, 1988). In one study, batterers underestimated the quality and number of caring gestures received from their wives. They saw themselves as "doing more and getting less" in the relationship (Langhinrichsen-Rohling, Smutzler, & Vivian, 1994). Holtzworth-Munroe and Hutchinson (1993) found analogous outcomes in responses of batterers to vignettes of problematic marital situations. Violent husbands attributed more negative intentions to their wives than did husbands in comparison groups. Similarly, when Neidig, Friedman, and Collins (1986) asked the question, "In your day-to-day dealings with other people, what percent of the time do you expect others might try to take advantage of you?" they found that batterers reported higher percentages than comparisons.

Margolin et al. (1988), using Conflict Tactics Scales (CTS; Straus, 1979) subscale scores, classified four groups of men as physically violent, verbally violent, withdrawing, or nonabusive and nondistressed. In a series of 10-minute, videotaped problem-solving discussions, physically violent men expressed more negative affect (offensive behaviors and harsh voice tones) than did nonviolent men (also see Smith & O'Leary, 1987; Vivian & O'Leary, 1987).

In a related study, Jacobson and Gottman (1993) unexpectedly discovered that during extremely belligerent verbal behaviors, such as yelling, threatening, and demeaning their female partners, batterers were *less* physiologically aroused than comparison groups of nonbattering male partners. This evaluation suggested that verbally combative behaviors may actually be calming, rather than upsetting, to maritally abusive men (see Jacobson et al., 1994).

Stress and Poor Problem-Solving Skills. Finn (1985) determined that the relationship between stressors and family violence involves elements such as financial problems, unemployment of males, alcohol problems, pregnancy problems, problems with children, and status inequality. On one measure of stressful events, the Impact of Event Scale (IOE; Horowitz, Wilxer, & Alverez, 1979), batterers had experienced a somewhat larger number of emotionally traumatic events than nonbatterers and had rated their responses to these events as more intense (Kishur, 1989).

Others have suggested that the stress of the relationship itself might trigger some spousal abuse (Rosenbaum & O'Leary, 1981a). Consistent with this supposition, one team of investigators demonstrated that 11 of 14 stress items (e.g., job trouble, small income) significantly differentiated the violent from the nonviolent groups. The primary stressor reported by the maritally violent men was the female partner (Barnett et al., 1991).

Several researchers have posited a relationship between victimization in childhood and subsequent stress vulnerability (Kishur, 1989; van der Kolk, 1988). MacEwen and Barling (1988) proposed that abuse during childhood predisposes individuals to react to stressors with violence (also see Katz & Gottman, 1995). Although the association between childhood abuse, adult stress, and marital violence seems valid, work by Seltzer and Kalmuss (1988) showed that even without exposure to childhood abuse, stress can trigger marital violence.

Results from several sources have shown that when compared to nonbatterers, batterers are poor problem solvers (e.g., Allen, Calsyn, Fehrenbach, & Benton, 1989; Hastings & Hamberger, 1988). In fact, ineffective conflict resolution strategies and high marital distress may serve as mediating factors between observing interparental violence and wife battering (Choice et al., 1995). In one study that subjected men to a variety of problematic marital vignettes, Holtzworth-Munroe and Anglin (1991) found that maritally violent men described less competent responses to a conflict than nonviolent men (cf. Morrison, Van Hasselt, & Bellack, 1987). In particular, maritally violent men exhibited the most difficulty generating adequate responses to situations involving rejection by the wife, challenges from the wife, and jealousy.

Power and Control. Issues of partner control seem to characterize most battering relationships (Tinsley, Critelli, & Ee, 1992). Explanations for the relationship between power and control and battering depend in part on one's theoretical perspective. Feminists contend that men use violence as a means of exerting power and control over their wives (Pence & Paymar, 1986). Learning theorists further point out that when aggression is instrumental in obtaining one's goal, it is reinforcing and therefore likely to increase (Felson, 1992). Others conjecture that feeling powerless in the relationship may serve as a precursor to violence for some men (e.g., Finkelhor, 1983) or that some people have a greater need for power than others (Dutton & Strachan, 1987).

Research on need for power, based on a modified Thematic Apperception Test and other scales, revealed that wife-assaultive men generate higher need-for-power themes than nonassaultive men (Dutton & Strachan, 1987). In another evaluation, batterers reported feeling powerless and had a very low tolerance for being controlled contrasted with normative data (Petrik, Petrik, & Subotnik, 1994; cf. Allen et al., 1989). In a third inquiry, male batterers' assessment of their female partners' ability to reward them (a measure of interpersonal control) was positively correlated with the severity of male-to-female violence as assessed by the CTS (Claes & Rosenthal, 1990). In their review of published research, Hotaling and Sugarman (1986) found need for power and dominance to be an inconsistent risk marker.

Individual Differences in Personality and Psychopathology

Because not all men batter, it is essential to look for individual differences in personality or other variables (O'Leary, 1993). Some have speculated, for example, that battering is a matter of terror about dyadic intimacy (Dutton, 1994). Others maintain that battering is an issue of control (Gondolf & Russell, 1986). Identifying specific problem areas, such as intimacy or control issues, plays an important function in equipping practitio-

ners with a basis for treatment. Some personality traits assessed by researchers are anger and hostility, low self-esteem, jealousy, emotional dependency, and depression. In addition, researchers have used more general personality inventories to assess a broader range of both normal and abnormal traits.

Anger and Hostility. Research on anger has been somewhat mixed. Two investigations using the Novaco Anger Scale (Novaco, 1975) did not find significantly higher scores for batterers compared with nonbatterers (Hastings & Hamberger, 1988; Offutt, 1988). In the Hastings and Hamberger (1988) study, male nonalcoholic batterers scored significantly lower than nonabusive males, and in the Offutt (1988) investigation, batterers' scores were higher but not significantly higher. Offutt did find, however, that anger is significantly correlated with CTS scores. The problem with these studies is that batterers may deny or minimize aggression when it is overtly assessed on an anger scale (see Hoshmond, 1987).

Barnett et al. (1991) investigated differences between groups of men who varied in terms of being violent toward female cohabitants, nonfamily members, or no one, and in terms of marital satisfaction level. On the Buss-Durkee Hostility-Guilt Inventory (Buss & Durkee, 1957), maritally violent men differed from maritally nonviolent men on five of the eight dimensions included in the scale: assault, indirect hostility, irritability, resentment, and verbal hostility. The maritally violent men were more hostile overall than any of the other groups (see also Maiuro et al., 1988).

In an analysis using videotaped arguments between a man and a women, wife assaulters reported more anger evoked in response to the scenario than comparison men, especially in scenes in which the female had verbal power and appeared to be abandoning the male (Dutton & Strachan, 1987).

Low Self-Esteem. One suggestion has been that batterers beat women because they are displeased with themselves. Two controlled studies using different instruments produced evidence of lower self-esteem in maritally violent men compared with nonmaritally violent men (Goldstein & Rosenbaum, 1985; Neidig et al., 1986).

Jealousy and Emotional Dependence. Many clinicians, researchers, and shelter workers have observed that male spouse abusers suffer from extreme jealousy (Pagelow, 1981a; Wasileski,

Callaghan-Chaffee, & Chaffee, 1982). Some women have reported such extreme levels that their jealous husbands did not allow them to leave their homes (Avni, 1991; Hilberman & Munson, 1978). In an inquiry of lesbian battering, Renzetti (1992) identified a significant relationship between level of jealousy and degree of psychological abuse of a partner.

A recent account by Barnett, Martinez, and Bleustein (1995), however, challenges the role of jealousy in spouse abuse. These investigators found that batterers were not significantly more jealous than a group of unhappily married men who did not beat their wives (see also Murphy, Meyer, & O'Leary, 1994). Instead, jealousy correlated highly with marital dissatisfaction. Maritally violent men in this study, however, did have stronger reasons (e.g., emotional dependence) for staying in their relationships. These findings are congruent with previous research showing that batterers have profound dependency needs (Dutton & Painter, 1993; Margolin et al., 1988) and are more sensitive to themes of abandonment (Holtzworth-Munroe & Hutchinson, 1993).

Deviations in "Normal" Personality Traits. Some investigators have tested batterers on personality inventories that assess "normal" personality traits and compared their scores with the test's published norms (e.g., Bersani, Chen, Pendleton, & Denton, 1992). These tests have indicated, for example, that batterers possess interaction styles that are primarily negative. Batterers are significantly less stable emotionally and less socially conforming (Barnett, Wood, Belmont, & Shimogori, 1982). They also are more withdrawn, compulsive, insensitive, and experience many negative emotions such as fear, anxiety, and anger (Schuerger & Reigle, 1988).

It is important to note, however, that research based on normative data (i.e., standardized test scores), rather than on data from comparison groups from the same population, is unreliable. Illustrative of this problem is the finding that when respondents in the comparison group (e.g., nonbattering men from a sample of men undergoing counseling) complete the same questionnaires as individuals in the target group (e.g., batterers undergoing counseling), for instance, the scores of the comparison individuals may not correspond to normative data either. Collectively, the populations sampled may vary from the normative sample in important ways (see Barnett & Hamberger, 1992; Rosenbaum, 1988).

In a study comparing batterers with two nonmaritally violent comparison groups, Barnett and Hamberger (1992) analyzed responses to the California Psychological Inventory (CPI; Gough, 1975). In this survey, batterers clearly displayed different personality traits than nonbatterers in three general areas: intimacy, impulsivity, and problem-solving skills. The implications of this study were that batterers are less well adjusted than nonviolent men. They seem to be rigid, stereotyped, and unresourceful in problem-solving techniques and seem to exhibit difficulty with developing close, intimate relationships anchored on mutuality. They are also likely to be moody, impulsive, self-centered, demanding, and aloof.

Depression. Two investigations using comparison groups to assess batterers' moods demonstrated that domestically violent men are substantially more depressed than nondomestically violent men (Hastings & Hamberger, 1988; Maiuro et al., 1988). The level of depression experienced by maritally violent men sometimes extends to suicidal feelings. In one inquiry, men who had killed a family member more frequently tried to kill themselves than men who had killed a non-family member (Anasseril & Holcomb, 1985). Similarly, a Kentucky account of homicide-suicide clusters disclosed that 85% involved family members, with the most likely perpetrator being the current male partner ("Homicides Followed by Suicide," 1991).

"Abnormal" Personality Traits. As early as 1974, Faulk demonstrated that homicidal batterers were frequently mentally disturbed (see also Vaselle-Augenstein & Ehrlich, 1992). In one noteworthy investigation, Flournoy and Wilson (1991) analyzed data from various scales on the Minnesota Multiphasic Personality Inventory (MMPI; Hathaway & McKinley, 1940). Their results determined that 44% of the sample of 56 batterers participating in a counseling program obtained scores indicating some deviation from normal, and 56% of the batterers clustered in the normal range (also see Caesar, 1988; Coates, Leong, & Lindsay, 1987).

Using a different assessment of psychopathology, the Millon Clinical Multiaxial Inventory (MCMI; Millon, 1983), Hamberger and Hastings (1986b) contrasted 43 nonviolent community volunteers with 78 alcoholic batterers and 47 nonalcoholic batterers. They were able to classify 88% of their batterer populations as suffering from some level of psychopathology, and they identified several types of personality disorders: passive dependent/compulsive, narcissistic/antisocial, and schizoidal/borderline (also see Offutt, 1988). The term *borderline* implies that there is no dominant pattern of deviance, but there are problems with impulsivity, instability of moods, and so forth. Antisocial disorder is characterized by long-standing problems, such as a disregard for the rights of others, irresponsibility, and resisting authority.

Studies of assaultive males have revealed that about 80% to 90% display diagnosable psychopathology, whereas estimates of psychopathology in the general population range from 15% to 20%. The greater the severity and chronicity of the violence, the greater the likelihood of psychopathology (see Dutton, 1994, for a review).

Antisocial Personality Disorder. A synthesis of the findings points to antisocial personality as one of the most typical personality dimensions typifying male batterers (Dutton & Starzomski, 1993; Hamberger & Hastings, 1986b). Research on the intergenerational transfer of abuse, assessment of biological traits, personality tests, and measures of psychopathology all implicate antisocial personality orientation/disorder.

According to the Simons et al. (1995) analysis of 451 two-parent families, for exam-ple, harsh punishment during childhood is linked with the development of an antisocial personality orientation. Antisocial personality orientation may be the key characteristic that is transmitted across generations and, in turn, results in the well-established link between childhood abuse and adult male battering (Dutton et al., 1995; Simons et al., 1995).

A different line of evidence arising from genetic investigations of criminals also reveals a strong genetic component of antisocial personality disorder underlying criminal behavior (Mednick et al., 1987). Because of the overlap between family and nonfamily violence (general violence), the results of genetic studies on antisocial personality disorder may, by logical extension, apply to maritally assaultive men (Dunford et al., 1990; Fagan et al., 1983; Shields et al., 1988).

Personality tests, of course, evaluate criminals as possessing antisocial tendencies (Megargee, 1966). On the CPI, batterers exhibited a number of characteristics related to antisocial personality disorder, such as inadequate impulse control and self-centeredness (Barnett & Hamberger, 1992). Last, inquiries using psychopathological measures have found evidence for diagnosable antisocial personality disorder in spouse abusers (Hamberger & Hastings, 1986b).

Intermediate Chapter Summary

In terms of socialization, it is clear that there are strong linkages between exposure to violence in one's childhood home and later marital violence. Men **learn to be aggressive,** and some men seem to learn that women are the most opportune targets for their violence. Newer research has been successful in illuminating how other childhood experiences, such as being shamed or anxiously attached, or learning **inadequate problem-solving skills** help mold personality characteristics typical of men who batter.

The male hormone testosterone is a major **biological influence** differentiating men and women. Testosterone is correlated with aggression, although socially moderated. **Genetic studies** demonstrate a genetic component of criminal and aggressive behavior. Last, problems such as trauma during birth influence aggression levels. For the most part, researchers have failed to apply these findings to male spouse abusers.

Research on interpersonal relationship factors has most often explored the role of marital dissatisfaction, lack of verbal skills, stress, poor problem-solving skills, and control issues related to battering. Evidence suggests that wife assaulters are often **maritally discordant.** They appear to be **unassertive in communications** and display considerable negative affect during discussions of conflict. They frequently express feelings of "getting a raw deal" and often misperceive the wife's intentions. Most research indicates that batterers experience **high levels of stress,** particularly in terms of their reactions to their wives. Some argue that batterers are more vulnerable to stress because of childhood abuse and are poor problem solvers. The implications of the research suggest that batterers **use violence to control women** and to get their own way. Although equivocal, some evidence attests to a need-for-power trait in batterers.

Researchers have obtained correlational data from an array of single and broad-based tests of individual, intrapersonal differences. **Personality tests** for the "normal" individual portray batterers as extremely hostile and stressed individuals who suffer from low self-esteem. Often, batterers are highly jealous and emotionally dependent. On the CPI, batterers exhibit trouble in establishing intimacy, are unresourceful in problem-solving areas, and have inadequate impulse control. They are likely to be moody, impulsive, self-centered, demanding, and aloof.

Research support for **depression** as a batterer trait is strong. It is also clear that a significant proportion of court-referred batterers can be classified as suffering from some form of **psychopathology,** such as borderline or antisocial personality disorder. Taken together, studies implicate **antisocial orientation** and **antisocial personality disorder** as the traits most typical of batterer behavior.

Treatment

For an abuser to make any real changes in his behavior, he must receive appropriate counseling (Dutton, 1986a). Men who batter often find it difficult to recognize verbal and psychological abuse as abuse, and they find it most difficult to change these kinds of behaviors. Much of the work that must be done in effective batterers' programs revolves around recognition of these forms of intimidation and halting nonphysical as well as physical abuse in the relationship.

Because practitioners charged with treating batterers initially had to "jump in feet first," they mainly applied familiar treatments like individual or group counseling. In the late 1970s and early 1980s, treatment programs were developing so rapidly that by the mid-1980s, over 200 such programs existed in the United States alone (Stordeur & Stille, 1989). Out of this fragmented beginning grew the need for program evaluation, and from these assessments came rudimentary principles of treatment.

Behind every batterer is a battered woman who may be in danger. The batterer's participation in counseling in no way guarantees safety for the battered woman with whom he lives. A compelling aspect of batterer treatment programs, therefore, includes consideration of the battered woman's safety (Hamberger & Barnett, 1995). Practitioners have the ethical and legal "duty to warn" and protect potential victims (*Tarasoff v. the Regents of the University of California*, 1976) while maintaining a therapist's primary obligation to protect the client's privacy (see Sonkin, 1989). In an effort to ensure accountability to the victim, some programs have initiated

a period of victim safety planning (Hamberger & Hastings, 1990). Victim safety planning includes assisting the battered female partner in thinking through various options that facilitate escape, such as having money hidden somewhere, having a bag packed, and locating a safe home where she and her children may reside temporarily (see Dutton-Douglas, 1991).

Approaches to Counseling

Practitioners' conceptualizations about the causes of battering (i.e., sociopolitical, interpersonal, and intrapersonal) influence their treatment mode. The goals of programs ordinarily include planning for the victim's safety; empowering men to live emotionally aware, violence-free lives; and preventing intergenerational transmission of violence (Carden, 1994). Caesar and Hamberger (1989) divided therapeutic models into four main categories: feminist, cognitive-behavioral, family, and integrated.

Feminist Approaches. Feminist theory views battering as an extreme action falling on a continuum of behaviors intended to allow men to control and oppress women. Followers want to resocialize men to abandon power and control tactics as well as sexist attitudes toward women. Batterers must learn to stop "choosing" violence (e.g., EMERGE, 1980). As an illustration, a man who beats his wife because dinner is late must first learn that he has no right to order his wife to make dinner or to make it on time (Pence & Paymar, 1986). This approach also capitalizes on criminal justice sanctions as an integral part of a successful program (e.g., Schechter, 1982).

Critics question its empirical foundation and consider it more of a political statement than a psychological treatment (Dutton, 1994).

In parallel fashion, feminist scholars have criticized psychological explanations on grounds that they serve as excuses for battering (e.g., the "abuse excuse"). They are outspoken in their belief that battering should not be viewed as just an individual problem but also as a social and political problem. Furthermore, they label some psychological treatments, such as training to overcome "skill deficits," as misguided because, in reality, battering stems from the patriarchal system (e.g., Adams, 1988; Goldner, Penn, Sheinberg, & Walker, 1990).

Cognitive-Behavioral Approaches. Therapists using a cognitive-behavioral approach apply learning principles to help clients modify behavior identified as problematic by empirically based trait assessments. Simply put, a therapist might be called on to help a client "restructure" his thinking as in the following three-stage example: Initially, a batterer encounters external stimuli such as a wife's failure to have dinner ready on time. He will then internally mediate (interpret) the event (e.g., in terms of past learning, current stress, or drunkenness) as "not caring about how he feels" and decide that he must respond to "force her to treat him better." In the final stage, his external response is to "throw the food in her face."

A cognitive-behavioral approach focuses on restructuring the batterer's thinking so that he will interpret his wife's late dinner differently (e.g., she was ill) and discover other behavioral options (e.g., take the family out to a fast-food restaurant). Other therapeutic techniques involve helping batterers accomplish goals such as managing adverse arousal and learning appropriate assertion and problem-solving skills (Hamberger & Lohr, 1989; Saunders, 1989a). Although evaluative research is clouded by high drop-out rates, studies have reported some success in treating batterers with this approach (e.g., Dutton, 1986a; Faulkner, Stoltenberg, Cogen, Nolder, & Shooter, 1992).

Couples and Systems Approaches. The least popular approach, systems theory, expands treatment to include marital dynamics and the whole family system as a context for marital violence. Underlying the systems approach is the value placed on preserving the family. From this stance, a batterer's violence is not isolated and ascribed to him alone but some-

how is attributable to the "relationship." Two assets of couples therapy are improving communication and allowing male and female therapists to model nonviolent behavior (Geffner & Rosenbaum, 1990).

Adams (1988) criticizes this approach because viewing abuse as an interactional problem of the couple runs the risk of reinforcing a batterer's belief that violence is not really his problem (Willbach, 1989). Critics further

---

Counselors should make a preliminary assessment of such things as patterns of alcohol use and social and legal problems and make appropriate plans for treatment.

---

point to the dearth of scientific studies documenting effectiveness of these programs and voice concern that violence and safety issues may lose priority (e.g., Edleson & Tolman, 1992). Others suggest that the process can be highly dangerous if it compels battered women to continue interaction with an abusive, controlling, and dangerous partner (Davis, 1984; Dutton-Douglas, 1991; Hansen, Harway, & Cervantes, 1991).

Treatment for Alcohol Abuse and Criminal Behavior. At the very least, counselors should make a preliminary assessment of such things as patterns of alcohol use and social and legal problems and make appropriate plans for treatment (Hamberger & Barnett, 1995). Therapists should assess the crime histories of wife assaulters by using a problem identification approach (Quinsey, Maguire, & Upfold, 1987). They should ask questions about arrest records, level of violence, and the selection of targets of violence.

Research consistently shows that spouse abusers have a number of alcohol-related problems (Gelles, 1993a). Both genetic (e.g., Bower, 1994) and learning components play a role in alcohol misuse (Vaillant & Milofsky, 1982). Because drunkenness can precipitate battering and be used as an excuse, practitioners must address alcohol treatment. One myth that Zubretsky and Digirolamo (1994) have tried to debunk, however, is that treatment of alcohol or substance abuse problems alone will concomitantly eliminate problems with domestic violence. A batterer trying to stop drinking, in fact, may be more abusive because of the new, added stress of attempting sobriety (see also A. Davidson, 1994). On the other hand, a treatment consisting of both behavioral marital therapy and treatment for alcoholism for alcoholic husbands and their wives has shown some promise in decreasing violence in men, especially in those who stopped drinking (O'Farrell & Murphy, 1995). These findings are just one more indication of the complexity of the alcohol-violence connection.

Counseling Outcomes for Group Treatments

A number of domestic violence experts are skeptical about the quality and permanence of behavioral changes made by abusers as a consequence of counseling (e.g., Gondolf, 1988b; Gondolf & Russell, 1986; Hart, 1988). Illustrative of just one problem is the tendency for batterers to enroll in a counseling program as a ploy to pressure the female partner into a reconciliation, only to drop the program as soon as the partner has returned (Bowker, 1983; Fagan, 1989). Although most counseling outcome studies use quasi-experimental designs (Carden, 1994), methodology has continually improved over the past decade (Edleson & Tolman, 1992). When discussing batterer treatment outcomes, the traditional catch-22 question, "Are you still beating your wife?" takes on new meaning.

Recidivism Outcome Studies. One of the first quasi-experimental studies to tackle this problem originated in Canada. Donald Dutton (1986a) compared postconviction rates over a 3-year period of 50 men who completed a 16-week court-mandated treatment program with those of a comparable group that did not receive treatment. Treated men had a 4% (police reports) or 16% (victim report) recidivism rate compared with nontreated assaulters, who had a 40% rate. In addition, CTS scores completed by both members of the couple demonstrated a significant drop in severe violence from 10.6 times per year before the treatment to 1.7 times per year following the treatment. Generalizability was limited by nonrandom selection of participants, by customary problems inherent in self-report data, and by uncontrollable variation in police decisions to rearrest. Overall, however, Dutton's work represented a striking improvement over anecdotal reports.

In one analysis of reports of female partners over a 2½-year posttreatment period, success rates for ending physical aggression were fairly high (Edleson & Grusznski, 1988). In another survey comparing 120 court-referred abusers with a group of 101 nonreferred abusers, court-referred abusers who attended 75% or more of the counseling sessions reduced recidivism (Chen, Bersani, Myers, & Denton, 1990). In a third investigation, 28% of 88 men who had completed a 12-session treatment program engaged in further acts of violence over a follow-up period of 1 year (Hamberger & Hastings, 1990).

Other Posttreatment Counseling Changes. Batterers may not only decrease their violence but also make other favorable posttreatment changes. In a 1-year follow-up study, Hamberger and Hastings (1989) reported a dramatic reduction in depressive symptoms following 12 cognitive-behavioral treatment sessions. A no-treatment comparison group, had it been available, would have clarified the findings further. Batterers, however, did not uniformly abandon psychologically abusive behaviors, nor did their scores on tests of pathology change (see also Sommer, 1990).

The Drop-Out Problem. The high rate of dropout in batterer programs is rather standard and undermines generalizability of results (e.g., Schuerger & Reigle, 1988). Illustrative of this problem are the results of a study by Gondolf and Foster (1991). They tracked the records of 200 inquiries into batterer programs. From inquiry to first intake session, the attrition rate was 73%. From inquiry to counseling attendance, attrition was 86%, and from inquiry to completion of 12 sessions, 93%. Altogether, only 1% completed the contracted 8-month treatment program.

One investigation following a 16-week spouse abuse abatement program compared violence-free completers with violence-repeating completers (Hamberger & Hastings, 1990). Violence-free completers had fewer alcohol and substance abuse problems during both pre- and posttreatment, and following treatment, they had lower scores for narcissism (self-centered and demanding). On the other hand, variation in outcomes generated by referral (self or mandated) and record of criminal activity failed to discriminate the two groups.

Court-Mandated Counseling. It is becoming evident that batterers who are court involved and ordered to treatment differ significantly on a number of dimensions from men who are not court involved and who voluntarily seek treatment. In one survey, for example, non-court-involved men had higher levels of education, employment, and income than court-involved men (e.g., mandated to counseling). Non-court-involved men also had higher levels of outside social support, for example, friends (Barrera et al., 1994). One researcher believes that there is no scientific evidence substantiating the effectiveness of any type of rehabilitative effort with offenders mandated to treatment (Berk, 1993).

Given what is currently known, it is probable that the court must remain involved in any mandated counseling orders. Criminal justice experts advise that diversion into a counseling program and out of the system should not occur before a plea is entered. As long as the abuser is under the control of the court, he can be sentenced without resetting the trial. According to the 1990 Family Violence Project (cited in Pagelow, 1992), without this leverage, a recalcitrant participant may be able to leave treatment with no record at all. Others are recommending longer jail time given that treatment is not uniformly effective (Shepard, 1992).

Effectiveness of Counseling Programs. The effectiveness of abuser counseling with or without mandatory arrest remains debatable (Gondolf & Russell, 1986; Neidig et al., 1986; Pirog-Good & Stets, 1986). Nonetheless, court-mandated treatment of wife assault is essential to the criminal justice system's objective of reducing recidivism (Dutton, 1988). If nothing else, arrest challenges a batterer's beliefs that his arrest and conviction were unjust and that his use of violence was justified (Ganley, 1981). It also places the responsibility for change on the batterer, a stance that is compatible with deterrence themes in the criminal justice system (Fagan, 1988). Court-ordered treatment is congruent with social-control models.

Syers and Edleson (1992) pinpointed two crucial variables affecting recidivism: number of previous arrests and duration of court-ordered counseling. Men arrested the first time the police visited the residence, and those mandated into counseling programs for a longer period of time, were significantly less likely to assault their female partners than men not arrested the first time or mandated into shorter counseling programs (see also Steinman, 1991).

The drop-out problem is an especially serious complication. As expected, recidivism is higher for dropouts than completers (e.g., Grusznski & Carrillo, 1988). Completers also diverge from noncompleters in other ways. One investigation found that dropouts were younger, had lower employment levels, and had higher pretreatment levels of police interaction for nonviolent offenses (Hamberger & Hastings, 1989). Pirog-Good and Stets (1986) noted that procedures like allowing clients not to pay for counseling and making use of criminal justice referrals led to higher retention levels than did alternative methods. Given the noticeable variety of outcomes across studies, Hilton (1994) believes that the next step should be to match arrest and treatment decisions to "type" of assaulter.

Community Intervention Projects

The critical situations encountered by many community agencies responding to wife assault have spawned a new type of organization, the community intervention project (CIP; Edleson & Tolman, 1992). The mutual interests of victims' rights advocates and women's groups converged to pressure police and to lobby legislatures to better protect battered women. A central tenet of CIPs is that society's response to domestic violence must change (see also Francis, 1993).

Historically, society has condoned, ignored, and concealed the behavior of batterers (Roy, 1982). Indeed, not everyone in the community believes that family violence is a crime or that the police should take action (see Choi & Edleson, 1995; Saunders & Size, 1986). What is new is the recognition that wife assault is a criminal offense (Barrera et al., 1994). Specific situational factors, such as severity and repetitiveness of the assault, underlie public opinion about whether police should respond and in what way (Choi & Edleson, 1995).

Women's advocates hold that abusers should suffer the same sanctions as other assaulters and that victims should not be held accountable to solve the problem. CIP staff and volunteers work with abusers, victims, police, prosecutors, probation officers, and social service agencies at every level to ameliorate domestic violence (Edleson, 1991). Two studies, in fact, have already shown that CIP involvement has significantly increased arrest rates, convictions, and court mandates to treatment (Gamache, Edleson, & Schock, 1988).

A 5-year follow-up study of men participating in a CIP used the criteria of reconviction, being a subject of a restraining order, or having been a police suspect in a domestic assault case to evaluate the effectiveness of the program. Using these criteria, Shepard (1992) found that perpetrator characteristics, rather than length or type of treatment, best predicted recidivism. "Men who had been abusive for a shorter period prior to the program, court ordered for chemical evaluation, in treatment for chemical dependency, abused as children, and previously convicted for nonassault crimes were more likely to be recidivists" (p. 167).

Summary

Some of the early representations of batterers about their tendencies to blame others and to minimize their own violence have been confirmed by subsequent research. Investigations of the breadth of violence in maritally assaultive men indicate that men arrested for wife assault have frequently been violent both in and out of the home. Violence may range on a continuum extending from family-only violent men who select their wives as a target to nonfamily-only violent men.

Childhood socialization experiences of maritally violent men appear to contrast with those of nonmaritally violent men. Research has documented inordinately high levels of violence in the childhood homes of batterers. It seems reasonable to assume that these early learning experiences (harsh discipline and parental conflict) have substantially influenced the development of antisocial behavior in batterers. It is conceivable that some batterers have also inherited unfavorable genetic predispositions like antisocial personality disorder, or have suffered from birth complications or head trauma.

Batterers and nonbatterers show many dissimilarities in personality and in interpersonal interaction styles. Batterers have tested positive for marital dissatisfaction, inadequate communication, high stress and faulty problem solving, and interpersonal control issues. Unidimensional personality tests have linked battering to anger and hostility, low self-esteem, jealousy and emotional dependence, and depression. More extensive, multidimensional personality inventories have tended to corroborate these findings. On tests assessing dimensions of psychopathology, a majority of batterers score in the abnormal range and are most likely to receive a diagnosis of borderline or antisocial personality disorder.

Practitioners acrimoniously debate the causes of battering and therefore the type of treatment most suitable. Victim safety concerns, however, have garnered near universal acceptance as the first priority for treatment programs. Feminists indict the sociopolitical system and emphasize antisexist education coupled with criminal justice sanctions. The cognitive-behavioral group assumes that individual variability scores as assessed on tests in personality and psychopathology accurately pinpoint problem areas and employs procedures premised on learning theory to modify behavior. Couples therapy presupposes that marital violence is a reflection of faulty interactions between the couple that allow violence to take place, and it focuses on techniques geared to improve communication and marital satisfaction. As stated previously, however, concerns for battered women's safety must dictate treatment decisions. Last, therapists must address problems with both alcohol and crime in batterers (Hamberger & Barnett, 1995).

Recidivism outcome studies following batterer treatment programs have shown promise in reducing violence and in ameliorating other symptoms like depression. Violence abatement programs, however, are not uniformly successful. The ongoing problem of counseling dropouts hampers generalizability of treatment strategies. Court-mandated counseling is a frequently selected judicial option, but this group of batterers should remain under court jurisdiction for the entire term of treatment. Relapse into violence remains high. Future research should focus on identifying treatment variables (e.g., length of treatment) and offender variables (e.g., alcohol abuse) that are associated with treatment outcomes to arrive at the best match.

Certainly, battering will continue as long as society delegates the solution to the victim. Community agencies must shoulder the responsibility for ending marital violence by working as a team. Some community intervention projects have made advances in combating marital violence, but much remains to be done if married couples are to live in violence-free homes.

Elder Abuse

CHAPTER CONTENTS

An Interview With Rosalie Wolf

"The message we give schoolchildren about elder abuse or family violence ought to be one of zero tolerance."

ROSALIE WOLF is an internationally recognized expert on aging and elder abuse. Currently, she is Executive Director of the Institute of Aging at the Medical Center of Central Massachusetts and Assistant Professor in the Departments of Medicine and Community Medicine and Family Practice at the University of Massachusetts Medical Center. She is the recipient of several notable grants that have allowed her to conduct innovative research in areas such as long-term care for elders, foster care for elders with mental retardation, and medical consent guardianship. As President of the National Committee for the Prevention of Elder Abuse, she has directed several projects, including Building Coalitions for the Prevention of Elder Abuse. She has coauthored two books with Karl Pillemer, Elder Abuse: Conflict in the Family *and* Helping Elderly Victims: The Reality of Elder Abuse. *She also serves as coeditor of the* Journal of Elder Abuse & Neglect. *She received her B.S. degree in chemistry from the University of Wisconsin, was a graduate student at Harvard Medical School (Radcliffe), and earned her Ph.D. in social welfare policy from Brandeis University in Massachusetts.*

Q: How did you become interested in elder abuse?

A: I served on an advisory committee to a local case management organization and their crisis intervention project in Massachusetts. Some of the clients had been abused and/or neglected. In 1980, the U.S. Administration on Aging (AoA) requested proposals for model projects on elder abuse. Because of my familiarity with the model and the research, I became involved in developing the proposal evaluation plan. When AoA decided to have all projects use the same evaluation procedures, they chose us to be the evaluators. The study was important because it included a larger group of older clients, which allowed for more in-depth analyses.

Q: What shaped your approach to the field?

A: I am a gerontologist, so I tend to view the situation from the broad perspective of ag-

ing. Elder abuse has gone through several conceptual transitions. First, abused elders were viewed as persons in need of services—the adult protective services [APS] approach. Second, they were seen as "victims of elder abuse," and then "victims of family violence." Because of recent political trends in response to violence and crime, abused elders are included as "victims of crime."

Q: What prevention efforts have been made in the field?

A: There is a strong emphasis toward public awareness, education, and professional training. Whatever small monies the federal government has allotted to the states to prevent elder abuse have gone into education and training. Elder abuse must be incorporated into all levels of education, beginning with the junior high schools. The message ought to be zero tolerance for family violence of all types, including elder abuse.

Q: What do you think is the greatest problem in the field?

A: Lack of research is a major gap. In contrast to the numbers of researchers who have worked on child and spouse abuse issues in the past decade or two, very few individuals have carried out research on elder abuse. We have not been able to attract either the money or the researchers.

Q: Does it seem to you that the public is much more outraged about child abuse than elder abuse?

A: Yes. Reports of elder abuse are often met with disbelief. People just don't think it happens. It's hidden. Elders do not talk about it. They often deny that it occurred; they feel ashamed, embarrassed, and humiliated, especially if it involves their children as per-petrators.

Q: Who should intervene? Adult protective services?

A: In most states, APS are authorized to in-vestigate and intervene. Elder abuse cases are complex, involving issues of health, men-tal health, substance abuse, housing—you name it. A multidisciplinary approach is needed that brings together the APS worker and representatives of the law, law enforce-ment, medicine, nursing, social work, and financial institutions.

Q: How can we best protect elders?

A: One of the best ways of protection is edu-cation: first, helping older persons to under-stand that abuse need not be tolerated and, second, giving them information about where to call for help.

Q: What should a researcher with a large grant do?

A: I believe a prevalence study should be a priority. There has not been one done as yet because the cost is almost prohibitive. Other needs include assessment of risk and inter-vention. Knowing what kinds of interven-tions work best is a challenge in the field of family violence. My interest is the variability of elders, families, and professionals in re-porting elder abuse.

Introduction

CASE HISTORY: JENNY AND JEFF, JR.—DWINDLING ASSETS, DWINDLING DEVOTION

Several years after my husband's death, my 91-year-old mother-in-law, Jenny, became unable to care for herself. She went to live with my brother-in-law, Jeff, Jr., and his wife, Marianne. Although my own aging mother was dying, I took time to visit Jenny, who had always been a loving mother-in-law.

Over the next year, Jeff, Jr. became Jenny's guardian, and she made out a new will giving one third of her estate to each of us—myself, Jeff, Jr., and Marianne. I didn't understand this sudden change from the previous division of half for each son, but I said nothing; after all, I was only a widowed daughter-in-law. As Jenny continued to deteriorate, I asked Jeff, Jr. if he were planning to put Jenny in a retirement home where she would

receive around-the-clock care. He said he couldn't afford to place her in a home and that he and Marianne would care for her at home. I was amazed. Jeff, Jr. had sold Jenny's home for a probable yield of $150,000 in cash. Jeff, Jr. and Marianne owned a mini-estate and stocks and bonds and were probably worth $2 million.

I was puzzled by what was going on with Jenny and Jeff, Jr., but then I became seriously con-cerned when I heard a number of rumors from Jenny's other relatives and friends. They said that Jeff, Jr. and Marianne had offered financial ad-vice to several other aging relatives. Each had changed his or her will to name Jeff, Jr. and Marianne the beneficiaries, and each had died shortly thereafter of neglect and malnutrition.

Over the next few months, I became alarmed when Jenny "refused to come to the phone to speak to me." Marianne told me that "Jenny couldn't walk far enough to get to the phone." After 2 weeks, I drove several hours to visit her. I was ap-palled. There was Jenny, sitting alone in a hot room that smelled like urine. She would not speak to me. She was in the maid's quarters, with no television and no phone. She was dirty and unkempt. There were no diapers in the room, only a piece of moldy bologna in the small refrigerator, and she had not taken her medications. Later, when I expressed my concern to Jeff, Jr., he said that he was going to hire an Asian couple to come in and take care of her. I left feeling some sense of relief that Jenny's ordeal would soon be over.

A week later, I received a call from the Asian couple. Frightened by Jenny's condition when they came over to care for her, they had called the paramedics, who took Jenny to the hospital, and then they called me. Doctors diagnosed her con-dition as malnutrition, dehydration, and neglect. The Asian couple said that Jeff, Jr. and Marianne had gone on a vacation, leaving no money for food or diapers, no instructions, no telephone numbers or itinerary, not even information about when they would return. Finally, I felt compelled to call the county Adult Protective Services, who said they would visit the premises, and they did. I also called some other relatives, who started mak-ing unscheduled visits to see Jenny.

Jeff, Jr. and Marianne continue taking unex-pected vacations to visit other aging relatives who may "need financial management services in the near future." I fear that Jeff, Jr. and Marianne hope to come home someday to find that Jenny had simply "passed away in her sleep." I am con-stantly uneasy about Jenny's situation. I frequently call Adult Protective Services to see if they can do something more, and I keep "popping in" to check up on Jenny when Jeff, Jr. and Marianne are away from home.

Jenny, by all accounts, is doing better now. She is clean and has food in the refrigerator. The Asian couple drops in every day briefly and brings in food and diapers on their own. Jenny is still alone most of the time and she seems too frightened to say much. As Jenny's life is slowly ending, I feel that my life is on hold. I wish I knew for sure that everything that could be done was being done to protect Jenny. It's in God's hands now. (Author's case history)

* * *

Violence against elders is a perpetual feature of American social history (Stearns, 1986). Like other forms of family violence, however, there has been an ebb and flow of its visibility and invisibility. During the 1980s, violence against elders received heightened attention, especially violence perpetrated by informal caretakers such as relatives (Department of Health Social Services Inspectorate, 1992). This interest, however, has only recently begun to attract scholarly attention. As a result, there is a surprising dearth of research on violence against elders. In fact, the totality of knowledge about elder abuse is analogous to the extent of knowledge about child abuse 20 years ago (Hirst & Miller, 1986). One reason for the lack of research is that there is no agreement on the degree to which elder abuse represents a serious problem for el-ders. Certainly, abuse presents an urgent problem to the victims, but it may not be their most severe problem (Callahan, 1988). According to Pillemer and Finkelhor's (1988) modified Conflict Tactics Scales (CTS; Straus, 1979) and neglect data, for example, the abuse rate of persons age 65 and over is 3.2%, whereas the poverty rate for this age group is 13.2% (Ward, 1984).

Any type of problem afflicting elders, of course, is likely to multiply with the rapid increase of this group in the population. Not only are people around the world living longer, but changing economic conditions, families, family mobility, women's roles, and traditional methods of elder care appear to have contributed to an increasing rate of elder abuse (see Kosberg & Garcia, 1995b; Kwan, 1995). The 1991 census counted 30 million elders (age 65+), 12.7% of the total population (U.S. Bureau of the Census, 1991). This figure, however, is apt to rise through this century and into the next. Even more significantly, the "frail elderly," those over 70 years of age, are the fastest growing segment of the elderly population; most of them are female.

Elder abuse occurs against a background of social change, such as fluctuating norms about who is responsible to give family care and who is eligible to receive family care. There are no clear norms or moral rules about who is responsible for elder care (Phillipson, 1993). Adult children are not legally required to help an elder parent in need; moreover, approximately 20% of elders are childless (Stone, Cafferata, & Sangl, 1987). Because there are no agreed-on moral or legal standards concerning responsibility for elders, therefore, it is difficult to know who should be held accountable for their care or neglect. This ambiguity places elders in an especially vulnerable position, easily forgotten and often neglected. With little agreement on who should care for elders and how they should be cared for, it should come as no surprise that there is little agreement on how elder abuse should be defined. Some scholars reserve the word *abuse* for discussions of physical violence, whereas others refer more broadly to psychological and emotional abuse. Taken together, these problems have generated a literature on elder abuse that lacks coherence and precision.

Further complicating matters is the fact that even in cases of interpersonal violence, it is often not clear who is the victim and who is the perpetrator. Some elder violence, in fact, can be categorized as mutual violence (e.g., Phillipson, 1992). An elder may strike out at the caregiver, for instance, in reaction to a loss of personal freedom when the caregiver finds it necessary to curtail the elder's behavior (e.g., not let the elder leave the house alone) (Meddaugh, 1990).

In sum, the nascency of research on elder abuse leaves numerous gaps in current knowledge and creates a large number of uncertainties. This chapter begins with perhaps the greatest uncertainty of all, namely, the lack of a clear definition and the resulting difficulty in assessing the forms and frequencies of elder abuse. Other important questions include the prevalence of abuse, the basic causes of elder abuse, identification of elder abusers, and treatment and prevention strategies.

Scope of the Problem

If an older father wishes to wear a food-stained jacket, is an offspring-caregiver supposed to enforce some sort of cleanliness standard to avoid being neglectful? What can

Table 11.1 Most Frequently Used Categories of Elder Abuse

Category	Description
Physical abuse	Lack of personal care, lack of supervision, visible bruises and welts, repeated beatings, withholding of food
Psychological abuse	Verbal assaults, isolation, threats, inducement of fear
Financial or material abuse	Misuse, appropriation, or theft of money or property
Unsatisfactory living environment	Unclean home, urine odor in home, hazardous living conditions
Violation of individual or constitutional rights	Reduction of personal freedom or autonomy, involuntary commitment guardianship, false imprisonment, "incompetence"

SOURCE: From "Elder Abuse," by F. A. Boudreau, 1993, in R. L. Hampton, T. P. Gullotta, G. R. Adams, E. H. Potter III, and R. P. Weissberg, *Family Violence: Prevention and Treatment*, p. 145. Copyright © 1993 by Sage. Reprinted by permission of Sage Publications, Inc.

a caregiver do if an elder decides to drink too much alcohol or to act foolishly? What if an adult son decides to let his increasingly dependent father fend for himself? Is the son an abuser? Is the father abused? In view of circumstances like these, definitions of elder abuse are even more diffuse and murky than those for child abuse and marital abuse (Hall, 1989; Phillips, 1989). Definitional disparity, along with other factors, has impeded research progress to such an extent that the scope of elder abuse is unknown.

What Is Elder Abuse?

The debate about what constitutes abuse is probably more pronounced in the area of elder abuse than in other subfields of abuse. In addition to previously mentioned problems associated with defining subjective terms like *abuse*, elder abuse encompasses additional problems in defining the meaning of elder (i.e., age requirements), dependency (i.e., incompetent to care for self), and concepts such as self-neglect. It can also include financial abuse.

Boudreau (1993) distinguishes five broad categories of abuse most frequently cited in the literature. They are physical, psychological, financial or material, unsatisfactory living environment (e.g., unclean home), and violation of individual or constitutional rights. Although there is a general consensus that physical violence constitutes abuse, there is far more controversy concerning terms like *psychological abuse* or *violation of constitutional rights*. At what point, for example, does an argument become a "verbal assault" or insist-

ing that an aging parent not walk outside alone after 10:00 p.m. become a violation of constitutional rights (Pillemer & Finkelhor, 1988)? The definitions offered by Boudreau, and those generally offered in the elder abuse literature, are vague. Refer to Table 11.1 for further explanations of Boudreau's (1993) groupings.

In a more widely acknowledged classification system, Hudson (1991) solicited opinions from 63 professionals in diverse specialties such as law, medicine, psychology, public health, and social work. Over three successive rounds of decision making, the experts attempted to reach a consensus about the appropriateness of certain theoretical definitions. In one series of judgments, for example, participants categorized mistreatment into two major classes (elder abuse or elder neglect), with two modes of intent (unintentional or intentional). Each round resulted in greater and greater specificity with more and more subdefinitions. The final taxonomy, consisting of four forms of elder mistreatment (physical, social, psychological, and financial), appears in Table 11.2. Note that the taxonomy excludes self-neglect and does not list sexual abuse separately (see boxed insert: "Is Self-Neglect a Form of Mistreatment?").

With one exception, senior adults in a follow-up study agreed with the results provided by experts. Whereas experts assumed "screaming and yelling" would have to occur several times to be abusive, seniors judged even one episode of such behavior as abusive (Hudson & Carlson, 1994).

The taxonomy's exclusion of sexual abuse as a separate category (and its inclusion within

Table 11.2 Theoretical Definition by Delphi Panel of Elder Mistreatment Experts

Level II

Elder mistreatment	Destructive behavior that is directed toward an older adult; occurs within the context of a relationship connoting trust; and is of sufficient intensity and/or frequency to produce harmful physical, psychological, social, and/or financial effects of unnecessary suffering, injury, pain, loss, and/or violation of human rights and poorer quality of life for the older adult.
Personal/social relationship	Persons in close personal relationships with an older adult connoting trust and some socially established behavioral norms, for example, relatives by blood or marriage, friends, neighbors, any "significant other."
Professional/business relationship	Persons in a formal relationship with an older adult that denotes trust and expected services, for example, physicians, nurses, social workers, nursing aides, bankers, lawyers, nursing home staff, home health personnel, and landlords.

Level III

Elder abuse	Aggressive or invasive behavior/action(s), or threats of same, inflicted on an older adult and resulting in harmful effects for the older adult.
Elder neglect	The failure of a responsible party(ies) to act so as to provide, or to provide what is prudently deemed adequate and reasonable assistance that is available and warranted to ensure that the older adult's basic physical, psychological, social, and financial needs are met, resulting in harmful effects for the older adult.

Level IV

Intentional	Abusive or neglectful behavior or acts that are carried out for the purpose of harming, deceiving, coercing, or controlling the older adult so as to produce gain for the perpetrator (often labeled *active* abuse/neglect in the literature).
Unintentional	Abusive or neglectful behavior or acts that are carried out, but *not* for the purpose of harming, deceiving, coercing, or controlling the older adult, so as to produce gain for the perpetrator (often labeled *passive* abuse/neglect in the literature).

Level V

Physical	Behavior(s)/action(s) in which physical force(s) is used to inflict the abuse; or available and warranted physical assistance is not provided, resulting in neglect.
Psychological	Behavior(s)/action(s) in which verbal force is used to inflict the abuse; or available and warranted psychological/emotional assistance/support is not provided, resulting in neglect.
Social	Behavior(s)/action(s) that prevents the basic social needs of an older adult from being met; or failure to provide available and warranted means by which an older adult's basic social needs can be met.
Financial	Theft or misuse of an older adult's funds or property; or failure to provide available and warranted means by which an older adult's basic material needs can be met.

SOURCE: From "Elder Mistreatment: A Taxonomy With Definitions by Delphi," by M. F. Hudson, 1991, *Journal of Elder Abuse & Neglect, 3*(2), p. 14. Copyright 1991 by Margaret F. Hudson. Reprinted with permission.

the physical abuse category) may be unfortunate, because sexual abuse represents a distinctive form of elder abuse. Direct forms of sexual abuse can include intercourse, molestations, sexualized kissing, oral or genital contact, and digital penetration. Indirect forms of abuse might include exhibitionism, forced viewing of pornography, unwanted sexual discussions, and exposed masturbation (see Ramsey-Klawsnik, 1991).

Estimates of Elder Abuse

Because elder abuse is particularly hidden, the acquisition of prevalence estimates

IS SELF-NEGLECT A FORM OF MISTREATMENT?

Johnson (1986) defined elder mistreatment as "self- or other-inflicted suffering unnecessary to the maintenance of the quality of life of the older person" (p. 180). The most controversial aspect of this definition, and others like it, is the inclusion of self-neglect as a form of mistreatment. Manifestations of self-neglect may include an unsatisfactory living environment, failure to seek or follow medical advice, failure to obtain psychological counseling, the abuse of alcohol and other drugs, and allowing financial exploitation of oneself (Sellers, Folts, & Logan, 1992).

The inclusion of self-neglect as a form of maltreatment raises several significant issues. First, there can be a tension between an appraisal of self-neglect and recognition of an elder's right to self-determination. Who is to say that behavior that seems foolish, like visiting a psychic weekly or concluding that one bath every 11 days is ideal, is actually self-neglect, or perhaps a form of mental illness?

Second, self-neglect does not fit a definition of abuse within a required interactional framework that includes a victim-and-perpetrator relationship (Hudson, 1994). Although self-neglect is a frequent problem for elders, it occurs without a perpetrator and often occurs in situations where the elder is legally competent, even though mentally or physically impaired (e.g., Tatara, 1993). Self-neglect, however, frequently occurs in plain view of family members and occasionally is aided and abetted by relatives' actions, such as buying liquor for an alcoholic elder. More commonly, however, self-neglect results from impairment and isolation, with no one to blame for the "maltreatment" except society.

Because elder advocates are primarily concerned with protecting elders from harm, it is apparent why self-neglect is increasingly considered a social problem (Mixson, 1991). In some cases, it also runs counter to an elder's right to make autonomous decisions about how to spend his or her remaining days.

---

has been complicated. Unlike children who go out of the house to school, elders who live alone and seldom leave the house are more invisible. They tend not to report their adversities, and professionals and paraprofessionals tend not to identify their abuse (Kosberg, 1988). According to Pillemer and Finkelhor's (1988) telephone survey of community elders, only 1 in 14 cases of elder abuse is reported to adult protective services (APS). Although more than half of the elder abuse cases reported are for self-neglect, generally APS receive reports about only the most serious cases of abuse. Elder abuse may actually be increasing, according to data collected by the U.S. House of Representatives, Select Committee on Aging (1990) and according to the number of cases reported to local agencies (Tatara, 1993).

In addition to the hidden nature of elder abuse, there are sample differences (e.g., random community vs. small clinical; abused elders vs. abusive caregivers), verification differences (e.g., police or agency verified vs. self-report), and divergence in the types of data gathered (e.g., agency records, interviews, and physical examinations). All these variations contribute to inconsistency between studies (Salend, Kane, Satz, & Pynoos, 1984).

Official Estimates. An analysis of the Comparative Homicide File (CHF) revealed that in comparison with other age groups, elderly persons are especially unlikely to be murdered and, moreover, are especially unlikely to be murdered by a family member (Bachman, 1993). Dawson and Langan (1994) of the Bureau of Justice Statistics found that only 11% of all homicide victims age 60 or older were killed by a son or daughter. Of those homicides involving children and elder parents, sons killed fathers (53%) about as often as mothers (47%), but daughters were much more likely to kill a father (81%) than a mother (19%).

The number of reported incidents (not victims) of intrafamily elder abuse and neglect reported to APS reached 227,000 in 1991. Data from investigative findings from 30 states indicated that 54.6% of the cases were substantiated (confirmed by authorities), whereas 38.2% were not; results from 7.3% cases were unknown. Of substantiated reports, 51.4% were for self-neglect, 44.6% were for abuse by others, and 4% were unknown. Of those abused by others (not self-neglect), 45% cases were for neglect, 19% for physical abuse, 17% for financial exploitation, 14% for psychological abuse, 1% for sexual abuse, and 4% for all other known types (Tatara, 1993).

Self-Report Surveys. Recognizing the need for more generalizable and inclusive data, Pillemer and Finkelhor (1988) conducted telephone interviews with 2,020 Boston area residents age 65 and older. They estimated the prevalence rate of three different kinds of elder abuse: physical, psychological, and neglect. They did not, however, assess financial abuse. Using a modified version of the CTS, they defined physical abuse as any violent act (e.g., pushed, grabbed, shoved, beat up) committed by a caregiver (spouse, child, or other coresident) since the respondent had turned 65. They defined neglect as withholding "activities of daily living" (e.g., meal preparation, housework) 10 or more times in the preceding year. Finally, they designated psychological abuse as "chronic verbal aggression" (e.g., insulted, swore at, threatened) occurring more than 10 times a year. Of the 2,020 elders interviewed, 63 (3.2%) reported being abused. Specifically, 2.0% reported being victimized by physical abuse (since turning 65), 1.1% reported psychological abuse, and 0.4% reported neglect (in the past year).

The National Crime Victimization Survey (NCVS) determined that elders (2.3/1,000) are especially unlikely to be victims of an assault compared to other age cohorts (26.7/1,000). On the other hand, for some time periods (e.g., 1987 to 1990), when they were assaulted, elders (13%) were proportionately more likely to be assaulted by family members than those under 65 (9%) (Bachman, 1993).

Intermediate Chapter Summary

The term *elder abuse* covers a wide variety of **omissions and commissions of various behaviors:** physical abuse, psychological abuse, material abuse, and neglect. Some authorities expand the terminology of elder abuse and neglect to encompass anomalous situations in which an elder lacks appropriate care (e.g., food, medicine) (Johnson, 1986). An elder who chooses to live alone, who refuses to bathe or take life-saving medication, is a victim of neglect. But who is the perpetrator? Without norms and laws governing who should care for elders, it is society that presumably must shoulder the blame. Another problem with definitions of elder abuse is that notions like "violations of individual constitutional rights" (e.g., preventing an elder from having visitors) are especially subjective and difficult to operationalize and may impinge on an adult's autonomy (e.g., Boudreau, 1993).

Depending on how an individual researcher chooses to define and assess elder abuse, the rate of abuse may be very high or very low. Because elders frequently face numerous personal problems (e.g., poverty, poor health, incompetence), **broad definitions** will produce very high rates of abuse. Data from APS, for example, included cases of substantiated and unsubstantiated abuse and cases of self-neglect, as well as cases of intrafamily violence. These data indicate that problems of elders are real and pervasive.

Scholars who focus more narrowly on perpetration of physical violence against elders obviously find considerably less elder abuse in society. In terms of physical violence, rates of abuse appear to be quite low. When compared to other age cohorts, elders are victims of relatively few family homicides. The best estimates of physical abuse come from Pillemer and Finkelhor (1988), whose CTS data revealed that only 2% of elders are victims of physical violence in any given year. **Inclusion of psychological abuse and neglect** (but not financial abuse) by others raised the annual rate to 3.2%. This rate indicates that elder abuse is among the least common forms of family violence. At the same time, however, a prevalence rate of 3.2% means that as many as 1 million elders are affected nationally.

Searching for Patterns: Who Is Abused and Who Are the Abusers?

Elder abuse researchers have tried to classify types of elders who may be especially vulnerable to abuse and types of individuals who abuse elders. They have examined issues of family relationship, gender, age, and race, as well as mental health and alcohol abuse. Given definitional, sampling, and methodological limitations of the research, observers accept identified patterns as preliminary in nature.

Characteristics of Abused Elders

Research on elder abuse has revealed few consistent differences between victims and nonvictims. If there is such an individual as a "typical" abused elder, it may be an older woman who is supporting a dependent adult child or a disabled or cognitively impaired spouse (Wolf & Pillemer, 1989).

Living Arrangements. Elders living alone (widowed, divorced, or never married) are less likely to be abused than elders who live with someone else (Pillemer & Finkelhor, 1988). Of those who do not live alone, elders who live with their spouses are less vulnerable than elders who live with grown offspring or other caretakers (Paveza et al., 1992). Research also suggests that abused elders are more isolated, in terms of number of contacts with family and friends, than nonabused elders (Wolf & Pillemer, 1989).

Gender. In regard to gender, results are contradictory. Official APS reports revealed that most abuse victims (68%) are female (Tatara, 1993), whereas data from the Boston self-report survey indicated that the majority of victims are male (52%) (Pillemer & Finkelhor, 1988). Even more important, the Boston study suggests that the victimization rate for men (5.1%) is double that for women (2.5%). Several explanations may account for these seemingly contradictory findings.

First, the elderly population is disproportionately female. In fact, an Australian researcher typified elder abuse as a "women's issue" because of gender disproportionality (Dunn, 1995). In the Boston study, for example, 65% of the respondents were women. Therefore, the absolute numbers of male and female victims might be similar even though the risk of being abused is much higher for men. This pattern also helps to explain, at least in part, why such a high proportion of cases reported to APS involve women. There are simply more elderly women. Another reason for the gender discrepancy is that women tend to sustain more serious abuse, and more serious cases of abuse are more likely to be reported to APS. Finally, the rate of abuse may be higher for men because they are more likely to be living with someone else (a risk factor for elder abuse) (Pillemer & Finkelhor, 1988). Living by oneself, which is more common for women, reduces the likelihood of abuse (Paveza et al., 1992).

Socioeconomic Status and Race. Research on socioeconomic status has revealed that poor elders in the United States are no more likely to be abused than middle-class elders (Boudreau, 1993), and retired elders are at no greater risk than those still working (Bachman & Pillemer, 1991).

Some studies have found no racial disparity in the rate of elder abuse (e.g., Pillemer & Finkelhor, 1988), whereas others have (e.g., Hall, 1986). In a study specifically designed to examine the minority status of 1,477 cases of agency-confirmed abuse, 35% of maltreatment reports came from minority elders, although only 21% of the population were minorities (Hall, 1986). Another study of 597 agency cases revealed that European Americans (whites) were more likely to suffer from self-neglect, African Americans from neglect by others, and both races equally from physical or financial abuse (Longres, 1992). Other studies suggest that races may differ more in their perceptions of behaviors they designate as abusive than in the actual frequency of abusive behaviors experienced (Moon & Williams, 1993).

Characteristics of Elder Abusers

Relationship to Victim. Statistics derived from APS files indicate that an elder abuser is most frequently a relative who lives with the elder and has cared for the elder for a long period of time (Taler & Ansello, 1985). A Los Angeles County study (January 1993 through June 1993) of 1,855 substantiated elder abuse and neglect cases found that two thirds of the suspected abusers were family members (35% offspring, 14% spouse, and 18% other relationship). Other suspects were care custodians (12%), health practitioners (3%), no relationship (14%), and unknown (4%) (Los Angeles County Department of Community and Senior Citizen Services, 1994). Another large-scale study across 18 states similarly found that family members were suspected in two thirds of the cases (32.5% adult children, 14.4% spouses, 4.2% grandchildren, 2.5% siblings, and 12.5% other relatives). Nonfamily-suspected abusers were 7.5% friends or neighbors, 6.3% service providers, 18.2% all other categories, and 2.0% unknown (Tatara, 1993).

In their telephone survey of Boston area elders, Pillemer and Finkelhor (1988) also found that abuse by nonfamily members is rare. Of the 3.2% of the sample of elders who were abused, 58% reported being abused by spouses, 24% by children, and 18% by others (grandchildren, siblings, boarders). This finding, according to Pillemer and Finkelhor, challenges the popular perception that abuse is most often perpetrated by adult offspring.

Marital Status and Age. Research in the United States (Pillemer & Finkelhor, 1988) and in several other countries (e.g., Halicka, 1995; Johns & Hydle, 1995) suggests that most elder abuse is spouse abuse. Many abusive caretakers in Pillemer and Finkelhor's (1988) study were over age 50 (75%) or even 70 (20%), and over 64% of the perpetrators were financially dependent on the victim (also see Wolf, Godkin, & Pillemer, 1986). Abusers who are elders themselves may suffer from dementia or other problems that render them less able to care for a dependent elder. Although some of their neglect may be conscious and premeditated, some may result from ignorance or incompetence. Accounting for intentionality of the abuse in such cases becomes an issue (Glendenning, 1993; Taler & Ansello, 1985).

Gender. Although women usually shoulder the major burden of elder care (Deitch, 1993),

they may not be the primary abusers. Concerning gender, Tatara (1993) found that among substantiated APS cases, 52% of the abusers were male, 42% were female, and 6% were unknown (also see Giordano & Giordano, 1984; Sengstock & Liang, 1982).

Related Problems of Abusers. On the whole, financial problems typify a number of abusers (Bendik, 1992; Stone et al., 1987; Wolf et

---

Abusers tend to be socially isolated and frequently have substance abuse problems, arrest records, and poor employment records.

---

al., 1986). Abusers also tend to be socially isolated and to receive low levels of social support (Bendik, 1992). They also frequently have substance abuse problems, arrest records, and poor employment records (see Anetzberger, 1987; Godkin, Wolf, & Pillemer, 1989; Greenberg, McKibben, & Raymond, 1990; Hickey & Douglass, 1981a; Kosberg, 1988; Stone et al., 1987). Some may have intellectual deficits (Kinderknecht, 1986).

Intermediate Chapter Summary

Elder abuse has only recently gained the attention of researchers, partially because of lack of agreement over definitions of such abuse and also over the degree to which elders are affected. With the rapid increase of elders in the population and with the proliferation of uncertainty and change in our world, there is a call for more attention to this area of study. It is often not even clear who is the victim and who is the perpetrator.

Official **adult protective services (APS) data** indicate that most elder abuse victims are female. One of the reasons that there are more female victims, however, is that the majority of elders are female. **Boston survey data** (i.e., random community sample) revealed that the rate of victimization is actually higher for men, but this study did not include self-neglect or financial exploitation.

Elders living with relatives are more likely to suffer abuse than elders living alone. Although some studies indicate low relationships between poor health indicators and abuse, others suggest that an elder's physical dependency clearly plays a role in vulnerability to abuse. What **sparse data** are available show no differences in socioeconomic status between abused and nonabused elders and provide no conclusive evidence about racial disparity.

APS data suggest that victims of elder abuse are predominantly females and abusers are primarily males. The Boston community study suggests the reverse gender differences. Data are inconsistent about whether most perpetrators are spouses or adult offspring. In either case, many **elder abusers** are relatively old themselves and suffer from mental and physical impairments, low levels of social support, and substance abuses. Many have arrest records and are unemployed. The implication of the research is that those who abuse and neglect elders often need help themselves.

It is useful to reiterate that when comparing various studies' findings about generalities, such as the gender of victims or perpetrators, that the data sources available (i.e., APS data vs. Boston study) may not be adequately comparable. Significant sample variations and other methodological problems indicate that any summarizing statements about patterns of elder abuse are still preliminary.

Explaining Elder Abuse

It is not known with any certainty why relatives abuse elders. Looking at abuse worldwide, Kosberg and Garcia (1995a) list several correlates of elder abuse: low socioeconomic level, marital status (married), substance abuse, personal problems of the caretakers, isolation, female gender, cultural heterogeneity, lack of housing, and societal acceptance of violence. The causal significance of these factors, however, remains unclear.

The three theories most widely advanced in the United States to explain elder abuse are social learning theory, social exchange theory (including situational stress and dependency), and psychopathology of the abuser (see Fulmer, 1991; Tomita, 1990).

Social Learning Theory

Because learning theory has received wide acceptance as one explanation for child abuse and spouse abuse, it seems reasonable to suggest that it may offer a viable account of elder abuse by adult offspring. This view holds that children exposed to violence are likely to grow up to adopt proabuse norms that eventually contribute to the abuse of their own parents or grandparents (Fulmer & O'Malley, 1987). Others see the learning connection more as a retaliatory response for past abuse (Rathbone-McCuan, 1980).

What scant research has been conducted, however, has thus far failed to substantiate a learning connection. One study that specifically tested the theory by comparing the childhoods of adult children who abuse their elder parents with those of parents who abuse their children found no overall differences using the CTS. On the severe violence items of the CTS, however, child abusers had significantly higher scores of being abused as children themselves than did elder abusers. The results suggested that the transgenera-tional theory of abuse is a more useful construct for explaining child abuse than for explaining elder abuse (Korbin, Anetzberger, & Austin, 1995). In another inquiry that examined retrospective accounts of their parental punishment of their children (not observation of marital violence), Wolf and Pillemer (1989) found no significant differences between abused elders and a comparison group of nonabused elders.

Social Exchange Theory

Social exchange postulates that elders have little to offer in the way of rewards. Interacting with them is costly and rarely "pays off." Taking care of an elder can be very time consuming and unpleasant and offers few benefits to the caregiver. Imagine the frustration of a wife who spends several hours cooking a birthday meal for her husband who is suffering from a severe memory impairment and decides that it is not his birthday, so he will not eat any dinner at all.

In one survey, 150 caregivers identified several types of "costs" resulting from the elder's impairment. Some of the difficulties, for example, were that the elder refused help or that the elder complained. Some of the "benefits" were an improved relationship with the elder or discovery of the caretaker's new strengths. Although research on exchange theory is limited, correlational analyses have revealed that a number of the difficulties enumerated by caregivers are associated with measures of their negative stress level and feelings of being burdened (Hinrichsen, Hernandez, & Pollack, 1992). Presumably, these costs, in combination with the few tangible rewards associated with elder care, could result in abuse.

Dependency Theory. A number of observers have speculated that the dependency of an elder functions as a cost for others and provokes abuse. This view suggests that an elder's impairments, such as being in a wheelchair, make him or her overly dependent on others. These caregivers eventually become overburdened by the elder's demands. The assumption, then, is that impaired elders would be victimized more frequently than nonimpaired elders.

Findings are inconsistent, however, about whether impaired or frail elders are more often abused than those who are not impaired (Biegel, Sales, & Schulz, 1991; Homer & Gilleard, 1990; Pedrick-Cornell & Gelles, 1982; Phillips, 1983; Pillemer & Suitor, 1992). In a study comparing abused and nonabused groups of elders, the abused group was not significantly more impaired in terms of illnesses or capacity to function than the nonabused group. Instead, it was the abusers who were significantly more dependent on their victims than their nonabusing counterparts. In fact, two thirds of the abusers were dependent on their victims in some way (housing, household repair, financial assistance, transportation) (Wolf & Pillemer, 1989).

Situational Stress. Proponents of the situational stress model contend that the stress often associated with elder care produces abusive behavior (Phillips, 1986). In fact, caregiver stress may be the major source of elder abuse (Steinmetz, 1993). One recent analysis of elders given flu vaccinations indicated that only 37% of elders providing care for a spouse with Alzheimer's disease mounted an effective immunological defense. Of the group of elders not comparably burdened, 50% responded appropriately in terms of an immunological response (cited in "Stress Undercuts," 1996).

As an illustration, Mace (1981) coined the term "36-hour day" to capture the laborious job of caring for an Alzheimer's patient, and others invented phrases like the "sandwich generation" to convey the burden of caring for one's own children while also caring for an aging parent (Brody, 1981; Preston, 1984; Steinmetz, 1993). The phrase "granny dumping" appeared when a few overburdened families left a sick and aging parent in a hospital emergency room (U.S. House of Representatives, Select Committee on Aging, 1990). Frequently, siblings designate another sibling (adult offspring) who lives near an aging parent as the caretaker. Instead of elder caretaking being a family matter, it becomes an individual responsibility of one child (Janosick & Green, 1992).

One study of external stressors experienced by families of abused and nonabused elders found that the main contrast arose from the stress engendered by the abuser's behavior (e.g., getting arrested), not by stress engendered by the care of the elder (Wolf &

Findings are inconsistent about whether impaired or frail elders are more often abused than those who are not impaired.

Pillemer, 1989). Sometimes, elder abuse is retaliatory. Caregivers are physically violent with elders who are violent toward them (Coyne, Reichman, & Berbig, 1993).

Individual (Intrapersonal) Trait Differences—Psychopathological Problems of Abusers

Many researchers have concluded that it is the characteristics of the caregivers, not the victims, that differentiate elderly victims from nonvictims (Bristowe & Collins, 1989; Kosberg, 1988; Pillemer & Finkelhor, 1989). This perspective holds that elder abusers tend to suffer from a variety of pathologies and mood disturbances (Bendik, 1992; Hickey & Douglass, 1981b; Movsas & Movsas, 1990; Pillemer & Finkelhor, 1989). In one study, for example, approximately 38% of abusers in three geographically different samples had a history of psychiatric illness and about 39% had alcohol problems (Wolf & Pillemer, 1988). The case history of Mohammed and Ahmed illustrates how the emotional and behavioral problems of an adult offspring can lead to elder abuse.

CASE HISTORY: MOHAMMED AND AHMED— "THE VOICES MADE ME DO IT"

Mohammed is a 79-year-old retired carpenter who currently lives with his son, Ahmed. Ahmed is a 53-year-old food server in a high school cafeteria, where he has worked for the school district for 20 years. At age 38, doctors diagnosed Ahmed as having paranoid schizophrenia. At 40, Ahmed went broke, spending most of his money on home security devices and car alarms that he "needed" for self-protection. Eventually, Ahmed's financial problems forced him to move back home with his father.

Mohammed's approach to Ahmed's problems was to "set Ahmed straight" whenever he told odd stories about his coworkers or neighbors. Mohammed accused Ahmed of "talking hogwash" and of "needing medicine because he was crazy." Ahmed's response was to try to argue with Mohammed to convince him that his stories about other people were true. The battle between the two loomed larger and larger until Ahmed's problems became the focal point of Mohammed's life.

To save himself the aggravation of dealing with Ahmed, Mohammed began staying in his room as much as possible. Ahmed reacted by standing in front of Mohammed's door, yelling and screaming at him to come out. One time, Ahmed got so mad that he ripped out the telephone so the neighbors could not tell Mohammed lies about him. Another time, he barricaded Mohammed into his room for a day and Mohammed had to break a window to escape. Mohammed sank into a deep depression. He loved Ahmed, but he felt humiliated, blamed, afraid, and all alone.

The next year, Mohammed slipped on the ice and broke his leg. At first, Ahmed was the dutiful son who took food to Mohammed, drove him to the doctor, and cleaned the apartment. Eventually, however, the voices told him that Mohammed was plotting to have him locked up in an insane asylum. One day, Ahmed beat Mohammed and pushed him out of his bed. There Mohammed lay on the floor for a day until a neighbor heard him groaning and called the police.

The police locked up Ahmed for a 3-day evaluation and called social services, who had Mohammed admitted to a nursing home temporarily. In the psychiatric hospital, doctors started Ahmed on strong antipsychotic drugs. Now, Ahmed is loving, kind, and "normal," as long as he takes his medicines. At the moment, things are better for both Mohammed and Ahmed, but no one knows for how long. (Author's case history)

* * *

An impressive amount of research has linked mental health risk factors and social characteristics to abusive caretakers: clinical depression (Paveza et al., 1992; Taler & Ansello, 1985), excessive dependency (Pillemer, 1993), anger and hostility (Coyne et al., 1993; Garcia & Kosberg, 1992), personality disorder (Lau & Kosberg, 1979), mood disturbance (Bendik, 1992), low self-esteem (Godkin et al., 1989), poor physical health (Bendik, 1992), inadequate communication skills (Greenberg et al., 1990; Stone et al., 1987; Wolf et al., 1986), and inadequate coping skills (Godkin et al., 1989).

Intermediate Chapter Summary

Experts have advanced several theories to explain elder abuse. **Social learning theory** accentuates acquisition of abusive behaviors during childhood and their manifestation in adulthood with the elder parent as victim. The scant data available so far have failed to substantiate this theory; it is too early to evaluate this explanation.

Social exchange theory, as applied to elder abuse, posits that just as aging parents (or spouses) need more and more care, they are less and less able to offer rewards or benefits to those who care for them. This imbalance implies that caring for an elder "doesn't pay," so a caretaker might just as well neglect the elder (Pedrick-Cornell & Gelles, 1982). Correlational analyses indicate this theory is valid, but, again, there is only limited research to date.

The dependency of an elder, brought about by impairments, raises the **"costs" of elder care** and may contribute to abuse. Research, however, finds little support for this viewpoint (Wolf & Pillemer, 1989). A very common theme is situational stress of the caregiver. Presumably, victims' needs create such powerful feelings of **stress in caregivers** that they may lose control and abuse their elderly relatives. Presumably, middle-aged offspring are caught between the demands of two generations and are vulnerable to caregiver stress.

The **individual differences (psychopathology of the abuser) theory** presumes elder abuse most likely results from the deviance and dependence of the abusers. A large body of evidence demonstrates that perpetrators do tend to have far-ranging problems such as alcohol abuse and emotional instability (Pillemer & Finkelhor, 1988). The psychological status of the abuser, in fact, may be a better predictor of elder abuse than the characteristics of the victim (e.g., Bendik, 1992).

Because all the theories have limitations, it may be necessary to identify a configuration of related factors or to **integrate theories** (Tomita, 1990). Situational stress, for example, in combination with particular personality types might set the stage for elder mistreatment (Bendik, 1992).

Conceptions of Elder Abuse in Other Countries

Research about elder abuse in other countries has lagged behind that in the United States. Cross-cultural conceptions about elder abuse are similar in some ways to those in the United States, but reveal some interesting cultural contrasts. Recognition of elder abuse worldwide rested primarily on its "discovery" in the United States and Britain (see Kosberg & Garcia, 1995a). At first, experts in other countries tended to deny its existence in their own countries. In Ireland, for instance, the minister of health was quoted as saying that "no cases of abuse of the elderly were formally reported to me in 1989 or 1990" (quoted in Horkan, 1995, pp. 131-132). By the mid-1980s, however, a few reports from other countries began to appear (Chan, 1985; Kivela, 1995). In Australia, the public may have been reluctant to recognize elder abuse until the 1990s (Dunn, 1995) (see boxed insert: "The Effect of Culture on Elder Abuse").

Responses to Elder Abuse

Increasingly, governmental agencies and community professional groups have identified elder abuse as a social problem. The U.S. Department of Social and Rehabilitation Services began funding National Protective Services in the late 1960s (Quinn, 1985). In 1978, the Subcommittee on Human Services of the House Select Committee held the first congressional investigation on elder abuse (Olinger, 1991). Following the hearings, Congress in 1981 recommended the establishment of the National Center for Adult Abuse (Filinson, 1989). By 1985, every state had some form of adult protection programs (Quinn, 1985), and by 1989, 42 states had enacted some form of mandatory elder abuse reporting law (General Accounting Office, 1991; Wolf & Pillemer, 1989). Nonetheless, neither in the United States nor in any other country are there formal APS agencies that provide surveillance over vulnerable elders (Kosberg & Garcia, 1995a).

Just as definitional ambiguity has hindered research, it has also hampered efforts to respond to elder abuse. Legal definitions of elder abuse not only vary from state to state but may also vary from the operating standards employed by APS agencies. This confusion thwarts detection of certain types of abuse (e.g., psychological abuse) and hampers intervention strategies (Valentin & Cash,, 1986). Compounding the problems of definitional ambiguity is a lack of knowledge about the causes of elder abuse.

Finally, many of the cases that APS investigate are similar to the case of Jenny and Jeff, Jr. described at the beginning of the chapter. Uncertainties abound: Would a judge find Jeff, Jr. and Marianne guilty of neglect? Is Jenny's situation serious enough to warrant her removal from their house? Would Jenny be happier living elsewhere? What is the former daughter-in-law's appropriate role in helping Jenny? Who should inherit the remainder of Jenny's estate when she dies? In the real world, there are no good answers, only more difficult questions.

More research is needed to answer many questions about elder abuse. In 1991, an interdisciplinary group of researchers formulated a national agenda of research priorities for elder abuse. They pinpointed the need to make the following determinations: (a) nature and extent of the problem, (b) etiology—the origin and root causes, (c) societal costs and consequences, (d) identification of abused elders, (e) prevention and treatment, and (f) legal concerns (Stein, 1991).

Legal Issues

Federal and state governments, and many county and city governments, have attempted to prevent elder abuse through legislation. In California, for example, Section 15610 of the Welfare and Institutions Code delineates elder abuse as physical abuse, neglect, aban-

THE EFFECT OF CULTURE ON ELDER ABUSE

Experts in other countries are likely to distinguish between elder abuse and elder mistreatment, or to include a category specified as the absence of quality care. Others suggest that fear of abuse and abandonment should be included as a type of abuse (Kosberg & Garcia, 1995a).

The conditions within a country greatly affect the rates of elder abuse. In South Africa, the general level of violence is so high that violence against elders is something of a "blip on a radar screen" (Eckely & Vilakazi, 1995). In countries like Hong Kong, strong emigration patterns have left an ever-growing number of older people alone with no family to offer care (Kwan, 1995). By contrast, immigration in Israel has created a population of elders who are predominantly foreign born (Lowenstein, 1995). In Australia, the Aboriginal population has a significantly lower life expectancy, thus lowering elder abuse rates.

In India, poverty, illiteracy, and female dependency play a strong part in elder abuse. Customs such as giving away one's property as preparation for the next world, as the last stage of life, make financial exploitation much easier (Shah, Veedon, & Vasi, 1995). In Finland, as many as 20% of the elders have no children or family of any sort to offer support (or abuse) (cited in Kivela, 1995). The multigenerational shared-housing situation in Poland seems to encourage neglect and psychological abuse (Halicka, 1995).

Data about elder abuse in other countries are sparse. Elder abuse in Australia, Canada, Great Britain, and Norway appears to approximate roughly estimates made in the United States (Kurrle & Sadler, 1993; Ogg & Bennett, 1992; Podkieks, 1992). In many countries (e.g., Hong Kong, India), abandonment and neglect seem more significant problems than physical abuse (e.g., Kwan, 1995; Pitsiou-Darrough & Spinellis, 1995; Shah et al., 1995). The number of Finnish elders seeking shelter from abuse was 3% to 6% (cited in Kivela, 1995). In Greece, the estimate for physical abuse was quite high, 15% (Pitsiou-Darrough & Spinellis, 1995).

In contrast to studies in the United States, studies in other countries show that low socioeconomic status is a definite risk factor for elder abuse. This is especially true when there are no government assistance programs for elders (Eckely & Vilakazi, 1995). Several international experts also seem relatively confident that elder abuse is most frequently (or very often) an extension of spouse abuse into old age (e.g., Halicka, 1995; Johns & Hydle, 1995).

Most foreign countries rely totally on informal care systems (i.e., family) for support and care of elders. In Finland, there are no government programs of any sort (cited in Kivela, 1995), and in Australia there are no adult protective services (Dunn, 1995). In Israel, only 15% of dependent elders receive help from public authorities, and 85% receive help from informal sources (Lowenstein, 1995). In Greece, elder abuse is "just one more problem," and victims must wait their turn for help (Johns & Hydle, 1995).

Laws regarding elder abuse vary throughout the world. Whereas laws sanction abuse of elders in Greece, for example, there are no laws protecting elders with diminished capacity from financial exploitation (Pitsiou-Darrough & Spinellis, 1995). In India, laws mandate legal responsibility for parental care to all financially able children (Shah et al., 1995). In Israel, there are no special provisions for elders, but they are protected under a general Protection of Helpless Persons law (Lowenstein, 1995). As of 1994, South Africa had no laws dealing with elder abuse (Eckely & Vilakazi, 1995). In Ireland, refusing to provide the necessities of life to any child, aged person, or sick person is a misdemeanor (Horkan, 1995).

donment, fiduciary abuse, isolation, and mental suffering (see Los Angeles County Medical Association, 1992). In general, elder abuse laws, like this one from California, lack specificity, in part because difficulties abound in defining who elders are and what constitutes elder abuse (Crystal, 1987).

There are those, however, who argue that criminalization of elder abuse is not fruitful. Formby (1992) believes that the criminalization of elder abuse may be counterproductive and may actually hamper efforts of APS workers who are required by law to report the abuse, but do not always do so. Confronting an abusive caregiver with criminal charges, for example, has the potential of being the most disruptive approach that can be taken (Phillips, 1989). More specifically, if legal authorities choose to separate and remove the elder from the abuser, it may cut the elder off from the only people who provide meaning in the elder's life (Sengstock, Hwalek, & Petrone, 1989). From this perspective, what elder abusers need is support, not punishment.

Another disagreement centers on the applicability of addressing elder abuse by adopting legislation modeled after child abuse laws (see Vinton, 1992). A number of experts have discussed the potentially negative consequences of this approach with its emphasis on victim incompetence and dependency (e.g., Bolton & Bolton, 1987; Finkelhor & Pillemer, 1988; Kosberg, 1988). These experts believe that it is demeaning to treat elders like children. It is also commonly assumed that abused elders, like abused spouses (but not abused children), seemingly have the option of living in a home separate from the abuser. Others maintain that elders often cannot care for themselves. In these cases, they need to be protected just as children need to be protected (Straus, Gelles, & Steinmetz, 1980).

Mandatory Reporting Laws. Those most frequently mandated to report abuse are health and mental health professionals and law enforcement personnel. Those most frequently mandated to receive the reports are social service departments (Wolf & Pillemer, 1989). The enactment of this type of legislation is controversial, not only because it treats elders like children but also because the definitions of abuse and victimization are so broad that they may violate the constitutional rights of elders (Faulkner, 1982; Lee, 1986). Along the same lines, some professionals are mandated both to report and to keep a client's communications confidential (Wolf & Pillemer, 1989).

Successful reporting often arises from collaborative efforts between agencies. The lack of interagency understanding about the role of law enforcement as opposed to the role of social service is at the core of many failures to report. Programs built on interagency cross-fertilization and training have potential for overcoming mistrust and establishing successful policy guidelines. Police, for example, help social service personnel define serious abuse and explain various possible police reactions to reports. In return, police learn they can rely on social service personnel to

serve as intermediaries when elders will not cooperate with them. Working together in one jurisdiction led to a 300% increase in reports (Reulbach & Tewksbury, 1994).

Legal Services Available to Elders. Generally, attorneys can provide services not available from other professionals, such as court and noncourt actions and nonlegal actions that have the potential to threaten court action (Sengstock & Barrett, 1986). By and large, elders most frequently need one of four types of legal interventions: (a) orders of protection to remove the abuser from the residence, (b) guardianship of the elder and his or her estate, (c) representative payeeships to safeguard certain types of the elder's income such as social security, and (d) protection against involuntary commitment (Segal & Iris, 1989).

Although elders may have many unmet legal needs (Hightower, Heckert, & Schmidt, 1990), they tend to make sparse use of legal resources for several reasons (Korbin, Anetzberger, Thomasson, & Austin, 1991). They may be reluctant to instigate and become involved in the legal process, especially if the case involves family members (Pollack, 1995). They may fear retaliation or be physically or financially unable to look for help (Gelles & Cornell, 1990). Elders also may feel offended by certain attitudes of attorneys and other professional workers toward them or be suspicious of outsiders (Griffith, Roberts, & Williams, 1993). Professionals may appear condescending or disinterested in an elder's problems. Elders also may not label their mistreatment as abuse, partly because definitions of elder abuse are overly technical and unclear.

Fortunately, a few alternative services have attempted to meet the needs of these vulnerable elders. A noteworthy volunteer project sponsored by the Los Angeles County Barristers Association helped approximately 1,125 elderly clients obtain restraining orders in 1993 (Beitiks, 1994).

Elders can help prevent their own abuse by completing a number of documents (e.g., durable powers of attorney) and keeping them updated (Overman, 1992). Elders need to plan for long-term illnesses and retirement. A primary, but difficult, task for elders is to retain power as long as possible (Sukosky, 1992). A durable power of attorney made during an elder's capacity, in anticipation of loss of capacity, is a wise legal move (Blunt, 1993). In many cases, financial abuse can be prevented.

Changes in the Court. Some believe that the limited powers of the court have played a role in elder abuse. Nolan (1990) recommends an expanded role for judges so that they might have the option in surrogate power cases to shape a remedy that best suits the elder's needs. Furthermore, judges need to implement good monitoring practices that

---

It is not uncommon for victims to receive services that they do not need, insufficient services, or even refusal by agency personnel to provide services requested.

---

include the following: (a) informing guardians of their responsibilities, (b) requiring guardians to submit informative reports, (c) checking reports, and (d) holding or having the option to hold a hearing on the reports (Zimny & Diamond, 1993).

Police Approaches. Collaboration between protective services and law enforcement is a growing trend (Reulbach & Tewksbury, 1994). In 1992, the Los Angeles Police Department formalized a unique Elder Person's Estate Unit within the Fiduciary Abuse Specialist Team (FAST) to curb financial exploitation of seniors. FAST includes a district attorney, stockbroker, bank trust officer, retired probate judge, and public guardian staff. Some of their duties include training APS representatives, public guardians, and ombudsmen on how to detect financial abuse. Acting as a fiduciary "SWAT team," they sweep into banks and other areas to safeguard the senior's assets by suggesting that administrators put a hold on the assets. This team has recovered $31 million in homes, vehicles, and life savings since it began informally in 1987 (Nerenberg, 1995).

Professional Practitioners

What may be more important than legislation is knowing what to do when a case of elder abuse is detected. Responding to elder mistreatment is a complex and confusing area of social work practice (Braun, Lenzer, Shumacher-Mukai, & Snyder, 1993). By law, most APS programs are concerned with *dependent* adults. As a result, abused elders who are functioning independently, but are abused or exploited, are not technically eligible for services. In fact, there may be no good interventions available (Penhale, 1993).

At the center of the problem is the continuing ambiguity concerning who is responsible for dependent elders and what kind of care (or lack of care) constitutes mistreatment. There is no one agency that oversees service delivery of abused, competent elders as there is for child abuse (Braun et al., 1993; Lachs & Pillemer, 1995). It is not uncommon for victims to receive services that they do not need, insufficient services, or even refusal by agency personnel to provide services requested. Because of this tangled web, it is probable that some service providers try not to recognize elder abuse when encountered and engage in referrals as their principal response (Block & Sinnott, 1979). Collectively, it is important to develop an orderly and systematic service delivery system to assist abused elders (Weiner, 1991).

Agency Responsibility. The agencies most commonly assigned responsibility for implementing legal policies are APS. APS have the duty to protect dependent elders regardless of whether the abuse they suffer meets some particular legal definition. APS keep agency files of reported cases and oversees the care of dependent elders.

Larger social service bureaus often incorporate APS as subcomponents of their organizations. One examination of the social services offered to 204 abused elders by the Department of Aging in Illinois provides a typical illustration of APS: case management (97.5%); homemaker assistance (34.8%); legal services (24.5%); medical care and therapy (16.2%); institutional placement (14.7%); supervision and reassurance (14.2%); counseling (13.2%); home health assistance (12.3%); meals and income assistance (16.7%); housing and relocation assistance (6.4%); police, court work, and protection orders (6.9%); guardianship (3.4%); and other (6.4%) (Sengstock et al., 1989).

Some agencies are more involved than others in responding to elder abuse. A survey of state public health departments indicated that only 20% had procedures in place for dealing with elder abuse (Ehrlich & Anetzberger, 1991). In contrast, a survey of 183 agencies for aging found that 95.6% provided information and referrals that helped reduce the incidence of family violence (Blakely & Dolon, 1991). Frequently undertaken activities included providing advocacy services (93.4%), working to increase public awareness (93.4%), and reporting suspected cases of elder abuse to APS (92.3%).

In one study of three model projects, staff rated "changes in living arrangements" as the most effective intervention strategy and "changes in the circumstances of the perpetrator" as the least effective approach. Of the 266 cases where data on resolutions were available, over one third judged the problem as "completely" resolved and another third believed that "some progress" in resolution had been made. Victim receptivity to intervention was a key variable in successful resolution, and perpetrator lack of receptivity was pivotal in unresolved cases (Wolf & Pillemer, 1989).

Elders Who Refuse Care. Some practitioners have become discouraged trying to help elders in need because they so frequently refuse service. In Fredriksen's (1989) survey of 115 elders referred to APS, the most frequent outcome was that clients refused services (26.4%). In a related study, 81% of elders who rejected intervention were women with no disabling characteristics whose sons were the caretakers and perpetrators (Vinton, 1991).

Family Caretakers. Professionals charged with making decisions about placement of elders needing care should not automatically assume that family members are fit caretakers (Kosberg, 1988). Professionals also need to weigh the advisability of family care in light of the difficulties encountered in discontinuing home care once it has begun (Deitch, 1993). Professionals should conduct a preplacement screening to identify high-risk elders and high-risk caretakers (Kosberg, 1988). Finally, professionals need to assist families with the burdens of caretaking (e.g., procurement of additional home services) even if they judge a family setting to be suitable.

In fact, some believe that the most effective way to combat elder abuse is to focus on prevention of caretaker stress (Steinmetz, 1988). Caretakers need to have support groups, short-term respite care, and household help (Deitch, 1993). Caretakers also need education to become aware of the potential for abuse. A particularly strong deterrent to elder abuse is the presence of an active social network that curbs the elder's and/or the caretaker's isolation. Interaction with others helps to define the boundaries of legitimate and illegitimate behaviors (Deitch, 1993).

The Medical Field

Doctors, nurses, and other medical personnel can also play a vital role in assisting elder abuse victims. Emergency rooms and medical centers have a protocol for identifying and reporting elder abuse. Most states have resource hotlines that doctors (or elders) can call for assistance in matters of abuse (Lachs & Pillemer, 1995). In recent years, the American Medical Association has recognized the problem and in 1992 increased its efforts to include family violence education in medical school training. Representative of these efforts are those made by the Los Angeles County Medical Association (1992) in conjunction with several other agencies (e.g., Los Angeles City Department of Aging). The association prepared a booklet to assist doctors on a number of issues regarding elder abuse, such as diagnosis and clinical findings, case management, intervention, and risk management. Included is a series of nine questions that doctors should ask older patients. Figure 11.1 lists these questions.

Research on the responses of medical personnel to elder abuse has suggested that these individuals are reluctant to report suspected cases (Blakely & Dolon, 1991). In one study, a significant number of the interviewed doctors (36%) and nurses (60%) interviewed cited lengthy court appearances as a major reason for their failure to comply with mandated reporting laws. Some were simply unaware of reporting laws (O'Malley, Segel, & Perez, 1979). Other frequent reasons may include beliefs that the problem is not serious enough, the evidence is insufficient, services are inadequate, and the report would disrupt family relationships (Clark-Daniels, Daniels, & Baumhover, 1989)

Physical and occupational therapists could play a role in the detection of elder abuse because their observation of elders with symptoms of abuse puts them in a good position to facilitate remedial and preventive services (Holland, Kasraian, & Leonardelli, 1987). Community health nurses, who go directly into homes, are other community service providers who by virtue of their function and responsibilities could become critical participants in the identification, prevention, and treatment of elder mistreatment (VanderMeer, 1992).

ASSESSMENT INTERVIEW (WITH PATIENT AND FAMILY)

When asking the patient more direct questions pertaining to mistreatment, first explain that such questions are routine because many families experience this problem but don't know where to turn for help. The following are examples of more direct questions that may be asked of patients, depending on the individual case.

— Has anyone at home ever hurt you?
— Has anyone ever touched you when you didn't want to be touched?
— Has anyone ever forced you to do something against your will?
— Has anyone taken anything that was yours without permission?
— Have you ever given anything away even though you really didn't want to? Why?
— Does anyone ever talk or yell at you in a way that makes you feel lousy or bad about yourself?
— Are you afraid of anyone?
— Has anyone ever threatened you?
— Has anyone ever failed to help you take care of yourself when you needed help?

Explore each of the above affirmative responses further: How did (does) mistreatment occur? How often? Has mistreatment increased or changed over time? Explain. What precipitates mistreatment? Why does the patient think mistreatment occurs? Is patient in danger as a result of the mistreatment? How serious is the danger? How serious are the consequences of mistreatment? Can the patient protect him- or herself? Does the patient want to prevent mistreatment? How? If not, why? Have there been previous efforts to prevent mistreatment? If so, who helped? What happened? What would be different this time? What does the patient want to happen now?

SOURCE: From *"Elder Mistreatment Guidelines for Health Care Professionals: Detection, Assessment, and Intervention,"* p. 14, 1988. Copyright by Mt. Sinai/Victim Services Agency, Elder Abuse Project. Reprinted with permission of Victim Services, New York and Mt. Sinai.

Other Innovations

Several authorities have advocated the establishment of emergency shelters for battered elders (Boudreau, 1993; Pillemer & Finkelhor, 1989). In a 1992 Florida survey of 6,026 women who were sheltered during the previous year, only 132 were over age 60 and, of those, 95% had been assaulted by a spouse. Special programming for older women existed in only 2 of 25 shelters (Vinton, 1992). Availability of battered women's shelters, however, may not be as helpful to elderly women as better access to elder care facilities.

One method of combating elder abuse or guardianship problems that is gaining increasing recognition is the formation of multidisciplinary community teams (Hwalek, Williamson, & Stahl, 1991; Nerenberg et al., 1990). Four types of teams have emerged: hospital based, family practice based including APS, the consortium-based team organized through informal networking among community professionals, and the community-based multidisciplinary team developed under the auspices of a single agency serving elder abuse victims. These teams call on the expertise of individuals in law enforcement, medical and legal fields, religion, and mental health (Nachman, 1991). After identifying a case of elder abuse or neglect, a team can jointly make decisions about the most effective methods of intervening and which agency is best suited to the task. Even identifying elder abuse lends itself to a team approach (Matlaw & Spence, 1994). A related type of team is a health care decision-making team to serve incapacitated elders (Fins, 1994).

Education and Training

The three most important group targets of elder abuse education should be professionals, community leaders, and elders themselves. States should require licensed professionals to take continuing education courses in health care, gerontology, and elder abuse. Psychologists should offer training programs for the so-called gatekeepers (i.e., mail carriers, storekeepers, neighbors, bus drivers, store clerks, church members, senior center members, veterans). Gatekeepers could help by becoming alert to any signs that an older person is in trouble (Deitch, 1993). Networking approaches between various community groups is the key component of successful educational programs (Weiner, 1991).

Summary

This chapter has briefly summarized current knowledge about elder abuse. Research conducted to date has been insufficient to determine the scope of elder abuse. First, the dilemma of defining elder abuse has dominated the field. In particular, the inclusion of self-neglect as an abuse category has confused the issue. Second, studies have frequently relied on small, nonrandom samples.

Estimates of elder abuse suggest that about 2% to 4% of elders experience abuse, but these estimates are constrained by definitional ambiguities and methodological limitations. Scales and interview methods for assessing abuse have been varied and often inadequate. Rarely are the results of elder abuse lethal. The most frequent abusers are family members, although it is unclear whether adult offspring or spouses more frequently perpetrate abuse.

Experts do not agree on the causes of elder abuse, and no single theory has proved satisfactory. Social learning may be one explanatory factor, but supportive evidence is currently lacking. Social exchange theory suggests that abusers may experience feelings that taking care of an elder is not worth the effort. Both the dependency of elder victims and the situational stress their care creates may provoke caregivers to abuse them, but evidence challenges this assumption. To the contrary, research suggests that elder abusers have psychological and social stressors of their own, such as mental illness, alcoholism, and unemployment, that render them dependent, stressed, and unable to cope with elderly relatives.

Cross-cultural studies show many similarities between elder abuse internationally and in the United States. The problem of defining elder abuse occurs around the world, but foreign countries tend to include a broad category of "mistreatment" to describe behaviors such as the withholding of quality care. Many interesting cultural differences affect rates, such as the degree to which children are legally responsible to care for their parents and whether extended families live together. Because elder abuse has only recently been recognized in other countries, very few professionals in the community respond to its occurrence.

During the past decade, elder abuse has gained greater recognition as a legal and social problem. Laws regarding elder abuse are vague, just as definitions are, and experts differ about whether criminalization of elder abuse is the most effective approach or whether laws protecting elders from abuse should parallel those for children. In 42 of the 50 states, there are laws that mandate reporting of elder abuse to either police or social service professionals. Attorneys have been comparatively active in providing services to elders (e.g., guardianship matters), but more advocacy seems necessary.

Community professionals have responded to elder abuse in a variety of ways. Legal bodies have enacted laws to criminalize elder abuse, but some experts criticize this approach, characterizing it as counterproductive. Mandatory reporting laws have met with some resistance and inadequate implementation but still hold potential for protecting elders. Others have pinpointed the complexity of protecting elders assumed to be capable of making their own decisions. Attorneys have increasingly attempted to intervene in the area of elder abuse by improving such services as guardianship provisions. Increasingly, police have developed expertise in recognizing and pursuing abusers and in collaborating with social workers.

Social workers, as the primary guardians of the aged, have attempted to identify elders at risk and to furnish various types of interventions such as homemaker services, counseling, and relocation of victims. One of the most effective intervention strategies may be to alter the elder's living arrangements (possibly by removing the perpetrator). Medical personnel have been relatively inactive in identifying and referring abused elders for treatment but are currently expanding their efforts to comply with mandatory reporting laws. Some advocate the establishment of shelters for abused elders. Probably the most innovative approach is the organization of community multidisciplinary teams composed of various community professionals charged with handling elder abuse. Professionals need more training themselves and when trained they should educate other community mem- bers. Alert citizens can help prevent elder abuse by reporting information about elders who may need assistance.

12

Looking Toward the Future

CHAPTER OUTLINE

An Interview With Robert Geffner

"We need to all become aware of the entire continuum of family violence. We need to increase awareness, cooperativeness, and interdisciplinary networking among all researchers, clinicians, and advocates in the field."

ROBERT GEFFNER is a leading family violence networking advocate who combines advocacy with work as a clinician and researcher. After serving for 17 years as Professor of Psychology at the University of Texas at Tyler (UT-Tyler), he assumed the position of Clinical Director of Counseling, Testing, and Psychiatric Services in the Tyler area. He is also Editor in Chief of the Trauma and Maltreatment Press for Haworth Press. In this capacity he will continue editing the Journal of Child Sexual Abuse and oversee the development of several new journals in the field, including the Journal of Emotional Abuse. He is also Founder and President of the Family Violence & Sexual Assault Institute (FVSAI) and edits its semiannual bulletin. The institute is an international resource center and has achieved unparalleled success in establishing a clearinghouse for articles, books, media, and other resources. Innovations include topical bibliographies on spouse, child, and elder abuse as well as training and research conferences. He received a B.S. in chemistry from the University of California, Los Angeles, an M.A. in psychology from San Jose State University, and a Ph.D. in psychology from the University of California, Santa Cruz.

Q: How did you get interested in the area of family violence?

A: When a local rape hotline was developing in 1979, the staff wanted a psychologist to serve on the board. I was the only one with any background, because of my previous experience as a volunteer in a rape crisis center. While I served on the board for the next 5 years, I helped convert this small, local rape hotline into a full-service regional crisis center, and as president of the board I helped build a shelter for battered women and children. From there, I became interested in developing programs for treating family violence victims and offenders.

My involvement just sort of expanded. By sitting in on some national task forces, it became clear that as professionals in the field, we needed better networking. Since no one was doing much about the problem, I obtained a seed grant to develop the Family Violence Research and Treatment Program at UT–Tyler. We started with spouse abuse and then gradually expanded into all the other areas of domestic violence and sexual assault. As our work evolved, we created computerized databases.

Q: Looking back, what have been your major contributions?

A: One of my major contributions has been to encourage and enhance integration of the various areas of family violence—child abuse, spouse abuse, and partner abuse—as well as to increase integration of research and intervention. In our research and clinical programs, for example, we look at how being a victim of one type of abuse makes the individual more vulnerable and at risk for other types of abuse. We study offenders in the same way.

Second, we have helped those working in a single area, such as child abuse, to become more knowledgeable about the work of those involved in different areas, but there is still much to be done to foster awareness of work across the whole field. We need to all become aware of the entire continuum of family violence. We need to increase the awareness, cooperativeness, and interdisciplinary networking among all researchers, clinicians, and advocates in the field. We here at FVSAI have tried to be at the forefront of this movement for many years. From the standpoint of networking, I have established some practical means, like the clearinghouse, by which people can become aware of each others' work and state-of-the-art knowledge in the field.

Q: What would you do with a large grant?

A: I would try to learn more about the effectiveness of intervention programs. We really don't have much data on program effectiveness in any areas of family violence. In particular, we need to gain information about long-term effects of treatment. Along with this, we need to obtain an integrated understanding of the long-term impact of violence on family members, especially on children.

Q: What should communities do to diminish family violence?

A: Based on task force recommendations, they should first create family violence coordinating councils to make sure that problems don't fall through the cracks and to ensure interdisciplinary networking to work on these matters in an objective, nonpoliticized manner. At the national level, government officials need to take a more proactive view to fund research, intervention, and prevention programs; to set guidelines for working in the field; and to recognize publicly that family violence is a problem of epidemic proportions that will affect future generations.

Introduction

Family violence encompasses a multitude of diverse negative interactions that occur between different family members and other intimates. Researchers have categorized family violence into several subtypes: physical child abuse (PCA), child sexual abuse (CSA), child neglect and maltreatment, children exposed to marital violence, courtship violence, marital violence (i.e., battered women and batterers), and elder abuse.

The boundaries that have come to separate these various forms of family violence have tended to obscure the commonalities and contributed to the lack of integration and unification of the field. Academic specifications notwithstanding, violent families rarely "specialize" in one form of violence. Husbands who physically assault their wives, for example, are likely to psychologically mistreat them and even rape them (e.g., Finkelhor & Yllo, 1987; Frieze, 1983). If one member of an intimate marital or dating dyad is

violent, the other is likely to be violent also (Gelles & Straus, 1988; Stets & Pirog-Good, 1987). Parents who are physically violent toward each other are more likely to be physically and sexually abusive toward their children (Paveza, 1988; Sirles & Franke, 1989). Children who are physically punished by a parent are more likely to be violent toward a sibling (Straus, 1991c). Furthermore, children who are abused and neglected are frequently exposed to many forms of child maltreatment, including combinations of physical and sexual abuse, child neglect, and psychological maltreatment (see Hughes, 1988; Ney, Fung, & Wickett, 1994).

Integrating Research Findings

A comprehensive approach to family violence that acknowledges the common patterns between subtypes and recognizes the interrelationships among subfields is needed to advance the entire field of family violence. A comprehensive approach would increase general knowledge and understanding about family violence and ultimately provide direction for efforts aimed at preventing family violence.

An integrated synthesis of research findings is helpful in looking back over past findings and looking toward new ways of thinking about family violence. One area in the family violence literature that reflects a growing integrated focus is research examining children who experience multiple forms of maltreatment. Maltreated children are likely to suffer from multiple forms of abuse (physical, sexual, emotional) and neglect (see Ney et al., 1994). This integrated approach adds to our understanding because it emphasizes the interactive nature of the various forms of maltreatment.

CASE HISTORY: MONA, A MULTIPLY MALTREATED CHILD

Mona was 6 years old when she was referred to an inpatient psychiatric ward. She had tried to kill her stepbrother with a knife. An interview with Mona's father and stepmother revealed that Mona had only recently been removed from her biological mother's custody due to sexual abuse, neglect, and emotional abuse.

Mona's mother frequently left Mona and her 2-year-old sister locked in their apartment for days at a time with nothing more than water and a few boxes of cereal to eat. She often returned home drunk with strange men, some of whom had sexually molested Mona.

Mona's mother confessed that she did not like Mona and wanted to be rid of her child, feelings she freely shared with Mona.

Forms of Abusive Behaviors

The term *family violence* applies to a continuum of behaviors including physical aggression, sexual assault, neglect, financial exploitation, and many forms of psychological maltreatment such as verbal denigration, terrorizing, rejection, and exposing other family members to the observation of violence.

Characteristics of Perpetrators and Victims

Abusive interactions typically involve an individual who, by virtue of his or her physical size, strength, gender, status, or position, abuses or neglects another family member or intimate. Although the population of victims and perpetrators of family violence is heterogeneous, representing all races, genders, socioeconomic classes, and ages, some similarities span the various subtypes (e.g., child abuse, wife abuse) of violence.

Demographic Similarities. Certain demographic characteristics, nonetheless, occur with enough regularity to serve as risk factors for most types of family violence. Age is one such risk marker. Young parents and spouses are much more likely than older parents and spouses to mistreat family members and to expose children to violence (see Gelles, 1993b; Straus, Gelles, & Steinmetz, 1980).

Low Socioeconomic Status. Low socioeconomic status (SES) or economic hardship is another risk factor that characterizes perpetrators and victims of physical and sexual abuse, emotional maltreatment and neglect, courtship violence, and marital violence (e.g., Belknap, 1989; Hotaling & Sugarman, 1986; Sedlak, 1991).

Childhood Victimization. A third well-documented risk factor for adult perpetration of family violence is victimization during childhood. Adults physically abused as children are more likely to abuse their own children than adults not abused as children (Greenfeld,

1996). The same is true of adults sexually abused as children. Even exposure to parental violence during childhood is a risk factor for adult perpetration of family violence (e.g., Egeland, 1993; Hotaling & Sugarman, 1986; Straus, 1991a; Webersinn, Hollinger, & DeLamatre, 1991).

Criminality. Evidence continues to mount suggesting that violence against family members at home is an impetus to violence against strangers in the community (Straus, 1991a). A well-recognized long-term effect of PCA is criminal behavior (Widom, 1989). In fact, Spaccarelli, Coatsworth, and Bowden (1995) found that violent adolescent offenders had higher rates of exposure to serious physical abuse, and weapons violence between adults, than control groups. Several aspects of social learning appear to be involved in these findings (e.g., Eron, Huesmann, Lefkowitz, & Walder, 1987; Patterson, Reid, & Dishion, 1992). This strong finding that children and adolescents exposed to family violence are far more antisocial than those not exposed holds true for adult male batterers (Dutton & Starzomski, 1993; Hamberger & Hastings, 1986b). Another connection is evident in the overlap between wife abuse and criminal behavior among identified batterers (Dunford, Huizinga, & Elliott, 1990; Shields, McCall, & Hanneke, 1988). Finally, elder abusers frequently have criminal records (e.g., Anetzberger, 1987; Godkin, Wolf, & Pillemer, 1989; Kosberg, 1988).

Methodological Issues: Conducting Better Research

Family violence research suffers from a number of methodological limitations. Much of the problem is the nature of the subject matter and the populations studied. Because most family violence is never reported, data from official sources typically lead to underestimates of its prevalence (e.g., Miller, Cohen, & Wiersema, 1996; Straus et al., 1980). Access to victims is usually difficult, and their vulnerability raises many ethical dilemmas in working with them (Melton, 1990; Ohlin & Tonry, 1989; Weis, 1989). Perpetrators are often reluctant to discuss their own violent behavior. In addition, ideal experimental research designs (e.g., multiple informants) are rarely feasible, and long-term longitudinal studies are difficult and costly to conduct (Rosenbaum, 1988; Weis, 1989).

Fortunately, family violence researchers are becoming increasingly aware of these methodological shortcomings, and most are working to ameliorate the problems (e.g., Koss, 1989). Government agencies, in particular, have made headway in accumulating more accurate statistics and in providing the kinds of data needed by family violence researchers (e.g., Bachman & Saltzman, 1995; Greenfeld, 1996; Miller et al., 1996). The Bureau of Justice Statistics (BJS), for example, has changed its categorization of violent offenders (i.e., stranger vs. nonstranger) to intimates, acquaintances, and strangers. According to David Finkelhor (personal communication, August 18, 1995), it is further advisable for researchers conducting the National Crime Victimization Surveys (NCVS) to expand their samples to include persons younger than 12 years of age.

Definitional Issues

The most consistent methodological weakness across all areas of family violence is the difficulty defining terms such as *abuse, neglect, psychological abuse,* and *battering*. The relative importance of explicit definitional criteria, such as the specific behaviors involved, the severity or frequency of the act, the consequences of the act, and the intent of the perpetrator, often varies from one expert to the next. Distinctions between illegitimate and legitimate violence are also inherently subjective.

The ambiguous nature of family violence definitions has hindered attempts to understand and alleviate the problem. Without definitional consensus, it is challenging to determine how often various forms of family violence occur in society (see Valentin & Cash, 1986). When researchers employ broad definitions, rates of victimization are higher. When they use more circumscribed parameters, rates are lower. Definitional ambiguity not only confounds the interpretations of individual studies but also adds to the problem of making comparisons across studies.

Other uncertainties abound as well. The designation of certain victim groups, such as abused elders, for instance, remains indeterminate. The variability of abuse terms used by professional groups demonstrates another area of definitional ambiguity. Social workers, clinicians, legal professionals, police, government agencies, and researchers may all independently customize the terminology of family violence to meet their specific needs, yet these groups do not function wholly independently from each other in the real world. Clearer definitions of abuse would certainly enhance collaborative efforts made between groups (e.g., Reulbach & Tewksbury, 1994).

At the very least, researchers need to clearly articulate operational definitions in any given study. One suggestion is that experts meet in Delphi panels, following Hudson's (1991) procedure within the elder abuse field, to establish meaning through consensus after which they follow through to create standards for acceptable assessment techniques.

Measurement Issues

The definitional ambiguity so characteristic of family violence research also undermines measurement. In fact, scientists generally hold that the true meaning of a term is completely dependent on its stated measurement. Nowhere have the problems in measurement been more apparent than in the ongoing debate over the validity of the Conflict Tactics Scales (CTS; Straus, 1979). Experts disagree, for example, on the specific questions married couples should be asked. In addition to the frequency of violence, for example, should surveys attempt to measure the motives one might have for engaging in violence (e.g., self-defense, interpersonal control) or the consequences of violence (see Barnett, Lee, & Thelen, 1995; Cascardi, Langhinrichsen, & Vivian, 1992; Margolin, 1987; Saunders, 1988)?

Because of definitional variations and subsequent problems in measurement, data originating from police reports, social service and government agencies, and researchers' surveys of general and clinical populations all vastly differ. Lack of standardization also arises from the types of questions posed and who asks them (e.g., Bachman & Taylor, 1994). Although there are inevitable differences in frequency estimates based on official, agency, and self-report survey data, other distinctions seem more avoidable.

BJS statisticians, as one example, have made significant headway in reaching consensus in the measurement of sexual assault and rape. Using NCVS data based on a modified test of Koss's (1989) sexual aggression questionnaire (Bachman & Taylor, 1994), Bachman and

Saltzman (1995) reported data far more comparable to Koss's (1989) than obtained in previous years (see Peters, Wyatt, & Finkelhor, 1986, for a comparable change in CSA questionnaires). The test revisions not only contribute to more uniform estimates of abuse but also bring greater unanimity of meaning to terms such as *sexual assault* and *rape*. Congruity of this sort should become a goal within every subfield of family violence and, thus, within the field as a whole.

Sampling Problems

Obtaining large representative samples of individuals involved in family violence is extremely difficult. Most family violence studies either employ samples of victims of abuse, neglect, or spousal battering or gather samples of perpetrators who have committed these offenses. Such individuals are more likely to represent the extreme ends of the family violence continuum and may not be representative of the total population of family violence victims and perpetrators (Straus, 1991b).

An additional sampling concern common to all areas of family violence research is the contamination of samples. Researchers often fail to distinguish between various subgroups of victims (and subgroups of perpetrators) who are psychologically and demographically quite heterogeneous. In terms of child maltreatment, for example, they may "lump" together physically abused children with those who are victims of child neglect. In the same way, they may include incestuous and nonincestuous men in a single sample of sexual abusers. Such classification systems probably obscure important distinctions between subgroups.

A separate but related problem is the inability of researchers to establish truly accurate databases. Official data sources, such as the Uniform Crime Reports, include only those crimes that are reported to the police. Because most family violence is not reported, these records are unable to capture the vast extent of family violence. Surveys of self-reported violence (e.g., the National Family Violence Surveys; Straus & Gelles, 1986) and victimization surveys (e.g., NCVS) presumably estimate the amount of violence more precisely but are criticized on other levels (see Miller et al., 1996).

Establishing Cause-Effect Relationships

Most research in family violence is retrospective and correlational. In child abuse research, for example, adults are often asked to recall their childhood experiences of abuse. These retrospective accounts of abuse are then correlated with measurements of current psychological dysfunctions. Two difficulties with this method stem from memory deficits and from memory reconstructions. Even when retrospective accounts are accurate, two variables such as childhood abuse and depression may be correlated without necessarily being causally related. Certainly, the fact that child abuse victims are more likely than nonvictims to suffer from adult depression lends some support to the hypothesis that child abuse causes depression.

It is important to note, however, that other factors, such as living in a chaotic family environment or living without one's father in the home, rather than childhood abuse, might be the actual determinants of levels of depression. It is possible, in other words, that the correlation between childhood victimization and depression is spurious (i.e., accidental). Although researchers often have little choice but to conduct correlational studies, more methodologically sophisticated studies are needed to establish direct cause-and-effect relationships.

Recommendations for Improving Research

Recommendations for improving research in family violence primarily encompass definitional consensus, data collection, research design, and statistical approaches. There are several ways to improve data collection.

Government Support. One suggestion made in 1984 by the Attorney General's Task Force on Family Violence was that the federal government should collect family violence data on prevalence, incidence, and correlates of family violence (U.S. Department of Justice, 1984). With federal funding, large representative cross-cultural surveys could be conducted (Gartner, 1993; Wyatt, 1994)). The government could also establish central registers for police reports with greater efforts expended in developing uniform reporting standards. Finally, the government could establish a repository for archiving family violence data to avoid needless costs in recurrent data collection (Ohlin & Tonry, 1989).

Complex Research Designs. Another way to improve research and to establish more causal connections is through more complex research designs that include actual experimentation (Farrington, Ohlin, & Wilson, 1986). Some interesting approaches to date have included laboratory attempts to frustrate or sexually arouse abusive participants and compare their responses to nonabused controls who are also frustrated or sexually aroused (Follingstad, Kalichman, Cafferty, & Vormbrock, 1992; Malamuth, 1989). As an alternative, researchers are conducting longitudinal studies in other areas of family violence research where experimental designs are not ethically possible. Longitudinal studies on the effects of child maltreatment (e.g., poor problem-solving skills), for example, have recently appeared that will help to isolate cause-and-effect relationships (Erickson, Egeland, & Pianta, 1989; Everson, Hunter, Runyon, & Edelson, 1989).

Statistical Applications. Finally, application of statistical innovations should bring greater clarity to findings. Increased use of meta-analysis, for example, would help to summarize disparate findings (Sugarman & Hotaling, 1989). Similarly, the use of multivariate statistical procedures, which are capable of evaluating the multidimensional nature of family violence, should contribute to a more comprehensive view of the numerous factors that are involved in family violence (see Appendix A for a checklist of research requirements).

Integrating Theories

Scholars have proposed many theories to explain the various forms of family violence. Some theories are more specific in scope, focusing on topics such as family dysfunction, the transmission of maltreatment from one generation to the next, and psychopathology or dysfunction in the offender. Other theories are broader and focus on cultural and structural factors.

Single-Factor Theories

A number of these single-factor (univariate) theories apply to more than one subtype (e.g., PCA, CSA) of family violence although not equally across the areas. The correlates (e.g., age) of victimization and perpetration of family violence also reveal commonalities across the various forms. It is possible to group these single-factor theories along a nature-nurture dichotomy. A tripartite classification of behavioral causation specifies *biological, environmental,* and *learning* factors. Nature (biological), environmental (e.g., poverty), and interactional stress (e.g., dyadic conflict) explanations appeared early in the development of the field. The paragraphs below attempt to clarify the learning component of the nurture interpretation by organizing these univariate theories within a cognitive learning framework. Such an expansion and synthesis of single-factor theories should help account for violence throughout the entire field.

BIOLOGICAL FACTORS

One understudied area that is receiving more consideration is the role of biological factors in family violence. Studies have so far shown physiological differences among two groups of family violence perpetrators. PCA perpetrators show elevated physiological reactivity when responding to both negative and positive child stimuli (Milner & Chilamkurti, 1991). Male spouse abusers, in contrast, show less physiologically arousal during a quarrel, instead of more (Jacobson & Gottman, 1993). Genetic predispositions may also differentiate violent from nonviolent individuals (e.g., Mednick, Gabrielli, & Hutchings, 1987). Future research should continue this line of inquiry.

ENVIRONMENTAL FACTORS

Environmental (Structural) Stress Factors. Stress associated with unemployment, poverty, poor housing, family demands, and lack of social support (i.e., social isolation) contribute to victimization patterns across the entire field (e.g., Barnett, Fagan, & Booker, 1991; Boudreau, 1993; Whipple & Webster-Stratton, 1991; Wolfe, Jaffe, Wilson, & Zak, 1985). In fact, some experts have theorized that stress levels in elder abusers may be a major cause of abuse (Hinrichsen, Hernandez, & Pollack, 1992). Other environmental factors such as lead poisoning are highly associated with violence in delinquents and may yet prove to contribute to family violence in adolescents (Bower, 1996). Lead poisoning also is associated with low intelligence, a characteristic of many PCA abusers and some elder abusers (see Hunter, Kilstrom, Kraybill, & Loda, 1978; Kinderknecht, 1986).

Interactional and Relationship Stress Factors. Research in several areas has corroborated the role of interactional or relationship stress in elevating family violence. Negative parent-child interactions (Bousha & Twentyman, 1984; Department of Health & Human Services [DHHS], 1993) often characterize the relationships of abusive parents and their children. Research has also revealed high dyadic stress levels in violent dating partners, maritally abusive couples, and elder abusers (see Babcock, Waltz, Jacobson, & Gottman, 1993; Halicka, 1995; Johns & Hydle, 1995; Makepeace, 1987; Margolin, John, & Gleberman, 1988; Marshall & Rose, 1987; Pillemer & Finkelhor, 1988).

SOCIAL LEARNING THEORY

The extent to which social learning theory can account for family violence remains unsettled. There is indeed a substantial body of research showing that growing up in a violent family increases the probability that an individual will be physically or sexually violent as an adult (Egeland, 1993; Laws & Marshall, 1990). The link between childhood abuse and adult male battering is well established (Dutton, Van Ginkel, & Starzomski, 1995; Simons, Wu, & Conger, 1995). On the other hand, the fact that most people who grow up in violent families do not become violent and that many people who are violent were not raised in violent homes serves as a reminder that factors other than learning contribute to family violence (Kaufman & Zigler, 1993; Widom, 1989). Some of these opposed findings stem from studies lacking control groups (Widom, 1989) or from studies in which the link did not show up in adolescence but later in adulthood (Rivera & Widom, 1990).

A MORE COMPREHENSIVE LEARNING THEORY

Expanding social learning theory to incorporate other aspects of learning may resolve some of these issues. In the past, social learning models have relied most heavily on modeling of violent behaviors as the basic component that propels this intergenerational cycle of abuse. A few also have included conditioning through reward and punishment (see Spaccarelli et al., 1995, for a review). Apparently, however, no one has advanced a strictly cognitive theory to explain battering, although clinicians have frequently applied a cognitive-behavioral model to treatment (e.g., Hamberger & Barnett, 1995).

A cognitive learning theory could embrace a large number of violence-promoting beliefs, attitudes, or cognitive styles. These cognitions may be learned directly or indirectly in childhood and later be associated with an adult's levels of interpersonal violence (MacEwen, 1994). Children may learn, for example, that violence is an acceptable response to overwhelming negative inner personal feelings (attitude), or they may fail to learn adequate problem-solving skills (cognitions) (e.g., Jaffe, Wolfe, & Wilson, 1990). Such beliefs are manifested in personality traits, socialization, and the like. Assuming a cognitive learning foundation as the basis for the eight single-factor theories described below makes it possible to formulate a broader learning model to account for family violence.

1. Individual Personality Traits. Certain attitudes and feelings about the self may be the result of learning, although genetic predispositions cannot be ruled out. Low self-esteem provides an excellent illustration of apparent generational transmission. Abused children and those exposed to violence suffer from measurable deficits in self-esteem (e.g., Fredrich & Wheeler, 1982; Hughes, 1992; McKay, 1987). Several groups of perpetrators exhibit low self-esteem: (a) PCA and CSA perpetrators (see Groth, Birnbaum, & Gary, 1982; Milner & Chilamkurti, 1991), (b) batterers (Goldstein & Rosenbaum, 1985; Neidig, Friedman, & Collins, 1986), and (c) elder abusers (Godkin et al., 1989). Victim groups seem similarly afflicted: (a) PCA and CSA victims (Beitchman et al., 1992; Gross & Keller, 1992), (b) date rape victims (Resick, 1993), and (c) battered women following experience with severe abuse (Bowker, 1993; Cascardi et al., 1992).

Similar relationships exist in both victim and perpetrator groups for some other personality traits such as depression, anger control problems, and impulse control problems (see Bowker, 1993; Hamberger & Hastings, 1988; Kenning, Merchant, & Tomkins, 1991; Paveza et al., 1992). On a large personality inventory, the California Psychological Inventory (CPI; Gough, 1975), Barnett and Hamberger (1992) found that batterers clearly displayed different personality traits than non-batterers in intimacy, impulsivity, and problem-solving ability. Browne and Finkelhor (1986) found that depression was the most common long-term effect for CSA victims.

2. Holding Misperceptions.
The tendency for perpetrators to hold misperceptions about their victims seems to run the gamut of family violence situations as well. In sexual abuse, perpetrators' misperceptions of a child's consent and/or enjoyment seem to occur (see Seidman, Marshall, Hudson, & Robertson, 1994). In dating relationships, men who become aggressive often report believing that women wanted more sexual contact, whereas women maintained that they wanted less (Muehlenhard & Linton, 1987). Finally, in spouse abuse, violent husbands appear to misperceive their wives' communication and intentions (Holtzworth-Munroe & Hutchinson, 1993; Margolin et al., 1988).

3. Psychopathology.
Certain kinds of psychopathology are also characteristic of family violence offenders. In one sample of batterers, 44% obtained scores indicating some deviation from normal on the Minnesota Multiphasic Personality Inventory (MMPI; Hathaway & McKinley, 1940), whereas 56% of the batterers clustered in the normal range (Flournoy & Wilson, 1991; also see Hamberger & Hastings, 1986b). Elder abusers similarly exhibit elevated scores on measures of psychopathology (Glendenning, 1993; Taler & Ansello, 1985). PCA and CSA victims exhibit high levels of psychopathology as well (see Briere & Runtz, 1988; Gomes-Schwartz, Horowitz, & Cardarelli, 1990).

Post-traumatic stress disorder (PTSD), one possible result of traumatic victimization, is frequently diagnosed in CSA victims (Kendall-Tackett, Williams, & Finkelhor, 1993), date rape victims (Jones & Muehlenhard, 1994; Resick, 1993; Santello & Leitenberg, 1993), and battered women (Houskamp & Foy, 1991; Saunders, 1994).

4. Attachment Theory.
If learning theory were extended even further, it could also accommodate attachment theory (e.g., Bowlby, 1980; Dutton, Saunders, Starzomski, & Batholomew, 1994; Goldner, Penn, Sheinberg, & Walker, 1990; Mayseless, 1991). Insecurely attached individuals are emotionally dependent on others, yet fearful and angry, with their feelings easily triggered by situational factors such as perceived abandonment (see Dutton et al., 1994; Mayseless, 1991; Seidman et al., 1994). Emotional dependency stemming from insecure attachment provides an excellent explanation for the coexistence of love and violence and the failure to leave abusive relationships (e.g., Billingham, 1987; Dutton & Painter, 1981). Furthermore, personality characteristics (e.g., low self-esteem) have a fertile field for development within insecure parent-child relationships. Similarly, mothers who are psychologically unavailable, perhaps as a result of battering, may be less able to form secure attachments with their infants (Elbow, 1982; Hart & Brassard, 1987).

5. Patriarchal Factors.
The causal significance of patriarchy continues to be vigorously debated among family violence theorists. Whereas some scholars (e.g., Yllö & Straus, 1990) see a clear connection between patriarchy and societal acceptance of abuse of women and children, others downplay the significance of patriarchy. Dutton (1994) has recently claimed that there is a basic fallacy in attempting to predict individual behavior on the basis of broad cultural features. He cites three lines of evidence that suggest patriarchal explanations are of limited usefulness. Findings that the rate of female-to-male violence is high, that the rate of lesbian and gay violence is at least equal to heterosexual battering, and that only a small minority of men actually beat their wives weigh heavily against patriarchal interpretations (see Letellier, 1994; Renzetti, 1992; Straus & Gelles, 1986).

6. Male Socialization Factors.
Another reflection of broad cultural forces that has increasingly attracted attention is male socialization. Male socialization may help explain greater male involvement in CSA and battering, for example (see Finkelhor & Lewis, 1988; Levant, 1994). Levant et al. (1992) identified a number of traditional norms of masculinity that emerged after World War II, including avoiding all things feminine; restricting emotion; and displaying toughness, aggression, and self-reliance. Grusznski and

Bankovics (1990) capture some of the ethic of male socialization as follows: "When they were children and pushed down on the playground, it was their job to come up with a handful of gravel rather than [a face full of] tears" (p. 209). In terms of battering potential, the devaluation of women that sometimes accompanies the traditional masculine role justifies aggression toward women. The problem of devaluation of women continues, according to a New York Times Poll (Lewin, 1994). A telephone poll of 1,055 teenagers aged 13 to 17 showed that 59% of the boys thought girls were "lesser than themselves."

The emerging emphasis on male socialization has prompted a number of unusual trends. Some college campuses began offering men's studies courses to raise awareness about men's socialization issues (Salholz, Uehling, & Raine, 1986). Another fast-growing, evangelical Christian movement, titled Promise Keepers, preaches a regimen of marital responsibility, sexual purity, racial harmony, and help to other men to keep their promises. This male-only group, led by former Colorado football coach Bill McCartney, rents arenas like the Houston Astrodome for revival-type meetings. In this setting, men are allowed to express their emotions freely (Neill & McGraw, 1995).

7. Female Socialization Factors. Women's socialization also plays a role in family violence in several ways. Many cultures expect women to hold traditional values, to marry, to take responsibility for the quality of their marital relationships, to provide a home for their children, and to stay with their husbands through "thick and thin" (Ferguson, 1980). Women also learn to be emotionally dependent on men (Kalmuss & Straus, 1982; Strube & Barbour, 1983), and they frequently are economically dependent on men as well (e.g., Strube & Barbour, 1983). Women are socialized to place a high value on their relationships (Johnson, Crowley, & Sigler, 1992), and part of their identity hinges on their ability to make and maintain relationships (Miller, 1976, p. 83). Altogether, these factors play a strong role in women's decisions to stay with a male partner, even if he is violent.

8. Powerlessness. Women's socialization, children's immaturity, men's dominance, and discrimination against minority groups and the aging all combine to place these groups in a relatively powerless social position (e.g., Coleman & Straus, 1986). It is commonly argued that powerlessness contributes to violence because there are few potential costs of violence for powerful people who victimize powerless people. That is, powerless people lack the "resources to inflict costs on their attackers" (Gelles, 1983, p. 159). For example, children, lacking the resources to protect themselves, must turn to society (e.g., government, churches, synagogues) when parents do not protect them from abuse. In general, the more a society values its children, the less it will tolerate the victimization, and the more actively it will seek to protect them (Wurtele & Miller-Perrin, 1992).

Collectively, it is possible to conceptualize each of these single-factor theories (i.e., individual personality traits, misperceptions, psychopathology, attachment, patriarchy, male socialization, female socialization, and powerlessness) as being at least, in part, cognitively based and therefore elements of a cognitive model. Along with social learning theory (modeling) and direct conditioning (e.g., rewards and punishments), the addition of a purely cognitive component could form a general learning theory. This general learning model, taken together with biological and environmental factors, would then constitute a more comprehensive model of the major causative factors of family violence.

Multifactor Interactional Theories

Although many single-factor theories have proved valuable in explaining certain aspects of family violence, no individual factor or univariate model can fully explain family violence. Lack of success with univariate models, along with growing awareness of the multidimensional nature of family violence, led several researchers to propose multifactor

> ### No individual factor or univariate model can fully explain family violence.

interactional models for several forms of family violence (Belsky, 1993; Dutton, 1988; Lundberg-Love & Geffner, 1989; Riggs & O'Leary, 1989; Wurtele & Miller-Perrin, 1992). These models describe the process of abuse as a complex pattern of behaviors involving multiple ecological levels (e.g., individual, family, society) that interact with one another to contribute to violence.

First, there are individual factors associated with both the abusive individual and the victim that are considered risk factors for abuse. For the abuser, risk factors might be unemployment, low SES, childhood history of abuse, or substance abuse (e.g., Wurtele & Miller-Perrin, 1992). Certain victim characteristics such as developmental disabilities in children serve as risk factors for family violence (Ammerman, Van Hasselt, Hersen, McGonigle, & Lubetsky, 1989). Family factors including marital discord, unhappy family life, and divorce might also contribute to family violence (e.g., Rosenbaum & O'Leary, 1981a). Finally, societal and cultural factors such as societal acceptance of violence, corporal punishment, exploitation (e.g., child pornography), and patriarchy are likely to promote abuse as well (Straus et al., 1980).

Society's expenses include victims' unpaid medical and mental health care costs as well as police, fire, social services, and criminal justice processing.

In addition to the contribution of multiple interacting risk factors, researchers have also proposed that the balance in a particular situation, between risk factors and protective supports, determines whether family violence is likely to occur (Belsky, 1980; Cicchetti & Carlson, 1989; Wurtele & Miller-Perrin, 1992) An abusive childhood experience of the adult perpetrator, for example, might serve as a risk factor and contribute to violence. In contrast, protective factors such as having satisfying adult relationships may decrease the probability of family violence (Egeland, Jacobvitz, & Sroufe, 1988). Future research should assess the explanatory power of multidimensional models while focusing on risk factors and protective factors associated with each ecological level.

Preventing Family Violence

Nearly every expert in the field emphasizes the importance of preventing family violence rather than reacting to it after the fact (e.g., U.S. Advisory Board on Child Abuse and Neglect [ABCAN], 1993). Social agencies have adopted a crisis management approach instead of developing preventive measures. In discussing the problems in the child protection system, for example, Melton and Barry (1994) recently concluded, "The system responds to allegations, not to needs" (p. 5). The same could probably be said for all forms of family violence (e.g., Deitch, 1993). The social service system, in general, focuses on reporting and investigation to the exclusion of treatment and prevention.

Costs of Family Violence

Intrafamily abuse nearly always results in adverse consequences for the victims. Victims' monetary costs are mainly out-of-pocket expenses (e.g., medical costs), reduced productivity (i.e., at work, home, school), and nonmonetary costs (e.g., pain, suffering, loss of quality of life) (see Miller et al., 1996, for a review). Society's expenses include victims' unpaid medical and mental health care costs as well as police, fire, social services, and criminal justice processing.

Out-of-Pocket Costs. Payment for services to crime victims by mental health specialists (e.g., social workers, psychiatrists, psychologists) is an understudied area. These costs are the largest component of tangible losses for most forms of child abuse and rape. The costs of mental health care for the typical child sexual abuse victim, for example, are estimated to be $5,800, one of the highest amounts for any category of crime victims. Revenues for mental health care providers treating crime victims represent 10% to 20% of U.S. mental health care spending. In 1991, victim-related revenues were estimated to be $5.8 billion to $6.8 billion. Approximately half this amount was caused by crimes that year and the other half by child abuse in previous years (Miller et al., 1996).

Physical injury normally results in expensive emergency room care and other medical expenses (e.g., treatment of venereal disease) ("The Billion-Dollar Epidemic," 1992). Average medical care costs for an incident of PCA victimization are $790. Mental health care costs per victimization are approximately $2,700.

Reduced Productivity. Individuals incapacitated or unable to work as a result of family violence suffer a loss of productivity not only for themselves but also for their employers. A parent or guardian who must leave work to take an abused child to a doctor loses productivity. Short-term productivity losses for the average assault victim are estimated to be $356, whereas long-term productivity losses are estimated to be $2,035.

Nonmonetary Costs. Nonmonetary costs entail factors (e.g., fear, pain) that are the most difficult to estimate. PTSD may evoke lifelong anxiety and somatic effects. Some estimates of these intangible costs are based on jury compensation awards. Other types of estimates derive from expenses incurred in securing one's safety (e.g., security alarms). Each rape victimization, for example, costs an estimated $103,400 in "quality of life" expenses.

Costs to Society. There are numerous costs to society in addition to victim-incurred losses. Calls for medical treatment, police, welfare services, shelters, housing, child protective services, and adult protective services all require extensive tax-paid government funding (see Zorza, 1991, 1994). Social and victim services costs for each PCA victimization, for example, are $2,100 (Miller et al., 1996).

Advocate Groups

At the forefront of the struggle to prevent family violence are a number of advocacy groups. These groups are active in education, treatment, deterrence, and policy development. Advocates try to increase social costs by speaking out against the behavior they find egregious. Murray Straus (1994), for example, hopes to increase societal condemnation of spanking. Lenore Walker (1979) hopes to increase societal condemnation of wife assault. Some of the most visible groups working to end family violence are listed in the boxed insert titled "Advocating Violence-Free Families."

It seems reasonable to expect that societal investment in prevention can significantly affect the rate of family violence. Despite the relative recency of the "discovery" of family violence, the changing societal response to this problem has been quite dramatic. Commitments need to be made in all areas of family violence. Advocates maintain that one of the most important social changes needed to combat marital violence is for society to stop condoning it. There is a great need for education that conveys the message that family violence will not be tolerated (Kaci, 1990). "Private Citizens, corporate citizens, courts, the government, we all have to deliver the message to abusers," argues Michael Dowd of Pace University ("Focus—Call for Help," 1994). "We're not going to tolerate it anymore. You will be a pariah among us if you abuse a woman. We are not doing that today, and we have to begin."

Preventing family violence begins with social awareness and the recognition that expertise, energy, and money are needed to alleviate the conditions that produce family violence. Many experts maintain, however, that society has not yet made these commitments and that communities direct most of their resources toward responding to, rather than preventing, family violence. Fortunately, commitment to the prevention of family violence is growing, as evidenced by the many prevention strategies that are beginning to appear.

Around the world, governments are acknowledging the victimization of vulnerable people, including children, women, and elders (e.g., Heise, 1989; Holloway, 1994; Kosberg & Garcia, 1995b). Several recent examples illustrate the point that politicians regard family violence as a problem worthy of their consideration. Advocates for elders, for instance, recently convened in Washington for a White House Conference on Aging. Their recommendations included the following:

1. Encourage public and private partnerships to develop research studies.
2. Develop uniform definitions and a uniform reporting system at the state level.
3. Establish public and private partnerships to initiate a national education campaign.
4. Develop and implement training and continuing education programs.
5. Expand authority and resources for the long-term care ombudsman program and elder protective services.
6. Urge Congress to fully fund the Older American Act.
7. Found an elder abuse reporting hotline in each state (see National Committee for the Prevention of Elder Abuse, 1995).

Protecting women has likewise been the focus of political attention. In 1990, Delaware Senator Joseph Biden introduced the

ADVOCATING VIOLENCE-FREE FAMILIES

Advocacy groups play a significant role in preventing family violence. They may raise awareness about a particular problem, mobilize people to do something about the problem, and sometimes contribute funds to help alleviate the problem. Advocacy groups have taken many forms and represent a number of different concerns and ideologies.

Government-related groups. The federal government supports a number of organizations, such as the National Center on Child Abuse and Neglect (NCCAN). This agency receives funding from the U.S. Department of Health and Human Services. It undertakes many tasks such as providing grants for research on child abuse and neglect, funding resource centers that identify and organize information on child abuse and neglect, and advocating for child protection. The federal government also funds certain specific projects related to abuse (e.g., the Consortium for Elder Abuse Prevention). Most recently, the federal government opened a domestic abuse hotline ("HHS Awards," 1995) (see Appendix B for a list of organizations concerned with family violence).

Domestic violence coalitions. Another type of advocacy group, the coalition, is represented by the National Coalition Against Domestic Violence (NCADV) and the National Coalition Against Sexual Assault (NCASA). The concerned citizens who establish and maintain coalitions may advocate for family violence in a number of ways. They frequently establish community shelters, provide 24-hour hotlines to handle crisis situations, offer support groups for victims, and provide counseling for victims and perpetrators. In addition, they usually sponsor training of professionals and community leaders. They may also attempt to procure special free or low-cost services for victims (e.g., dental or medical care). Many such advocates help provide research participants, and others work with universities to offer supervised clinical internships and volunteer activities. They often hold conferences and publish educational newsletters and pamphlets. Because funding for these services is nearly always meager, coalitions usually recruit dues-paying members, hold rallies, solicit donations, and sell items such as Christmas cards.

Specialized organizations. Closely allied to the coalitions are organizations focused on particular problems. One such group is the National Organization for Victim Assistance (NOVA). This group lists as its major goal advocacy for victims of crime and crises so that victims are treated with compassion and respect. NOVA offers direct assistance to victims and training for service providers and allied professionals. Activities are funded through membership dues, donations, silent auctions, guest appearances by celebrities, book signings, and the like (see Appendix B for a list of domestic violence resources).

Law and policy groups. Lawyers and other individuals concerned with legislative approaches to the prevention of family violence occasionally form law and policy centers. Many of these groups attempt to track current laws (often state by state) and to evaluate their implementation and outcomes. They focus on divorce and mediation laws, rape laws, and laws concerning orders of protection. Based on their findings, such groups usually formulate new policies and accompanying legislation. They work with legislative advocates who lobby in state legislatures. They also recruit attorneys for pro bono work and collaborate with academicians and others to publish books and articles. To pay for their activities, these groups might recruit members, send newsletters, sell bibliographies, and address community and professional gatherings.

Sometimes, formal organizations appoint subcommittees to investigate specific problems. One prominent policy center is the American Bar Association, Center on Children and Law. The explicit goal of the center is to protect children and to strengthen the family through its influence on public policy. The center recently launched a new 3-year project (funded by the Freddie Mac Foundation) to assist court systems throughout the United States in assessing their performance in child abuse and neglect cases, and to implement plans that will result in court proceedings that are speedier and more fair ("ABA Center," 1995).

Clearinghouses. Some advocacy groups specialize in providing information through clearinghouses. One of the most notable efforts is the Family Violence and Sexual Assault Institute in Tyler, Texas. This clearinghouse categorizes both published and unpublished research articles, reviews books and media, sells some books and pamphlets, announces conferences and grants, produces specialized bibliographies, publishes articles, and operates a speaker's bureau.

Specialized professional groups. Although not truly advocacy groups, some professionals are responding to the problem of domestic violence by volunteering their expertise. Illustrative of this activity is a group of plastic surgeons who have banned together to repair women's faces damaged by battering (Reed, Weinstein, & Bane, 1996).

RECENT IMPROVEMENTS IN
RESPONDING TO FAMILY VIOLENCE

1. All 50 states have enacted mandatory reporting laws for suspected child abuse (Myers & Peters, 1987).
2. Two thirds of children report "involvement" in victimization prevention programs (Finkelhor & Dziuba-Leatherman, 1994).
3. A 1995 child care bill will provide $20 million for improving state criminal history records to facilitate background checks of persons seeking work in child care centers ("Child Care Bill," 1995).
4. Some states are assembling a photo index of convicted child molesters to give the public more access to information about sex offenders in their communities (see Boxall, 1996).
5. All but 3 of the 50 states have eliminated marital exemption laws for rape (Small & Tetreault, 1990).
6. Many states now mandate arrest in domestic violence cases (Ford, 1991).
7. The Violence Against Women Act, a $1.6 billion inclusion in the Clinton administration's 1994 crime bill, has provided funding to bolster the criminal justice system's response to violence against women ("Washington Report," 1995).
8. Researchers and governments in other nations have become more involved during the past decade (Kosberg & Garcia, 1995b).

Violence Against Women Act, legislation designed to raise awareness about the "national tragedy" of violence against women (Biden, 1993). This legislation, which was ultimately included in the Clinton administration's crime bill, provides $1.6 billion to various endeavors designed to protect women from victimization ("Crime Bill," 1994). The United Nations Convention on the Rights of the Child also recently addressed the issue of child protection worldwide (Krugman, 1995). (See boxed insert: "Recent Improvements in Responding to Family Violence.")

It is possible that these factors and others may have contributed to decreasing rates of many forms of family violence. Support for this statement comes, at least in part, from an analysis of the historical record of past maltreatment of women and children (DeMause, 1974; Dobash & Dobash, 1979; Pleck, 1987). Additional confirmation comes from the National Violence Surveys, which suggest a decrease in the rate of self-reported child abuse and marital violence from 1975 to 1985 (Straus & Gelles, 1986). The topic is controversial, nonetheless, because the volume of official reports continues to soar (Bloom, 1996).

Targeting Potential Victims and Perpetrators

There are many ongoing prevention efforts that are representative of current approaches directed at potential victims and perpetrators, at-risk families, and society more generally.

School-Based Programs for Children. During the 1980s, school-based empowerment programs to help children avoid and report victimizations became popular (Finkelhor & Dziuba-Leatherman, 1994). School-based programs generally teach children knowledge and skills believed to be important in protecting themselves from a variety of dangerous situations. Such programs have obvious appeal because they are an inexpensive, easy way to reach most school-age children, who for the most part are eager to learn (Daro & McCurdy, 1994). In 1991, Breen, Daro, and Romano (cited in Finkelhor, Asdigian, & Dziuba-Leatherman, 1995) reported the results of a 1990 survey of elementary school districts, which revealed that 85% of districts offered education programs, with 65% of those education programs mandated. Finkelhor and Dziuba-Leatherman (1995) conducted the National Youth

Victimization Intervention Study, a telephone survey of 2,000 children and their caretakers, and found that 67% of children reported being exposed to victimization programs, with 37% of the children reporting participation within the past year.

Research evaluations of school-based programs suggest that, in general, exposure to victimization programs increases knowledge and protection skills (Daro & McCurdy, 1994; Wurtele & Miller-Perrin, 1992). The National Youth Victimization Prevention Study, for example, found that children who were exposed to comprehensive school-based prevention programs, compared with children who had not been exposed or who were only minimally exposed, were more knowledgeable about the dangers of sexual abuse and more effectively equipped with protection strategies. Unfortunately, no research has demonstrated a decline in the actual number of victimizations (Finkelhor et al., 1995). There is also speculation, but little evidence, that school-based victimization programs might lead to increased disclosures by victimized children (Daro & McCurdy, 1994; Wurtele & Miller-Perrin, 1992).

Educating Young Adults About Partner Violence and Date Rape. A number of women's advocates have conjectured about where prevention of courtship violence, date rape, and later marital violence should begin. For some, the obvious starting point is in the schools (Levy, 1991). Exposing high school and college students to courtship violence awareness programs, for example, may be a feasible approach to preventing family violence, in general, and later marital violence, in particular (Cate, Henton, Koval, Christopher, & Lloyd, 1982; Murphy & O'Leary, 1987; Roscoe & Benaske, 1985). Most campus educational programs focus on attitude change, hoping to communicate that violence should not be an accepted element of interpersonal relationships and that nonviolent resolution strategies are available (Roscoe & Benaske, 1985).

Advocates suggest several specific ways these goals might be accomplished, including human relations workshops to teach nonviolent conflict resolution tactics, creation of shelters and dating violence hotlines, and education of student services personnel to better identify individuals at risk of being involved in dating violence (Sugarman & Hotaling, 1989). According to Billingham (1987), broader intervention strategies might begin with raising awareness among college

staff (e.g., housing directors, administrators, students) through media campaigns. He further suggests that conducting a survey of the level of violence on campus would be beneficial in making the problem relevant to a particular campus—"It's happening here and now." General information programs such as workshops, guest lectures, posters, brochures, and newspaper articles are techniques that are increasingly being employed in an attempt to educate the campus community about why dating violence occurs and where to find help.

Some experts believe that educational programs have the potential to reduce rates of date rape. Increased awareness of date rape and its causes could potentially promote inhibition factors and increase victims' resistance (Lundberg-Love & Geffner, 1989). Muehlenhard and Linton (1987), for instance, urge that campus programs present educational information, including sex education; endeavor to enhance women's self-defense strategies; and offer assertiveness training. Others maintain that programs aimed at male collegians should attempt to alter rape tolerance and acceptance of rape myths (Lenihan, Rawlins, Eberly, Buckley, & Masters, 1992). Individuals who do not accept rape myths are less likely to blame rape victims, and myths often excuse culpability in the mind of the rapist (Janssens & Kopper, 1993; Lonsway & Fitzgerald, 1994).

Presently, researchers have evaluated very few education programs. One program that has undergone systematic appraisal is a Canadian high school prevention program that used a half-day workshop format featuring 22 topics such as date rape, male issues in relationships, and anger control. Workshops and auditorium programs featured various videos, enactments, and classroom discussions. Students selected and attended two of the workshops. Pretest-posttest differences showed positive knowledge and many appropriate changes in attitudes toward behaviors like forced sex (Sudermann & Jaffe, 1993). A similar program with Canadian high school students achieved similar results (Lavoie, Vezina, Piche, & Boivin, 1995). Without doubt, more assessment research is necessary (see Seidman, 1987).

Education for Elder Abuse Prevention. One slightly different educational effort is centered in communities. Groups of professionals meet with elders to inform them about the existence of elder abuse, how to avoid it (e.g., writing wills, fraud protection), and what to do about it (Weiner, 1991).

Training Professionals. More and more, experts are urging that mental health professionals obtain more training to encourage them to be on the alert for family violence. When professionals encounter a child with poor social skills, for example, they might ask about the possibility of family violence and, at the very least, inform parents about its negative consequences for children (Kenning et al., 1991). Several problems came to light in Chapter 6 about children exposed to marital violence that were related to inadequate training of professionals (Tomkins et al., 1994). One omission was that shelter workers seldom refer clients to child protective services because the protective agencies are already overloaded with abused children (Carlson, 1984). Even if told about a child's exposure, shelter workers seldom notify police because police so frequently hold the opinion that this type of abuse is not a real problem (Tomkins et al., 1994).

Training is especially needed in terms of promoting interagency collaboration (Nerenberg, 1995; Reulbach & Tewksbury, 1994; Tomkins et al., 1994). When police, lawyers, and mental health professionals work together, the improvement in outcomes is dramatic. In a study of elder abuse, for example, interagency collaboration led to a 300% increase in reports (Reulbach & Tewksbury, 1994). In 1995, a special government publication summarized productive collaborations between police, district attorneys, physicians, and child protective services personnel handling child abuse cases in San Diego, California (Smith, 1995).

Another group of professionals in need of training are judges working with family violence cases (ABCAN, 1995). In terms of spouse abuse, judges have not only displayed a hands-off policy but also a gender bias that works against women (Hofford & Harrell, 1993; National Center on Women and Family Law, Inc., 1994). Judges supervising elder guardianship cases need to establish better monitoring practices that protect elders' financial assets (Zimny & Diamond, 1993). Custody issues are another area where judges need training (Pagelow, 1992). Fortunately, the National Council of Juvenile and Family Court Judges is an excellent resource for pamphlets and books for educating the judiciary (National Council of Juvenile and Family Court Judges, 1995).

Increasing Perpetrator Costs (Deterrence). As noted throughout the book, the costs of family violence have historically been quite low. Before the 20th century, in fact, there were few social or legal consequences for family violence. Although the costs to the offender have undoubtedly risen in recent years, there is reason to believe that family violence still remains one of the least costly violent crimes in America. Experts estimate that less than 10% of all domestic assaults, for example, are reported to the police. This pattern holds even for cases where serious injury is involved. All too often, critics continue to argue, police approach domestic violence cases with the intent of "handling the situation" rather than enforcing the law (Buzawa & Buzawa, 1993).

The social costs of family violence are also low. Although there is considerable social stigma attached to designations like child molester, child abuser, or wife batterer, most family abusers manage to avoid stigmatizing labels (see Greenfeld, 1996). The history of violence between O.J. and Nicole Simpson serves as a good example of the limited social costs associated with family violence. There was no outcry of public condemnation when

---

> **When police, lawyers, and mental health professionals work together, the improvement in outcomes is dramatic.**

O.J. pleaded no contest to spousal assault in 1989. He was not, at least in society's eye, a "wife beater." In July of the same year, in fact, NBC hired Simpson as a football analyst and the Hertz rental car company retained Simpson as an advertising spokesperson. Would society's reaction toward O.J. Simpson have been different had he been accused of using marijuana, or revealed that he was homosexual, or used a racial slur, or assaulted someone other than his wife?

Most researchers and advocates agree that increasing social costs of family violence would result in decreasing rates of family violence. There is little agreement, however, concerning exactly how the costs should be increased.

The value of increasing legal costs to the perpetrator is also a matter of considerable dispute. The debate centering around the

Minneapolis Police Experiment and the subsequent replication has produced more questions than answers (Berk, Campbell, Klap, & Western, 1992; Dunford et al., 1990; Sherman, Smith, Schmidt, & Rogan, 1992). Although imprisonment may have an insufficient deterrent effect, it seems premature to abandon completely a deterrence strategy to family violence prevention. There is some evidence that arrest deters violent offenders who have a lot to lose such as marital status or employment (Sherman et al., 1992). Although arrest may have little measurable effect on the behavior of an individual perpetrator, efforts to increase the costs of family violence in general (e.g., social and legal costs) may ultimately lead to a decrease in family violence in general.

A society that refuses to tolerate a behavior is likely to produce fewer people who engage in the behavior. Therefore, as society increasingly condemns normative violence in society and in the family (as it has increasingly condemned the exploitation of women, children, and elders), and as it increasingly sanctions violent family offenders, the cumulative effect should be less violence in the family (Williams, 1992).

Providing More Victim Support. Victim support groups and shelters for battered women are also important in preventing family violence. These groups serve to educate and empower victims who might feel trapped in abusive relationships (Johnson, 1980; Sedlak, 1988b).

Targeting At-Risk Families

CASE HISTORY: EMMANUELLE'S LACK OF SUPPORT

Emmanuelle, an 18-year-old high school senior, was desperate. The father of her child had abandoned her, she was unable to support herself and her child with her waitressing job, and her family was unwilling to help. With nowhere to turn, she left her 2½-year-old child at a Brooklyn hospital with a note:

"To Whom It May Concern: I am an 18-year-old student and I also work. I can't handle the pressure. I sometimes take it out on her. I love her and would not like to hurt her. Please find her a good home where she'll have the love she deserves."

The next day, Emmanuelle realized she had made a mistake and called the hospital to ask for her baby back. When she arrived, she was arrested and charged with child abandonment (Fontana & Moohnan, 1994).

* * *

For Fontana and Moohnan (1994), the case of Emmanuelle illustrates the need for intervention rather than punishment. Emmanuelle was a young mother with no support. When her cries for help were not heard, she chose to abandon her baby. With help, she might have been able to care for her child, whereas prosecuting her merely put "one more young woman in jail and another child in the city's already overstretched foster care system" (p. 229). In addition, Emmanuelle's situation sent a message to other needy parents: "Don't dare come out and ask for help, because you'll be thrown into prison and your baby will be taken away! Stay in your closet and beat up your kid or get rid of her. You'll be safer that way!" (p. 229).

From this perspective, perhaps the best way to prevent family violence is to meet the needs of at-risk families (see Earle, 1995). This is an especially popular perspective for child abuse because many abusive and neglectful parents may not know how to be good parents. They may be young and immature, have economic pressures, and be socially isolated. Maritally violent couples may be similarly afflicted.

Parental Competency Programs. Parental competency programs, or home visitation programs, connect parents with a mentor who can provide social support and parenting suggestions. Most programs attempt to identify high-risk parents (i.e., young, low income) and intervene before the first child is born (Daro & McCurdy, 1994). Parental competency programs are gaining considerable support (for a review, see Daro & McCurdy, 1994; Wurtele & Miller-Perrin, 1992). ABCAN cited home visitation as the one policy that the government could implement right now that could make a difference (Krugman, 1995). In 1992, the National Committee to Prevent Child Abuse teamed up with the Ronald McDonald Children's Charities and started the Healthy Families of America (HFA) program. HFA, a home visitation program that is active in 60 communities, is an important part of the long-term family support strategy in many states. HFA services, which are provided by volunteers, generally begin before birth, are intensive (at least once a week), and provide social support for parents as well as instruction on parenting and child development ("Healthy Families," 1994).

Encouraging Violence-Free Relationships. Those who focus on marital violence prevention have likewise suggested that prevention efforts occur as early as possible (i.e., before people are in a position to be violent) (Levy, 1984). For example, Skills for Violence Free Relationships (SVFR), which targets 13- to 18-year-olds, challenges sex-role attitudes and teaches nonviolent conflict resolution strategies (Rybarik, Dosch, Gilmore, & Krajewski, 1995). Jaffe, Suderman, Reitzel, and Killip (1992) documented favorable changes in attitudes, behavior, and intentions following a large-scale, secondary school primary prevention program for violence in intimate relationships. Jaffe, Hastings, and Reitzel (1992) make several recommendations for schools such as training personnel to recognize the behavior of children exposed to domestic abuse and teaching children conflict resolution skills. Because of the possibility of child endangerment, schools may give greater attention to children from violent homes by offering special marital violence classes (Stagg, Wills, & Howell, 1989).

Awareness Within Society

Prevention of family violence begins with its recognition by society. The origin of violence often remains invisible because family members are reluctant to report it and professionals do not detect it, or often fail to report it when they do realize it has occurred (Kosberg, 1988). Societal-level solutions are often the most difficult to articulate as well as to implement. It is commonly argued, for example, that family violence solutions must begin with an emphasis on the various social ills that directly or indirectly influence family violence like poverty, unemployment, and inadequate housing (Gelles & Straus, 1988). It is reasonable to assume that a societal commitment to eliminating these problems would be, at least indirectly, a commitment to eliminating family violence (Pearl, 1994).

Although a discussion of large-scale economic and social causes of marital violence is beyond the scope of this chapter, there are a few significant broad cultural solutions worth noting. There appears to be considerable agreement, at least on a theoretical level, that "violence begets violence." That is, societal acceptance and glorification of violence, the victimization of children, and marital violence all contribute to the level of violence in society (see Eron et al., 1987). Although there is considerable debate about the specifics of the "violence begets violence" thesis, there are numerous examples that appear to confirm its principles.

1. Children who grow up in a climate of violence, either as abused children or as observers of abuse, are more likely to commit acts of violence when compared to children who have not grown up in a climate of violence (Spaccarelli et al., 1995; "Violence in Families," 1995).
2. Abused children are more aggressive toward their peers than comparison children (Graziano & Mills, 1992).
3. The more children are spanked, the more likely they are to be violent toward their siblings, commit juvenile delinquency and serious crimes, and to be abusive spouses or abusive parents (Straus, 1991c).
4. Children and young adults who are exposed to violent television display more aggression than children in control groups (Eron et al., 1987).

Like so many other areas, of social science research, the causal pathway between societal ills and family violence is difficult to establish definitively. Does media violence, for example, cause societal violence or is it merely a reflection of society's interest in violence? Despite some degree of uncertainty surrounding the relationship between social acceptance of violence and victimization, many authors argue that targeting societal acceptance of violence and victimization is necessary to help prevent family violence (e.g., Gelles & Straus, 1988).

Media Violence. It is impossible to determine how much of the responsibility for family violence should be placed on the media. On the one hand, explanations of family violence that reduce the problem of violence in the media are oversimplifying a very complex issue. As research on the relationship between television and violence increases, however, the potential causal significance of the media becomes more difficult to ignore.

According to Comstock and Strasburger (1990), the "now-sizable literature—over 1,000 articles, including reviews—gives considerable empirical support to the hypothesis that exposure to TV violence increases the likelihood of subsequent aggressive or antisocial behavior" (p. 32).

This conclusion has gained considerable support, and today it is common to hear politicians of all persuasions denounce media violence. In February 1996, President Bill Clinton signed into law a telecommunications bill that, among other things, will require that all television sets be equipped with a "V chip." The V chip will allow parents to block violent television programming they deem unacceptable (Zoglin, 1996). Of course, use of the V chip may not immediately reduce violence, but for those who decry the effects of television violence, it is seen as a step in the right direction.

Spanking. Spanking is another form of culturally accepted violence that is so common that it remains largely unnoticed. In one survey of 679 college students, the overwhelming majority of the respondents had been spanked (93%), believed spanking works (69%), believed parents should have the right to spank (85%), and plan to spank their own children (83%) (Graziano & Namaste, 1990). Despite this overwhelming societal acceptance, social scientists and advocates have shown an increasing willingness to condemn its use, not only because it may contribute to subsequent violence, but also because it is wrong in and of itself (see Finkelhor & Dziuba-Leatherman, 1994; Graziano, 1994; Straus, 1994).

Experts point to several specific problems with spanking (see boxed insert: "Ten Myths That Perpetuate Corporal Punishment"). For some, there is an inherent contradiction between the ideal of the loving parent and the purposeful violence of corporal punishment (Graziano, 1994; Straus, 1994). In addition, corporal punishment can and often does become abuse when parents are especially angry or stressed. Other parents may be punishing their children in ways they deem acceptable, but that society might condemn. This definitional vagueness provides parents substantial latitude that some maintain contributes to abuse (Graziano, 1994). Perhaps most significant of all, legitimate forms of violence (e.g., corporal punishment) may "spill over" into other condemned forms of violence (Straus, 1994).

There are signs that the general public is listening to these criticisms of corporal punishment. Although the level of acceptance of corporal punishment remains high, the trend is for fewer and fewer parents to spank their children. Daro and Gelles (1992) surveyed a nationally representative sample of 1,250 adults each year between 1987 and 1992. Results indicated that the majority (71%-75%) of the public view physical punishment as harmful to children. Although 53% of parents reported spanking or hitting their children in 1992, rates of spanking or hitting declined 17% between 1988 and 1992. In addition, most states have banned corporal punishment in the public schools, and in some Scandinavian countries it is even criminalized (Finkelhor & Dziuba-Leatherman, 1994).

Social Service Agencies. Responding to abuse is a challenging assignment for social work practitioners (Braun, Lenzer, Shumacher-Mukai, & Snyder, 1993). Underfunding of social service agencies has led to a crisis in care for victims and abusers (Goldsmith, 1996). According to ABCAN (1993), the system is failing. At least 21 states are under court supervision because they failed to take proper care of children who had been abused or neglected (Pear, 1996). Referring specifically to child abuse, for example, Wekerle and Wolfe (1993) argue that "current laws and priorities across North America are such that protection agencies have fewer and fewer resources to assist those families who have not, as yet, been identified as being in violation of any common standards" (p. 502).

Additionally, laws and policies are sometimes counterproductive. Several experts, for example, have advised against family unification as a major goal (Gelles, 1993b). The true story of 6-year-old Elisa Izquierdo (in boxed insert titled "Personalizing Family Violence Research" in Chapter 1) exemplifies the tragedies that can result (Van Biema, 1995). Although uncommon at this level, mistreatment of children by their foster parents does occur (Spencer & Knudsen, 1992).

Resources for Those Needing Help and Survivors

Brief overviews of professional treatment modalities for victims and offenders have appeared throughout the chapters. Victims themselves, friends of victims, and even pro-

TEN MYTHS THAT PERPETUATE CORPORAL PUNISHMENT

In his recent book *Beating the Devil Out of Them: Corporal Punishment in American Families,* Murray Straus (1994) offers the most comprehensive statement to date on the problems of spanking as a discipline technique. A summary of the myths surrounding corporal punishment is provided below.

Myth 1: Spanking works better. According to Straus, there is no evidence that spanking works better than other forms of discipline. What little research has been conducted, in fact, suggests that spanking may be less effective than nonviolent forms of discipline (e.g., "time out" or a lost privilege).

Myth 2: Spanking is needed as a last resort. If one accepts the argument that spanking is no better than other forms of discipline, then it stands to reason that there would be no situations when spanking would be necessary. Straus argues that much of the time parents resort to hitting, they are doing so out of their own frustration. Essentially, they are sending a message to the child that if one is angry, hitting is justified.

Myth 3: Spanking is harmless. According to Straus, hitting is so firmly entrenched in our culture that it is very difficult for us to admit that it is wrong. To do so would be to admit that our parents were wrong or we were wrong. The evidence suggests, however, that on average, spanking does more harm than good. Certainly, most people who were spanked "turn out fine," but this fact does not disprove the general pattern. The fact that most smokers do not die of lung cancer does not disprove the evidence on the harmful effects of smoking.

Myth 4: One or two times won't cause any damage. It is true that the evidence suggests that spanking is most harmful when it is frequent and severe. However, if spanking is harmful in large quantities, how can it be good in small quantities?

Myth 5: Parents can't stop without training. Eliminating spanking would be easy, Straus maintains, if society would embrace the belief that a child should never be hit. Parent educators and social scientists are reluctant to take this stand, however, because of the belief that parents cannot be expected to stop unless they are presented with alternative parenting techniques. Straus maintains, however, that parents do not need training in alternative parenting techniques; they simply need to embrace the belief that spanking is wrong. Everyone agrees, for example, that demeaning or insulting language (i.e., psychological abuse) is wrong and no one argues that parents cannot be expected to change without training. "Rather than arguing that parents need to learn certain skills before they can stop using corporal punishment," Straus (1994) argues, "I believe that parents are more likely to use and cultivate those skills if they decide or are required to stop spanking" (p. 156).

Myth 6: If you don't spank, your children will be spoiled or run wild. It is true that some children who are not spanked run wild, but it is equally true that some children who are spanked run wild. The key to having well-behaved children is being a consistent disciplinarian, not a physical disciplinarian.

Myth 7: Parents spank rarely or only for serious problems. It is true that many parents perceive that they reserve spanking for serious problems, but Straus maintains that parents simply do not realize how often they hit their child. This is especially true for parents who use spanking as their primary discipline technique.

Myth 8: By the time a child is a teenager, parents have stopped. The National Family Violence Surveys indicate that over one half of parents of 13- and 14-year-olds had hit their child in the previous 12 months. With teenagers, the punishment is more likely to be a slap to the face than to the bottom.

Myth 9: If parents don't spank, they will verbally abuse their children. Parents who spank frequently are actually more likely to be verbally abusive.

Myth 10: It is unrealistic to expect parents never to spank. Straus asks why it is unrealistic to expect husbands not to hit their wives. Why is violence unacceptable among strangers, but acceptable between a parent and child? Criminalizing spanking is probably not feasible, but progress can be made "by showing parents that spanking is dangerous, that their children will be easier to bring up if they do not spank, and by clearly saying that a child should never, under any circumstances, be spanked" (Straus, 1994, p. 162).

OLD QUESTIONS—NEW FRONTIERS

Legal Frontiers
1. *Children who kill.* A child kills an abusive parent after years of abuse and is tried for murder. What should be society's response?
2. *Elder care responsibility.* Who is responsible to ensure the well-being of parents, especially abusive parents?
3. *Battered women's rights.* Can battered women, as a class, be denied health care or insurance? Can battered women be fired because of their abuse?
4. *Child molesters' continued incarceration.* Is it legal for a panel of experts or a jury to determine that a molester is too dangerous to be released to society after he or she has served a prison term for conviction ("Sexual Predator," 1996)?

Ethical Dilemmas: Conflicts Related to Parent-Parent or Parent-Child Rights
1. *Parental kidnapping.* One parent kidnaps a child from the other. A child is taken without prior knowledge or consent of the custodial parent.
2. *Adoptive versus biological parents' rights.* A biological parent tries to reclaim a child after abandonment and subsequent adoption of the child (Alexander, 1996).
3. *Conception rights.* A woman conceives under unusual circumstances, such as by using sperm from a sperm bank. A surrogate parent gives birth to a nonbiological child.
4. *A child's rights to adoption after abandonment by a biological parent.* A biological parent prevents a child he or she has previously abandoned or been unable to care for from being adopted or from having an adoptive family.

Lesser-Known Frontiers
1. *Sibling abuse.* Brothers and sisters abuse each other. Very little is known about sibling abuse. Should society overlook sibling abuse as normative?
2. *Adolescent physical and sexual abuse offenders.* An adolescent in the family physically abuses or sexually molests a younger relative.
3. *Child-to-parent abuse.* An adolescent physically abuses a parent.

fessionals, however, may profit from knowing about other available resources (see Berry, 1996). In addition to access to national organizations and state coalitions, there are a number of professional and popular books and manuals. Some of these references center on the needs of particular groups, like abusive men, individuals involved in gay and lesbian battering, and victims within various ethnic groups. Others focus on special problems, like health issues, legal concerns, or government policies (see Appendix C for a list of related books).

Anticipating Tomorrow's Research Topics

Although this text has covered a wide spectrum of topics and presented numerous research findings, there appear to be a number of additional questions yet to be resolved. Several problems related to family violence require new research, as well as the adoption of national and international policies. The boxed insert titled "Old Questions—New Frontiers" presents a brief list of what lies ahead.

One area of study just over the horizon is children who kill their parents. These children most often come from violent families. Because such children are most often teenagers, parricide will probably fall within the

---

ADOLESCENT PARRICIDE

Adolescent parricide is a rare event that most often occurs in extremely dysfunctional, abusive, and alcoholic families where the adolescent cannot escape. Psychopathology in such families is almost routine (Toch, 1995). Very frequently, offenders have seriously considered murdering their parents for several years before they finally do.

Between 1977 and 1986, more than 300 parents were killed annually, according to Heide's (1987) search of the FBI Supplementary Homicide Reports. Somewhat less than a third of all (male and female) adolescent parricide offenders (APOs) are under 18 years of age (Daly & Wilson, 1988). The most typical APO is a white, non-Hispanic male under the age of 30.

Even so, it is ill advised to assume that APOs are all the same. One system classifies APOs into three typologies: (a) the severely abused child, (b) the severely mentally ill child, and (c) the dangerously antisocial child. Although one of these typologies may be paramount in a particular case, the classifications are not mutually exclusive (Heide, 1995).

The most typical scenario is the case of the severely abused adolescent living in an intolerable situation who sees no other way out (Morris, 1985). All too often, children with documented abuse histories have been returned to their parents. According to Metz (1994), court documents "show with heartbreaking redundancy the failed efforts of children to get help from authorities" (p. 36) before they murdered a parent. One Arizona judge totally disregarded the plight of a teenage girl whose father had sexually assaulted her before he went to bed. The judge stated that whatever the father did before he retired was "immaterial" to the daughter's defense. Children under age 16 who would prefer leaving to murdering cannot really survive on their own. They cannot work and they must go to school (Wadlington, Whitebread, & Davis, 1983).

One of the most widely publicized cases of parricide involved 16-year-old Richard and 17-year-old Deborah Jahnke of Cheyenne, Wyoming. The two teenagers premeditated the murder of their father and killed him on his arrival home from an anniversary dinner with his wife of 20 years. Richard Jahnke, an IRS agent, physically abused the entire family, terrorized them with guns and threats and sexually abused Deborah. Richard had previously sought relief by contacting a child protective agency, but the agency mishandled the case.

Despite Richard's conviction of involuntary manslaughter, over 4,000 community residents wrote to the judge, and 10,000 signed a petition urging leniency in sentencing the youths. The judge remained unswayed by public opinion. He sentenced Richard to 5 to 15 years and Deborah to 3 to 8 years in prison. The Supreme Court of Wyoming upheld the sentences, but Governor Ed Herschler commuted both sentences and ordered psychiatric evaluation and treatment ("It Made Terrible Sense," 1982).

The newest trends in judicial processing of parricide cases indicate increasing compassion toward the APO (Ewing, 1990a). Courts are finally waking up to the fact that children do not commit parricide unless something is terribly wrong, according to Los Angeles defense attorney Paul Mones (1989). The first case in which extreme PTSD symptoms led to the acceptance of the battered-child defense for an APO occurred in 1989 (Kackzor, 1989).

---

area of adolescent victim-offenders. The boxed insert titled "Adolescent Parricide" presents a brief overview of known information (Heide, 1995).

Concluding Comments

This chapter points out that the boundaries that often separate the many forms of family violence and maltreatment tend to obscure the many similarities of types of abuse. The important methodological issues, etiological models, and prevention strategies tend to be comparable across all forms of family violence. Unfortunately, many methodological problems have hindered family violence research, and family violence theory is not well developed. In the future, researchers should intensify their endeavor to uncover the multiple interacting risk factors that contribute to family violence, along with the preventive factors that decrease the probability of violence.

Society will need to extend its efforts broadly, if family violence is to end. Given the history of family violence, where family victimization has been allowed to flourish behind closed doors, such a community commitment is not only desirable but necessary. It is our hope that the students reading this book will become part of the community dedicated to ending family violence.

Appendix A

<hr>

Suggestions for Improving Research

1. *Define abuse operationally.* Terms to define include types of abuse, severity of abuse, frequency of abuse, and chronicity of abuse. Specify the tests used to assess the abuse and methods of data collection. Use continuous rather than categorical measurement scales whenever possible.
   a. *Physical child abuse.* Behaviors to count include slaps, pushes, shoves, minor hits, violent hits, choking, blows to head, use of weapons, shaken baby syndrome, abandonment, killing, and multiple forms of abuse.
   b. *Child sexual abuse.* Behaviors to count include acts of child pornography; exposing children to adult genitalia; kissing and fondling; touching of child's genitals; digital penetration; vaginal, oral, and anal intercourse; cunnilingus; and fellatio.
   c. *Child neglect.* Behaviors qualifying as neglect might include failing to seek medical care for a sick child, failing to keep the child clean, failure to provide food, allowing the child to be exposed to household chemicals or broken windows, failure to clean the house, failure to provide housing, maintaining a chaotic household, leaving a baby locked in a car, leaving a child out alone at night, allowing truancy, failure to praise and encourage a child, and teaching a child to sell drugs.

d. *Child psychological maltreatment.* Behaviors that represent psychological abuse include rejecting, degrading or humiliating, frightening and threatening, isolating, missocializing (e.g., teaching the child to beat up other children), exploiting, emotional withdrawal, and restricting a child's movements.
   e. *Child exposure to parental violence.* Behaviors to count include various observed forms of abuse, seeing or hearing abuse, seeing the outcomes of abuse (e.g., bruises or cuts), observing other outcomes of abuse (e.g., arrival of the police or arrest of a parent), changing residences, living in a shelter, being questioned by professionals, providing testimony in court, and being forced into visitation with an abusive or even deadly parent.
   f. *Interpartner abuse.* Interpartner abuse includes many of the same abuses visited upon children. Emotional or psychological abuse includes verbal abuse, threats, humiliation, destruction of property, control of the victim's actions, and confinement. Other abuses might include abandonment, withdrawal of financial support, and abuse of one's children or pets. Physical abuse includes minor abuses such as pushing and shoving, intermediate abuses such as hitting and kicking, and more serious forms of assault such as choking and the use of weapons. Sexual abuse includes a variety of unwanted sexual activities, such as rape or sodomy, and exposure to health-threatening diseases.
2. *Describe victims and perpetrators comprehensively.* Provide information about victims' and perpe-

trators' age; gender; race, ethnicity, or cultural identification; socioeconomic status; income; family relationship; and marital relationship, including sexual orientation. Include other information when relevant, such as the victim's and the perpetrator's grade in school, occupation, employment status, religious affiliation, or affiliation with other groups such as sororities. Include information about the victim's and the perpetrator's possible involvement with the criminal justice system in terms of arrests and orders of protection against him or her.

3. *Collect data from a wide range of informants.*

   a. *Family informants* should include victims, perpetrators, intimate partners, family members, and other witnesses (e.g., housekeepers). Provide information about the informant's age; gender; and race, ethnicity, or cultural identification. Specify the informant's relationship to victim, such as family member or marital partner (including sexual orientation). When relevant, determine the informant's socioeconomic status, income, educational level, occupation, employment status, religious affiliation, or affiliation with other groups such as sororities or fraternities.

   b. *Involved professional informants* should include individuals such as teachers, shelter workers, medical personnel, police, or mental health professionals. For professionals, include information about their training, experience, and areas of expertise.

4. *Define and describe all current (or past) risk factors.* Describe all risk factors for victims, perpetra-

tors, and any others involved. Risk factors for children might include age, gender, poverty, inadequate housing, inadequate medical care, absence from school, trauma, PTSD, illnesses and disabilities, neglect, unstable home or single-parent home, presence of stepparents, availability, dangerous living conditions, other factors, and multiple factors. For adults, additional factors might include drug and alcohol use, poor education, job loss, social isolation, and discrimination.

5. *Comprehensively define interventions used to eliminate or reduce the abuse and outcomes of interventions.* Describe any clinical programs, including their orientation, content, length, and inclusion of other participants. Describe other interventive strategies such as educational or prevention programs. Describe the circumstances of the intervention, such as court ordered, voluntary, shelter bound, individual, group or family, paid or unpaid. Describe the outcomes of interventions and their effectiveness.

6. *Research design and statistical analyses.* Strive to conduct longitudinal studies whenever appropriate. Clearly describe all tests and questionnaires as well as the methods of data collection. Specify if the data are self-report or other report. For reliability and validity, try to compare data from multiple informants (e.g., both husband and wife) and compare a target group's responses with an appropriate comparison group(s). Describe statistical tests selected and the rationale for their selection when useful. Use multivariate statistical techniques whenever appropriate.

Appendix B

Organizations Concerned With Family Violence

National Domestic Violence Hotline
800-799-7233

This number responds to emergency crisis calls from battered individuals, women, and others involved in family violence. It also provides referrals to local batterer programs.

Family Resources (family, child, women, men, and elders)

FAMILY RESOURCES

Family Resource Coalition (FRC)
200 S. Michigan Ave., 16th Fl.
Chicago, IL 60604
312-341-0900

This organization tries to strengthen family services through prevention. FRC is also a clearinghouse and provides technical assistance.

Health Resource Center on Domestic Violence
The Family Violence Prevention Fund
383 Rhode Island St., Ste. 304
San Francisco, CA 94103-5133
415-252-8900
800-313-1310

This group attempts to strengthen the health care response to family violence. It provides publications and technical assistance.

National Clearinghouse on Families and Youth (NCFY)
P.O. Box 13505
Silver Spring, MD 20911-3505
301-608-8098

The NCFY individualizes research, provides networking, and provides updates on youth initiatives.

National Council to Prevent Child Abuse and Family Violence
1155 Connecticut Ave., NW, Ste. 400
Washington, DC 20036
202-429-6695
800-222-2000

The United Way sponsors some local counseling programs for physically and sexually abusive parents and others involved in family violence (e.g., Parents Anonymous).

CHILD ABUSE ORGANIZATIONS

Center for the Prevention of Sexual and Domestic Violence
936 N. 34th St., Ste. 200
Seattle, WA 98193
206-634-1903

This group focuses on marital and date rape. It provides rape prevention education through speakers, publications, and consultation. It also holds training for ministers.

Child Welfare League of America (CWLA)
440 First St. NW, Ste. 310
Washington, DC 20001-2085
202-638-2952

Kempe National Center for the Prevention and Treatment of Child Abuse and Neglect
1205 Oneida St.
Denver, CO 80220
303-321-3963

National Coalition Against Domestic Violence (NCADV)
(membership information)
P.O. Box 34103
Washington, DC 20043-4103
202-638-6388

This coalition works to end domestic violence against children and women. It provides technical assistance, newsletters, and publications.

National Association of Counsel for Children (NACC)
1205 Oneida St.
Denver, CO 80220
303-322-2260

This organization is for professional lawyers and other professionals who represent children.

National Center for Missing and Exploited Children (NCMEC)
2101 Wilson Blvd., Ste. 550
Arlington, VA 22201
703-235-3900
800-843-5678

The NCMEC is a clearinghouse and resource center funded by the Office of Juvenile Justice and Delinquency Prevention (OJJDP). It provides a number of useful publications (government agency).

National Committee to Prevent Child Abuse (NCPCA)
332 S. Michigan Ave., Ste. 1600
Chicago, IL 60604
312-663-3520

The NCPCA provides many resources, including statistical survey information across the 50 states.

World Health Organization (WHO)
Geneva, Switzerland
Fax: 41 (22) 791-4189
e-mail: belsey@who.ch

In 1996, WHO is working with other groups to assist in sponsoring and hosting several international meetings: First World Congress Against Commercial Sexual Exploitation of Children, International Campaign to End Child Prostitution in Asian Tourism (ECPAT), and the Nongovernment Organization (NGO) Group on the Convention on the Rights of the Child.

WOMAN ABUSE GROUPS

Center for the Prevention of Sexual and Domestic Violence
936 N. 34th St., Ste. 200
Seattle, WA 98193
206-634-1903

This group provides rape prevention education through speakers, publications, and consultation. It provides information about marital and date rape.

Center for Women's Policy Studies
2000 P St., NW, Ste. 508
Washington, DC 20036
202-872-1770

Minnesota Program Development
Domestic Abuse Intervention Project (DAIP)
206 W. Fourth St., Rm. 201
Duluth, MN 55806
218-722-2781
Fax: 218-722-1545

This organization distributes training materials and conducts training seminars. It provides specialized training materials for those working with Native American families.

National Coalition Against Domestic Violence (NCADV)
(membership information)
P.O. Box 34103
Washington, DC 20043-4103
202-638-6388

This coalition works to end domestic violence against children and women. It provides technical assistance, newsletters, and publications.

National Coalition Against Domestic Violence (NCADV)
(to order publications)
P.O. Box 18749
Denver, CO 80218-0749
303-839-1852

This coalition works to end domestic violence against children and women. It provides technical assistance, newsletters, and publications.

Young Women's Christian Association (YWCA)
624 9th St., NW
Washington, DC 20001
202-626-0700

Local organizations offer a variety of services such as exercise, fitness, infant care, children's programs, food banks, and abuse counseling. Telephone the local YWCA in your area only.

MEN'S GROUPS

Abusive Men Exploring New Directions (AMEND)
777 Grant St., Ste. 600
Denver, CO 80203
303-832-6363

Domestic Abuse Intervention Project (DAIP)
206 W. Fourth St., Rm. 201
Duluth, MN 55806
218-722-2781
218-722-4134
Fax: 218-722-1545

EMERGE: Counseling and Education to Stop Violence
18 Hurley St., Ste. 100
Cambridge, MA 02141
617-422-1550

EMERGE provides technical assistance and training. It also distributes publications.

Men Overcoming Violence (MOVE)
54 Mint St., Ste. 300
San Francisco, CA 94103
415-777-4496

National Organization for Changing Men (RAVEN)
7314 Manchester, 2nd Fl.
St. Louis, MO 63143
314-645-2075

ELDER ABUSE

National Academy of Elder Law Attorneys (NAELA)
1604 N. Country Club Rd.
Tucson, AZ 85716
602-881-4005

This is a professional organization of attorneys concerned with improving the availability of legal services to older persons. NAELA is striving to define the area of practice, establish practice standards, and create an information network among elder law attorneys. It distributes some publications.

National Center on Elder Abuse
810 First St., NE, Ste. 500
Washington, DC 20002-4267
202-682-2470

National Committee for the Prevention of Elder Abuse
UCSF/Mt. Zion Center on Aging
3330 Geary Blvd., 3rd Fl.
San Francisco, CA 94118
Fax: 415-750-4136

Legal Services

American Bar Association (ABA) Center on Children and the Law
740 15th St. NW
Washington, DC 20005
202-662-1720

This group provides training and technical assistance to prosecutors handling child abuse cases. State statutes, case law, and other resources are available. Court reform is a goal of this group. Publications are available.

American Bar Association (ABA) IOLTA Clearinghouse
541 N. Fairbanks Court
Chicago, IL 60611-3314
312-988-5748

This ABA group collects funds and distributes them for programs and for support of legal personnel in special projects.

Battered Women's Justice Project
4032 Chicago Ave., South
Minneapolis, MN 55407
612-824-8768
800-903-0111

This organization studies abused women in the criminal justice system, provides information to attorneys, and advocates for battered women or others working with them.

Legal Council for the Elderly (LCE)
P.O. Box 96474
Washington, DC 20090
202-434-2152
Legal Hotline: 800-424-3410

This organization is a unit of the American Association of Retired Persons (AARP) that provides technical assistance, publications, training (e.g., guardianship), and referrals (some pro bono). The hotline connects callers with an attorney who will try to resolve the issues or advise the caller where to obtain help.

National Academy of Elder Law Attorneys (NAELA)
1604 North Country Club Rd.
Tucson, AZ 85716
602-881-4005

This is a professional organization of attorneys concerned with improving the availability of legal services to older persons. NAELA is striving to define the area of practice, establish practice standards, and create an information network among elder law attorneys. It distributes some publications.

National Association of Counsel for Children (NACC)
1205 Oneida St.
Denver, CO 80220
303-322-2260

The NACC is a professional organization for lawyers and other practitioners who represent children in court, and it publishes a variety of materials relating to children's legal rights as well as sponsoring child abuse training.

National Battered Women's Law Project at the National Center on Women and Family Law
799 Broadway, Ste. 402
New York, NY 10003
212-741-9480

This project serves as a clearinghouse for information for legal professionals and advocates. It addresses a number of specific issues such as child custody. It provides information about case law, model briefs and statistics.

National Center for Prosecution of Child Abuse American Prosecutors Research Institute (APRI)
99 Canal Center Plaza, Ste. 510
Alexandria, VA 22314
703-739-0321

APRI has on-staff attorneys who offer technical assistance to attorneys and other professionals working in the field of child abuse. They also provide training and publications.

National Center on Women and Family Law. Inc.
275 7th Ave., Ste. 1206
New York, NY 10001
212-741-9480

This organization publishes a newsletter and serves as a clearinghouse on legal issues related to family violence.

National Clearinghouse for the Defense of Battered Women
125 S. 9th St., Ste. 302
Philadelphia, PA 19107
215-351-0010

This organization provides information and resources to legal personnel and assists battered women charged with crimes. It is especially concerned with women who kill in self-defense. It publishes a newsletter and networks.

NOW Legal Defense and Educational Fund
99 Hudson St., 12th Fl.
New York, NY 10013
212-925-6635

This sister organization to NOW focuses on litigation and education in areas of gender discrimination and related issues. It sponsors women's legal rights, among other legal problems.

Project Assist
Legal Aid of Western Missouri
1005 Grand Ave., Ste. 600
Kansas City, MO 64106
816-474-6750

Quincy District Court Domestic Violence Prevention Program
Quincy Division District Court Department
One Dennis F. Ryan Parkway
Quincy, MA 02169
617-471-1650

Resource Center on Child Custody and Protection National
Council of Juvenile and Family Court Judges
Family Violence Project
P.O. Box 8970
Reno, NV 89507
702-784-6012
800-527-3223
Fax: 702-784-6160

This group provides a number of publications (e.g., model codes and court programs) to assist judges and others on family violence.

Medical Resources

American Academy of Pediatrics. Department C
P.O. Box 927, SW
Elk Grove Village, IL 60009-2188
708-228-5005

The academy publishes information on issues such as child sexual abuse, identification, and effects on victims.

American College of Obstetricians and Gynecologists
409 12th St.
Washington, DC 20024
202-638-5577

This group provides a pamphlet about abused women patients.

American Medical Association (AMA)
Department of Mental Health
515 N. State St.
Chicago, IL 60610
312-464-5066

This association of doctors provides referrals and brochures containing help for doctors treating family violence victims.

Domestic Violence Project of the American Academy of
Facial Plastic and Reconstructive Surgery (AAFPRS)
1110 Vermont Ave., NW, Ste. 220
Washington, DC 20005
800-842-4546
NCADV
202-638-6388

This group, along with the National Coalition Against Domestic Violence (NCADV), provides some free facial and reconstructive and plastic surgery for victims of family violence.

Health Resource Center and Domestic Violence
Family Violence Prevention Fund
383 Rhode Island St., Ste. 304
San Francisco, CA 94103-5133
415-252-8900
800-313-1310
Fax: 415-252-8991

This organization attempts to strengthen the health care response to domestic violence. It provides publications and technical assistance.

Culture-Specific Information

Black Battered Women's Project
Minnesota Institute on Black Chemical Abuse
2616 Nicollet Ave. South
Minneapolis, MN 55408

Center for Child Protection and Family Support
People of Color Leadership Institute (POCLI)
714 G St., SE
Washington, DC 20003
202-544-3144

This group attempts to improve cultural competence in child welfare systems that serve children and families of color. It publishes a cultural competence training guide and a bibliography of publications.

Family Crisis Center
Alternatives to Violence: East Hawaii
P.O. Box 10448
Hilo, HI 96721-7798
808-969-7798

Hawaii Family Court
First Circuit
777 Punch Bowl St.
Honolulu, HI 96813
808-528-5959

Special Resources for Immigrant and Refugee Women
Immigrant Assistance Line
415-554-244 (English and Spanish)
415-554-2454 (Cantonese, Mandarin, and Vietnamese)

Women of Nations
P.O. Box 4637
St. Paul, MN 55104
612-222-5830

Provides information on American Indian women involved in domestic violence.

CANADA

London Family Court Clinic
Ste. 200
254 Pall Mall St.
London, Ontario N6A 5P6
Canada
519-679-7250

This clinic provides educational pamphlets on violence prevention for schoolchildren and teenagers.

Men's Groups Toward a National Lifting
Glebe New Men's Group
32 Morris St.
Ottawa, Ontario K1F 4A7
Canada
613-233-7376
Contact: Ken Fisher

National Clearing House on Family Violence
Family Violence Prevention Division in Health Canada
Social Service Programs, Health Canada
1st Fl., Finance Bldg.
Tunney's Pasture
Ottawa, Ontario K1A 1B5
Canada
800-267-1291

Gay and Lesbian Organizations

Help for Battered Gays and Lesbians
Lesbian Battering Intervention Project
Minnesota Coalition for Battered Women
1619 Dayton Ave., Ste. 303
St. Paul, MN 55104
612-646-6177

National Coalition Against Domestic Violence (NCADV)
P.O. Box 18749
Denver, CO 80218-0749
303-839-1852

National Gay and Lesbian Domestic Violence Victim's Network
3506 S. Ouray Circle
Aurora, CO 80013
303-266-3477

Provides support for victims and publishes a handbook on same-sex domination.

Substance Abuse and Self-Help Groups

Black Battered Women's Project
Minnesota Institute on Black Chemical Abuse
2616 Nicollet Ave., South
Minneapolis, MN 55408

Children of Alcoholics Foundation
555 Madison Ave., 20th Fl.
New York, NY 10022
212-754-0656
800-359-2623

The foundation promotes public and professional awareness of children of alcoholics' problems and develops programs and materials to break the cycle of family alcoholism.

National Clearinghouse for Alcohol and Drug Information (NCADI)
11426 Rockville Pike, Ste. 200
Rockville, MD 20852
301-468-2600
800-729-6686

NCADI is the Center for Substance Abuse Prevention. It provides information on research, publications, and prevention.

Miscellaneous Resources

HOTLINES

To locate a hotline, look in the nonbusiness sections of a telephone directory under Social Service Agencies, Shelters, and Women's Organizations.

Legal Council for the Elderly (LCE)
Legal Hotline: 800-424-3410

The hotline connects callers with an attorney who will try to resolve the issues or advise the caller where to obtain help.

National Battered Woman's Hotline
c/o Texas Council on Family Violence
8701 North MoPac Expressway, Ste. 450
Austin, TX 78759
512-794-1133
800-525-1978

This organization, along with state coalitions and many local shelters, have hotlines. Some hotlines have counselors who are fluent in a second language (e.g., Spanish).

National Domestic Violence Hotline
800-799-7233

This number responds to emergency crisis calls from battered individuals, women, and others involved in family violence. It also provides referrals to local batterer programs.

HOUSING

National Coalition for Low-Income Housing
1012 14th St., NW, Ste. 1200
Washington, DC 20005
202-662-1530

Shelters provide temporary housing to appropriate clients when they have vacancies and some help with extended housing. Some have staff who are able to speak a second language (e.g., Spanish).

RELIGIOUS INFORMATION

California Professional Society on Abuse of Children (CAPSAC). (1996). *Anthology of sermons.* Orange, CA: Author. [Call 619-773-1649.]

Center for the Prevention of Sexual and Domestic Violence
936 N. 34th St., Ste. 200
Seattle, WA 98193
206-634-1903

This center provides educational materials for religious organizations preparing sermons for clergy and lessons for Sunday school classes. It educates clergy about child abuse and inappropriate behaviors of clergy.

Promise Keepers
10200 W. 44th Ave.
Wheatridge, CO 80033
303-964-7600
800-501-0211

This interfaith Christian group for men only has a number of local organizations that hold conventions. The purpose of the organization is to encourage male bonding and to provide sermons about the commitments of men to their families.

GENERAL CRIME VICTIM ORGANIZATIONS

National Organization for Victim Assistance
1757 Park Road, NW
Washington, DC 20010
202-232-6682

This group runs public education programs, provides direct services to victims, and develops public policy and training programs for policymakers and health care providers.

National Victim Center
555 Madison Ave., Ste. 2001
New York, NY 10022
800-FYI-CALL

This organization provides research, education, training, advocacy, and resources for those working with crime victims. It networks through an INFOLINK line. It has some publications (e.g., on stalking).

Research, Statistics, and Clearinghouses (Publications)

RESEARCH AND STATISTICS

American Humane Association. American Association for Protecting Children (AAPC)
63 Inverness Dr. East
Englewood, CO 80112-5117
800-227-4645
Fax: 303-792-5333

The AAPC promotes child protection services through training, education, and consultation. It provides national statistics on child abuse issues. It operates the National Resource Center on Child Abuse and Neglect (government agency).

National Center for Missing and Exploited Children (NCMEC)
2101 Wilson Blvd., Ste. 550
Arlington, VA 22201
703-235-3900
800-843-5678

The NCMEC is a clearinghouse and resource center funded by the Office of Juvenile Justice and Delinquency Prevention (OJJDP). It provides a number of useful publications (government agency).

National Center on Child Abuse and Neglect (NCCAN)
U.S. Department of Health and Human Services
P.O. Box 1182
Washington, DC 20013
703-385-7565
800-394-3366

NCCAN publishes manuals for professionals involved in the child protection system and to enhance community collaboration and the quality of services provided to children and families. NCCAN conducts research, collects information, and provides assistance to states and communities on child abuse issues.

National Committee to Prevent Child Abuse (NCPCA)
332 S. Michigan Ave., Ste. 1600
Chicago, IL 60604
312-663-3520

The NCPCA provides many resources (e.g., educational pamphlets), including statistical survey information across the 50 states.

National Institute of Justice
U.S. Department of Justice
National Criminal Justice Reference Service
P.O. Box 6000
Rockville, MD 20849-6000
301-251-5500
800-851-3420
e-mail: askncjrs@ncjrs.aspensys.com

The National Institute of Justice develops research and collects information about crime. It is part of the U.S. Department of Justice. It provides the largest clearinghouse of criminal justice information in the world and many related services. NCJRS will provide electronic versions of many documents.

CLEARINGHOUSES

Boulder County Safehouse
P.O. Box 4157
Boulder, CO 80306
303-449-8623

This group publishes books in English and Spanish on children and family violence. These books

are especially useful to parents, teachers, and health care workers.

Clearinghouse on Child Abuse and Neglect Information
P.O. Box 1182
Washington, DC 20012
703-385-7565
800-394-3366

This clearinghouse offers annotated bibliographies and can provide statistics.

Family Resource Coalition (FRC)
200 S. Michigan Ave., 16th Fl.
Chicago, IL 60604
312-341-0900

This group attempts to strengthen families through prevention and maintains a clearinghouse.

Family Violence and Sexual Assault Institute (FVSAI)
1310 Clinic Dr.
Tyler, TX 75701
903-595-6799
Fax: 903-595-6799

FVSAI has a large number of available unpublished articles (e.g., convention papers) and references to published articles. The organization prepares special bibliographies and treatment manuals and publishes a quarterly newsletter. It reviews books and media and announces conferences.

The Higher Education Center Against Violence and Abuse
386 McNeal Hall
1985 Buford Ave.
St. Paul, MN 55108-6142
612-624-0721
800-646-2282 (within Minnesota)
Fax: 612-625-4288
e-mail: mincava@umn.edu

This Minnesota-based organization provides training for professionals in higher education. The group provides technical assistance, plans conferences, and helps fund pilot projects. It provides an electronic clearinghouse for colleges, universities, and career schools.

National Battered Women's Law Project at the National Center on Women and Family Law
799 Broadway, Ste. 402
New York, NY 10003
212-741-9480

This project serves as a clearinghouse for information for legal professionals and advocates. It addresses a number of specific issues, such as child custody. It provides information about case law, model briefs, and statistics.

National Clearinghouse for Alcohol and Drug Information (NCADI)
11426 Rockville Pike, Ste. 200
Rockville, MD 20852
301-468-2600
800-729-6686

This group is a communications service of the Center for Substance Abuse Prevention. NCADI provides information on research, publications, prevention and education resources, and prevention programs, and a catalog is available on request.

National Clearinghouse for the Defense of Battered Women
125 S. 9th St., Ste. 302
Philadelphia, PA 19107
215-351-0010

National Clearinghouse on Families and Youth (NCFY)
P.O. Box 13505
Silver Spring, MD 20911-3505
301-608-8098

This organization tailors research for clients and networks.

National Clearinghouse on Marital and Date Rape
Berkeley, CA 94708-1697
510-524-1582

Offers fee-based phone consultations ($15 individuals, $30 organizations, $7.50/minute). State Law Chart 3.

National Coalition Against Domestic Violence (NCADV)
(to order publications)
P.O. Box 18749
Denver, CO 80218-0749
303-839-1852

This coalition works to end domestic violence against children and women. It provides technical assistance, newsletters, and publications.

National Resource Center on Domestic Violence
6400 Flank Dr., Ste. 1300
Harrisburg, PA 17112-2778
800-537-2238
Fax: 717-545-9456

This center furnishes information and resources to advocates and policymakers.

The National Self-Help Clearinghouse
Graduate School of City University of New York
25 W. 43rd St., Rm. 620
New York, 10036
212-354-8525
212-642-2944

This organization lists self-help groups and makes referrals to national self-help groups.

Appendix C

Related Readings for Victims, Professionals, and Others

The following references vary in their appropriateness for different readers. Some focus on different victim groups and others address more tangential issues. Some address issues of importance to practitioners and others address research concerns.

Individuals involved in family violence are best served in making reading selections by consulting with a mental health professional familiar with their situation.

Ackerman, R. J., & Pickering, S. E. (1995). *Before it's too late.* Deerfield Park, FL: Health Communications.

Agtuca, J. R. (1994). *A community secret: For the Filipina in an abusive relationship.* Seattle, WA: Seal.

Alsdurf, J., & Alsdurf, P. (1989). *Battered into submission.* Madison, MN: University Christian Fellowship.

Ammerman, R. T., & Hersen, M. (1992). *Assessment of family violence: A clinical and legal sourcebook.* New York: Wiley.

Aris, B. (1994, April). Battered women who kill: The law still denies us a hearing. *Glamour,* p. 160.

Bachman, R. (1992). *Death and violence on the reservation: Homicide, family violence, and suicide in American Indian populations.* New York: Auburn House.

Barnett, O. W., & LaViolette, A. D. *It could happen to anyone: Why battered women stay.* Newbury Park, CA: Sage.

Bart, P. B., & Moran, E. G. (Eds.). (1993). *Violence against women.* Newbury Park, CA: Sage.

Bergen, R. K. (1996). *Wife rape.* Newbury Park, CA: Sage.

Berry, D. B. (1995). *The domestic violence sourcebook.* Los Angeles: Lowell House.

Biden, J. J. (1993). Violence against women: The congressional response. *American Psychologist, 48,* 1059-1061.

Bottoms, B. L., & Goodman, G. S. (1996). *International perspectives on child abuse and children's testimony: Psychological research and law.* Newbury Park, CA: Sage.

Boulder County Safehouse. (1990). *We can't play at my house: Children and domestic violence* (Handbook for teachers, Bk. 2). Boulder, CO: Author.

Buzawa, E. S., & Buzawa, C. G. (1996). *Do arrest and restraining orders work.* Newbury Park, CA: Sage.

Brier, J. N. (1992). *Child abuse trauma.* Newbury Park, CA: Sage.

California Professional Society on Abuse of Children (CAPSAC). (1996). *Anthology of sermons.* Orange: Author. Call 619-773-1649.

Campbell, J. C. (Ed.). (1995). *Assessing dangerousness.* Newbury Park, CA: Sage.

Clark, D. (1987). *Loving someone gay.* Berkeley, CA: Celestial Arts.

Clunis, D. M., & Green, G. D. (1995). *The lesbian parenting book.* Seattle, WA: Seal.

Cochran-Berry, B., with Parrent, J. (1995). *Life after Johnnie Cochran: Why I left the sweetest-talking, most successful Black lawyer in L.A.* New York: Basic Books.

Cohen, D., & Eisdorfer, C. (1995). *Caring for your aging parents.* New York: Putnam.

deBecker, G. (1992). *Security recommendations.* Albuquerque: Gavin deBecker/CLC of New Mexico.

Dutton, D. G. (1995). *The batterer.* New York: HarperCollins.

Engel, B. (1990). *The emotionally abused woman.* New York: Ballantine.

Evans, P. (1996). *The verbally abusive relationship.* Holbrook, MA: Adam Media.

Evans, R. M. (1995). *Childhood hurts.* New York: Bantam.

Fairstein, L. A. (1993). *Sexual violence: Our war against rape.* New York: William Morrow.

Fedders, C., & Elliott, L. (1987). *Shattered dreams.* New York: Harper & Row.

Ferrato, D., with Jones, A. (1991). *Living with the enemy.* New York: Aperture Foundation.

Flannery, R. B., Jr. (1992). *Post trauma stress disorder.* New York: Crossword.

Fontes, L. A. (Ed.). (1995). *Sexual abuse in nine North American cultures: Treatment and prevention.* Thousand Oaks, CA: Sage.

Forward, S. D. (1989). *Toxic parents.* New York: Bantam.

Fredrickson, R. (1992). *Repressed memories.* New York: Fireside/Parkside.

Gardiner, J. (1994, April). Why did I take it? *Mademoiselle,* p. 153.

Gelles, R., & Loeske, D. R. (1993). *Current controversies on family violence.* Newbury Park, CA: Sage.

Gelles, R. J. (1996). *The book of David: How preserving families can cost children's lives.* New York: Basic Books.

Gelles, R. J., & Cornell, C. P. (1990). *Intimate violence in families* (2nd ed.). Newbury Park, CA: Sage.

Greenberg, K. E. (1994). *Family abuse: Why do people hurt each other?* New York: Twenty-First Century.

Hamberger, L. K., & Renzetti, C. M. (Eds.). (1996). *Domestic partner abuse: Expanding paradigms for understanding and intervention.* New York: Springer.

Hampton, R. L. (1991). *Black family violence: Current research and theory.* Lexington, MA: Lexington.

Herman, J. L. (1992). *Trauma and recovering.* New York: HarperCollins.

Hilton, Z. N. (1993). *Legal responses to wife assault: Current trends and evaluation.* Newbury Park, CA: Sage.

Horton, A. L., & Williamson, J. A. (1988). *Abuse and religion: When praying isn't enough.* Lexington, MA: Lexington.

Hunter, N. (1991). *Abused boys.* New York: Fawcett.

Island, D., & Letellier, P. (1991). *Men who beat men who love them: Battered gay men and domestic violence.* New York: Harrington Park.

Jaffe, P. G., Wolfe, D. A., & Wolfe, S. K. (1990). *Children of battered women.* Newbury Park, CA: Sage.

Jensen, R. H. (1994, September/October). A day in court. *Ms., 2*(2), 48-49.

Johnson, T. F. (Ed.). (1996). *Elder mistreatment.* Binghamton, NY: Haworth.

Jones, A. (1994). *Next time she'll be dead.* Boston: Beacon.

Kanuha, V. (1990). Compounding the triple jeopardy: Battering in lesbian of color relationships. *Women and Therapy, 9,* 169-184.

Kinports, K., & Fischer, K. (1993). Orders of protection in domestic violence cases: An empirical assessment of the impact of the reform statutes. *Texas Journal of Women and the Law, 2,* 163.

Kosberg, J. I., & Garcia, J. L. (Eds.). (1995). *Elder abuse: International and cross-cultural perspectives.* New York: Haworth.

Lardner, G., Jr. (1995). *The stalking of Kristin: A father investigates the murder of his daughter.* New York: Atlantic Monthly Press.

Ledray, L. (1994). *Recovery from rape.* New York: Henery Hill.

Levant, R. F., with Kopecky, G. (1995). *Masculinity reconstructed.* New York: Dutton (Penguin).

Levy, B. (1991). *Dating violence.* Seattle, WA: Seal.

Levy, B. (1992). *In love and danger: A teen's guide to breaking free of abusive relationships.* Seattle, WA: Seal.

Loftus, E., & Ketcham, K. (1994). *The myth of repressed memory.* New York: St. Martin's.

Marwick, C. (1994). Health and justice professionals set goals to lessen domestic violence. *Journal of the American Medical Association, 271,* 15, 1147-1148.

Melody, P., Miller, A. W., & Miller, J. K. (1992). *Facing love addiction.* New York: HarperCollins.

Mones, P. (1991). *When a child kills: Abused children who kill their parents.* New York: Pocket Books.

Neidhardt, E. R., & Allen, J. A. (1993). *Family therapy with the elderly.* Newbury Park, CA: Sage.

Newell, B. (1993, Winter). Children's rights [Special issue]. *NCADV Voice.*

NiCarthy, G., Gottlieb, N., & Coffman, S. (1993). *You don't have to take it.* Seattle, WA: Seal.

Noel, N. L., & Yam, M. (1992, December). Domestic violence: The pregnant battered woman. *Women's Health, 27,* 871-883.

Parker, B. (1993). Abuse of adolescents: What can we learn from pregnant teenagers? *AWHONN's Clinical Issues, 4,* 363-370.

Paymar, M. (1993). *Violent no more: Helping men end domestic abuse.* Alameda, CA: Hunter House.

Renzetti, C. M. (1992). *Violent betrayal: Partner abuse in lesbian relationships.* Newbury Park, CA: Sage.

Robertson, R. (1992). *Abusive husband.* Lake Oswego, OR: Heritage Park.

Robson, R. (1992). *Lesbian (out)law: Survival under the rule of law.* Ithaca, NY: Firebrand.

Roy, M. (1988). *Children in crossfire.* Deerfield Beach, FL: Health Communications.

Russell, M. N. (1995). *Confronting abusive beliefs.* Newbury Park, CA: Sage.

Russianoff, P. (1993). *Why do I think I am nothing without a man.* New York: Bantam.

Salter, A. C. (1995). *Transforming trauma.* Newbury Park, CA: Sage.

Sanders, T. L. (1991). *Male survivors.* Freedom, CA: Crossing.

Shepard, M., & Pence, E. (1988). The effect of battering on the employment status of women. *Affilia, 3*(2), 56-61.

Stanko, E. (1990). *Everyday violence.* New York: HarperCollins.

Stark, E., & Flitcraft, A. (1996). *Women at risk.* Newbury Park, CA: Sage.

Statman, J. B. (1995). *The battered woman's survival guide: Breaking the cycle.* Dallas, TX: Taylor.

Steinman, M. (Ed.). (1991). *Woman battering: Policy responses.* Cincinnati, OH: Anderson Publishing and Criminal Justice Sciences.

Stordeur, R. A., & Stille, R. (1989). *Ending men's violence against their partners: One road to peace.* Newbury Park, CA: Sage.

Tapp, A., Banks, H., Stark, F. G., Funk, R. E., Adams, E., & Houseal, D. (1992, Fall). Men's role in the battered women's movement [Special issue]. *NCADV Voice.*

Thompson, R. A. (1995). *Preventing child maltreatment through social support.* Newbury Park, CA: Sage.

Tomkins, A. J., Steinman, M., Kenning, M. K., Somaia, M., & Afrank, J. (1992). Children who witness woman battering. *Law & Policy, 14*(2/3), 169-181.

Truscott, D. (1992). Intergenerational transmission of violent behavior in adolescent males. *Aggressive Behavior, 18,* 327-335.

Turner, T., with Loder, K. (1986). *Tina.* New York: Morrow.

Vedral, J. L. (1993). *Get rid of him.* New York: Warner.

Walker, L. (1979). *The battered woman.* New York: Harper & Row.

Wallace, H. (1996). *Family violence: Legal, medical, and social perspectives.* Boston: Allyn and Bacon.

Warshar, R. (1994). *I never called it rape.* New York: HarperCollins.

Whitaker, L. C., & Pollard, J. W. (1996). *Campus violence: Kinds, causes, and cures.* New York: Haworth.

White, E. C. (1985). *Chain, chain, change: For Black women dealing with physical and emotional abuse.* Seattle, WA: Seal.

Wiehe, V. R. (1996). *A primer for working with child abuse and neglect.* Newbury Park, CA: Sage.

Wiklund, P. (1995). *Sleeping with a stranger—How I survived marriage to a child molester.* Holbrook, MA: Adam Media.

Wolf, R. S., & Pillemer, K. A. (1989). *Helping elderly victims.* New York: Columbia University Press.

Wolfe, D. A. (1996). *The youth relationships manual.* Newbury Park, CA: Sage.

Zorza, J. (1991). Woman battering: A major cause of homelessness. *Clearinghouse Review* [Special issue], *61,* 421-429.

NOTE: Some Barnes & Noble bookstores have a separate section of books listed under *abuse.*

References

ABA center on children starts project to help court systems in child abuse cases. (1995). *Family Violence & Sexual Assault Bulletin, 11*(3-4), 38.

Abel, G. G., Becker, J. V., & Cunningham-Rathner, J. (1984). Complications, consent, and cognitions in sex between children and adults. *International Journal of Law and Psychiatry, 7,* 89-103.

Abel, G. G., Becker, J. V., & Skinner, L. J. (1986). Behavioral approaches to treatment of the violent sex offender. In L. H. Roth (Ed.), *Clinical treatment of the violent person* (pp. 100-123). New York: Guilford.

Abel, G. G., Gore, D. K., Holland, C. L., Camp, N., Becker, J. V., & Rathner, J. (1989). The measurement of the cognitive distortions of child molesters. *Annals of Sex Research, 2,* 135-153.

Abel, G. G., & Rouleau, J. L. (1990). The nature and extent of sexual assault. In W. L. Marshall, D. R. Laws, & H. E. Barbaree (Eds.), *Handbook of sexual assault: Issues, theories, and treatment of the offender* (pp. 9-21). New York: Plenum.

Abramson, J. H., Terespolsky, L., Brook, J. G., & Kark, L. (1965). Cornell Medical Index as a health measure in epidemiological studies: A test of the validity of a health questionnaire. *British Journal of Preventive Medicine, 16,* 103-110.

Abramson, L. (1994, July 25). Unequal justice. *Newsweek, 124*(4), 25.

Achenbach, T. M., & Edelbrock, C. S. (1983). *Manual for the Child Behavior Checklist and Revised Child Behavior Profile.* Burlington: University of Vermont Press.

Achenbach, T. M., & Edelbrock, C. S. (1987). *Manual for the youth self-report and profile.* Burlington: University of Vermont Press.

Adams, D. C. (1986, August). *Counseling men who batter: A profeminist analysis of five treatment mod-*

els. Paper presented at the annual meeting of the American Psychological Association, Washington, DC.

Adams, D. C. (1988). Treatment models of men who batter: A profeminist analysis. In K. Yllö & M. Bograd (Eds.), *Feminist perspectives on wife abuse* (pp. 176-199). Newbury Park, CA: Sage.

Adams, S. L., Isaac, N. E., Cochran, D., & Brown, M. E. (1996). Dating violence among adolescent batterers: A profile of restraining order defendants in Massachusetts. *Domestic Violence Report, 1*(2), 1-2, 7, 12-13.

Adler, J., Carroll, G., Smith, V., & Rogers, P. (1994, November). Innocents lost. *Newsweek,* pp. 26-30.

Ageton, S. S. (1983). *Sexual assault among adolescents.* Lexington, MA: D. C. Heath.

Aguilar, R. J., & Nightingale, N. N. (1994). The impact of specific battering experiences on the self-esteem of abused women. *Journal of Family Violence, 9,* 35-45.

Aguirre, B. E. (1985). Why do they return? Abused wives in shelters. *Social Work, 30,* 350-354.

Ainsworth, M. D. S. (1973). The development of infant-mother attachment. In B. Caldwell & H. Ricciuti (Eds.), *Review of child development research* (Vol. 3, pp. 1-94). Chicago: University of Chicago Press.

Ainsworth, M. D. S., & Bowlby, J. (1991). An ethological approach to personality development. *American Psychologist, 46,* 331-341.

Aldarondo, E. (1996). Cessation and persistence of wife assault: A longitudinal analysis. *American Journal of Orthopsychiatry, 66,* 141-151.

Alessandri, S. M. (1991). Play and social behavior in maltreated pre-schoolers. *Development and Psychopathology, 3,* 191-205.

Alessi, J. J., & Hearn, K. (1984). Group treatment of children in shelters for battered women. In A. R. Roberts (Ed.), *Battered women and their families* (pp. 49-61). New York: Springer.

Alexander, M. B. (1996, April 11). Foster dad, birth mom renew war. *Daily News*, p. 3.

Alexander, P. C., & Follette, V. M. (1992). Dating violence: Current and historical correlates. *Behavioral Assessment, 14,* 39-52.

Alexander, P. C., & Lupfer, S. L. (1987). Family characteristics and long-term consequences associated with sexual abuse. *Archives of Sexual Behavior, 16,* 235-245.

Alexander, R. C., Surrell, J. A., & Cohle, S. D. (1987). Microwave oven burns to children: An unusual manifestation of child abuse. *Pediatrics, 79*(2), 255.

Alfaro, J. D. (1981). Report on the relationship between child abuse and neglect and later socially deviant behavior. In R. J. Hunter & Y. E. Walker (Eds.), *Exploring the relationship between child abuse and delinquency* (pp. 175-219). Montclair, NJ: Allanheld, Osmun.

Allen, C. M., & Straus, M. A. (1980). Resources, power and husband-wife violence. In M. A. Straus & G. T. Hotaling (Eds.), *The social causes of husband-wife violence* (pp. 188-208). Minneapolis: University of Minnesota Press.

Allen, D. M., & Tarnowski, K. J. (1989). Depressive characteristics of physically abused children. *Journal of Abnormal Child Psychology, 17,* 1-11.

Allen, K., Calsyn, D. A., Fehrenbach, P. A., & Benton, G. (1989). A study of interpersonal behaviors of male batterers. *Journal of Interpersonal Violence, 4,* 79-89.

Allen, R. E., & Oliver, J. M. (1982). The effects of child maltreatment on language development. *Child Abuse & Neglect, 6,* 299-305.

Alsdurf, J. M. (1985). Wife abuse and the church: The response of pastors. *Response, 8*(1), 9-11.

American Association for Protecting Children. (1985). *Highlights of official child neglect and abuse reporting, 1983.* Denver, CO: American Humane Association.

American Association for Protecting Children. (1986). *Highlights of official child neglect and abuse reporting, 1984.* Denver, CO: American Humane Association.

American Association for Protecting Children. (1988). *Highlights of official child neglect and abuse reporting, 1986.* Denver, CO: American Humane Association.

American Association for Protecting Children. (1989). *Highlights of official child neglect and abuse reporting, 1987.* Denver, CO: American Humane Association.

American Humane Association. (1976). *National analysis of official child neglect and abuse reporting.* Denver, CO: Author.

American Humane Association. (1981). *Annual report, 1980: National analysis of official child neglect and abuse reporting.* Denver, CO: Author.

American Humane Association. (1984). *Highlights of official child abuse and neglect reporting—1982.* Denver, CO: Author.

American Psychiatric Association. (1987). *Diagnostic and statistical manual of mental disorders* (3rd ed., rev.). Washington, DC: Author.

American Psychiatric Association. (1994). *Diagnostic and statistical manual of mental disorders* (4th ed.). Washington, DC: Author.

Ammerman, R. T. (1991). The role of the child in physical abuse: A reappraisal. *Violence and Victims, 6,* 87-101.

Ammerman, R. T., Van Hasselt, V. B., Hersen, M., McGonigle, J. J., & Lubetsky, M. J. (1989). Abuse and neglect in psychiatrically hospitalized multihandicapped children. *Child Abuse & Neglect, 13,* 335-343.

Amundson, M. J. (1989). Family crisis care: A home-based intervention program for child abuse. *Issues in Mental Health Nursing, 10,* 285-296.

Anasseril, D., & Holcomb, W. (1985). A comparison between men charged with domestic and nondomestic homicide. *Bulletin of the American Academy of Psychiatry and Law, 13,* 233-241.

Anderson, K. E., Lytton, H., & Romney, D. M. (1986). Mothers' interactions with normal and conduct-disordered boys: Who affects whom? *Developmental Psychology, 22,* 604-609.

Anderson, S. C. (1993). Anti-stalking laws: Will they curb the erotomanic's obsessive pursuit? *Law and Psychology Review, 17,* 171-185.

Andrews, B., & Brewin, C. R. (1990). Attributions of blame for marital violence: A study of antecedents and consequences. *Journal of Marriage and the Family, 52,* 757-767.

Anetzberger, G. J. (1987). *The etiology of elder abuse by adult offspring.* Springfield, IL: Charles C Thomas.

Apt, C., & Hurlbert, D. F. (1993). The sexuality of women in physically abusive marriages: A comparative study. *Journal of Family Violence, 8,* 57-69.

Arias, I., & Johnson, P. (1989). Evaluation of physical aggression among intimate dyads. *Journal of Interpersonal Violence, 4,* 298-307.

Arias, I., Samios, M., & O'Leary, K. D. (1987). Prevalence and correlates of physical aggression during courtship. *Journal of Interpersonal Violence, 2,* 82-90.

Armstrong, L. (1978). *Kiss daddy goodnight: A speakout on incest.* New York: Hawthorn.

Arroyo, W., & Eth, S. (1995). Assessment following violence-witnessing trauma. In E. Peled, P. G. Jaffe, & J. L. Edleson (Eds.), *Ending the cycle of violence: Community responses to children of battered women* (pp. 27-42). Thousand Oaks, CA: Sage.

Asbury, J. (1987). African American women in violent relationships. In R. Hampton (Ed.), *Violence in the Black family: Correlates and consequences* (pp. 89-105). Lexington, MA: Lexington Books.

Asbury, J. (1993). Violence in families of color in the United States. In R. L. Hampton, T. P. Gullotta, G. R. Adams, E. H. Potter, III, & R. P. Weissberg (Eds.), *Family violence: Prevention and treatment* (pp. 159-178). Newbury Park, CA: Sage.

Asher, S. J. (1990, August). *Primary, secondary, and tertiary prevention of violence against women.* Paper presented at the annual meeting of the American Psychological Association, Boston.

Astin, M. C., Lawrence, K. J., & Foy, D. W. (1993). Posttraumatic stress disorder among battered women: Risk and resiliency factors. *Violence and Victims, 8,* 17-28.

Atkins, E. (1992). Reporting fetal abuse through California's child abuse and neglect reporting act. *Southwestern University Law Review, 21*(1), 105-123.

Avni, N. (1991). Battered wives: The home as a total institution. *Violence and Victims, 6,* 137-149.

Ayoub, C. C., & Milner, J. S. (1985). Failure to thrive: Parental indicators, types, and outcomes. *Child Abuse & Neglect, 9,* 491-499.

Azar, S. T. (1988). Methodological considerations in treatment outcome research. In G. T. Hotaling, D. Finkelhor, J. T. Kirkpatrick, & M. A. Straus (Eds.), *Coping with family violence* (pp. 288-298). Newbury Park, CA: Sage.

Azar, S. T., Barnes, K. T., & Twentyman, C. T. (1988). Developmental outcomes in abused children: Consequences of parental abuse or a more general breakdown in caregiver behavior? *Behavior Therapist, 11,* 27-32.

Azar, S. T., & Wolfe, D. A. (1989). Child abuse and neglect. In E. J. Mash & R. A. Barkley (Eds.), *Treatment of childhood disorders* (pp. 451-489). New York: Guilford.

Azrin, N. H., Holz, W. C., & Hake, D. F. (1963). Fixed-ratio punishment. *Journal of Experimental Analysis of Behavior, 6,* 141-148.

Babcock, J. C., Waltz, J., Jacobson, N. S., & Gottman, J. M. (1993). Power and violence: The relation between communication patterns, power discrepancies, and domestic violence. *Journal of Consulting and Clinical Psychology, 61,* 40-50.

Bachman, R. (1993). The double edged sword of violent victimization against the elderly: Patterns of family and stranger perpetration. *Journal of Elder Abuse & Neglect, 5*(4), 59-76.

Bachman, R., & Coker, A. L. (1995). Police involvement in domestic violence: The interactive effects of victim injury, offender's history of violence, and race. *Violence and Victims, 10,* 91-106.

Bachman, R., & Pillemer, K. A. (1991). Retirement: Does it affect marital conflict and violence? *Journal of Elder Abuse & Neglect, 3*(2), 75-88.

Bachman, R., & Saltzman, L. E. (1996). *Violence against women: Estimates from the redesigned survey* (Bureau of Justice Statistics special report).

Rockville, MD: U.S. Department of Justice. (NCJ No. 154348)

Bachman, R., & Taylor, B. M. (1994). The measurement of family violence and rape by the redesigned National Crime Victimization Survey. *Justice Quarterly, 11,* 499-512.

Bagarozzi, D., & Giddings, C. (1983). Conjugal violence: A critical review of current research and clinical practices. *American Journal of Family Therapy, 11,* 3-15.

Bagley, C. (1990). Is the prevalence of child sexual abuse decreasing? Evidence from a random sample of 750 young adult women. *Psychological Reports, 66,* 1037-1038.

Bagley, C. (1991). The prevalence and mental health sequels of child abuse in a community sample of women aged 18-27. *Canadian Journal of Community Mental Health, 10*(1), 103-116.

Bagley, C., & Ramsay, R. (1986). Sexual abuse in childhood: Psychological outcomes and implications for social work practice. *Journal of Social Work and Human Sexuality, 4,* 33-47.

Baily, T. F., & Baily, W. H. (1986). *Operational definitions of child emotional maltreatment: Final report* (National Center on Child Abuse and Neglect, DHHS Publication No. 90-CA-0956). Washington, DC: Government Printing Office.

Bakan, D. (1971). *Slaughter of the innocents: A study of the battered child phenomenon.* San Francisco: Jossey-Bass.

Bakwin, H. (1949). Emotional deprivation in infants. *Journal of Pediatrics, 35,* 512-521.

Balos, B., & Trotzky, K. (1988). Enforcement of domestic abuse act in Minnesota: A preliminary study. *Law and Inequality, 6,* 83-107.

Bandura, A. (1971). *Social learning theory.* Morristown, NJ: General Learning.

Bandura, A., Ross, D., & Ross, S. A. (1961). Transmission of aggression through imitation of aggressive models. *Journal of Abnormal and Social Psychology, 67,* 575-582.

Bane, V., Grant, M., Alexander, B., Kelly, K., Brown, S. A., Wegher, B., & Feldon-Mitchell, L. (1990, December 17). Silent no more. *People,* pp. 94-97, 99-100, 102, 104.

Barbaree, H., Marshall, W., & Hudson, S. (Eds.). (1993). *The juvenile sex offender.* New York: Guilford.

Bard, M. (1970). Role of law enforcement in the helping system. In J. Monahan (Ed.), *Community mental health and the criminal justice system* (pp. 99-109). Elmsford, NJ: Pergamon.

Bard, M., & Zacker, J. (1974). Assaultiveness and alcohol use in family disputes. *Criminology, 12,* 281-292.

Barling, J., O'Leary, K. D., Jouriles, E. N., Vivian, P., & MacEwen, K. E. (1987). Factor similarity of the Conflict Tactics Scale across samples, spouses, and sites: Issues and implications. *Journal of Family Violence, 2,* 37-54.

Barnett, O. W., & Fagan, R. W. (1993). Alcohol use in male spouse abusers and their female partners. *Journal of Family Violence, 8,* 1-25.

Barnett, O. W., Fagan, R. W., & Booker, J. M. (1991). Hostility and stress as mediators of aggression in violent men. *Journal of Family Violence, 6,* 219-241.

Barnett, O. W., & Hamberger, L. K. (1992). The assessment of maritally violent men on the California Psychological Inventory. *Violence and Victims, 7,* 15-28.

Barnett, O. W., & LaViolette, A. D. (1993). *It could happen to anyone: Why battered women stay.* Newbury Park, CA: Sage.

Barnett, O. W., Lee, C. Y., & Thelen, R. E. (1995, July). *Gender differences in forms, outcomes, and attributions for interpartner aggression.* Paper presented at the 4th International Family Violence Research Conference, Durham, NH.

Barnett, O. W., & Lopez-Real, D. I. (1985, November). *Women's reactions to battering and why they stay.* Paper presented at the annual meeting of the American Society of Criminology, San Diego, CA.

Barnett, O. W., Martinez, T. E., & Bleustein, B. W. (1995). Jealousy and anxious romantic attachment in maritally violent and nonviolent males. *Journal of Interpersonal Violence, 10,* 473-486.

Barnett, O. W., Martinez, T. E., & Keyson, M. (1996). The relationship between violence, social support, and self-blame in battered women. *Journal of Interpersonal Violence, 11,* 221-233.

Barnett, O. W., & Planeaux, P. S. (1989, January). *A hostility-guilt assessment of counseled and uncounseled batterers.* Paper presented at the Responses to Family Violence Research Conference, Purdue University, Purdue, IN.

Barnett, O. W., & Ryska, T. A. (1986, November). *Masculinity and femininity in male spouse abusers.* Symposium presented at the annual meeting of the American Society of Criminology, Atlanta, GA.

Barnett, O. W., Wood, C., Belmont, J., & Shimogori, Y. (1982, November). *Characteristics of spouse abusers.* Paper presented at the annual meeting of the American Society of Criminology, Toronto.

Barone, V. J., Greene, B. F., & Lutzker, J. R. (1986). Home safety with families being treated for child abuse and neglect. *Behavioral Modification, 14,* 230-254.

Barrera, M., Palmer, S., Brown, R., & Kalaher, S. (1994). Characteristics of court-involved men and non-court-involved men who abuse their wives. *Journal of Family Violence, 9,* 333-345.

Barshis, V. R. G. (1983). The question of marital rape. *Women's Studies International Forum, 6,* 383-393.

Barton, K., & Baglio, C. (1993). The nature of stress in child-abusing families: A factor analytic study. *Psychological Reports, 73,* 1047-1055.

Bass, E., & Davis, L. (1988). *The courage to heal.* New York: Harper & Row.

Bath, H. I., & Haapala, D. A. (1993). Intensive family preservation services with abused and neglected children: An examination of group differences. *Child Abuse & Neglect, 17,* 213-225.

The battered woman: Breaking the cycle of abuse. (1989, June 15). *Emergency Medicine, 15,* 104-115.

Bauer, W. D., & Twentyman, C. T. (1985). Abusing, neglectful, and comparison mothers' responses to child-related and non-child-related stressors. *Journal of Consulting and Clinical Psychology, 53,* 335-343.

Baumann, E. A. (1989). Research rhetoric and the social construction of elder abuse. In J. Best (Ed.), *Images of issues: Typifying contemporary social problems* (pp. 55-74). New York: Aldine de Gruyter.

Baumeister, R. F., Stillwell, A., & Wotman, S. R. (1990). Victim and perpetrator accounts of interpersonal conflict: Autobiographical narratives about anger. *Journal of Personality and Social Psychology, 59,* 994-1005.

Bauserman, S. A. K., & Arias, I. (1992). Relationships among marital investment, marital satisfaction, and marital commitment in domestically victimized and nonvictimized wives. *Violence and Victims, 7,* 287-296.

Bays, J. (1990). Substance abuse and child abuse: Impact of addiction on the child. *Pediatric Clinics of North America, 37,* 881.

Bays, J., & Chadwick, D. (1993). Medical diagnosis of the sexually abused child. *Child Abuse & Neglect, 17,* 91-110.

Beaver, E. D., Gold, S. R., & Prisco, A. G. (1992). Priming macho attitudes and emotions. *Journal of Interpersonal Violence, 7,* 321-333.

Becker, H. W. (1963). *Outsiders.* New York: Free Press.

Becker, J. V. (1994). Offenders: Characteristics and treatment. *Future of Children, 4,* 176-197.

Becker, J. V., Kaplan, M. S., Cunningham-Rathner, J., & Kavoussi, R. (1986). Characteristics of adolescent sexual perpetrators: Preliminary findings. *Journal of Family Violence, 1,* 85-87.

Beitchman, J. H., Zucker, K. J., Hood, J. E., daCosta, G. A., & Akman, D. (1991). A review of the short-term effects of child sexual abuse. *Child Abuse & Neglect, 15,* 537-556.

Beitchman, J. H., Zucker, K. J., Hood, J. E., daCosta, G. A., Akman, D., & Cassavia, E. (1992). A review of the long-term effects of child sexual abuse. *Child Abuse & Neglect, 16,* 101-118.

Beitiks, K. O. (1994, August). Violence on the homefront: A tiny step to alleviate dangers. *California Bar Journal,* pp. 1, 6.

Belknap, J. (1989). The sexual victimization of unmarried women in nonrelative acquaintances. In M. A. Pirog-Good & J. E. Stets (Eds.), *Violence in dating relationships: Emerging social issues* (pp. 205-218). New York: Praeger.

Bell, R. Q. (1977). Socialization findings reexamined. In R. Q. Bell & L. V. Harper (Eds.), *Child effects on adults* (pp. 53-85). Hillsdale, NJ: Lawrence Erlbaum.

Bell, R. Q., & Chapman, M. (1986). Child effects in studies using experimental or brief longitudinal approaches to socialization. *Developmental Psychology, 22,* 595-603.

Belsky, J. (1980). Child maltreatment: An ecological integration. *American Psychologist, 35,* 320-335.

Belsky, J. (1993). Etiology of child maltreatment: A developmental-ecological analysis. *Psychological Bulletin, 114,* 413-434.

Benatar, P., Geraldo, N., & Capps, R. (1981). *Hell is for children* [Record]. Rare Blue Music, Inc./Neil Geraldo (ASCAP), Red Admiral Music Inc./Big Tooth Music Co. (BMI), Rare Blue Music Inc./Muscletone Music (ASCAP). (1980)

Bendik, M. F. (1992). Reaching the breaking point: Dangers of mistreatment in elder caregiving situations. *Journal of Elder Abuse & Neglect, 4*(3), 39-59.

Benedict, M., White, R., Wulff, L., & Hall, B. (1990). Reported maltreatment in children with multiple disabilities. *Child Abuse & Neglect, 14,* 207-217.

Bennett, L. W., Tolman, R. M., Rogalski, C. J., & Srinivasaraghavan, J. (1994). Domestic abuse by male alcohol and drug addicts. *Violence and Victims, 9,* 359-368.

Berger, A. (1985). Characteristics of abusing families. In L. L'Abate (Ed.), *The handbook of family psychology and therapy* (pp. 900-936). Homewood, IL: Dorsey.

Bergman, B., Larsson, G., Brismar, B., & Klang, M. (1988). Aetiological and precipitating factors in wife battering. *Acta Psychiatric Scandinavia, 77,* 338-345.

Bergman, L. (1992). Dating violence among high school students. *Social Work, 37,* 21-27.

Berk, R. A. (1986). What a difference a day makes: An empirical study of the impact of shelters for battered women. *Journal of Marriage and the Family, 48,* 481.

Berk, R. A. (1993). What the scientific evidence shows: On average, we can do no better than arrest. In R. J. Gelles & D. R. Loseke (Eds.), *Current controversies on family violence* (pp. 323-336). Newbury Park, CA: Sage.

Berk, R. A., Campbell, A., Klap, R., & Western, B. (1992). The deterrent effect of arrest in incidents of domestic violence: A Bayesian analysis of four field experiments. *American Sociological Review, 57,* 698-708.

Berk, R. A., Fenstermaker, S., & Newton, P. J. (1990). An empirical analysis of police responses to incidents of wife battery. In G. T. Hotaling, D. Finkelhor, J. T. Kirkpatrick, & M. A. Straus (Eds.), *Coping with family violence* (pp. 158-168). Newbury Park, CA: Sage.

Berk, R. A., & Newton, P. J. (1985). Does arrest really deter wife battery? An effort to replicate the findings of the Minneapolis spouse abuse experiment. *American Sociological Review, 50,* 253-262.

Berk, R. A., Newton, P., & Berk, S. F. (1986). What a difference a day makes: An empirical study of the impact of shelters for battered women. *Journal of Marriage and the Family, 48,* 481-490.

Berlin, F. S., & Meinecke, C. F. (1981). Treatment of sex offenders with anti-androgenic medication: Conceptualization, review of treatment modalities and preliminary findings. *American Journal of Psychiatry, 138,* 601-607.

Berliner, L. (1991). Clinical work with sexually abused children. In C. R. Hollin & K. Howells (Eds.), *Clinical approaches to sex offenders and their victims* (pp. 209-228). New York: John Wiley.

Berliner, L. (1994). The problem with neglect. *Journal of Interpersonal Violence, 9,* 556.

Berliner, L., & Conte, J. R. (1990). The process of victimization: The victim's perspective. *Child Abuse & Neglect, 14,* 29-40.

Bernard, C., & Schlaffer, E. (1992). Domestic violence in Austria: The institutional response. In E. C. Viano (Ed.), *Intimate violence: An interdisciplinary perspective* (pp. 243-254). Bristol, PA: Taylor & Francis.

Bernard, J. L., Bernard, S. L., & Bernard, M. L. (1985). Courtship violence and sex typing. *Family Relations, 34,* 573-576.

Bernard, M. L., & Bernard, J. L. (1983). Violent intimacy: The family as a model for love relationships. *Family Relations, 32,* 283-286.

Berry, D. B. (1996). *The domestic violence sourcebook.* Los Angeles: Lowell House.

Berry, M. (1991). The assessment of imminence of risk of placement: Lessons from a family preservation program. *Children and Youth Services Review, 13,* 239-256.

Bersani, C. A., Chen, H. T., Pendleton, B. F., & Denton, R. (1992). Personality traits of convicted male batterers. *Journal of Family Violence, 7,* 123-134.

Berson, N., & Herman-Giddens, M. (1994). Recognizing invasive genital care practices: A form of child sexual abuse. *The APSAC Advisor, 7*(1), 13-14.

Besharov, D. (1990). *Recognizing child abuse.* New York: Free Press.

Besharov, D. (1991). Reducing unfounded reports. *Journal of Interpersonal Violence, 6,* 112-115.

Besharov, D. J. (1985). "Doing something" about child abuse: The need to narrow the grounds for state intervention. *Harvard Journal of Law and Public Policy, 3,* 539-589.

Best, J. (Ed.). (1989). *Images of issues: Typifying contemporary social problems.* New York: Aldine de Gruyter.

Beutler, L. E., Williams, R. E., & Zetzer, H. A. (1994). Efficacy of treatment for victims of child sexual abuse. *Future of Children, 4*(2), 156-175.

Biden, J. R. (1993). Violence against women. *American Psychologist, 48,* 1059-1061.

Biegel, D. E., Sales, E., & Schulz, R. (1991). *Family caregiving in chronic illness: Alzheimer's disease, cancer, heart disease, mental illness, and stroke.* Newbury Park, CA: Sage.

Billingham, R. E. (1987). Courtship violence: The patterns of conflict resolution strategies across seven levels of emotional commitment. *Family Relations, 36,* 283-289.

The billion-dollar epidemic. (1992, January 6). *American Medical News, 35*(1), 7.

Biology and family, partners in crime. (1996, July 6). *Science News, 150*(1), 11.

Birns, B., Cascardi, M., & Meyer, S. (1994). Sex-role socialization: Developmental influences on wife abuse. *American Journal of Orthopsychiatry, 64,* 50-59.

Birns, B., & Meyer, S. L. (1993). Mothers' role in incest: Dysfunctional women or dysfunctional theories? *Journal of Child Sexual Abuse, 2*(3), 127-135.

Black, D. (1980). *The manners and customs of the police.* New York: Academic Press.

Black, D., & Kaplan, T. (1988). Father kills mother: Issues and problems encountered by a child psychiatric team. *British Journal of Psychiatry, 153,* 624-630.

Black, M., Schuler, M., & Nair, P. (1993). Prenatal drug exposure: Neurodevelopmental outcome and parenting environment. *Journal of Pediatric Psychology, 18,* 605-620.

Blake-White, J., & Kline, C. M. (1985). Treating the dissociative process in adult victims of childhood incest. *Social Casework, 66,* 394-402.

Blakely, B. E., & Dolon, R. (1991). Area agencies on aging and the prevention of elder abuse: The results of a national study. *Journal of Elder Abuse & Neglect, 3*(2), 21-40.

Blankenhorn, D. (1994, December 19). Not orphanages or prisons, but responsible fathers. *Los Angeles Times,* p. 7.

Block, M. R., & Sinnott, J. D. (1979). *The battered elder syndrome: An exploratory.* Baltimore: University of Maryland, Center on Aging.

Bloom, D. (1996, March 23). Child-abuse reports soar in L.A. *Daily News,* p. 4.

Blunt, A. P. (1993). Financial exploitation of the incapacitated. *Journal of Elder Abuse & Neglect, 5*(1), 19-32.

Bograd, M. (1988). Feminist perspectives on wife abuse: An introduction. In K. Yllö & M. Bograd (Eds.), *Feminist perspectives on wife abuse* (pp. 11-26). Newbury Park, CA: Sage.

Bograd, M. (1990). Why we need gender to understand human violence. *Journal of Interpersonal Violence, 5,* 132-135.

Bograd, M. (1992). Values in conflict: Challenges to family therapists' thinking. *Journal of Marital and Family Therapy, 18,* 245-256.

Bologna, M. J., Waterman, C. K., & Dawson, L. J. (1987, July). *Violence in gay male and lesbian relationships: Implications for practitioners and policy makers.* Paper presented at the Third National Family Violence Research Conference, Durham, NH.

Bolton, F. G., & Bolton, S. R. (1987). *Working with violent families.* Newbury Park, CA: Sage.

Bolton, F. G., Laner, R. H., Gai, D. G., & Kane, S. P. (1981). The study of child maltreatment: When is research . . . research? *Journal of Family Issues, 2,* 535-539.

Bonfante, J., Cole, W., Gwynne, S. C., & Kamlani, R. (1994, June 6). Oprah! Oprah in the court. *Time, 143*(23), 30-31.

Bookwala, J., Frieze, I. H., Smith, C., & Ryan, K. (1992). Predictors of dating violence: A multivariate analysis. *Violence and Victims, 7,* 297-311.

Bools, C., Neale, B., & Meadow, R. (1994). Munchausen syndrome by proxy: A study of psychopathology. *Child Abuse & Neglect, 18,* 773-788.

Booth, A. B., & Osgood, D. W. (1993). The influence of testosterone on deviance in adulthood: Assessing and explaining the relationship. *Criminology, 31,* 93-117.

Boudreau, F. A. (1993). Elder abuse. In R. L. Hampton, T. P. Gullotta, G. R. Adams, E. H. Potter, III, & R. P. Weissberg (Eds.), *Family violence: Prevention and treatment* (pp. 142-158). Newbury Park, CA: Sage.

Bourg, S., & Stock, H. V. (1994). A review of domestic violence arrest statistics in a police department using a pro-arrest police: Are pro-arrest policies enough? *Journal of Family Violence, 9,* 177-192.

Bourque, L. (1989). *Defining rape.* Durham, NC: Duke University Press.

Bousha, D. M., & Twentyman, C. T. (1984). Mother-child interactional style in abuse, neglect, and control groups: Naturalistic observations in the home. *Journal of Abnormal Psychology, 93,* 106-114.

Bouza, A. (1991). Responding to domestic violence. In M. Steinman (Ed.), *Woman battering: Policy responses* (pp. 191-102). Cincinnati, OH: Anderson.

Bowen, N. H. (1982). Guidelines for career counseling with abused women. *Vocational Guidance Quarterly, 31,* 123-127.

Bower, B. (1993a). Sudden recall: Adult memories of child abuse spark heated debate. *Science News, 144,* 177-192.

Bower, B. (1993b). The survivor syndrome. *Science News, 144,* 202-204.

Bower, B. (1994). Alcoholism exposes its "insensitive" side. *Science News, 145,* 118.

Bower, B. (1996, February 10). Excess lead linked to boys' delinquency. *Science News, 149*(6), 81-96.

Bowker, L. H. (1983). *Beating wife beating.* Lexington, MA: Lexington Books.

Bowker, L. H. (1993). A battered woman's problems are social, not psychological. In R. J.

Gelles & D. R. Loseke (Eds.), *Current controversies on family violence* (pp. 154-165). Newbury Park, CA: Sage.

Bowker, L. H., Arbitell, M., & McFerron, J. R. (1988). On the relationship between wife beating and child abuse. In K. Yllö & M. Bograd (Eds.), *Feminist perspectives on wife abuse* (pp. 158-174). Newbury Park, CA: Sage.

Bowker, L. H., & Mauer, L. (1986). The effectiveness of counseling services utilized by battered women. *Women and Therapy, 5,* 65-82.

Bowlby, J. (1980). *Attachment and loss: Loss* (Vol. 3). London: Hogarth.

Boxall, B. (1996, February 10). Photo index of convicted child molester unveiled. *Los Angeles Times, 17,* 1.

Bradford, J. (1990). The antiandrogen and hormonal treatment of sex offenders. In W. L. Marshall, D. R. Laws, & H. E. Barbaree (Eds.), *Handbook of sexual assault: Issues, theories, and treatment of the offender* (pp. 297-327). New York: Plenum.

Brassard, M. R., Germain, R., & Hart, S. N. (1987a). The challenge: To better understand and combat psychological maltreatment of children and youth. In M. R. Brassard, R. Germain, & S. N. Hart (Eds.), *Psychological maltreatment of children and youth* (pp. 3-24). New York: Pergamon.

Brassard, M. R., Germain, R., & Hart, S. N. (1987b). *Psychological maltreatment of children and youth.* New York: Pergamon.

Brassard, M. R., Hart, S. N., & Hardy, D. (1991). Psychological and emotional abuse of children. In R. T. Ammerman & M. Hersen (Eds.), *Case studies in family violence* (pp. 255-270). New York: Plenum.

Brassard, M. R., Hart, S. N., & Hardy, D. (1993). The psychological maltreatment rating scales. *Child Abuse & Neglect, 17,* 715-729.

Braun, K., Lenzer, A., Shumacher-Mukai, C., & Snyder, P. (1993). A decision tree for managing elder abuse and neglect. *Journal of Elder Abuse & Neglect, 5*(3), 89-103.

Braun, S., & Pasternak, J. (1994, September 2). Life of violence catches up to suspected murderer, 11. *Los Angeles Times,* pp. A1, A18.

Breines, G., & Gordon, L. (1983). The new scholarship on family violence. *Signs: Journal of Women in Culture and Society, 8,* 490-531.

Bremner, R. H. (1971). *Children and youth in America: A documentary history: Vol. 2. 1866-1932.* Cambridge, MA: Harvard University Press.

Bresee, P., Stearns, G. B., Bess, B. H., & Packer, L. S. (1986). Allegations of child sexual abuse in child custody disputes: A therapeutic assessment model. *American Journal of Orthopsychiatry, 56,* 560-569.

Brice-Baker, J. R. (1994). Domestic violence in African-American and African-Caribbean families. *Journal of Social Distress and the Homeless, 3,* 23-38.

Bridges, G. S., & Weis, J. G. (1985). *Study design and its effects on correlates of violent behavior.* Seattle: University of Washington, Center for Law and Justice.

Briere, J. (1987). Predicting self-reported likelihood of battering: Attitudes and childhood experiences. *Research in Personality, 21,* 61-69.

Briere, J. (1992a). *Child abuse trauma: Theory and treatment of the lasting effects.* Newbury Park, CA: Sage.

Briere, J. (1992b). Methodological issues in the study of sexual abuse effects. *Journal of Consulting and Clinical Psychology, 60,* 196-203.

Briere, J., & Conte, J. (1993). Self-reported amnesia for abuse in adults molested as children. *Journal of Traumatic Stress, 6,* 21-31.

Briere, J., & Elliott, D. M. (1994). Immediate and long-term impacts of child sexual abuse. *Future of Children, 4*(2), 54-69.

Briere, J., & Runtz, M. (1987). Post sexual abuse trauma: Data and implications for clinical practice. *Journal of Interpersonal Violence, 2,* 367-379.

Briere, J., & Runtz, M. (1988). Multivariate correlates of childhood psychological and physical maltreatment among university women. *Child Abuse & Neglect, 12,* 331-341.

Briere, J., & Runtz, M. (1989). The Trauma Symptoms Checklist (TSC-33): Early data on a new scale. *Journal of Interpersonal Violence, 4,* 151-163.

Briere, J., & Runtz, M. (1990). Differential adult symptomatology associated with three types of child abuse histories. *Child Abuse & Neglect, 14,* 357-364.

Briere, J., & Zaidi, L. Y. (1989). Sexual abuse histories and sequelae in female psychiatric emergency room patients. *American Journal of Psychiatry, 146,* 1602-1606.

Brinkerhoff, M. B., & Lupri, E. (1988). Interpersonal violence. *Canadian Journal of Sociology, 13,* 407-434.

Bristowe, E., & Collins, J. B. (1989). Family mediated abuse of noninstitutionalized frail elderly men and women in British Columbia. *Journal of Elder Abuse & Neglect, 1*(1), 45-64.

Brody, E. M. (1981). "Women in the middle" and family help to older people. *Gerontologist, 21,* 471-480.

Brommer, S. (1993, October 13). Domestic abuse law requires medical reporting. *Daily News,* p. 4.

Broude, G. J., & Greene, S. J. (1983). Cross-cultural codes on husband-wife relationship. *Ethnology, 22,* 263-280.

Brower, M., & Sackett, R. (1985, November 4). Split. *People Magazine,* pp. 108, 111.

Brown, J. K. (1992). Introduction: Definitions, assumptions, themes, and issues. In D. A. Counts, J. K. Brown, & J. C. Campbell (Eds.), *Sanctions and sanctuary: Cultural perspectives on the beating of wives* (pp. 1-18). Boulder, CO: Westview.

Browne, A. (1983, March). *Self-defensive homicides by battered women: Relationships at risk.* Paper presented at the meeting of the American Psychology-Law Society, Chicago.

Browne, A. (1987). *When battered women kill.* New York: Free Press.

Browne, A. (1990, December 11). *Assaults between intimate partners in the United States: Incidence, prevalence, and proportional, risk for women and men.* Testimony before the United States Senate, Committee on the Judiciary, Washington, DC.

Browne, A., & Finkelhor, D. (1986). Impact of child sexual abuse: A review of the research. *Psychological Bulletin, 99,* 66-77.

Browning, J., & Dutton, D. (1986). Assessment of wife assault with the Conflict Tactics Scale: Using couple data to quantify the differential reporting effect. *Journal of Marriage and the Family, 48,* 375-379.

Brownmiller, S. (1975). *Against our will: Men, women, and rape.* New York: Bantam.

Bruce, D. A., & Zimmerman, R. A. (1989). Shaken impact syndrome. *Pediatric Annals, 18,* 482-494.

Bruch, C. S. (1988). And how are the children? The effects of ideology and mediation on child custody law and children's well-being in the United States. *International Journal of Law and the Family, 2,* 106-126.

Brunk, M., Henggeler, S. W., & Whelan, J. P. (1987). Comparison of multi-systemic therapy and parent training in the brief treatment of child abuse and neglect. *Journal of Consulting and Clinical Psychology, 55,* 171-178.

Brush, L. D. (1990). Violent acts and injurious outcomes in married couples: Methodological issues in the National Survey of Families and Households. *Gender & Society, 4,* 56-67.

Brustin, S. L. (1995). Legal responses to dating violence [Special issue]. *Family Law Quarterly, 29,* 331-356.

Bryan, J. W., & Freed, F. W. (1982). Corporal punishment: Normative data and sociological and psychological correlates in a community population. *Journal of Youth and Adolescence, 11,* 77-87.

Bryer, J. B., Nelson, B. A., Miller, J. B., & Krol, P. A. (1987). Childhood sexual and physical abuse as factors in adult psychiatric illness. *American Journal of Psychiatry, 144,* 1426-1430.

Budin, L. E., & Johnson, C. F. (1989). Sex abuse prevention programs: Offenders' attitudes about their efficacy. *Child Abuse & Neglect, 13,* 77-87.

Burcky, W. D., & Reuterman, N. A. (1989). Dating violence in high school: A profile of the victims. *Psychology: A Journal of Human Behavior, 26,* 1-9.

Bureau of Justice Statistics. (1992). *Criminal victimization in the United States, 1991.* Washington, DC: U.S. Department of Justice, Bureau of Justice Statistics. (NCJ No. 139563)

Burge, S. K. (1995, August). *Stop the abuse: Teaching physicians to intervene with family violence.* Paper presented at the annual meeting of the American Psychological Association, New York.

Burgess, A. W. (1995). Rape trauma syndrome. In P. Searles & R. J. Berger (Eds.), *Rape and society: Readings on the problem of sexual assault* (pp. 239-245). Boulder, CO: Westview.

Burke, A. (1995, July 31). Valley needs more shelter beds. *Daily News,* p. 6.

Burke, P. J., Stets, J. E., & Pirog-Good, M. A. (1989). Gender identity, self-esteem, and physical and sexual abuse in dating relationships. In M. A. Pirog-Good & J. E. Stets (Eds.), *Violence in dating relationships: Emerging social issues* (pp. 72-93). New York: Praeger.

Burman, B., Margolin, G., & John, R. S. (1993). America's angriest home videos: Behavioral contingencies observed in home reenactment of marital conflict. *Journal of Consulting and Clinical Psychology, 61,* 28-39.

Burnam, M. A., Stein, J. A., Golding, J. M., Siegel, J. M., Sorenson, S. B., Forsythe, A. B., & Telles, C. A. (1988). Sexual assault and mental disorders in a community population. *Journal of Consulting and Clinical Psychology, 56,* 843-850.

Burt, M. R. (1980). Cultural myths and support for rape. *Journal of Personality and Social Psychology, 38,* 217-230.

Burt, M. R. (1991). Rape myths and acquaintance rape. In A. Parrot & L. Bechhofer (Eds.), *Acquaintance rape: The hidden crime* (pp. 26-40). New York: John Wiley.

Bushman, B. J., & Cooper, H. M. (1990). Effects of alcohol on human aggression: An integrative research review. *Psychological Bulletin, 107,* 341-354.

Business Publishers, Inc. (1996). *Directory of aging resources* (3rd ed.). Thousand Oaks, CA: Sage.

Buss, A., & Durkee, A. (1957). An inventory for assessing different kinds of hostility. *Journal of Consulting Psychology, 2,* 343-349.

Butler, K. (1994, June). Clashing memories, mixed messages. *Los Angeles Times Magazine,* p. 12.

Buzawa, E. S., & Buzawa, C. G. (1990). *Domestic violence: The criminal justice response.* Newbury Park, CA: Sage.

Buzawa, E. S., & Buzawa, C. G. (1993). The scientific evidence is not conclusive. In R. J. Gelles & D. R. Loseke (Eds.), *Current controversies on family violence* (pp. 337-356). Newbury Park, CA: Sage.

Byrne, C. A., Arias, I., & Lyons, C. M. (1993, March). *Attributions for partner behavior in violent and nonviolent couples.* Paper presented at the annual meeting of the Southeastern Psychological Association, Atlanta, GA.

Cabrino, J. (1978). The elusive crime of emotional abuse. *Child Abuse & Neglect, 2,* 89-99.

Caesar, P. L. (1988). Exposure to violence in the families-of-origin among wife abusers and maritally nonviolent men. *Violence and Victims, 3,* 49-63.

Caesar, P. L., & Hamberger, L. K. (Eds.). (1989). *Treating men who batter.* New York: Springer.

Cahill, C., Llewelyn, S. P., & Pearson, C. (1991). Treatment of sexual abuse which occurred in childhood: A review. *British Journal of Clinical Psychology, 30,* 1-12.

Cahn, N. R., & Lerman, L. G. (1991). Prosecuting woman abuse. In M. Steinman (Ed.), *Woman battering: Policy responses* (pp. 95-112). Cincinnati, OH: Anderson.

Caliso, J. A., & Milner, J. S. (1994). Childhood physical abuse, childhood social support, and adult child abuse potential. *Journal of Interpersonal Violence, 9,* 27-44.

Callahan, J. J. (1988). Elder abuse: Some questions for policymakers. *Gerontologist, 28,* 453-458.

Campbell, J. C. (1989a). A test of two explanatory models of women's responses to battering. *Nursing Research, 38*(1), 18-24.

Campbell, J. C. (1989b). Women's responses to sexual abuse in intimate relationships. *Health Care for Women International, 8,* 335-347.

Campbell, J. C. (1990, December). Battered woman syndrome: A critical review. *Violence Update, 1*(4), 1, 4, 10-11.

Campbell, J. C., & Alford, P. (1989). The dark consequences of marital rape. *American Journal of Nursing, 87,* 946-949.

Campbell, J. C., & Sheridan, D. J. (1989). Emergency nursing interventions with battered women. *Journal of Emergency Nursing, 15,* 12-17.

Candell, S., Frazier, P., Arikan, N., & Tofteland, A. (1993, August). *Legal outcomes in rape cases: Case attrition and postrape recovery.* Paper presented at the annual meeting of the American Psychological Association, Toronto.

Cantos, A. L., Neidig, P. H., & O'Leary, K. D. (1994). Injuries of women and men in a treatment program for domestic violence. *Journal of Family Violence, 9,* 113-124.

Cappell, C., & Heiner, R. B. (1990). The intergenerational transmission of family aggression. *Journal of Family Violence, 5,* 135-152.

Carden, A. D. (1994). Wife abuse and the wife abuser: Review and recommendations. *Counseling Psychologist, 22,* 539-582.

Caringella-MacDonald, S. (1988). Parallels and pitfalls: The aftermath of legal reform for sexual assault, marital rape, and domestic violence victims. *Journal of Interpersonal Violence, 3,* 174-189.

Carlisle-Frank, P. (1991, July). Do battered women's beliefs about control affect their decisions to remain in abusive environments. *Violence Update, 1*(11), 1, 8, 10-11.

Carlson, B. E. (1984). Children's observations of interparental violence. In A. R. Roberts (Ed.), *Battered women and their families* (pp. 147-167). New York: Springer.

Carlson, B. E. (1990). Adolescent observers of marital violence. *Journal of Family Violence, 5,* 285-299.

Carlson, B. E. (1996). Dating violence: Student beliefs about the consequences. *Journal of Interpersonal Violence, 11,* 3-18.

Carlson, V., Cicchetti, D., Barnett, D., & Braumwald, K. (1989). Disorganized/disoriented attachment relationships in maltreated infants. *Developmental Psychology, 25,* 525-531.

Carmody, D. C., & Williams, K. R. (1987). Wife assault and perceptions of sanctions. *Violence and Victims, 2,* 25-38.

Carroll, C. A., & Haase, C. C. (1987). The function of protective services in child abuse and neglect. In R. Helfer & R. Kempe (Eds.), *The battered child* (4th ed., pp. 137-151). Chicago: University of Chicago Press.

Cascardi, M., Langhinrichsen, J., & Vivian, D. (1992). Marital aggression, impact, injury, and health correlates for husbands and wives. *Archives of Internal Medicine, 152,* 1178-1184.

Cassady, L., Allen, B., Lyon, E., & McGeehan, D. (1987, July). *The child-focused intervention program: Treatment and program evaluation for children in a battered women's shelter.* Paper presented at the Third National Family Violence Research Conference, Durham, NH.

Cate, R. M., Henton, J. M., Koval, J., Christopher, F. S., & Lloyd, S. (1982). Premarital abuse: A social psychological perspective. *Journal of Family Issues, 3,* 79-90.

Cate, R. M., & Lloyd, S. A. (1992). *Courtship.* Newbury Park, CA: Sage.

Cavaiola, A. A., & Schiff, M. (1988). Behavioral sequelae of physical and/or sexual abuse in adolescents. *Child Abuse & Neglect, 12,* 181-188.

Cavaliere, F. (1995). Parents killing kids: A nation's shame. *APA Monitor, 26*(2), 34.

Ceci, S., & Bruck, M. (1993). Suggestibility of the child witness: A historical review and synthesis. *Psychological Bulletin, 113,* 403-439.

Celano, M. P. (1990). Activities and games for group psychotherapy with sexually abused children. *International Journal of Group Psychotherapy, 40,* 419-429.

Chadhuri, M., & Daly, K. (1991). Do restraining orders help? Battered women's experiences with male violence and the legal process. In E. S. Buzawa & C. G. Buzawa (Eds.), *Domestic violence: The changing criminal justice response* (pp. 227-252). Westport, CT: Greenwood.

Chaffin, M. (1994). Research in action: Assessment and treatment of child sexual abusers. *Journal of Interpersonal Violence, 9,* 224-237.

Chan, P. H. T. (1985). Report of elder abuse at home in Hong Kong. Hong Kong Council of Social Services and Hong Kong Polytechnic.

Chang, D. B. K. (1989). An abused spouse's self-saving process: A theory of identity transformation. *Sociological Perspectives, 32,* 535-550.

Chapman, J., & Smith, B. (1987). *Child sexual abuse: An analysis of case processing.* Washington, DC: American Bar Association.

Chen, H., Bersani, C., Myers, S. C., & Denton, R. (1990). Evaluating the effectiveness of a court sponsored abuser treatment program. *Journal of Family Violence, 4,* 309-322.

Chesler, P. (1986). *Mothers on trial: The battle for children and custody.* Seattle, WA: Seal.

Chester, B., Robin, R. W., Koss, M. P., Lopez, M. P., & Goldman, D. (1994). Grandmother dishonored: Violence against women by male partners in American Indian communities. *Violence and Victims, 9,* 249-258.

Child care bill has $20 million for criminal history check. (1995, December 1). *Criminal Justice Newsletter, 24*(23), 6.

Child Welfare League of America. (1986). *Too young to run: The status of child abuse in America.* New York: Author.

Children's Safety Network. (1992). *Domestic violence: A directory of protocols for health care providers.* Newton, MA: Education Development Center.

Chiriboga, C. A. (1993). Fetal effects. *Neurologic Clinics, 3,* 707-728.

Choi, A., & Edleson, J. L. (1995). Advocating legal intervention in wife assaults: Results from a national survey of Singapore. *Journal of Interpersonal Violence, 10,* 243-258.

Choice, P., Lamke, L. K., & Pittman, J. F. (1995). Conflict resolution strategies and marital distress as mediating factors in the link between witnessing interparental violence and wife battering. *Violence and Victims, 10,* 107-119.

Christensen, A., Margolin, G., & Sullaway, M. (1992). Interparental agreement on child behavior problems. *Psychological Assessment, 4,* 419-425.

Christopoulos, C., Bonvillian, J. D., & Crittenden, P. M. (1988). Maternal language input and child maltreatment. *Infant Mental Health Journal, 9,* 272-286.

Christopoulos, C., Cohn, A. D., Shaw, D. S., Joyce, S., Sullivan-Hanson, J., Kraft, S. P., & Emery, R. E. (1987). Children of abused women: I. Adjustment at time of shelter residence. *Journal of Marriage and the Family, 49,* 611-619.

Chu, J. A., & Dill, D. L. (1990). Dissociative symptoms in relation to childhood physical and sexual abuse. *American Journal of Psychiatry, 147,* 887-892.

Churchill, S. D. (1993). The lived meanings of date rape: Seeing through the eyes of the victim. *Family Violence and Sexual Assault Bulletin, 9*(1), 20-23.

Cicchetti, D., & Barnett, D. (1991). Toward the development of a scientific nosology of child maltreatment. In D. Cicchetti & W. Grove (Eds.), *Thinking clearly about psychology: Essays in honor of Paul E. Meehl* (pp. 346-377). Minneapolis: University of Minnesota Press.

Cicchetti, D., & Carlson, V. (Eds.). (1989). *Child maltreatment: Theory and research on the causes and consequences of child abuse and neglect.* New York: Cambridge University Press.

Cicchetti, D., & Rizley, R. (1981). Developmental perspectives on the etiology, intergenera-

tional transmission, and sequelae of child maltreatment. In D. Cicchetti & R. Rizley (Eds.), *New directions for child development: Developmental perspectives on child maltreatment* (pp. 31-55). San Francisco: Jossey-Bass.

Cicchetti, D., Toth, S., & Bush, M. (1988). Developmental psychopathology and incompetence in childhood: Suggestions for intervention. In B. Lahey & A. Kazdin (Eds.), *Advances in clinical child psychology* (pp. 1-71). New York: Plenum.

Claerhout, S., Elder, J., & Janes, C. (1982). Problem-solving skills of rural battered women. *American Journal of Community Psychology, 10,* 605-612.

Claes, J. A., & Rosenthal, D. M. (1990). Men who batter women: A study in power. *Journal of Family Violence, 5,* 215-224.

Clark-Daniels, C. L., Daniels, R. S., & Baumhover, L. A. (1989). Physicians' and nurses' responses to abuse of the elderly: A comparative study of two surveys in Alabama. *Journal of Elder Abuse & Neglect, 1*(4), 57-72.

Claussen, A. H., & Crittenden, P. M. (1991). Physical and psychological maltreatment: Relations among types of maltreatment. *Child Abuse & Neglect, 15,* 5-18.

Clearinghouse on Child Abuse and Neglect Information. (1992). *Reporting drug-exposed infants.* Fairfax, VA: Caliber Associates.

Coates, C. J., Leong, D. J., & Lindsay, M. (1987, July). *Personality differences among batterers voluntarily seeking treatment and those ordered to treatment by the court.* Paper presented at the Third National Family Violence Research Conference, Durham, NH.

Cohen, J. A., & Mannarino, A. P. (1993). A treatment model for sexually abused preschoolers. *Journal of Interpersonal Violence, 8,* 115-131.

Cohn, A. H., & Daro, D. (1987). Is treatment too late: What ten years of evaluation research tell us. *Child Abuse & Neglect, 11,* 433-442.

Coleman, D. H., & Straus, M. A. (1983). Alcohol abuse and family violence. In E. Gottheil, A. Durley, I. F. Skolada, & H. M. Waxman (Eds.), *Alcohol, drug abuse, and aggression* (pp. 104-123). Springfield, MA: Charles C Thomas.

Coleman, D. H., & Straus, M. A. (1986). Marital power, conflict, and violence in a nationally representative sample of American couples. *Violence and Victims, 1,* 141-157.

Collins, J. J., & Schlenger, W. E. (1988). Acute and chronic effects of alcohol use on violence. *Journal of Studies on Alcohol, 49,* 516-521.

Comstock, G., & Strasburger, V. C. (1990). Deceptive appearances: Television violence and aggressive behavior. *Journal of Adolescent Health Care, 11,* 31-44.

Conaway, L. P., & Hansen, D. J. (1989). Social behavior of physically abused and neglected children: A critical review. *Clinical Psychology Review, 9,* 627-652.

Conger, R. D., Burgess, R., & Barrett, C. (1979). Child abuse related to life change and perceptions of illness: Some preliminary findings. *Family Coordinator, 28,* 73-78.

Conrad, P., & Schneider, J. W. (1992). *Deviance and medicalization: From badness to sickness: With a new afterword by the authors.* Philadelphia: Temple University Press.

Conte, J. R. (1993). Sexual abuse of children. In R. L. Hampton, T. P. Gullotta, G. R. Adams, E. H. Potter, III, & R. P. Weissberg (Eds.), *Family violence: Prevention and treatment* (pp. 56-85). Newbury Park, CA: Sage.

Conte, J. R., & Schuerman, J. R. (1987). Factors associated with an increased impact of child sexual abuse. *Child Abuse & Neglect, 11,* 201-211.

Conte, J. R., Wolf, S., & Smith, T. (1989). What sexual offenders tell us about prevention strategies. *Child Abuse & Neglect, 13,* 293-301.

Corder, B. F., Haizlip, T., & DeBoer, P. A. (1990). A pilot study for a structured, time-limited therapy group for sexually abused pre-adolescent children. *Child Abuse & Neglect, 14,* 243-251.

Cornell, C. P., & Gelles, R. J. (1982). Adolescent to parent violence. *Urban Social Change Review, 15,* 8-14.

Corse, S., Schmid, K., & Trickett, P. (1990). Social network characteristics of mothers in abusing and nonabusing families and their relationships to parenting beliefs. *Journal of Community Psychology, 18,* 44-59.

Corvo, K. N. (1992). Attachment and violence in the families-of-origin of domestically violent men. *Dissertation Abstracts International, 54,* 1950A. (UMI No. 9322595)

Courtois, C., & Watts, C. (1982). Counseling adult women who experienced incest in childhood or adolescence. *Personnel and Guidance Journal, 60,* 275-279.

Coyne, A. C., Reichman, W. E., & Berbig, L. J. (1993). The relationship between dementia and elder abuse. *American Journal of Psychiatry, 150,* 643-663.

Crime bill contains billions for state and local agencies (Violence Against Women Act). (1994, August). *Criminal Justice Newsletter, 26*(6), 6-7.

Crimmins, D. B., Bradlyn, A. S., St. Lawrence, J. S., & Kelly, J. A. (1984). In-clinic training to improve the parent-child interaction skills of a neglectful mother. *Child Abuse & Neglect, 8,* 533-539.

Crittenden, P. M. (1982). Abusing, neglecting, problematic, and adequate dyads: Differentiating patterns of interaction. *Merrill-Palmer Quarterly, 27,* 201-218.

Crittenden, P. M. (1988). Distorted patterns of relationship in maltreating families: The role of internal representation models. *Journal of Reproductive and Infant Psychology, 6,* 183-199.

Crittenden, P. M. (1990). Internal representational models of attachment relationships. *Infant Mental Health Journal, 11,* 259-277.

Crittenden, P. M. (1992). Children's strategies for coping with adverse home environments: An interpretation using attachment theory. *Child Abuse & Neglect, 16,* 329-343.

Crittenden, P., & Ainsworth, M. (1989). Child maltreatment and attachment theory. In D. Cicchetti & V. Carlson (Eds.), *Child maltreatment: Theory and research on the causes and consequences of child abuse and neglect* (pp. 432-463). New York: Cambridge University Press.

Cronin, C. (1995). Adolescent reports of parental spousal violence in military and civilian families. *Journal of Interpersonal Violence, 10,* 117-122.

Crouch, J. L., & Milner, J. S. (1993). Effects of child neglect on children. *Criminal Justice and Behavior, 20,* 49-65.

Crystal, S. (1987). Elder abuse: The latest crisis. *Public Interest, 88,* 56-66.

Culp, R. E., Culp, A. M., Soulis, J., & Letts, D. (1989). Self-esteem and depression in abusive, neglecting, and nonmaltreating mothers. *Infant Mental Health Journal, 10,* 243-251.

Culp, R. E., Little, V., Letts, D., & Lawrence, H. (1991). Maltreated children's self-concept: Effects of a comprehensive treatment program. *American Journal of Orthopsychiatry, 61*(1), 114-121.

Cummings, N. (1990). Issues of the 1990s. *Response, 13*(1), 4.

Curtis, A. (1992, December 1). Some on ritual abuse task force say satanists are poisoning them. *Los Angeles Times,* pp. B1, B4.

Dalto, C. A. (1983). Battered women: Factors influencing whether or not former shelter residents return to the abusive situation. *Dissertation Abstracts International, 44,* 1277B. (UMI No. 8317463)

Daly, M., & Wilson, M. (1988, October 28). Evolutionary social psychology. *Science, 242,* 519-524.

Damon, L., Todd, J., & MacFarlane, K. (1987). Treatment issues with sexually abused young children. *Child Welfare, 116,* 125-137.

Daro, D. (1988). *Confronting child abuse: Research for effective program design.* New York: Free Press.

Daro, D., & Alexander, R. (1994). Preventing child abuse fatalities: Moving forward. *The APSAC Advisor, 7*(4), 49-50.

Daro, D., & Gelles, R. J. (1992). Public attitudes and behaviors with respect to child abuse prevention. *Journal of Interpersonal Violence, 7,* 517-531.

Daro, D., & McCurdy, K. (1991). *Current trends in child abuse and reporting fatalities: The results of the 1990 annual fifty state survey.* Chicago: National Center on Child Abuse Prevention Research.

Daro, D., & McCurdy, K. (1994). Preventing child abuse and neglect: Programmatic interventions. *Child Welfare, 73,* 405-430.

Davidson, A. (1994). Alcohol, drugs, and family violence. *Violence Update, 4*(5), 5-6.

Davidson, H. (1994). *The impact of domestic violence on children: A report to the president of the American Bar Association* (2nd rev. ed.). Chicago: American Bar Association. (Report No. 549-0248)

Davidson, T. (1978). *Conjugal crime: Understanding and changing the wife beating pattern.* New York: Hawthorne.

Davies, P. T., & Cummings, E. M. (1994). Marital conflict and child adjustment: An emotional security hypothesis. *Psychological Bulletin, 116,* 387-411.

Davis, L. (1991). Murdered memory. *Health, 5,* 79-84.

Davis, L. V. (1984, May-June). Beliefs of service providers about abused women and abusing men. *Social Work,* pp. 243-250.

Davis, L. V., & Carlson, B. E. (1987). Observation of spouse abuse—What happens to the children? *Journal of Interpersonal Violence, 2,* 278-291.

Davis, R. C., & Brickman, E. (1991). Supportive and unsupportive responses of others to rape victims: Effects on concurrent victim adjustment. *American Journal of Community Psychology, 19,* 443-451.

Davis, S. P., & Fantuzzo, J. W. (1989). The effects of adult and peer social initiations on the social behavior of withdrawn and aggressive maltreated preschool children. *Journal of Family Violence, 4,* 227-248.

Dawson, B., DeArmas, A., McGrath, M. L., & Kelly, J. A. (1986). Cognitive problem-solving training to improve the child-care judgment of child neglectful parents. *Journal of Family Violence, 1,* 209-221.

Dawson, J. M., & Langan, P. A. (1994). *Murder in families.* Annapolis Junction, MD: Bureau of Justice Statistics. (NCJ No. 143498)

DeAngelis, T. (1993). APA panel is examining memories of child abuse. *APA Monitor, 24,* 44.

Deitch, I. (1993, August). *Alone, abandoned, assaulted: Prevention and intervention of elder abuse.* Paper presented at the annual meeting of the American Psychological Association, Toronto.

DeKeseredy, W. S., & Kelly, K. D. (1993). The incidence and prevalence of woman abuse in Canadian university and college dating relationships. *Canadian Journal of Sociology, 18,* 137-159.

DeLozier, P. (1992). Attachment theory and child abuse. In C. M. Parks & J. Stevenson-Hinde (Eds.), *The place of attachment in human behavior* (pp. 95-117). New York: Basic Books.

DeMaris, A. (1987). The efficacy of a spouse abuse model in accounting for courtship violence. *Journal of Family Issues, 8,* 291-305.

DeMaris, A. (1992). Male versus female initiation of aggression: The case of courtship violence.

In E. C. Viano (Ed.), *Intimate violence: Interdisciplinary perspectives* (pp. 111-120). Bristol, PA: Taylor & Francis/Hemisphere.

DeMause, L. (1974). *A history of childhood.* New York: Psychotherapy Press.

Dembo, R., Williams, L., Wothke, W., Schmeidler, J., & Brown, C. H. (1992). The role of family factors, physical abuse, and sexual victimization experiences in high-risk youths' alcohol and other drug use and delinquency: A longitudinal model. *Violence and Victims, 7,* 245-266.

Denham, S. A., Renwick, S. M., & Holt, R. W. (1991). Working and playing together: Prediction of preschool social-emotional competence from mother-child interaction. *Child Development, 62,* 242-249.

Denzin, N. K. (1984). Toward a phenomenology of domestic, family violence. *American Journal of Sociology, 90,* 483-513.

Department of Health and Human Services. (1981). *Study findings: National study of the incidence and severity of child abuse and neglect* (DHHS Publication No. OHDS 81-30325). Washington, DC: Government Printing Office.

Department of Health and Human Services. (1988). *Study findings: Study of national incidence and prevalence of child abuse and neglect* (DHHS Publication No. ADM 20-01099). Washington, DC: Government Printing Office.

Department of Health and Human Services. (1993). *A report on the maltreatment of children with disabilities* (DHHS Publication No. 105-89-1630). Washington, DC: Government Printing Office.

Department of Health and Human Services. (1994). *Child maltreatment 1992: Reports from the states to the National Center on Child Abuse and Neglect.* Washington, DC: Government Printing Office.

Department of Health Social Services Inspectorate. (1992). *Confronting elder abuse: An SSI London Region Survey.* London: Her Majesty's Stationery Office.

DePaul, A. (1992, January). New laws in California aid women victimized by violence. *Criminal Justice Newsletter, 23*(2), 5-6.

de Paul, J., & Arruabarrena, M. I. (1995). Behavior problems in school-aged physically abused and neglected children in Spain. *Child Abuse & Neglect, 19,* 409-418.

Dibble, U., & Straus, M. A. (1980). Some social determinants of inconsistency between attitudes and behavior: The case of family violence. *Journal of Marriage and the Family, 42,* 71-80.

DiLalla, L. F., & Gottesman, I. (1991). Biological and genetic contributors to violence. Widom's untold tale. *Psychological Bulletin, 109,* 125-129.

Disbrow, M. A., Doerr, H., & Caulfield, C. (1977). Measuring the components of parents' potential for child abuse and neglect. *Child Abuse & Neglect, 1,* 279-296.

Dobash, R. E., & Dobash, R. P. (1978). Wives: The "appropriate" victims of marital violence. *Victimology: An International Journal, 2,* 426-442.

Dobash, R. E., & Dobash, R. P. (1979). *Violence against wives: A case against patriarchy.* New York: Free Press.

Dobash, R. E., & Dobash, R. P. (1988). Research as social action: The struggle for battered women. In K. Yllö & M. Bograd (Eds.), *Feminist perspectives on wife abuse* (pp. 51-74). Newbury Park, CA: Sage.

Dobash, R. P., Dobash, R. E., Wilson, M., & Daly, M. (1992). The myth of sexual symmetry in marital violence. *Social Problems, 39,* 71-91.

Dodge, K. A. (1991). Emotion and social information processing. In J. Garber & K. A. Dodge (Eds.), *The development of emotion regulation and dysregulation* (pp. 159-181). New York: Cambridge University Press.

Dodge, K. A., Bates, J. E., & Pettit, G. S. (1990). Mechanisms in the cycle of violence. *Science, 250,* 1678-1682.

Dodge, M., & Greene, E. (1991). Juror and expert conceptions of battered women. *Violence and Victims, 6,* 271-282.

Doll, L., Joy, D., & Bartholow, B. (1992). Self-reported childhood and adolescent sexual abuse among homosexual and bisexual men. *Child Abuse & Neglect, 16,* 855-864.

Dollard, J., Doob, L. W., Miller, N. E., & Sears, R. R. (1939). *Frustration and aggression.* New Haven, CT: Yale University Press.

Domestic violence in the courts. (1989). *Response, 12*(4), 3-6. (Excerpted from *Gender Bias in the Courts,* report of the Maryland Special Joint Committee on Gender Bias in the Courts, 1989, Annapolis, MD)

Dore, M. M., Doris, J, & Wright, P. (1995). Identifying substance abuse in maltreating families: A child welfare challenge. *Child Abuse & Neglect, 19,* 531-543.

Douglas, M. A. (1987). The battered woman syndrome. In D. J. Sonkin (Ed.), *Domestic violence on trial: Psychological and legal dimensions of family violence* (pp. 39-54). New York: Springer.

Doumas, D., Margolin, G., & John, R. S. (1994). The intergenerational transmission of aggression across three generations. *Journal of Family Violence, 9,* 157-175.

Dowdney, L., & Pickles, A. R. (1991). Expression of negative affect within disciplinary encounters: Is there dyadic reciprocity? *Developmental Psychology, 27,* 606-617.

Downs, W. R., Miller, B. A., & Panek, D. D. (1993). Differential patterns of partner-to-woman violence: A comparison of samples of community, alcohol-abusing, and battered women. *Journal of Family Violence, 8,* 113-135.

Drotar, D., Eckerle, D., Satola, J., Pallotta, J., & Wyatt, B. (1990). Maternal interactional behavior with nonorganic failure-to-thrive in-fants: A case comparison study. *Child Abuse & Neglect, 14,* 41-51.

Dubowitz, H. (1994). Neglecting the neglect of neglect. *Journal of Interpersonal Violence, 9,* 556-560.

Dubowitz, H., Black, M., Harrington, D., & Verschoore, A. (1993). A follow-up study of behavior problems associated with child sexual abuse. *Child Abuse & Neglect, 17,* 743-754.

Dubowitz, H., Black, M., Starr, R., & Zuravin, S. (1993). A conceptual definition of child neglect. *Criminal Justice and Behavior, 20,* 8-26.

Dubowitz, H., Hampton, R. L., Bithoney, W. G., & Newberger, E. H. (1987). Inflicted and noninflicted injuries: Differences in child and familial characteristics. *American Journal of Orthopsychiatry, 57,* 525-535.

Dunford, F. W., Huizinga, D., & Elliott, D. S. (1990). The role of arrest in domestic assault: The Omaha police experiment. *Criminology, 28,* 183-206.

Dunn, P. F. (1995). "Elder abuse" as an innovation to Australia: A critical overview. In J. I. Kosberg & J. L. Garcia (Eds.), *Elder abuse: International and cross-cultural perspectives* (pp. 13-30). Binghamton, NY: Haworth.

Durfee, M. (1994). History and status of child death review teams. *The APSAC Advisor, 7*(4), 4-5.

Dutton, D. G. (1986a). The outcome of court-mandated treatment for wife assault: A quasi-experimental evaluation. *Violence and Victims, 1,* 163-175.

Dutton, D. G. (1986b). Wife assaulters' explanations for assault: The neutralization of self-punishment. *Canadian Journal of Behavioral Sciences, 18,* 381-390.

Dutton, D. G. (1988). *The domestic assault of women.* Boston: Allyn & Bacon.

Dutton, D. G. (1994). Patriarchy and wife assault: An ecological fallacy. *Violence and Victims, 9,* 167-182.

Dutton, D. G., & Hemphill, K. J. (1992). Patterns of socially desirable responding among perpetrators and victims of wife assault. *Violence and Victims, 7,* 29-39.

Dutton, D. G., & Painter, S. L. (1981). Traumatic bonding: The development of emotional attachments in battered women and other relationships of intermittent abuse. *Victimology: An International Journal, 6*(1-4), 139-155.

Dutton, D. G., & Painter, S. L. (1993a). The battered woman syndrome: Effects of severity and intermittency of abuse. *American Journal of Orthopsychiatry, 63,* 614-622.

Dutton, D. G., & Painter, S. L. (1993b). Emotional attachments in abusive relationships: A test of traumatic bonding theory. *Violence and Victims, 8,* 105-120.

Dutton, D. G., & Starzomski, A. J. (1993). Borderline personality in perpetrators of psychological and physical abuse. *Violence and Victims, 8,* 327-337.

Dutton, D. G., & Strachan, C. E. (1987). Motivational needs for power and spouse-specific assertiveness in assaultive and nonassaultive men. *Violence and Victims, 2,* 145-156.

Dutton, D. G., Saunders, K., Starzomski, A., & Batholomew, K. (1994). Intimacy-anger and insecure attachment as precursors of abuse in intimate relationships. *Journal of Applied Social Psychology, 24,* 1367-1386.

Dutton, D. G., Van Ginkel, C., & Starzomski, A. (1995). The role of shame and guilt in the intergenerational transmission of abusiveness. *Violence and Victims, 10,* 121-131.

Dutton-Douglas, M. A. (1991). Counseling and shelter services for battered women. In M. Steinman (Ed.), *Woman battering: Policy responses* (pp. 113-130). Cincinnati, OH: Anderson.

Dutton-Douglas, M. A., & Dione, D. (1991). Counseling and shelter services for battered women. In M. Steinman (Ed.), *Woman battering: Policy responses* (pp. 113-130). Cincinnati, OH: Anderson.

D'Zurilla, T. J. (1986). *Problem-solving therapy: A social competence approach to clinical intervention.* New York: Springer.

Eagly, A. H., & Steffen, V. J. (1986). Gender and aggressive behavior: A meta-analytic review of the social psychological literature. *Psychological Bulletin, 100,* 309-330.

Earle, R. B. (1995, October). *Helping to prevent child abuse—and future criminal consequences.* Washington, DC: U.S. Department of Justice. (NCJ No. 156216)

Eckely, S. C. A., & Vilakazi, P. A. C. (1995). Elder abuse in South Africa. In J. I. Kosberg & J. L. Garcia (Eds.), *Elder abuse: International and cross-cultural perspectives* (pp. 171-182). Binghamton, NY: Haworth.

Eckenrode, J., & Doris, J. (1991). *The academic effects of child abuse and neglect* [Progress report]. Washington, DC: National Center on Child Abuse and Neglect.

Edleson, J. L. (1991). Coordinated community responses. In M. Steinman (Ed.), *Woman battering: Policy response* (pp. 203-220). Cincinnati, OH: Anderson.

Edleson, J. L., & Brygger, M. P. (1986). Gender differences in reporting of battering incidents. *Family Relations, 35,* 377-382.

Edleson, J. L., & Grusznski, R. J. (1988). Treating men who batter: Four years of outcome data from the Domestic Abuse Project. *Journal of Social Science Research, 12,* 3-22.

Edleson, J. L., & Tolman, R. M. (1992). *Intervention for men who batter.* Newbury Park, CA: Sage.

Egan, K. (1983). Stress management with abusive parents. *Journal of Clinical Child Psychology, 12,* 292-299.

Egeland, B. (1991). From data to definition. *Development and Psychopathology, 3,* 37-43.

Egeland, B. (1993). A history of abuse is a major risk factor for abusing the next generation. In R. J. Gelles & D. R. Loseke (Eds.), *Current controversies on family violence* (pp. 197-208). Newbury Park, CA: Sage.

Egeland, B., Jacobvitz, D., & Sroufe, A. (1988). Breaking the cycle of child abuse. *Child Development, 59,* 1080-1088.

Egeland, B., & Sroufe, A. (1981). Developmental sequelae of maltreatment in infancy. *New Directions for Child Development, 11,* 77-92.

Egeland, B., Sroufe, L. A., & Erickson, M. F. (1983). The developmental consequences of different patterns of maltreatment. *Child Abuse & Neglect, 7,* 459-469.

Ehrlich, P., & Anetzberger, G. J. (1991). Survey of state public health departments on procedures for reporting elder abuse. *Public Health Reports, 106,* 151-154.

Eigenberg, H., & Moriarty, L. (1991). Domestic violence and local law enforcement in Texas. *Journal of Interpersonal Violence, 6,* 102-109.

Eisikovits, Z. C., Guttmann, E., Sela-Amit, M., & Edleson, J. L. (1993). Woman battering in Israel: The relative contributions of interpersonal factors. *American Journal of Orthopsychiatry, 63,* 313-317.

Elbow, M. (1977). Theoretical considerations of violent marriages. *Social Casework, 58,* 515-526.

Elbow, M. (1982). Children of violent marriages: The forgotten victims. *Social Casework: The Journal of Contemporary Social Work, 63,* 465-471.

Elder mistreatment guidelines for health care professionals: Detection, assessment, and intervention. (1988). New York: Mt. Sinai/Victim Services Agency, Elder Abuse Project.

Ellerstein, N. S., & Canavan, W. (1980). Sexual abuse of boys. *American Journal of Diseases of Children, 134,* 255-257.

Elliott, M. (1993). *Female sexual abuse of children.* New York: Guilford.

Elliott, M. (1994). Impaired object relations in professional women molested as children. *Psychotherapy, 31,* 79-86.

Elliott, M., & Briere, J. (1992). Sexual abuse trauma among professional women: Validating the Trauma Symptom Checklist-40 (TSC-40). *Child Abuse & Neglect, 16,* 391-398.

Elliott, M., Browne, K., & Kilcoyne, J. (1995). Child sexual abuse prevention: What offenders tell us. *Child Abuse & Neglect, 19,* 579-594.

Ellis, D. (1992). Woman abuse among separated and divorced women: The relevance of social support. In E. C. Viano (Ed.), *Intimate violence: Interdisciplinary perspectives* (pp. 177-189). Bristol, PA: Taylor & Francis/Hemisphere.

Elwell, M. E., & Ephross, P. H. (1987). Initial reactions of sexually abused children. *Social Casework, 68,* 109-116.

Emans, R. L. (1988). Psychology's responsibility in false accusations of child abuse. *Journal of Clinical Psychology, 44,* 1000-1004.

EMERGE. (1980). *Do you feel like beating up on somebody?* Boston: Author.

Emery, B. C., Lloyd, S. A., & Castleton, A. (1989, November). *Why women hit: A feminist perspective.* Paper presented at the annual conference of the National Conference on Family Relations, New Orleans, LA.

Emery, R. E. (1989). Family violence. *American Psychologist, 44,* 321-328.

Erez, E. (1986). Intimacy, violence and the police. *Human Relations, 39,* 265-281.

Ericksen, J. R., & Henderson, A. D. (1992). Witnessing family violence: The children's experience. *Journal of Advanced Nursing, 17,* 1200-1209.

Erickson, M. F., & Egeland, B. (1987). A developmental view of the psychological consequences of maltreatment. *School Psychology Review, 16,* 156-168.

Erickson, M. F., Egeland, B., & Pianta, R. (1989). The effects of maltreatment on the development of young children. In D. Cicchetti & V. Carlson (Eds.), *Child maltreatment: Theory and research on the causes and consequences of child abuse and neglect* (pp. 647-684). New York: Cambridge University Press.

Erickson, S. K., & McKnight, M. S. (1990). Mediating spousal abuse divorces [Special issue: Mediation and spouse abuse]. *Mediation Quarterly, 7,* 377-388.

Eron, L. D., Huesmann, L. R., Lefkowitz, M. M., & Walder, L. O. (1987). How learning conditions in early childhood—including mass media—relate to aggression in later adolescence. *Psychological Reports, 9,* 291-334.

Ethier, L. S., Lacharite, C., & Couture, G. (1995). Childhood adversity, parental stress and depression of negligent mothers. *Child Abuse & Neglect, 19,* 619-632.

Ethier, L. S., Palacio-Quintin, E., & Jourdan-Ionescu, C. (1992, June). Abuse and neglect: Two distinct forms of maltreatment. *Canada's Mental Health,* pp. 13-19.

Everson, M. D., & Boat, B. W. (1989). False allegations of sexual abuse by children and adolescents. *American Academy of Child and Adolescent Psychiatry, 28,* 230-235.

Everson, M. D., & Boat, B. W. (1990). Sexualized doll play among young children: Implications for the use of anatomical dolls in sexual abuse evaluations. *Journal of the American Academy of Child and Adolescent Psychiatry, 29,* 736-742.

Everson, M. D., Hunter, W. M., Runyon, D. K., & Edelson, G. A. (1989). Maternal support following disclosure of incest. *American Journal of Orthopsychiatry, 59,* 198-207.

Everson, M. D., Hunter, W. M., Runyon, D., & Edelson, G. A. (1990). Maternal support following disclosure of incest. *Annual Progress in Child Psychiatry and Child Development, 9,* 292-306.

Ewigman, B., Kivlahan, C., & Land, G. (1993). The Missouri Child Fatalities Study: Underreporting of maltreatment fatalities among children younger than five years of age, 1983 through 1986. *Pediatrics, 91,* 330-337.

Ewing, C. P. (1990a). *Kids who kill.* Lexington, MA: Lexington Books.

Ewing, C. P. (1990b). Psychological self-defense. *Law and Human Behavior, 14,* 579-594.

Ewing, C. P., & Aubrey, M. (1987). Battered women and public opinion: Some realities about myths. *Journal of Family Violence, 2,* 257-264.

Fagan, J. A. (1988). Contributions of family violence research to criminal justice policy on wife assault: Paradigms of science and social control. *Violence and Victims, 3,* 159-186.

Fagan, J. A. (1989). Cessation of family violence: Deterrence and dissuasion. In L. Ohlin & M. Tonry (Eds.), *Family violence* (pp. 377-425). Chicago: University of Chicago Press.

Fagan, J. A., Stewart, D., & Hansen, K. (1983). Violent men or violent husbands? Background factors and situational correlates. In D. Finkelhor, R. J. Gelles, G. T. Hotaling, & M. A. Straus (Eds.), *The dark side of families: Current family violence research* (pp. 49-67). Beverly Hills, CA: Sage.

Faller, K. C. (1988). *Child sexual abuse: An interdisciplinary manual for diagnosis, case management, and treatment.* New York: Columbia University Press.

Faller, K. C. (1989). Why sexual abuse? An exploration of the intergenerational hypothesis. *Child Abuse & Neglect, 13,* 543-548.

Faller, K. C. (1993). Research on false allegations of sexual abuse in divorce. *The APSAC Advisor, 6*(1), 7-10.

Fantuzzo, J. W. (1990). Behavioral treatment of the victims of child abuse and neglect. *Behavior Modification, 14,* 316-39.

Fantuzzo, J. W., DePaola, L. M., Lambert, L., Martino, T., Anderson, G., & Sutton, S. (1991). Effects of interparental violence on the psychological adjustment and competencies of young children. *Journal of Consulting and Clinical Psychology, 59,* 258-265.

Fantuzzo, J. W., & Lindquist, C. U. (1989). The effects of observing conjugal violence on children: A review and analysis of research methodology. *Journal of Family Violence, 4,* 77-94.

Fantuzzo, J. W., Stovall, A., Schachtel, D., Goins, C., & Hall, R. (1987). The effects of peer social initiations on social behavior of withdrawn maltreated preschool children. *Journal of Behavior Therapy and Experiential Psychiatry, 18,* 357-363.

Farrell, D., & Hall, C. (1994, June 15). Friends recall Simpsons as a vibrant couple. *Los Angeles Times,* pp. A1, A18.

Farrington, D. P., Ohlin, L. E., & Wilson, J. Q. (1986). *Understanding and controlling crime: Toward a new research strategy.* New York: Springer-Verlag.

Farrington, K. M. (1980). Stress and family violence. In M. A. Straus & G. T. Hotaling (Eds.), *The social causes of husband-to-wife violence* (pp. 94-114). Minneapolis: University of Minnesota Press.

Faulk, M. (1974). Men who assault their wives. *Medicine, Science, and the Law, 14,* 180-183.

Faulkner, K., Stoltenberg, C. D., Cogen, R., Nolder, M., & Shooter, E. (1992). Cognitive-behavioral group treatment for male spouse abusers. *Journal of Family Violence, 7,* 37-55.

Faulkner, L. R. (1982). Mandating the reporting of suspected cases of elder abuse: An inappropriate, ineffective, and ageist response to the abuse of older adults. *Family Law Quarterly, 16*(1), 69-91.

Federal Bureau of Investigation. (1978-1987). *Crime in the United States (1977-1986).* Washington, DC: Government Printing Office.

Feinauer, L. L. (1989). Comparison of long-term effects of child abuse by type of abuse and by relationship of the offender to the victim. *American Journal of Family Therapy, 17,* 48-56.

Feld, S. L., & Straus, M. A. (1989). Escalation and desistance of wife assault in marriage. *Criminology, 27,* 141-161.

Feldman, W., Feldman, E., Goodman, J. T., McGrath, P. J., Pless, R. P., Corsini, L., & Bennett, S. (1991). Is childhood sexual abuse really increasing in prevalence? An analysis of the evidence. *Pediatrics, 88*(1), 29-33.

Feldman-Summers, S., & Pope, K. S. (1994). The experience of forgetting childhood abuse: A national survey of psychologists. *Journal of Consulting and Clinical Psychology, 62,* 636-639.

Felson, R. B. (1992). "Kick 'em when they're down": Explanation of the relationship between stress and interpersonal aggression and violence. *Sociological Quarterly, 33,* 1-16.

Fenstermaker, S. (1989). Acquaintance rape on campus: Responsibility and attributions of crime. In M. A. Pirog-Good & J. E. Stets (Eds.), *Violence in dating relationships: Emerging social issues* (pp. 257-271). New York: Praeger.

Ferguson, K. E. (1980). *Self, society, and womankind: The dialectic of liberation.* Westport, CT: Greenwood.

Ferraro, K. J. (1981). Battered women and the shelter movement. *Dissertation Abstracts International, 42,* 879A. (UMI No. 8115605)

Ferraro, K. J. (1989). Policing woman battering. *Social Problems, 36,* 61-74.

Ferraro, K. J., & Johnson, J. M. (1984, August). *The meanings of courtship violence.* Paper presented at the Second National Conference of Family Violence Researchers, Durham, NH.

Fields, M. (1978). Wife beating: Government intervention policies and practices. In U.S. Commission on Civil Rights, *Battered women: Issues of public policy.* Washington, DC: U.S. Commission on Civil Rights.

Filinson, R. (1989). Introduction. In R. Filinson & S. R. Ingman (Eds.), *Elder abuse: Practice and policy* (pp. 17-34). New York: Human Sciences Press.

Finkelhor, D. (1979). *Sexually victimized children.* New York: Free Press.

Finkelhor, D. (1981). The sexual abuse of boys. *Victimology: An International Journal, 6,* 76-84.

Finkelhor, D. (1983). Common features of family abuse. In D. Finkelhor, R. J. Gelles, G. T. Hotaling, & M. A. Straus (Eds.), *The dark side of families: Current family violence research* (pp. 17-30). Beverly Hills, CA: Sage.

Finkelhor, D. (1984). *Child sexual abuse: New theory and research.* New York: Free Press.

Finkelhor, D. (1986). *A sourcebook on child sexual abuse.* Beverly Hills, CA: Sage.

Finkelhor, D. (1990). Is child abuse overreported? The data rebut arguments for less intervention. *Public Welfare, 48,* 23-29.

Finkelhor, D. (1993). Epidemiological factors in the clinical identification of child sexual abuse. *Child Abuse & Neglect, 17,* 67-70.

Finkelhor, D. (1994a). Current information on the scope and nature of child sexual abuse. *Future of Children, 4*(2), 31-53.

Finkelhor, D. (1994b). The international epidemiology of child sexual abuse. *Child Abuse & Neglect, 18,* 409-417.

Finkelhor, D., Asdigian, N., & Dziuba-Leatherman, J. (1995). The effectiveness of victimization prevention instruction: An evaluation of children's responses to actual threats and assaults. *Child Abuse & Neglect, 19,* 141-153.

Finkelhor, D., & Baron, L. (1986). High risk children. In D. Finkelhor (Ed.), *A sourcebook on child sexual abuse* (pp. 60-88). Beverly Hills, CA: Sage.

Finkelhor, D., & Dziuba-Leatherman, J. (1994). Victimization of children. *American Psychologist, 49,* 173-183.

Finkelhor, D., & Dziuba-Leatherman, J. (1995). Victimization prevention programs: A national survey of children's exposure and reactions. *Child Abuse & Neglect, 19,* 129-139.

Finkelhor, D., Hotaling, G., Lewis, I. A., & Smith, C. (1990). Sexual abuse in a national survey of adult men and women: Prevalence, characteristics, and risk factors. *Child Abuse & Neglect, 14,* 19-28.

Finkelhor, D., & Lewis, I. A. (1988). An epidemiologic approach to the study of child molestation. *Annals of the New York Academy of Sciences, 528,* 64-78.

Finkelhor, D., & Pillemer, K. A. (1988). Elder abuse: Its relationship to other forms of domestic violence. In G. T. Hotaling, D. Finkelhor, J. T. Kirkpatrick, & M. A. Straus (Eds.), *Family abuse and its consequences: New directions in research* (pp. 244-254). Newbury Park, CA: Sage.

Finkelhor, D., Williams, L., & Burns, N. (1988). *Nursery crimes: Sexual abuse in daycare.* London: Sage.

Finkelhor, D., & Yllö, K. (1987). *License to rape: Sexual abuse of wives.* New York: Free Press.

Finn, J. (1985). The stresses and coping behavior of battered women. *Social Casework: The Journal of Contemporary Social Work, 66*, 341-349.

Finn, P. (1991). Civil protection orders: A flawed opportunity for intervention. In M. Steinman (Ed.), *Woman battering: Policy responses* (pp. 155-189). Cincinnati, OH: Anderson.

Fins, D. L. (1994). Health care decision-making for incapacitated elders: An innovative social service agency model. *Journal of Elder Abuse & Neglect, 6*(2), 39-51.

Fish-Murray, C. C., Koby, E. V., & van der Kolk, B. A. (1987). Evolving ideas: The effect of abuse on children's thought. In B. A. van der Kolk (Ed.), *Psychological trauma* (pp. 89-109). Washington, DC: American Psychiatric Association.

Flanagan, T. J., & Maguire, K. (Eds.). (1992). *Sourcebook of criminal justice statistics—1991.* Washington, DC: U.S. Department of Justice, Bureau of Justice Statistics. (NCJ No. 137369)

Flanzer, J. P. (1993). Alcohol and other drugs are key causal agents of violence. In R. J. Gelles & D. R. Loseke (Eds.), *Current controversies on family violence* (pp. 171-181). Newbury Park, CA: Sage.

Fleisher, L. D. (1987). Wrongful birth: When is there liability for prenatal injury? *American Journal of Diseases in Children, 141*, 1260.

Flournoy, P. S., & Wilson, G. L. (1991). Assessment of MMPI profiles of male batterers. *Violence and Victims, 6*, 309-320.

Flynn, C. P. (1990). Sex roles and women's response to courtship violence. *Journal of Family Violence, 5*, 83-94.

Foa, E. B., Rothbaum, B. O., & Steketee, G. S. (1993). Treatment of rape victims. *Journal of Interpersonal Violence, 8*, 256-276.

Focus—Call for help. (1994, June 23). *MacNeil/Lehrer news hour* [Transcript]. Overland Park, KS: Strictly Business.

Follingstad, D. R., Brennan, A. F., Hause, E. S., Polek, D. S., & Rutledge, L. L. (1991). Factors moderating physical and psychological symptoms of battered women. *Journal of Family Violence, 6*, 81-95.

Follingstad, D. R., Hause, E. S., Rutledge, L. L., & Polek, D. S. (1992). Effects of battered women's early responses on later abuse patterns. *Violence and Victims, 7*, 109-128.

Follingstad, D. R., Kalichman, S. C., Cafferty, T. P., & Vormbrock, J. K. (1992). Aggression levels following frustration of abusing versus nonabusing college males. *Journal of Interpersonal Violence, 7*, 3-18.

Follingstad, D. R., Rutledge, L. L., Polek, D. S., & McNeill-Hawkins, K. (1988). Factors associated with patterns of dating violence toward college women. *Journal of Family Violence, 3*, 169-182.

Fontana, V., & Alfaro, J. (1987). *High risk factors associated with child maltreatment fatalities.* New York: Mayor's Task Force on Child Abuse and Neglect.

Fontana, V. J., & Moohnan, V. (1994). Establish more crisis intervention centers. In D. Bender & B. Leone (Eds.), *Child abuse: Opposing viewpoints* (pp. 227-234). San Diego, CA: Greenhaven.

Foo, L., & Margolin, G. (1995). A multivariate investigation of dating aggression. *Journal of Family Violence, 10*, 351-377.

Ford, D. A. (1991). Preventing and provoking wife battery through criminal sanctions: A look at the risks. In D. D. Knudson & J. L. Miller (Eds.), *Abused and battered: Social and legal responses to family violence* (pp. 191-209). New York: Aldine de Gruyter.

Forehand, R., Long, N., & Brody, G. (1988). Divorce and marital conflict: Relationship to adolescent competence and adjustment in early adolescence. In E. M. Heatherington & J. D. Arasteh (Eds.), *Impact of divorce, single parenting and stepparenting on children* (pp. 155-167). Hillsdale, NJ: Lawrence Erlbaum.

Formby, W. A. (1992). Should elder abuse be decriminalized? A justice system perspective. *Journal of Elder Abuse & Neglect, 4*(4), 121-130.

Fornek, S., & O'Donnell, M. (1994, December 19). State addresses orphanage idea. *Chicago Sun-Times.*

Forsstrom-Cohen, B., & Rosenbaum, A. (1985). The effects of parental marital violence on young adults: An exploratory investigation. *Journal of Marriage and the Family, 47*, 467-472.

Fortin, A., & Chamberland, C. (1995). Preventing the psychological maltreatment of children. *Journal of Interpersonal Violence, 10*, 275-295.

Fowler, W. E., & Wagner, W. G. (1993). Preference for and comfort with male versus female counselors among sexually abused girls in individual treatment. *Journal of Counseling Psychology, 40*, 65-72.

Francis, W. M. (1993). Integrated responses to family violence: Implications for law enforcement. *Family Violence and Sexual Assault Bulletin, 9*(3), 25-28.

Frankel, K. A., & Bates, J. E. (1990). Mother-toddler problem solving: Antecedents in attachment, home behavior, and temperament. *Child Development, 61*, 810-819.

Frazier, P. A. (1991). Self-blame as a mediator of postrape depressive symptoms. *Journal of Social and Clinical Psychology, 10*, 47-57.

Fredrich, W. N., & Wheeler, K. K. (1982). The abusing parent revisited: A decade of psychological research. *Journal of Nervous and Mental Disease, 10*, 577-587.

Fredriksen, K. I. (1989). Adult protective services: A caseload analysis. *Journal of Interpersonal Violence, 4*, 245-250.

Freud, S. (1961). On the origins of psychoanalysis. In J. Strachey (Ed. and Trans.), *The standard edition of the complete psychological works of Sigmund Freud* (Vol. 1). London: Hogarth. (Original work published 1895)

Freund, K., & Langevin, R. (1976). Bisexuality in homosexual pedophilia. *Archives of Sexual Behavior, 5,* 415-423.

Freund, K., McKnight, C. K., Langevin, R., & Cibiri, S. (1972). The female child as a surrogate object. *Archives of Sexual Behavior, 2,* 119-133.

Friedman, L. (1991). Cost-effective compassion. *NOVA Newsletter, 15*(9), 7.

Friedrich, W. N. (1990). *Psychotherapy of sexually abused children and their families.* New York: Norton.

Friedrich, W. N. (1993). Sexual victimization and sexual behavior in children: A review of recent literature. *Child Abuse & Neglect, 17,* 59-66.

Friedrich, W. N., Berliner, L., Urquiza, A. J., & Beilke, R. L. (1988). Brief diagnostic group treatment of sexually abused boys. *Journal of Interpersonal Violence, 3,* 331-343.

Friedrich, W. N., & Boriskin, J. A. (1976). The role of the child in abuse: A review of the literature. *American Journal of Orthopsychiatry, 46*(4), 580-590.

Friedrich, W. N., Enbender, A. J., & Luecke, W. J. (1983). Cognitive and behavioral characteristics of physically abused children. *Journal of Consulting and Clinical Psychology, 51,* 313-314.

Friedrich, W. N., Grambusch, P., Damon, L. (1992). The Child Sexual Behavior Inventory: Normative and clinical findings. *Journal of Consulting and Clinical Psychology, 60,* 303-311.

Friedrich, W. N., Luecke, W. M., Beilke, R. L., & Place, V. (1992). Psychotherapy outcome of sexually abused boys. *Journal of Interpersonal Violence, 7,* 396-409.

Friedrich, W. N., Urquiza, A. J., & Beilke, R. (1986). Behavioral problems in sexually abused young children. *Journal of Pediatric Psychology, 11,* 47-57.

Friedrich, W. N., & Wheeler, K. K. (1982). The abusing parent revisited: A decade of psychological research. *Journal of Nervous and Mental Disease, 10,* 577-587.

Frieze, I. H. (1983). Investigating the causes and consequences of marital rape. *Signs: Journal of Women in Culture and Society, 8,* 532-553.

Frieze, I. H., & Browne, A. (1989). Violence in marriage. In L. Ohlin & M. Tonry (Eds.), *Family violence* (pp. 163-218). Chicago: University of Chicago Press.

Frieze, I. H., Hymer, S., & Greenberg, M. S. (1984). Describing the victims of crime and violence. In A. S. Kahn (Ed.), *Final report of the American Psychological Association Task Force on the Victims of Crime and Violence* (pp. 19-78). Washington, DC: American Psychological Association.

Frisch, M. B., & MacKenzie, C. J. (1991). A comparison of formerly and chronically battered women on cognitive and situational dimensions. *Psychotherapy, 28,* 339-344.

Frodi, A., & Lamb., M. (1980). Child abusers' responses to infant smiles and cries. *Child Development, 51,* 238-241.

Fromuth, M. E. (1986). The relationship of child sexual abuse with later psychological adjustment in a sample of college women. *Child Abuse & Neglect, 10,* 5-15.

Fulmer, T. T. (1990). The debate over dependency as a relevant predisposing factor in elder abuse and neglect. *Journal of Elder Abuse & Neglect, 2*(1-2), 51-71.

Fulmer, T. T. (1991). Elder mistreatment: Progress in community detection and intervention. *Family & Community Health, 14*(2), 26-34.

Fulmer, T. T., & O'Malley, T. A. (1987). *Inadequate care of the elderly.* New York: Springer.

Furstenberg, F. F., Morgan, S. P., & Allison, P. D. (1987). Paternal participation and children's well-being after marital dissolution. *American Sociological Review, 52,* 695-701.

Gagan, R. J., Cupoli, J. M., & Watkins, A. H. (1984). The families of children who fail to thrive: Preliminary investigations of parental deprivation among organic and nonorganic cases. *Child Abuse & Neglect, 8,* 93-103.

Gamache, D. J., Edleson, J. L., & Schock, M. D. (1988). Coordinated police, judicial and social service response to woman battering: A multi-baseline evaluation across communities. In G. T. Hotaling, D. Finkelhor, J. T. Kirkpatrick, & M. A. Straus (Eds.), *Coping with family violence: Research and policy perspectives* (pp. 193-209). Newbury Park, CA: Sage.

Gamache, E. (1991). Domination and control: The social context of dating violence. In B. Levy (Ed.), *Dating violence: Young women in danger* (pp. 69-83). Seattle, WA: Seal.

Ganaway, G. K. (1989). Historical versus narrative truth: Clarifying the role of exogenous trauma in the etiology of MPD and its variants. *Dissociation, 2,* 205-220.

Ganley, A. L. (1981). *Court mandated counseling for men who batter: A three-day workshop for mental health professional* [Participants' manual]. Washington, DC: Center for Women's Policy Studies.

Ganley, A. L. (1989). Integrating feminist and social learning analyses of aggression: Creating multiple models for intervention with men who batter. In P. L. Caesar & L. K. Hamberger (Eds.), *Treating men who batter: Theory, practice, and programs* (pp. 195-235). New York: Springer.

Garbarino, J., & Crouter, A. (1978). Defining the community context for parent-child relations: The correlates of child maltreatment. *Child Development, 49,* 604-616.

Garbarino, J., & Gilliam, G. (1980). *Understanding abusive families.* Lexington, MA: Lexington Books.

Garbarino, J., Guttman, E., & Seely, J. (1986). *The psychologically battered child.* San Francisco: Jossey-Bass.

Garcia, J. L., & Kosberg, J. I. (1992). Understanding anger: Implications for formal and informal caregivers. *Journal of Elder Abuse & Neglect, 4*(4), 87-99.

Garmezy, N. (1983). Stressors of childhood. In N. Garmezy & M. Rutter (Eds.), *Stress, coping, and development of children* (pp. 43-84). New York: McGraw-Hill.

Garner, J., & Clemmer, E. (1986). *Danger to police in domestic disturbances—A new look*. Washington, DC: U.S. Department of Justice, National Institute of Justice.

Garrett-Gooding, J., & Senter, R. (1987). Attitudes and acts of sexual aggression on a university campus. *Sociological Inquiry, 57,* 348-371.

Garrison, M. (1991). Good intentions gone awry: The impact of New York's equitable distribution law on divorce outcomes. *Brooklyn Law Review, 57,* 621-754.

Garrity-Rokous, F. E. (1994). Punitive legal approaches to the problem of prenatal drug exposure. *Infant Mental Health Journal, 15,* 218-237.

Gartner, R. (1993). Methodological issues in cross-cultural large-survey research on violence. *Violence and Victims, 8,* 199-215.

Gates, D. (1994, December). History of the orphanage. *Newsweek,* pp. 12, 33.

Gaudin, J. M. (1993). Effective intervention with neglectful families. *Criminal Justice and Behavior, 20,* 66-89.

Gaudin, J. M., Jr., Wodarski, J. S., Arkinson, M. K., & Avery, L. S. (1990). Remedying child neglect: Effectiveness of social network interventions. *Journal of Applied Social Sciences, 15,* 97-123.

Geffner, R. (1987). Director's comments. *Family Violence Bulletin, 3*(1), 1.

Geffner, R. (1990). Family abuse, the judicial system, and politics. *Family Violence Bulletin, 6*(3), 1.

Geffner, R., & Pagelow, M. D. (1990a). Mediation and child custody issues in abusive relationships. *Behavioral Sciences and the Law, 8,* 151-159.

Geffner, R., & Pagelow, M. D. (1990b). Victims of spouse abuse. In R. T. Ammerman & M. Hersen (Eds.), *Treatment of family violence: A sourcebook* (pp. 81-97). New York: John Wiley.

Geffner, R., & Rosenbaum, A. (1990). Characteristics and treatment of batterers. *Behavioral Sciences and the Law, 8,* 131-140.

Gelles, R. (1973). Child abuse as psychopathology: A sociological critique and reformulation. *American Journal of Orthopsychiatry, 43,* 611-621.

Gelles, R., & Hargreaves, E. (1981). Maternal employment and violence towards children. *Journal of Family Issues, 2,* 509-530.

Gelles, R. J. (1976). Abused wives: Why do they stay? *Journal of Marriage and the Family, 38,* 659-668.

Gelles, R. J. (1980). A profile of violence toward children in the United States. In G. Gerbner, C. J. Ross, & E. Zegler (Eds.), *Child abuse: An agenda for action* (pp. 82-105). New York: Oxford University Press.

Gelles, R. J. (1983). An exchange/social control theory. In D. Finkelhor, R. J. Gelles, G. T. Hotaling, & M. A. Straus (Eds.), *The dark side of families: Current family violence research* (pp. 151-165). Beverly Hills, CA: Sage.

Gelles, R. J. (1989). Child abuse and violence in single-parent families: Parent absence and economic deprivation. *American Journal of Orthopsychiatry, 59*(4), 492-501.

Gelles, R. J. (1993a). Alcohol and other drugs are associated with violence—They are not its cause. In R. J. Gelles & D. R. Loseke (Eds.), *Current controversies on family violence* (pp. 182-196). Newbury Park, CA: Sage.

Gelles, R. J. (1993b). Constraints against family violence. *American Behavioral Scientist, 36,* 575-586.

Gelles, R. J. (1993c). The doctrine of family reunification: Child protection or risk? *The APSAC Advisor, 6*(2), 9-10.

Gelles, R. J. (1993d). Through a sociological lens: Social structure and family violence. In R. J. Gelles & D. J. Loseke (Eds.), *Current controversies on family violence* (pp. 31-46). Newbury Park, CA: Sage.

Gelles, R. J., & Cornell, C. P. (1985). *Intimate violence in families.* Newbury Park, CA: Sage.

Gelles, R. J., & Cornell, C. P. (1990). *Intimate violence in families* (2nd. ed.). Newbury Park, CA: Sage.

Gelles, R. J., & Harrop, J. (1989a). *The risk of abusive violence among children with non-biological parents.* Paper presented at the annual meetings of the National Council on Family Relations, New Orleans, LA.

Gelles, R. J., & Harrop, J. W. (1989b). Violence, battering, and psychological distress among women. *Journal of Interpersonal Violence, 4,* 400-420.

Gelles, R. J., & Loseke, D. R. (1993). Conclusions: Social problems, social policy, and controversies on family violence. In R. J. Gelles & D. R. Loseke (Eds.), *Current controversies on family violence* (pp. 357-366). Newbury Park, CA: Sage.

Gelles, R. J., & Straus, M. A. (1979). Determinants of violence in the family: Toward a theoretical integration. In W. R. Burr, R. Hill, F. I. Nye, & I. Reiss (Eds.), *Contemporary theories about the family* (pp. 549-581). New York: Free Press.

Gelles, R. J., & Straus, M. A. (1987). Is violence toward children increasing? A comparison of 1975 and 1985 national survey rates. *Journal of Interpersonal Violence, 2,* 212-222.

Gelles, R. J., & Straus, M. A. (1988). *Intimate violence.* New York: Simon & Schuster.

General Accounting Office. (1991). *Elder abuse: Effectiveness of report laws and other factors.* Washington, DC: Government Printing Office. (HRD-91-74)

Gentemann, K. (1984). Wife beating: Attitudes of a nonclinical population. *Victimology: An International Journal, 9,* 109-119.

Gentry, C. E., & Eaddy, V. B. (1980). Treatment of children in spouse abusive families. *Victimology: An International Journal, 2-4,* 240-250.

George, R., Wulczyn, F., & Fanshel, D. (1994). A foster care research agenda for the 90s. *Child Welfare, 73,* 525-549.

Gerow, J. R. (1989). *Psychology: An introduction* (2nd ed.). Glenville, IL: Scott, Foresman.

Getter, H., & Nowinski, J. (1981). A free response test of interpersonal effectiveness. *Journal of Personality Assessment, 45,* 301-308.

Giarretto, H. (1982). A comprehensive child sexual abuse treatment program. *Child Abuse & Neglect, 6,* 263-278.

Gibbs, J. (1975). *Crime, punishment, and deterrence.* New York: Elsevier.

Gibbs, N. (1993, January 18). 'Til death do us part. *Time,* pp. 38, 40-45.

Gibson, J. W., & Gutierrez, L. (1991). A service program for safe-home children [Special issue: Family violence]. *Families in Society, 72,* 554-562.

Gil, D. G. (1970). *Violence against children: Physical child abuse in the United States.* Cambridge, MA: Harvard University Press.

Gil, E., & Johnson, T. C. (1993). *Sexualized children: Assessment and treatment of sexualized children and children who molest.* Rockville, MD: Launch.

Gilbert, N. (1993). Examining the facts: Advocacy research overstates the incidence of date and acquaintance rape. In R. J. Gelles & D. R. Loseke (Eds.), *Current controversies on family violence* (pp. 120-132). Newbury Park, CA: Sage.

Giles-Sims, J. (1983). *Wife battering: A systems theory approach.* New York: Guilford.

Gilgun, J. F. (1988). Self-centeredness and the adult male perpetrator of child sexual abuse. *Contemporary Family Therapy, 10,* 216-242.

Gilgun, J. F., & Connor, T. M. (1989). How perpetrators view child sexual abuse. *Social Work, 34,* 249-251.

Ginsburg, H., Wright, L. S., Harrell, P. M., & Hill, D. W. (1989). Childhood victimization: Desensitization effects in the later lifespan. *Child Psychiatry and Human Development, 20,* 59-71.

Giordano, N. H., & Giordano, J. A. (1984). Elder abuse: A review of the literature. *Social Work, 29,* 232-236.

Gleason, W. J. (1993). Mental disorders in battered women: An empirical study. *Violence and Victims, 8,* 53-68.

Gleason, W. J. (1995). Children of battered women: Developmental delays and behavioral dysfunction. *Violence and Victims, 10,* 153-160.

Glendenning, F. (1993). What is elder abuse and neglect? In P. Decalmer & F. Glendenning (Eds.), *The mistreatment of elderly people* (pp. 1-34). London: Sage.

Godkin, M. A., Wolf, R. S., & Pillemer, K. A. (1989). A case-comparison analysis of elder abuse and neglect. *International Journal of Aging and Human Development, 28,* 207-225.

Goetting, A. (1989). Patterns of marital homicide: A comparison of husbands and wives. *Journal of Comparative Family Studies, 20,* 341-354.

Goetting, A. (1991). Female victims of homicide: A portrait of their killers and the circumstances of their deaths. *Violence and Victims, 6,* 159-168.

Gold, C. A. (1993). Long-term consequences of childhood physical and sexual abuse. *Archives of Psychiatric Nursing, 7*(3), 163-173.

Goldberg-Ambrose, C. (1992). Unfinished business in rape law reform. *Society for the Psychological Study of Social Issues, 48,* 173-185.

Goldenson, R. M. (1984). *Longman dictionary of psychology and psychiatry.* New York: Longman.

Goldner, V., Penn, P., Sheinberg, M., & Walker, G. (1990). Love and violence: Gender paradoxes in volatile attachments. *Family Process, 29,* 343-364.

Goldsmith, S. (1996, April 10). Social workers decry child abuse caseloads. *Daily News,* pp. 1, 6.

Goldstein, D., & Rosenbaum, A. (1985). An evaluation of self-esteem of maritally violent men. *Family Relations, 34,* 425-428.

Gomes-Schwartz, B., Horowitz, J. M., & Cardarelli, A. P. (1990). *Child sexual abuse: The initial effects.* Newbury Park, CA: Sage.

Gondolf, E. W. (1988a). *Battered women as survivors: An alternative to treating learned helplessness.* Lexington, MA: Lexington Books.

Gondolf, E. W. (1988b). The effect of batterer counseling on shelter outcome. *Journal of Interpersonal Violence, 3,* 275-289.

Gondolf, E. W. (1990). The human rights of women survivors. *Response, 13*(2), 6-8.

Gondolf, E. W. (1992). Discussion of violence in psychiatric evaluations. *Journal of Interpersonal Violence, 7,* 334-349.

Gondolf, E. W., Fisher, E., & McFerron, J. R. (1988). Racial differences among shelter residents: A comparison of Anglo, Black, and Hispanic battered. *Journal of Family Violence, 3,* 39-51.

Gondolf, E. W., & Foster, R. A. (1991). Pre-program attrition in batterer programs. *Journal of Family Violence, 6,* 337-349.

Gondolf, E. W., McWilliams, J., Hart, B., & Stuehling, J. (1994). Court responses to petitions for civil protection orders. *Journal of Interpersonal Violence, 9,* 503-517.

Gondolf, E. W., & Russell, D. (1986). The case against anger control treatment for batterers. *Response, 9*(3), 2-5.

Goodchilds, J. D., & Zellman, G. L. (1984). Sexual signaling and sexual aggression in adolescent relationships. In N. M. Malamuth & E. Donnestein (Eds.), *Pornography and sexual aggression* (pp. 233-243). Orlando, FL: Academic Press.

Goodman, G., Bottoms, B., Schwartz-Kenney, B., & Rudy, L. (1991). Children's memory of a stressful event: Improving children's reports. *Journal of Narrative Life History, 1,* 69-99.

Goodman, G. S., Levine, M., Melton, G. B., & Ogden, D. W. (1991). Child witnesses and the confrontation clause: The American Psychological Association brief in *Maryland v. Craig. Law and Human Behavior, 15,* 13-29.

Goodman, G. S., Taub, E. P., Jones, D. P. H., England, T., Port, L. K., Rudy, L., & Prado, L. (1992). Testifying in criminal court. *Monograph of the Society for Research in Child Development, 57*(5), 1-141.

Gorney, B. (1989). Domestic violence and chemical dependency: Dual problems, dual interventions. *Journal of Psychoactive Drugs, 21,* 229-238.

Gough, H. G. (1975). *Manual for the California Psychological Inventory.* Palo Alto, CA: Consulting Psychologists Press.

Graham, D. L. R., Rawlings, E. I., Ihms, K., Latimer, D., Foliano, J., Thompson, A., Suttman, K., Farrington, M., & Hacker, R. (1995). A scale for identifying "Stockholm syndrome" reactions in young dating women: Factor structure, reliability, and validity. *Violence and Victims, 10,* 3-22.

Graham, D. L. R., Rawlings, E., & Rimini, E. (1988). Survivors of terror: Battered women, hostages, and the Stockholm syndrome. In K. Yllö & M. Bograd (Eds.), *Feminist perspectives on wife abuse* (pp. 217-233). Newbury Park, CA: Sage.

Graham, P., Dinwall, R., & Wolkind, S. (1985). Research issues in child abuse. *Social Science Medicine, 21,* 1217-1228.

Grasmick, H. G., Blackwell, B. S., Bursik, R. J., Jr., & Mitchell, S. (1993). Changes in perceived threats of shame, embarrassment, and legal sanctions for interpersonal violence, 1982-1992. *Violence and Victims, 8,* 313-325.

Gray, E. (1993). *Unequal justice: The prosecution of child sexual abuse.* New York: Free Press.

Graziano, A. M. (1994). Why we should study subabusive violence against children. *Journal of Interpersonal Violence, 9,* 412-419.

Graziano, A. M., & Mills, J. (1992). Treatment for abused children: When is a partial solution acceptable? *Child Abuse & Neglect, 16,* 217-228.

Graziano, A. M., & Namaste, K. A. (1990). Parental use of physical force in child discipline: A survey of 679 college students. *Journal of Interpersonal Violence, 5,* 449-463.

Greenberg, J. R., McKibben, M., & Raymond, J. A. (1990). Dependent adult children and elder abuse. *Journal of Elder Abuse & Neglect, 2*(1-2), 73-86.

Greenblat, C. S. (1983). Wife battering: A systems theory approach. In D. Finkelhor, R. J. Gelles, G. T. Hotaling, & M. A. Straus (Eds.), *The dark side of families: Current family violence research* (pp. 235-260). Beverly Hills, CA: Sage.

Greenfeld, L. A. (1996, March). *Child victimizers: Violent offenders and their victims.* Washington, DC: U.S. Department of Justice, Bureau of Justice Statistics. (NCJ No. 153258)

Griffith, A., Roberts, G., & Williams, J. (1993). Elder abuse and the law. In P. Decalmer & F. Glendenning (Eds.), *The mistreatment of elderly people* (pp. 62-75). London: Sage.

Gross, A. B., & Keller, H. R. (1992). Long-term consequences of childhood physical and psychological maltreatment. *Aggressive Behavior, 18,* 171-185.

Grossier, D. (1986). *Child witness to family violence: Social problem-solving skills and behavior adjustment.* Unpublished doctoral dissertation, University of Denver, Denver, CO.

Groth, A. N. (1979). Sexual trauma in the life histories of rapists and child molesters. *Victimology: An International Journal, 4,* 10-16.

Groth, A. N., Birnbaum, H. J., & Gary, T. S. (1982). The child molester: Clinical observations. In J. R. Conte & D. A. Shorte (Eds.), *Social work and child abuse* (pp. 129-144). New York: Haworth.

Groth, A. N., Hobson, W. F., & Gary, T. S. (1982). The child molester: Clinical observations. In J. Conte & D. A. Shorte (Eds.), *Social work and child sexual abuse* (pp. 129-144). New York: Haworth.

Gruber, K. J., & Jones, R. J. (1983). Identifying determinants of risk of sexual victimization of youth: A multivariate approach. *Child Abuse & Neglect, 7,* 17-24.

Grusznski, R. J., & Bankovics, G. (1990). Treating men who batter: A group approach. In D. Moore & F. Leafgren (Eds.), *Problem solving strategies and interventions for men in conflict* (pp. 201-211). Alexandria, VA: American Association for Counseling and Development.

Grusznski, R. J., Brink, J. C., & Edleson, J. L. (1988). Support and education groups for children of battered women. *Child Welfare, 67,* 431-444.

Grusznski, R. J., & Carrillo, T. P. (1988). Who completes batterer treatment programs? An empirical question. *Journal of Family Violence, 3,* 141-150.

Gustkey, E. (1994, June 18). USC, ex-teammates reel from shock, disbelief. *Los Angeles Times,* pp. A8, A9.

Gwartney-Gibbs, P. A., Stockard, J., & Bohmer, S. (1987). Learning courtship aggression: The influence of parents, peers, and personal experiences. *Family Relations, 36,* 276-282.

Gwinn, C. G. (1994, January). *Children and domestic violence.* Paper presented at the San Diego Conference on Responding to Child Maltreatment, San Diego, CA.

Gyrch, J. H., & Fincham, F. D. (1990). Marital conflict and children's adjustment: A cognitive-contextual framework. *Psychological Bulletin, 108,* 267-290.

Haapala, D. A., & Kinney, J. M. (1988). Avoiding out-of-home placement of high-risk status offenders through the use of intensive family preservation services. *Criminal Justice and Behavior, 15,* 334-348.

Hadeed, A. J., & Siegel, S. R. (1989). Maternal cocaine use during pregnancy: Effect on the newborn infant. *Pediatrics, 84,* 205.

Hahn, J. (1994, June). A death in Los Angeles. *California Lawyer, 14*(6), 19.

Haj-Yahia, M. M., & Edleson, J. L. (1994). Predicting the use of conflict resolution tactics among engaged Arab-Palestinian men in Israel. *Journal of Family Violence, 9,* 47-62.

Hale, M. (1874). *The history of the pleas of the crown.* Philadelphia: Robert H. Small. (Original work published 1736)

Halicka, M. (1995). Elder abuse and neglect in Poland. In J. I. Kosberg & J. L. Garcia (Eds.), *Elder abuse: International and cross-cultural perspectives* (pp. 157-169). Binghamton, NY: Haworth.

Hall, P. A. (1986). Minority elder maltreatment: Ethnicity, gender, age, and poverty. *Ethnicity and Gerontological Social Work, 9*(4), 53-72.

Hall, P. A. (1989). Elder maltreatment items, subgroups, and types: Policy and practice implications. *International Journal of Aging and Human Development, 28,* 191-205.

Hamberger, L. K. (1991, August). *Research concerning wife abuse: Implications for training physicians and criminal justice personnel.* Paper presented at the annual meeting of the American Psychological Association, San Francisco.

Hamberger, L. K. (1994). Introduction—Domestic partner abuse: Expanding paradigms for understanding and intervention. *Violence and Victims, 9,* 91-94.

Hamberger, L. K., & Arnold, J. (1989). Dangerous distinctions among "abuse," "courtship violence," and "battering." *Journal of Interpersonal Violence, 4,* 520-522.

Hamberger, L. K., & Arnold, J. (1991). The impact of mandatory arrest on domestic violence perpetrator counseling services. *Family Violence Bulletin, 6*(1), 11-12.

Hamberger, L. K., & Barnett, O. W. (1995). Assessment and treatment of men who batter. In L. VandeCreek, S. Knapp, & T. L. Jackson (Eds.), *Innovations in clinical practice: A source book* (Vol. 14, pp. 31-54). Sarasota, FL: Professional Resource Press.

Hamberger, L. K., & Hastings, J. E. (1986a). Characteristics of spouse abusers. *Journal of Interpersonal Violence, 1,* 363-373.

Hamberger, L. K., & Hastings, J. E. (1986b). Personality correlates of men who abuse their partners: A cross-validation study. *Journal of Family Violence, 1,* 323-341.

Hamberger, L. K., & Hastings, J. E. (1988). Characteristics of male spouse abusers consistent with personality disorders. *Hospital and Community Psychiatry, 39,* 763-770.

Hamberger, L. K., & Hastings, J. E. (1989). Counseling male spouse abusers: Characteristics of treatment completers and dropouts. *Violence and Victims, 4,* 275-286.

Hamberger, L. K., & Hastings, J. E. (1990). Recidivism following spouse abuse abatement counseling: Treatment implications. *Violence and Victims, 5,* 157-170.

Hamberger, L. K., & Lohr, J. M. (1989). Proximal causes of spouse abuse: A theoretical analysis for cognitive-behavioral interventions. In P. L. Caesar & L. K. Hamberger (Eds.), *Treating men who batter: Theory, practice, and programs* (pp. 53-76). New York: Springer.

Hampton, R. L. (1987). Race, class, and child maltreatment. *Journal of Comparative Family Studies, 18*(1), 113-126.

Hampton, R. L., & Newberger, E. H. (1988). Child abuse incidence and reporting by hospitals: Significance of severity, class, and race. In G. T. Hotaling, D. Finkelhor, J. T. Kirkpatrick, & M. A. Straus (Eds.), *Coping with family violence: Research and policy perspectives* (pp. 212-221). Newbury Park, CA: Sage.

Hanneke, C. R., Shields, N. M., & McCall, G. J. (1986). Assessing the prevalence of marital rape. *Journal of Interpersonal Violence, 1,* 350-362.

Hansen, D. J., Pallotta, G. M., Tishelman, A. C., Conaway, L. P., & MacMillan, V. M. (1989). Parental problem-solving skills and child behavior problems: A comparison of physically abusive, neglectful, clinic, and community families. *Journal of Family Violence, 4,* 353-368.

Hansen, M., Harway, M., & Cervantes, N. (1991). Therapists' perceptions of severity in cases of family violence. *Violence and Victims, 6,* 225-235.

Hanson, H., Sawyer, D. D., Hilton, J., & Davis, S. F. (1992, August). *Reported death anxiety in battered and nonbattered women.* Paper presented at the annual meeting of the American Psychological Association, Washington, DC.

Hanson, R. K., Gizzarelli, R., & Scott, H. (1994). The attitudes of incest offenders. *Criminal Justice and Behavior, 21,* 187-202.

Harrell, A. D., Smith, B., & Newmark, L. (1993). *Court processing of restraining orders for domestic violence victims.* Washington, DC: Urban Institute.

Harrington, N. T., & Leitenberg, H. (1994). Relationship between alcohol consumption and victim behaviors immediately preceding sexual aggression by an acquaintance. *Violence and Victims, 9,* 315-324.

Harris, M. B. (1991). Effects of sex of aggressor, sex of target, and relationship on evaluations of physical aggression. *Journal of Interpersonal Violence, 6,* 174-186.

Harry, J. (1989). Parental physical abuse and sexual orientation in males. *Archives of Sexual Behavior, 18*(3), 251-261.

Hart, B. (1986). Lesbian battering: An examination. In K. Lobel (Ed.), *Naming the violence* (pp. 173-189). Seattle, WA: Seal.

Hart, B. J. (1988). *Safety for women: Monitoring batterers' programs.* Harrisburg: Pennsylvania Coalition Against Domestic Violence.

Hart, B. J. (1990). Gentle jeopardy: The further endangerment of battered women and children in custody mediation [Special issue: Mediation and spouse abuse]. *Mediation Quarterly, 7,* 317-330.

Hart, P. D. (1994, February 9). *The January 1994 Wall Street Journal/NBC poll* (No. 4045). Washington, DC: Hart-Teeter.

Hart, S. N., & Brassard, M. R. (1987). A major threat to children's mental health: Psychological maltreatment. *American Psychologist, 42,* 160-165.

Hart, S. N., & Brassard, M. (1989). *Developing and validating operationally defined measures of emotional maltreatment: A multimodal study of the relationships between caretaker behaviors and child characteristics across three developmental levels* (Grant No. DHHS 90CA1216). Washington, DC: Department of Health and Human Services and National Center on Child Abuse and Neglect.

Hart, S. N., & Brassard, M. R. (1990). Psychological maltreatment of children. In R. T. Ammerman & M. Hersen (Eds.), *Treatment of family violence: A sourcebook* (pp. 77-112). New York: John Wiley.

Hart, S. N., & Brassard, M. R. (1991). Psychological maltreatment: Progress achieved. *Development and Psychopathology, 3,* 61-70.

Hart, S. N., & Brassard, M. R. (1993). Psychological maltreatment. *Violence Update, 3*(7), 4, 6-7, 11.

Hart, S. N., Germain, R., & Brassard, M. R. (1987). The challenge: To better understand and combat psychological maltreatment of children and youth. In M. R. Brassard, R. Germain, & S. N. Hart (Eds.), *Psychological maltreatment of children and youth* (pp. 3-24). New York: Pergamon.

Hartman, C. R., & Burgess, A. W. (1988). Information processing of trauma. *Journal of Interpersonal Violence, 3,* 443-457.

Hastings, J. E., & Hamberger, L. K. (1988). Personality characteristics of spouse abusers: A controlled comparison. *Violence and Victims, 3,* 31-48.

Hathaway, P. (1989, May). Failure to thrive: Knowledge for social workers. *Health and Social Work,* pp. 122-126.

Hathaway, S. R., & McKinley, J. C. (1940). A multiphasic personality schedule (Minnesota) I: Construction of the schedule. *Journal of Psychology, 10,* 249-254.

Haugaard, J. J., & Reppucci, N. D. (1988). *The sexual abuse of children.* San Francisco: Jossey-Bass.

Hay, T., & Jones, L. (1994). Societal interventions to prevent child abuse and neglect. *Child Welfare, 73,* 379-403.

Hayashino, D. S., Wurtele, S. K., & Klebe, K. J. (1995). Child molesters: An examination of cognitive factors. *Journal of Interpersonal Violence, 10,* 106-116.

Haynes, C., Cutler, C., Gray, J., O'Keefe, K., & Kempe, R. (1983). Nonorganic failure to thrive: Decision for placement and videotaped evaluations. *Child Abuse & Neglect, 7,* 309-319.

Hazzard, A. (1993). Trauma-related beliefs as mediators of sexual abuse impact in adult women survivors: A pilot study. *Journal of Child Sexual Abuse, 2,* 55-69.

Healthy families in America. (1994). *Violence Update, 5*(2), 1-4.

Heath, L., Kruttschnitt, C., & Ward, D. A. (1986). Family violence, television viewing habits, and other adolescent experiences related to violence criminal behavior. *Criminology, 24,* 235-267.

Hechler, D. (1988). *The battle and the backlash: The child sexual abuse war.* Lexington, MA: Lexington Books.

Heger, R. L., & Yungman, J. J. (1989). Toward a causal typology of child neglect. *Child Youth Services Review, 11,* 203-220.

Hegar, R. L., Zuravin, S. J., & Orme, J. G. (1994). Factors predicting severity of physical child abuse injury. *Journal of Interpersonal Violence, 9,* 170-183.

Heide, K. M. (1987, November). *Parricide: Nationwide incidence and correlates.* Paper presented at the annual meeting of the American Society of Criminology, Montreal, Canada.

Heide, K. M. (1995). *Why kids kill parents.* Thousand Oaks, CA: Sage.

Heim, N., & Hursch, C. J. (1979). Castration for sex offenders: A review and critique of recent European literature. *Archives of Sexual Behavior, 8,* 281-304.

Heise, L. (1989). International dimensions of violence against women. *Response, 12*(1), 3-11.

Helfer, R. E. (1990, June). The neglect of our children. *The World & I,* pp. 531-541.

Henning, K., Leitenberg, H., Coffey, P., Turner, T., & Bennett, R. T. (1996). Long-term psychological and social impact of witnessing physical conflict between parents. *Journal of Interpersonal Violence, 11,* 35-51.

Hensey, O. J., Williams, J. K., & Rosenbloom, L. (1983). Intervention in child abuse: Experiences in Liverpool. *Developmental Medicine and Neurology, 25,* 606-611.

Henton, J. M., Cate, R. M., Koval, J., Lloyd, S., & Christopher, F. S. (1983). Romance and violence in dating relationships. *Journal of Family Issues, 4,* 467-481.

Heppner, M. J. (1978). Counseling the battered wife: Myths, facts, and decisions. *Personnel and Guidance Journal, 47,* 522-524.

Heppner, P. P., & Gonzales, D. S. (1987). Men counseling men. In M. Scher, G. Stevens, G. Good, & G. A. Eichenfield (Eds.), *Handbook of counseling and psychotherapy* (pp. 30-38). Newbury Park, CA: Sage.

Herdt, G. (1987). *The Sambia: Ritual and gender in New Guinea.* New York: Holt, Rinehart and Winston.

Herman, J. L. (1986). Histories of violence in an outpatient population: An exploratory study. *American Journal of Orthopsychiatry, 56,* 137-141.

Herman, J. L. (1992). *Trauma and recovery.* New York: Basic Books.

Herman, J. L., & Schatzow, E. (1987). Recovery and verification of memories of childhood sexual trauma. *Psychoanalytic Psychology, 4,* 1-14.

Herrenkohl, E. C., Herrenkohl, R. C., Rupert, L. J., Egolf, B. P., & Lutz, J. G. (1995). Risk factors for behavioral dysfunction: The relative impact of maltreatment, SES, physical health problems, cognitive ability, and quality of parent-child interaction. *Child Abuse & Neglect, 19,* 191-203.

Herrenkohl, R. C., Herrenkohl, E. C., Egolf, B. P., & Wu, P. (1991). The developmental consequences of abuse: The Lehigh longitudinal study. In R. H. Starr & D. A. Wolfe (Eds.), *The effects of child abuse and neglect: Issues and research* (pp. 57-85). New York: Guilford.

Hershorn, M., & Rosenbaum, A. (1985). Children of marital violence: A closer look at the unintended victims. *American Journal of Orthopsychiatry, 55,* 260-266.

Herzberger, S. D. (1991). The Conflict Tactics Scales. In D. J. Keyser & R. C. Sweetland (Eds.), *Test critiques, 8* (pp. 98-105). Kansas City, MO: Test Corporation of America.

HHS awards $1 million VAWA grant for national domestic abuse hotline. (1995). *Family Violence & Sexual Assault Bulletin, 11*(3-4), 38.

Hickey, T., & Douglass, R. L. (1981a). Mistreatment of the elderly in the domestic setting: An exploratory study. *American Journal of Public Health, 71,* 500-507.

Hickey, T., & Douglass, R. L. (1981b). Neglect and abuse of older family members: Professionals' perspectives and case experiences. *Gerontologist, 21,* 171-176.

Hickox, A., & Furnell, J. R. G. (1989). Psychosocial and background factors in emotional abuse of children. *Child: Care, Health and Development, 15,* 227-240.

Hightower, D., Heckert, A., & Schmidt, W. (1990). Elderly nursing home residents' need for public guardianship services in Tennessee. *Journal of Elder Abuse & Neglect, 2*(3-4), 105-122.

Hilberman, E., & Munson, K. (1978). Sixty battered women. *Victimology: An International Journal, 2,* 460-470.

Hilton, Z. N. (1992). Battered women's concerns about their children witnessing wife assault. *Journal of Interpersonal Violence, 7,* 77-86.

Hilton, Z. N. (1994). The failure of arrest to deter wife assault: What now? *Violence Update, 4*(5), 1-2, 4, 10.

Hinchey, F. S., & Gavelak, J. R. (1982). Empathic responding in children of battered mothers. *Child Abuse & Neglect, 6,* 395-401.

Hinrichsen, G. A., Hernandez, N. A., & Pollack, S. (1992). Difficulties and rewards in family care of depressed older adults. *Gerontologist, 32,* 486-492.

Hirschel, J. D., & Hutchison, I. (1991). Police-preferred arrest policies. In M. Steinman (Ed.), *Woman battering: Policy responses* (pp. 49-72). Cincinnati, OH: Anderson.

Hirschel, J. D., Hutchison, I., Dean, C. W., & Mills, A. M. (1992). Review essay on the law enforcement response to spouse abuse: Past, present, and future. *Justice Quarterly, 9,* 247-283.

Hirschi, T. (1969). *Causes of delinquency.* Berkeley: University of California Press.

Hirst, S. P., & Miller, J. (1986). The abused elderly. *Journal of Psychosocial Nursing & Mental Health Services, 24*(10), 28-34.

Ho, T. P., & Kwok, W. M. (1991). Child sexual abuse in Hong Kong. *Child Abuse & Neglect, 15,* 597-600.

Hockenberry, S. L., & Billingham, R. E. (1993). Psychological reactance and violence within dating relationships. *Psychological Reports, 73,* 1203-1208.

Hoffman, K. L., Demo, D. H., & Edwards, J. N. (1994). Physical wife abuse in a non-Western society: An integrated theoretical approach. *Journal of Marriage and the Family, 56,* 131-146.

Hoffman-Plotkin, D., & Twentyman, C. T. (1984). A multimodal assessment of behavioral and cognitive deficits in abused and neglected preschoolers. *Child Development, 55,* 794-802.

Hofford, M., & Harrell, A. D. (1993, October). *Family violence: Interventions for the justice system. Program brief.* Washington, DC: Bureau of Justice Assistance.

Holden, G. W., & Ritchie, K. L. (1991). Linking extreme marital discord, child rearing, and child behavior problems: Evidence from battered women. *Child Development, 62,* 311-327.

Holiman, M. J., & Schilit, R. (1991). Aftercare for battered women: How to encourage the maintenance of change. *Psychotherapy, 28,* 345-353.

Holland, L. R., Kasraian, K. R., & Leonardelli, C. A. (1987). Elder abuse: An analysis of the current problem and potential role of the rehabilitation professional. *Physical & Occupational Therapy in Geriatrics, 5*(3), 41-50.

Holloway, M. (1994, August). Trends in women's health—A global view. *Scientific American,* pp. 76-83.

Holmes, W. M. (1993). Police arrests for domestic violence. *American Journal of Police, 12,* 101-125.

Holtzworth-Munroe, A. (1988). Causal attribution in marital violence: Theoretical and methodological issues. *Clinical Psychology Review, 8,* 331-344.

Holtzworth-Munroe, A., & Anglin, K. (1991). The competency of responses given by maritally violent versus nonviolent men to problematic marital situations. *Violence and Victims, 6,* 257-269.

Holtzworth-Munroe, A., & Hutchinson, G. (1993). Attributing negative intent to wife behavior: The attributions of maritally violent versus nonviolent men. *Journal of Abnormal Psychology, 102,* 206-211.

Holtzworth-Munroe, A., Monaco, V., Waltz, J., Jacobson, N. S., Fehrenbach, P. A., & Gottman, J. M. (1992). Recruiting nonviolent men as control subjects for research on marital violence: How easily can it be done? *Violence and Victims, 7,* 79-88.

Holtzworth-Munroe, A., & Stuart, G. L. (1994). Typologies of male batterers: Three subtypes and the differences among them. *Psychological Bulletin, 116,* 476-497.

Homer, A. C., & Gilleard, C. (1990). Abuse of elderly people by their caretakers. *British Medical Journal, 301,* 1359-1362.

Homicides followed by suicide—Kentucky, 1985-1990. (1991, September 27). *Morbidity and Mortality Weekly Report, 40,* 652-653, 659.

Hong, S. M., & Page, S. (1989). A Psychological Reactance Scale: Development, factor structure and reliability. *Psychological Reports, 64,* 1323-1326.

Horkan, E. M. (1995). Elder abuse in the Republic of Ireland. In J. I. Kosberg & J. L. Garcia (Eds.), *Elder abuse: International and cross-cultural perspectives* (pp. 119-137). Binghamton, NY: Haworth.

Horowitz, M., Wilxer, N., & Alverez, W. (1979). Impact of Event scale: A measure of subjective stress. *Psychosomatic Medicine, 41,* 3.

Horton, A. L., & Johnson, B. L. (1993). Profile and strategies of women who have ended abuse. *Families in Society: The Journal of Contemporary Human Services, 74,* 481-492.

Horton, A. L., Simonidis, K. M., & Simonidis, L. L. (1987). Legal remedies for spousal abuse: Victim characteristics, expectations, and satisfaction. *Journal of Family Violence, 2,* 265-279.

Hoshmond, L. S. T. (1987). Judgment of anger problems by clients and therapists. *Journal of Interpersonal Violence, 2,* 251-263.

Hotaling, G. T., Straus, M. A., & Lincoln, A. J. (1990). Intrafamily violence and crime and violence outside the family. In M. A. Straus & R. J. Gelles (Eds.), *Physical violence in American families: Risk factors and adaptations to violence in 8,145 families* (pp. 431-470). New Brunswick, NJ: Transaction Books.

Hotaling, G. T., & Sugarman, D. B. (1986). An analysis of risk markers in husband to wife violence: The current state of knowledge. *Violence and Victims, 1,* 101-124.

Hotaling, G. T., & Sugarman, D. B. (1990). A risk marker analysis of assaulted wives. *Journal of Family Violence, 5,* 1-13.

Houskamp, B. M., & Foy, D. W. (1991). The assessment of post-traumatic stress disorder in battered women. *Journal of Interpersonal Violence, 6,* 367-375.

Howell, M. J., & Pugliesi, K. L. (1988). Husbands who harm: Predicting spousal violence by men. *Journal of Family Violence, 3,* 15-27.

Howes, C., & Eldredge, R. (1985). Responses of abused, neglected, and non-maltreated children to the behaviors of their peers. *Journal of Applied Developmental Psychology, 6,* 261-270.

Hudson, M. F. (1991). Elder mistreatment: A taxonomy with definitions by Delphi. *Journal of Elder Abuse & Neglect, 3*(2), 1-20.

Hudson, M. F. (1994). Elder abuse: Its meaning to middle-aged and older adults—Part II: Pilot results. *Journal of Elder Abuse & Neglect, 6*(1), 55-82.

Hudson, M. F., & Carlson, J. (1994). Elder abuse: Its meaning to middle-aged and older adults—Part I: Instrument development. *Journal of Elder Abuse & Neglect, 6*(1), 29-54.

Hughes, H. M. (1986). Research with children in shelters: Implications for clinical services. *Children Today,* pp. 21-25.

Hughes, H. M. (1988). Psychology and behavior correlates of family violence in child witnesses and victims. *American Journal of Orthopsychiatry, 58,* 77-90.

Hughes, H. M. (1992). Impact of spouse abuse on children of battered women: Implications for practice. *Violence Update, 2*(17), 1, 9-11.

Hughes, H. M., & Barad, S. J. (1983). Psychological functioning of children in battered women's shelter: A preliminary investigation. *American Journal of Orthopsychiatry, 53,* 525-531.

Hughes, H. M., Parkinson, D., & Vargo, M. (1989). Witnessing spouse abuse and experiencing physical abuse: A "double whammy"? *Journal of Family Violence, 4,* 197-209.

Hughes, H. M., Vargo, M. C., Ito, E. S., & Skinner, S. K. (1991). Psychological adjustment of children of battered women: Influences of gender. *Family Violence Bulletin, 7*(1), 15-17.

Hunter, J. A., Goodwin, D. W., & Becker, J. V. (1994). The relationship between phallometrically measured deviant sexual arousal and clinical characteristics in juvenile sexual offenders. *Behavior Research and Therapy, 32,* 533-538.

Hunter, R., & Kilstrom, N. (1979). Breaking the cycle in abusive families. *American Journal of Psychiatry, 136,* 1320-1322.

Hunter, R. S., Kilstrom, N., Kraybill, E. N., & Loda, F. (1978). Antecedents of child abuse and neglect in premature infants: A prospective study in a newborn intensive care unit. *Pediatrics, 61,* 629-635.

Hutchison, I. W., Hirschel, J. D., & Pesackis, C. E. (1994). Family violence and police utilization. *Violence and Victims, 9,* 299-313.

Hwalek, M., Williamson, D., & Stahl, C. (1991). Community-based m-team roles: A job analysis. *Journal of Elder Abuse & Neglect, 3*(3), 45-71.

Ieda, R. (1986). The battered woman. *Women & Therapy, 5,* 167-176.

Irvine, J. (1990). Lesbian battering: The search for shelter. In P. Elliott (Ed.), *Confronting lesbian battering* (pp. 25-30). St. Paul: Minnesota Coalition for Battered Women.

Island, D., & Letellier, P. (1991). *Men who beat the men who love them*. New York: Harrington Park.

It made terrible sense. (1982, December). *Newsweek*, *105*(50), 34.

Jackson, B. (1985, February 25). John Fedders of SEC is pummeled by large and personal problems. *Wall Street Journal*, pp. 1, 24.

Jackson, J., Calhoun, K., Amick, A., Maddever, H., & Habif, V. (1990). Young adult women who report childhood intrafamilial sexual abuse: Subsequent adjustment. *Archives of Sexual Behavior, 19*, 211-221.

Jacobson, N. S. (1994). Rewards and dangers in researching domestic violence. *Family Process, 33*, 81-85.

Jacobson, N. S., & Gottman, J. M. (1993, August). *New picture of violent couples emerges from UW study*. Paper presented at the annual meeting of the American Psychological Association, Toronto.

Jacobson, N. S., Gottman, J. M., Waltz, J., Rushe, R., Babcock, J. C., & Holtzworth-Munroe, A. (1994). Affect, verbal content and psychophysiology in the arguments of couples with a violent husband. *Journal of Consulting and Clinical Psychology, 62*, 982-988.

Jaffe, P. G., Austin, G., Lescheid, A., & Sas, L. (1981). Critical issues in the development of custody and access dispute resolution services. *Canadian Journal of Behavioural Science, 19*, 405-417.

Jaffe, P. G., Hastings, E., & Reitzel, D. (1992). Child witnesses of woman abuse: How can schools respond? *Response, 79*(2), 12-15.

Jaffe, P. G., Sudermann, M., Reitzel, D., & Killip, S. M. (1992). An evaluation of a secondary school primary prevention program on violence in intimate relationships. *Violence and Victims, 7*, 129-146.

Jaffe, P. G., Wilson, S. K., & Wolfe, D. A. (1986). Promoting changes in attitudes and understanding of conflict resolution among child witnesses of family violence. *Canadian Journal of Behavioral Science, 18*, 356-380.

Jaffe, P. G., Wilson, S. K., & Wolfe, D. A. (1989). Specific assessment and intervention strategies for children exposed to wife battering: Preliminary investigation. *Canadian Journal of Community Mental Health, 7*, 157-163.

Jaffe, P. G., Wolfe, D. A., Telford, A., & Austin, G. (1986). The impact of police charges in incidents of wife abuse. *Journal of Family Violence, 1*, 37-49.

Jaffe, P. G., Wolfe, D. A., & Wilson, S. K. (1990). *Children of battered women*. Newbury Park, CA: Sage.

Jaffe, P. G., Wolfe, D. A., Wilson, S. K., & Zak, L. (1986a). Family violence and child adjustment: A comparative analysis of girls' and boys' behavioral symptoms. *American Psychiatric Association, 143*, 74-77.

Jaffe, P. G., Wolfe, D. A., Wilson, S. K., & Zak, L. (1986b). Similarities in behavioral and social

maladjustment among child victims and witnesses to family violence. *American Journal of Orthopsychiatry, 56*, 142-146.

Janoff-Bulman, R. (1985). Criminal vs. noncriminal victimization: Victims' reactions. *Victimology: An International Journal, 10*, 498-511.

Janosick, E., & Green, E. (1992). *Family life*. Boston: Jones and Bartlett.

Janssens, L. A., & Kopper, B. A. (1993, August). *The role of victim blame following sexual assaults*. Paper presented at the annual meeting of the American Psychological Association, Toronto.

Jeffords, C. R. (1984). Prosecutorial discretion in cases of marital rape. *Victimology: An International Journal, 9*, 415-425.

Jehu, D., Klasen, C., & Gazan, M. (1986). Cognitive restructuring of distorted beliefs associated with childhood sexual abuse. *Journal of Social Work and Human Sexuality, 4*, 49-69.

Jenkins, J. M., Smith, M. A., & Graham, P. J. (1989). Coping with parental quarrels. *Journal of the American Academy of Child and Adolescent Psychologists, 28*, 182-189.

Jensen, G. F., & Karpos, M. (1993). Managing rape: Exploratory research on the behavior of rape statistics. *Criminology, 31*, 363-385.

Johns, S., & Hydle, I. (1995). Norway: Weakness in welfare. In J. I. Kosberg & J. L. Garcia (Eds.), *Elder abuse: International and cross-cultural perspectives* (pp. 139-156). Binghamton, NY: Haworth.

Johnson, B., & Morse, H. (1968). *The battered child: A study of children with inflicted injuries*. Denver, CO: Denver Department of Welfare.

Johnson, I. M. (1988). Wife abuse: Factors predictive of the decision-making process of battered women. *Dissertation Abstracts International, 48*, 3202A. (UMI No. 8803369)

Johnson, I. M., Crowley, J., & Sigler, R. T. (1992). Agency response to domestic violence: Services provided by battered women. In E. C. Viano (Ed.), *Intimate violence: An interdisciplinary perspective* (pp. 191-202). Bristol, PA: Taylor & Francis.

Johnson, J. M. (1980). Official cooptation of the battered women's shelter movement. *American Behavioral Scientist, 24*, 827-843.

Johnson, T. C. (1989). Female child perpetrators: Children who molest other children. *Child Abuse & Neglect, 13*, 571-585.

Johnson, T. F. (1986). Critical issues in the definition of elder mistreatment. In K. A. Pillemer & R. S. Wolf (Eds.), *Elder abuse: Conflict in the family* (pp. 167-196). Dover, MA: Auburn House.

Johnston, J. R., & Campbell, L. E. G. (1993). A clinical typology of interparental violence in disputed-custody divorces. *American Journal of Orthopsychiatry, 63*, 190-199.

Jones, D. P. H. (1986). Individual psychotherapy for the sexually abused child. *Child Abuse & Neglect, 10*, 377-385.

Jones, D. P. H. (1991). Ritualism and child sexual abuse. *Child Abuse & Neglect, 15,* 163-170.

Jones, D. P. H. (1994). Editorial: The syndrome of Munchausen by proxy. *Child Abuse & Neglect, 18,* 769-771.

Jones, D. P. H., & McGraw, J. M. (1987). Reliable and fictitious accounts of sexual abuse to children. *Journal of Interpersonal Violence, 2,* 27-45.

Jones, E. D., & McCurdy, K. (1992). The links between types of maltreatment and demographic characteristics of children. *Child Abuse & Neglect, 16,* 201-215.

Jones, J. M., & Muehlenhard, C. L. (1994, August). *The consequences of men's use of verbal and physical sexual coercion of women.* Paper presented at the annual meeting of the American Psychological Association, Los Angeles.

Jones, R. L., & Jones, J. M. (1987). Racism as psychological maltreatment. In M. R. Brassard, R. Germain, & S. N. Hart (Eds.), *Psychological maltreatment of children and youth* (pp. 146-158). New York: Pergamon.

Jouriles, E. N., Barling, J., & O'Leary, D. K. (1987). Predicting child behavior problems in maritally violent families. *Journal of Abnormal Child Psychology, 15,* 165-173.

Jouriles, E. N., Murphy, C. M., & O'Leary, K. D. (1989). Interpersonal aggression, marital discord, and child problems. *Journal of Consulting and Clinical Psychology, 57,* 453-455.

Jurik, N. C., & Winn, R. (1990). Gender and homicide: A comparison of men and women who kill. *Violence and Victims, 5,* 227-242.

Justice, B., & Justice, R. (1979). *The broken taboo.* New York: Human Sciences Press.

Justice Department announces plans for sex offender notification. (1995). *Criminal Justice Newsletter, 26*(8), 3-4.

Kaci, J. H. (1990). Issues of the 1990s. *Response, 13*(1), 4.

Kackzor, B. (1989, July 1). Precedent-setting defense gets girl cleared in slaying. *Tampa Tribune,* pp. B1, B5.

Kalichman, S. C., Craig, M. E., & Follingstad, D. R. (1989). Factors influencing the reporting of father-child sexual abuse: Study of licensed practicing psychologists. *Professional Psychology: Research and Practice, 20,* 84-89.

Kalmuss, D. S. (1984). The intergenerational transmission of marital aggression. *Journal of Marriage and the Family, 46,* 11-19.

Kalmuss, D. S., & Straus, M. A. (1982). Wife's marital dependency and wife abuse. *Journal of Marriage and the Family, 44*(1-4), 277-286.

Kalmuss, D. S., & Straus, M. A. (1990). Wife's marital dependency and wife abuse. In M. A. Straus & R. J. Gelles (Eds.), *Physical violence in American families: Risk factors and adaptations to violence in 8,145 families* (pp. 369-382). New Brunswick, NJ: Transaction Books.

Kalu, W. J. (1993). Battered spouses as a social concern in work with families in two semi-rural

communities in Nigeria. *Journal of Family Violence, 8,* 361-373.

Kandel, E., & Mednick, S. A. (1991). Perinatal complications predict violent offending. *Criminology, 29,* 519-529.

Kandel-Englander, E. (1992). Wife battering and violence outside the family. *Journal of Interpersonal Violence, 7,* 462-470.

Kaner, A., Bulik, C. M., & Sullivan, P. F. (1993). Abuse in adult relationships of bulimic women. *Journal of Interpersonal Violence, 8,* 52-63.

Kanin, E. J. (1957). Male aggression in dating-courting relations. *American Journal of Sociology, 63,* 197-204.

Kantor, G., & Straus, M. A. (1990). The "drunken bum" theory of wife beating. In M. A. Straus & R. J. Gelles (Eds.), *Physical violence in American families* (pp. 203-224). New Brunswick, NJ: Transaction.

Kantor, G. K., Jasinski, J. L., & Aldarondo, E. (1994). Sociocultural status and incidence of marital violence in Hispanic families. *Violence and Victims, 9,* 207-222.

Kasian, M., & Painter, S. L. (1992). Frequency and severity of psychological abuse in a dating population. *Journal of Interpersonal Violence, 7,* 350-364.

Katz, L. F., & Gottman, J. M. (1995). Vagal tone protects children from marital conflict. *Development and Psychopathology, 7,* 83-92.

Katz, R. C. (1990). Psychosocial adjustment in adolescent child molesters. *Child Abuse & Neglect, 14,* 567-575.

Kaufman, G. K., & Straus, M. A. (1990). Response of victims and the police to assaults on wives. In M. A. Straus & R. J. Gelles (Eds.), *Physical violence in American families: Risk factors and adaptations to violence in 8,145 families* (pp. 756-766). New Brunswick, NJ: Transaction Books.

Kaufman, J. (1991). Depressive disorders in maltreated children. *Journal of the American Academy of Child and Adolescent Psychiatry, 30,* 257-265.

Kaufman, J., & Cicchetti, D. (1989). The effects of maltreatment on school-aged children's socioemotional development: Assessments in a day-camp setting. *Developmental Psychology, 25,* 516-524.

Kaufman, J. & Zigler, E. (1987). Do abused children become abusive parents? *American Journal of Orthopsychiatry, 57,* 186-192.

Kaufman, J., & Zigler, E. (1993). The intergenerational transmission of abuse is overstated. In R. J. Gelles & D. R. Loseke (Eds.), *Current controversies on family violence* (pp. 209-221). Newbury Park, CA: Sage.

Kavanagh, C. (1982). Emotional abuse and mental injury. *Journal of the American Academy of Child Psychiatry, 21,* 171-177.

Kawamura, G., & Carroll, C. A. (1976). Managerial and financial aspects of social service programs. In R. Helfer & C. Kempe (Eds.), *Child abuse and neglect: The family and the community* (pp. 293-309). Cambridge, MA: Ballinger.

Kazdin, A. E. (1987). *Conduct disorders in childhood and adolescence.* Newbury Park, CA: Sage.

Keilitz, S. L. (1994). Legal report—Civil protection orders: A viable justice system tool for deterring domestic violence. *Violence and Victims, 9,* 79-84.

Kelly, E. E., & Warshafsky, L. (1987, July). *Partner abuse in gay male and lesbian couples.* Paper presented at the Third National Family Violence Research Conference, Durham, NH.

Kelsey, T., & Roscoe, B. (1986). Dating violence among high school students. *Psychology, A Quarterly Journal of Human Behavior, 23,* 53-59.

Kempe, C., & Helfer, R. (1972). *Helping the battered child and his family.* Philadelphia: J. B. Lippincott.

Kempe, C. H., Silverman, F. N., & Steele, B. F. (1962). The battered child syndrome. *Journal of the American Medical Association, 181,* 17-24.

Kempe, C. H., Silverman, F. N., Steele, B. F., Droegemueller, W., & Silver, H. K. (1962). The battered child syndrome. *Journal of the American Medical Association, 181,* 107-112.

Kempe, R. S., Cutler, C., & Dean, J. (1980). The infant with failure-to-thrive. In C. H. Dempe & R. E. Helfer (Eds.), *The battered child* (3rd ed., pp. 163-182). Chicago: University of Chicago Press.

Kempe, R. S., & Goldbloom, R. B. (1987). Malnutrition and growth retardation ("failure to thrive") in the context of child abuse and neglect. In R. E. Helfer & R. S. Kempe (Eds.), *The battered child* (4th ed., pp. 312-335). Chicago: University of Chicago Press.

Kendall-Tackett, K. A., Williams, L. M., & Finkelhor, D. (1993). Impact of sexual abuse on children: A review and synthesis of recent empirical studies. *Psychological Bulletin, 113,* 164-180.

Kenning, M., Merchant, A., & Tomkins, A. (1991). Research on the effects of witnessing parental battering: Clinical and legal policy implication. In M. Steinman (Ed.), *Woman battering: Policy responses* (pp. 237-261). Cincinnati, OH: Anderson.

Kercher, G., & McShane, M. (1984). The prevalence of child sexual abuse victimization in an adult sample of Texas residents. *Child Abuse & Neglect, 8,* 495-501.

Keronac, S., Taggart, M. E., Lescop, J., & Fortin, M. F. (1986). Dimensions of health in violent families. *Health Care for Women International, 7,* 413-426.

Kilpatrick, D. G., & Veronen, L. J. (1983). Treatment for rape related problems: Crisis intervention is not enough. In L. H. Cohen, W. L. Claiborn, & C. A. Spector (Eds.), *Crisis intervention* (pp. 165-185). New York: Human Sciences Press.

Kim, K. I., & Cho, Y. G. (1992). Epidemiological survey of spousal abuse in Korea. In E. C.

Viano (Ed.), *Intimate violence: An interdisciplinary perspective* (pp. 277-282). Bristol, PA: Taylor & Francis.

Kinard, E. M. (1982). Experiencing child abuse: Effects on emotional adjustment. *American Journal of Orthopsychiatry, 52,* 82-91.

Kinderknecht, C. (1986). In home social work with abused or neglected elderly: An experimental guide to assessment and treatment. *Journal of Gerontological Social Work, 9,* 29-42.

Kirkham, M. A., Schinke, S. P., Schilling, R. F., Meltzer, N. J., & Norelius, K. L. (1986). Cognitive-behavioral skills, social supports, and child abuse potential among mothers of handicapped children. *Journal of Family Violence, 1,* 235-245.

Kishur, G. R. (1989). The male batterer: A multidimensional exploration of conjugal violence. *Dissertation Abstracts International, 49,* 2409A. (UMI No. 8814496)

Kivela, S. L. (1995). Elder abuse in Finland. In J. I. Kosberg & J. L. Garcia (Eds.), *Elder abuse: International and cross-cultural perspectives* (pp. 31-44). Binghamton, NY: Haworth.

Klaus, P. A., & Rand, M. R. (1984). *Family violence* (Bureau of Justice Statistics special report). Rockville, MD: Bureau of Justice Statistics. (NCJ No. 93449)

Klein, C. F. (1995). Full faith and credit: Interstate enforcement of protection orders under the Violence Against Women Act of 1994 [Special issue]. *Family Law Quarterly, 29,* 253-271.

Kneisl, C. R. (1991). Healing the wounded, neglected inner child of the past. *Nursing Clinics of North America, 26,* 745-755.

Knight, R. A., & Hatty, S. E. (1992). Violence against women in Australia's capital. In E. C. Viano (Ed.), *Intimate violence: An interdisciplinary perspective* (pp. 255-264). Bristol, PA: Taylor & Francis.

Knopp, F., Freeman-Longo, R., & Stevenson, W. (1992). *Nationwide survey of juvenile and adult sex-offender treatment programs and model.* Orwell, VT: Safer Society.

Kolko, D. J. (1987). Treatment of child sexual abuse: Programs, progress, and prospects. *Journal of Family Violence, 2,* 303-318.

Kolko, D. J. (1992). Characteristics of child victims of physical violence. *Journal of Interpersonal Violence, 7,* 244-276.

Koop, C. E. (1989, May). *Violence against women—A global problem.* Paper presented at the Pan American Health Organization, Geneva, Switzerland.

Korbin, J. E., Anetzberger, G., & Austin, C. (1995). The intergenerational cycle of violence in child and elder abuse. *Journal of Elder Abuse & Neglect, 7*(1), 1-15.

Korbin, J. E., Anetzberger, G. J., Thomasson, R., & Austin, C. (1991). Abused elders who seek legal recourse against their adult offspring: Findings from an exploratory study. *Journal of Elder Abuse & Neglect, 3*(3), 1-18.

Kosberg, J. I. (1988). Preventing elder abuse: Identification of high risk factors prior to placement decisions. *Gerontologist, 28,* 43-50.

Kosberg, J. I., & Garcia, J. L. (1995a). Common and unique themes on elder abuse from a world-wide perspective. In J. I. Kosberg & J. L. Garcia (Eds.), *Elder abuse: International and cross-cultural perspectives* (pp. 183-197). Binghamton, NY: Haworth.

Kosberg, J. I., & Garcia, J. L. (1995b). Introduction to the book. In J. I. Kosberg & J. L. Garcia (Eds.), *Elder abuse: International and cross-cultural perspectives* (pp. 1-12). Binghamton, NY: Haworth.

Koski, P. (1987). Family violence and nonfamily deviance: Taking stock of the literature. *Marriage and Family Review, 12,* 23-46.

Koss, M. P. (1985). The hidden rape victim: Personality, attitudinal, and situational characteristics. *Psychology of Women Quarterly, 9,* 193-212.

Koss, M. P. (1989). Hidden rape: Sexual aggression and victimization in a national sample of students in higher education. In M. A. Pirog-Good & J. E. Stets (Eds.), *Violence in dating relationships: Emerging social issues* (pp. 145-168). New York: Praeger.

Koss, M. P. (1992). Defending date rape. *Journal of Interpersonal Violence, 7,* 122-126.

Koss, M. P. (1993). Detecting the scope of rape. *Journal of Interpersonal Violence, 8,* 198-222.

Koss, M. P., & Cook, S. L. (1993). Facing the facts: Date and acquaintance rape are significant problems for women. In R. J. Gelles & D. R. Loseke (Eds.), *Current controversies on family violence* (pp. 104-119). Newbury Park, CA: Sage.

Koss, M. P., & Dinero, T. E. (1989). Discriminant analysis of risk factors for sexual victimization. *Family Relations, 57,* 242-250.

Koss, M. P., Giarretto, C. A., & Wisniewski, N. (1987). The scope of rape: Incidence and prevalence of sexual aggression and victimization in a national sample of higher education students. *Journal of Consulting and Clinical Psychology, 55,* 162-170.

Koss, M. P., & Gidycz, C. A. (1985). Sexual Experiences Survey: Reliability and validity. *Journal of Consulting and Clinical Psychology, 50,* 455-457.

Koss, M. P., Goodman, L. A., Browne, A., Fitzgerald, L. F., Puryear-Keita, G., & Russo, N. F. (1994a). *Male violence against women at home, at work, and in the community.* Washington, DC: American Psychological Association.

Koss, M. P., Goodman, L. A., Browne, A., Fitzgerald, L. F., Puryear-Keita, G. K., & Russo, N. F. (1994b). *No safe haven.* Washington, DC: American Psychological Association.

Koss, M. P., Koss, P., & Woodruff, W. J. (1991). Deleterious effects of criminal victimization on women's health and medical utilization. *Archives of Internal Medicine, 151,* 342-357.

Kovacs, M. (1981). Rating scales to assess depression in school-age children. *Acta Paedopsychiatry, 46,* 305-315.

Kratcoski, P. C. (1984). Perspectives on intra-family violence. *Human Relations, 37,* 443-453.

Kroll, P. D., Stock, D. F., & James, M. E. (1985). The behavior of adult alcoholic men abused as children. *Journal of Nervous and Mental Disease, 173,* 689-693.

Krugman, R. D. (1995). Future directions in preventing child abuse. *Child Abuse & Neglect, 19,* 272-279.

Krugman, S., Mata, L., & Krugman, R. (1992). Sexual abuse and corporal punishment during childhood: A pilot retrospective survey of university students in Costa Rica. *Pediatrics, 90,* 157-161.

Kruttschnitt, C., & Dornfeld, M. (1992). Will they tell? Assess preadolescents' reports of family violence. *Journal of Research on Crime and Delinquency, 29,* 136-147.

Kruttschnitt, C., Heath, L., & Ward, D. A. (1986). Family violence, television viewing habit, and other adolescent experiences related to violent criminal behavior. *Criminology, 24,* 235-267.

Kurrle, S. E., & Sadler, P. M. (1993). Australian service providers: Responses to elder abuse. *Journal of Elder Abuse & Neglect, 5*(1), 57-76.

Kurtz, P. D., Gaudin, J. M., Howing, P. T., & Wodarski, J. S. (1993). The consequences of physical abuse and neglect on the school age child: Mediating factors. *Children and Youth Services Review, 15,* 85-104.

Kurz, D. (1990). Interventions with battered women in health care settings. *Violence and Victims, 5,* 243-256.

Kurz, D. (1993). Physical assaults by husbands: A major social problem. In R. J. Gelles & D. R. Loseke (Eds.), *Current controversies on family violence* (pp. 88-103). Newbury Park, CA: Sage.

Kurz, D., & Stark, E. (1988). Not-so-benign neglect: The medical response to battering. In K. Yllö & M. Bograd (Eds.), *Feminist perspectives on wife abuse* (pp. 249-266). Newbury Park, CA: Sage.

Kwan, A. Y. (1995). Elder abuse in Hong Kong. In J. I. Kosberg & J. L. Garcia (Eds.), *Elder abuse: International and cross-cultural perspectives* (pp. 65-80). Binghamton, NY: Haworth.

LaBell, L. S. (1979). Wife abuse: A sociological study of battered women and their mates. *Victimology: An International Journal, 4,* 257-267.

Lacayo, R. (1996, January 29). Law and order. *Time,* pp. 29-33.

Lacey, K. A., & Parkin, J. M. (1974). The normal short child. *Archives of Disabled Children, 49,* 417.

Lachenmeyer, J. R., & Davidovicz, H. (1987). Failure to thrive: A critical review. In B. B. Lahey & A. E. Kazdin (Eds.), *Advances in clinical psychology* (Vol. 10, pp. 335-359). New York: Plenum.

Lachnit, C. (1991, April). "Satan trial": Jurors rule for two sisters. *Orange County Register, 1,* 26.

Lachs, M. S., & Pillemer, K. A. (1995). Abuse and neglect of elderly persons. *New England Journal of Medicine, 332,* 437-443.

LaFave, W. (1965). *Arrest: The decision to take a suspect into custody.* New York: Little, Brown.

Lahey, B. B., Conger, R. D., Atkeson, B. M., & Treiber, F. A. (1984). Parenting behavior and emotional status of physically abusive mothers. *Journal of Consulting and Clinical Psychology, 52,* 1062-1071.

Landenburger, K. (1989). A process of entrapment in and recovery from an abusive relationship. *Issues in Mental Health Nursing, 10,* 209-227.

Landsman, M. J., Nelson, K., Allen, M., & Tyler, M. (1992). *The self-sufficiency project: Final report.* Iowa City, IA: National Resource Center on Family Based Services.

Lane, G., & Russell, T. (1989). Second-order systemic work with violent couples. In P. L. Caesar & L. K. Hamberger (Eds.), *Treating men who batter* (pp. 134-162). New York: Springer.

Laner, M. R. (1983). Courtship abuse and aggression: Contextual aspects. *Sociological Spectrum, 3,* 69-83.

Laner, M. R. (1990). Violence or its precipitators: Which is more likely to be identified as a dating problem? *Deviant Behavior, 11,* 319-329.

Laner, M. R., & Thompson, J. (1982). Abuse and aggression in courting couples. *Deviant Behavior, 3,* 229-244.

Lang, R. A., & Frenzel, R. R. (1988). How sex offenders lure children. *Annals of Sex Research, 1,* 303-317.

Langan, P. A., & Innes, C. A. (1986). *Preventing domestic violence against women* (Bureau of Justice Statistics special report). Washington, DC: U.S. Department of Justice. (NCJ No. 102037)

Langhinrichsen-Rohling, J., Neidig, P., & Thorn, G. (1995). Violent marriages: Gender differences in levels of current violence and past abuse. *Journal of Family Violence, 10,* 159-176.

Langhinrichsen-Rohling, J., Smutzler, N., & Vivian, D. (1994). Positivity in marriage: The role of discord and physical aggression against wives. *Journal of Marriage and the Family, 56,* 69-79.

Lanktree, C. B., Briere, J., & Zaidi, L. Y. (1991). Incidence and impacts of sexual abuse in a child outpatient sample: The role of direct inquiry. *Child Abuse & Neglect, 15,* 447-453.

Lanning, K. V. (1991). Ritual abuse: A law enforcement view or perspective. *Child Abuse & Neglect, 15,* 171-173.

Lanning, K. V., & Burgess, A. W. (1984, January). Child pornography and sex rings. *FBI Law Enforcement Bulletin,* pp. 10-16.

Larrance, D. T., & Twentyman, C. T. (1983). Maternal attributions and child abuse. *Journal of Abnormal Psychology, 92,* 449-457.

Larson, C. S., Terman, D. L., Gomby, D. S., Quinn, L. S., & Behrman, R. E. (1994). Sexual abuse of children: Recommendations and analysis. *Future of Children, 4*(2), 4-30.

Last, J. M. (1983). *A dictionary of epidemiology.* New York: Oxford University Press.

Lau, E. E., & Kosberg, J. I. (1979). Abuse of the elderly by informal care providers. *Aging, 299,* 10-15.

Launius, M. H., & Jensen, B. L. (1987). Interpersonal problem-solving skills in battered, counseling, and control women. *Journal of Family Violence, 2,* 151-162.

Lavoie, F., Vezina, L., Piche, C., & Boivin, M. (1995). Evaluation of a prevention program for violence in teen dating relationships. *Journal of Interpersonal Violence, 10,* 516-524.

Laws, D. R., & Marshall, W. L. (1990). A conditioning theory of the etiology and maintenance of deviant sexual preferences and behavior. In W. L. Marshall, D. R. Laws, & H. E. Barbaree (Eds.), *Handbook of sexual assault: Issues, theories, and treatment of the offender* (pp. 209-229). New York: Plenum.

Lawson, C. (1993). Mother-son sexual abuse: Rare or underreported? A critique of the research. *Child Abuse & Neglect, 17,* 261-269.

Lawson, L., & Chaffin, M. (1992). False negatives in sexual abuse disclosure interviews. *Journal of Interpersonal Violence, 7,* 532-542.

Layzer, J. I., Goodson, B. D., & DeLange, C. (1986). Children in shelters. *Response, 9*(2), 2-5.

Lee, D. (1986). Mandatory reporting of elder abuse: A cheap but ineffective solution to the problem. *Fordham Urban Law Journal, 14,* 725-771.

Lehnen, R. G., & Skogan, W. G. (1981). *The National Crime Survey: Working papers, Vol. 1, current and historical perspectives.* Washington, DC: U.S. Department of Justice.

LeJeune, C., & Follette, V. (1994). Taking responsibility: Sex differences in reporting dating violence. *Journal of Interpersonal Violence, 9,* 133-140.

Lenihan, G., Rawlins, M., Eberly, C., Buckley, B., & Masters, B. (1992). Gender differences in rape supportive attitudes before and after a date rape education intervention. *Journal of College Student Development, 33,* 331-338.

Leonard, K. E., & Jacob, T. (1988). Alcohol, alcoholism, and family violence. In V. B. Van Hasselt, R. L. Morrison, A. S. Bellack, & M. Hersen (Eds.), *Handbook of family violence* (pp. 383-406). New York: Plenum.

Lerman, L. G. (1984). Mediation of wife abuse cases: The adverse impact of informal dispute resolution on women. *Harvard Women's Law Journal, 1,* 57-113.

Letellier, P. (1994). Gay and bisexual male domestic violence victimization: Challenges to feminist theory and responses to violence. *Violence and Victims, 9,* 95-106.

Levant, R. F. (1994, August). *Male violence against female partners: Roots in male socialization and development*. Paper presented at the annual meeting of the American Psychological Association, Los Angeles.

Levant, R. F., Hirsch, L. S., Celentano, E., Cozza, T. M., Hill, S., MacEachern, M., Marty, N., & Schendker, J. (1992). The male role: An investigation of contemporary norms. *Journal of Mental Health Counseling, 14,* 325-337.

Levesque, R. J. R. (1994). Sex differences in the experience of child sexual victimization. *Journal of Family Violence, 9,* 357-369.

Levinger, G. (1966). Sources of marital dissatisfaction among applicants for divorce. *American Journal of Orthopsychiatry, 36,* 803-807.

Levinson, D. (1988). Family violence in a cross-cultural perspective. In V. B. Van Hasselt, R. L. Morrison, A. S. Bellack, & M. Hersen (Eds.), *Handbook of family violence* (pp. 435-456). New York: Plenum.

Levy, B. (1984). *Skills for violence-free relationships.* Long Beach: Southern California Coalition for Battered Women. (Curriculum for Young People Ages 13-18)

Levy, B. (1991). *Dating violence: Young women in danger.* Seattle, WA: Seal.

Lewin, T. (1994, July 11). Poll of teenagers: Battle of the sexes on roles in family. *New York Times,* pp. A1, B7.

Lie, G., Schlitt, R., Bush, J., Montagne, M., & Reyes, L. (1991). Lesbians in currently aggressive relationships: How frequently do they report aggressive past relationships? *Violence and Victims, 6,* 121-135.

Lieber, J., & Steptoe, S. (1994, June 27). Fatal attraction. *Sports Illustrated,* pp. 15-31.

Limbaugh, R. (1994, January 24). No tears for Lorena. *Newsweek,* p. 56.

Lindberg, M. (1991). An interactive approach to assessing the suggestibility and testimony of eyewitnesses. In J. Doris (Ed.), *The suggestibility of children's recollections: Implications for eyewitness testimony* (pp. 47-55). Washington, DC: American Psychological Association.

Lipovsky, J. A., & Elliott, A. N. (1993). Individual treatment of the sexually abused child. *The APSAC Advisor, 6*(3), 15-18.

Lloyd, J. C., & Sallee, A. L. (1994). The challenge and potential of family preservation services in the public child welfare system. *Protecting Children, 10*(3), 3-6.

Lloyd, S. A. (1988, November). *Conflict and violence in marriage.* Paper presented at the annual meeting of the National Council on Family Relations, Philadelphia.

Lloyd, S. A. (1991). The darkside of courtship: Violence and sexual exploitation. *Family Relations, 40,* 14-20.

Lloyd, S. A., Koval, J. E., & Cate, R. M. (1989). Conflict and violence in dating relationships. In M. A. Pirog-Good & J. E. Stets (Eds.), *Vio-*

lence in dating relationships: Emerging social issues (pp. 126-142). New York: Praeger.

Lo, W. A., & Sporakowski, M. J. (1989). The continuation of violent dating relationships among college students. *Journal of College Student Development, 30,* 432-439.

Locke, H. J., & Wallace, K. M. (1957). Short marital adjustment and prediction tests: Their reliability and validity. *Journal of Marriage and Family Living, 21,* 251-255.

Lockhart, L. L., White, B. W., Causby, V., & Isaac, A. (1994). Letting out the secret: Violence in lesbian relationships. *Journal of Interpersonal Violence, 9,* 469-492.

Loftus, E., & Ketcham, K. (1991). *Witness for the defense.* New York: St. Martin's.

Loftus, E. F. (1993). The reality of repressed memories. *American Psychologist, 48,* 518-537.

Long, G. M., & McNamara, J. R. (1989). Paradoxical punishment as it relates to the battered woman syndrome. *Behavior Modification, 13,* 192-205.

Longres, J. F. (1992). Race and type of maltreatment in an elder abuse system. *Journal of Elder Abuse & Neglect, 4*(3), 61-83.

Lonsway, K. A., & Fitzgerald, L. A. (1994). Rape myths: In review. *Psychology of Women Quarterly, 18,* 133-164.

Loring, M. T. (1994). *Emotional abuse.* New York: Lexington Books.

Los Angeles County Department of Community and Senior Citizen Services. (1994). *Abuse by others—1/93 through 6/93.* Los Angeles: Author.

Los Angeles County Medical Association. (1992). *Diagnostic and treatment guidelines on elder abuse and neglect.* Los Angeles: Author.

Loulan, J. (1987). *Lesbian passion.* San Francisco: Spinsters/Aunt Lute.

Lowenstein, A. (1995). Elder abuse in a forming society: Israel. In J. I. Kosberg & J. L. Garcia (Eds.), *Elder abuse: International and cross-cultural perspectives* (pp. 81-100). Binghamton, NY: Haworth.

Lujan, C., DeBruyn, L. M., May, P. A., & Bird, M. E. (1989). Profile of abused and neglected American Indian children in the Southwest. *Child Abuse & Neglect, 13,* 449-461.

Lundberg-Love, P., & Geffner, R. (1989). Date rape: Prevalence, risk factors, and a proposed model. In M. A. Pirog-Good & J. E. Stets (Eds.), *Violence in dating relationships: Emerging social issues* (pp. 169-184). New York: Praeger.

Lutzker, J. R. (1990). Behavioral treatment of child neglect. *Behavior Modification, 14,* 301-315.

Lutzker, J. R., Campbell, R. V., & Watson-Perczel, M. (1984). Using the case study method to treat several problems in a family indicated for child neglect. *Education and Treatment of Children, 7,* 315-333.

Lutzker, J. R., Megson, D. A., Dachman, R. S., & Webb, M. E. (1985). Validating and training adult-child interaction skills to professionals and to parents indicated for child abuse and neglect. *Journal of Child and Adolescent Psychotherapy, 2,* 91-104.

Lutzker, S. Z., Lutzker, J. R., Braunling-McMorrow, D., & Eddleman, J. (1987). Prompting to increase mother-baby stimulation with single mothers. *Journal of Child and Adolescent Psychotherapy, 4,* 3-12.

Lynch, M. A., & Roberts, J. (1982). *Consequences of child abuse.* London: Academic Press.

Lyons, T. J., & Oates, R. K. (1993). Falling out of bed: A relatively benign occurrence. *Pediatrics, 92,* 125.

MacAndrew, C., & Edgerton, R. B. (1969). *Drunken comportment: A social explanation.* Chicago: Aldine.

Mace, N. L. (1981). *The 36-hour day: A family guide to caring for persons with Alzheimer's disease, related dementing illness, and memory loss in later life.* Baltimore: Johns Hopkins University Press.

MacEwen, K. E. (1994). Refining the intergenerational transmission hypothesis. *Journal of Interpersonal Violence, 9,* 350-365.

MacEwen, K. E., & Barling, J. (1988). Multiple stressors, violence in the family of origin, and marital aggression: A longitudinal investigation. *Journal of Family Violence, 3,* 73-87.

Maertz, K. F. (1990). Self-defeating beliefs of battered women (Doctoral dissertation, University of Alberta, Canada). *Dissertation Abstracts International, 51,* 5580B. (UMI No. 8814496)

Maguire, K., & Pastore, A. L. (Eds.). (1994). *Sourcebook of criminal justice statistics—1993.* Washington, DC: U.S. Department of Justice, Bureau of Justice Statistics.

Maier, S. F., & Seligman, M. E. P. (1976). Learned helplessness: Theory and evidence. *Journal of Experimental Psychology: General, 105,* 3-46.

Maiuro, R. D., Cahn, T. S., & Vitaliano, P. P. (1986). Assertiveness deficits and hostility in domestically violent men. *Violence and Victims, 1,* 279-289.

Maiuro, R. D., Cahn, T. S., & Vitaliano, P. P. (1988). Anger, hostility, and depression in domestically violent versus generally assaultive men and nonviolent control subjects. *Journal of Consulting and Clinical Psychology, 56,* 17-23.

Makepeace, J. M. (1981). Courtship violence among college students. *Family Relations, 30,* 97-102.

Makepeace, J. M. (1986). Gender differences in courtship violence victimization. *Family Relations, 30,* 97-102.

Makepeace, J. M. (1987). Social factor and victim-offender differences in courtship violence. *Family Relations, 36,* 87-91.

Malamuth, N. M. (1989). Predictors of naturalistic sexual aggression. In M. A. Pirog-Good & J. E. Stets (Eds.), *Violence in dating relationships: Emerging social issues* (pp. 219-240). New York: Praeger.

Malatack, J. J., Wiener, E. S., Gartner, J. C., Zitelli, B. J., & Brunetti, E. (1985). Munchausen by proxy: A new complication of central venous catheterization. *Pediatrics, 75,* 523-525.

Malinosky-Rummell, R., & Hansen, D. J. (1993). Long-term consequences of childhood physical abuse. *Psychological Bulletin, 114,* 68-79.

Mannarino, A. P., Cohen, J. A., Smith, J. A., & Moore-Motily, S. (1991). Six- and twelve-month follow-up of sexually abused girls. *Journal of Interpersonal Violence, 6,* 494-511.

Margolin, G. (1979). Conjoint marital therapy to enhance anger management and reduce spouse abuse. *American Journal of Family Therapy, 7,* 13-23.

Margolin, G. (1987). The multiple forms of aggressiveness between marital partners: How do we identify them? *Journal of Marital and Family Therapy, 13,* 77-84.

Margolin, G., & Burman, B. (1993). Wife abuse versus marital violence: Different terminologies, explanations, and solutions. *Clinical Psychology Review, 13,* 59-73.

Margolin, G., Burman, B., & John, R. S. (1989). Home observations of married couples reenacting naturalistic conflicts. *Behavioral Assessment, 11,* 101-118.

Margolin, G., & Fernandez, V. (1987). The "spontaneous" cessation of marital violence: Three case examples. *Journal of Marital and Family Therapy, 13,* 241-250.

Margolin, G., John, R. S., & Gleberman, L. (1988). Affective responses to conflictual discussions in violent and nonviolent couples. *Journal of Consulting and Clinical Psychology, 56,* 24-33.

Margolin, L., & Craft, J. L. (1990). Child abuse by adolescent caregivers. *Child Abuse & Neglect, 14,* 365-373.

Margolin, L., Moran, P. B., & Miller, M. (1989). Social approval for violations of sexual consent in marriage and dating. *Violence and Victims, 4,* 45-55.

Marques, J., Nelson, C., West, M. A., & Day, D. M. (1994). The relationship between treatment goals and recidivism among child molesters. *Behavior Research and Therapy, 32,* 577-588.

Marshall, L. L. (1987, June). *Partnership abuse: Comparison of two studies using college students.* Paper presented at the Iowa Conference on Personal Relationships.

Marshall, L. L. (1994). Physical and psychological abuse. In W. R. Cupach & B. H. Spitzberg (Eds.), *The dark side of interpersonal communication* (pp. 281-311). Edison, NJ: Lawrence Erlbaum.

Marshall, L. L., & Rose, P. (1987). Gender, stress and violence in the adult relationships of a sample of college students. *Journal of Social and Personal Relationships, 4,* 299-316.

Marshall, L. L., & Rose, P. (1988). Family of origin violence and courtship abuse. *Journal of Counseling and Development, 66,* 414-418.

Marshall, L. L., & Rose, P. (1990). Premarital violence: The impact of family of origin violence, stress, and reciprocity. *Violence and Victims, 5,* 51-64.

Marshall, W., & Eccles, A. (1993). Pavlovian conditioning processes in adolescent sex offenders. In H. Barbaree, W. Marshall, & S. Hudson (Eds.), *The juvenile sex offender* (pp. 118-142). New York: Guilford.

Marshall, W., & Pithers, W. (1994). A reconsideration of treatment outcome with sex offenders. *Criminal Justice and Behavior, 21,* 10-27.

Marshall, W. L., & Barbaree, H. E. (1988). The long-term evaluation of a behavioral treatment program for child molesters. *Behavior Research and Therapy, 26,* 499-511.

Marshall, W. L., Barbaree, H. E., & Butt, J. (1988). Sexual offenders against male children: Sexual preferences. *Behavior Research and Therapy, 26,* 383-391.

Marshall, W. L., Barbaree, H. E., & Christophe, D. (1986). Sexual offenders against female children: Sexual preferences for age of victims and type of behavior. *Canadian Journal of Behavioral Science, 18,* 424-439.

Marshall, W. L., Jones, R., Ward, T., Johnston, P., & Barbaree, H. E. (1991). Treatment outcome with sex offenders. *Clinical Psychology Review, 11,* 465-485.

Martin, D. (1978). Battered women: Society's problem. In J. R. Chapman & M. Gates (Eds.), *The victimization of women* (pp. 111-141). Beverly Hills, CA: Sage.

Martin, P. Y., & Hummer, R. A. (1995). Fraternities and rape on campus. In P. Searles & R. J. Berger (Eds.), *Rape and society: Readings on the problem of sexual assault* (pp. 139-151). Boulder, CO: Westview.

Martin, S. E. (1989). Research note: The response of the clergy to spouse abuse in a suburban county. *Violence and Victims, 4,* 217-225.

Mash, E. J., Johnston, C., & Kovitz, K. (1983). A comparison of the mother-child interactions of physically abused and non-abused children during play and task situations. *Journal of Clinical Child Psychology, 12,* 337-346.

Matlaw, J. R., & Spence, D. M. (1994). The hospital elder assessment team: A protocol for suspected cases of elder abuse and neglect. *Journal of Elder Abuse & Neglect, 6*(2), 23-37.

Matthews, W. J. (1984). Violence in college couples. *College Student Journal, 18,* 150-158.

Mayseless, O. (1991). Adult attachment patterns and courtship violence. *Family Relations, 40,* 21-28.

McClung, J. J., Murray, R., & Braden, N. J. (1988). Intentional ipecac poisoning in children. *American Journal of Diseases in Children, 142,* 637-639.

McCord, J. (1983). A forty year perspective on effects of child abuse and neglect. *Child Abuse & Neglect, 7,* 265-270.

McCurdy, K., & Daro, D. (1994a). Child maltreatment: A national survey of reports and fatalities. *Journal of Interpersonal Violence, 9,* 75-94.

McCurdy, K., & Daro, D. (1994b). Current trends in child abuse reporting and fatalities: The results of the 1993 annual fifty state survey. (Available from the National Committee to Prevent Child Abuse, 332 South Michigan Ave., Suite 1600, Chicago, IL 60604)

McGee, R. A., & Wolfe, D. A. (1991). Psychological maltreatment: Toward an operational definition. *Development and Psychopathology, 3,* 3-18.

McGuire, T., & Feldman, K. (1989). Psychological morbidity of children subjected to Munchausen syndrome by proxy. *Pediatrics, 83,* 289-292.

McKay, E. J. (1987, July). *Children of battered women.* Paper presented at the Third National Family Violence Research Conference, Durham, NH.

McKay, M. M. (1994). The link between domestic violence and child abuse: Assessment and treatment considerations. *Child Welfare, 73,* 29-39.

McKeel, A. J., & Sporakowski, M. J. (1993). How shelter counselors' views about responsibility for wife abuse relate to services they provide. *Journal of Family Violence, 8,* 101-112.

McLaughlin, I. G., Leonard, K. E., & Senchak, M. (1992). Prevalence and distribution of premarital aggression among couples applying for a marriage license. *Journal of Family Violence, 4,* 309-319.

McLeer, S. V., & Anwar, R. (1989). A study of battered women presenting in an emergency department. *American Journal of Public Health, 79,* 65-66.

McNair, D. M., Lorr, M., & Doppleman, L. F. (1981). *Profile of Mood States manual.* San Diego, CA: Educational and Industrial Testing Service.

Meadow, R. (1977). Munchausen syndrome by proxy: The hinterland of child abuse. *Lancet, 2,* 343-345.

Meadow, R. (1990). Suffocation, recurrent apnea, and sudden infant death. *Journal of Pediatrics, 117,* 351-356.

Meddaugh, D. I. (1990). Reactance: Understanding aggressive behavior in long-term care. *Journal of Psychosocial Nursing and Mental Health Services, 28*(4), 28-33.

Mednick, S. A., Gabrielli, W. F., & Hutchings, B. (1987). Genetic factors in the etiology of criminal behavior. In S. A. Mednick, T. E. Moffitt, & S. S. Stack (Eds.), *The causes of crime* (pp. 74-91). Cambridge: Cambridge University Press.

Megargee, E. I. (Ed.). (1966). Undercontrolled and overcontrolled personality types in extreme antisocial aggression. *Psychological Monographs: General and Applied, 80*(3, Whole No. 611).

Meichenbaum, D. (1977). *Cognitive-behavior modification: An integrative approach.* New York: Plenum.

Melton, G. B. (1990). Certificates of confidentiality under the public service act: Strong protection but not enough. *Violence and Victims, 5,* 67-70.

Melton, G. B., & Barry, F. D. (1994). Neighbors helping neighbors: The vision of the U.S. Advisory Board on Child Abuse and Neglect. In G. B. Melton & F. D. Barry (Eds.), *Protecting children from abuse and neglect* (pp. 1-13). New York: Guilford.

Mennen, F. E., & Meadow, D. (1994). A preliminary study of the factors related to trauma in childhood sexual abuse. *Journal of Family Violence, 9,* 125-142.

Mennen, F. E., & Meadow, D. (1995). The relationship of abuse characteristics to symptoms in sexually abused girls. *Journal of Interpersonal Violence, 10,* 259-274.

Menon, R. (1990). Unsafe at any age: A preliminary discussion of child rape in India. *Canadian Woman's Studies, 13,* 27-29.

Meredith, W. H., Abbot, D. A., & Adams, S. L. (1986). Family violence: Its relation to marital and parental satisfaction and family strengths. *Journal of Family Violence, 1,* 299-305.

Merriam-Webster's collegiate dictionary (10th ed.). (1993). Springfield, MA: Merriam-Webster.

Mertin, P. G. (1992). An adaptation of the Conflict Tactics Scales. *Australian Journal of Marriage and the Family, 13,* 166-169.

Metz, H. (1994, May). The sins of the fathers. *Student Lawyer,* pp. 32-36.

Meyer, J. (1994, June 17). Police records detail 1989 beating that led to charge. *Los Angeles Times,* p. A24.

Michaelson, R. (1993, September). Context needed for study of child abuse and neglect. *APA Monitor, 24*(9), 12-13.

Miller, D. T., & Porter, C. A. (1983). Self-blame in victims of violence. *Journal of Social Issues, 39,* 139-152.

Miller, J. B. (1976). *Toward a new psychology of women.* Boston: Beacon.

Miller, S. L. (1989). Unintended side effects of pro-arrest policies and their race and class implications for battered women: A cautionary note. *Criminal Justice Policy Review, 3,* 299-316.

Miller, T. R., Cohen, M. A., & Wiersema, B. (1996, February). *Victim costs and consequences: A new look* (Final summary report presented to the National Institute of Justice). Washington, DC: U.S. Department of Justice. (NCJ No. 155282)

Miller-Perrin, C. L. (1996). *Sexually abused children's perceptions of sexual abuse: A preliminary analysis and comparison across ages.* Manuscript submitted for publication, Pepperdine University.

Millon, T. (1983). *Millon Clinical Multiaxial Inventory manual.* Minneapolis, MN: Interpretive Scoring Systems.

Mills, T. (1985). The assault on the self: Stages in coping with battering husbands. *Qualitative Sociology, 8,* 103-123.

Milner, J. S., & Chilamkurti, C. (1991). Physical child abuse perpetrator characteristic: A review of the literature. *Journal of Interpersonal Violence, 6,* 336-344.

Milner, J. S., & Robertson, K. R. (1990). Comparison of physical child abusers, intrafamilial sexual child abusers, and child neglecters. *Journal of Interpersonal Violence, 5,* 37-48.

Milner, J. S., & Wimberly, R. C. (1980). Prediction and explanation of child abuse. *Journal of Clinical Psychology, 36,* 875-888.

Miner, M., Marques, J., Day, D., & Nelson, C. (1990). Impact of relapse prevention in treating sex offenders: Preliminary findings. *Annals of Sex Research, 3,* 165-185.

Mitchel, L. (1989). Report on fatalities from National Committee for Prevention of Child Abuse. *Protecting Children, 6,* 3-5.

Mixson, P. M. (1991). Self-neglect: A practitioner's perspective. *Journal of Elder Abuse & Neglect, 3*(1), 35-42.

Model law on family violence includes strict arrest policy. (1994, May). *Criminal Justice Newsletter, 25*(10), 1-2.

Monahan, J., Appelbaum, P. S., Mulvey, E. P., Robbins, P. C., & Lidz, C. W. (1993). Ethical and legal duties in conducting research on violence: Lessons from the MacArthur risk assessment study. *Violence and Victims, 8,* 387-396.

Mones, P. (1989, November). *A comparison of children who kill family members and children who kill non-related persons.* Paper presented at the annual meeting of the American Society of Criminology, Reno, NV.

Montoya, J. (1993). Something not so funny happened on the way to conviction: The pretrial interrogation of child witnesses. *Arizona Law Review, 35,* 927.

Moon, A., & Williams, O. J. (1993). Perceptions of elder abuse and help-seeking patterns among African-American, Caucasian American, and Korean-American elderly women. *Gerontologist, 33,* 386-395.

Moore, T., Pepler, D., Mae, R., & Kates, M. (1989). Effects of family violence on children: New directions for research and intervention. In B. Pressman, G. Cameron, & M. Rothery (Eds.), *Intervening with assaulted women: Current theory, research, and practice.* Hillsdale, NJ: Lawrence Erlbaum.

Morash, M. (1986). Wife battering. *Criminal Justice Abstracts, 18,* 252-271.

Morency, N. L., & Krauss, R. M. (1982). The nonverbal encoding and decoding of affect in first and fifth graders. In R. S. Feldman (Ed.),

Development of nonverbal behavioral skill. New York: Springer-Verlag.

Morganthau, T., Springen, K., Smith, V. E., Rosenberg, D., Beals, G., Bogert, C., Gegax, T. T., & Joseph, N. (1994, December 12). The orphanage. *Newsweek*, pp. 28-32.

Morris, G. (1985). *The kids next door. Sons and daughters who kill their parents.* New York: William Morrow.

Morrison, J. (1989). Childhood sexual histories of women with somatization disorder. *American Journal of Psychiatry, 146,* 239-241.

Morrison, R. L., Van Hasselt, V. B., & Bellack, A. S. (1987). Assessment of assertion and problem-solving skills in wife abusers and their spouses. *Journal of Family Violence, 2,* 227-256.

Movsas, T. Z., & Movsas, B. (1990). Abuse versus neglect: A model to understand the causes of and treatment strategies for mistreatment of older persons. *Issues in Law & Medicine, 6,* 163-173.

Mowbray, C. T. (1988). Post-traumatic therapy for children who are victims of violence. In F. M. Ochberg (Ed.), *Post-traumatic therapy for children who are victims of violence* (pp. 196-212). New York: Brunner/Mazel.

Muehlenhard, C. L. (1989). Misinterpreted dating behaviors and the risk of date rape. In M. A. Pirog-Good & J. E. Stets (Eds.), *Violence in dating relationships: Emerging social issues* (pp. 241-256). New York: Praeger.

Muehlenhard, C. L., & Linton, M. A. (1987). Date rape and sexual aggression in dating situations: Incidence and risk factors. *Journal of Counseling Psychology, 34,* 186-196.

Muldary, P. S. (1983). Attribution of causality of spouse assault. *Dissertation Abstracts International, 44,* 1249B. (UMI No. 8316576)

Mulhurn, S. (1991). Satanism and psychotherapy: A rumor in search of an inquisition. In J. Richardson, J. Best, & D. Bromley (Eds.), *The satanism scare* (pp. 145-174). New York: Aldine de Gruyter.

Munkel, W. I. (1994). Neglect and abandonment. In A. E. Brodeur & J. A. Monteleone (Eds.), *Child maltreatment: A clinical guide and reference* (pp. 241-257). St. Louis, MO: Medical Publishing.

Murdock, R. L. (1992). *Suffer the children: A pediatrician's reflections on abuse.* Santa Fe, NM: Health Press.

Murphy, C. M., & Cascardi, M. (1993). Psychological aggression and abuse in marriage. In R. L. Hampton, T. P. Gullotta, G. R. Adams, E. H. Potter, III, & R. P. Weissberg (Eds.), *Family violence: Prevention and treatment* (pp. 86-112). Newbury Park, CA: Sage.

Murphy, C. M., Meyer, S. L., & O'Leary, K. D. (1994). Dependency characteristics of partner assaultive men. *Journal of Abnormal Psychology, 103,* 729-735.

Murphy, C. M., & O'Leary, K. D. (1987, July). *Verbal aggression as a predictor of physical aggression in early marriage.* Paper presented at the Third National Family Violence Research Conference, Durham, NH.

Murrin, M. R., & Laws, D. R. (1990). The influence of pornography on sexual crimes. In W. L. Marshall, D. R. Laws, & H. E. Barbaree (Eds.), *Handbook of sexual assault: Issues, theories, and treatment of the offender* (pp. 73-91). New York: Plenum.

Murty, K. S., & Roebuck, J. B. (1992). An analysis of crisis calls by battered women in the city of Atlanta. In E. C. Viano (Ed.), *Intimate violence: Interdisciplinary perspectives* (pp. 61-81). Bristol, PA: Taylor & Francis.

Mydans, S. (1994, June). Prosecutors are rebuked on child sex abuse case. *New York Times*, p. A7.

Myers, J. E. B. (1992). *Evidence in child abuse and neglect cases.* New York: John Wiley.

Myers, J. E. B. (1993). Commentary: A call for forensically relevant research. *Child Abuse & Neglect, 17,* 573-579.

Myers, J. E. B. (1994). Adjudication of child sexual abuse cases. *Future of Children, 4*(2), 84-101.

Myers, J. E. B., & Peters, W. D. (1987). *Child abuse reporting and legislation in the 1980s.* Denver, CO: American Humane Association.

Myers, J. E. B., Tikosh, M. A., & Paxson, M. A. (1992). Domestic violence prevention statutes. *Violence Update, 3*(4), 3, 5-9.

Nachman, S. (1991). Community-based m-team roles: A job analysis. *Journal of Elder Abuse & Neglect, 3*(3), 45-71.

Nasjleti, M. (1980). Suffering in silence: The male incest victim. *Child Welfare, 59,* 269-275.

National Center for Prosecution of Child Abuse. (1993). *Legislation requiring sex offenders to register with a government agency.* Alexandria, VA: Author.

National Center on Child Abuse and Neglect. (1978). *Child sexual abuse: Incest, assault, and sexual exploitation, a special report.* Washington, DC: Author.

National Center on Women and Family Law, Inc. (1994). *The effects of woman abuse on children: Psychological and legal authority* (2nd ed.). New York: Author.

National Committee for the Prevention of Elder Abuse. (1995, July). *President's message.* Washington, DC: National Center on Elder Abuse.

National Council of Juvenile and Family Court Judges. (1995, August 21). *Notice of available publications and technical assistance.* Reno, NV: Author.

National Victims Center. (1992, April 23). *Rape in America: A report to the nation.* Arlington, VA: Author.

Neff, J. A., Holamon, B., & Schluter, T. D. (1995). Spousal violence among Anglos, Blacks, and Mexican Americans: The role of demographic variables, psychosocial predictors, and alcohol consumption. *Journal of Family Violence, 10,* 1-21.

Neidig, P., Friedman, D., & Collins, B. (1986). Attitudinal family violence characteristics of men who have engaged in spouse abuse. *Journal of Family Violence, 1,* 223-233.

Neill, M., & McGraw, D. (1995, July 31). Old ways, new men. *People, 46*(5), 46-48.

Nelson, B. J. (1984). *Making an issue of child abuse: Political agenda setting for social problems.* Chicago: University of Chicago Press.

Nelson, K., Saunders, E., & Landsman, M. J. (1990). *Chronic neglect in perspective: A study of chronically neglecting families in a large metropolitan county.* Oakdale: National Resource Center on Family Based Services, University of Iowa School of Social Work.

Nerenberg, L. (1995, June). LAPD's fiduciary SWAT team. *Nexus, 1*(2), 4-5.

Nerenberg, L., Hanna, S., Harshbarger, S., McKnight, R., McLaughlin, C., & Parkins, S. (1990). Linking systems and community services: The interdisciplinary team approach. *Journal of Elder Abuse & Neglect, 2*(1-2), 101-135.

Newman, G. R. (1979). *Understanding violence.* New York: J. B. Lippincott.

Newmark, L., Harrell, A., & Salem, P. (1995). Domestic violence and empowerment in custody and visitation in custody and visitation cases [Special issue]. *Family and Conciliation Courts Review, 33,* 30-62.

Ney, P. G. (1989). Child mistreatment: Possible reasons for its transgenerational transmission. *Canadian Journal of Psychiatry, 34,* 594-601.

Ney, P. G., Fung, T., & Wickett, A. R. (1994). The worst combinations of child abuse and neglect. *Child Abuse & Neglect, 18,* 705-714.

NiCarthy, G. (1982). *Getting free: A handbook for women in abusive relationships* (2nd ed.). Seattle, WA: Seal.

NiCarthy, G. (1987). *The ones who got away.* Seattle, WA: Seal.

Nisonoff, L., & Bitman, I. (1979). Spouse abuse: Incidence and relationship to selected demographic variables. *Victimology: An International Journal, 4,* 131-139.

Nolan, B. S. (1990). A judicial menu: Selecting remedies for the incapacitated elder. *Journal of Elder Abuse & Neglect, 2*(3-4), 73-88.

Nomellini, S., & Katz, R. C. (1983). Effects of anger control training on abusive parents. *Cognitive Therapy and Research, 7,* 57-68.

Novaco, R. (1975). *Anger control: The development and evaluation of an experimental treatment.* Lexington, MA: Lexington Books.

Nurius, P. S., Furrey, J., & Berliner, L. (1992). Coping capacity among women with abusive partners. *Violence and Victims, 7,* 229-243.

Nuttall, R., & Jackson, H. (1994). Personal history of childhood abuse among clinicians. *Child Abuse & Neglect, 18,* 455-472.

Oates, R. K., & Bross, D. C. (1995). What have we learned about treating child physical abuse? A literature review of the last decade. *Child Abuse & Neglect, 19,* 463-474.

O'Brien, M., John, R. S., Margolin, G., & Erel, O. (1994). Reliability and diagnostic efficacy of parent's reports regarding children's exposure to marital aggression. *Violence and Victims, 9,* 45-62.

O'Brien, M., Margolin, G., John, R. S., & Krueger, L. (1991). Mothers' and sons' cognitive and emotional reactions to simulated marital and family conflict. *Journal of Consulting and Clinical Psychology, 59,* 692-703.

O'Farrell, T. J., & Murphy, C. M. (1995). Marital violence before and after alcoholism treatment. *Journal of Consulting and Clinical Psychology, 63,* 256-262.

Office of Juvenile Justice and Delinquency Prevention. (1995). *OJJDP fact sheet (No. 21).* Rockville, MD: Juvenile Justice Clearing House.

Offutt, R. A. (1988). Domestic violence: Psychological characteristics of men who batter. *Dissertation Abstracts International, 49,* 3452B. (UMI No. 8818887)

Ogg, J., & Bennett, G. C. J. (1992). Elder abuse in Britain. *British Medical Journal, 305,* 998-999.

O'Hagan, K. (1993). *Emotional and psychological abuse of children.* Toronto: University of Toronto Press.

O'Hagan, K. P. (1995). Emotional and psychological abuse: Problems of definition. *Child Abuse & Neglect, 19,* 449-461.

Ohlin, L., & Tonry, M. (1989). Family violence in perspective. In L. Ohlin & M. Tonry (Eds.), *Violence in marriage* (pp. 1-18). Chicago: University of Chicago Press.

O.J. Simpson. (1994, June 27). *Newsweek,* pp. 12-27.

O'Keefe, M. (1994a). Adjustment of children from maritally violent homes. *Families in Society, 75,* 403-415.

O'Keefe, M. (1994b). Linking marital violence, mother-child/father-child aggression, and child behavior problems. *Journal of Family Violence, 9,* 63-78.

O'Keefe, N. K., Brockopp, K., & Chew, E. (1986). Teen dating violence. *Social Work, 31,* 465-468.

Okun, L. E. (1983). A study of woman abuse: 300 battered women taking shelter, 119 woman-batterers in counseling. *Dissertation Abstracts International, 44,* 1972B. (UMI No. 8324256)

Okun, L. E. (1986). *Woman abuse: Facts replacing myths.* Albany: State University of New York Press.

O'Leary, K. D. (1993). Through a psychological lens: Personality traits, personality disorders, and levels of violence. In R. J. Gelles & D. R. Loseke (Eds.), *Current controversies on family violence* (pp. 7-30). Newbury Park, CA: Sage.

O'Leary, K. D., Barling, J., Arias, I., Rosenbaum, A., Malone, J., & Tyree, A. (1989). Prevalence and stability of physical aggression between spouses: A longitudinal analysis. *Journal of Consulting and Clinical Psychology, 57,* 263-268.

O'Leary, K. D., Curley, A., Rosenbaum, A., & Clarke, C. (1985). Assertion training for abused wives: A potentially hazardous treatment. *Journal of Marital and Family Therapy, 11,* 319-322.

O'Leary, K. D., & Curley, A. D. (1986). Assertion and family violence: Correlates of spouse abuse. *Journal of Marital and Family Therapy, 12,* 281-289.

Olinger, J. P. (1991). Elder abuse: The outlook for federal legislation. *Journal of Elder Abuse & Neglect, 3*(1), 43-52.

Olweus, D. (1979). Stability of aggressive reaction patterns in males: A review. *Psychological Bulletin, 86,* 852-875.

O'Malley, H. C., Segel, H. D., & Perez, R. (1979). *Elder abuse in Massachusetts: Survey of professionals and paraprofessionals.* Boston: Legal Research and Services to the Elderly.

Orava, T. A., McLeod, P. J., & Sharpe, D. (1996). Perceptions of control, depressive symptomatology, and self-esteem of women in transition from abusive relationships. *Journal of Family Violence, 11,* 167-186.

Orloff, L. E., Jang, D., & Klein, C. F. (1995). With no place to turn: Improving legal advocacy for battered immigrant women [Special issue]. *Family Law Quarterly, 29,* 313-329.

Overholser, J. C., & Beck, S. J. (1989). The classification of rapists and child molesters. *Journal of Offender Counseling, Services & Rehabilitation, 13,* 15-25.

Overholser, J. C., & Moll, S. H. (1990). Who's to blame: Attributions regarding causality in spouse abuse. *Behavioral Sciences and the Law, 8,* 107-120.

Overman, W. H. (1992). Preventing elder abuse and neglect through advance legal planning. *Journal of Elder Abuse & Neglect, 3*(4), 5-21.

Owens, D. M., & Straus, M. A. (1975). The social structure of violence in childhood and approval of violence as an adult. *Aggressive Behavior, 1,* 193-211.

Pagelow, M. (1984). *Family violence.* New York: Praeger.

Pagelow, M. D. (1981a). *Woman-battering: Victims and their experiences.* Beverly Hills, CA: Sage.

Pagelow, M. D. (1981b). *Women and crime.* New York: Macmillan.

Pagelow, M. D. (1992). Adult victims of domestic violence. *Journal of Interpersonal Violence, 7,* 87-120.

Paget, K. D., Philp, J. D., & Abramczyk, L. W. (1993). Recent developments in child neglect. In T. H. Ollendick & R. J. Prinz (Eds.), *Advances in clinical child psychology* (Vol. 15, pp. 121-174). New York: Plenum.

Painter, S. L., & Dutton, D. G. (1985). Patterns of emotional bonding in battered women: Traumatic bonding. *International Journal of Women's Studies, 57,* 101-110.

Pape, K. T., & Arias, I. (1995). Control, coping, and victimization in dating relationship. *Violence and Victims, 10,* 43-54.

Parish, R. A., Myers, P. A., Brandner, A., & Templin, K. H. (1985). Developmental milestones in abused children, and their improvement with a family-oriented approach to the treatment of child abuse. *Child Abuse & Neglect, 9,* 245-250.

Parke, R. D., & Collmer, C. W. (1975). Child abuse: An interdisciplinary analysis. In E. M. Hetherington (Ed.), *Review of child development research* (Vol. 5, pp. 509-590). Chicago: University of Chicago Press.

Parker, K. (1996, January 10). Managed care being applied to wife beating. *Daily News,* p. 13.

Parry, R., Broder, E. A., Schmitt, E. A. G., Saunders, E. B., & Hood, E. (Eds.). (1986). *Custody disputes: Evaluation and intervention.* Toronto: Lexington Books.

Passantino, G., Passantino, B., & Trott, J. (1990). Satan's sideshow. *Cornerstone, 90,* 24-28.

Pate, A. M., & Hamilton, E. E. (1992). Formal and informal deterrents to domestic violence: The Dade County spouse assault experiment. *American Sociological Review, 57,* 671-697.

Patterson, G. R. (1982). *Coercive family process.* Eugene, OR: Castalia.

Patterson, G. R., Reid, J. B., & Dishion, T. D. (1992). *Antisocial boys: A social interaction approach* (Vol. 4). Eugene, OR: Castalia.

Paveza, G. J. (1988). Risk factors in father-daughter child sexual abuse: A case-control study. *Journal of Interpersonal Violence, 3,* 290-306.

Paveza, G. J., Cohen, D., Eisdorfer, C., Freels, S., Semla, T., Ashford, J. W., Gorelick, P., Hirschman, R., Luchins, D., & Levy, P. (1992). Severe family violence and Alzheimer's disease: Prevalence and risk factors. *Gerontologist, 32,* 493-497.

Pear, R. (1996, March 17). Child-protection programs found deficient. *Daily News,* pp. 1, 24.

Pearl, P. S. (1994). Emotional abuse. In A. E. Brodeur & J. A. Monteleone (Eds.), *Child maltreatment: A clinical guide and reference* (pp. 259-283). St. Louis, MO: Medical Publishing.

Pedrick-Cornell, C., & Gelles, R. J. (1982). Elder abuse: The status of current knowledge. *Family Relations: Journal of Applied Family and Child Studies, 31,* 457-469.

Peled, E. (1993). Children who witness women battering: Concerns and dilemmas in the construction of a social problem. *Children and Youth Services Review, 15,* 43-52.

Peled, E., & Davis, D. (1995). *Groupwork with children: A practitioner's manual.* Thousand Oaks, CA: Sage.

Peled, E., & Edleson, J. L. (1992). Multiple perspectives on groupwork with children of battered women. *Violence and Victims, 7,* 327-346.

Peled, E., Jaffe, P. J., & Edleson, J. L. (1994). *Ending the cycle of violence: Community response to children of battered women.* Thousand Oaks, CA: Sage.

Pelton, L. H. (1994). The role of material factors in child abuse and neglect. In G. B. Melton & F. D. Barry (Eds.), *Protecting children from abuse and neglect* (pp. 166-181). New York: Guilford.

Peltoniemi, T. (1982). Current research on family violence in Finland and Sweden. *Victimology: An International Journal, 7,* 252-255.

Pemberton, D. A., & Benady, D. R. (1973). Consciously rejected children. *British Journal of Psychiatry, 123,* 575-578.

Pence, D., & Wilson, C. (1994). *Team investigation of child sexual abuse: Uneasy alliance.* Newbury Park, CA: Sage.

Pence, E., & Paymar, M. (1986). *Power and control: Tactics of men who batter.* Duluth: Minnesota Program Development.

Penhale, B. (1993). The abuse of elderly people: Considerations for practice. *British Journal of Social Work, 23,* 95-112.

Perilla, J. L., Bakeman, R., & Norris, F. H. (1994). Culture and domestic violence: The ecology of abused Latinas. *Violence and Victims, 9,* 325-339.

Perry, N. & McAuliff, B. (1993). The use of videotaped child testimony: Public policy implications. *Notre Dame Journal of Law, Ethics, and Public Policy, 7,* 387.

Perry, N. W. (1992). How children remember and why they forget. *The APSAC Advisor, 5,* 1-2, 13-16.

Petchers, M. K. (1995, July). *Child maltreatment among children in battered mothers' households.* Paper presented at the 4th International Family Violence Research Conference, Durham, NH.

Peters, J., Dinsmore, J., & Toth, P. (1989). Why prosecute child abuse? *South Dakota Law Review, 34,* 649-659.

Peters, J. M. (1989). Criminal prosecution of child abuse: Recent trends. *Pediatric Annals, 18,* 505-509.

Peters, S. D., Wyatt, G. E., & Finkelhor, D. (1986). Prevalence. In D. Finkelhor (Ed.), *A sourcebook on child sexual abuse* (pp. 15-39). Beverly Hills, CA: Sage.

Petrik, N. D., Petrik, R. E., & Subotnik, L. S. (1994). Powerlessness and the need to control. *Journal of Interpersonal Violence, 9,* 278-285.

Pfouts, J. H., Schopler, J. H., & Henley, C. H. (1982). Forgotten victims of family violence. *Social Work, 27,* 367-368.

Phillips, L. R. (1983). Abuse and neglect of the frail elderly at home: An exploration of theoretical relationships. *Journal of Advanced Nursing, 8,* 379-392.

Phillips, L. R. (1986). Theoretical explanations of elder abuse: Competing hypotheses and unresolved issues. In K. A. Pillemer & R. S. Wolf (Eds.), *Elder abuse: Conflict in the family* (pp. 197-217). Dover, MA: Auburn House.

Phillips, L. R. (1989). Issues involved in identifying and intervening in elder abuse. In F. Filin-

son & S. R. Ingman (Eds.), *Elder abuse: Practice and policy* (pp. 86-93). New York: Human Sciences Press.

Phillipson, C. (1992). Confronting elder abuse: Fact and fiction. *Generations Review, 2,* 3.

Phillipson, C. (1993). Abuse of older people: Sociological perspectives. In P. Decalmer & F. Glendenning (Eds.), *Mistreatment of elderly people* (pp. 88-101). Newbury Park, CA: Sage.

Piers, M. W. (1978). *Infanticide: Past and present.* New York: Norton.

Pillemer, K. A. (1986). Risk factors in elder abuse: Results from a case-control study. In K. A. Pillemer & R. S. Wolf (Eds.), *Elder abuse: Conflict in the family* (pp. 236-263). Dover, MA: Auburn House.

Pillemer, K. A. (1993). The abused offspring are dependent: Abuse is caused by the deviance and dependence of abusive caregivers. In R. J. Gelles & D. R. Loseke (Eds.), *Current controversies on family violence* (pp. 237-249). Newbury Park, CA: Sage.

Pillemer, K. A., & Finkelhor, D. (1988). The prevalence of elder abuse: A random sample survey. *Gerontologist, 28,* 51-57.

Pillemer, K. A., & Finkelhor, D. (1989). Causes of elder abuse: Caregiver stress versus problem relatives. *American Journal of Orthopsychiatry, 59,* 179-187.

Pillemer, K. A., & Suitor, J. J. (1992). Violence and violent feelings: What causes them among family caregivers? *Journal of Gerontology, 47,* S165-S172.

Pirog-Good, M. A., & Stets, J. (1986). Programs for abusers: Who drops out and what can be done. *Response, 9*(2), 17-19.

Pirog-Good, M. A., & Stets, J. E. (1989). The help-seeking behavior of physically and sexually abused college students. In M. A. Pirog-Good & J. E. Stets (Eds.), *Violence in dating relationships: Emerging social issues* (pp. 108-125). New York: Praeger.

Pistole, M. C. (1989). Attachment in adult romantic relationships: Style of conflict resolution and relationship satisfaction. *Journal of Social and Personal Relationships, 6,* 505-510.

Pithers, W., & Kafka, M. (1990). Relapse prevention with sex aggressors: A method for maintaining therapeutic gain and enhancing external supervision. In W. L. Marshall, D. R. Laws, & H. E. Barbaree (Eds.), *Handbook of sexual assault: Issues, theories, and treatment of the offender* (pp. 343-361). New York: Plenum.

Pitsiou-Darrough, E. N., & Spinellis, C. D. (1995). Mistreatment of the elderly in Greece. In J. I. Kosberg & J. L. Garcia (Eds.), *Elder abuse: International and cross-cultural perspectives* (pp. 45-64). Binghamton, NY: Haworth.

Pizzey, E. (1974). *Scream quietly or the neighbors will hear.* London: Penguin.

Plass, P. S., & Straus, M. A. (1987, July). *Intra-family homicide in the United States: Incidence, trends, and differences by region, race, and gender.* Paper presented at the Third National Family Violence Research Conference, Durham, NH.

Pleck, E. (1978). The battered data syndrome: A comment on Steinmetz's article. *Victimology: An International Journal, 2,* 680-683.

Pleck, E. (1987). *Domestic tyranny: The making of American sound policy against family violence from colonial times to present.* New York: Oxford University Press.

Plotkin, R. C., Azar, C. S., Twentyman, C. T., & Perri, M. G. (1981). A critical evaluation of the research methodology employed in the investigation of causative factors of child abuse and neglect. *Child Abuse & Neglect, 5,* 449-455.

Podkieks, E. (1992). National survey on abuse of the elderly in Canada. *Journal of Elder Abuse & Neglect, 4*(5), 5-58.

Polansky, N. A., Ammons, P. W., & Gaudin, J. M. (1985, January). Loneliness and isolation in child neglect. *Social Casework: The Journal of Contemporary Social Work,* pp. 38-47.

Polansky, N. A., Ammons, P. W., & Weathersby, B. L. (1983, September-October). Is there an American standard of child care? *Social Work,* pp. 341-346.

Polansky, N. A., Chalmers, M. A., & Williams, D. P. (1987). Assessing adequacy of rearing: An urban scale. *Child Welfare, 57,* 439-448.

Polansky, N. A., Gaudin, J. M., Ammons, P. W., & Davis, K. B. (1985). The psychological ecology of the neglectful mother. *Child Abuse & Neglect, 9,* 265-275.

Polansky, N. A., & Williams, D. P. (1978). Class orientation to child neglect. *Social Work,* pp. 397-401.

Pollack, D. (1995). Elder abuse and neglect cases reviewed by appellate courts. *Journal of Family Violence, 10,* 413-424.

Porter, B., & O'Leary, K. D. (1980). Marital discord and childhood behavior problems. *Journal of Abnormal Child Psychology, 8,* 287-295.

Poteat, G. M., Grossnickle, W. F., Cope, J. G., & Wynne, D. C. (1990). Psychometric properties of the wife abuse inventory. *Journal of Clinical Psychology, 48,* 828-834.

Powers, J. L., & Eckenrode, J. (1988). The maltreatment of adolescents. *Child Abuse & Neglect, 12,* 189-199.

Powers, J. L., Eckenrode, J., & Jaklitsch, B. (1990). Maltreatment among runaway and homeless youth. *Child Abuse & Neglect, 14,* 87-98.

Prange, R. C. (1985). Battered women and why they return to the abusive situation: A study of attribution-style, multiple-dimensional locus of control and social-psychological factors. *Dissertation Abstracts International, 46,* 4026B. (UMI No. 8522840)

Prendergast, W. E. (1979). The sex offender: How to spot him before it is too late. *Sexology,* pp. 46-51.

Preston, S. (1984). Children and elderly in the U.S. *Scientific American, 251*(6), 44-49.

Prino, C. T., & Peyrot, M. (1994). The effect of child physical abuse and neglect on aggressive, withdrawn, and prosocial behavior. *Child Abuse & Neglect, 18,* 871-884.

Procci, W. R. (1990). *Medical aspects of human sexuality.* New York: Cahners.

Ptacek, J. (1988). Why do men batter their wives? In K. Yllö & M. Bograd (Eds.), *Feminist perspectives on wife abuse* (pp. 133-157). Newbury Park, CA: Sage.

Putnam, F. W. (1991). The satanic ritual abuse controversy. *Child Abuse & Neglect, 15,* 175-179.

Pynoos, R. S., & Eth, S. (1985). Children traumatized by witnessing acts of personal violence: Homicide, rape, or suicide behavior. In S. Eth & R. S. Pynoos (Eds.), *Post-traumatic stress disorder in children* (pp. 19-43). Los Angeles: American Psychiatric Association.

Quinn, M. J. (1985). Elder abuse and neglect. *Generations, 10*(2), 22-25.

Quinsey, V. L., Chaplin, T. C., & Carrigan, W. F. (1979). Sexual preferences among incestuous and nonincestuous child molesters. *Behavior Therapy, 10,* 562-565.

Quinsey, V. L., Harris, G. T., Rice, M. E., & Lalumière, M. L. (1993). Assessing treatment efficacy in outcome studies of sex offenders. *Journal of Interpersonal Violence, 8,* 512-523.

Quinsey, V. L., Maguire, A., & Upfold, D. (1987). The behavioral treatment of rapists and child molesters. In E. K. Morris & C. J. Braukmann (Eds.), *Behavioral approaches to crime and delinquency* (pp. 363-382). New York: Plenum.

Rabb, J., & Rindfleisch, N. (1985). A study to define and assess severity of institutional abuse/neglect. *Child Abuse & Neglect, 9,* 285-294.

Rabinowitz, D. (1990, May). From the mouths of babes to a jail cell: Child abuse and the abuse of justice: A case study. *Harper's Magazine,* pp. 52-63

Ragg, D. M., & Webb, C. (1992). Group treatment for the preschool child witness of spouse abuse. *Journal of Child and Youth Care, 7,* 1-19.

Ramsey-Klawsnik, H. (1991). Elder sexual abuse: Preliminary findings. *Journal of Elder Abuse & Neglect, 3*(3), 73-90.

Randolf, M. K., & Conkle, L. K. (1993). Behavioral and emotional characteristics of children who witness parental violence. *Family Violence and Sexual Assault Bulletin, 9*(2), 23-27.

Rasche, C. E. (1988). Minority women and domestic violence: The unique dilemmas of battered women of color. *Journal of Contemporary Criminal Justice, 4,* 150-174.

Rathbone-McCuan, E. (1980). Elderly victims of family violence and neglect. *Social Casework, 61,* 296-304.

Ray, K. C., Jackson, J. L., & Townsley, R. M. (1991). Family environments of victims of intrafamilial and extrafamilial child sexual abuse. *Journal of Family Violence, 6,* 365-374.

Reece, R. M. (1990). Unusual manifestations of child abuse. *Pediatric Clinics of North America, 37,* 905-921.

Reed, S., Weinstein, F., & Bane, V. (1996, April 27). The kindest cut. *People,* pp. 67, 69-70.

Regehr, C. (1990). Parental responses to extrafamilial child sexual assault. *Child Abuse & Neglect, 14,* 113-120.

Reid, J. B., Kavanaugh, K., & Baldwin, D. V. (1987). Abusive parents' perceptions of child problem behavior: An example of parental bias. *Journal of Abnormal Child Psychology, 15,* 451-466.

Reidy, T. J. (1977). The aggressive characteristics of abused and neglected children. *Journal of Clinical Psychology, 33,* 1140-1145.

Reno, J. (1994). Foreword. *The APSAC Advisor, 7*(4), 1.

Renzetti, C. M. (1992). *Violent betrayal: Partner abuse in lesbian relationships.* Newbury Park, CA: Sage.

Resick, P. A. (1993). The psychological impact of rape. *Journal of Interpersonal Violence, 8,* 223-255.

Resick, P. A., & Reese, D. (1986). Perception of family social climate and physical aggression. *Journal of Family Violence, 1,* 71-83.

Reulbach, D. M., & Tewksbury, J. (1994). Collaboration between protective services and law enforcement: The Massachusetts model. *Journal of Elder Abuse & Neglect, 6*(2), 9-21.

Reuterman, N. A., & Burcky, W. D. (1989). Dating violence in high school: A profile of the victims. *Psychology: A Journal of Human Behavior, 26,* 1-9.

Rew, L., & Esparza, D. (1990). Barriers to disclosure among sexually abused male children. *Journal of Child and Adolescent Psychiatric and Mental Health Nursing, 3,* 120-127.

Richardson, J., Best, J., & Bromley, D. (Eds.). (1991). *The satanism scare.* New York: Aldine de Gruyter.

Rigakos, G. S. (1995). Constructing the symbolic complainant: Police subculture and the nonenforcement of protection orders for battered women. *Violence and Victims, 10,* 227-247.

Riggs, D. S. (1993). Relationship problems and dating aggression: A potential treatment target. *Journal of Interpersonal Violence, 8,* 18-35.

Riggs, D. S., Kilpatrick, D. G., & Resnick, H. S. (1992). Long-term psychological distress associated with marital rape and aggravated assault: A comparison to other crime victims. *Journal of Family Violence, 7,* 283-296.

Riggs, D. S., Murphy, C. M., & O'Leary, K. D. (1989). Intentional falsification in reports of interpartner aggression. *Journal of Interpersonal Violence, 4,* 220-232.

Riggs, D. S., & O'Leary, K. D. (1989). A theoretical model of courtship aggression. In M. A. Pirog-Good & J. E. Stets (Eds.), *Violence in dating relationships: Emerging social issues* (pp. 53-71). New York: Praeger.

Riggs, D. S., O'Leary, K. D., & Breslin, F. C. (1990). Multiple correlates of physical aggression in dating couples. *Journal of Interpersonal Violence, 5,* 61-73.

Ringwalt, C., & Caye, J. (1989). The effect of demographic factors on perceptions of child neglect. *Children and Youth Services Review, 11,* 133-144.

Rivera, B., & Widom, C. S. (1990). Childhood victimization and violent offending. *Violence and Victims, 5,* 19-35.

Roberts, A. R. (1987). Psychosocial characteristics of batterers: A study of 234 men charged with domestic violence offenses. *Journal of Family Violence, 2,* 81-93.

Roberts, R. N., Wasik, B. H., Casto, G., & Ramey, C. T. (1991). Family support in the home: Programs, policy, and social change. *American Psychologist, 46,* 131-137.

Rodenburg, F. A., & Fantuzzo, J. W. (1993). The measure of wife abuse: Steps toward the development of a comprehensive assessment technique. *Journal of Family Violence, 8,* 203-228.

Rohrbeck, C. A., & Twentyman, C. T. (1986). Multimodal assessment of impulsiveness in abusing, neglecting, and nonmaltreating mothers and their preschool children. *Journal of Consulting and Clinical Psychology, 54,* 231-236.

Romer, S. (1990). Child sexual abuse in custody and visitation disputes: Problems, progress, and prospects. *Golden Gate University Law Review, 20,* 647-680.

Romero, J., & Williams, L. (1985). Recidivism among convicted sex offenders: A 10-year follow-up study. *Federal Probation, 49*(1), 58-64.

Roscoe, B., & Benaske, N. (1985). Courtship violence experiences by abused wives: Similarities in pattern of abuse. *Family Relations, 34,* 419-424.

Roscoe, B., Goodwin, M. P., & Kennedy, D. (1987). Sibling violence and agonistic interactions experienced by early adolescents. *Journal of Family Violence, 2*(2), 121-137.

Rosen, K. H., & Stith, S. M. (1995, July). *Surviving abusive dating relationships: Processes of leaving, healing and moving on.* Paper presented at the 4th International Family Violence Research Conference, Durham, NH.

Rosenbaum, A. (1986). Of men, macho, and marital violence. *Journal of Family Violence, 1,* 121-129.

Rosenbaum, A. (1988). Methodological issues in marital violence research. *Journal of Family Violence, 3,* 91-104.

Rosenbaum, A., & Hoge, S. K. (1989). Head injury and marital aggression. *American Journal of Psychiatry, 146,* 1048-1051.

Rosenbaum, A., & O'Leary, K. D. (1981a). Children: The unintended victims of marital violence. *American Journal of Orthopsychiatry, 51,* 692-699.

Rosenbaum, A., & O'Leary, K. D. (1981b). Marital violence: Characteristics of abusive couples. *Journal of Consulting and Clinical Psychology, 49,* 63-76.

Rosenberg, D. A. (1987). Web of deceit: A literature review of Munchausen syndrome by proxy. *Child Abuse & Neglect, 11,* 547-563.

Rosenberg, M. S. (1987). Children of battered women: The effects of witnessing violence on their social problem-solving abilities. *Behavior Therapies, 10,* 85-89.

Rosenfeld, A. A., Bailey, R., Siegel, B., & Bailey, G. (1986). Determining incestuous contact between parent and child: Frequency of children touching parents' genitals in a nonclinical population. *Journal of the American Academy of Child Psychiatry, 25,* 481-484.

Rosenfeld, A. A., Siegel, B., & Bailey, R. (1987). Familial bathing patterns: Implications for cases of alleged molestation and for pediatric practice. *Pediatrics, 79,* 224-229.

Rosenfield-Schlichter, M. D., Sarber, R. E., Bueno, G., Greene, B. F., & Lutzker, J. R. (1983). Maintaining accountability for an ecobehavioral treatment for one aspect of child neglect: Personal cleanliness. *Education and Treatment of Children, 6,* 153-164.

Rosenthal, J. A., Motz, J. K., Edmonson, D. A., & Groze, V. (1991). A descriptive study of abuse and neglect in out-of-home placement. *Child Abuse & Neglect, 15,* 249-260.

Rossman, B. B. R. (1994). Children in violent families: Current diagnostic and treatment considerations. *Family Violence and Sexual Assault Bulletin, 10*(3-4), 29-34.

Rossman, B. B. R., Bingham, R. D., Cimbora, D. M., Dickerson, L. K., Dexter, R. M., Balog, S. A., & Mallah, K. (1993, August). *Relationships of trauma severity to trauma symptoms for child witnesses.* Paper presented at the annual meeting of the American Psychological Association, Toronto.

Rouse, L. P. (1984). Models, self-esteem, and locus of control of factors contributing to spouse abuse. *Victimology: An International Journal, 9,* 130-141.

Rouse, L. P. (1991). College students and the legacy of spouse abuse. *New Directions for Student Services, 54*(Summer), 51-62.

Rouse, L. P., Breen, R., & Howell, M. (1988). Abuse in intimate relationships: A comparison of married and dating college students. *Journal of Interpersonal Violence, 3,* 414-429.

Rowe, B. R., & Lown, J. M. (1990). The economics of divorce and remarriage for rural Utah families. *Journal of Contemporary Law, 16,* 301-332.

Roy, M. (1982). *The abusive partner: An analysis of domestic battering.* New York: Van Nostrand.

Roy, M. (1988). *Children in the crossfire: Violence in the home—How does it affect our children?* Deerfield Beach, FL: Health Communications.

Rubin, A. (1991). The effectiveness of outreach counseling and support groups for battered women: A preliminary evaluation. *Research on Social Work Practice, 1,* 332-357.

Rumptz, M. H., Sullivan, C. M., Davidson, W. S., II, & Basta, J. (1991). An ecological approach to tracking battered women over time. *Violence and Victims, 3,* 237-244.

Rush, F. (1980). *The best kept secret: Sexual abuse of children.* Englewood Cliffs, NJ: Prentice Hall.

Russell, D. E. (1983a). The incidence and prevalence of intrafamilial and extrafamilial sexual abuse of female children. *Child Abuse & Neglect, 7,* 133-146.

Russell, D. E. (1983b). The prevalence and incidence of forcible rape and attempted rape of females. *Victimology: An International Journal, 7,* 81-93.

Russell, D. E. H. (1982). *Rape in marriage.* New York: Macmillan.

Russell, M. N., Lipov, E., Phillips, N., & White, B. (1989). Psychological profiles of violent and nonviolent maritally distressed couples. *Psychotherapy, 26,* 81-87.

Russo, N. F. (Ed.). (1985). *A women's mental health agenda.* Washington, DC: American Psychological Association.

Rust, J. O., & Troupe, P. A. (1991). Relationships of treatment of child sexual abuse with school achievement and self-concept. *Journal of Early Adolescence, 11,* 420-429.

Rutter, M. (1979). Protective factors in children's responses to stress and disadvantage. In M. W. Kent & J. E. Rolf (Eds.), *Primary prevention of psychopathology: Vol 3. Promoting social competence and coping in children* (pp. 49-74). Hanover, NH: University Press of New England.

Rutter, M., & Giller, H. (1983). *Juvenile delinquency: Trends and perspectives.* New York: McGraw-Hill.

Ryan, G., & Lane, S. (Eds.). (1991). Juvenile sexual offending. Lexington, MA: Lexington Books.

Rybarik, M. F., Dosch, M. F., Gilmore, G. D., & Krajewski, S. S. (1995). Violence in relationships: A seventh grade inventory of knowledge and attitudes. *Journal of Family Violence, 10,* 223-251.

Salend, E., Kane, R. A., Satz, M., & Pynoos, J. (1984). Elder abuse reporting: Limitations of statutes. *Gerontologist, 24,* 61-69.

Salholz, E., Uehling, M. D., & Raine, G. (1986, April). The book on men's studies—Rambo goes to college. *Newsweek, 112*(18), 79.

Salter, A. C. (1988). *Treating child sex offenders and victims: A practical guide.* Newbury Park, CA; Sage.

Saltzman, L. E., Mercy, J. A., Rosenberg, M. L., Elsea, W. R., Napper, G., Sikes, R. K., & Waxweiler, R. J. (1990). Magnitude and patterns of family and intimate assault in Atlanta, Georgia, 1984. *Violence and Victims, 5,* 3-17.

Salzinger, S., Feldman, R. S., Hammer, M., & Rosario, M. (1993). The effects of physical abuse on children's relationships. *Child Development, 64,* 169-187.

Salzinger, S., Kaplan, S., Pelcovitz, D., Samit, C., & Krieger, R. (1984). Parent and teacher assessment of children's behavior in child maltreating families. *Journal of the American Academy of Child Psychiatry, 23,* 459-464.

Santello, M. D., & Leitenberg, H. (1993). Sexual aggression by an acquaintance: Methods of coping and later psychological adjustment. *Violence and Victims, 8,* 91-104.

Sapiente, A. A. (1988). Locus of control and causal attributions of maritally violent men. *Dissertation Abstracts International, 50,* 758B. (UMI No. 8822697)

Sarber, R. E., Halasz, M. M., Messmer, M. C., Bickett, A. D., & Lutzker, J. R. (1983). Teaching menu planning and grocery shopping to a mentally retarded mother. *Mental Retardation, 21,* 101-106.

Sariola, H., & Uutela, A. (1994). The prevalence and context of child sexual abuse in Finland. *Child Abuse & Neglect, 18,* 827-835.

Sato, R. A., & Heiby, E. M. (1992). Correlates of depressive symptoms among battered women. *Journal of Family Violence, 7,* 229-245.

Saunders, D. G. (1988). Wife abuse, husband abuse, or mutual combat? A feminist perspective on the empirical findings. In K. Yllö & M. Bograd (Eds.), *Feminist perspectives on wife abuse* (pp. 99-113). Newbury Park, CA: Sage.

Saunders, D. G. (1989a). Cognitive and behavioral interventions with men who batter: Applications and outcome. In P. L. Caesar & L. K. Hamberger (Eds.), *Treating men who batter: Theory, practice and programs* (pp. 77-100). New York: Springer.

Saunders, D. G. (1989b, November). *Who hits first and who hurts most? Evidence for the greater victimization of women in intimate relationships.* Paper presented at the annual meeting of the American Society of Criminology, Reno, NV.

Saunders, D. G. (1992). A typology of men who batter: Three types derived from cluster analysis. *American Journal of Orthopsychiatry, 62,* 264-275.

Saunders, D. G. (1994). Posttraumatic stress symptom profiles of battered women: A comparison of survivors in two settings. *Violence and Victims, 9,* 31-44.

Saunders, D. G. (1995). The tendency to arrest victims of domestic violence: A preliminary analysis of office characteristics. *Journal of Interpersonal Violence, 10,* 147-158.

Saunders, D. G., & Size, P. B. (1986). Attitudes about woman abuse among police officers, victims, and victim advocates. *Journal of Interpersonal Violence, 1,* 25-42.

Saywitz, K. J., Goodman, G. S., Nicholas, E., & Moan, S. F. (1991). Children's memories of a physical examination involving genital touch: Implications for reports of child sexual abuse. *Journal of Consulting and Clinical Psychology, 59,* 682-691.

Saywitz, K. J., & Nathanson, R. (1993). Children's testimony and their perceptions of stress in and out of the courtroom. *Child Abuse & Neglect, 17,* 613-622.

Saywitz, K., & Snyder, L. (1993). Improving children's testimony with preparation. In G. S. Goodman & B. L. Bottoms (Eds.), *Child victims, child witnesses: Understanding and improving testimony* (pp. 117-146). New York: Guilford.

Scavo, R. R. (1989, February). Female adolescent sex offenders: A neglected treatment group. *Social Casework: The Journal of Contemporary Social Work,* pp. 114-117.

Schechter, S. (1982). *Women and male violence: The visions and struggles of the battered women's movement.* Boston: South End.

Schechter, S. (1988). Building bridges between activists, professionals, and researchers. In K. Yllö & M. Bograd (Eds.), *Feminist perspectives on wife abuse* (pp. 299-312). Newbury Park, CA: Sage.

Scher, M. (1980). Men and intimacy. *Counseling and Values, 25,* 62-68.

Schetky, D. H., & Green, A. H. (1988). *Child sexual abuse: A handbook for health care and legal professionals.* New York: Brunner/Mazel.

Schmitt, B. D. (1987). The child with nonaccidental trauma. In R. Helfer & R. Kempe (Eds.), *The battered child* (4th ed., pp. 178-196). Chicago: University of Chicago Press.

Schneider, E. M. (1986). Describing and changing: Women's self-defense work and the problem of expert testimony on battering. *Women's Rights Law Reporter, 9*(3-4), 195-222.

Schreier, H. A., & Libow, J. A. (1993). Munchausen syndrome by proxy: Diagnosis and prevalence. *American Journal of Orthopsychiatry, 63*(2), 318-321.

Schuerger, J. M., & Reigle, N. (1988). Personality and biographic data that characterize men who abuse their wives. *Journal of Clinical Psychology, 44,* 75-81.

Schuller, R. A., & Vidmar, N. (1992). Battered woman syndrome evidence in the courtroom: A review of the literature. *Law and Human Behavior, 16,* 273-291.

Schulman, M. A. (1979, July). *A survey of spousal abuse against women in Kentucky* (Study No. 792701, conducted for the Kentucky Commission on Women, sponsored by the U.S. Department of Justice, Law Enforcement Assistance Administration). Washington, DC: Government Printing Office.

Schwartz, I. M., AuClaire, P., & Harris, L. J. (1991). Family preservation services as an alternative to out-of-home placement of adolescents. In K. Wells & D. E. Biegel (Eds.), *Family preservation services: Research and evaluation* (pp. 33-46). Newbury Park, CA: Sage.

Schwartz, M. D., & DeKeseredy, W. S. (1993). The return of the "battered husband syndrome" through the typification of women as violent. *Crime, Law and Social Change, 20*, 249-265.

Schwendinger, H., & Schwendinger, J. (1981). *Rape and inequality.* Beverly Hills, CA: Sage.

Schwendinger, H., & Schwendinger, J. S. (1985). *Adolescent subcultures and delinquency: Research edition.* New York: Praeger.

Scutt, J. A. (1983). *Even in the best of homes: Violence in the family.* Melbourne: Penguin.

Seawell, A. A. F., IV. (1984). The caring relationship in violent marriages: A descriptive study of love and pair attraction. *Dissertation Abstracts International, 45*, 1063B. (UMI No. 8413722)

Sedlak, A. J. (1988a). Prevention of wife abuse. In V. B. Van Hasselt, R. L. Morrison, A. S. Bellack, & M. Hersen (Eds.), *Handbook of family violence* (pp. 319-358). New York: Plenum.

Sedlak, A. J. (1988b). The use and psychosocial impact of a battered women's shelter. In G. T. Hotaling, D. Finkelhor, J. T. Kirkpatrick, & M. A. Straus (Eds.), *Coping with family violence* (pp. 122-128). Newbury Park, CA: Sage.

Sedlak, A. J. (1990). *Technical amendment to the study findings—National incidence and prevalence of child abuse and neglect: 1988.* Rockville, MD: Westat.

Sedlak, A. J. (1991). *National incidence and prevalence of child abuse and neglect: 1988. Revised report.* Rockville, MD: Westat.

Segal, S. R., & Iris, M. A. (1989). Strategies for service provision: The use of legal interventions in a systems approach to casework. In R. Filinson & S. R. Ingman (Eds.), *Elder abuse: Practice and policy* (pp. 104-116). New York: Human Sciences Press.

Segal, Z. V., & Stermac, L. E. (1990). The role of cognition in sexual assault. In W. L. Marshall, D. R. Laws, & H. E. Barbaree (Eds.), *Handbook of sexual assault: Issues, theories, and treatment of the offender* (pp. 161-174). New York: Plenum.

Seidman, B. T., Marshall, W. L., Hudson, S. M., & Robertson, P. J. (1994). An examination of intimacy and loneliness in sex offenders. *Journal of Interpersonal Violence, 9*, 518-534.

Seidman, E. (1987). Toward a framework for primary prevention research. In J. Steinberg & M. Silverman (Eds.), *Preventing mental disorders: A research perspective* (Report No. ADM 87-1192, pp. 2-18). Rockville, MD: Department of Health and Human Services.

Seligman, M. E. P. (1975). *Helplessness: On depression, development and death.* San Francisco: Freeman.

Sellers, C. S., Folts, W. E., & Logan, K. M. (1992). Elder mistreatment: A multidimensional problem. *Journal of Elder Abuse & Neglect, 4*(4), 5-23.

Seltzer, J. A., & Kalmuss, D. S. (1988). Socialization and stress explanations for spouse abuse. *Social Forces, 67*, 473-491.

Sengstock, M. C., & Barrett, S. (1986). Elderly victims of family abuse, neglect, and maltreat-

ment: Can legal assistance help? *Journal of Gerontological Social Work, 9*, 43-60.

Sengstock, M. C., Hwalek, M., & Petrone, S. (1989). Services for aged abuse victims: Service types and related factors. *Journal of Elder Abuse & Neglect, 1*(4), 37-56.

Sengstock, M. C., & Liang, J. (1982). *Identifying and characterizing elder abuse.* Detroit, MI: Wayne State University, Institute of Gerontology. (ERIC Document Reproduction Service No. ED 217368)

Serra, P. (1993). Physical violence in the couple relationship: A contribution toward the analysis of context. *Family Process, 32*, 21-33.

Sexual predator law upheld. (1996, February 10). *Daily News*, p. 5.

Sgroi, S. M. (1982). Family treatment of child sexual abuse. *Journal of Social Work and Human Sexuality, 1*, 109-128.

Shah, G., Veedon, R., & Vasi, S. (1995). Elder abuse in India. In J. I. Kosberg & J. L. Garcia (Eds.), *Elder abuse: International and cross-cultural perspectives* (pp. 101-118). Binghamton, NY: Haworth.

Shainess, N. (1979). Vulnerability to violence: Masochism as process. *American Journal of Psychotherapy, 33*, 174-189.

Shepard, M. (1992). Predicting batterer recidivism five years after community intervention. *Journal of Family Violence, 7*, 167-178.

Shepard, M., & Pence, E. (1988). The effect of battering on the employment status of women. *Affilia, 3*(2), 55-61.

Shepard, M. F., & Campbell, J. A. (1992). The Abusive Behavior Inventory: A measure of psychological and physical abuse. *Journal of Interpersonal Violence, 7*, 291-305.

Shepherd, J. (1990). Victims of personal violence: The relevance of Symonds' model of psychological response and loss theory. *British Journal of Social Work, 20*, 309-332.

Sherman, L. W. (1992). *Policing domestic violence: Experiments and dilemmas.* New York: Free Press.

Sherman, L. W., & Berk, R. (1984). The specific deterrent effects of arrest for domestic assault. *American Sociological Review, 49*, 261-272.

Sherman, L. W., Smith, D. A., Schmidt, J. D., & Rogan, D. P. (1992). Crime, punishment, and stake in conformity: Legal and informal control of domestic violence. *American Sociological Review, 57*, 680-690.

Shields, N. M., McCall, G., & Hanneke, C. R. (1988). Patterns of family and nonfamily violence: Violent husbands and violent men. *Violence and Victims, 3*, 83-97.

Shotland, R. L. (1992). A theory of the causes of courtship rape: Part 2. *Journal of Social Issues, 48*, 127-143.

Shotland, R. L., & Straw, M. K. (1976). Bystander response to an assault: When a man attacks a woman. *Journal of Personality and Social Psychology, 34*, 990-999.

Showalter, S. M., & Bevill, K. L. (1996, April). *Factors associated with nonparticipation in a courtship violence study.* Paper presented at the annual meeting of the Western Psychological Association, San Jose, CA.

Siegel, J. M., Sorenson, S. B., Golding, J. M., Burnam, M. A., & Stein, J. A. (1987). The prevalence of childhood sexual assault: The Los Angeles Epidemiologic Catchment Area Project. *American Journal of Epidemiology, 126,* 1141-1153.

Siegel, L. J. (1995). *Criminology.* St. Paul, MN: West.

Sigelman, C. K., Berry, C. J., & Wiles, K. A. (1984). Violence in college students' dating relationships. *Journal of Applied Social Psychology, 5,* 530-548.

Sigler, R. T. (1989). *Domestic violence in context: An assessment of community attitudes.* Lexington, MA: Lexington Books.

Silvern, L., & Kaersvang, L. (1989). The traumatized children of violent marriages. *Child Welfare, 68,* 421-436.

Silvern, L., Karyl, J., & Landis, T. Y. (1995). Individual psychotherapy for the traumatized children of abused women. In E. Peled, P. G. Jaffe, & J. L. Edelson (Eds.), *Ending the cycle of violence: Community responses to children of battered women* (pp. 43-76). Thousand Oaks, CA: Sage.

Silvern, L., Karyl, J., Waelde, L., Hodges, W. F., Starek, J., Heidt, E., & Min, K. (1995). Retrospective reports of parental partner abuse: Relationships to depression, trauma symptoms and self-esteem among college students. *Journal of Family Violence, 10,* 177-202.

Simons, R. L., Wu, C. I., & Conger, R. D. (1995). A test of various perspectives on the intergenerational transmission of domestic violence. *Criminology, 33,* 141-170.

Sirles, E. A., & Franke, P. J. (1989). Factors influencing mothers' reactions to intrafamily sexual abuse. *Child Abuse & Neglect, 13,* 131-139.

Skinner, B. F. (1938). *The behavior of organisms.* New York: Appleton-Century-Crofts.

Small, M. A., & Tetreault, P. A. (1990). Social psychology, "marital rape exemptions," and privacy. *Behavioral Sciences and the Law, 8,* 141-149.

Smith, B., Hillenbrand, S., & Govestsky, S. (1990). *The problem response to child sexual abuse offender: How is it working?* Chicago: American Bar Association.

Smith, B. E. (1995, June). *Prosecuting child physical abuse cases: A case study in San Diego.* Washington, DC: U.S. Department of Justice, Office of Juvenile Justice and Delinquency Prevention. (NCJ No. 152978)

Smith, D. A., & O'Leary, K. D. (1987, July). *Affective components of problem-solving communication and their relationships with interspousal aggression.* Paper presented at the Third National Family Violence Research Conference, Durham, NH.

Smith, E. O., & Byrd, L. (1987). External and internal influences on aggression in captive group-living monkeys. In R. J. Gelles & J. Lancaster (Eds.), *Child abuse and neglect: Biosocial dimensions* (pp. 175-199). Hawthorne, NY: Aldine de Gruyter.

Smith, J. P., & Williams, J. G. (1992). From abusive household to dating violence. *Journal of Family Violence, 7,* 153-165.

Smith, M., & Pazder, L. (1980). *Michelle remembers.* New York: Crongdon & Lattes.

Smith, M. D. (1987). The incidence and prevalence of woman abuse in Toronto. *Violence and Victims, 2,* 33-47.

Smith, M. D. (1990). Patriarchal ideology and wife beating: A test of a feminist hypothesis. *Violence and Victims, 5,* 257-273.

Smith, S. (1975). *The battered child syndrome.* London: Butterworths.

Smith, S. M., Hanson, R., & Noble, S. (1974). Social aspects of the battered baby syndrome. *British Journal of Psychiatry, 125,* 568-582.

Smith, W. L. (1994). Abusive head injury. *The APSAC Advisor, 7*(4), 16-19.

Smolowe, J. (1994, July 4). Family violence hits home. *Time,* pp. 18-25.

Smolowe, J. (1995, December 11). Making the tough calls. *Time,* pp. 40-44.

Snell, J. E., Rosenwald, R. J., & Robey, A. (1964). The wifebeater's wife: A study of family interaction. *Archives of General Psychiatry, 11,* 107-113.

Snyder, D. K., & Scheer, N. S. (1981). Predicting disposition following brief residence at a shelter for battered women. *American Journal of Community Psychology, 9,* 559-566.

Sokol, R., & Clarren, S. K. (1989). Guidelines for use of terminology describing the impact of prenatal alcohol on the offspring. *Alcoholism: Clinical and Experimental Research, 13,* 597-598.

Solomon, Z., Mikulincer, M., & Flum, H. (1988). Negative life events, coping responses, and combat-related psychopathology: A prospective study. *Journal of Abnormal Psychology, 97,* 302-307.

Sommer, J. A. (1990). Men who batter: Attitudes toward women. *Dissertation Abstracts International, 51,* 5592B. (UMI No. 9107514)

Sonkin, D. J. (Ed.). (1989). *Domestic violence on trial: Psychological and legal dimensions of family violence.* New York: Springer.

Sonkin, D. J., Martin, D., & Walker, L. E. (1985). *The male batterer: A treatment approach.* New York: Springer.

Sorenson, S. B., Stein, J. A., Siegel, J. M., Golding, J. M., & Burnam, M. A. (1987). Prevalence of adult sexual assault: The Los Angeles Epidemiologic Catchment Area Study. *American Journal of Epidemiology, 126,* 1154-1164.

Sorenson, S. B., & Telles, C. A. (1991). Self-reports of spousal violence in a Mexican-American and non-Hispanic White population. *Violence and Victims, 6,* 3-15.

Sorenson, S. B., & White, J. C. (1992). Adult sexual assault: Overview of research. *Journal of Social Issues, 48,* 1-8.

Spaccarelli, S., Coatsworth, J. D., & Bowden, B. S. (1995). Exposure to serious family violence among incarcerated boys: Its association with violent offending and potential mediating variables. *Violence and Victims, 10,* 163-182.

Spaccarelli, S., Sandler, I. N., & Roosa, M. (1994). History of spouse violence against mother: Correlated risks and unique effects in child mental health. *Journal of Family Violence, 9,* 79-98.

Spanier, G. B. (1976). Measuring dyadic adjustment: New scales for assessing the quality of marriage and similar dyads. *Journal of Marriage and the Family, 38,* 15-28.

Spector, M., & Kitsuse, J. I. (1977). *Constructing social problems.* Menlo Park, CA: Benjamin Cummings.

Spence, J. T., Helmreich, R., & Stapp, J. (1973). A short version of the Attitudes Toward Women Scale (AWS). *Bulletin of the Psychonomic Society, 2,* 219-220.

Spencer, J. W., & Knudsen, D. D. (1992). Out-of-home maltreatment: An analysis of risk in various settings for children. *Children and Youth Services Review, 14,* 485-492.

Spitz, R. A. (1945). Hospitalism. *Psychoanalytic Study of the Child, 1,* 53-74.

Spohn, C., & Horney, J. (1991). "The laws's the law, but fair is fair." Rape shield laws and officials' assessment of sexual history evidence. *Criminology, 29,* 137-161.

Springs, F. E., & Friedrich, W. N. (1992). Health risk behaviors and medical sequelae of childhood sexual abuse. *Mayo Clinic Proceedings, 67,* 527-532.

Stafne, G. (1989). *The Wisconsin mandatory arrest monitoring project: Final report.* Madison: Wisconsin Coalition Against Domestic Violence.

Stagg, V., Wills, G. D., & Howell, M. (1989). Psychopathology in early childhood witness of family violence. *Topics in Early Childhood Special Education, 9,* 73-87.

Stanton, E. C., Anthony, S. B., & Gage, M. J. (Eds.). (1889). *History of women suffrage: Vol. 1. 1848-1861.* New York: Fowler & Wells. (Reprint of 1881 edition)

Star, B. C., Clark, C. G., Goetz, K. M., & O'Malia, L. (1979). Psychosocial aspects of wife beating. *Journal of Contemporary Social Casework, 60,* 479-487.

Stark, E., & Flitcraft, A. H. (1985). Spouse abuse. In *Surgeon General's Workshop on Violence and Public Health source book.* Atlanta, GA: U.S. Public Health Service.

Stark, E., & Flitcraft, A. H. (1988). Women and children at risk: A feminist perspective on child abuse. *International Journal of Health Services, 18,* 97-118.

Stark, E., Flitcraft, A., Zuckerman, D., Gray, A., Robinson, J., & Frazier, W. (1981). *Wife assault in the medical setting: An introduction for health personnel* (Monograph Series No. 7). Washington, DC: Department of Health and Human Services, National Clearinghouse on Domestic Violence.

State of Oregon Children's Services Division. (1991). *Mental injury: The hidden hurt* [Brochure]. Salem: Author.

Stearns, P. J. (1986). Old age family conflict: The perspective of the past. In K. A. Pillemer & R. S. Wolf (Eds.), *Elder abuse: Conflict in the family* (pp. 3-24). Dover, MA: Auburn House.

Steele, B. J., & Pollock, C. (1968). A psychiatric study of parents who abuse infants and small children. In R. Helfer & C. H. Kempe (Eds.), *The battered child* (pp. 89-133). Chicago: University of Chicago Press.

Steiger, H., & Zanko, M. (1990). Sexual traumata among eating disordered, psychiatric, and normal female groups: Comparison of prevalence and defense styles. *Journal of Interpersonal Violence, 5,* 74-86.

Stein, K. (1991). A national agenda for elder abuse and neglect research: Issues and recommendations. *Journal of Elder Abuse & Neglect, 3*(3), 91-108.

Stein, T. J. (1993). Legal perspectives on family violence against children. In R. L. Hampton, T. P. Gullotta, G. R. Adams, E. H. Potter, III, & R. P. Weissberg (Eds.), *Family violence: Prevention and treatment* (pp. 179-197). Newbury Park, CA: Sage.

Steinman, M. (1991). The public policy process and woman battering: Problems and potentials. In M. Steinman (Ed.), *Woman battering: Policy responses* (pp. 1-18). Cincinnati, OH: Anderson.

Steinmetz, S. K. (1977). The battered husband syndrome. *Victimology: An International Journal, 2,* 499-509.

Steinmetz, S. K. (1982). A cross-cultural comparison of sibling violence. *International Journal of Family Psychiatry, 2,* 337-351.

Steinmetz, S. K. (1987). Family violence: Past, present, and future. In M. B. Sussman & S. K. Steinmetz (Eds.), *Handbook of marriage and the family* (pp. 725-765). New York: Plenum.

Steinmetz, S. K. (1988). Elder abuse by family caregivers: Processes and intervention strategies [Special issue: Coping with victimization]. *Contemporary Family Therapy: An International Journal, 10,* 256-271.

Steinmetz, S. K. (1993). The abused elderly are dependent: Abuse is caused by the perception of stress associated with providing care. In R. J. Gelles & D. R. Loseke (Eds.), *Current controversies on family violence* (pp. 222-236). Newbury Park, CA: Sage.

Stermac, L., Hall, K., & Henskens, M. (1989). Violence among child molesters. *Journal of Sex Research, 26,* 450-459.

Sternberg, K. J., Lamb, M. E., Greenbaum, C., Cicchetti, D., Dawud, S., Cortes, R. M., Krispin, O., & Lorey, F. (1993). Effects of domestic violence on children's behavior problems and depression. *Developmental Psychology, 29,* 44-52.

Stets, J. E. (1990). Verbal and physical aggression in marriage. *Journal of Marriage and the Family, 52,* 501-514.

Stets, J. E. (1991). Psychological aggression in dating relationships: The role of interpersonal control. *Journal of Family Violence, 6,* 97-114.

Stets, J. E., & Henderson, D. (1991). Contextual factors surrounding conflict resolution while dating: Results from a national study. *Family Relations, 40,* 29-36.

Stets, J. E., & Pirog-Good, M. A. (1987). Violence in dating relationship. *Social Psychology Quarterly, 50,* 237-246.

Stets, J. E., & Pirog-Good, M. A. (1989). Patterns of physical and sexual abuse for men and women in dating relationships: A descriptive analysis. *Journal of Family Violence, 4,* 63-76.

Stets, J. E., & Pirog-Good, M. A. (1990). Interpersonal control and courtship aggression. *Journal of Social and Personal Relationships, 7,* 371-394.

Stets, J. E., & Straus, M. A. (1989). The marriage license as a hitting license: A comparison of assaults in dating, cohabiting, and married couples. In M. A. Pirog-Good & J. E. Stets (Eds.), *Violence in dating relationship: Emerging social issues* (pp. 33-52). New York: Praeger.

Stets, J. E., & Straus, M. A. (1990). Gender differences in reporting marital violence and its medical and psychological consequences. In M. A. Straus & R. J. Gelles (Eds.), *Physical violence in American families: Risk factors and adaptations to violence in 8,145 families* (pp. 151-166). New Brunswick, NJ: Transaction Books.

Stevens, M., & Gebhart, R. (1985). *Rape education for men: Curriculum guide.* Columbus: Ohio State University Rape Education Prevention Project.

Stone, R. G., Cafferata, G. L., & Sangl, J. (1987). Caregivers of the frail elderly: A national profile. *Gerontologist, 27,* 616-616.

Stordeur, R. A., & Stille, R. (1989). *Ending men's violence against their partners: One road to peace.* Newbury Park, CA: Sage.

Stouthamer-Loeber, M., van Kammen, W., & Loeber, R. (1992). Researchers' forum: The nuts and bolts of implementing large-scale longitudinal studies. *Violence and Victims, 7,* 63-78.

Stratford, L. (1988). *Satan's underground.* Eugene, OR: Harvest House.

Straus, M. (1980). A sociological perspective on the causes of family violence. In M. R. Green (Ed.), *Violence and the family* (pp. 7-31). Boulder, CO: Westview.

Straus, M. A. (1974). Foreword. In R. J. Gelles (Ed.), *The violent home: Study of physical aggression between husbands and wives* (pp. 13-17). Beverly Hills, CA: Sage.

Straus, M. A. (1976). Sexual inequality, cultural norms, and wife beating. *Victimology: An International Journal, 1,* 54-76.

Straus, M. A. (1977a). Societal morphogenesis and intrafamily violence in cross-cultural perspective. *Annals of the New York Academy of Sciences, 285,* 717-730.

Straus, M. A. (1977b). Wife beating: How common and why? *Victimology: An International Journal, 1,* 54-76.

Straus, M. A. (1979). Measuring intrafamily conflict and aggression: The Conflict Tactics Scale (CT). *Journal of Marriage and the Family, 41,* 75-88.

Straus, M. A. (1980a). Societal stress and marital violence in a national sample of American families. In F. Wright, C. Bahn, & R. W. Rieber (Eds.), *Annals of the New York Academy of Sciences: Vol. 347. Forensic psychology and psychiatry* (pp. 229-250). New York: New York Academy of Sciences.

Straus, M. A. (1980b). Victims and aggressors in marital violence. *American Behavioral Scientist, 23,* 681-704.

Straus, M. A. (1983). Ordinary violence, child abuse, and wife beating: What do they have in common? In D. Finkelhor, R. J. Gelles, G. T. Hotaling, & M. A. Straus (Eds.), *The dark side of families* (pp. 213-234). Beverly Hills, CA: Sage.

Straus, M. A. (1986). Medical care costs of intrafamily assault and homicide. *Bulletin of the New York Academy of Medicine, 62,* 556-561.

Straus, M. A. (1990a). The Conflict Tactics Scale and its critics: An evaluation and new data on the validity and reliability. In M. A. Straus & R. J. Gelles (Eds.), *Physical violence in American families: Risk factors and adaptations to violence in 8,145 families* (pp. 49-73). New Brunswick, NJ: Transaction Books.

Straus, M. A. (1990b). The National Family Violence Surveys. In M. A. Straus & R. J. Gelles (Eds.), *Physical violence in American families: Risk factors and adaptations to violence in 8,145 families* (pp. 3-16). Brunswick, NJ: Transaction Books.

Straus, M. A. (1991a, September). *Children as witness to marital violence: A risk factor for life-long problems among a nationally representative sample of American men and women.* Paper presented at the Ross Roundtable titled "Children and Violence," Washington, DC.

Straus, M. A. (1991b). Conceptualization and measurement of battering: Implications for public policy. In M. Steinman (Ed.), *Woman battering: Policy responses* (pp. 19-47). Cincinnati, OH: Anderson.

Straus, M. A. (1991c). Discipline and deviance: Physical punishment of children and violence and other crime in adulthood. *Social Problems, 38,* 133-154.

Straus, M. A. (1991d). New theory and old canards about family violence research. *Social Problems, 38,* 180-197.

Straus, M. A. (1993). Physical assaults by wives—A major social problem. In R. J. Gelles & D. J.

Loseke (Eds.), *Current controversies on family violence* (pp. 67-87). Newbury Park, CA: Sage.

Straus, M. A. (1994). *Beating the devil out of them: Corporal punishment in American families.* New York: Lexington Books.

Straus, M. A., & Gelles, R. J. (1986). Societal change and change in family violence from 1975 to 1985 as revealed by two national surveys. *Journal of Marriage and the Family, 48,* 465-479.

Straus, M. A., & Gelles, R. J. (1990). *Physical violence in American families.* New Brunswick, NJ: Transaction Books.

Straus, M. A., Gelles, R. J., & Steinmetz, S. K. (1980). *Behind closed doors: Violence in the American Family.* Garden City, NY: Doubleday.

Straus, M. A., Hamby, S. L., Boney-McCoy, S., & Sugarman, D. B. (1995). *The revised Conflict Tactics Scales (CTS2): Development and preliminary psychometric data.* Durham, NH: Family Violence Research Laboratory.

Straus, M. A., & Smith, C. (1990). Family patterns of primary prevention of family violence. In M. A. Straus & R. J. Gelles (Eds.), *Physical violence in American families: Risk factors and adaptations to violence in 8,145 families* (pp. 507-526). New Brunswick, NJ: Transaction Books.

Straus, M. B. (1988). Abused adolescents. In M. B. Straus (Ed.), *Abuse and victimization across the lifespan* (pp. 107-123). Baltimore, MD: Johns Hopkins University Press.

Straus, R. B. (1995). Supervised visitation and family violence [Special issue]. *Family Law Quarterly, 29,* 229-252.

Stress undercuts flu shots. (1996, April). *Science News, 149*(15), 231.

Strube, M. J., & Barbour, L. S. (1983). The decision to leave an abusive relationship: Economic dependence and psychological commitment. *Journal of Marriage and the Family, 45,* 785-793.

Strube, M. J., & Barbour, L. S. (1984). Factors related to the decision to leave an abusive relationship. *Journal of Marriage and the Family, 46,* 837-844.

Stubbing, E. (1990). Police who think family homicide is preventable are pointing the way. *Response, 13*(1), 8.

Studer, M. (1984). Wife-beating as a social problem: The process of definition. *International Journal of Women's Studies, 7,* 412-422.

Sturgeon, V. H., & Taylor, J. (1980). Report of a five year follow-up study of mentally disordered sex offenders released from Atascadero State Hospital in 1973. *Criminal Justice Journal, 4,* 41-63.

Sudermann, M., & Jaffe, P. (1993, August). *Violence in teen dating relationships: Evaluation of a large scale primary prevention program.* Paper presented at the annual meeting of the American Psychological Association, Toronto.

Sudia, C. (1986). Preventing out-of-home placement of children: The first steps to permanency planning. *Children Today, 15*(6), 4-5.

Sugarman, D. B., & Frankel, S. L. (1993, August). *A meta-analytic study of wife assault and patriarchal beliefs.* Paper presented at the annual meeting of the American Psychological Association, Toronto.

Sugarman, D. B., & Hotaling, G. T. (1989). Dating violence: Prevalence, context, and risk markers. In M. A. Pirog-Good & J. E. Stets (Eds.), *Violence in dating relationship: Emerging social issues* (pp. 3-32). New York: Praeger.

Sugg, N. K., & Inui, T. (1992). Primary care physician's response to domestic violence. *Journal of the American Medical Association, 23,* 3157-3160.

Suh, E. K., & Abel, E. M. (1990). The impact of spousal violence on the children of the abuse. *Journal of Individual Social Work, 4,* 27-34.

Sukosky, D. G. (1992). Elder abuse: A preliminary profile of abusers and the abused. *Family Violence and Sexual Assault Bulletin, 8*(4), 23-26.

Sullivan, C. M. (1991, August). Battered women as active helpseekers. *Violence Update, 1*(12), 1, 8, 10-11.

Sullivan, P. M., Brookhouser, P., Scanlan, J. M., Knutson, J. F., & Schulte, L. E. (1992). Demographic and behavioral characteristics of abused handicapped children. In F. L. Parker, R. Robinson, S. Sambrano, & C. Piotrkowski (Eds.), *New directions in child and family research: Shaping Head Start in the 90's* (pp. 238-240). Washington, DC: Department of Health and Human Services.

Swett, C., Surrey, J., & Cohen, C. (1990). Sexual and physical abuse histories and psychiatric symptoms among male psychiatric outpatients. *American Journal of Psychiatry, 147,* 632-636.

Syers, M., & Edleson, J. L. (1992). The combined effects of coordinated criminal justice intervention in woman abuse. *Journal of Interpersonal Violence, 7,* 490-502.

Szinovacz, M. E. (1983). Using couple data as a methodological tool: The case of marital violence. *Journal of Marriage and the Family, 45,* 633-644.

Taler, G., & Ansello, E. F. (1985). Elder abuse. *Association of Family Physicians, 32,* 107-114.

Tan, C., Basta, J., Sullivan, C. M., & Davidson, W. S. (1995). The role of social support in the lives of women exiting domestic violence shelters. *Journal of Interpersonal Violence, 10,* 437-451.

Tang, C. S. K., Critelli, J. W., & Porter, J. F. (1993). Motives in sexual aggression: The Chinese context. *Journal of Interpersonal Violence, 8,* 435-445.

Tarasoff v. the Regents of the University of California, 529 P.2d 553 (Cal. 1974), *vac.,* reheard in bank and *aff'd,* 131 Cal Rptr. 14, 551 P.2d 334 (1976).

Tatara, T. (1993). Understanding the nature and scope of domestic elder abuse with the use of state aggregate data: Summaries of the key findings of a national survey of state APS and aging services. *Journal of Elder Abuse & Neglect, 5*(4), 35-57.

Telch, C. F., & Lindquist, C. U. (1984). Violent versus non-violent couples: A comparison of patterns. *Psychotherapy, 2,* 242-248.

Terr, L. (1991). Child traumas: An outline and overview. American *Journal of Psychiatry, 50,* 15-19.

Teske, R. H. C., Jr., & Parker, M. L. (1983). *Spouse abuse in Texas: A study of women's attitudes and experiences.* Huntsville, TX: Sam Houston State University, Criminal Justice Center, Survey Research Program.

Thigpen, S. M., & Bonner, B. L. (1994). Child death review teams in action. *The APSAC Advisor, 7*(4), 5-8.

Thoennes, N., Salem, P., & Pearson, J. (1995). Mediation and domestic violence: Current policies and practices [Special issue]. *Family and Conciliation Courts Review, 33,* 6-29.

Thompson, C. (1989). Breaking through walls of isolation: A model for churches in helping victims of violence. *Pastoral Psychology, 38,* 35-38.

Thurman v. City of Torrington, 595 F. Supp. 1521 (D. Conn. 1984).

Tiff, L. L. (1993). *Battering of women: The failure of intervention and the case for prevention.* Boulder, CO: Westview.

Tilden, V. P. (1989). Response of the health care delivery system to battered women. *Issues in Mental Health Nursing, 10,* 309-320.

Tilden, V. P., & Shepherd, P. (1987). Battered women: The shadow side of families. *Holistic Nursing Practice, 1,* 25-32.

Timnick, L. (1985, August). 22% in survey were child abuse victims. *Los Angeles Times,* p. 1.

Tinsley, C. A., Critelli, J. W., & Ee, J. S. (1992, August). *The perception of sexual aggression: One act, two realities.* Paper presented at the annual meeting of the American Psychological Association, Washington, DC.

Tjaden, P., & Thoennes, N. (1992). Predictors of legal intervention in child maltreatment cases. *Child Abuse & Neglect, 16,* 807-821.

Toch, H. (1995). Foreword. In K. M. Heide (Ed.), *Why kids kill parents* (pp. ix-xii). Thousand Oaks, CA: Sage.

Tolman, R. M. (1989). The development of a measure of psychological maltreatment of women by their male partners. *Violence and Victims, 4,* 159-178.

Tomita, S. K. (1990). The denial of elder mistreatment by victims and abusers: The application of neutralization theory. *Violence and Victims, 5,* 171-184.

Tomkins, A. J., Mohamed, S., Steinman, M., Macolini, R. M., Kenning, M. K., & Afrank, J. (1994). The plight of children who witness woman battering: Psychological knowledge and policy implications. *Law and Psychology Review, 18,* 137-187.

Tontodonato, P., & Crew, B. K. (1992). Dating violence, social learning theory, and gender: A multivariate analysis. *Violence and Victims, 7,* 3-14.

Trainor, C. (1984). *A description of officially reported adolescent maltreatment and its implications for policy and practice.* Denver, CO: American Humane Association.

Travis, C. (1993, January). Beware the incest-survivor machine. *New York Times,* p. 1.

Trickett, P. K., & Kuczynski, L. (1986). Children's misbehaviors and parental discipline strategies in abusive and nonabusive families. *Developmental Psychology, 22,* 115-123.

Trimpey, M. L. (1989). Self-esteem and anxiety: Key issues in an abused women's support group. *Issues in Mental Health Nursing, 10,* 297-308.

Truesdell, D. L., McNeil, J. S., & Deschner, J. (1986, March-April). The incidence of wife abuse in incestuous families. *Social Work,* pp. 138-140.

Truscott, D. (1992). Intergenerational transmission of violent behavior in adolescent males. *Aggressive Behavior, 18,* 327-335.

Tsai, M., & Wagner, N. (1978). Therapy groups for women sexually abused as children. *Archives of Sexual Behaviour, 7,* 417-427.

Turner, S. F., & Shapiro, C. H. (1986). Battered women: Mourning the death of a relationship. *Social Work, 31,* 372-376.

Tuteur, J. M., Ewigman, B. E., Peterson, L., & Hosokawa, M. C. (1995). The maternal observation matrix and Mother-Child Interaction Scale: Brief observational screening instruments for physically abusive mothers. *Journal of Clinical Child Psychology, 24*(1), 55-62.

Twentyman, C. T., & Plotkin, R. C. (1982). Unrealistic expectations of parents who maltreat their children: An educational deficit that pertains to child development. *Journal of Clinical Psychology, 38,* 497-503.

$26 million in grants announced for the Violence Against Women Act. (1995, March). *Criminal Justice Newsletter, 26*(6), 6-7.

Ulbrich, P., & Huber, J. (1981). Observing parental violence: Distribution and effects. *Journal of Marriage and the Family, 38,* 623-631.

Urquiza, A. J., & Goodlin-Jones, B. L. (1994). Child sexual abuse and adult revictimization with women of color. *Violence and Victims, 9,* 223-232.

U.S. Advisory Board on Child Abuse and Neglect. (1990). *First report of the U.S. Advisory Board on Child Abuse and Neglect.* Washington, DC: Department of Health and Human Services and National Council on Child Abuse and Neglect.

U.S. Advisory Board on Child Abuse and Neglect. (1993). *Neighbors helping neighbors: A new national strategy for the protection of children.* Washington, DC: Government Printing Office.

U.S. Advisory Board on Child Abuse and Neglect. (1995). *A nation's shame: Fatal child abuse and neglect in the United States.* Washington, DC: Department of Health and Human Services and National Council on Child Abuse and Neglect.

U.S. Bureau of the Census. (1991). *Statistical abstract of the United States 1991* (111th ed.). Washington, DC: U.S. Department of Commerce.

U.S. Bureau of the Census. (1994). *Statistical abstract of the United States 1994* (114th ed.). Washington, DC: Author.

U.S. Department of Justice. (1984). *Attorney General's Task Force on Family Violence* (Final report). Washington, DC: Author.

U.S. Department of Justice [FBI]. (1992). *Crime in the United States, 1991.* Washington, DC: Government Printing Office.

U.S. House of Representatives, Select Committee on Aging. (1990, May 1). *Elder abuse: A decade of shame and inaction* (Hearings). Washington, DC: Government Printing Office.

Vaillant, G. E., & Milofsky, E. S. (1982). The etiology of alcoholism: A prospective viewpoint. *American Psychologist, 37,* 494-503.

Valentin, D., & Cash, T. (1986). A definitional discussion of elder mistreatment. *Journal of Gerontological Social Work, 9*(3), 17-28.

Van Biema, D. (1995, December 11). Abandoned to her fate. *Time, 146*(24), 32-36.

van der Kolk, B. A. (1987). The psychological consequences of overwhelming life experiences. In B. A. van der Kolk (Ed.), *Psychological trauma* (pp. 1-30). Washington, DC: American Psychiatric Association.

van der Kolk, B. A. (1988). Trauma in men: Effects on family life. In M. B. Straus (Ed.), *Abuse and victimization across the lifespan* (pp. 170-185). Baltimore, MD: Johns Hopkins University Press.

VanderMeer, J. L. (1992). Elder abuse and the community health nurse. *Journal of Elder Abuse & Neglect, 4*(4), 37-45.

Van Hasselt, V. B., Morrison, R. L., & Bellack, A. S. (1985). Alcohol use in wife abusers and their spouses. *Addictive Behavior, 10,* 127-135.

Varvaro, F. F. (1991). Using a grief response assessment questionnaire in a support group to assist battered women in their recovery. *Response, 13*(4), 17-20.

Vaselle-Augenstein, R., & Ehrlich, A. (1992). Male batterers: Evidence for psychopathology. In E. C. Viano (Ed.), *Intimate violence: Interdisciplinary perspectives* (pp. 139-154). Bristol, PA: Taylor & Francis.

Vass, J. S., & Gold, S. R. (1995). Effects of feedback on emotion in hypermasculine males. *Violence and Victims, 10,* 217-226.

Vaughn, D. (1987, July). The long goodbye. *Psychology Today,* pp. 37-38, 42.

Victor, J. S. (1993). *Satanic panic.* Chicago: Open Court.

Vinton, L. (1991). Factors associated with refusing services among maltreated elderly. *Journal of Elder Abuse & Neglect, 3*(2), 89-103.

Vinton, L. (1992). Battered women's shelters and older women: The Florida experience. *Journal of Family Violence, 7,* 63-72.

Violence in families leads to delinquency, OJJDP study finds. (1995, February). *Criminal Justice Newsletter, 26*(3), 6-7.

Vissing, Y. M., Straus, M. A., Gelles, R. J., & Harrop, J. W. (1991). Verbal aggression by parents and psychosocial problems of children. *Child Abuse & Neglect, 15,* 223-238.

Vivian, D., & O'Leary, K. D. (1987, July). *Communication patterns in physically aggressive engaged couples.* Paper presented at the Third National Family Violence Research Conference, Durham, NH.

Vogt, W. P. (1993). *Dictionary of statistics and methodology: A nontechnical guide for the social sciences.* Newbury Park, CA: Sage.

Vondra, J., Barnett, D., & Cicchetti, D. (1990). Self-concept, motivation, and competence among preschoolers from maltreating and comparison families. *Child Abuse & Neglect, 14,* 525-540.

Waaland, P., & Keeley, S. (1985). Police decision making in wife abuse: The impact of legal and extralegal factors. *Law and Human Behavior, 9,* 355-366.

Wadlington, W., Whitebread, C. H., & Davis, S. M. (1983). *Children in the legal system.* New York: Foundation.

Wagar, J. M., & Rodway, M. R. (1995). An evaluation of a group treatment approach for children who have witnessed wife abuse. *Journal of Family Violence, 10,* 295-306.

Waldner-Haugrud, L. K., & Magruder, B. (1995). Male and female sexual victimization in dating relationships: Gender differences in coercion techniques and outcomes. *Violence and Victims, 10,* 203-215.

Walker, A. G. (1993). Questioning young children in court. *Law and Human Behavior, 17,* 59-81.

Walker, C. E., Bonner, B. L., & Kaufman, K. L. (1988). *The physically and sexually abused child.* New York: Pergamon.

Walker, E., Downey, G., & Bergman, A. (1989). The effects of parental psychopathology and maltreatment on child behavior: A test of the diathesis-stress model. *Child Development, 60,* 15-24.

Walker, L. E. (1977). Battered women and learned helplessness. *Victimology: An International Journal, 2,* 525-534.

Walker, L. E. (1979). *The battered woman.* New York: Harper & Row.

Walker, L. E. (1983). The Battered Woman Syndrome Study. In D. Finkelhor, R. J. Gelles, G. T. Hotaling, & M. A. Straus (Eds.), *The dark side of families* (pp. 31-48). Beverly Hills, CA: Sage.

Walker, L. E. (1984). *The battered woman syndrome.* New York: Springer.

Walker, L. E. (1985, June 7). *Psychology of battered women.* Symposium conducted at the Laguna

Human Options Conference, Laguna Beach, CA.

Walker, L. E. (1993). The battered woman syndrome is a psychological consequence of abuse. In R. J. Gelles & D. R. Loseke (Eds.), *Current controversies on family violence* (pp. 133-153). Newbury Park, CA: Sage.

Walker, L. E., & Edwall, G. E. (1987). Domestic violence and determination of visitation and custody in divorce. In D. J. Sonkin (Ed.), *Domestic violence on trial: Psychological and legal dimensions of family violence* (pp. 127-152). New York: Springer.

Wallace, R., & Nosko, A. (1993). Working with shame in the group treatment of male batterers. *International Group Psychotherapy, 43,* 45-61.

Walsh, J. (1995, September 11). Born to be second class. *Time,* pp. 48-51.

Walters, G. D. (1992). A meta-analysis of the gene-crime relationship. *Criminology, 30,* 595-613.

Walton, E., Fraser, M. W., Lewis, R. E., & Pecora, P. (1993). In-home family-focused reunification: An experimental study. *Child Welfare, 72,* 473-487.

Ward, R. A. (1984). *The aging experience.* New York: Harper and Row.

Warnken, W. J., Rosenbaum, A., Fletcher, K. E., Hoge, S. K., & Adelman, S. A. (1994). Head-injured males: A population at risk for relationship aggression. *Violence and Victims, 9,* 153-166.

Warshaw, R. (1988). *I never called it rape.* New York: Simon & Schuster.

Wasileski, M., Callaghan-Chaffee, M. E., & Chaffee, R. B. (1982). Spousal violence in military homes: An initial survey. *Military Medicine, 147,* 761-765.

Watson, J. B., & Raynor, R. (1920). Conditioned emotional reactions. *Journal of Experimental Psychology, 3,* 1-14.

Watts, D. L., & Courtois, C. A. (1981). Trends in the treatment of men who commit violence against women. *Personnel and Guidance Journal, 60,* 245-249.

Wauchope, B. A., & Straus, M. A. (1990a). Age, gender, and class differences in physical punishment and physical abuse of American children. In M. A. Straus & R. J. Gelles (Eds.), *Physical violence in American families: Risk factors and adaptations to violence in 8,145 families* (pp. 133-148). New Brunswick, NJ: Transaction Books.

Wauchope, B. A., & Straus, M. A. (1990b). Physical punishment and physical abuse of American children: Incidence rates by age, gender, and occupational class. In M. A. Straus & R. J. Gelles (Eds.), *Physical violence in American families: Risk factors and adaptations to violence in 8,145 families* (pp. 133-148). New Brunswick, NJ: Transaction Books.

Weber, T. (1991, April 13). Tearful jurors say they'll never forget horrifying testimony. *Orange County Register,* p. 26.

Webersinn, A. L., Hollinger, C. L., & DeLamatre, J. E. (1991). Breaking the cycle of violence: An examination of factors relevant to treatment follow-through. *Psychological Reports, 68,* 231-240.

Webster, R. L., Goldstein, J., & Alexander, S. (1985). A test of the explanatory value of alternative models of child abuse. *Journal of Comparative Family Studies, 16,* 295-317.

Weinberg, S. K. (1955). *Incest behavior.* New York: Citadel.

Weiner, A. (1991). A community-based education model for identification and prevention of elder abuse. *Journal of Gerontological Social Work, 16*(3-4), 107-119.

Weis, J. G. (1989). Family violence research methodology and design. In L. Ohlin & M. Tonry (Eds.), *Family violence* (pp. 117-162). Chicago: University of Chicago Press.

Weise, D., & Daro, D. (1995). *Current trends in child abuse reporting and fatalities: The results of the 1994 annual fifty state survey.* Chicago: National Committee to Prevent Child Abuse. (332 South Michigan Ave., Suite 1600, Chicago, IL 60604)

Wekerle, C., & Wolfe, D. A. (1993). Prevention of child abuse and neglect: Promising new directions. *Clinical Psychology Review, 13,* 501-540.

Wells, R. D., McCann, J., Adams, J., Voris, J., & Ensign, J. (1995). Emotional, behavioral, and physical symptoms reported by parents of sexually abused, nonabused, and allegedly abused prepubescent females. *Child Abuse & Neglect, 19,* 155-163.

Wells, S. J. (1994a). Child protective services: Research for the future. *Child Welfare League of America, 123,* 431-447.

Wells, S. J. (1994b). The role of child protective services in responding to and preventing child deaths. *The APSAC Advisor, 7*(4), 31-34.

Wesch, D., & Lutzker, J. R. (1991). A comprehensive 5-year evaluation of Project 12-Ways: An ecobehavioral program for treating and preventing child abuse and neglect. *Journal of Family Violence, 6,* 17-35.

Westra, B., & Martin, H. P. (1981). Children of battered women. *Maternal Child Nursing, 10,* 41-54.

Wetzel, L., & Ross, M. A. (1983). Psychological and social ramifications of battering: Observations leading to a counseling methodology for victims of domestic violence. *Personnel and Guidance Journal, 61,* 423-428.

Whatley, M. A., & Riggio, R. E. (1991, August). *Attributions of blame for female and male victims.* Paper presented at the annual meeting of the American Psychological Association, San Francisco.

Whipple, E. E., & Webster-Stratton, C. (1991). The role of parental stress in physically abusive families. *Child Abuse & Neglect, 15,* 279-291.

White, J. W. (1983). Sex and gender issues in aggression research. In R. G. Geen & E. I.

Donnerstein (Eds.), *Aggression: Theoretical and empirical reviews* (Vol. 2, pp. 1-26). New York: Academic Press.

White, J. W., & Koss, M. P. (1991). Courtship violence: Incidence in a national sample of higher education students. *Violence and Victims, 6,* 247-256.

Whiteman, M., Fanshel, D., & Grundy, J. F. (1987). Cognitive behavioral interventions aimed at anger of parents at risk of child abuse. *Social Work, 32,* 469-474.

Widom, C. S. (1989). Does violence beget violence? A critical examination of the literature. *Psychological Bulletin, 106,* 3-28.

Widom, C. S. (1995, March). Victims of childhood sexual abuse—Later criminal consequences. *National Institute of Justice,* pp. 1-8.

Widom, C. S. (1989). Child abuse, neglect, and violent criminal behavior. *Criminology, 27,* 251-271.

Wiehe, V. R. (1990). *Sibling abuse: Hidden physical, emotional, and sexual trauma.* Lexington, MA: Lexington Books.

Wild, N. J. (1989). Prevalence of child sex rings. *Pediatrics, 83,* 553-558.

Wildin, S. R., Williamson, W., & Wilson, G. S. (1991). Children of battered women: Developmental and learning profile. *Clinical Pediatrics, 30,* 299-302.

Willbach, D. (1989). Ethics and family therapy: The case management of family violence. *Journal of Marital and Family Therapy, 15,* 43-52.

Williams, K. R. (1992). Social sources of marital violence and deterrence: Testing an integrated theory of assaults between partners. *Journal of Marriage and the Family, 54,* 620-629.

Williams, L. M. (1992). Adult memories of childhood abuse: Preliminary findings from a longitudinal study. *The APSAC Advisor, 5,* 19-21.

Williams, L. M. (1994). Recall of childhood trauma: A prospective study of women's memories. *Journal of Consulting and Clinical Psychology, 62,* 1167-1176.

Williams, L. M., & Finkelhor, D. (1990). The characteristics of incestuous fathers: A review of recent studies. In W. L. Marshall, D. R. Laws, & H. E. Barbaree (Eds.), *Handbook of sexual assault: Issues, theories, and treatment of the offender* (pp. 231-255). New York: Plenum.

Williams, M. B. (1993). Assessing the traumatic impact of child sexual abuse: What makes it more severe? *Journal of Child Sexual Abuse, 2,* 41-59.

Williamson, J. M., Borduin, C. M., & Howe, B. A. (1991). The ecology of adolescent maltreatment: A multilevel examination of adolescent physical abuse, sexual abuse, and neglect. *Journal of Consulting and Clinical Psychology, 59,* 449-457.

Wilson, D. G., & Wilson, A. V. (1991). *Spousal abuse cases: Perceptions and attitudes of service providers* (Report prepared for the Attorney General's Task Force on Domestic Violence Crime). Louisville: Kentucky Criminal Justice Statistical Analysis Center.

Wilson, J., & Herrnstein, R. (1985). *Crime and human nature.* New York: Simon & Schuster.

Wilson, M. N., Baglioni, A. J., Jr., & Downing, D. (1989). Analyzing factors influencing readmission to a battered women's shelter. *Journal of Family Violence, 4,* 275-284.

Wilson, S. K., Cameron, S., Jaffe, P. G., & Wolfe, D. A. (1989). Children exposed to wife abuse: An intervention model. *Social Casework: The Journal of Contemporary Social Work, 70,* 180-184.

Wincze, J. P., Bansal, S., & Malamud, M. (1986). Effects of medroxyproesterone acetate on subjective arousal, arousal to erotic stimulation and nocturnal penile tumescence in male sex offenders. *Archives of Sexual Behavior, 15,* 293-305.

Wind, T. W., & Silvern, L. (1992). Type and extent of child abuse as predictors of adult functioning. *Journal of Family Violence, 7,* 261-281.

Witt, D. D. (1987). A conflict theory of family violence. *Journal of Family Violence, 2,* 291-301.

Wodarski, J. S., Kurtz, P. D., Gaudin, J. M., & Howing, P. T. (1990). Maltreatment and the school age child: Major academic, socioemotional, and adaptive outcomes. *Social Work, 35,* 506-513.

Wolf, R. S., Godkin, M. A., & Pillemer, K. A. (1986). Maltreatment of the elderly: A comparative analysis. *Pride Institute Journal of Long Term Home Health Care, 5,* 10-17.

Wolf, R. S., & Pillemer, K. A. (1988). Intervention, outcome, and elder abuse. In G. T. Hotaling, D. Finkelhor, J. T. Kirkpatrick, & M. A. Straus (Eds.), *Coping with family violence* (pp. 257-274). Newbury Park, CA: Sage.

Wolf, R. S., & Pillemer, K. A. (1989). *Helping elderly victims: The reality of elder abuse.* New York: Columbia University Press.

Wolfe, D. A. (1987). *Child abuse: Implications for child development and psychopathology.* Newbury Park, CA: Sage.

Wolfe, D. A. (1991). *Preventing physical and emotional abuse of children.* New York: Guilford.

Wolfe, D. A., Edwards, B., Manion, I., & Koverola, C. (1988). Early intervention for parents at risk of child abuse and neglect: A preliminary investigation. *Journal of Consulting and Clinical Psychology, 56,* 40-47.

Wolfe, D. A., Jaffe, P. G., Wilson, S. K., & Zak, L. (1985). Children of battered women: The relation of child behavior to family violence and maternal stress. *Journal of Consulting and Clinical Psychology, 53,* 657-665.

Wolfe, D. A., & Mosk, M. D. (1983). Behavioral comparisons of children from abusive and distressed families. *Journal of Consulting and Clinical Psychology, 51,* 702-708.

Wolfe, D. A., & Sandler, J. (1981). Training abusive parents in effective child management. *Behavior Modification, 5,* 320-335.

Wolfe, D. A., St. Lawrence, J. S., Graves, K., Brehony, K., Bradlyn, A. S., & Kelly, J. A. (1982). Intensive behavioral parent training for a child abusive mother. *Behavior Therapy, 13,* 438-451.

Wolfe, D. A., & Wekerle, C. (1993). Treatment strategies for child physical abuse and neglect: A critical progress report. *Clinical Psychology Review, 13,* 473-500.

Wolfe, D. A., Wolfe, V. V., & Best, C. L. (1988). Child victims of sexual abuse. In V. B. Van Hasselt, R. L. Morrison, A. S. Bellack, & M. Hersen (Eds.), *Handbook of family violence* (pp. 157-185). New York: Plenum.

Wolfe, D. A., Zak, L., Wilson, S. K., & Jaffe, P. G. (1986). Child witnesses to violence between parents: Critical issues in behavioral and social adjustment. *Journal of Abnormal Child Psychology, 14,* 95-104.

Wolfgang, M. E., & Ferracuti, F. (1972). *Delinquency in a birth cohort.* London: Tavistock.

Wolfner, G. D., & Gelles, R. J. (1993). A profile of violence toward children: A national study. *Child Abuse & Neglect, 17,* 197-212.

Wolman, B. J. (1973). *Dictionary of behavioral science.* New York: Van Nostrand Reinhold.

Wolock, T., & Horowitz, B. (1984). Child maltreatment as a social problem: The neglect of neglect. *American Journal of Orthopsychiatry, 54,* 530-542.

Worling, J. R. (1995). Adolescent sibling-incest offenders: Differences in family and individual functioning when compared to adolescent nonsibling sex offenders. *Child Abuse & Neglect, 19,* 633-643.

Worth, D. M., Matthews, P. A., & Coleman, W. R. (1990). Sex role, group affiliation, family background, and courtship violence in college students. *Journal of College Student Development, 31,* 250-254.

Wozencraft, T., Wagner, W., & Pellegrin, A. (1991). Depression and suicidal ideation in sexually abused children. *Child Abuse & Neglect, 15,* 505-511.

Wurtele, S. K., & Miller-Perrin, C. L. (1992). *Preventing child sexual abuse: Sharing the responsibility.* Lincoln: University of Nebraska Press.

Wyatt, G. E. (1985). The sexual abuse of Afro-American and White-American women in childhood. *Child Abuse & Neglect, 9,* 507-519.

Wyatt, G. E. (1994). Sociocultural and epidemiological issues in the assessment of domestic violence. *Journal of Social Distress and the Homeless, 3,* 7-21.

Yanagida, E. H., & Ching, J. W. (1993). MMPI profiles of child abusers. *Journal of Clinical Psychology, 49,* 569-576.

Yegidis, B. L. (1992). Family violence: Contemporary research findings and practice issues. *Community Mental Health Journal, 28,* 519-529.

Yegidis, B. L., & Renzy, R. B. (1994). Battered women's experiences with a preferred arrest policy. *Affilia, 9,* 60-70.

Yesavage, J. A., & Widrow, L. (1985). Early parental discipline and adult self-destructive acts. *Journal of Nervous and Mental Disease, 17,* 74-77.

Yllö, K. A., & Straus, M. A. (1990). Patriarchy and violence against wives: The impact of structural and normative factors. In M. A. Straus & R. J. Gelles (Eds.), *Physical violence in American families: Risk factors and adaptations to violence in 8,145 families* (pp. 383-399). New Brunswick, NJ: Transaction Books.

Yorukoglu, A., & Kemph, J. P. (1966). Children not severely damaged by incest with a parent. *Journal of American Academy of Child Psychiatry, 5,* 111-124.

Yoshihama, M., & Sorenson, S. B. (1994). Physical, sexual, and emotional abuse by male intimates: Experiences of women in Japan. *Violence and Victims, 9,* 63-77.

Young, R. E., Bergandi, T. A., & Titus, T. G. (1994). Comparison of the effects of sexual abuse on male and female latency-aged children. *Journal of Interpersonal Violence, 9,* 291-306.

Youngblade, L. M., & Belsky, J. (1990). Social and emotional consequences of child maltreatment. In R. T. Ammerman & M. Hersen (Eds.), *Children at risk: An evaluation of factors contributing to child abuse and neglect* (pp. 109-140). New York: Plenum.

Yuan, Y. T., & Struckman-Johnson, D. L. (1991). Placement outcomes for neglected children with prior placements in family preservation programs. In K. Wells & D. E. Biegel (Eds.), *Family preservation services: Research and evaluation* (pp. 92-118). Newbury Park, CA: Sage.

Zeanah, C. H., & Zeanah, P. D. (1989). Intergenerational transmission of maltreatment: Insights from attachment. *Psychiatry, 52,* 177-195.

Zigler, E. (1977, Fall). Supreme Court on spanking: Upholding discipline or abuse? *Society for Research in Child Development Newsletter,* pp. 1-3.

Zigler, E., & Hall, N. W. (1989). Child abuse in America. In D. Cicchetti & V. Carlson (Eds.), *Child maltreatment: Theory and research on the causes and consequences of child abuse and neglect* (pp. 38-75). San Francisco: Jossey-Bass.

Zimny, G. H., & Diamond, J. A. (1993). Judicial evaluation of recommendations for improving monitoring of guardians. *Journal of Elder Abuse & Neglect, 5*(3), 51-67.

Zingraff, M. T., Leiter, J., Myers, K. A., & Johnsen, M. C. (1993). Child maltreatment and youthful problem behavior. *Criminology, 31*(2), 173-202.

Zoglin, R. (1996, February 19). Chips ahoy. *Time, 147*(8), 42-45.

Zorza, J. (1991). Woman battering: A major cause of homelessness. *Clearinghouse Review, 61,* 421-429.

Zorza, J. (1992). The criminal law of misdemeanor domestic violence, 1970-1990. *Journal of Criminal Law and Criminology, 46,* 46-72.

Zorza, J. (1994). Woman battering: High costs and the state of the law [Special issue]. *Clearinghouse Review, 28,* 383-395.

Zorza, J. (1995). Recognizing and protecting the privacy and confidentiality needs of battered women [Special issue]. *Family Law Quarterly, 29,* 273-311.

Zorza, J., & Woods, L. (1994a). *Analysis and policy implications of the new domestic violence police studies.* Washington, DC: National Center on Women and Family Law.

Zorza, J., & Woods, L. (1994b). *Mandatory arrest.* Washington, DC: National Center on Women and Family Law.

Zubretsky, T. M., & Digirolamo, K. M. (1994, March). Adult domestic violence: The alcohol connection. *Violence Update, 4*(7), 1-2, 4, 8.

Zuckerman, B., & Bresnahan, K. (1991). Developmental and behavioral consequences of prenatal drug and alcohol exposure. *Pediatric Clinics of North America, 38,* 1387-1406.

Zumwalt, R. E., & Hirsch, C. S. (1987). Pathology of fatal child abuse and neglect. In R. Helfer & R. Kempe (Eds.), *The battered child* (4th ed., pp. 247-285). Chicago: University of Chicago Press.

Zuravin, S. J. (1986). Residential density and urban child maltreatment: An aggregate analysis. *Journal of Family Violence, 1,* 307-322.

Zuravin, S. J. (1988a). Child abuse, child neglect, and maternal depression: Is there a connection? In National Center on Child Abuse and Neglect (Ed.), *Child neglect monograph: Proceedings from a symposium.* Washington, DC: Clearinghouse on Child Abuse and Neglect Information.

Zuravin, S. J. (1988b). Child maltreatment and teenage first births: A relationship mediated by chronic sociodemographic stress? *American Journal of Orthopsychiatry, 50,* 91-103.

Zuravin, S. J. (1989). The ecology of child abuse and neglect: Review of the literature and presentation of data. *Violence and Victims, 4*(2), 101-120.

Zuravin, S. J. (1991). Research definitions of child physical abuse and neglect: Current problems. In R. H. Starr, Jr. & D. A. Wolfe (Eds.), *The effects of child abuse and neglect: Research issues* (pp. 100-128). New York: Guilford.

Zuravin, S. J., & DiBlasio, F. A. (1992). Child-neglecting adolescent mothers: How do they differ from their nonmaltreating counterparts? *Journal of Interpersonal Violence, 7,* 471-487.

Zuravin, S. J., & Grief, G. L. (1989). Normative and child-maltreating AFDC mothers. *Social Casework: The Journal of Contemporary Social Work, 74,* 76-84.

Zuravin, S. J., & Taylor, R. (1987). *Family planning behaviors and child care adequacy, final report.* Washington, DC: Department of Health and Human Services, Office of Population Affairs.

Author Index

Subject Index

About the Authors

Ola W. Barnett is Professor of Psychology in the Social Science Division, Pepperdine University, Malibu, California. She received her doctorate at the University of California, Los Angeles, specializing in learning. Her major research and publication areas are the characteristics of maritally violent men, the assessment of marital violence, and battered women. She coordinates a student volunteer program for a battered women's shelter and has served as a volunteer facilitator for a batterers' group. She is the recipient of the Charles B. Luckman Distinguished Teaching Fellows Award. She has coauthored (with Alyce D. LaViolette) a best-selling book, *It Could Happen to Anyone: Why Battered Women Stay.*

Cindy Miller-Perrin is Associate Professor of Psychology at Pepperdine University in Malibu, California. She received her doctorate in clinical psychology from Washington State University. Following her doctoral studies, she completed a postdoctoral fellowship at the University of Washington, where she was involved in research and clinical work with developmentally delayed children. She has had a variety of clinical experiences working with maltreated children and their families. Her major research and publications are in the area of child sexual abuse, including a book titled *Child Sexual Abuse: Sharing the Responsibility* (coauthored with S. Wurtele).

Robin Perrin is Associate Professor of Sociology at Pepperdine University in Malibu, California. He received his doctorate in sociology from Washington State University in 1989. Following his doctoral studies, he was Assistant Professor of Sociology at Seattle Pacific University in Seattle, Washington. His research interests and publications are in the area of the sociology of religion and deviant behavior. He has written a book titled *Social Deviance: Being Behaving and Branding* (coauthored with David Ward and Tim Carter) and has served as Assistant Editor of the *Journal for the Scientific Study of Religion.*